Bill Ball

SAMS
Teach Yourself
Linux®
in 24 Hours

SECOND EDITION

SAMS

A Division of Macmillan Computer Publishing
201 West 103rd St., Indianapolis, Indiana, 46290 USA

Sams Teach Yourself Linux® in 24 Hours, Second Edition

Copyright © 1999 by Sams Publishing

International Standard Book Number: 0-672-31526-2

Library of Congress Catalog Card Number: 98-88372

Printed in the United States of America

First Printing: April 1999

00   99   99   4   3   2

Trademarks

Warning and Disclaimer

EXECUTIVE EDITOR
Jeff Koch

ACQUISITIONS EDITOR
Gretchen Ganser

DEVELOPMENT EDITOR
Sean Dixon

MANAGING EDITOR
Brice Gosnell

PROJECT EDITOR
Gretchen Uphoff

COPY EDITOR
Kristine Simmons
Kelly Talbot

INDEXER
Robert Saigh

PROOFREADER
Andrew Beaster

TECHNICAL EDITOR
Kurt Wall

SOFTWARE DEVELOPMENT SPECIALIST
Michael Hunter

INTERIOR DESIGN
Gary Adair

COVER DESIGN
Aren Howell

LAYOUT TECHNICIANS
Ayanna Lacey
Heather Hiatt Miller
Amy Parker

Contents at a Glance

Introduction   1

PART I INSTALLATION AND CONFIGURATION   **5**

Hour 1 Preparing to Install Linux   7
      2 Installing Linux   23
      3 Post-Installation Issues   41

PART II LEARNING LINUX BASICS   **67**

Hour 4 Reading and Navigation Commands   69
      5 Manipulation and Searching Commands   93
      6 Using the Shell   117
      7 Using the X Window System   143
      8 Exploring the K Desktop Environment   177

PART III CONNECTING TO THE OUTSIDE WORLD   **197**

Hour 9 Using Communications Programs   199
     10 Connecting to the Internet   223
     11 Configuring Internet Email   249
     12 Configuring Internet News   269
     13 Internet Downloading and Browsing   289

PART IV USING LINUX PRODUCTIVELY   **311**

Hour 14 Text Processing   313
     15 Preparing Documents   337
     16 Graphics Tools   359
     17 Learning Math and Financial Tools   381
     18 Personal Productivity Tools   399
     19 Home Office Management with StarOffice   415
     20 Relaxation and Playing Linux Games   435

PART V ADMINISTERING YOUR SYSTEM   **449**

Hour 21 Basic System Administration   451

    22 Handling Files and Your File System   479

    23 Backing Up and Restoring Your System   509

    24 Using Scheduling to Automate System Management   523

       Index   531

Table of Contents

INTRODUCTION   **1**

PART I INSTALLATION AND CONFIGURATION   **5**

HOUR 1 PREPARING TO INSTALL LINUX   **7**

What is Linux? 8
What is OpenLinux? 9
What Equipment is Required? 10
What Equipment is Supported? 10
What Equipment Doesn't Work? 11
    Winprinters 11
    Winmodems 12
    Infrared Ports 12
What Equipment Do I Have? 13
How Do I Plan for the Installation? 14
    Booting the Install from CD-ROM 15
    Booting the Install from Floppies 16
    Other Ways 17
Planning Your Boot Process 17
Preparing Your Hard Drive 18
    Preparing Your Hard Drive from Windows 19
Summary 21
Q&A 22
Exercises 22

HOUR 2 INSTALLING LINUX   **23**

Beginning the Installation 24
Finishing Your Linux Installation 31
    Logging in to Linux 35
    Rebooting and Shutting Down 38
Summary 38
Q&A 39
Exercises 39

HOUR 3 POST-INSTALLATION ISSUES   **41**

The X Window System 42
    How the X Window System is Configured 42
    The XF86Config File 45
    Bypassing or Disabling the kdm Login Display 48
    Starting an X11 Session 49

Configuring Sound for OpenLinux..50
    Loading Sound Modules 50
    Testing Your Sound Configuration 53
    Configuring Sound with COAS...53
    A Quick Recording Script..56
    Configuring Sound the Easy Way 57
Enabling PCMCIA Cards 57
Configuring Network Information with COAS 61
    Configuring Your Ethernet Interface 61
Using an Iomega Zip Drive with OpenLinux..64
Summary 65
Q&A 65
Exercises 66

PART II LEARNING LINUX BASICS   **67**

HOUR 4 READING AND NAVIGATION COMMANDS   **69**

Getting Help with the man Command 69
Navigating and Searching the File System...72
    Moving to Different Directories with the cd Command 72
    Knowing Where You Are with the pwd Command 73
    Searching Directories for Matching Files with the find Command 74
    Finding Files with the whereis Command 75
    Locating Files with the locate Command 76
    Getting Command Summaries with whatis and apropos 76
Reading Directories and Files...78
    Listing Directories with the ls Command 78
    Listing Directories with the dir and vdir Commands 82
    Listing and Combining Files with the cat Command 84
    Reading Files with the more Command 86
    Browsing Files with the less Command 87
Reading the Beginning or End of Files with the head and tail Commands 88
Summary..90
Q&A 91
Exercises 91

HOUR 5 MANIPULATION AND SEARCHING COMMANDS   **93**

Manipulating Files or Directories...93
    Creating Files with the touch Command.......................................94
    Deleting Files with the rm Command 95
    Creating Directories with the mkdir Command............................96

Removing Directories with the `rmdir` Command 97

Renaming Files with the `mv` Command..98

Copying with the `cp` Command 100

Creating Hard and Symbolic Links with the `ln` Command 102

Handling Files with the Midnight Commander Program 104

Searching Files 105

What Are Regular Expressions? 106

Searching Inside Files with the `grep` Commands 108

Compressing and Uncompressing Files 110

Creating Archives with the Tape Archive Command 110

Creating `cpio` Archives..113

Compressing Files with the `gzip` Command 114

Compressing Files with the `compress` Command.................................114

Summary 115

Q&A 115

Exercises 116

HOUR 6   USING THE SHELL   117

What is a Shell? 117

What Shells are Available? 118

Features of `ash` 119

Features of the Default Linux Shell—`bash` 120

The Public Domain Korn Shell—`pdksh` 121

Features of the csh-Compatible Shell—`tcsh`...122

`zsh`...122

Understanding the Shell Command Line 123

Customizing Your Shell...127

Running Programs in the Background 131

How to Use Pipes 134

Building Shell Scripts...136

Summary 140

Q&A 140

Exercises 141

HOUR 7   USING THE X WINDOW SYSTEM   143

Starting X 144

Starting X11 with Different Color Depths 145

Using Virtual Consoles with X11 147

Starting Multiple X11 Sessions...148

Logging in to OpenLinux and X11 with xdm..149

X11 Window Managers 150

Configuring the `fvwm` Window Manager 151

Starting AfterStep 155

Starting the `twm` Window Manager 156

X11 Terminal Programs 157
    Changing the xterm Terminal Settings 158
    Using the Memory-Efficient rxvt Terminal....................................159
Learning X11 Basic Operations 160
    Using X11 Client Geometry Settings 160
    Setting Background and Foreground Colors for X11 Clients.....................161
    Setting X11 Client Resources 162
    Changing X11 Mouse and Cursor Modes..164
    How to Copy and Paste in X11 165
    Capturing and Dumping X11 Windows 167
    Customizing the X11 Root Window and Using Screen savers.....................168
Exploring X11 Programs 172
    Listing X11 Fonts with xlsfonts 172
    Getting Window Information with the xwininfo Client 173
    Making a Sticky Note Calendar with the xmessage Client....................174
    Keeping Time with X11 Clocks 174
Summary...175
Q&A 176
Exercises 176

HOUR 8 EXPLORING THE K DESKTOP ENVIRONMENT   **177**

Starting KDE..179
Features of the KDE Desktop...180
    Performing Basic Desktop Actions 180
    Using Desktop panel 181
    Editing the KDE Panel Menu 182
    Using the kfm File Manager 183
Configuring KDE with the KDE Control Center 184
    Using Display Manager Options..185
    Changing Your Desktop's Wallpaper...187
    Changing Your Screensaver..188
    Changing Default Fonts..189
    Installing System Sounds 190
    Changing Keyboard and Mouse Settings 191
    Changing Window Buttons, Properties, and Title Bars.......................193
    Controlling Cursor Movement Through Desktops 195
Summary...195
Q&A 196
Exercises 196

PART III CONNECTING TO THE OUTSIDE WORLD   **197**

   HOUR 9 USING COMMUNICATIONS PROGRAMS   **199**

     Setting Up and Testing Your Modem 200
       Creating /dev/modem with the lisa Command 201
     Dialing Out with Communications Programs 203
       Setting Up and Calling Out with minicom...204
       Setting Up and Calling Out with the seyon X11 Client 206
       Setting Up Your Linux System for Dialing In...208
     Sending and Receiving Faxes..211
       Faxing with the efax System 211
       Sending Fax Documents with the ksendfax Client............................216
       Sending Fax Documents with mgetty+sendfax 218
     Summary..220
     Q&A 221
     Exercises 221

   HOUR 10 CONNECTING TO THE INTERNET   **223**

     Hardware You Need 224
     Linux Software You Need..226
     Information You Need from Your ISP 228
     Setting Up a PPP Connection Manually...229
       Editing the resolv.conf File 229
       Editing the PPP Connection Scripts 230
     Manually Starting and Stopping PPP Connections 232
       Using minicom to Connect..232
       Using Your ppp-on Script to Connect 233
       Stopping the PPP Connection 234
     Configuring a PPP Connection with kppp 234
       Configuring Your kppp Connection 235
       Starting and Stopping PPP with kppp 239
     Configuring a PPP Connection with xisp 240
       Configuring a New xisp Account 241
       Starting and Stopping PPP with xisp 243
     Checking the Connection 243
       Using the ifconfig Command 243
       Using the netstat Command 244
       Using the ping Command 245
       Using the route Command 245
       Reading Your System Log...246
     Summary..247
     Q&A 247
     Exercises 248

HOUR 11 CONFIGURING INTERNET EMAIL   **249**

Setting Up and Getting Your Email 249
    Retrieving Your Email with `fetchmail` 251
Sending Mail with Mail Programs 253
    Using the `mail` Program 253
    Configuring and Using the `elm` Mail Program 255
    Configuring and Using the `pine` Mail Program 257
    Configuring and Using Netscape Messenger for Email 260
    Subscribing to Mailing Lists 263
Configuring `procmail` and Writing Recipes to Fight Spam 264
Summary 267
Q&A 267
Exercises 268

HOUR 12 CONFIGURING INTERNET NEWS   **269**

Reading Usenet News with the `tin` Newsreader 271
Reading Usenet News with the `slrn` Newsreader 274
Reading Usenet News with the `krn` Client..278
Reading Usenet News with Netscape Discussions....................................282
Before Posting to a Usenet Group 285
Summary 286
Q&A 286
Exercises 287

HOUR 13 INTERNET DOWNLOADING AND BROWSING   **289**

Using File Transfer Protocol Programs to Get Files 290
    Retrieving Files with the `ftp` Command..290
    Downloading with the `ncFTP` Program 297
Browsing the World Wide Web with Linux Browsers 298
    Fast Browsing with the `lynx` Command 299
    Exploring Netscape Communicator 300
Chatting with Internet Relay Chat 304
Installing and Configuring AOL Instant Messenger................................306
Connecting with Other Computers with the `telnet` Command........................308
Summary 309
Q&A 310
Exercises 310

PART IV USING LINUX PRODUCTIVELY **311**

HOUR 14 TEXT PROCESSING **313**

Word Processors in the Linux Environment...313
Features of the XEmacs Environment..315
Variants of the VIsual iMproved Editor —vim 317
Features of Pine's pico Editor..319
Five Editors in One—joe 321
Configuring the jed Editor 321
Using the kedit Editor Client 322
Using the CRiSPlite Editor 324
StarOffice's StarWriter 324
Corel's WordPerfect for Linux 326
Applix Words..327
Changing Text with sed and Other Filters 329
Spell Checking Your Documents 332
Correcting Documents with the ispell Command 332
Single Word Lookup and Other Tricks 334
Summary 335
Q&A 335
Exercises 336

HOUR 15 PREPARING DOCUMENTS **337**

Formatting Text...337
Formatting Text Using Text Filters 338
Formatting Text with the groff Formatter 342
Formatting Text with TeX 346
Printing Text Documents 347
Printing Documents with the LPRng Printing System 349
Configuring Your Printer with the lisa Command...........................351
Configuring WordPerfect for Printing..354
Summary 356
Q&A 356
Exercises 357

HOUR 16 GRAPHICS TOOLS **359**

Understand Linux Graphics File Formats 360
Converting and Viewing Graphics 367
Graphics Editing with GIMP..369
Graphics Editing with ImageMagick 373
Using the xv Command to View Graphics 374
Using the gv Command to View PostScript Files 376

A Word About Digital Cameras and Scanners 377

Summary 379

Q&A 379

Exercises 379

HOUR 17 LEARNING MATH AND FINANCIAL TOOLS   **381**

Calculators 382

    Doing Desk Calculations with the dc Command 382

    Calculating with the X11 xcalc Client 383

    Calculating with the kcalc Client 383

    Performing Unit Conversions with the units Command 385

    Programming Calculators with the bc Language Interpreter 386

Spreadsheets 387

    Using the Public Domain sc Spreadsheet 387

    Using the slsc Spreadsheet 389

    Finding the Free Wingz Spreadsheet 390

    Features of the StarCalc Spreadsheet Program 391

    Commercial Features of the Applixware Spreadsheet Program 393

Using gnuplot to Graph Mathematical Formulas 394

Summary 396

Q&A 396

Exercises 397

HOUR 18 PERSONAL PRODUCTIVITY TOOLS   **399**

Scheduling Personal Reminders and Tasks with the at Command 400

Scheduling Regular Reminders with the crontab Command 403

Creating Appointment Reminders with the X11 ical Client.............................405

Checking the Calendar and Keeping Appointments with emacs 409

Setting Alarms with the knotes Client 411

Summary 412

Q&A 413

Exercises 413

HOUR 19 HOME OFFICE MANAGEMENT WITH STAROFFICE   **415**

Installing and Configuring StarOffice 416

    Starting StarOffice 419

    Customizing StarOffice 420

    Installing a Printer for StarOffice 421

Using StarOffice 421

    Creating Documents with StarWriter 423

    Spellchecking and Saving StarWriter Documents 426

    Calculating with StarCalc 428

    Graphing with StarCalc 431

Summary 432

Q&A 433

Exercises 433

HOUR 20 RELAXATION AND PLAYING LINUX GAMES   **435**

Playing Music CDs with the kscd and xplaycd Clients...............................435

    Playing Music with the xplaycd Client...438

Games for the Console 439

    Playing emacs Games 441

Games for the X Window System 442

    Playing Chess with the xboard Client..442

    Playing X11 Solitaire 443

    Playing Backgammon for X11 444

    Playing Galaga for X11...444

    Breakout the Fun with the X11 Client xboing 445

    Playing Quake for X Windows...445

Summary 447

Q&A 447

Exercises 448

PART V ADMINISTERING YOUR SYSTEM   **449**

HOUR 21 BASIC SYSTEM ADMINISTRATION   **451**

Running as the root Operator with the su Command...........................452

Getting Disk Space Information 454

    Getting Filesystem Statistics with the df Command 454

    Getting Filesystem Disk Usage with the du Command 455

    Checking Symbolic Links with the symlinks Command 457

    Saving Disk Space...458

Getting Memory Information 460

    Memory Reporting with the free Command 461

    Virtual Memory Reporting with the vmstat Command 461

    Viewing Your Shell's "Ulimit"ations...462

    Reclaiming Memory with the kill Command 463

Getting System Load Information with the top and xload Commands............464

    Determining How Long Linux Has Been Running with the uptime and

    w Commands 466

    Getting Network and Mail Information with the pppstats and mailstats

    Commands 467

    Monitoring Your Serial Ports with the statserial Command....................468

Managing User Access 468

Creating Users with the adduser Command 469

Managing Users with the lisa Command 469

Changing Passwords with the passwd Command 470

Restricting Logins 472

Setting Disk Quotas..473

Summary..476

Q&A 476

Exercises 477

HOUR 22 HANDLING FILES AND YOUR FILE SYSTEM   479

How OpenLinux Is Organized 480

Using the mount Command to Access Other Filesystems 482

Understanding the Filesystem Table, /etc/fstab 482

Formatting a Floppy 484

Formatting Floppies with the KFloppy Client 488

The mtools Package 489

Managing File Ownership and Permissions..491

Understanding Linux File Types 492

Reading File Permissions Flags 492

Changing File Permissions with the chmod Command.......................................494

Changing File Ownership with the chown Command. 496

Changing Groups and Ownerships with the chgrp and newgrp Commands 497

Managing Linux Software with rpm, lisa, and kpackage 499

Using the rpm Command 499

Using kpackage 502

Using the lisa Command 505

Summary..507

Q&A 508

Exercises 508

HOUR 23 BACKING UP AND RESTORING YOUR SYSTEM   509

Considerations Before Performing Backups and Restores....................................509

Configuring the BRU Backup System for Backups and Restores 511

Backing Up Your System with the tar Command 515

Using the cpio Command to Backup and Restore 517

Using the taper Script for Tape Drive Backups and Restores 518

Summary..520

Q&A 520

Exercises 521

HOUR 24 USING SCHEDULING TO AUTOMATE SYSTEM MANAGEMENT **523**

Using the cron Daemon 524
    Managing User cron Scheduling..525
    Setting Schedules with the crontab Command 525
Managing User Scheduling with the atrun Command 527
    Controlling the batch and at Commands...528
Summary..530
Q&A 530
Exercises 530

INDEX **531**

About the Author

Bill Ball is the author of several best-selling books about Linux: *Sams Teach Yourself Linux in 24 Hours*, Que's *Using Linux*, *Sams Red Hat Linux Unleashed*, and *Sams How to Use Linux*. He is a technical writer, editor, and magazine journalist and has been working with computers for the past 20 years. He first started working with Linux, beginning with kernel version .99, after moving from BSD4.3 Machten for the Apple Macintosh. He has published articles in magazines such as Computer Shopper and MacTech Magazine and first started editing books for Que in 1986. An avid fly fisherman, he builds bamboo fly rods and fishes on the nearby Potomac River when he's not driving his vintage MG sports cars. He lives in the Shirlington area of Arlington County, Virginia.

Dedication

To my lovely wife Cathy for her kindness, understanding—and most importantly, killer coffee in the morning.

Acknowledgments

Thanks are due to the following people at Macmillan: Theresa Ball (for books), Lynette Quinn (for being my mentor), Tracy Williams (for finding lost contracts), Gretchen Ganser (for making me chill out), Sean Dixon (a great development editor), Jeff Koch (for the opportunities), and Eric Goldfarb (for keeping mcp.com online all the time). Special thanks to Kurt Wall—without his technical expertise, edits, and advice, I'd look like an idiot. Thanks are also due to the kind folks at Caldera Systems, Inc. and the Northern Virginia Linux Users Group, especially Gregory J. Pryzby! Thanks to Linus Torvalds for Linux, Richard M. Stallman for the GNU GPL, and Eric S. Raymond (esr) for carrying forward the Open Source Software banner. Finally, thanks to Bill Gates for making Linux more popular than ever.

Tell Us What You Think!

As the reader of this book, *you* are our most important critic and commentator. We value your opinion and want to know what we're doing right, what we could do better, what areas you'd like to see us publish in, and any other words of wisdom you're willing to pass our way.

As the executive editor for the Operating Systems team at Macmillan Computer Publishing, I welcome your comments. You can fax, email, or write me directly to let me know what you did or didn't like about this book—as well as what we can do to make our books stronger.

Please note that I cannot help you with technical problems related to the topic of this book and that due to the high volume of mail I receive, I might not be able to reply to every message.

When you write, please be sure to include this book's title and author as well as your name and phone or fax number. I will carefully review your comments and share them with the author and editors who worked on the book.

Fax: 317.581.4663

Email: opsys@mcp.com

Mail: Executive Editor
          Operating Systems
          Macmillan Computer Publishing
          201 West 103rd Street
          Indianapolis, IN 46290 USA

Introduction

Welcome to Linux! You hold in your hands everything you need to install and use one of the most powerful computer operating systems in the world. This book is designed to help guide you through the process of learning about Linux. To make the task even easier, this book uses one of the best Linux distributions on the market today—OpenLinux from Caldera Systems, Inc.

Although the title of this book is *Teach Yourself Linux in 24 Hours*, you won't be alone while you learn. As you're taken from installation through system administration to playing games, you'll find advice, tips, and hints to help you along the way. Before you know it, you'll be familiar with the terms, topics, and technical concepts dealing with the hottest and newest operating system in the world—Linux!

Teach Yourself Linux in 24 Hours is designed to help you learn quickly. You'll find it an indispensable guide to installing Linux and getting right to work. This helps you overcome technical obstacles, explains complex subjects in simple language, and shows you some neat tricks to make your computing experience easier.

Each section of this book gives you an hour's worth of knowledge and examples you can run as you learn. By the way, this book was created, developed, and edited using the software included on the book's CD-ROM. I hope you enjoy teaching yourself Linux!

What is Linux?

Linux (pronounced lih-nuks) is a UNIX-like operating system that runs on many different computers. Although many people might refer to Linux as the operating system and included software, strictly speaking, Linux is the operating system *kernel*, which comes with a *distribution* of software. The Linux distribution included with this book is Caldera Systems, Inc. OpenLinux and features special software not included with other distributions (see the section "What's Included on the CD-ROM?" later in the "Introduction").

Linux was first released in 1991 by its author, Linus Torvalds, at the University of Helsinki. Since then, it has grown tremendously in popularity as programmers around the world embraced his project of building a free operating system, adding features, and fixing problems.

Linux is popular with today's generation of computer users for the same reasons early versions of the UNIX operating system enticed fans more than 20 years ago. Linux is portable, which means you'll find versions running on name-brand or clone PCs, Apple Macintoshes, Sun workstations, or Alpha-based computers. Linux also comes with source code, so you can change or customize the software to adapt to your needs. Finally, Linux is a great operating system that is rich in features adopted from other versions of UNIX. Soon you'll become a fan, too!

Why Teach Yourself Linux?

You should teach yourself Linux for a number of good reasons. You'll expand your knowledge of your computer's hardware, which can be handy in troubleshooting problems. You'll also learn the basics of using a UNIX-like operating system loaded with state-of-the-art features. When you combine this knowledge of hardware and software, you'll be well on your way to becoming a "power" computer user.

Use this book as a starting point in learning Linux basics. You'll learn all the skills you need to build and run a powerful and productive Linux workstation. Although you won't learn how to program in Java, administer a wide-area network, or manage a Web server, you will learn these things:

- Using Linux is a great way to connect to the Internet for emailing, file downloading, or World Wide Web browsing.
- You can get to work right away, as this book's Linux distribution (on CD-ROM) comes with a rich assortment of popular productivity tools, such as word processors, calendars, emailers, or graphics programs. More than 2,000 programs are included!
- You can have fun with some wacky arcade games.
- In no time at all, you'll be on your way to joining the worldwide community of Linux users.

Who is This Book For?

This book is for someone who wants to quickly master the basics of how to install, run, and maintain Linux on an Intel-based personal computer. All the tools you need are included.

Your computer should have a monitor (display), keyboard, mouse, hard drive, floppy drive, and CD-ROM drive. Although you can jump right in and install Linux on your hard drive, you should have some technical information about your computer and its hardware on hand before you start.

What's Included on the CD-ROM?

Everything you need! Included with this book is a CD-ROM from Caldera Systems, Inc. containing the latest and one of the most popular distributions of Linux—OpenLinux. This distribution includes the Linux kernel, more than 2,000 programs, and nearly 20,000 pages of documentation. As you read through this book and install or configure software, you'll see Caldera's OpenLinux distribution was chosen to help you learn. Some of its advantages are:

- OpenLinux is easy to install.
- OpenLinux uses a convenient software management system based on packages and includes several programs to help you add or remove software.
- OpenLinux includes the K Desktop Environment for the X Window System and has been specially configured to work "out of the box" so you can get to work right away.
- OpenLinux includes the highly popular StarOffice office suite of programs for word processing, graphics presentations, and spreadsheet forecasting.
- OpenLinux uses graphic tools to help you administer and maintain your system.
- OpenLinux software updates, patches, and bug fixes are available for free on the Internet through Caldera System's FTP and Web site.

How to Use This Book

This book is designed to teach you the latest version of the Caldera OpenLinux operating system in 24 one-hour sessions. You will learn how to install OpenLinux on your computer, how to use the Linux commands, how to use various windowing systems with OpenLinux, how to connect to the Internet, and how to use Linux to increase your productivity.

Each hour, or session, starts with an overview of the topic to inform you of what to expect in each lesson. This overview helps you determine the nature of the lesson and whether the lesson is relevant to your current needs.

Each lesson has a main section that discusses the lesson topic in a clear, concise manner by breaking the topic down into logical component parts and explaining each component clearly.

Interspersed in each lesson are special elements, called Tips, Cautions, and Notes, that provide additional information.

A *Tip* informs you of a trick or element that is easily missed by most new Linux users. Feel free to skip these hints and additions; however, if you skip reading them, you might miss a shorter or more efficient way to accomplish a task described in the main text.

A *Caution* deserves at least as much attention as the body of the lesson, because these point out a problematic element of the operating system or a "gotcha" you want to avoid while using the operating system. Ignoring the information contained in a Caution could have adverse effects on the stability of your computer. Be careful to read every Caution you run across.

A Note is designed to clarify the concept being discussed. Notes also contain additional information that might be slightly off-topic but interesting nonetheless. Notes elaborate on the subject, and if you're comfortable with your understanding of the subject, you can read these to add to your knowledge or bypass them with no danger.

Each lesson concludes with a Summary of what you have just learned, a Q&A section that answers the questions users new to Linux most frequently ask about that particular lesson's subject, and a Workshop containing exercises that will advance the reader in a further, hands-on study of that lesson's topic.

PART I

Installation and Configuration

Hour

1   Preparing to Install Linux

2   Installing Linux

3   Post-Installation Issues

HOUR 1

Preparing to Install Linux

Welcome to the wonderful world of Linux! This hour is the best place to start reading *before* attempting to install OpenLinux. There are several good reasons, especially for new Linux users, to sit down, take a deep breath, relax, and collect some thoughts before jumping into an installation.

Intrepid or experienced Linux users, such as those migrating from other distributions and installations such as Red Hat, Debian, or S.U.S.E. might feel tempted to rip the CD-ROM out of the back of this book and launch the installation. Hey, go for it! The CD-ROM boots, and you can easily use your existing Linux partitions. I think you'll be quite pleased with the treasure trove of software and the carefully crafted Caldera configuration of Linux.

For those of you coming into the light from the Dark Side—welcome! Consider some of the topics covered in this hour:

- What is Linux? (Or what isn't it?)
- What is OpenLinux? (And how is it different from other Linux distributions?)
- What equipment is required? (Do I have everything?)

- What equipment is supported? (Will my stuff work?)
- What equipment doesn't work? (Uh oh! What am I going to miss?)
- What equipment do I have? (Do I know about my computer?)
- How do I plan for the installation? (What do I need to know?)
- How is Linux installed? (Count me the ways!)
- How do I plan to boot OpenLinux? (How can I boot Linux?)

After these introductory sections, you then get directions on how to prepare your hard drive for OpenLinux. So, if you're an experienced user, skip this hour. Heck, you can skip the next two hours! But if you want to know a little more about Linux and how OpenLinux is different, read on! First-time Linux installers and users definitely need to read what follows.

What is Linux?

NEW TERM   Linux is the *kernel* of an operating system that runs on many different types of computers. This is the core piece of software that provides an interface between the command line or program and your computer's hardware. The Linux kernel manages such things as memory, how and when files are opened or closed, and what *process*, or program, has the full attention of your computer's Central Processing Unit (CPU).

Linux, a clone of the UNIX operating system, was first released on October 5, 1991 by its author, Linus Torvalds, at the University of Helsinki. Linux supports all the features of a modern operating system, including (but not limited to) the following:

- All major networking protocols
- Disk quota support
- Full source code
- Internationalization for fonts and keyboards
- Job control
- Math co-processor emulation
- Memory protection
- Multiple platforms
- Multiple processors
- Multiple users
- Multitasking
- Shared libraries

- Support for more than a dozen filesystems
- Virtual consoles
- Virtual memory

Linux is distributed as copyrighted software, or, because it is under the GNU General Public License (GPL), "copyleft" software. Basically, this license states that you can modify or give away copies of Linux, even sell it for profit, as long as you recognize the original author(s)' copyright and provide the source code.

Not all the software included on this book's CD-ROM is distributed under the GNU GPL. Always read any COPYRIGHT or LICENSE file included with a program. For more information about the GNU GPL, browse to: http://www.fsf.org/copyleft/gpl.html.

Linux inherits more than 25 years of UNIX experience, source code, and support. This makes Linux, even though one of the newest operating systems, far more mature than current commercial offerings. Linux is also a bargain. You have to spend nearly $5,000 for a 50-user license for Windows NT at the time of this writing, whereas you can get much more (including more than 1,000 programs) from Linux for the cost of this book.

There are versions of Linux for computers not based on the Intel chip, such as those from Sun Microsystems (SPARC) or computers using other central processing units (CPUs), such as the Alpha chip. To read more about other distributions of Linux for computers besides those based on the x86 architecture, browse to http://metalab.unc.edu/LDP.

Linux is not shareware. Linux is not in the public domain. Linux is not a "toy" operating system suitable only for longhaired hackers. Linux is a viable, alternative platform for high-end network server operations as well as a desktop operating system.

What is OpenLinux?

NEW TERM OpenLinux is a Linux *distribution*, or collection of specially tweaked software, configuration files, and utilities, pressed on a CD-ROM by Caldera Systems, Inc. You can find a CD-ROM chock-full of software in the back of this book that contains everything you need to start teaching yourself Linux.

Caldera Systems, Inc. (derived from its parent company, Caldera, Inc.) first produced a Linux distribution in 1994. The OpenLinux distribution has several features not provided in other distributions, such as Est, Inc.'s BRU-2000 backup and restore client, DR-DOS, NetWare 3.x and 4.x utilities, the NetWare NDS client, Corel's WordPerfect 8 for Linux, and the latest StarOffice office suite. Caldera also preconfigured the desktop panel of the K Desktop Environment to work specifically with the programs installed from this book's CD-ROM.

 BRU-2000 and StarOffice 5.0 are not actually included in the version of OpenLinux 2.2 included on the CD-ROM for the book, both both are available for free download from the Web.

Another outstanding feature of this Linux distribution is that Caldera has made the process of installing Linux easier than ever by including limited editions of Power Quest's PartitionMagic and Boot Magic on the CD-ROM. You'll be pleasantly surprised!

What Equipment is Required?

If you can run DOS or Windows on your computer, you can probably install and run OpenLinux. The general requirements for installing OpenLinux are the following:

- 386 or better equivalent CPU
- 16 megabytes of random access memory (RAM)—although Linux can work with 8 megabytes (32 is the recommended minimum when using StarOffice)
- 1.44MB 3.5 inch floppy drive
- CD-ROM drive
- Minimum of 300 megabytes to one gigabyte of hard drive space for a complete installation of the contents of this book's CD-ROM

What Equipment is Supported?

The best and definitive place to check what computer hardware is supported out of the box by OpenLinux is at this site:

http://www.calderasystems.com/products/openlinux/hardware.html

There are listings of supported hard disk and CD-ROM drive interfaces (such as IDE, XT, or SCSI), parallel-port CD-ROM drives, supported serial boards, mouse pointing devices (rodentiometers), tape drives, networking cards, and PCMCIA cards.

Video cards, or video chipsets for laptop users, are listed under the
/usr/X11R6/lib/X11/doc directory after you install OpenLinux and the X Window
System. To read an online list of supported cards for X11 (and which X11 server to use),
browse to this site:

http://www.xfree86.org/cardlist.html

Laptop users definitely need to browse the Linux Laptop Pages. There are specific directions on how to install and configure Linux and X11 for your laptop. Look for your laptop model listed at this site:

http://www.cs.utexas.edu/users/kharker/linux-laptop/

What Equipment Doesn't Work?

With the explosion of the personal computer market in the last few years, more and more
homes and businesses are either buying computers for the first time or upgrading older
computers. Believe it or not, you'll probably have fewer problems installing Linux with
one- to three-year-old hardware than if you're on the latest and greatest PC. This is
because although Linux is supported by the efforts of programmers around the world, not
many PC manufacturers support Linux (yet!) by releasing the specifications of their
hardware. Without these techincal details, programmers can have a difficult time writing
software. If your computer's hardware is not supported by Linux, complain to its manufacturer!

Fortunately, the list of unsupported hardware, or hardware with problems, is much
smaller than supported hardware. For example, you might have trouble with older 486-
based AMD CPUs, older Cyrix CPUs, and Microchannel-based PCs. There is little support for parallel-port tape drives and some Xircom ethernet cards with the current Linux
software.

Winprinters

Winprinters, or printers that depend on operating system-specific drivers, such as the
Hewlett-Packard 710, 720, 820, and 1000-series printers, are not supported by software
included on this book's CD-ROM. However, you can find support for some of these
printers through the use of special software, located at this site:

http://www.rpi.edu/~normat/technical/ppa

Other problems crop up with printing support for Epson Stylus color printers. You can
find some answers from Caldera at the following site:

http://www.calderasystems.com/support/techguide/styluscolor.html

Winmodems

Winmodems (part of a disgusting recent trend by PC and laptop manufacturers trying to save a few pennies per unit) are operating system-specific and will probably never be supported by Linux. These modems, which use less hardware than "real" modems, work through the use of software drivers (it's cheaper to offload all the work on your computer's CPU; besides, if you use Windows 9x, you're only doing one thing at a time anyway, right?). If you buy a PC or laptop with one of these modems, you're at the mercy of the manufacturer whether the modem is supported in the future or whether it works with another operating system.

> Beware! Many manufacturers tout these modems as "56K ITU V.90 modems," but fail to mention they are winmodems. Ask if the modem can be used with DR-DOS, PCDOS, or MSDOS. If not, it's a winmodem. To be safe, buy an external modem that can be used with any computer operating system.

Infrared Ports

Although software to support your computer's infrared port isn't included on this book's CD-ROM, the good news is that there is full infrared support for OpenLinux. This means that if you have a laptop or desktop with an IR port, you can now network, print to an IR printer (such as an HP 340Cbi or Canon BJC80), and even transfer or back up your 3Com Palm PDA without cables! Browse to this site:

```
http://www.cs.uit.no/~dagb/irda/irda.html
```

There are directions on how to download, install, and configure IR support for Linux. For complete directions in a HOWTO document format, browse to this site:

```
http://www.userpage.fu-berlin.de/~r2d2c3po/ir_howto.cgi
```

> If you own a 3Com Palm Pilot Professional or Palm III, there are nearly two dozen Pilot support utilities included with OpenLinux. Kenneth Albanowski's pilot-xfer command makes backing up a Palm III as easy as this:
>
> ```
> pilot-xfer /dev/pilot -b pilotbackupdirectory
> ```
>
> If you use KDE, use the Kpilot client, installed from the /col/install/RPMS directory on your OpenLinux CD-ROM. This is a graphical interface to administering your Palm computer.

What Equipment Do I Have?

You need to know a little about your computer before installing OpenLinux. Get out your paper and pencil, and then fill out as much information as you can in this section's following checklist. If your PC or laptop manufacturer didn't document all the technical details of your computer, you might have to browse the manufacturer's Web site or call for the information.

- Type of CPU (386, and so on)
- Amount of system RAM (in megabytes)
- Total size of hard drive (in megabytes)
- Hard drive space needed for the Linux swap partition (twice the size of system memory, or your computer's RAM; see Hour 2, "Installing Linux")
- Size of hard drive you want for OpenLinux (in megabytes, depending on the type of installation; see Hour 2)
- Type of hard drive controller (for example, IDE/SCSI)
- Type of CD-ROM controller (for example, ATAPI)
- Number of serial ports (note: there is no Universal Serial Bus, or USB, support for Linux at the time of this writing)
- Type of keyboard (PS/2, most likely)
- Number of keys (101, 102, 104, and so on)
- Type of mouse (PS/2, serial, and so on)
- Infrared port (COM1–COM4, IRQs used, shared, and so on)
- Serial port assignments (COM1–COM4, IRQs used)
- Type of modem (Fax class support, such as Class 1, 2.0, voice, and so on)
- Parallel port assignment (0x378, IRQ 5, and so on)
- Model and type of printer (Epson, HP, PostScript, HPCL, and so on)
- PC cards used (modem, network, flash memory, and so on)
- Type of PCMCIA controller (TI, for example)
- Type of sound card (SoundBlaster, ESS, and so on)
- I/O address of sound card (such as 0x220)
- DMA values (0, 1, and so on)
- Sound card IRQ (such as 5 or 7)
- Miscellaneous addresses (such as for MPU)

- Type of graphics card (chipset used, such as TGUI9680, Cirrus Logic, ATI Rage II, and so on)
- Amount of video memory (1MB, 2MB, 4MB, and so on)
- Color depth capability (256, 16-bit, 24-bit, and so on)
- Monitor Horizontal Refresh (such as 31.5–60, 31.4, and so on)
- Monitor Vertical Refresh (70–100, for example)
- Monitor Maximum Resolution (800×600, 1024×768, 1280×1024, and so on)

You might not need all this information to install OpenLinux, but sooner or later these details come in handy when you install PC cards, set up sound, or configure X11.

How Do I Plan for the Installation?

Many new OpenLinux users easily install Linux by themselves. If you experience a problem, don't be disappointed, and don't give up! Here are the four basic hurdles to a successful OpenLinux installation:

1. Partitioning the hard drive—This is one of the reasons many people think Linux is hard to install. How many computer users today have partitioned a hard drive or even installed an operating system? Don't be intimidated by this step, which merely makes room for OpenLinux on your hard drive. Just make sure to back up important documents or files before you begin. See Table 1.1 for the size requirements of different installations, and then write down your requirements. Many experienced OpenLinux users don't bother with this step at all and simply install Linux as the sole operating system. Installing Linux is a breeze if you don't have to deal with creating or resizing hard drive partitions.

TABLE 1.1 CALDERA OPENLINUX INSTALLATION REQUIREMENTS

Size in Megabytes	Installation Description
300	Small system (with X11 and KDE) with programs suitable to use your computer as a server
500	Standard system (the default); includes development tools and other programs suitable for a server and workstation
1024	Full installation (everything)

1

2. Configuring the X Window System—X11 is the default graphical interface for OpenLinux—but it is *not* Linux. X runs on many different types of computers and operating systems, which is why there is such a wealth of graphical programs for Linux. You have a better chance of configuring X11 to work with your graphics hardware if you have a graphics card that's been on the market for at least two years. You'll configure X11 during your OpenLinux installation. Details about configuring X can be found under the `/usr/X11R6/lib/X11/doc` directory after OpenLinux is installed.

3. Configuring sound—OpenLinux comes with loadable code modules you can use to get sound working, or you can recompile the Linux kernel to work with your sound card (some details can be found at `http://www.calderasystems.com/support/techguide.html`). If you don't want to hassle with kernel modules or rebuilds, browse to `http://www.4front-tech.com/oss.html`, and download an evaluation copy of the Open Sound System drivers. This inexpensive set of sound drivers supports hundreds of different sound systems. Using OSS is one of the easiest ways to configure sound cards for Linux. See Hour 20, "Relaxation and Playing Linux Games," for tips on configuring OpenLinux for sound.

4. Getting connected—Connecting to the Internet using OpenLinux is an important step. To make the job of connecting to the Internet easier, use the Red Hat `netcfg` tool, the `kppp` client, or the `xisp` client to set up your account. Make sure to read the PPP HOWTO and ISP Hookup HOWTO under the `/usr/doc/HOWTO` directory if you have trouble. Hour 9, "Using Communications Programs," has the details about using a modem with OpenLinux. See Hour 10, "Connecting to the Internet," for information about how to establish a PPP connection.

You next have to decide how to install OpenLinux. I don't cover installing Linux using a network or a Parallel Line (PLIP) interface (for details about these methods, see `http://www.calderasystems.com/support/techguide.html`).

Booting the Install from CD-ROM

The easiest way to install OpenLinux is to insert the OpenLinux CD-ROM in your computer, reboot, and follow the prompts. Booting from a CD-ROM drive might require you to reset your computer's BIOS to change the order of boot disk recognition (usually done by pressing a particular F key (or key sequence) after starting your computer—see your computer's manual for details).

Booting the Install from Floppies

You can create a boot floppy diskette, then insert your OpenLinux CD-ROM, and boot from your floppy to start an installation. The easiest way to create a boot floppy is to install the OpenLinux utilities under Windows (see this chapter's later section "Preparing Your Hard Drive from Windows"). You can then click on the Create Install Diskette icon in the OpenLinux program folder on your Start menu.

You can also use the RAWRITE3.COM program under DOS to create the floppy if you cannot boot the OpenLinux CD-ROM. First, note the drive letter (such as D or E) for your CD-ROM. To create a boot floppy, do the following:

1. Insert the OpenLinux CD-ROM, and then reboot to DOS. At the DOS command line, type the drive letter of your CD-ROM, change the directory to the \col\launch\floppy directory, and start the RAWRITE3 command like this:

   ```
   D:
   CD \COL\LAUNCH\FLOPPY
   RAWRITE3
   ```

2. After the RAWRITE3 program starts, it asks you to enter the source file name. Type **INSTALL.144**, and press Enter.

3. RAWRITE3 then asks you to enter the destination drive (A or B); type the drive letter of your floppy, such as **A**, and press Enter.

4. RAWRITE3 then asks you to install the target diskette in the disk drive. Insert a blank diskette into your drive, and press Enter.

5. RAWRITE3 copies the file INSTALL.144 to your floppy.

6. When you finish, remove and label the diskette.

> If you have a PCMCIA CD-ROM drive or need other specialized support, repeat the preceding steps with a separate floppy, but use MODULES.144 instead of INSTALL.144. This creates a second disk with software you need to help OpenLinux recognize your external CD-ROM or PC cards during the first installation steps.

Label and keep your boot floppies in a safe place. You'll need them (if you don't boot from CD-ROM) in Hour 2.

Other Ways

A number of hardware vendors also offer Linux preinstalled on a new hard drive, laptop, or computer. If you want a computer completely configured out of the box, this is the way to go. Browse to `http://metalab.unc.edu/LDP/HOWTO/VAR-HOWTO.html`.

You can always ask a friend with Linux experience to come over and install OpenLinux for you! This is a great way to share information, and having someone on hand to help can make the installation process easier. Alternatively, go to a Linux User Group (LUG) InstallFest! Browse to `http://www.linux.org/users/index.html` to find a LUG near you. LUGs regularly hold installation meetings, and you can have OpenLinux installed and configured in no time at all!

Planning Your Boot Process

There are many different ways to start Linux. You have to decide whether you want to start Linux from a boot prompt, a command line in DOS, from floppy diskette, or a commercial software program.

1. LILO—The Linux loader (LILO) is a small program used to jumpstart Linux or other operating systems. You can install LILO in the Master Boot Record of a DOS partition or in the root partition of a Linux partition on your hard drive directly after the install process.

Install OpenLinux and LILO after you have installed Windows. With typical disregard, other operating system installs wipe out LILO (although it can be restored by booting with a Linux boot diskette and rerunning the `lilo` command found under the `/sbin` directory.

2. `LOADLIN.EXE`—Use the LOADLIN program from DOS to boot Linux. You do not have to install LILO if you use this program. You need to copy the Linux kernel onto a DOS partition or floppy. Booting from DOS has the advantage of enabling certain hardware (such as an Mwave adapter) to work with OpenLinux.

3. Boot diskette—A boot diskette can also be used to start Linux. You can save LILO on a diskette and then boot Linux, DOS, or other operating systems.

4. Floppy—Want to try Linux from a floppy before installing OpenLinux? Browse to `http://metalab.unc.edu/LDP/devel.html` and search for Linux distributions that fit on a floppy. You can boot to Linux with a single floppy (but you don't get the X Window System).

5. System Commander—This is a commercial program you can use to boot multiple operating systems. Browse to `http://www.systemcommander.com` for details.

6. BootMagic—Included with PowerQuest Corp.'s PartitionMagic, BootMagic can be used to boot multiple operating systems, such as Windows NT and IBM's OS2. The commercial version of PartitionMagic also includes a DOS utility named PQBoot, which lists active, bootable partitions and can be used to boot other operating systems, such as Linux. Browse to `http://www.powerquest.com` for details.

Preparing Your Hard Drive

NEW TERM The first step in the installation process (after making boot floppies, if needed) is to partition, or create room on your hard drive. If you only want to use OpenLinux on your computer, skip the rest of this hour and proceed directly to Hour 2. But if you want to use a *dual-boot* computer, or boot at least two different operating systems, you need to create a partition on your hard drive with enough room for your OpenLinux software.

NEW TERM Partitions are nothing more than a special way to look at a hard drive and how it is divided up. There are two types of partitions: *primary* and *extended*. Your hard drive can contain four primary partitions. If you need to further divide or map your hard drive, you can designate one of these primary partitions as an extended partition (which can then be divided up even more).

NEW TERM These partitions generally contain a *filesystem*. A filesystem is how files or directories are written to the hard drive. DOS and older versions of Windows use a filesystem called FAT16. Newer versions of Windows use FAT32. Linux uses two types of filesystems: ext2 (for storing files) and swap (for temporarily storing memory).

Fortunately, Caldera's OpenLinux CD-ROM contains everything you need to partition your hard drive for OpenLinux! This CD-ROM contains limited editions of PowerQuest's PartitionMagic and Boot Magic. You'll be able to set up your Linux partitions directly from Windows after you install these utilities (read on to learn how).

During the installation process, some laptop and desktop users might find a small partition used by the computer's BIOS for "Save to Disk" operations (such as putting the computer to sleep). This partition is generally the same size as the amount of system memory, or RAM, installed in your computer. Generally speaking, leave this partition alone. Also note that if you increase your computer's RAM, the partition might need to be resized to match the new size of internal memory (which could cause some interesting juggling or resizing of other partitions).

Preparing Your Hard Drive from Windows

The first step to preparing your hard drive to support booting Windows and OpenLinux is to install Caldera's and Power Quest's utilities. Start your computer. When the Windows desktop appears, insert your OpenLinux CD-ROM. The OpenLinux Welcome screen should appear, as shown in Figure 1.1.

FIGURE 1.1

The OpenLinux Welcome dialog box is the starting point for your OpenLinux adventure!

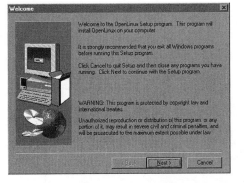

If the install process doesn't begin automatically, double-click your computer's CD-ROM icon under the My Computer folder.

Follow the prompts, and this setup procedure will create an OpenLinux program folder in your Start menu. This folder will contain Shortcuts to creating installation (boot) floppies, installing Boot Magic (to support booting Windows and Linux), and partitioning your hard drive and installing Linux. After the setup finishes, double-click the Partition and Install Linux icon (as shown in Figure 1.2).

FIGURE 1.2

Double-click the Partition and Install Linux program to begin your installation.

This will start the PartitionMagic Caldera Edition setup program, as shown in Figure 1.3. Follow the prompts, and the setup will create a PowerQuest program folder on your hard drive. A PartitionMagic program folder for your Start menu will also be created.

FIGURE 1.3

To start your installation, you must first install the PartitionMagic Caldera Edition program.

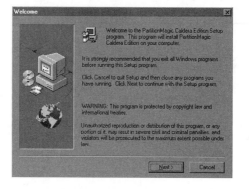

After the installation, the setup program will then ask you to click a Finish button. This will shut down Windows and run PartitionMagic. You'll be asked, as shown in Figure 1.4, to remove your OpenLinux CD-ROM before continuing. This is because you must first create your Linux partitions before you install Linux. (Your computer could reboot directly to installing OpenLinux if the CD-ROM is still inserted.)

FIGURE 1.4

Don't forget to remove your CD-ROM before continuing your installation!

If you already have a Linux installation and use LILO, your computer will reboot to LILO at this point. To continue the installation, boot to Windows from LILO. However, the installation procedure will not recognize your existing Linux partitions. After you install OpenLinux, you'll find a Delete Linux icon in the PartitionMagic program folder you can use to delete Linux partitions. The best way to install OpenLinux on an existing Linux setup is to reboot and install OpenLinux using the installation floppies or directly from CD-ROM. See Hour 2, "Installing Linux," for details.

PartitionMagic Caldera Edition will only recognize your first hard drive and will only create three different sized partitions: 300 megabytes, 500 megabytes, and one gigabyte. When its dialog box appears, click the desired Linux partition size, and click the OK button. You then see PartitionMagic's dialog box, which shows the partitioning progress. After the partitioning is complete, insert your OpenLinux boot floppy diskette and/or your OpenLinux CD-ROM, and reboot your computer to start the installation.

If you want to use more hard drive space than the maximum one gigabyte afforded by the limited edition of PartitionMagic, boot directly to the OpenLinux installation with a boot floppy and/or the OpenLinux CD-ROM. During the initial installation, choose the Custom partitioning scheme. Note, however, that you must have an available existing or empty partition; this partition will be formatted for Linux.

Summary

This hour introduced you to some basic concepts about Linux, OpenLinux, and how to prepare for a Linux installation.

Q&A

Q I'm confused! What's the best way to install OpenLinux?

A Although it all depends on your computer's hardware and how you plan to use
OpenLinux, the simplest, most direct way to install OpenLinux is to boot with the
OpenLinux CD-ROM from the back of this book. You can overwrite any existing
data and install OpenLinux as the primary operating system.

Q I want to use NT and OpenLinux! What do I do?

A Install NT first. But when installing OpenLinux, install LILO in the Linux root
partition (see Hour 2).

**Q I have the commercial version PartitionMagic. Can I use this program instead
of the Caldera Edition?**

A Yes. You'll have a bit more flexibility, as PartitionMagic can create any size partition from your existing hard drive space. Caldera included a special edition of
PartitionMagic to make the job of making room on your hard drive a bit easier, but
the commercial version of PartitionMagic offers many, many additional features.

**Q I have 32 megabytes of RAM. How large of a swap space should I plan for?
What's the largest swap space I can use?**

A If you have 32 megabytes of RAM, plan on creating a 64-megabyte swap partition.
In general, create a swap partition at least twice the amount of your computer's
RAM (or larger if you plan to run memory-intensive programs, such as graphics
editors).

Exercises

1. Create your OpenLinux installation boot floppies. Make sure to label them correctly.

2. Install OpenLinux and PowerQuest's Caldera Systems Edition PartitionMagic.
Note which program folders are used for OpenLinux and PartitionMagic in your
Start menu.

3. Sit down and calculate the amount of hard drive space you want to use with
OpenLinux. Don't forget to include the swap space required!

Hour **2**

Installing Linux

This hour shows you how to install OpenLinux. At this point, you should know how much hard drive space you want to devote to OpenLinux. You should also have filled out the checklist presented in Hour 1, "Preparing to Install Linux," and have this information on hand during and after the installation process. You also need the OpenLinux boot disks if your computer cannot boot from a CD-ROM drive. Take your time during the installation, and don't proceed until you're sure of the information presented in the installation dialog boxes.

If you've installed OpenLinux or other Linux distributions, be prepared for a pleasant surprise! The latest version of Caldera OpenLinux offers the fastest and easiest Linux installation ever! The folks at Caldera have made the chore of installing Linux a pleasant task with features such as the following:

- A complete graphical interface to the install process
- Point-and-click hard drive partitioning for experts
- Background installation of packages from CD-ROM while continuing the system configuration process

- Automatic detection of graphics cards for configuring the X Window System
- A pleasant diversion while the installation continues

> You have backed up any important documents or files, right? Don't proceed to install OpenLinux unless you're absolutely sure you won't lose any important data. If you're installing OpenLinux on a brand new desktop or notebook computer, make sure you have a restore CD-ROM or have followed the manufacturer's recommendations on backing up critical device drivers. Granted, you might be able to get most of the important files from the manufacturer's Web site, but unfortunately, many computer manufacturers don't provide a restore CD-ROM and still require end users to back up included software to diskette. You have been warned!

Beginning the Installation

Experienced installers might have skipped the installation instructions in Hour 1. If so, the first step is to set your computer to boot from its CD-ROM drive. This might require you to restart your computer and then press and hold down a function key during the restart to enter your computer's BIOS manager. Set your computer's BIOS to change the order of the recognized boot device so the CD-ROM drive is recognized first. You probably have to then save these changes and restart your computer. Then, do the following:

1. Insert the OpenLinux CD-ROM in your computer, and reboot.
2. If you followed the directions in Hour One and inserted your CD-ROM, when your computer restarts, you see Caldera's splash screen.
3. OpenLinux starts booting. You see various lines of technical information flash by on the screen as OpenLinux determines the various components installed on your computer (such as the hard drive, floppy, serial ports, keyboard, or CD-ROM) and attempts to load various software components.
4. At the dialog box Shown in Figure 2.1, click to select the type of mouse installed on your system. Test your mouse buttons by moving your cursor to the labeled test area and then clicking the left, right, or middle mouse buttons. When you finish, click the Next button.

FIGURE 2.1

OpenLinux should automatically detect your mouse, but you can use the Set Up Mouse dialog to test your mouse buttons.

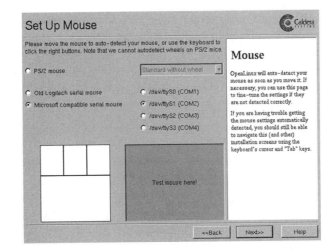

5. You're asked to select where Linux should be installed. If you partitioned your hard drive with Partition Magic, OpenLinux automatically highlights the Prepared Partitions button—click Next to continue. (Partition Magic will have automatically created a large, single Linux partition and a smaller Linux swap partition for the installation process.)

> The Caldera Edition of Partition Magic implements a simple partitioning scheme using a single Linux native and a single swap partition. This is the easiest and fastest way to install OpenLinux, but it might not suit the needs of more advanced users. For a quick digression on partitioning, read Eric S. Raymond's Installation HOWTO (under the /usr/doc/HOWTO directory), especially Section 6.4, "Creating partitions for Linux."

If you'd rather use the entire hard drive, click Entire Hard disk to format and install Linux.

> If you select Entire Hard disk, OpenLinux formats your entire drive. Make sure this is what you want to do! Always back up important information before installing Linux (or any other operating system)!

If you want to create several Linux partitions from an existing spare partition, click Custom (Expert only!), and click the Next button. You see a dialog box you can use to split up an existing partition to create different partitions for different parts of your OpenLinux installation (many experienced Linux users create separate partitions for programs, users, or temporary storage). Use the Custom (Expert only!) dialog box to create Linux partitions from existing Linux, Windows, or DOS hard drive partitions. By using the Edit button in the Expert mode, you can change the size of a partition and designate mounting points for Linux partitions. When you finish with the Expert mode, click the Write button to save your changes, and then click the Next button to continue.

6. OpenLinux now displays the Linux partition information, as shown in Figure 2.2. You should see at least one Root Partition (with a "/" Mount Point) and a Virtual Memory (or swap) partition. If you're satisfied, click the Format Chosen Partitions button to continue.

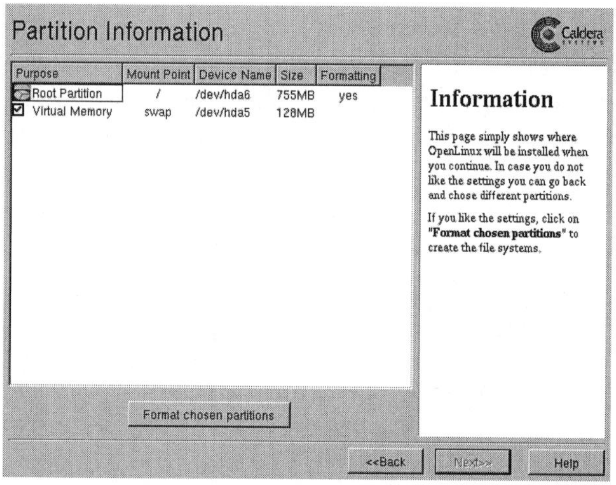

FIGURE 2.2

Format your Linux partitions prior to installing OpenLinux

7. OpenLinux now formats your new Linux partitions. When the formatting is finished, the Next button becomes active. Click Next to continue.

8. You're now asked to select an installation. There are four choices: a minimum set (about 300 megabytes for a server installation with the X Window System); all recommended packages (about 500 megabytes for a server and workstation installation with the X Window System and development packages); all recommended plus commercial packages; and all packages (about one gigabyte for a complete installation of all the software included on your CD-ROM). Click the desired package to install, and then click the Next button to continue.

OpenLinux doesn't enable you to try to choose an installation larger than the available space on your Linux partition. You have to choose a smaller installation. If you have the hard drive space, you can back through the installation dialog boxes by pressing the Back button to create a larger Linux partition or create additional Linux partitions later.

2

9. OpenLinux now shows a dialog box and asks you to select a keyboard model and layout. Scroll through the list of keyboards, and click your model. Next, select a keyboard layout (such as U.S. English). To test the selected keyboard, click in the Test here field and type some text. When you finish, click the Next button to continue. Also, note that the package installation continues copying files to your Linux partition while you continue the configuration process!

10. OpenLinux now asks you to select your video card, as shown in Figure 2.3. This is a critical step in the installation process and ensures that you'll be able to run the X Window System at the best possible resolution with your computer's video card and monitor. Look at the Card Type field to see if your computer's video card is correctly listed. Next, click the amount of video RAM installed on your video card (such as 2MB). Even if your video card is correctly listed, click the Probe button to get more accurate information. This runs the XF86_SVGA X11 server to probe your graphics card for setup information.

FIGURE 2.3

OpenLinux should automatically detect your video card, but you can click the Probe button to get a more specific setting.

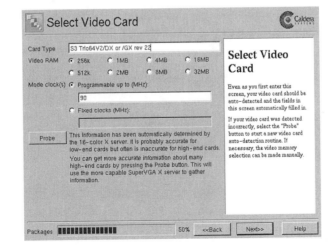

11. After you click the Probe button, a dialog box appears, asking you to confirm the probe. Click the Probe button to continue or the Abort button to cancel the probe.

12. Your screen blanks and a dialog box with an OK button appears if the probe is successful. Click OK to close the dialog box, and then click Next to continue configuring the X Window System.

13. You now see a Select Monitor dialog box with a list of monitors and horizontal and vertical sync ranges, as shown in Figure 2.4. Scroll through the list of monitors, and click the model used with your system. If you do not see your monitor listed, enter your monitor's name and sync ranges below the scrolling list. Click the Monitor name field, and then type a name. Enter the low and high horizontal sync ranges by clicking on the up and down arrows, and then do the same for the low and high vertical sync ranges. When you finish, click the Next button.

FIGURE 2.4

Scroll through the list of monitors and either pick a specific monitor, or type in details about your computer's monitor.

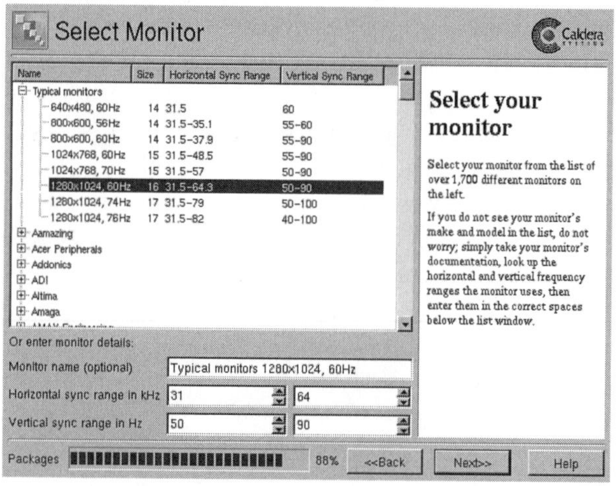

Make sure to enter correct sync values for your monitor! You can possibly damage your display with incorrect settings! You have been warned!

14. The next dialog box asks for your preferred video mode, as shown in Figure 2.5. Click a desired resolution, such as 800×600, which represents the number of pixels available across and down your display. Don't choose a resolution outside of your monitor's capabilities! Next, click a desired display depth from the list in the upper-right corner of your screen. When finished, click the Test This Mode button to test your settings.

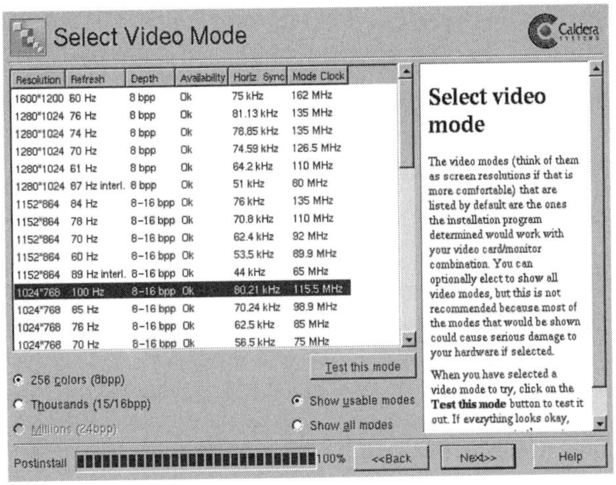

FIGURE 2.5

The Select Video Mode dialog is used to pick the best resolution and color depth for your monitor and graphics card.

15. A confirm dialog box appears. Click OK to continue. The screen clears, and a representative X11 display appears for about 10 seconds, as shown in Figure 2.6. When the installation dialog box reappears, click the Next button to continue.

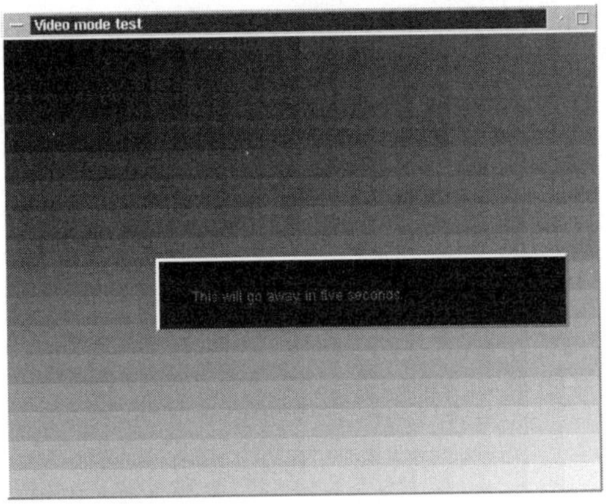

FIGURE 2.6

During your X11 configuration, OpenLinux lets you test your graphics card and monitor to make sure your settings are correct.

16. OpenLinux now asks you to set the root password. This is the password for the system administrator—you! Type in a password, then press Enter, and type it in again. Don't forget this password! You need this password to perform important configuration tasks during your OpenLinux sessions. When you finish, click the Next button.

Good passwords have a minimum of eight characters and contain a mix of
letters and numbers.

17. The next dialog box asks you to add at least one new user to your OpenLinux system, as shown in Figure 2.7. Start by clicking the Real Name field, and enter your
name. Press Enter, and then type in a Login name. Press Enter, and then type in a
password. Press Enter, and then again enter the password. Next, click bash, tcsh,
or zsh to select a Login Shell. When you finish, click the Add User button. To
continue, click the Next button.

FIGURE 2.7

*The Set Login Name(s)
dialog is used to cre-
ate new users during
your OpenLinux
installation. (Other
users may be added
or deleted after
installation.*

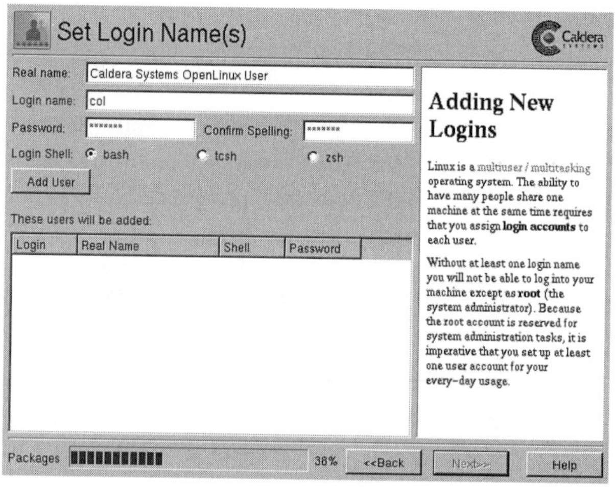

Login names are generally the first letter of a person's name, followed by
the last name. For example, Julie Lewis would have a login name of jlewis,
and Jeff Goldfarb would have a login name of jgoldfarb.

18. You can now set up networking in the dialog shown in Figure 2.8. If your computer is attached to a network and you have a network card installed, enter the IP
Address (such as 192.168.1.2), Hostname (such as wishbone.erols.com),
Netmask, and Gateway of your network. If your network has a Domain Name
server, enter its IP address. If you don't have a network card, click the Next button
to continue.

FIGURE 2.8

If you have a network card installed, use the Set Up Networking dialog to enter networking information, such as the Internet Protocol, or IP, address number of your computer.

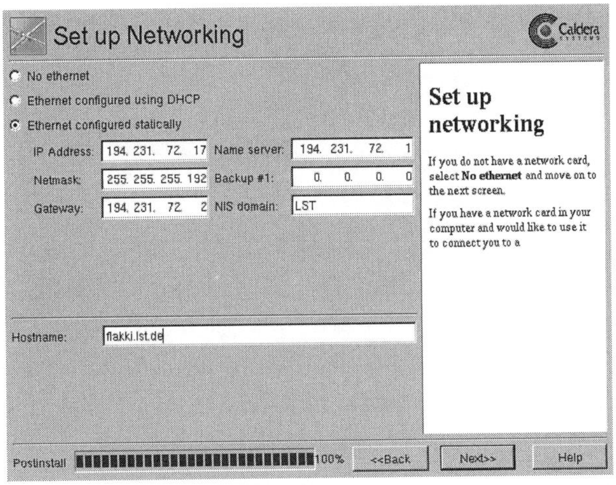

If you skip this, you can always add and configure a networking card later. See Hour 3, "Post-Installation Issues," for details.

19. To make sure OpenLinux keeps accurate track of time, you're now asked to select your time zone. Scroll through the list of zones, and then click your time zone. If your computer's hardware clock is set to local time, click the Hardware Clock Runs in Local Time item, and then click Next to continue.

20. Now relax! It's time to play a familiar game of falling blocks while OpenLinux continues to copy files to your hard drive. Click New Game to start the action. Use your cursor keys to rotate, shift, or drop the blocks into place. While you play, the progress bar along the bottom of the screen helps you monitor the installation. When the install finishes, click the Finish button.

Finishing Your Linux Installation

Congratulations! Hang in there because you're almost finished installing OpenLinux! After you click Finish, OpenLinux reboots your computer to the K Desktop Environment's K display manager login screen (as shown in Figure 2.9).

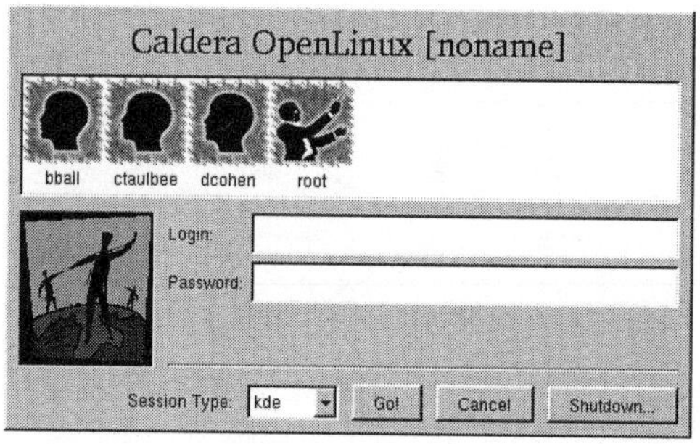

FIGURE 2.9

Your first peek at OpenLinux is at the K display manager, where you must log in to Linux.

Caldera OpenLinux [noname]

bball   ctaulbee   dcohen   root

Login:

Password:

Session Type: [kde ▾]   [Go!]   [Cancel]   [Shutdown...]

Although you can log in now if you want to, there's still an important step left in the installation! If you want to boot to Linux, you must first shut down, restart, and then install BootMagic from Windows.

Experienced Linux users might want to use LILO, but should know that at this point, unlike previous OpenLinux installs, LILO has been installed, and the default /etc/lilo.conf configuration file is configured to start LILO from the root Linux partition. This might not be what you want, but it is the proper configuration to support commercial boot loaders such as System Commander or the included version of Boot Magic. Although experienced LILO users might either use a boot floppy or install LILO in the Master Boot Record of the DOS partition, the MBR is needed by Boot Magic. At this point you have to decide if you want to use BootMagic or LILO. If you decide to use LILO, log in to OpenLinux as root, then edit /etc/lilo.conf to point to the MBR, and insert an entry to support booting DOS. (One is not included by default, and you might have noticed that the installation process does not offer you the opportunity to configure LILO.) If you decide to not use LILO by itself, BootMagic then uses LILO (installed on your Linux partition) to boot OpenLinux. For more information, see the file README under the /usr/doc/lilo directory.

Click the Shutdown button, then select Shutdown, and restart to reboot to Windows. When the Windows desktop appears, click the Post Install Boot Magic menu item from the OpenLinux folder on the Start menu. Make sure your OpenLinux CD-ROM is inserted in your computer. The BootMagic setup window appears, as shown in Figure 2.10.

FIGURE 2.10

To enable booting DOS, Windows, or Linux, you must install a boot loader, such as BootMagic.

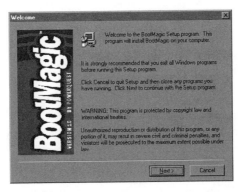

Follow the prompts to install BootMagic, entering your name and acknowledging the licensing agreements. When prompted to create a BootMagic boot diskette, insert a blank floppy in your computer, and follow the prompts. This is an important safety step that enables you to recover and boot your computer in case your drive's MBR becomes corrupted.

You can also make a BootMagic boot diskette later by clicking the Create BootMagic diskette icon in the BootMagic program folder on your Start menu.

BootMagic then installs on your computer, placing a boot loader in the MBR of your hard drive. After the installation finishes, you see the BootMagic Configuration window on your desktop, as shown in the Figure 2.11.

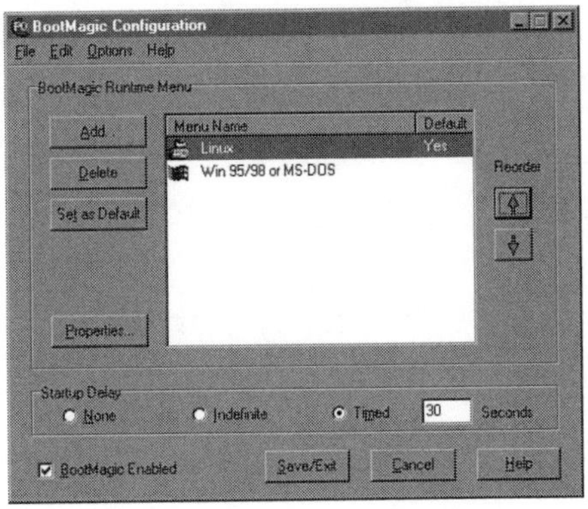

FIGURE 2.11

The BootMagic Configuration window is used to set the default operating system, reorder your booting list, or set startup delays.

BootMagic recognizes that you have created and installed a Linux partition on your hard drive. Click the Linux menu name, and then click the Reorder button to move Linux up in the list (where it rightfully belongs). Next, click the Set as Default button to make Linux the default operating system to boot.

BootMagic's Startup Delay buttons and Timed delay field enable you to boot immediately, wait for a mouse click on an operating system name, or set a delay from 1 to 99 seconds before booting. Make sure the BootMagic Enabled checkbox is checked. When you finish configuring BootMagic, click the Save/Exit button to save your changes.

To boot to Linux and log in, restart your computer. BootMagic then loads and displays its boot menu, listing Linux and then Windows. Booting starts according to the delay you set in its configuration window. You then see Caldera's customized LILO message screen (from the file message under the /boot directory), as shown in Figure 2.12.

FIGURE 2.12

BootMagic uses LILO to boot Linux.

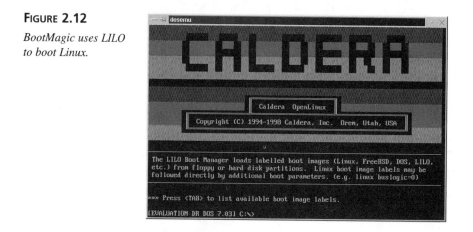

Type **linux** at the boot prompt to start your OpenLinux session. If you do nothing, OpenLinux boots after 50 seconds.

The boot delay can be changed by editing the file /etc/lilo.conf and rerunning the lilo command.

Logging in to Linux

After OpenLinux boots, you again see the kdm client's login screen. At the login prompt, type **root**, and then press Enter. Then, enter the password you used during the install process.

The screen clears, and you start your first OpenLinux session using the X Window System with the K Desktop Manager (discussed in Hour 8, "Exploring the K Desktop Environment"), as shown in Figure 2.13.

FIGURE 2.13

The first view of an OpenLinux X11 KDE session.

The main window on the desktop is the KDE configuration manager, which offers a one-time time configuration of KDE *themes*, or how you want KDE's windows, buttons, and colors to appear. Click the Next button to continue to the themes setup, and you see a selection of themes, as shown in Figure 2.14.

Click a theme icon (such as KDE, MacOS, Windows, or BeOS), and KDE automatically sets the theme for your KDE sessions. Then, click on the Next button to proceed to the next screen, as shown in Figure 2.15.

FIGURE 2.14

Select a window theme from KDE's configuration menu by clicking on a theme icon.

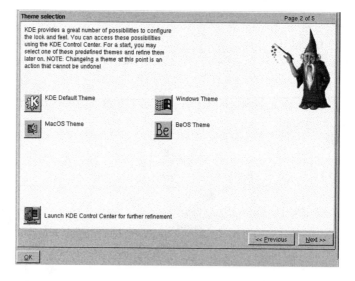

FIGURE 2.15

KDE's setup automatically creates convenient floppy and CD-ROM icons on your desktop.

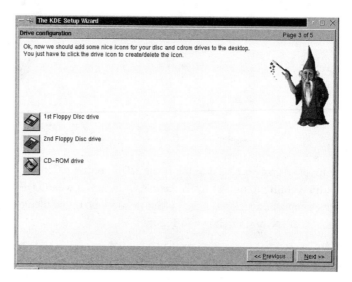

Click on each desired icon, and KDE puts each on your root desktop. These icons provide an easy way to view the contents of a floppy disk or can be used as drag-and-drop icons for copying. For example, if you have a floppy inserted in your computer, you can later drop a file onto the floppy icon to copy the file to diskette.

When you finish, click the Next button. The next screen asks if you want a printer icon.
When you finish, click the Next button again to configure convenient hypertext links for
your desktop (as shown in Figure 2.16).

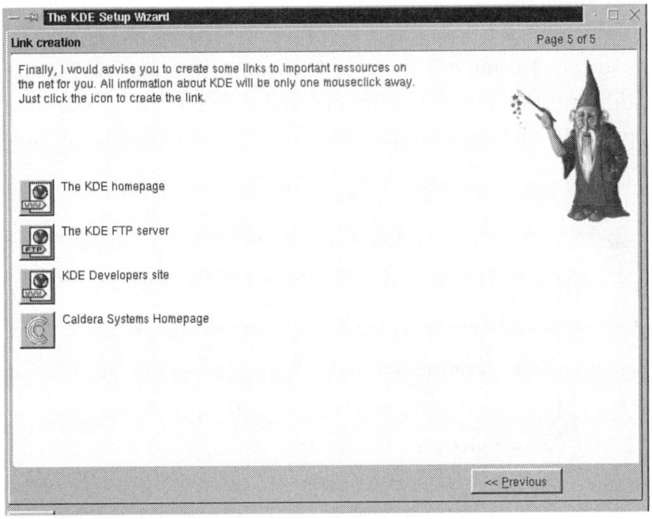

FIGURE 2.16

*KDE creates Internet
and hypertext links on
your desktop during
setup.*

After you finish, click the OK button. Your screen appears as shown in Figure 2.17
(depending on the theme you chose during setup).

FIGURE 2.17

*A KDE-themed KDE
desktop after configu-
ration.*

Rebooting and Shutting Down

At this point, you can exit your first KDE session by clicking the small icon above the padlock on the KDE panel (as shown in Figure 2.17) or by clicking the Application Starter button (the large "K") and clicking the logout menu item. KDE asks you to confirm the logout. Click the logout button; the screen clears, and you again see the kdm login screen. To shut down and restart your computer, click the Shutdown button, select Shutdown or Shutdown and Restart, and then click OK. Your computer shuts down or reboots to BootMagic.

Linux also offers a way to shut down or reboot from the command line of a terminal. After typing **su** and pressing enter to switch to superviser mode, use the `shutdown` command, along with its `-r` (reboot) option, followed by the word now, like this:

```
# shutdown -r now
```

Alternatively, you can use the number **0**, like this:

```
# shutdown -r 0
```

This reboots your computer. Use the `shutdown` command along with its `-h` (halt) option, followed by the word now, like this:

```
# shutdown -h now
```

Alternatively, you can use the number **0**, like this:

```
# shutdown -h 0
```

This shuts down OpenLinux. When you see the message "System is halted." you can turn off your computer.

Summary

This hour detailed a step-by-step simple OpenLinux installation session. Installing OpenLinux is a major hurdle in using Linux but is usually an easy accomplishment. Although some computer users might be disconcerted by having to partition a hard drive to install a dual-boot computer, most find the process relatively painless. Welcome to Linux!

Q&A

Q **I screwed up my LILO installation! My system won't boot to OpenLinux!**

A This is probably an error in the /etc/lilo.conf file. Use the OpenLinux boot diskette to reboot your computer. At the command line, type **linux root=/dev/*your_hard_drive*** (such as /dev/hda1). See the BootPrompt-HOWTO under the /usr/doc/HOWTO directory.

Q **What are some good documents to read about installing OpenLinux?**

A Although you can find many different documents installed under the /usr/doc/HOWTO or /usr/doc/HOWTO/mini directories, such as Linux+Win95, Loadlin+Win95, or the Linux Installation Guide, you should first read the technical documents, FAQs, and errata at http://support.calderasystems.com/caldera or http://www.calderasystems.com/support/techguide.html.

Exercises

1. Try rebooting your computer. Press the Tab key at the LILO boot prompt. What happens?

2. At the LILO boot prompt, type **vga=ask**, and press Enter. What happens?

3. After pressing Enter in the previous exercise and starting the boot process to OpenLinux, what happens next?

HOUR **3**

Post-Installation Issues

This hour shows you how to configure OpenLinux to work with various hardware and software components. You'll learn how to disable or bypass X11 and the kdm graphical login, change the default color depth of your X11 server, configure OpenLinux to use your sound card, set and configure an Ethernet network interface, enable PCMCIA card service, and use a Zip drive.

If you've partitioned your hard drive, installed OpenLinux, and have successfully logged in and out of Linux, congratulations! Most of the hard work is done. This hour might help you finish your installation by showing you how to configure different computer hardware to work with OpenLinux.

All the configuration tasks described in this hour require you to be logged in as the root operator. Make sure you proceed slowly, and always make a backup copy of important files before editing the original!

The X Window System

The X Window System is the default graphical interface for Linux—but it is *not* OpenLinux. Originally developed by a consortium of computer companies and the Massachusetts Institute of Technology (MIT) , The X Window System, known as X11 or X, is a network windowing system that runs along with Linux to provide graphics services . The main task in configuring X11 is to choose the correct X11 server (included on your OpenLinux CD-ROM) and then to properly configure this server to work with your computer's graphics card.

Configuring X11 is one of the major hurdles new OpenLinux users face when installing OpenLinux. X11 runs on many different types of computers and works with many different types of graphics cards. You have a much better chance of configuring X11 to work with your graphics hardware if you have a graphics card that's been around in the market for at least two years. Having the latest and greatest graphics card lessens your chances of being able to use X—although you can still use Linux.

The version of X11 included on your OpenLinux CD-ROM comes from The Xfree86 Project, Inc. , a group of programmers from around the world who have worked very hard to provide a free graphical interface for Linux (and other operating systems , such as BSD). These folks deserve a big vote of thanks. To read more about The XFree86 Project, browse to http://www.xfree86.org.

How the X Window System is Configured

This section introduces you to X11's configuration file for OpenLinux: the XF86Config file, found under the /etc directory. During your OpenLinux installation, X11 used a graphical interface by starting an X11 server named XF86_VGA16 . Hopefully, your OpenLinux desktop now takes the best advantage of your computer's monitor and graphics card with a properly selected X server and configuration file. However, if you need to reconfigure X11 because you install a new graphics card or if X11 isn't working to your satisfaction, you can reconfigure X11.

The `xf86config` command configures X11 through a text-based interface . Before you begin, take some time to read documentation under the `/usr/X11R6/lib/X11/doc` directory. This directory, summarized in Table 3.1, contains numerous documents with information about accelerated video graphics , different video monitors , various graphics chipsets , different video modes , and several helpful text files filled with tips on configuring X11.

TABLE 3.1 XFREE86 DOCUMENTATION

File	Description
AccelCards	List of tested accelerated graphics cards
BUILD	How to compile the XFree86 X distribution from source
COPYRIGHT	Copyright statement
Devices	Old file of contributed XF86Config Device sections
Monitors	Old file of contributed XF86Config Monitor sections
QuickStart.doc	Quick-start guide to setting up XFree86
README	General information about the current XFree86 release
README.Config	Detailed, step-by-step guide to configuring XFree86
README.DECtga	Information for DEC 21030 users
README.DGA	How to program for the XFree86 DGA interface
README.LinkKit	Specific information on how to build XFree86 from scratch
README.Linux	Good information for Linux users about installing and using XFree86
README.MGA	Information about the Matrox Millennium & Mystique video cards
README.Mach32	Information about the Mach32 XFree86 X server
README.Mach64	Release notes about the Mach64 XFree86 X server
README.NVIDIA	Notes for NVidia NV1, SGS-Thomson STG2000, and RIVA 128 video cards
README.Oak	Notes for Oak Technologies Inc. chipset users
README.P9000	Release notes for the P9000 XFree86 X server
README.S3	Notes for S3 chipset users
README.S3V	Notes for S3 ViRGE, ViRGE/DX, ViRGE/GX, ViRGE/MX, and ViRGE/VX users
README.SiS	Notes for Sis chipset users
README.Video7	Readme file about Video7 drivers

continues

TABLE 3.1 CONTINUED

File	Description
README.W32	Notes for W32 and ET6000 chipset users
README.WstDig	Notes for Western Digital chipset users
README.agx	Information about the AGX XFree86 X server
README.apm	Notes about the Alliance Promotion chipset
README.ark	Notes for ARK Logic chipset users
README.ati	Information about XFree86's ATI Adapters video drivers
README.chips	Notes about Chips and Technologies chipsets
README.cirrus	Information about XFree86 support for Cirrus Logic chipset
README.clkprog	Programming info about external video clock setting programs
README.cyrix	Information about Cyrix chipsets
README.epson	Information about EPSON SPC8110 (laptop) chipsets
README.mouse	Details about XFree86's X11 mouse support
README.neo	Information about NeoMagic (laptop) chipsets
README.rendition	Information about the Rendition chipset
README.trident	Notes for Trident chipset users
README.tseng	Notes for Tseng chipset users
RELNOTES	Definitive release notes for XFree86
ServersOnly	How your directories should look when building XFree86 X servers
VGADriver.Doc	HOWTO on adding an SVGA or VGA drive to XFree86
VideoModes.doc	Eric S. Raymond's comprehensive treatise on building `XF86Config` modelines
xinput	General info on input device (such as joystick) support in XFree86

Before you use the `xf86config` command to reconfigure X11, log in as the root operator, and make a backup copy first, like so:

```
# cp /etc/XF86Config /etc/XF86Config.org
```

You can then start the command by typing it on the command line of a terminal window like this:

```
# xf86config
```

After you press Enter, follow the prompts to configure your graphics card and monitor for X11. The xf86config command generates a new XF86Config file in the /etc directory.

The XF86Config File

The XF86Config file is used to properly feed font, keyboard, mouse, video chipset, monitor capabilities, and color depth setting information to your selected X11 display server. XF86Config is a single text file that consists of several sections that are summarized in Table 3.2.

You can page through your system's XF86Config file by using the less command (discussed in Hour 4, "Reading and Navigation Commands"). At the command line of a terminal, use less, followed by the path to XF86Config, like this:

 # less /etc/XF86Config

You can then use the cursor keys to browse through the file. Press the Q key when you finish reading.

TABLE 3.2 MAJOR SECTIONS OF THE *XF86Config* FILE

Section	Purpose
Files	Tells the X server where colors, fonts, or specific software modules are located
Module	Tells the X server what special modules should be loaded
ServerFlags	Contains on/off flags to enable or deny special actions, such as core dumps , keyboard server shutdown , video-mode switching , video tuning , and mouse and keyboard configuration
Keyboard	Tells the X server what keyboard to expect and what settings to use
Pointer	Tells the X server what pointer to use and how buttons are handled
Xinput	Special section for devices, such as graphics pads , styli, and so on
Monitor	Specifies details and settings for your monitor , such as name, horizontal sync ranges , vertical sync ranges , and modelines (one for each video resolution , such as 640×480, 800×600, 1024×768, and so on)
Device	Provides details about your video chipset , such as RAM , clockchips , and so on
Screen	Specifies what X server to use, the color depth (such as 8-, 16-, 24-, or 32-bits per pixel), screen size (such as 640×480, 800×600, 1024×768, and so on), and the size of the virtual screen

Do not use an XF86Config from someone who does not have the same graphics card and monitor as you! Incorrect settings can damage your monitor. Do not use monitor settings outside you monitor's specifications . You have been warned! The *only* exception to this rule might be for PC notebook users with *exactly* the same components.

Before you try to start an X11 session using your new XF86Config settings , as the root operator , open the file in your favorite text editor , disable line wrapping , and check the settings. It is essential, especially for laptop users , to do this to check the created settings, enable or disable some X server options , enter the correct amount of video memory , and fine-tune monitor settings.

The XF86Config Files Section

The Files section tells the X server the location of the color name database and system fonts .

The XF86Config ServerFlags Section

Several parts of this section can be used to configure special actions enabled by your XFree86 X server . Enable a particular action by removing the pound sign (#) in front of the specific flag. Most users do not disable the DontZap feature because it provides a quick way to exit an X session . The DontZoom feature can be disabled if you use X in only one video resolution , such as 800×600 pixels.

The XF86Config Keyboard Section

The Keyboard section tells the X server what type of keyboard to expect and settings to use, such as language type , key character layout , and manufacturer.

The XF86Config Pointer Section

The Pointer section tells the X server what pointer, or mouse, to use and how the buttons are handled. Some Protocol settings are Auto for a serial mouse and BusMouse for a bus mouse. The Device entry, /dev/mouse, is a symbolic link to the actual device (such as /dev/ttys0 for a serial mouse).

Two-button mouse users definitely want to enable the three-button emulator , in which simultaneously depressing both buttons simulates pressing the middle button, or button 2. One common use of button 2 is to paste text or graphics. For more information about configuring a mouse, see the file README.mouse under the /usr/X11R6/lib/X11/doc directory.

The `XF86Config` Monitor Section

Although the first several parts of the XF86Config file are easy to understand , if you're an XFree86 user whose initial XF86Config file does not work, pay specific attention to the Monitor section, the Device section, and the Screen section. The Monitor section contains specific details and settings for your monitor, such as your monitor's name, its horizontal and vertical sync ranges, and critical modelines (one for each video resolution, such as 640×480, 800×600, 1024×768, and so on). Understanding the modeline is the key to fine-tuning your X11 display.

For the best details, see the files VideoModes.doc and README.Config under the /usr/X11R6/lib/X11/doc directory before fine-tuning modeline s in your XF86Config file. Another good tutorial is the XFree86-Video-Timings-HOWTO under the /usr/doc/HOWTO directory.

3

The basic parts of a modeline are 10 different values representing the following (from left to right):

- A label of the screen resolution , such as 800×600
- A video frequency in MHz
- The number of visible dots per line on your display
- The Start Horizontal Retrace value (number of pulses before video sync pulse starts)
- The End Horizontal Retrace value (end of sync pulse)
- The total number of visible and invisible dots on your display
- The Vertical Display End value , or number of visible lines of dots on your display
- The Start Vertical Retrace value (number of lines before the sync pulse starts)
- The End Vertical Retrace value (number of lines at the end of the sync pulse)
- The Vertical Total value , or total number of visible and invisible lines on your display

The `XF86Config` Device Section

The Device section contains details about your video chipset , such as RAM , clockchips , and so on. Note that even though you tell xf86config or XF86Setup that you have two megabytes of video RAM , these values are commented out with a pound sign (#). To properly configure for X, you need to remove the pound sign in front of the VideoRam setting in this part of the XF86Config file.

This section of your XF86Config file is critical. The device definition is used to tell the X server exactly what type of video chipset and options to support. For a list of device identifiers and options , see the README file under the /usr/X11R6/lib/X11/doc directory corresponding with your chipset.

The XF86Config Screen Section

The Screen section tells what X server to use , the color depth (such as 8-, 16-, 24- or 32-bits per pixel), screen size (such as 640×480, 800×600, or 1024×768, and so on), and the size of the virtual screen .

This section contains directions for your chosen X server (the XF86_SVGA or other color server , the 4-bit, or 16-color XF86_VGA16 server , or the monochrome server , XF86_Mono) on what resolutions and virtual screen size to support.

For example, if you're using the 8-bit, or 256-color, mode of the XF86_SVGA server , you might have the choice of a 640×480 display (with an 800×600 virtual screen) or an 800×600 display. Resolutions can be toggled during your X session by holding down the **Ctrl+Alt** keys and depressing the plus (**+**) or minus (**-**) keys on your keypad. Laptop users need to use the NumLock key before switching resolutions.

Bypassing or Disabling the kdm Login Display

The default OpenLinux configuration uses X11 and the kdm client to provide a log-in screen. However, you can bypass this screen and go directly to a log-in prompt for a text-only console (without X11) by pressing Ctrl+Alt+F2. You then see a log-in prompt. To return to the kdm login, press Alt+F1.

Alt+F1 or Alt+F2 are known as *virtual consoles*. This means that with Linux, you can have up to six different logins from the keyboard of the same computer at the same time. See Hour 7, "Using the X Window System," for details about using virtual consoles and X11.

If you don't want Linux to start X11 or use the kdm graphical login display, you can configure OpenLinux not to use kdm after booting. First, log in as the root operator, and make a copy of the file inittab under the /etc directory with the cp command like this:

```
# cp /etc/inittab /etc/inittab.org
```

Next, use a favorite text editor (discussed in Hour 14, "Text Processing"), open the file, and look for the following line:

```
id:5:initdefault
```

Change the number 5 (which is the X11 runlevel) in the line to a 3 (which is the multi-user runlevel without X), like this:

```
id:3:initdefault
```

Save the file, then reboot your computer. After Linux reboots, wait until OpenLinux has reported the booting progress, and then press Alt+F2. You see a log-in prompt.

However, a much safer way to not use X11 is to tell OpenLinux to boot directly to multi-user mode at the LILO boot prompt, like this:

```
linux 3
```

After you press Enter, OpenLinux boots without using X11 or kdm.

Starting an X11 Session

If you've configured OpenLinux not to use X11, you can start an X11 session by typing **startx** at the command line after you log in. To start an X session using the K Desktop Environment , type **kde** at the command line. To start an X session using more than 256 colors, use **startx** or **kde** , as in the following two examples (you can also try substituting 24 or 32):

```
# startx -- -bpp 16
```

```
# kde -- -bpp 16
```

You can also change the default color depth used when you boot OpenLinux and start X11. Open your system's XF86Config file, and look in the Screen section for the following line:

```
DefaultColorDepth 16
```

This entry tells the default X server to use thousands of colors for the display. If you know your computer can use millions of colors (from testing during your OpenLinux install), change the setting to the following:

```
DefaultColorDepth 32
```

Save the file, and restart X11 from the command line or through the kdm Shutdown button.

Your graphics card and monitor must be capable of supporting more than 256 colors to use greater color depths, such as 16, 24, or 32. Incorrect settings will result in the X server repeatedly trying to use bad settings and will make logging into Linux nearly impossible. Test your graphics card and monitor when you install OpenLinux; you'll then know what default settings you can use.

Configuring Sound for OpenLinux

Configuring OpenLinux to use your computer's sound system can be considered one of the last major hurdles in a successful Linux installation. Of course, if playing music, watching Internet TV, or participating in recreational death matches with Quake is important to you, sound configuration is an important task.

The good news is that over the last several years, Linux has evolved to make the job of configuring sound a lot easier. In the past, configuring Linux to use sound involved a potentially frustrating cycle of configuring kernel source code, compiling, and testing. Today, however, the kernel uses loadable code modules to provide sound support for your computer.

Even better news is that most computers today follow common protocols when playing sound. You can easily configure OpenLinux to play sound through your computer's sound card.

Loading Sound Modules

OpenLinux comes with nearly 30 loadable code sound modules, found under the /lib/modules/2.2.3/sound directory, where 2.2.3 is the version of your OpenLinux kernel (or the output of the uname command with the -r option). See the following example:

```
# uname -r
2.2.3
# ls /lib/modules/2.2.3/sound
aci.o              gus.o              opl3sa2.o          soundlow.o
ad1816.o           mad16.o            pas2.o             sscape.o
ad1848.o           maui.o             pss.o              trix.o
adlib_card.o       mpu401.o           sb.o               uart401.o
aedsp16.o          msnd.o             sgalaxy.o          uart6850.o
awe_wave.o         msnd_classic.o     softoss2.o         v_midi.o
cs4232.o           msnd_pinnacle.o    sonicvibes.o       wavefront.o
es1370.o           opl3.o             sound.o
es1371.o           opl3sa.o           soundcore.o
```

These code modules support sound cards configured for a stock OpenLinux 2.2 kernel. You can read about the specific configuration of your kernel by looking at the WHATSIN-2.2.3-modular document (where 2.2.3 is the version of your Linux kernel) under the /boot directory. Table 3.3 lists just some of the cards (and compatibles) and modules supported by OpenLinux.

TABLE 3.3   OPENLINUX 2.2 KERNEL MODULE SOUND SUPPORT

Name	Module(s)
Crystal CS4232 (PnP)	cs4232.o, ad1848.o
Ensoniq ES1370	es1370.o
Ensoniq ES1371	ES1371.O
Ensoniq SoundScape	sscape.o
Generic OPL2/OPL3 FM synthesizer	opl3.o
Gravis Ultrasound	gus.o
MediaTrix AudioTrix Pro	trix.o
MPU-401	mpu401.o
OPTi MAD16, Mozart	mad16.o
ProAudioSpectrum 16	pas2.o
PSS, ECHO-ADI2111	pss.o
Rockwell Wave Artist (Netwinder)	waveartist.o
SoftOSS software wave table	softoss2.o
Sound Blaster compatibles, Aztec Sound Galaxy, SB16/32/64/AWE, ESS, Jazz16	sb.o
Sound card support	sound.o, sbcard.o
Turtle Beach Wave Front, Maui, Tropez	wavefront.o, maui.o
Yamaha OPL3-SA1	opl3.o

Before you can begin, find and write down the I/O port addresses, IRQ, and DMA channel number for your computer's sound system. You have this information if you followed the recommendations in Hour 1, "Preparing to Install Linux."

If you performed a full installation of OpenLinux from the CD-ROM (which includes the source code for Linux), you can find an excellent tutorial, along with details about configuring OpenLinux to work with sound cards. Look at the directory /usr/src/linux/Documentation/sound, and definitely read the file README.modules. The /usr/src/linux/drivers/sound directory contains the source code to the sound modules. Also read the Sound-HOWTO under the /usr/doc/HOWTO directory.

Log in as the root operator. At the command line of your console or an X11 terminal window, use the `insmod` command to load the sound kernel modules. This procedure should work for most computers with SoundBlaster or equivalent cards. Type the following, and replace the `io`, `irq`, and `dma` values with those for your computer:

```
# insmod sound
# insmod uart401
# insmod sb io=0x220 irq=5 dma=1
```

You can then see if the sound modules were loaded with the `lsmod` command, like this:

```
# lsmod
Module                  Size  Used by
sb                     32660   1
uart401                 5936   1  [sb]
sound                  58584   0  (autoclean) [sb uart401]
soundcore               2404   5  (autoclean) [sb sound]
soundlow                 300   0  (autoclean) [sound]
...
```

You can also try looking at the output of the `/dev/sndstat` device, like this (your output might look different):

```
# cat /dev/sndstat
OSS/Free:3.8s2++-971130
Load type: Driver loaded as a module
Kernel: Linux noname.nodomain.nowhere 2.2.3 #1 Tue Mar 9 23:27:39 MST 1999
i586
Config options: 0

Installed drivers:

Card config:

Audio devices:
0: ESS ES1688 AudioDrive (rev 11) (3.1)

Synth devices:

Midi devices:

Timers:
0: System clock

Mixers:
0: Sound Blaster
```

Testing Your Sound Configuration

Try to play a sound included in the KDE distribution. Use the `play` command to test your sound card by playing `ktalkd.wav` (the sound of a phone ringing), like this:

```
# play /opt/kde/share/sounds/ktalkd.wav
```

If your sound configuration does not work the first time, or if you enter an incorrect setting, use the `rmmod` command, followed by the name of the driver, to unload each sound module from system memory and try again. If the sound works, great!

You can find numerous sound utilities for OpenLinux installed from this book's CD-ROM. Some handy utilities include `kmix` for KDE and `xmixer` to control the balance and source of your system's sound.

Configuring Sound with COAS

OpenLinux comes with a new utility, the Caldera Open Administration System, or COAS, that you can use to administer and configure Linux. COAS can be used to control many different features of your OpenLinux system, including the following:

- Ethernet interfaces, such as the Internet Protocol (IP) address of your computer
- Filesystems, such as mounting options for local or remote storage devices
- Hostname resolution, such as where your computer looks up the names and addresses of other computers
- Kernel module boot-time control to load or unload kernel modules, such as those for sound, from memory (more than 350 kernel modules are included with OpenLinux)
- Mail, such as setting how your email messages are sent or received
- Network services, such as the Network Information Service
- Peripheral controls for configuring your keyboard, mouse, or printer
- Software management to control the types of software, such as scientific or text processing packages, installed on your computer
- System resource information to provide information about your computer's Central Processing Unit (CPU)
- System services, such as what services to start when booting (for example, printing)
- Time, such as setting your system's clock and timezone (useful when traveling)
- User management, such as adding, deleting, or renaming users and passwords

3

COAS is a "work in progress." This means that not all functions might be
enabled with the version included on your CD-ROM. Check
http://www.calderasystems.com and browse through the news and support
areas for information about your version of OpenLinux.

When you have sound working, start COAS by clicking the Application Starter button on
your K Desktop Environment's panel; select COAS, and then click the Kernel menu
item, as shown in Figure 3.1.

FIGURE 3.1

*The COAS client can
be used to configure
OpenLinux kernel
modules.*

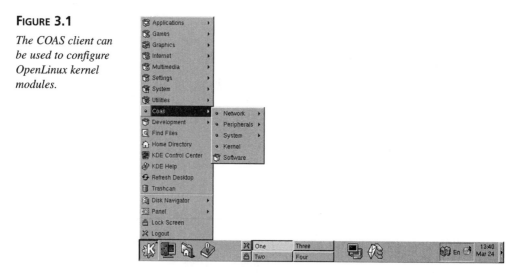

You see a short welcome dialog box. Click the OK button or press Enter to continue. You
then see a dialog box, shown in Figure 3.2, with a list of currently loaded kernel modules
on the right, and available modules on the left.

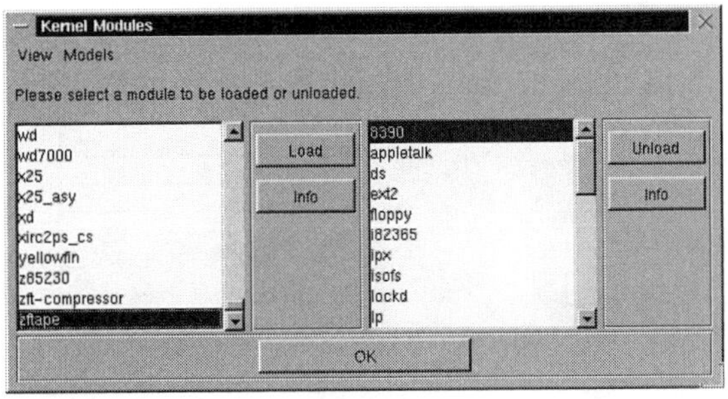

FIGURE 3.2

Configure your system's kernel modules by clicking the module's name in the left (unloaded) or right (loaded) dialog box list.

Using this previous example, scroll through the list of modules on the left, then select the sound module, and click the Load button. A dialog box appears, as shown in figure 3.3.

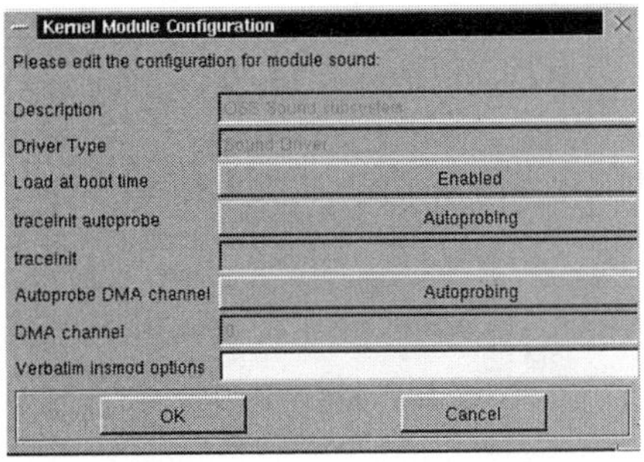

FIGURE 3.3

Configure how or when a kernel module is loaded with COAS.

Because no options are needed (for this example), make sure the **Load at boot time** button is enabled. Click the OK button. Next, scroll through the list of modules on the left, select the uart401 module, and click the Load button. Again, ensure loading at boot time, and click OK. To finish configuring for sound, scroll through the list of modules, and select the sb module. Click the Load button, and you see a dialog box similar to the one in Figure 3.4.

FIGURE 3.4

*Configure
SoundBlaster-
compatible card kernel
modules easily for
Linux with COAS!*

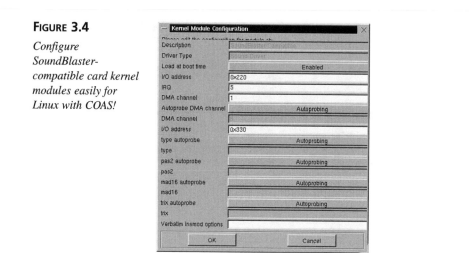

Click in the I/O address, IRQ, and DMA fields, and enter your sound card's addresses.
Make sure boot-time loading is enabled, and click the OK button. The module loads
(you might hear a slight "click"), and your card is configured! To exit COAS, click the
OK button.

A Quick Recording Script

Here's a short recording script you can use to record sound with a built-in or attached
microphone. The script works by using the dd command to save and convert a specified
amount of data (in seconds) to your hard drive. Type the script in Listing 3.1 in a file
using your favorite text editor:

LISTING 3.1   THE RECORDER SCRIPT

```
#! /bin/sh
# recorder - record sound to disk file
# usage: recorder [n] soundfilename
echo -ne "recording "
echo -ne $1
echo -ne " seconds of sound to "
echo $2.au
/bin/dd bs=8k count=$1 </dev/audio >$2.au
```

Save the file with a name, such as recorder, and then use the chmod command to make
the script executable, like this:

chmod +x recorder

First, use `kmix` or `xmixer` to set your microphone's input level. To record a sound, type `recorder`, followed by a number in seconds, like this:

```
# recorder 5 myfirstsound
```

The script responds with the following:

```
recording 5 seconds of sound to myfirstsound.au
5+0 records in
5+0 records out
```

Play the sound by sending it to your audio device, like this:

```
# cat myfirstsound.au >/dev/audio
```

Configuring Sound the Easy Way

Of course, there's an even easier way to configure OpenLinux for sound. Browse to `http://www.opensound.com/linux.html`, and download a copy of the Open Sound System, or OSS. You can find links to detailed technical procedures for manual sound configuration, or you can use the commercial version of OSS, which supports more than 200 sound cards (and which saves you a *lot* of time and effort).

OSS installs using a shell script. When you buy OSS online, you receive a license message by email. You can also use a 30-day demonstration version to try out the software. If you're having a hard time configuring sound on your system, give OSS a try!

Enabling PCMCIA Cards

If you installed OpenLinux on your laptop, one of the first tasks you should perform is enabling your PC card slots. Nearly all laptops come with a Type III or Type II PC card slot, which is typically used for a modem or Ethernet network card. However, there are many different types of PC cards used for functions, such as the following:

- ATA/IDE card drives (Flash cards, interfaces)
- ATA/IDE CD-ROM interfaces
- Ethernet interface
- Ethernet/modem combination cards
- Fast Ethernet interface
- Modems
- SCSI interfaces
- Serial interfaces
- Token-ring interface
- Wireless network interfaces

You can find a list of more than 275 cards supported by David Hind's PCMCIA Card Services package, which is a collection of kernel modules that automatically load and recognize inserted PC cards during the boot process. Read the file SUPPORTED.CARDS under the /usr/doc/pcmcia directory.

Even if your card is not listed, it might work, especially if it is a modem card.

> Winmodem PC cards, such as several models in the MegaHertz line or from other manufacturers, do **not** work under Linux. Do not purchase a winmodem modem or PC card for Linux.

Although the Card Services package is distributed only in source form through links at http://hyper.stanford.edu/HyperNews/get/pcmcia/home.html or Linux download sites, such as ftp://metalab.unc.edu/pub/Linux/kernel/pcmcia, you can find installed binaries of the modules on your OpenLinux system under the /lib/modules/2.2.3/pcmcia directory. However, Caldera OpenLinux (and indeed, no other distribution) does not have a laptop option for enabling Card Services. You must manually configure OpenLinux for your laptop's PC card controller.

> Make sure that Card Services is installed on your computer. If you do not see a /usr/doc/pcmcia-cs-3.0.9 directory on your system, chances are that Card Services is not installed. To install card services, insert your OpenLinux CD-ROM in your computer, and then mount the CD-ROM like this:
>
> # mount /mnt/cdrom
>
> Next, use the rpm command to install the software like this:
>
> # rpm -i /mnt/cdrom/col/install/RPMS/pcmcia*.rpm
>
> This installs the necessary software and documentation.

To enable the Card Services package for PCMCIA support, use your favorite text editor, and open the file pcmcia under the /etc/sysconfig directory. It looks like this:

```
PCMCIA=yes
PCIC=
PCIC_OPTS=
CARDMGR_OPTS="-f "
```

If you want to disable Card Services, type the word **no** in the PCMCIA= line. However, in order to use Card Services, you must enter the type of PCMCIA controller used for your laptop in the PCIC= entry. For many users the value **i82365** or **tcic** works. Your entry might look like this:

```
PCMCIA=yes
PCIC=i82365
PCIC_OPTS=
CARDMGR_OPTS="-f "
```

Save the file and exit your text editor. You can then reboot OpenLinux or start Card Services like this:

```
# /etc/rc.d/init.d/pcmcia start
Starting PCMCIA services: modules cardmgr
```

Card Services starts and reports that cardmgr, the PCMCIA device manager, has been activated. This device manager monitors your PC card slots for card inserts or removals. If you have a modem card inserted, you should then be able to use the modem. Other cards, such as Ethernet interfaces, will be recognized but cannot be used until you properly configure OpenLinux for networking.

After starting Card Services, you can check its status in at least three ways. First, you can use the dmesg command, like this:

```
# dmesg
…
Linux PCMCIA Card Services 3.0.9
  kernel build: 2.2.3 #1 Tue Mar 9 05:22:33 MET 1999
  options:  [pci] [cardbus]
Intel PCIC probe:
  TI 1131 PCI-to-CardBus at bus 0 slot 10, mem 0x68000000,
   2 sockets
    host opts [0]: [ring] [pci + serial irq] [no pci irq]
    [lat 168/176] [bus 32/34]
    host opts [1]: [ring] [pci + serial irq] [no pci irq]
    [lat 168/176] [bus 35/37]
    ISA irqs (scanned) = 3,4,7,9 status change on irq 9
cs: IO port probe 0x1000-0x17ff: clean.
cs: IO port probe 0x0100-0x04ff: excluding 0x330-0x337
0x378-0x37f 0x388-0x38f 0x408-0x40f 0x480-0x48f 0x4d0-0x4d7
cs: IO port probe 0x0a00-0x0aff: clean.
cs: memory probe 0xa0000000-0xa0ffffff: clean.
eth0: NE2000 Compatible: port 0x300, irq 3, hw_addr 00:E0:98:04:AA:D5
…
```

Not all the dmesg output is shown here, but you can see that the service has been loaded and that an Ethernet PC card was found by Card Services.

Another way to check is to look at your OpenLinux system log, a file named messages found under the /var/log directory. Use the less pager, followed by the pathname to the file, like this:

 # less /var/log/messages

```
...
Mar 23 22:20:32 noname kernel: Linux PCMCIA Card Services 3.0.9
Mar 23 22:20:32 noname kernel:   kernel build: 2.2.3 #1 Tue Mar 9
05:22:33 MET 1999
Mar 23 22:20:32 noname kernel:   options: [pci] [cardbus]
Mar 23 22:20:32 noname kernel: Intel PCIC probe:
Mar 23 22:20:32 noname kernel:   TI 1131 PCI-to-CardBus at bus 0
slot 10, mem 0x68000000, 2 sockets
Mar 23 22:20:32 noname kernel:     host opts [0]: [ring] [pci +
serial irq] [no pci irq] [lat 168/176] [bus 32/34]
Mar 23 22:20:32 noname kernel:     host opts [1]: [ring] [pci +
serial irq] [no pci irq] [lat 168/176] [bus 35/37]
Mar 23 22:20:32 noname kernel:     ISA irqs (scanned) = 3,4,7,9 status
change on irq 9
Mar 23 22:20:32 noname cardmgr[991]: starting, version is 3.0.9
Mar 23 22:20:32 noname cardmgr[991]: watching 2 sockets
Mar 23 22:20:32 noname kernel: cs: IO port probe 0x1000-0x17ff: clean.
Mar 23 22:20:32 noname kernel: cs: IO port probe 0x0100-0x04ff: excluding
0x330-0x337 0x378-0x37f 0x388-0x38f 0x408-0x40f 0x480-0x48f 0x4d0-0x4d7
Mar 23 22:20:32 noname kernel: cs: IO port probe 0x0a00-0x0aff: clean.
Mar 23 22:20:33 noname cardmgr[991]: initializing socket 0
Mar 23 22:20:33 noname kernel: cs: memory probe 0xa0000000-0xa0ffffff:
clean.
Mar 23 22:20:33 noname cardmgr[991]: socket 0: Linksys EtherFast 10/100
Fast
Ethernet
Mar 23 22:20:33 noname cardmgr[991]: executing: 'insmod
/lib/modules/2.2.3/net/8390.o'
Mar 23 22:20:33 noname cardmgr[991]: executing: 'modprobe net/8390'
Mar 23 22:20:33 noname cardmgr[991]: executing: 'insmod
/lib/modules/2.2.3/pcmcia/pcnet_cs.o'
Mar 23 22:20:33 noname kernel: eth0: NE2000 Compatible: port 0x300, irq 3,
hw_addr 00:E0:98:04:AA:D5
Mar 23 22:20:33 noname cardmgr[991]: executing: './network start eth0'
Mar 23 22:20:33 noname cardmgr[991]: + eth0: configuration file not found.
Mar 23 22:20:33 noname cardmgr[991]: start cmd exited with status 1
Mar 23 22:20:33 noname cardmgr[991]: exiting
...
```

Not all the output is shown here, but you can see that additional information, such as the model of your recognized card (in this case a Linksys EtherFast 10/100 card), is shown. Looking at your system's log is also a good way to diagnose other problems.

A third way to diagnose, check, or reset your PC cards, if you're using X11, is with David Hind's `cardinfo` client. Start `cardinfo` from the command line of a terminal window like this:

```
# cardinfo
```

After you press Enter, you see a window somewhat like that in Figure 3.5.

FIGURE 3.5

The cardinfo X11 client can be used to monitor, reset, suspend, eject, or insert PC cards with OpenLinux.

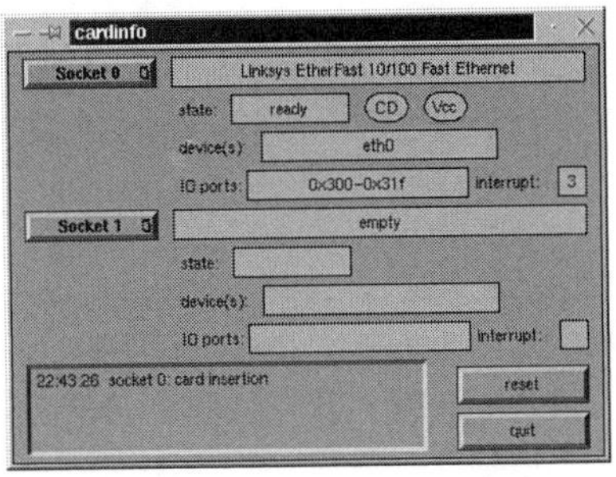

A small log window in the lower left of the `cardinfo` dialog box lists PC card events, such as insertion or removal. To control a card, press and hold down a card's Socket button. You'll see a small menu enabling you to reset, eject, or insert a card.

Configuring Network Information with COAS

Although you were asked for network information during your OpenLinux installation, this is not your only opportunity to configure an interface. If you didn't enter network information during the installation, you don't have to perform a re-install just to configure networking! Use the COAS utility to configure your interface's address.

Configuring Your Ethernet Interface

To configure your interface, click the Application Starter button in your KDE desktop, select COAS and then Network, and click on Ethernet Interfaces, as shown in Figure 3.6.

You then see a welcome dialog box. Click the OK button (or press Enter) to continue.
The Ethernet Interface Configuration dialog box appears, as shown in Figure 3.7.

To configure your interface, click in the Interface address field, and enter your computer's IP address (such as 192.168.1.20). When you finish, click the OK button. The
dialog box disappears. You can then check the status of your interface with the ifconfig
command, like this:

```
# ifconfig
lo        Link encap:Local Loopback
          inet addr:127.0.0.1  Mask:255.0.0.0
          UP LOOPBACK RUNNING  MTU:3924  Metric:1
          RX packets:56 errors:0 dropped:0 overruns:0 frame:0
          TX packets:56 errors:0 dropped:0 overruns:0 carrier:0
          collisions:0 txqueuelen:0
```

```
eth0       Link encap:Ethernet  HWaddr 00:E0:98:04:AA:D5
           inet addr:192.1.2.34  Bcast:192.1.2.0  Mask:255.255.255.0
           UP BROADCAST RUNNING MULTICAST  MTU:1500  Metric:1
           RX packets:5 errors:0 dropped:0 overruns:0 frame:0
           TX packets:5 errors:0 dropped:0 overruns:0 carrier:0
           collisions:0 txqueuelen:100
           Interrupt:3 Base address:0x300
```

If you do not see an active local loopback (lo) interface, use the ifconfig command with the lo and up options like this:

```
# ifconfig lo up
```

3

As you can see, you now have an active Ethernet interface (eth0) and address (in this case, 192.1.2.34). If you're connected to a local network, use the ping command to try to test your connection. Type ping on the command line of a terminal window, followed by the IP address of another computer, like this:

```
# ping 192.1.2.36
PING 192.1.2.36 (192.1.2.36): 56 data bytes
64 bytes from 192.1.2.36: icmp_seq=0 ttl=64 time=0.6 ms
64 bytes from 192.1.2.36: icmp_seq=1 ttl=64 time=0.5 ms
64 bytes from 192.1.2.36: icmp_seq=2 ttl=64 time=0.5 ms
64 bytes from 192.1.2.36: icmp_seq=3 ttl=64 time=0.5 ms
64 bytes from 192.1.2.36: icmp_seq=4 ttl=64 time=0.5 ms

--- 192.1.2.36 ping statistics ---
5 packets transmitted, 5 packets received, 0% packet loss
round-trip min/avg/max = 0.5/0.5/0.6 ms
```

Press Ctrl+C to stop the ping command, which sends and records the time it takes (in thousandths of a second) for a "packet" of 64 characters to be sent and echoed back from a remote computer. The remote computer can be on a local network or halfway across the world.

SETTING THE HOSTNAME

If you didn't set the hostname for your computer during the OpenLinux installation, you can add it later by using the Hostname menu item under the COAS System menu, or editing the file network under the /etc/ sysconfig directory. To manually change your hostname, use your favorite text editor and open the ~~sysconfig~~ file (which should look like this):
NETWORK

```
NETWORKING="yes"
HOSTNAME=noname.nodomain.nowhere
```

Change the HOSTNAME entry to the hostname of your computer, save the file, and exit your editor. You can then verify your new hostname with the host-name command.   *REBOOT*

Using an Iomega Zip Drive with OpenLinux

There are now at least three different Iomega parallel-port Zip drives available for Linux (not including internal IDE, USB, or SCSI drives): the original Zip drive, the Zip Plus drive, and the new Zip 250.

For the very latest development information about Linux and parallel-port devices, such as the Zip drive, browse to http://www.torque.net/ linux-pp.html.

The following steps (tested with an original Zip drive) will enable you to mount and use a Zip disk:

1. Turn on and connect your Zip drive to your computer's parallel port.

2. Insert a Zip disk into your Zip drive.

3. Create the directory (such as /mnt/zip) where you'd like to access the contents of your Zip disk, like this:

    ```
    # mkdir /mnt/zip
    ```

4. Use the insmod command to load kernel module support for the Zip drive, like this:

    ```
    # insmod scsi_mod
    # insmod sd_mod
    # insmod parport
    # insmod parport_pc
    # insmod ppa
    ```

This loads SCSI support (the Zip drive uses a low-level SCSI protocol), support for sharing the parallel port, and support for the Zip drive. After you load the `ppa` module, you should hear your Zip drive activate. You can then use the `mount` command, along with a filesystem type, device name (`/dev/sda`), and mount point, like this:

```
# mount -t vfat /dev/sda4 /mnt/zip
```

5. To unmount the Zip disk, use the `umount` command, followed by the mount point, like this:

```
# umount /mnt/zip
```

> Users of the Iomega Zip Plus or Zip 250 drive will need to use the `imm.o` module and will not be able to share the parallel port with a printer when using the Zip drive. If you use an original Zip parallel-port drive, you can use the Zip disk and print at the same time.

After you've verified that your Zip drive works, you can then use the Kernel utility under COAS to load your Zip drive's modules when booting.

Summary

This hour provided a step-by-step approach to configuring X11 for your computer's video card and monitor. Use this hour as the starting point for fine-tuning your X11 configuration.

Q&A

Q Help! My XFree86 only gives me a resolution of 320 by 200!

A It's possible that you picked the wrong resolution during your OpenLinux installation. Make sure to test various X11 modes during the OpenLinux install to get the best resolution possible with the most colors. You can also try reconfiguring X11 with the `xf86config` command and start X11 again. Pay close attention to the values you enter for your monitor's horizontal and vertical frequencies, and don't forget to edit your `XF86Config` file's `Device` section to set the correct amount of video RAM. If you have one of the latest and greatest video cards, the card might not be supported by XFree86 just yet. Chances are also good that the next release of XFree86's X11 distribution will contain fixes for your graphics cards.

Exercises

1. Start the `xvidtune` client , and then use its controls to fine-tune your X11 settings . See if you can get a better image on your display.

2. Try starting an X11 session at different color depths. Does your display look any different?

3. Try mounting, reading from, and writing to a Zip drive. Navigate to `http://www.torque.net/`.

4. Scroll through your `XF86Config` file while reading the `XF86Config` man page.

PART II
Learning Linux Basics

Hour

4 Reading and Navigation Commands

5 Manipulation and Searching Commands

6 Using the Shell

7 Using the X Window System

8 Exploring the K Desktop Environment

Hour 4

Reading and Navigation Commands

This hour introduces you to the basic Linux commands used for navigating, searching, and reading files and directories of the *file system*, your Linux partition's collection of directories. After working through the material, you'll know how to get help on commands, find out where you are in Linux, and find files on your hard drive. The hour starts with navigating and searching your directory, and then moves on to show you how to read directories and files. But first, you'll learn how to help yourself with the man command.

Getting Help with the man Command

One of the first things to know about Linux is that help is never far away. Like most implementations of UNIX, your Linux distribution comes with manual pages for most programs, utilities, commands, and programming system calls. You can get information about nearly any command, including man. For example, read the manual page for the man command by typing the following:

```
# man man
```

Manual pages started as one-page UNIX command summaries. The file for each manual page is named with a single-digit extension and placed in a subdirectory under /usr/man. Manual pages for many OpenLinux commands are copied to your computer's hard drive during the initial installation process or when you later install an individual program. For example, the manual page for man is named and found as follows:

/usr/man/man1/man.1.gz

The name of the manual page for the man command is man.1, but the extension .gz indicates that the man.1 file has been compressed with the gzip command. The man command automatically decompresses the file before displaying the manual page. For more information about compressed files, see the section "Compressing and Uncompressing Files" in Hour 5, "Manipulation and Searching Commands."

There are more than 1,000 manual page files under the /usr/man/man1 directory. But if, for example, you want to understand the format and placement of manual pages, you don't find this information in man.1 but in man.7 under /usr/man/man7. Look at Table 4.1 to see the location and contents of each manual section.

TABLE 4.1 THE LINUX MANUAL SECTIONS

Directory	Contents
/usr/man/man1	Commands—Commands you run from within a shell
/usr/man/man2	System calls—Documentation for kernel functions
/usr/man/man3	Library calls—Manual pages for libc functions
/usr/man/man4	Special files—Information about files in the /dev directory
/usr/man/man5	File formats—Details of formats for /etc/passwd and other files
/usr/man/man6	Games
/usr/man/man7	Macro packages—Descriptions of the Linux file system, manual pages, and others
/usr/man/man8	System management—Manual pages for root operator utilities
/usr/man/man9	Kernel routines—Documentation on Linux kernel source routines or kernel module specifications

Each manual page traditionally has a number of sections; the documentation for the command also breaks down into sections. Look at Table 4.2 for the organization of a manual page.

TABLE 4.2 ORGANIZATION OF A MANUAL PAGE

Section	Description
Name	The name of the command and a brief description
Synopsis	How to use the command and command-line options
Description	An explanation of the program and its options
Files	A list of files used by the command and their location
See also	A list of related man pages
Diagnostics	A description of unusual output
Bugs	Known problems
Author	The program's main author and other contributors

Online manual pages contain special typesetting codes for the nroff text formatting program, using special macros(as documented in man.7) that control how the manual page is displayed or printed. For more information on the nroff text formatting program, see Hour 15, "Preparing Documents." The nroff format also is critically important for other programs, such as makewhatis, whatis, and apropos, which you'll learn about later in this chapter. These programs expect manual pages to have a consistent format so that information can be properly displayed during search operations or properly stored when building an information database about your OpenLinux system's programs.

You can also find more detailed documentation for Linux commands and other subjects under the /usr/doc directory, which contains files called Frequently Asked Questions, or FAQs, and How-To documents, or HOWTOs. Additionally, the Free Software Foundation, which releases the GNU software packages, puts much of its documentation in a special hypertext info format. Many of the commands discussed in this book are GNU programs.

Much of the software for Linux comes from the Free Software Foundation, founded by Richard Stallman, author of the emacs editor (see Hour 14, "Text Processing"). The FSF distributes its software under the GNU General Public License, or GPL. Part of the success and popularity of Linux and GNU software is because of the terms of the GPL. If you want more information about the GNU software programs for Linux, the FSF, or the GNU GPL, you can try the info command, which is a reader for the GNU hypertext documentation found under the /usr/info directory. You can also use the man command like so:

```
man GPL
```

The man command normally searches for manual pages according to instructions detailed in the man.conf file under the /etc directory. These instructions define the default directories in which to look for manual pages. The default places to look for these pages are as follows:

```
MANPATH  /usr/man

MANPATH  /usr/TeX/man

MANPATH  /usr/local/man

MANPATH  /usr/X11R6/man

MANPATH  /usr/openwin/man
```

A graphic version of the man command, called xman, is available for the X Window System. You can use xman not only to read manual pages, but also to see directories of manual page entries. If you use the K Desktop Environment with X11 (introduced in Hour 8, "Exploring the K Desktop Environment"), you find that KDE manual pages are in Hypertext Markup Language, or HTML format.

Navigating and Searching the File System

This section introduces you to the basic navigational commands and shows you how to move around your Linux file system, find files, and build file information databases, such as those for use with the whatis command. You'll learn about alternative approaches and programs and how to speed up searches to find files quickly.

Moving to Different Directories with the cd Command

NEW TERM The cd (change directory) command is the basic navigation tool for moving to different parts of the Linux file system. After you log in to OpenLinux, you are in your home directory. This directory has a name, or *pathname*, beginning with /home/ followed by your username.

You can move directly to a different directory by typing the command followed by a pathname. For example, the following command moves you to the /usr/bin directory:

 # cd /usr/bin

When you're in that directory, you can move up to the /usr directory with the following command:

 # cd ..

You can also move to the root directory, or /, while in the /usr/bin directory by using the following command:

```
# cd ../..
```

Finally, you can always go back to your home directory (where your files are) by using the command

```
# cd
```

or

```
# cd ~
```

> If you try to use the man command to read the cd man page, you won't find one. Why? Because cd is built into the shell, which interprets your command line after you press Enter. See bash in Hour 6, "Using the Shell," for more details.

Knowing Where You Are with the pwd Command

The pwd (print working directory) command tells you where you are and prints the working (current) directory. For example, if you execute

```
# cd /usr/bin
```

and then type

```
# pwd
```

you see

```
/usr/bin
```

Although there's a man page for the pwd command, chances are that when you use pwd, you're using a pwd built into your shell. How do you tell? If you try calling pwd with the following command, you see only the current working directory printed:

```
# pwd --help
```

Instead, try using the pwd command in the /bin directory as follows:

```
# /bin/pwd --help
```

This runs the pwd command in the /bin directory and not the pwd built into your shell. You see a short help file for the pwd command and not the current directory. If you're ever in doubt about where you are, use the pwd command under the /bin directory.

Searching Directories for Matching Files with the find Command

The find command is a powerful searching utility you can use to find files on your hard drive. You can search your hard drive for files easily with a simple find command line. For example, to search for the spell command under the /usr directory, you use the following:

```
# find /usr -name spell -print
```

You can use the find command to find files by date, and you can also specify a range of times. For example, to find programs in the /usr/bin directory that you have not used in the last 100 days, you can try the following:

```
# find /usr/bin -type f -atime +100 -print
```

The -atime option is followed by a number representing days. To find any files, either new or modified, that are one or fewer days old in the /usr/bin directory, you can use the following option:

```
# find /usr/bin -type f -mtime -1 -print
```

The -mtime option, followed by a number in days (in this case one or less), looks for modified files. The find command also accepts wildcards (such as * or ?) in search strings, which you'll learn about in Hour 5. As a simple example, you can use find to show you all the PostScript files in your /usr directory with the following:

```
# find /usr -name '*.ps' -print
```

The section "Understanding Graphics Formats" in Hour 16, "Graphics Tools," covers PostScript files.

-xdev is one of the find command's handy options. The examples so far show searches limited to the /usr directory. But what if you want to search starting at the root (/) directory? -xdev limits searches to the current file system, which in this case is Linux. Without it, find merrily continues its search through any mounted CD-ROMs or your DOS or Windows partition, possibly finding files you're not interested in, slowing down the search, and cluttering up the search printout.

For example, you can use the -xdev option to limit your find command search to a Windows partition. To find all files ending in .sys on a mounted Windows partition under the /mnt/dos directory, use the -xdev option like this:

```
# find /mnt/dos -name *.sys -print -xdev
```

The find command has many different options and uses.

> You can also send the find command on search-and-destroy missions to delete selected files from your computer. See "Saving Disk Space" in Hour 21, "Basic System Administration," for details.

Although find rapidly searches your hard drive and file systems, there are other ways of quickly finding files, especially programs. Read on to find out more!

Finding Files with the `whereis` Command

The whereis command can quickly find files, and it shows you where the file's binary, source, and manual pages reside. For example, the following command shows that the find command is in the /usr/bin directory, and its man page is in the /usr/man/man1 directory:

```
# whereis find
find: /usr/bin/find /usr/man/man1/find.1.gz
```

You can also use whereis to find only the binary version of the program with the following:

```
# whereis -b find
find: /usr/bin/find
```

This is handy if you only want to see where a program is located and not its documentation. If whereis cannot find your request, you get an empty return string, for example:

```
# whereis foo
foo:
```

Part of the problem could also be that the file is not in any of the directories the whereis command searches. The directories whereis looks in are hard-coded into the program. Although this might seem like a drawback, limiting searches to known directories such as /usr/man, /usr/bin, or /usr/sbin can speed up the task of finding files.

Although whereis is faster than using find to locate programs or manual pages, there's an even faster search utility you can use, called locate, discussed in the next section.

Locating Files with the `locate` Command

One way to speed up searches for files is not to search your file directories! You can do this by using a program like `locate`. `locate` uses a single database of filenames and locations and saves time by looking in a single file instead of traversing your hard drive. Finding a file using `locate` is much faster than the `find` command because `locate` goes directly to the database file, finds any matching filenames, and displays its results.

`Locate` is easy to use. For example, to find all the PostScript files on your system, you can enter the following:

```
# locate *.ps
```

Almost instantly, the files appear on your screen. You might even find the `locate` command line a little easier to use than the `find` command. However, there is a catch: `find` works "right out of the box," whereas `locate` requires a database of all the files on your system. But don't worry—the procedure is almost automatic.

After you install OpenLinux, the `locate` database is updated every day at 5:50 a.m. To create an updated version of the `locate` database right away, you need to use the `updatedb` command. Make sure that you're logged in as the root operator, or use the `su` command (see Hour 21). At the prompt, enter the following:

```
# updatedb
```

It might take a minute or so for the `updatedb` command to finish its work, but when it's done, the database for `locate`, `locatedb`, resides in the `/var/state` directory. `locatedb` is about 700,000 characters in size for 900MB worth of files. The only downside to using the `locate` command is that over time, its database can become outdated as you add or delete files to your system. Fortunately, OpenLinux automatically updates the locate database; to find out how, see Hour 24, "Scheduling," for details.

Getting Command Summaries with `whatis` and `apropos`

As you first explore your OpenLinux system, you might come across programs whose function is not clear. Many Linux programs are designed to give at least a little help with a `?`, `-help` or `--help` option on the command line, but you generally shouldn't run a program without knowing what it does.

The whatis command might be able to help you quickly find out what a program is with a summary line derived from the program's manual page. For example, to find out what is who, you can enter the following:

```
# whatis who
```

Your screen clears, and the whatis command displays a summary like so:

```
who (1)     - show who is logged on
```

Press Q to quit the whatis command. However, unlike the locate command, you must first build a database of the command summaries with the makewhatis command, which is found under the /usr/sbin directory. To do this, make sure you're logged in as root, and enter the following:

```
# makewhatis
```

The makewhatis command, like the updatedb command, takes a few minutes to build the whatis database, which is called whatis and is found under the /usr/man/man1 directory. The makewhatis command has several options but does not have a manual page. To see a quick summary, use the following:

```
# makewhatis -?
```

4

You need to periodically update the whatis database to keep track of any newly installed programs. See Hour 24 for tips on how to make OpenLinux do this automatically.

Now you see how whereis and whatis can help you find programs or figure out what they do. But what if you want to do something but can't remember which program does what? In this case, you can turn to the apropos command.

For example, if you can't remember which command searches for files, you can enter the following:

```
# apropos search
apropos (1)            - search the whatis database for strings
badblocks (8)          - search a device for bad blocks
bsearch (3)            - binary search of a sorted array.
conflict (8)           - search for alias/password conflicts
find (1)               - search for files in a directory hierarchy
hcreate, hdestroy, hsearch (3) - hash table management
lfind, lsearch (3)     - linear search of an array.
lkbib (1)              - search bibliographic databases
lookbib (1)            - search bibliographic databases
lsearch (n)            - See if a list contains a particular element
manpath (1)            - determine user's search path for man pages
strpbrk (3)            - search a string for any of a set of characters
strspn, strcspn (3)    - search a string for a set of characters
tsearch, tfind, tdelete, twalk (3) - manage a binary tree
```

```
whatis (1)              - search the whatis database for complete words.
zgrep (1)               - search possibly compressed files for
➥ a regular expression
zipgrep (1)             - search possibly zip files for

➥ a regular expression
```

You see a list of programs from the whatis database on your screen. Press the Q key when you finish reading the list. The apropos command uses this database to search for the keyword you entered. If you keep your whatis database up-to-date, you're able to use apropos to help you find the program you need.

You can also use the man command's -K option to do the same thing as apropos, but the search is slow and presents each manual page in the search result. For example, to search for any programs dealing with PostScript, you can try the following:

 # man -K PostScript

This can result in the following output, before you quit with Q:

```
/usr/man/man7/unicode.7? [ynq] n
/usr/man/man7/suffixes.7? [ynq] n
/usr/man/man7/groff_char.7? [ynq] n
/usr/man/man1/convert.1x? [ynq] n
/usr/man/man1/xv.1? [ynq] n
/usr/man/man1/xdvi.1? [ynq] n
/usr/man/man1/dvips.1? [ynq] n
/usr/man/man1/afm2tfm.1? [ynq] n
/usr/man/man1/ps2pk.1? [ynq] n
/usr/man/man1/ps2frag.1? [ynq] q
```

Reading Directories and Files

Now that you know about directory navigation, searching for files, and how to find more information about programs, I'll introduce you to other basic Linux commands you can use. This section shows you how to list the contents of directories, make a catalog of your hard drive, and read the contents of files. You'll learn the basic forms of these commands to help get you started.

Listing Directories with the ls Command

The ls (list directory) command is one of the most often used programs. In its simplest form, ls lists nearly all the files in the current directory. But this command, which has such a short name, probably has more command-line options (more than 75 at last count) than any other program!

Why are there so many Linux commands, and why do they have such short names? If you're not familiar with Linux, you'll soon find hundreds of programs with short, initially cryptic names like cd, pwd, df, du, ps, ls, as, ar, at, w, and so on. Don't be intimidated! Instead, be thankful that Linux has inherited this rich assortment of traditional UNIX tools. The UNIX philosophy is that a good program is small and does one thing very well; the power of the operating system comes from combining the output of several programs in concert. Many of the command names were chosen to save typing. Why enter a long program name when one or two letters suffice? Also, many early UNIX users communicated with remote UNIX computers over very slow (110-baud) terminal lines, and short, precise commands were transmitted a lot faster. To better appreciate the short command names, read Hour 6.

In the simple form, ls lists the files in the current directory as in the following example:

```
[home/bball]$ ls
News          axhome        nsmail        search
author.msg    documents     reading       vultures.msg
auto          mail          research
```

The example lists files in my home directory.

You can also list the files as a single line, with comma separations, using the -m option:

```
# ls -m
News, author.msg, auto, axhome, documents, mail, nsmail, reading,
➥ research, search, vultures.msg
```

If you don't like this type of with the ls Commandlisting, you can have your files sorted horizontally, instead of vertically (the default) with the -x option, as follows:

```
# ls -x
News          author.msg    auto          axhome        documents
mail          nsmail        reading       research      search
vultures.msg
```

Are all these just files, or are there several directories? One way to find out is to use the -F option:

```
# ls -F
News/         axhome/       nsmail/       search*
author.msg    documents/    reading/      vultures.msg
auto/         mail/         research/
```

As you can see, the -F option causes the ls command to show the directories, each with a / character appended to the filename. The asterisk (*) shows that the file search is an executable program. But are these all the files in this directory? If you want to see everything, you can use the -a option with -F, as follows:

4

```
# ls -aF
./                  .dt/                .neditdb            auto/
../                 .dtprofile*         .netscape/          axhome/
.Xauthority         .festival_history   .newsrc             documents/
.Xdefaults          .forward            .oldnewsrc          mail/
.addressbook        .fvwm2rc95*         .pinerc             nsmail/
.addressbook.lu     .index/             .procmail/          reading/
.bash_history       .mailcap            .procmailrc         research/
.bash_logout        .mailrc             .tin/               search*
.bash_profile       .mime.types         .xinitrc*           vultures.msg
.bashrc             .ncftp/             News/
.desksetdefaults    .nedit              author.msg
```

As you can see, files or directories whose names begin with a period (.) are not displayed by ls unless you explicitly request all files. Using the -F option is one way to see the files and directories in your listings, but if you have a color monitor or use X11 in color, you can tell ls to show files, directories, or executable files in different colors. To do this, use the --color option like this:

```
# ls --color
```

In X11, using the xterm terminal, directories are blue, programs are green, and regular files are black. You can also customize which colors are used for different types of files.

For example, to have all graphics files, such as PCX or GIF graphics, appear in red and all text files ending in .txt appear in purple, create a shell *environment variable*, or system- or user-defined value, named LS_COLORS, define the colors, and export the variable like this:

```
# LS_COLORS="*pcx=31:*gif=31:*txt=35";export LS_COLORS
```

> The ls man page lists the default colors. You can put your custom definition in your .bashrc file for use the next time you log in to OpenLinux. As the root operator, you can also specify systemwide default colors for all users. See Hour 6 to see how to define LS_COLORS and other environment variables for use by all users on your OpenLinux system.

Long Directory Listing

Would you like even more information about your files? You can use the long format listing by using the ls -l option, for example:

```
# ls -l
total 2086
-rw-r--r--   1 bball     users       256302 Dec 30 15:42 162317art.zip
drwx------   6 bball     users         1024 Dec 17 22:35 Desktop
drwxr-xr-x  24 bball     users         1024 Dec  2 15:09 Office40
```

```
drwxr-xr-x  22 bball      users         1024 Dec  2 11:23 Office50
-rw-r--r--   1 bball      users        29360 Dec 30 14:38 Sheet.as
-rw-r--r--   1 bball      users          705 Dec 30 15:15 Sheet.wk3
-rw-r--r--   1 bball      users         2360 Dec 30 15:15 Sheet.xl4
-rw-r--r--   1 bball      users         5632 Dec 30 15:20 Sheet.xl5
-rw-r--r--   1 bball      users         2958 Dec 17 20:37 XWp
drwxr-xr-x   5 bball      users         1024 Mar 24  1998 aim
drwxr-xr-x   4 bball      users         1024 Dec 30 15:15 axhome
drwxr-xr-x   2 bball      users         1024 Dec 23 23:15 documents
drwxr-xr-x   2 bball      users         1024 Dec 11 11:06 graphics
drwxr-xr-x   6 bball      users         1024 Dec  1 11:19 lg
drwxrwxrwt   2 bball      users         1024 Dec  9 16:34 mail
drwx------   2 bball      users         1024 Nov  8 10:56 nsmail
drwxr-xr-x   3 bball      users         1024 Nov 10 16:22 rvplayer5.0
drwxr-xr-x   5 bball      users         1024 Nov  4 10:49 so50
drwxr-xr-x   2 bball      users         3072 Dec 30 15:43 tyl2
-rwxr-xr-x   1 bball      users        12004 Dec 30 12:37 worth.as
-rw-r--r--   1 bball      users         1533 Dec 30 13:09 worth.csv
-rw-r--r--   1 bball      users       227985 Dec 30 13:08 worth.dif
-rw-r--r--   1 bball      users         4905 Dec 30 13:12 worth.sc
-rw-r--r--   1 bball      users         6110 Dec 30 13:09 worth.slk
-rw-r--r--   1 bball      users         1533 Dec 30 13:09 worth.txt
```

As you can see, there are eight different columns. The first column is the file's permission flags, which are covered in Hour 22, "Handling Files and Your File System." These flags generally show the file's type, and who can read, write (modify or delete), or run the file.

The next column shows the number of links, which are discussed in Hour 5. Next is the owner name, followed by the group name. Owners and groups are discussed in Hour 22. The file size is listed next, followed by a timestamp stating when the file or directory was created or last modified. The last column, obviously, is each file's name.

Specifying Other Directories

You can also use the `ls` command to view the contents of other directories by specifying the directory or pathname on the command line. For example, if you want to see all the files in the /usr/bin directory (you'll probably see a lot more than these), use the following:

```
# ls /usr/bin
```

arch	dd	gzip	netstat	stty
ash	df	hostname	nisdomainname	su
awk	dmesg	kill	ping	sync
basename	dnsdomainname	ksh	ps	tar
bash	doexec	ln	pwd	tcsh
bsh	domainname	login	red	touch
cat	echo	ls	rm	true
chgrp	ed	mail	rmdir	umount
chmod	egrep	mkdir	rpm	uname

chown	false	mknod	sed	ypdomainname
cp	fgrep	more	setserial	zcat
cpio	gawk	mount	sh	
csh	grep	mt	sleep	
date	gunzip	mv	sort	

NEW TERM   *Regular expressions* are a language of special string specification patterns. The
ls command supports using wildcards and regular expressions, which means you
can use options similar to and much more complex than the examples you saw with the
find and locate commands. For example, if you only want to search for text files in the
current directory, you can use the following:

 # ls *.txt

Finally, if you want to see all the files on your system, you can use the ls -R option,
which recursively descends directories to show you their contents. Although you can use
this approach to search for files and build a catalog of the files on your system, be
warned that it might take several minutes to list your files. The listing might also include
files you don't want listed or files on other operating system file systems, such as DOS
or Windows, especially if you use the following:

 # ls -R /

A better approach might be to use the -d option with -R to list only a certain number of
directory levels. For example, the following command searches three directory levels
along the root (/) directory:

 # ls -Rd /*/*/*

However, there's a much better utility for getting a picture of the directory structure of
your system—tree—which is discussed in the following section.

> Do you like how ls -aF shows your directories? Do you prefer ls to use col-
> ors all the time? If you want the ls command to always show this sort of
> detail, see Hour 6.

Listing Directories with the `dir` and `vdir` Commands

If you just can't get the hang of using ls to list your directories, you can use the dir or
vdir commands. These commands have only about 45 command-line options compared
to ls, but they're just as capable. They work like ls but with certain defaults.

The dir command works like the default ls command, listing the files in sorted columns
as in the following example:

```
# dir
01_hyph.dat     49_thes.dat      bin          help          store
01_spell.dat    Desktop          config       install.ini   template
01_thes.dat     LICENSE          database     instdb.ins    wordbook
44_hyph.dat     README           download     kino          xp3
44_spell.dat    addin            explorer     l_soffice.xpm
44_thes.dat     autotext         filter       lib
49_hyph.dat     backup           fonts        s_soffice.xpm
49_spell.dat    basic            gallery      sofficerc
```

The vdir command works like the ls -l option and presents a long format listing by
default as follows:

```
# vdir
total 3659
-rw-rw-rw-   1 bball     users        65605 Oct 27 10:00 01_hyph.dat
-rw-rw-rw-   1 bball     users       313015 Oct 27 10:00 01_spell.dat
-rw-rw-rw-   1 bball     users       375808 Oct 27 10:00 01_thes.dat
-rw-r--r--   1 bball     users        65605 Oct 27 10:00 44_hyph.dat
-rw-r--r--   1 bball     users       313015 Oct 27 10:00 44_spell.dat
-rw-r--r--   1 bball     users       380928 Oct 27 10:00 44_thes.dat
-rw-rw-rw-   1 bball     users        51765 Oct 27 10:00 49_hyph.dat
-rw-rw-rw-   1 bball     users       602497 Oct 27 10:00 49_spell.dat
-rw-rw-rw-   1 bball     users      1191936 Oct 27 10:00 49_thes.dat
drwxr-xr-x   2 bball     users         1024 Dec  2 11:21 Desktop
-rw-r--r--   1 bball     users        11631 Oct 27 10:00 LICENSE
-rw-r--r--   1 bball     users         8435 Oct 27 10:00 README
drwxr-xr-x   3 bball     users         1024 Dec  2 11:21 addin
drwxr-xr-x   2 bball     users         1024 Dec  2 11:21 autotext
drwxr-xr-x   2 bball     users         1024 Dec 30 15:41 backup
drwxr-xr-x   2 bball     users         1024 Dec 17 11:43 basic
drwxr-xr-x   2 bball     users         2048 Dec  2 11:22 bin
drwxr-xr-x  11 bball     users         3072 Jan  4 09:52 config
drwxr-xr-x   2 bball     users         1024 Dec  2 11:30 database
drwxr-xr-x   2 bball     users         1024 Dec  2 11:20 download
drwxr-xr-x   5 bball     users         1024 Dec  2 11:28 explorer
drwxr-xr-x   2 bball     users         1024 Dec  2 11:22 filter
drwxr-xr-x   4 bball     users         1024 Dec  2 11:20 fonts
drwxr-xr-x  14 bball     users         2048 Dec  2 11:22 gallery
drwxr-xr-x   4 bball     users         1024 Dec  2 11:21 help
-rwxr-xr-x   1 bball     users        15569 Dec  2 11:22 install.ini
-rw-r--r--   1 bball     users       274209 Dec 17 11:20 instdb.ins
drwxr-xr-x   2 bball     users         1024 Dec  2 11:21 kino
-rw-r--r--   1 bball     users         5199 Oct 27 10:00 l_soffice.xpm
drwxr-xr-x   2 bball     users         3072 Dec  2 11:21 lib
-rw-r--r--   1 bball     users          812 Oct 27 10:00 s_soffice.xpm
-rwxr-xr-x   1 bball     users         8406 Jan  4 09:52 sofficerc
drwxr-xr-x   3 bball     users         1024 Dec  2 11:38 store
```

4

```
drwxr-xr-x  13 bball    users         1024 Dec 17 11:43 template
drwxr-xr-x   2 bball    users         1024 Dec  2 12:08 wordbook
drwxr-xr-x   5 bball    users         1024 Dec  2 11:20 xp3
```

Although you don't find separate manual pages for `dir` or `vdir` (they're mentioned in the `ls` man page), you can get help with each command by using the `--help` option.

Listing and Combining Files with the `cat` Command

NEW TERM The `cat` (concatenate file) command is used to send the contents of files to your screen. You can also use this command to send files' contents into other files, too, using a process called *output redirection*. This section shows you some basic uses for this command. See Hour 6 for more about standard input, standard output, and redirection. Although `cat` can be useful for reading short files, it is usually used either to combine, create, overwrite, or append files. To use `cat` to look at a short file, you can enter the following:

```
# cat test.txt
This text file was created by the cat command.
Cat could be the world's simplest text editor.
If you read this book, you'll learn how to use cat.
This is the last line of text in this file.
```

The cat command also has a number of options. If you'd like to see your file with line numbers, perhaps to note a specific phrase, you can use the `-n` option:

```
# cat -n test.txt
     1  This text file was created by the cat command.
     2  Cat could be the world's simplest text editor.
     3  If you read this book, you'll learn how to use cat.
     4  This is the last line of text in this file.
```

You can also use cat to look at several files at once because `cat` accepts wildcards:

```
# cat -n test*
     1  This text file was created by the cat command.
     2  Cat could be the world's simplest text editor.
     3  If you read this book, you'll learn how to use cat.
     4  This is the last line of text in this file.
     5  This is the first line of test2.txt.
     6  This file was also created by cat.
     7  This is the last line of test2.txt.
```

As you can see, cat also includes a second file in its output and numbers each line of the output, not each file. Note that you can also see both files with the following:

```
# cat test.txt test2.txt
```

The output is exactly the same as if you used a wildcard.

But looking at several files is only one way to use cat. You can also use the cat command with the redirection operator (>) to combine files. For example, if you want to combine test.txt and test2.txt into a third file called test3.txt, you can use the following:

```
# cat test* > test3.txt
```

You can check the result as follows:

```
# ls -l test*
-rw-r--r--  1 bball    users        190 Jan  4 16:06 test.txt
-rw-r--r--  1 bball    users        108 Jan  4 16:07 test2.txt
-rw-r--r--  1 bball    users        298 Jan  4 16:07 test3.txt
```

But what if you want to combine test.txt and test2.txt without creating a larger, third file? In this case, you first decide whether you want the contents of test.txt to go into test2.txt or the contents of test2.txt to go into test.txt. Then, using cat with the >> redirection operator, you type the following:

```
# cat test.txt >> test2.txt
```

This appends the contents of test.txt to the end of the test2.txt. To check the results, use cat again:

```
# cat test2.txt
This is the first line of test2.txt.
This file was also created by cat.
This is the last line of test2.txt.
This text file was created by the cat command.
Cat could be the world's simplest text editor.
If you read this book, you'll learn how to use cat.
This is the last line of text in this file.
```

Note that you can instead enter the command as follows:

```
# cat -n test.txt >> test2.txt
```

Now the test2.txt file looks like this:

```
# cat test2.txt
This is the first line of test2.txt.
This file was also created by cat.
This is the last line of test2.txt.
     1  This text file was created by the cat command.
     2  Cat could be the world's simplest text editor.
     3  If you read this book, you'll learn how to use cat.
     4  This is the last line of text in this file.
```

4

Finally, here's a trick you can use if you want to create a short text file without running a word processor or text editor. Because the cat command can read the standard input, you can make the cat command create a file and fill it with your keystrokes. To do so, first type the following, using myfile.txt as the example file:

```
# cat > myfile.txt
```

Now enter some text, such as the following:

```
This is the cat word processor.
This is the end of the file.
```

Now press Ctrl+D to close the file. To see if this works, try the following:

```
# ls -l myfile.txt
-rw-r--r--   1 bball     users              61 Jan  4 16:11 myfile.txt

# cat myfile.txt
This is the cat word processor.
This is the end of the file.
```

The cat command prints out the contents of any file, not just text files. Although cat can be useful to look at one or several short files, what do you do when you want to read longer text files? Read on and learn about pager commands, which make life easier when reading longer files.

Reading Files with the more Command

NEW TERM The more command is one of a family of Linux commands called *pagers*. Pager commands let you browse through files, reading a screen or line at a time. This can be extremely helpful, especially if you read a lot of manual pages, because the man command uses a pager to display each page.

The more command is a traditional pager in the sense that it provides the basic features of early pagers. You can use more on the command line as follows:

```
# more longfile.txt
```

If you need help, you can press the H key to see a help screen. You can also run other commands from inside more by using the exclamation character (!). Reading through a text file is easy because you can advance one screen by pressing the Spacebar and go backward one screen by pressing the B key.

The more command also has a number of command-line options. You can customize the screen prompt (more displays the current percentage of the file you're reading), set the screen size (the number of lines shown when going forward or backward through your file), use multiple filenames or wildcards, and turn scrolling on or off, in addition to other options.

Although you might find the `more` command to be more than adequate in reading files, you might really like the `less` pager.

Browsing Files with the `less` Command

`less` is more or less like `more`, but `less` is also much more than `more`. Confused? Don't be, because `less`, like `more`, is also a pager command. Its author, Mark Nudelman, improved on a number of features in the `more` command and added many others.

The `less` command offers a number of advantages over `more`:

- You can scroll backwards and forwards through text files using your cursor keys.
- You can navigate through files with bookmarks by line numbers or by percentages of file.
- You have sophisticated searches, pattern options, and highlighting through multiple files.
- Keystrokes are compatible with word processing programs, such as `emacs`.
- The `less` command doesn't quit on you when you reach the end of a file or the end of the standard input.
- The information prompt at the bottom of the screen is more customizable and offers more information.
- There are loads of options, including a separate key setup program, `lesskey`, so you can customize which keys control `less`.

When you install Linux, the `less` pager is the default pager used by a number of programs, such as the `man` command. If you need to read compressed files (those with a `.gz` extension, and about which you'll learn in Hour 5), you can use the `zless` command found under the `/usr/bin` directory.

As an example, I first create a text file containing a list of all the OpenLinux commands in the `/usr/bin` directory with the `ls` command, as follows:

```
# ls /usr/bin >programs.txt
```

This command line creates a text file called `programs.txt`. To read this file, use the `less` command as in the following:

```
# less programs.txt
```

4

The `less` command loads the file and displays lines starting at the beginning of the file. To advance a single screen, press the Spacebar. To go back a single screen, press the B key. You can also use the cursor keys to move forward, backward, and even left and right! Normally, the `less` command prompt is a colon (:) at the bottom left of your screen. However, you can use the `-M` command-line option to view more information about your file, as follows:

```
# less -M programs.txt
```

Now when you browse through your file, the `less` command prints the file's name, the current and total line numbers, and a percentage number representing the current position in the file. The prompt looks something like the following:

```
programs.txt line 91/1221 8%
```

This shows that you're reading the file `programs.txt`, with the 91st line of 1221 lines displayed at the top of the screen. If you want to run another program, such as the `wc`, or word count program, type an exclamation mark, followed by your command line, and press Enter, as follows:

```
! wc programs.txt
```

The `wc` command echoes the number of lines, words, and characters for the file `programs.txt` back to your screen. After the command finishes, the `less` command prints the word `done` and asks you to press Enter.

You can also quickly search through a text file using a `less` search command. Press the forward slash (/) and then type part of a word or phrase. The `less` command searches through your file and highlights the first found instance of the search string. To search for the same phrase, just press / followed by the Enter key. To quit reading the file, press the Q key, and you return to your shell's command line.

Reading the Beginning or End of Files with the `head` and `tail` Commands

Although the `head` and `tail` commands are not pagers per se, they can make life a lot easier when all you want to do is read the beginning or end of a file. Although these programs, like most Linux commands, are designed to do only one or two things, they do these tasks well.

The `head` command has a number of options besides the traditional `-n` *x*, which prints the first *x* lines of a file. The `head` command in your Linux distribution, which is part of the GNU text utilities, also prints any number of 512-character, 1-kilobyte (1024 bytes), or megabyte-sized blocks from the beginning of a file. Like the `cat` command, `head` can handle binary files.If you use head in the traditional way, you strip off lines from the beginning of one or several files. For example, if you want to see the first two lines of each HTML file for the Linux Installation Guide, use head with the option -n 2, followed by the path to the files, as follows:

```
# head -n 2 /usr/doc/LDP/install-guide/install-guide-3.2.html/*.html
==> /usr/doc/LDP/install-guide/install-guide-3.2.html/
➥footnode.html <==
<!DOCTYPE HTML PUBLIC "-//IETF//DTD HTML 2.0//EN">
<!--Converted with LaTeX2HTML 96.1-h (September 30, 1996) by Nikos
➥Drakos (nikos@cbl.leeds.ac.uk), CBLU, University of Leeds -->

==> /usr/doc/LDP/install-guide/install-guide-3.2.html/gs.html <==
<!DOCTYPE HTML PUBLIC "-//IETF//DTD HTML 2.0//EN">
<!--Converted with LaTeX2HTML 96.1-h (September 30, 1996) by Nikos
➥Drakos (nikos@cbl.leeds.ac.uk), CBLU, University of Leeds -->
```

Note that I only include the output for the first two files and that the default output from the head command is to include the filename (enclosed by ==> and <==). If you prefer just to have the information with no filenames, use the -q option, as follows:

```
# head -n 2 /usr/doc/LDP/install-guide/install-guide-3.2.html/*.html
<!DOCTYPE HTML PUBLIC "-//IETF//DTD HTML 2.0//EN">
<!--Converted with LaTeX2HTML 96.1-h (September 30, 1996) by Nikos
➥Drakos (nikos@cbl.leeds.ac.uk), CBLU, University of Leeds -->

<!DOCTYPE HTML PUBLIC "-//IETF//DTD HTML 2.0//EN">
<!--Converted with LaTeX2HTML 96.1-h (September 30, 1996) by Nikos
➥Drakos (nikos@cbl.leeds.ac.uk), CBLU, University of Leeds -->
```

The tail command is especially useful when you face the task of reading through large files where the most useful information is at the end of the file. One example task is to look at the system messages for errors. One message file, located in /var/log, contains details of system operations, but the log is updated at the end of the message file. In other words, text is appended, so the most recent messages are at the end of the file. To look at the last 12 lines in the message file using tail, make sure you're logged in as root, and type the following:

```
# tail -n 12 /var/log/messages
Nov 12 21:02:02 localhost cardmgr[152]: initializing socket 0
Nov 12 21:02:02 localhost cardmgr[152]: socket 0: ATA/IDE
➥Fixed Disk Card
Nov 12 21:02:02 localhost cardmgr[152]: executing: 'insmod /
➥lib/modules/2.0.30/p
cmcia/fixed_cs.o'
Nov 12 21:02:03 localhost kernel: hdc: SunDisk SDCFB-4,
➥ 3MB w/1kB Cache, LBA, CH
S=123/2/32
Nov 12 21:02:03 localhost kernel: ide1 at 0x100-0x107,0x10e on irq 3
```

```
Nov 12 21:02:03 localhost kernel:  hdc: hdc1
Nov 12 21:02:03 localhost cardmgr[152]: executing:
➥'./fixed start hdc'
Nov 12 21:02:03 localhost cardmgr[152]: initializing socket 1
Nov 12 21:02:03 localhost cardmgr[152]: socket 1: Serial or
➥Modem Card
Nov 12 21:02:03 localhost kernel: tty01 at 0x02f8 (irq = 5)
➥is a 16550A
Nov 12 21:02:03 localhost cardmgr[152]: executing:
➥'insmod /lib/modules/2.0.30/p
cmcia/serial_cs.o'
Nov 12 21:30:17 localhost PAM_pwdb[556]: (su) session opened
➥for user root by bball(uid=0)
```

If you try this example, OpenLinux might report the following:

`tail: /var/log/messages: Permission denied`

This means that you're not logged in as the root operator! For security reasons, OpenLinux prevents casual users from reading your system logs. Instead, try using the su command as follows:

`su -c "tail -n 12 /var/log/messages`

After you press Enter, su asks for the root password. Type in the root operator's password and press Enter again to see the information. This is a handy way to run commands as root.

Being able to read large files in this way is convenient, considering that the system messages can grow to more than a million characters.

Summary

This hour introduces more than a dozen basic commands you use during your OpenLinux sessions. Knowing how to get help, read files, list directories, and navigate through your file system are important skills. You use many of these commands repeatedly as you learn how to use OpenLinux.

Q&A

Q **I've found files with names like README under different directories under the /usr/doc directory. How do I read a README file?**

A Use the less pager from the command line, followed by the complete pathname to the desired file. For example, to read the README file for the pdksh shell, type a command line with less as follows and press Enter:

```
less /usr/doc/pdksh-5.2.13/README
```

Q **Some pathnames are really long! Is there an easier way to read or list a file?**

A Using the previous example, you can use an asterisk (*) in the pathname as follows:

```
less /usr/doc/pdksh*/README.
```

Q **I typed the previous example but used an asterisk as follows:**

```
less /usr/doc/p*/README
```

The less command says that it is reading file 1 of 25! What happened, and how do I read the other files?

A There are at least 37 different directories under the /usr/doc directory with names that begin with the letter p. Obviously, 25 of these directories contain a file called README. In the less pager, to jump to the next file, type a colon (:) and press the N key.

Q **How do I list just directory names? For example, I want to see the names of all directories under the /usr/doc directory that begin with the letter z.**

A Use the -d, or directory command-line option with the ls command. To see all the directories with names beginning with the letter z, type the command as follows:

```
ls -d /usr/doc/z*
```

Exercises

1. Use the cd command to go to the /usr/bin directory. Then type cd and press Enter. Where are you?

2. Again, use the cd command, but this time go to the / directory. Type cd ~ and press Enter. Next, type cd - and press Enter. Where are you?

3. The cat command's -n option numbers lines displayed to your screen. How can you number lines in files you read with the less command?

HOUR 5

Manipulation and Searching Commands

In this hour, you'll learn about creating, copying, deleting, and moving files and directories. You'll also learn about searching files and how to compress and decompress files. This information builds on information you learned in the preceding hour, and the commands you learn here are used later in this book.

Manipulating Files or Directories

Using Linux isn't different from using any other computer operating system. You create, delete, and move files on your hard drive in order to organize your information. This section shows you how to do these tasks quickly and easily.

Although the graphical interface for Linux, the X Window System, might offer drag-and-drop capabilities or multiple selections in order to copy or delete files, many of the commands you learn here form the base of these operations. It is worth knowing how these programs work, even if you don't use Linux in the console mode.

Creating Files with the touch Command

The touch command is easy to use, and generally, there are two reasons to use it. The first reason is to create a file, and the second is to update a file's modification date. The touch command is part of the GNU file utilities package and has several options.

To create a file with touch, use the following:

```
# touch newfile
# ls -l newfile
-rw-r--r--   1 bball     users            0 Jan  5 12:40 newfile
```

As you can see, touch creates a file with a length, or size, of zero. You can also use the following:

```
# > newfile2
# ls -l new*
-rw-r--r--   1 bball     users            0 Jan  5 12:40 newfile
-rw-r--r--   1 bball     users            0 Jan  5 12:41 newfile2
```

Like touch, this creates a file with a length of zero. So why use touch if you can do this at the command line? Because touch can update a file's date or time. You can even use touch to change a file's date or time to the past or the future, for example:

```
# touch newfile2
# ls -l newfile2
-rw-r--r--   1 bball     users            0 Jan  5 12:44 newfile2
```

As you can see, the file newfile2 now has a timestamp 3 minutes younger (12:44 instead of 12:41). You can also set the time and date of a file to an arbitrary time and date by using the touch command's -t option, followed by a string of numbers representing the month, day, time, and year, for example:

```
# touch -t 1225130000 newfile2
# ls -l --full-time new*
-rw-r--r--   1 bball     users            0 Tue Jan 05 12:40:14 1999 newfile
-rw-r--r--   1 bball     users            0 Mon Dec 25 13:00:00 2000 newfile2
```

The --full-time option and long format listing of the ls command show that the file newfile2 now has a timestamp of 1 p.m., Christmas Day, 2000 (which appears to be, and is indeed, a Monday).

One use for touch is during backup operations. Either before or after backing up a series of files or directories, you can use touch to update the timestamps of your files so that the backup program has a reference time for the next backup session. Another use for touch is to either delete or retain log files on your system during automated file cleanup by scheduled programs managed by cron (see the section "Using the cron Daemon" in Hour 24, "Using Scheduling to Automate System Management"). If you make a log file old enough, it is deleted. If you update it, the file is retained.

Deleting Files with the rm Command

The rm command deletes files. This command has several simple options but should be used cautiously. Why? Because when rm deletes a file, it is gone. (You might be able to recover portions of text files, though; see the mc command later this hour for pointers.)

> Always running Linux while logged in as the root operator and using the rm command has caused many untold tales of woe and grief. Why? Because with one simple command, you can wipe out not only your Linux system, but also any mounted file systems including DOS partitions, flash RAM cards, or removable hard drives, as follows:
>
> `# rm -fr /*`
>
> This command removes all files and directories recursively with the -r option, starting at the root (/) directory. If you must run Linux as root, make sure to back up your system, and read Hour 23, "Backing Up and Restoring Your System."

The rm command deletes one or several files from the command line. You can use any of the following:

```
# rm file
# rm file1 file2 file3
# rm file*
```

The first command line deletes a single file named file, the second command line deletes three files, and the third command line deletes any file in the current directory with a filename beginning with the letters file. One of the safer ways to use rm is through the -i, or interactive, option where you're asked if you want to delete the file, for example:

```
# rm -i new*
rm: remove `newfile'? y
rm: remove `newfile2'? y
```

5

You can also force file deletion by using the `-f` option, as in the following:

```
# rm -f new*
```

If you use the `-f` option and no files match the `new*` pattern, the `rm` command fails without displaying an error message. However, if `rm` finds a directory, even if it is empty, it does not delete the directory, and it complains, even if you use `-f`, as in the following:

```
# rm -f temp*
rm: temp: is a directory
rm: temp2: is a directory
```

When you combine the `-f` and `-r` options, you can delete directories and all files or directories found within, provided you own them or have permission; see Hour 22, "Handling Files and Your File System." `-f` and `-r` can be combined as in the following example:

```
# rm -fr temp*
```

The `-fr` option also makes `rm` act like the `rmdir` command (discussed later this hour). Be extremely careful when you use this option! Generally, when you delete a file in OpenLinux, the file is gone forever!

Some X window environments, such as KDE, or productivity suites, like StarOffice, offer "trash can" approaches to deleting files—files are not really deleted, just moved to a temporary directory. This is a safe, but not fail-safe, approach to deleting or recovering files. If you really need help with recovering a file, you might be able to use the `mc`, or Midnight Commander, command discussed later this hour.

Creating Directories with the `mkdir` Command

Use the `mkdir` command to create one or several directories. You might be surprised to know that `mkdir` can also create a whole hierarchy of directories, including parents and children, with a single command line.

This command is one of the basic tools, along with `cp` and `mv`, you can use to organize your information. Take a look at some examples. The following simple command line creates a single directory:

```
# mkdir temp
```

But you can also create multiple directories, as follows:

```
# mkdir temp2 temp3 temp4
```

You can also type the following to make a directory named `child` under `temp`:

```
# mkdir temp/child
```

This works because the `temp` directory exists (you just created it). But, suppose you type the following:

```
# mkdir temp5/child
mkdir: cannot make directory `temp5/child': No such file or directory
```

As you can see, `mkdir` complains because the `temp5` directory does not exist. To build a hierarchy of directories with `mkdir`, you must use the `-p`, or parent, option, as in the following example:

```
# mkdir -p temp5/parent/child
# tree temp5
temp5
`-- parent
    `-- child

2 directories, 0 files
```

As you can see, not only does `mkdir` create the `temp5` directory, but also a subdirectory called `parent`, and a subdirectory under parent called `child`.

Now that you know how to create directories, take a look at how to remove them.

Removing Directories with the `rmdir` Command

The `rmdir` command removes directories. To remove a directory, all you have to do is type the following:

```
# rmdir tempdirectory
```

But there's a catch: the directory must be empty first! If you try to delete a directory containing any files, you get an error message like this:

```
# rmdir temp5
rmdir: temp5: Directory not empty
```

In this example, `temp5` contains other directories. The `rmdir` command also complains if a directory contains only files and not directories. You can use the `rm` command to remove the files first (remember to be careful if you use the `-fr` option), move the files somewhere else, or rename the directory with the `mv` command, which is discussed next.

The `rmdir` command, like `mkdir`, has a `-p` option. You can use this option to remove directory hierarchies, as follows:

```
# rmdir -p temp5
rmdir: temp5: Directory not empty
```

Hmm... That doesn't work! How about the following:

```
# rmdir -p temp5/parent
rmdir: temp5/parent: Directory not empty
```

Hey! That doesn't work either. Now try this:

```
# rmdir -p temp5/*
rmdir: temp5/parent: Directory not empty
```

This is getting frustrating! Try it one more time:

```
# rmdir -p temp5/parent/child
```

Finally! As you can see, you must specify the complete directory tree to delete it. If you use the same command line without the `-p` option, only the child directory is deleted. But what if there are two or more subdirectories, as in the following example:

```
# mkdir -p temp5/parent/child
# mkdir temp5/parent/child2
# tree temp5
temp5
`-- parent
    |-- child
    `-- child2

3 directories, 0 files
```

In order to delete the entire directory system of `temp5`, you need to use the following:

```
# rmdir temp5/parent/*
```

Now you know how to create and remove directories. Next, you learn about the `mv` command, which you can use to move or rename files and directories.

Renaming Files with the `mv` Command

The `mv` command, called the rename command, indeed renames files or directories—but it is also known to many as a move command that moves files or directories around your file system.

Actually, in the technical sense, the files or directories are not really moved. If you insist on knowing all the gory details, read the *Linux System Administrator's Guide*, or the SAG, available through the following site:

```
http://metalab.unc.edu/LDP/LDP/sag/index.html
```

Don't want to read the SAG online? You can probably find a copy installed on your OpenLinux system. Try using the lynx text-only web browser, as follows:

```
lynx /usr/doc/LDP/system-admin-guide/sag-0.6-html/sag.html
```

For more information about using the lynx browser, see Hour 13, "Internet Downloading and Browsing."

In its simplest form, mv can rename files, for example:

```
# touch file1
# mv file1 file2
```

This command renames file1 to file2. Besides renaming files, mv can rename directories, whether they are empty or not. For example, even if you create a directory structure with the mkdir command, you can use the mv command to rename the new top-level directory, like so:

```
# mkdir -p temp/temp2/temp3
# mv temp newtemp
```

Although mv has nine different options, this section concentrates on the two most commonly used, -b (backup) and -i (interactive). These options enable you to use mv in a fairly safe way—mv not only renames but also overwrites quickly and silently (without asking)! The first option, -b, creates a backup of any file or directory you rename to an existing name, for example:

```
# touch uno deux tres
# ls uno deux tres
deux   tres   uno
# mv uno deux
# ls uno deux tres
ls: uno: No such file or directory
deux   tres
```

As you can see, without using -b, mv not only renames the file uno to deux, but deletes the file deux in the process. Is this dangerous? You bet! Now, try the -b option:

```
# touch uno
# ls uno deux tres
deux   tres   uno
# mv -b uno deux
# ls deux* tres
deux    deux~   tres
```

5

This example shows that although the file uno is renamed replacing the file deux, a backup of deux with a default extension of the tilde (~) is created.

The mv command can work silently, or as with rm, you can use the -i option, for example:

```
# touch file2 file3
# mv file2 file3
# touch file2
# mv -i file2 file3
mv: replace `file3'? y
```

Here, I create two files, and then rename the file file2 to file3, which deletes the original file3. However, I then use the -i option, and the mv command asks if I want to overwrite the file. The mv command does not ask for permission if no overwriting takes place, even if you use -i. You can also combine the -b and -i options as follows:

```
# mv -bi file2 file3
```

Now that you know how to delete, rename, or move your files, how do you copy files?

Copying with the cp Command

The cp, or copy, command copies files or directories. This command has nearly 40 command-line options. They aren't all covered here, but you learn about some of the most commonly used options, which save you time and trouble.

You'll most likely first use cp in its simplest form, for example:

```
# cp file1 file2
```

This copies file1 to create file2 and, unlike mv, leaves file1 in place. But you must be careful when using cp because you can copy a file onto a second file, effectively replacing it! In this regard, cp can act like mv. To show you how this can happen, try creating three files, each with a line of text, using the cat command:

```
# cat > file1
this is file1
# cat > file2
this is file 2
# cat > file3
this is the third file
# ls -l file*
-rw-r--r--   1 bball     users          14 Jan  5 13:29 file1
-rw-r--r--   1 bball     users          15 Jan  5 13:29 file2
-rw-r--r--   1 bball     users          23 Jan  5 13:29 file3
```

Now, copy a file onto another file, and then check the file sizes and the contents of the new file, as follows:

```
# cp file1 file2
# ls -l file*
-rw-r--r--  1 bball     users          14 Jan  5 13:29 file1
-rw-r--r--  1 bball     users          14 Jan  5 13:31 file2
-rw-r--r--  1 bball     users          23 Jan  5 13:29 file3
# cat file2
this is file1
```

It should be obvious that file1 replaces file2. To avoid this problem (unless you really want to overwrite the file), you can use the -b or -i options, which work like mv. Here's an example:

```
# cp -i file1 file2
cp: overwrite `file2'? n
# cp -bi file1 file2
cp: overwrite `file2'? y
# ls file*
file1   file2   file2~  file3
```

Note that file2, which is overwritten, is backed up.

The cp command can also copy a number of files at one time. The following example shows how to copy all the files in directory tempdir1 to directory tempdir2:

```
# cp tempdir1/* tempdir2
# tree tempdir2
tempdir2
|-- temp1file1
|-- temp1file2
`-- temp1file3

0 directories, 3 files
```

Like the rm command, cp also has an -r, or recursive, option. You can use this option to copy one directory into another. For example, to copy the tempdir1 directory and its files into tempdir2, use this syntax:

```
# cp -r tempdir1 tempdir2
# tree tempdir2
tempdir2
|-- temp1file1
|-- temp1file2
|-- temp1file3
`-- tempdir1
    |-- temp1file1
    |-- temp1file2
    `-- temp1file3

1 directory, 6 files
```

5

Finally, the cp command has the -p option, which is similar to mkdir's -p option. Normally, when you copy a file inside several directories into another directory, only the file is copied. The following example only copies temp1file1 into tempdir3:

```
# tree tempdir2
tempdir2
|-- temp1file1
|-- temp1file2
|-- temp1file3
`-- tempdir1
    |-- temp1file1
    |-- temp1file2
    `-- temp1file3

1 directory, 6 files
# cp tempdir2/tempdir1/temp1file1 tempdir3
```

However, what if you want to copy a file along with its directory structure? To do this, you can use the -P option:

```
# cp -P tempdir2/tempdir1/temp1file1 tempdir3
# tree tempdir3
tempdir3
`-- tempdir2
    `-- tempdir1
        `-- temp1file1

2 directories, 1 file
```

Not only does cp copy the single file, but it has also creates the subdirectory structure.

Creating Hard and Symbolic Links with the ln Command

Linux supports both hard and symbolic links. Although it is not important that you understand how links in Linux work, you need to understand the difference between these two types of links, and how to use links while you use Linux. To create hard or symbolic links, use the ln, or link, command.

NEW TERM   The ln command creates both types of links and links files with other files (including directories, which under OpenLinux are simply files, too). The important difference is that *hard* links directly link two files on only the same file system. On the other hand, you can use a *symbolic* link between directories or files that span different file systems. Hard links also have other advantages. If you use the ln command to create a hard link, you specify a second file on the command line you can use to reference the original file, as in the following example:

```
# cat > file1
This is file1
# ln file1 file2
# ls -l file*
-rw-r--r--   2 bball     users          14 Jan  5 13:32 file1
-rw-r--r--   2 bball     users          14 Jan  5 13:32 file2

# cat file2
This is file1
```

You can see that file2 is exactly the same as file1. If you delete file1, file2 remains. If you make changes to file1, such as adding text, these changes appear in file2, and if you make changes to file2, file1 is also updated. Although you can see two files, each 14 characters in size, only 14 characters of hard drive space are used for the original file (okay, technically more than that, but it depends on the block size of the partition or type of hard drive).

On the other hand, although symbolic links are useful, they have a drawback. The next examples show you why. First, to create a symbolic link, use the ln command's -s option:

```
# cat >file1
This is file1
# ln -s file1 file2
# ls -l file*
-rw-r--r--   1 bball     users          14 Jan  5 13:48 file1
lrwxrwxrwx   1 bball     users           5 Jan  5 13:48 file2 -> file1
```

Note the arrow pointing from file2 to file1. This tells you that file2 is a symbolic link to file1. Also note that file2 is smaller in length than file1. Symbolic links are different from hard links in that a symbolic link is merely an alias for the original file. Nothing happens to the original file if you delete the symbolic link. However, if you delete the original file, your symbolic link can't help you at all:

```
# rm -f file1
# cat file2
cat: file2: No such file or directory
```

Because the original file, file1, no longer exists, you can't access its contents through the symbolic link, file2. However, symbolic links do have an advantage over hard links. You can use a symbolic link to point to a directory on your OpenLinux file system or even another file system. In the following example, if you try to create a hard link to the /usr/local/games directory, the ln command complains and quits:

```
# ln /usr/local/games play
ln: /usr/local/games: hard link not allowed for directory
```

5

But you can use a symbolic link, as follows:

```
# ln -s /usr/local/games play
# ls -l play
lrwxrwxrwx  1 bball  users   16 Jan  5 14:12 play -> /usr/local/games
```

Now, instead of typing a long command like

```
# cd /usr/local/games
```

you can use

```
# cd play
```

 Symbolic links to other directories on other file systems, such as a DOS or Windows partition, can be handy. For example, having a directory called dos in your home directory that is linked to /mnt/dos/windows/desktop makes copying or moving files to and from Linux and Windows a lot easier. For example, if you want to have a linked directory named dos in your home directory and your DOS file system is mounted under the /mnt/dos directory, first make sure that the DOS file system is mounted, and then use the ln command to create a symbolic link, like so:

```
# ln -s /mnt/dos/windows/desktop dos
```

See Hour 22 for details about mounting other file systems.

So far, you've learned about using the command line. If you're familiar with more graphical interfaces for manipulating files, you'll like the next program, mc.

Handling Files with the Midnight Commander Program

The mc program, called Midnight Commander, is a graphical interface for handling files (see Figure 5.1). It is a visual shell (you'll learn more about shells in the next hour, "Using the Shell"). To start mc, type the following at the command line:

```
# mc
```

This section does not cover all the details of the mc program. Here are the highlights of its features:

- Provides a visual interface to two directories at a time
- Enables directory browsing with mouse clicks
- Enables menu-driven file operations with dialog boxes, mouse, keyboard and function key support

- Has an open command line to your shell

- Runs commands through mouse clicks

- Has extensive, built-in hypertext help screens

- Emulates and supports the ls, cp, ln, mv, mkdir, rmdir, rm, cd, pwd, find, chown, chgrp, and tree commands

- Compares directory contents

- Uses customized menus so you can build your own commands

- Can use network links for telnet or FTP operations (see Hour 13)

- Offers mouse-click decompression of files (see the section "Compressing Files with the gzip Command" later this hour)

- Can undelete files if your Linux file system is configured to support this capability

Midnight Commander is a handy and convenient tool to use for file handling and directory navigation. You have to invest some time learning how to use this program, but if you've used similar file-management interfaces, you'll feel right at home.

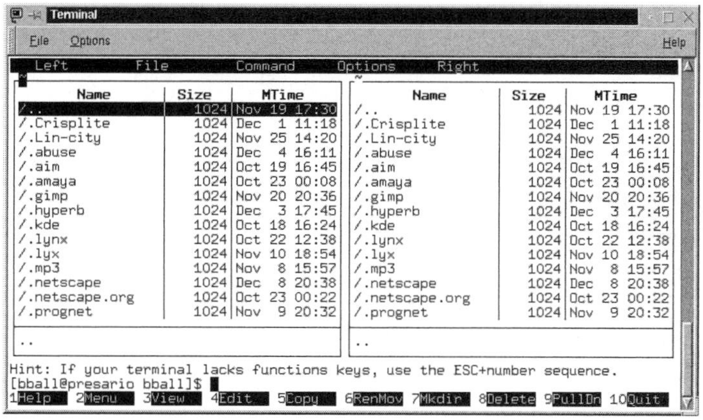

FIGURE 5.1

The Midnight Commander visual shell displays a graphical interface to Linux file commands.

Searching Files

This section introduces you to the use of sophisticated wildcards, or regular expressions, along with short examples of file searches using the grep family of programs. If you understand and use these expressions, you can create refined search techniques you can use again and again. You'll save time and effort during your work, and your learning investment will pay big dividends throughout your Linux experience.

What Are Regular Expressions?

NEW TERM *Regular expressions* are patterns that use special syntax to match strings (usually in text in files, unless your search is for filenames). There are also extended regular expressions that can use additional operators in the search patterns. The difference, important for syntax, should not deter you from learning how to construct patterns that accurately match your desired search targets. This is important if you're looking for text in files and critical if you're performing potentially dangerous tasks, such as multiple file deletions across your system.

You can build an infinite number of regular expressions using only a small subset of pattern characters. Table 5.1 contains a short list of some of these characters. You should be familiar with at least one (the asterisk) from the previous examples.

TABLE 5.1 COMMON REGULAR EXPRESSIONS

Expression	Matching
*	Any character
? or .	A single character
{x}	Preceding character x times
{x,y}	Preceding character at least x times but no more than y
{x,}	Preceding character at least x times
(xxx) ¦ (XXX)	String xxx or XXX
[xxx] or [x-x]	A character in a range of characters
[XYZ]+	X, Y, or Z at least once
\x	A character such as ? or \
^pattern	pattern at the beginning of a line
$pattern	pattern at the end of a line

This is not a comprehensive list of pattern characters. For more details, you can read the ed manual page (the ed command is discussed in Hour 14, "Text Processing"). For now, try several simple examples using different patterns.

The asterisk is useful for finding matches to all characters. For example, if you want to find all the text files in your directory with an extension of .txt, you can use the following:

```
# ls *.txt
14days.txt    96hours.txt   datalog.txt   datebook.txt  day67.txt
```

But suppose you want a list of all the ?files in your directory with numbers in the file-name? You can try to string multiple searches on the ls command line, like this:

```
# ls *0* *1* *2* *3* *4* *5* *6* *7* *8* *9*
08100097.db        14days.txt         backup001.file     phonelog.111597
08100097.db        32days.msg         day67.txt          phonelog.111597
08100097.db        32days.msg         day67.txt          phonelog.111597
08100097.db        96hours.txt        message.76
08100097.db        96hours.txt        message.76
14days.txt         backup001.file     phonelog.111597
```

Obviously, this is not the result you want because the multiple searches have printed duplicate filenames. To find exactly what you want, use a regular expression that tells ls to list any file that has a number appearing in the file's name, as follows:

```
# ls *[0123456789]*
0001file.0009      32days.msg         day67.txt
08100097.db        96hours.txt        message.76
14days.txt         backup001.file     phonelog.111597
```

This shows all the files containing numbers in the filename because you specify a range of characters or, in this case, numbers in your search pattern. You can also use a regular expression shorthand to build a shorter expression to do the same thing, for example:

```
# ls *[0-9]*
0001file.0009      32days.msg         day67.txt
08100097.db        96hours.txt        message.76
14days.txt         backup001.file     phonelog.111597
```

How you specify your pattern characters in your expression is important. If you only want a list of files ending in a number, you can use the following:

```
# ls *[0-9]
0001file.0009      message.76         phonelog.111597
```

If you only want a list of files beginning with a number, you can use this:

```
# ls [0-9]*
0001file.0009  08100097.db    14days.txt     32days.msg     96hours.txt
```

Here's a fun exercise: What if you want to list those files with numbers only inside or on both ends of a filename? Try these:

```
# ls *[-a-z][0-9]*
backup001.file  day67.txt
# ls [0-9]*[a-z]*[0-9]
0001file.0009
```

5

Finally, how do you match patterns when the pattern you're looking for contains a pattern-matching character? Easy! Use the backslash to *escape* the character, for example:

```
#  ls *\?*
cathy?.message
```

As you can see, using regular ?expressions can take some practice, b-ut your efforts are well rewarded. Try experimenting with different expressions to see if you can come up with results similar to the examples shown in this section.

Searching Inside Files with the grep Commands

This section introduces you to the family of grep commands. You'll learn about grep, egrep, and fgrep. In order to use these commands, you should know how to use some of the pattern-matching techniques already discussed. You'll use these commands to search through files and extract text. Each of these programs works by searching each line in a file. You can search single files or a range of files.

Each of the grep commands is basically the same and has nearly 20 different command-line options. The only real difference is that egrep uses a slightly different syntax for its pattern matching, whereas fgrep uses fixed strings. You'll see examples of each program and use some of the common options. For specific details about the pattern-matching capabilities of these programs, see the grep manual page.

To show you the difference in each program's search pattern syntax, I'll look for different patterns in Matt Welsh's *Linux Basic Installation Guide* (available at http://metalab.unc.edu/LDP or on your OpenLinux system in the /usr/doc/ LDP directory). For example, if you want to find all the lines in the guide that begin with a number, use the following syntax:

```
# grep ^[0-9] guide.txt
1 Introduction to Linux                             1
2 Obtaining and Installing Linux                   40
3 Linux Tutorial                                   85
4 System Administration                           137
...
# egrep ^[0-9] guide.txt
1 Introduction to Linux                             1
2 Obtaining and Installing Linux                   40
3 Linux Tutorial                                   85
4 System Administration                           137
...
# fgrep ^[0-9] guide.txt
```

You can see that `grep` and `egrep` returned a search (I deleted all the output except the first four lines). Note, however, that `fgrep` can not handle regular expressions. You must use fixed patterns or strings with the `fgrep` command, for example:

```
# fgrep friend guide.txt
large extent  by the  window manager.   This friendly  program is in
copy Linux from a friend who may already have the software,  or share
(Unfortunately, the system was being unfriendly.)
```

Now use `egrep` to try searching for the pattern of the letter (b) in the file:

```
# egrep "\([b]\)" guide.txt
(see Section 1.8 for a list of compatible boards), or (b) there is an
connect to the  network, or  (b) you  have a  ``dynamic'' IP address,
```

You see that exactly two lines in the file match (b). See what happens when you search with grep:

```
# grep "\([b]\)" guide.txt
This is version 2.2.2 of the book, "Linux Installation and Getting
to PostScript printers. This document was generated by a set of tools
from LaTeX source, so there may be a number of formatting problems.
This is not the "official" version of the book! Please see
...
```

Whoa! Not exactly what you wanted, is it? As you can see, grep does not use the same syntax as the `egrep` command. But you can use a simpler approach:

```
# grep "(b)" guide.txt
(see Section 1.8 for a list of compatible boards), or (b) there is an
connect to the  network, or  (b) you  have a  ``dynamic'' IP address,
```

This pattern works with grep and fgrep. If you try this pattern with egrep, you get the same results as if you tried extended regular expressions with grep (each line with a (b)).

Each grep program accepts nearly the same set of command-line options. One popular option is `-n`, or line numbering. This is handy because you see which lines in the file contain matches. This example works for each grep program:

```
# egrep -n "friend" guide.txt
1242:large extent by the window manager.  This friendly  program is
1942:copy Linux from a friend who may already have the software, or
5161:(Unfortunately, the system was being unfriendly.)
```

You can see that matches were made on lines 1242, 1942, and 5161. Another feature of these programs is that you don't have to retype your patterns each time you want to search. As a simple example, if you need to repeatedly search files for different words, you can put these into a file for grep to use. First, create a text file and then use the `-f` option to specify the file, as follows:

5

```
# cat > mywords
wonderful
Typewriter
War
# grep -nf mywords guide.txt
574:Typewriter Used to represent screen interaction, as in
617:software since the original Space War,  or, more recently, Emacs
1998:Now you must be convinced  of how wonderful Linux  is, and all
2549:inanimate object is a wonderful  way to relieve the occasional
3790:   Warning:  Linux  cannot currently  use 33090  sectors of
7780:to wear the magic hat when it is not needed, despite wonderful
10091:wonderful programs and configurations are available with a bit
```

Because you also use the line-numbering option, you should note that it has to come before the -f, or file, option, or grep reports an error, complains it can't find file n, and quits.

You can make grep act like fgrep with the -F option or like egrep with the -E option. You can also find a unique version of grep on your system, called zgrep, which you can use to search compressed files, the topic of the next section.

Compressing and Uncompressing Files

This section introduces you to the basics of archiving and compressing files. However, for details concerning using these programs for the purpose of system management or backing up your system, see Hour 23. Read on, and you'll learn how to build your own archives and save disk space.

Creating Archives with the Tape Archive Command

The tar (tape archive) program has its roots in the early days of computing before floppy drives, hard disks, and CD-ROMs. Software was distributed and backed up on large reels of magnetic tape, so one of the first programs to run on computers was a tape reader. Over time, the tar program proved its merit as a convenient way to transport files, and many programs for Linux come packaged in tar archives (your OpenLinux CD-ROM uses the rpm program to package files; see Hour 22).

Using tar, you can create an archive file containing multiple directories and files. The version of tar installed on your system also supports a -z option to use the gzip program to compress your archive. (gzip is discussed later in this chapter.)

The tar command has a bewildering array of options, but it's not hard to use. You can quickly and easily create an archive of any desired directory.

First, create a directory with three files, and then create a subdirectory with another three files:

```
# mkdir mydir
# cd mydir
# touch file1 file2 file3
# mkdir mydir2
# cd mydir2
# touch file21 file22 file23
# cd ../..
# tree mydir
mydir
|-- file1
|-- file2
|-- file3
`-- mydir2
    |-- file21
    |-- file22
    `-- file23

1 directory, 6 files
```

Now that you have a directory and files, create a tar archive using the c (create) and f (file) options with this command:

```
# tar cf mydir.tar mydir
# ls -l *.tar
-rw-r--r--  1 bball    users        10240 Jan  5 15:01 mydir.tar
```

Notice that your original directory is left untouched. By default, tar does not delete the original directories or files. You can use the --remove-files option if you want to do this, but it's not recommended. If you want to see what's going on, you can use the v option, like this:

```
# tar cvf mydir.tar mydir
mydir/
mydir/file1
mydir/file2
mydir/file3
mydir/mydir2/
mydir/mydir2/file21
mydir/mydir2/file22
mydir/mydir2/file23
```

The tar command shows you what directories and files are being added. Does this mean you have to add all the files in your directories? No! You can use the w, or interactive option, and have tar ask if you want each file added. This can be handy for selectively backing up small directories, for example:

```
# tar cwf mydir.tar mydir
add mydir?y
add mydir/file1?n
add mydir/file2?y
add mydir/file3?n
add mydir/mydir2?y
add mydir/mydir2/file21?y
add mydir/mydir2/file22?n
add mydir/mydir2/file23?y
```

Here I left out file1, file3, and file22 from this archive. But how can you make sure? One way is to use two tar options, t to list an archive's contents and f to specify a tar archive to use, for example:

```
# tar tf mydir.tar
mydir/
mydir/file2
mydir/mydir2/
mydir/mydir2/file21
mydir/mydir2/file23
```

Note that if options are placed in the wrong order (like the grep example), tar complains and quits. Now that you know how to create and see the contents of an archive, you can learn how to extract the whole archive or a single file. To extract everything, you can use the -x, or extract, option with -f. Just so you know what's going on, include the -v option, too:

```
# tar xvf mydir.tar
mydir/
mydir/file2
mydir/mydir2/
mydir/mydir2/file21
mydir/mydir2/file23
```

If you want only a few files from your archive, you can again use the w option:

```
# tar xvwf mydir.tar
extract mydir/?y
mydir/
extract mydir/file2?y
mydir/file2
extract mydir/mydir2/?y
mydir/mydir2/
extract mydir/mydir2/file21?y
mydir/mydir2/file21
extract mydir/mydir2/file23?y
mydir/mydir2/file23
```

Here, I went through the archive interactively extracting files. If you want a single file from an archive, you can specify the file on the command line. For this example, the original mydir is removed, and I'm using an empty directory:

```
# tar xf mydir.tar mydir/mydir2/file23
# tree mydir
mydir
`-- mydir2
    `-- file23

1 directory, 1 file
```

As you can see, only one file is extracted. Be careful, though! The tar command doesn't overwrite whole directories, but it does overwrite files with the same name.

Try experimenting with tar before you start building archives. Some other features to try are selectively deleting files from an archive or adding a file to an existing archive, which is something the next program, cpio, can do, too.

> You can use other programs, such as BRU-2000 or the taper script to back up your file system or selected files and directories. OpenLinux can also create file archives automatically through cron scheduling. See Hour 23 for information on BRU-2000 and the taper script; see Hour 24 for details on cron scheduling.

Creating cpio Archives

The cpio command copies files in and out of tar or cpio archives. Because cpio is compatible with tar, this section doesn't go into all the details of how it works, but it has some features that tar does not, such as the following:

- Support for both cpio and tar archives
- Support for a number of older tape formats
- The capability to read files' names from a pipe (which you'll learn about in the next hour)

Very few, if any, software packages for Linux are distributed in cpio format. Chances are you won't run across any cpio archives in your search for new software across the Internet. But if you're interested in the details about cpio, see its man page. For an example of how to use cpio to back up specific files, see Hour 23.

5

Compressing Files with the `gzip` Command

The `gzip` command compresses files. This program is not only handy for saving disk space by compressing large, less often used files, but could be, in combination with `tar`, the most popular compressed file format for Linux. You'll often find files with the `.tgz` or `.tar.gz` format while searching for new Linux software across the Internet.

You'll also find that much of the documentation under your `/usr/doc/HOWTO` directory was compressed with `gzip`. This can save a lot of space. According the Free Software Foundation folks in `gzip`'s manual page, `gzip` has a 60–70%compression rate for text files.

The `gzip` command is easy to use. To compress a file or tape archive, enter the following:

```
# gzip mydir.tar
```

By default, `gzip` compresses your file, appends a `.gz` extension, and deletes your original file. To uncompress your file, you can use the `gzip` companion program, `gunzip`, or the `gzip -d` (decompress) option. You have to make sure the file has a `.gz` (or `.Z`, `-gz`, `.z`, `-z`, or `_z`) extension, or both `gzip` and `gunzip` complain. If you want to specify your own extension, use the `-S` (suffix) option. For example, to compress a tape archive with the extension `.gzipped`, use `gzip` and its `-S` option, like so:

```
# gzip -S .gzipped mydir.tar
```

The `gzip` command also handles zipped, compressed, or pack compressed files. If you want more information during compression or decompression, you can use `-l`, or list option, to see the compressed or decompressed sizes of files. After compressing the directory `mydir` from the previous example, use the `gzip` to get statistics like this:

```
# gzip -l mydir.tar.gz
compressed   uncompr. ratio uncompressed_name
     239      10240  97.9% mydir.tar
```

Finally, `gzip` also has a helpful option, `-t`, to test the integrity of a compressed file. If the file is okay, `gzip` reports nothing. If you need to see `OK`, use `-tv` when you test a file.

Compressing Files with the `compress` Command

The `compress` command does just that: it compresses files. This is one of the earlier compression utilities for the UNIX world.

Files created with `compress` traditionally have a `.Z` extension. To compress a file, enter the following:

```
# compress file
```

To uncompress a file, use this:

```
# uncompress file.Z
```

As with `gzip`, you must specify a filename with a `.Z` extension, or `compress` will complain.

> Interested in other compression utilities for Linux? Look on your system for `zip`, `unzip`, `zipcloak`, `zipnote`, `zipsplit`, `zless`, `zcat`, `znew`, `zmore`, `zcmp`, `pack`, `compact`, `shar`, `unshar`, or `zforce`. You might not find all these installed, but you can find versions at favorite Linux software sites (such as `http://metalab.unc.edu/pub/Linux`) that work with OpenLinux.

Summary

This hour introduced the basic OpenLinux commands needed to create, delete, move, copy, search, save, and compress files and directories. As you learn more about OpenLinux during your sessions, you'll build on your basic knowledge to create more complex and custom commands.

Q&A

Q Are there any other file compression programs for OpenLinux?

A Yes. You might be able to get even better compression with the `bzip2` command. This program uses a different compression algorithm than `gzip` and is included with OpenLinux under the `/bin` directory. You can recognize these archives by the `.bz2` extension.

Q I've seen some files with an extension of `.uu` and wonder if these are compressed files?

A No. A file with a `.uu` extension has been converted from a binary format to plain text by the `uuencode` command. To convert the file back to its original form, use the `uudecode` command like so:

```
uudecode somefile.uu
```

These commands are used by some users to prepare artwork, programs, or other binary format files for transmission by electronic mail or for posting in a Usenet newsgroup message (see Hour 12, "Configuring Internet News," for more information about Usenet news).

5

Q **How can I look at what's inside a binary file? If I try to use the cat or less commands, I see a lot of garbage.**

A Try using the strings command. To see how to use strings with less, see Hour 6, "Using the Shell."

Q **How do I get more information about each file inside a tape archive? I know that the t option shows the file and directory names.**

A Use the v option along with t on the tar command line to view the permissions, owner, group, file size, date, time, and name of each item in a tape archive.

Exercises

1. The tar program can perform file compression during archiving operations. Create a compressed tape archive of a test directory using tar.

2. There are several other compression programs included with OpenLinux. What are their names? (Hint: Use whatever command you think is "apropos"priate!)

3. How can you find all the compressed files included with your OpenLinux distribution?

HOUR 6

Using the Shell

In this hour you're introduced to the shell. Although the trend in personal computing in the last 10 years has been to move away from the command line to a point-and-click interface, the shell is still very much alive in Linux and is used by many Linux programs.

This hour doesn't go into a detailed history of Linux or UNIX shells or take sides in a debate over which computing interface is easier or better to use. Nor does this hour delve into shell programming—there's not enough room in this hour (or even this book) to do so. This hour does, however, discuss the different shells you can find on your OpenLinux CD-ROM, show you how to use the shell to make your Linux experience more enjoyable, and highlight some of the basics of using the shell and the command line.

What is a Shell?

If you're not using the X Window System, the shell is one of the most important programs you use. The shell provides the interface to Linux so you can run programs. In fact, the shell is just another Linux program.

Although you can set up and run Linux without a shell (see Hour 21, "Basic System Administration," for details), even if you use graphical interface programs, you might find that you need to use the shell's command line.

The shell is a command interpreter that can be used to start, suspend, stop, or even write programs. The shell is an integral part of Linux and is part of the design of Linux and UNIX. If you imagine the Linux kernel as the center of a sphere, the shell is the outer layer surrounding the kernel. When you pass commands from the shell or other programs to Linux, the kernel (usually) responds appropriately.

There are many types of shells, but at least five (not counting the visual shell Midnight Commander, discussed in Hour 5, "Manipulation and Searching Commands") are on your CD-ROM. You can determine which shell you use when you log in to Linux by either looking at the contents of the /etc/passwd file or by searching the file for your username. Look at the following example:

```
# fgrep bball /etc/passwd
bball:x:100:100:William H. Ball,,,,:/home/bball:/bin/bash
```

Your shell is listed at the end of your passwd file entry (/bin/bash in the fgrep search example).

What Shells are Available?

This section lists the shells available for OpenLinux, along with some unique features of each to get you started. Each of these shells runs programs, and you might want to explore each to see how it works. This section also highlights some of the differences among the shells and points out important configuration files.

All these shells support changing directories with a built-in cd, or change directory, command. Interestingly, the ash and tcsh shells do not have a built-in pwd, or print working directory, command and must instead rely on the pwd command found under the /bin directory.

You chose a specific shell to use during your OpenLinux sessions when you first installed OpenLinux. If you want to change this default shell, use the chsh command, followed by the complete pathname of the shell you want to use. For example, to change your default to bash, use chsh, along with its -s option, like so:

```
# chsh -s /bin/bash
```

These shells, listed in Table 6.1, have many, many features. Read the manual pages for each in detail. Some of the features to look for and explore include the following:

- What are the shell's built-in commands?
- How is job control (or background processes, discussed later this chapter in the section, "Running Programs in the Background") handled?
- Does the shell support command-line editing?
- Does the shell support command-line history?
- What are the important startup or configuration files?
- What environmental variables are important for each shell?
- What command-line prompts can I use?
- What programming constructs are supported?

 There are several other shells that are included with OpenLinux: tclsh, a simple shell and Tcl interpreter; wish, a windowing shell for X11; scotty, a Tcl interpreter and shell; and rsh, a remote shell for running commands over a network. For details, see the tclsh, wish, scotty, and rsh manual pages.

TABLE 6.1 SHELLS INCLUDED IN THE OPENLINUX DISTRIBUTION

Name	Description
ash	Compact sh-compatible shell
bash	Bourne Again Shell (ksh- and sh- compatible)
csh	symbolic link to tcsh
ksh	pdksh, public domain Korn (ksh- compatible) shell
sh	symbolic link to bash
tcsh	csh-compatible shell
zsh	Z-shell; a csh-, ksh-, and sh- compatible shell

Features of ash

The ash shell, by Kenneth Almquist, is one of the smallest shells available for Linux. This shell has 24 different built-in commands and 10 different command-line options. The ash shell supports most of the common shell commands, such as cd, along with most of the normal command-line operators (discussed later this chapter in the section, "Understanding the Shell Command Line").

This is a popular shell that is generally used when you boot OpenLinux in the single-user mode (typing linux single at the LILO boot prompt) or for rescue mode or diskette versions of Linux. The small executable size, generally one-tenth of the bash shell, makes ash an ideal shell for small file systems.

Features of the Default Linux Shell—bash

The bash, or Bourne Again Shell, by Brian Fox and Chet Ramey, is one of the most popular shells for OpenLinux. It features 48 built-in commands and a dozen command-line options. The bash shell works just like the sh shell and has a symbolic link under the /bin directory, called sh, that points to the bash shell.

Not only does bash work like the sh shell, but it also has features of the csh and ksh shells. Because bash is so widely used, it is used for the examples in this hour. Later you're shown how to customize your command-line prompt using the bash shell.

The bash shell has many features. You can scroll through your previous commands with the arrow keys (a history feature), you can edit a command line, and if you forget the name of program, you can even ask the shell for help by using filename completion. You do this by typing part of a command and then pressing the Tab key. For example, if you type **l** and press the Tab key, you see the following:

```
# l<TAB>
laser       less         listres      locale       look         lsac
last        lesskey      lkbib        localedef    lookbib      lsattr
lastb       let          lmorph       locate       lpq          lsc
latex       lex          ln           lockfile     lpr          lsl
lbxproxy    lha          lndir        logger       lprm         lynx
ld          lightning    loadkeys     login        lptest       lz
ld86        lisa         loadunimap   logname      ls
ldd         lispmtopgm   local        logout       lsa
```

The bash shell responds by listing all known commands beginning with the letter l (or any executable file in the current directory). This can be very handy if you can't remember complex command names.

The bash shell also has built-in help and lists all the built-in commands, as well as help on each command. For example:

```
# help
GNU bash, version 1.14.7(1)
Shell commands that are defined internally. Type `help' to see this list.
Type `help name' to find out more about the function `name'.
Use `info bash' to find out more about the shell in general.
```

A star (*) next to a name means that the command is disabled.

```
%[DIGITS ¦ WORD] [&]                . filename
:                                   [ arg... ]
alias [ name[=value] ... ]          bg [job_spec]
bind [-lvd] [-m keymap] [-f filena  break [n]
builtin [shell-builtin [arg ...]]   case WORD in [PATTERN [¦ PATTERN].
cd [dir]                            command [-pVv] [command [arg ...]]
continue [n]                        declare [-[frxi]] name[=value] ...
...
while COMMANDS; do COMMANDS; done   { COMMANDS }
```

To get help with a particular command, type the command name after the help command. For example, to get help with help, type the following:

 # help help
```
help: help [pattern ...]
     Display helpful information about builtin commands.  If PATTERN is
     specified, gives detailed help on all commands matching PATTERN,
     otherwise a list of the builtins is printed.
```

NEW TERM The bash shell has several important files called *resource*, *run configuration*, and *shell startup* files. These files are used when you first log in to OpenLinux to define or share predefined values or definitions, such as the type of terminal used, default editor and printer, or location of executable programs. The /etc/profile initialization file is used systemwide (for all users) to set options, such as environment variables (discussed later) or to send a message (such as "Welcome to OpenLinux!") when you first log in. You can also use a .bashrc login file in your home directory for personalizing how your bash shell starts or handles different keystrokes (such as Backspace), and a .profile resource file (also in your home directory), which is used to tell your shell which resource file to use after you log in to OpenLinux.

For more information about the bash shell, there are a manual page, info pages you can browse with the info command, and documentation under the /usr/doc/bash directory.

The Public Domain Korn Shell—pdksh

6

The pdksh, or public domain Korn shell, originally created by Eric Gisin, features 42 built-in commands and 20 command-line options. This shell is found under the /bin directory, but a symbolic link also exists under the /usr/bin directory.

The pdksh shell is named ksh in your Linux system and like the bash shell, reads the shell initialization script /etc/profile if a file called .profile does not exist in your home directory. Unfortunately, this shell does not support the same command-line prompts as the bash shell. However, this shell does support job control (discussed later this hour), so you can suspend, background, recall, or kill programs from the command line.

This shell is nearly compatible with commercial versions of the Korn shell included with commercial UNIX distributions. Documentation for this shell is in the ksh manual page and in the pdksh directory (under the /usr/doc/pdksh directory).

Features of the csh-Compatible Shell—tcsh

The tcsh shell, by William Joy (and 47 other contributors), features 53 built-in commands and 18 command-line options. This shell emulates the csh shell but has many more features, including a command-line editor with spelling correction.

This shell is not only compatible with the bash shell prompts; it offers more prompt options than bash. tcsh uses the file csh.cshrc under the /etc/directory (much like bash's /etc/profile) if the .tcshrc or .cshrc resource files do not exist in your home directory. Like the bash shell, you can scroll through commands you've entered and edit the command line.

Get a list of the tcsh commands by using the builtins command (tcsh does not have help like the bash shell), as follows:

```
# builtins
:            @           alias      alloc      bg         bindkey    break
breaksw      builtins    case       cd         chdir      complete   continue
default      dirs        echo       echotc     else       end        endif
endsw        eval        exec       exit       fg         filetest   foreach
glob         goto        hashstat   history    hup        if         jobs
kill         limit       log        login      logout     ls-F       nice
nohup        notify      onintr     popd       printenv   pushd      rehash
repeat       sched       set        setenv     settc      setty      shift
source       stop        suspend    switch     telltc     time       umask
unalias      uncomplete  unhash     unlimit    unset      unsetenv   wait
where        which       while
```

For more information about this shell, read the tcsh manual page, or look in the tcsh directory under the /usr/doc/tcsh directory to see a Frequently Asked Questions (FAQ) file and other text files.

zsh

The zsh shell, originally created by Paul Falstad, is one of the largest shells for Linux and features 84 built-in commands. The zsh shell has more than 50 different command-line options and also emulates the sh and ksh shell commands.

Like the bash and tcsh shells, the zsh shell enables you to scroll through previous commands and complete, edit, or spell-check the command line. It also enables you to use job control to manage running programs. This shell features advanced command-line options for searching or matching file patterns.

Systemwide startup files for this shell are in the /etc directory:

```
/etc/zlogin
/etc/zlogout
/etc/zshenv
/etc/zshrc
```

These files are parsed if the zsh shell cannot find equivalent files, but with a leading period, such as .zlogin, in your home directory. This shell also has more command-line prompt options than other shells, such as bash or tcsh. This shell has features similar to all other shells and can emulate the sh or ksh shells when called as a symbolic link (although your OpenLinux system has the sh shell linked to the bash shell).

There's a lot of information for this shell: 10 manual page files, along with a /usr/doc/zsh directory filled with help files, examples, and other up-to-date and useful information.

Understanding the Shell Command Line

When you use the shell to start a program at the command line, the shell interprets your command, and the command echoes its output back to your screen. Using the shell, you can have the program's output sent elsewhere, such as to a file. In fact, nearly everything under OpenLinux is a file; this includes devices such as terminals, printers, and even many programs that can accept input from other files. The shell can also use one program's output as the input for another program or even tell a program to read its input from a file. For example, you can redirect the standard output of the ls command to a file:

```
# touch /tmp/trash/file1 /tmp/trash/file2 /tmp/trash/file3
➥/tmp/trash/file4
# ls -w 1 /tmp/trash/* >trashfiles.txt
```

NEW TERM The first command line creates four files in the /tmp/trash directory. The second command line creates a text file using the ls command's output and containing the names of the files under the /tmp/trash directory. The greater than (>) character is called a *standard output redirection operator* and is used to redirect the output of a command somewhere else. You also can use the less than (<) character, or *standard input redirection operator*, to feed information to other programs.

6

The examples used in the rest of this hour use the bash shell. If you want to try some of these command lines, type **bash** and press Enter at the command line to use the bash shell. When finished, type **exit**, press Enter, and you're returned to your original shell.

As a trivial example, you can use the file containing filenames created to build an archive using the cpio command. You do this by using the standard input to feed the file names into the cpio command:

```
# cpio -o <trashfiles.txt >trash.cpio
1 block
```

This command line causes the cpio command to read a list of files from the standard input, the trashfiles.txt file, and then creates an archive by sending its output through the standard output to a file called trash.cpio.

The cpio command is used, like the tar and dump commands, to archive or back up OpenLinux files. See Hour 23, "Backing Up and Restoring Your System," to learn how to use backup programs.

Generally, most programs you run from the shell command line have the capability to read from the standard input and write to the standard output. Along with the standard input and standard output, there is also a standard error output (which almost always prints to your display). Using the previous example, if the list of files fed into the cpio command contains an error, the cpio command complains and sends an error message to your screen:

```
# rm -fr /tmp/trash/file3
# cpio -o < trashfiles.txt >trash.cpio
cpio: /tmp/trash/file3: No such file or directory
1 block
```

One of the existing files has been deleted, but the input file, trashfiles.txt, which still contains the list of files, is not changed. When you try to use the list as a valid input to build an archive, the cpio command complains and sends an error message to your screen (but still builds the archive).

The shell assigns each input and output file a file number. For the standard input, the number is zero (0). For the standard output, the number is one (1), and for the standard error (where programs usually send error messages), the number is two (2). Knowing this, you can run cpio silently and can cause any errors to be sent to a file. Do this by combining the standard output redirection operator and the standard error's file number, as shown in the following example.

```
# cpio -o < trashfiles.txt >trash.cpio 2>cpio.errors
# cat cpio.errors
cpio: /tmp/trash/file3: No such file or directory
1 block
```

As you can see, the cpio command sent its errors, which normally are sent to the standard error output (your display), to a file called cpio.errors.

Normally, each time you redirect output to a file, either the named file is created, or if it exists, the named file is overwritten and its previous contents are irrevocably lost.

You should use file redirection carefully. If you redirect output to an existing file, you lose the original file, which might not be what you want.

If you want to retain the original contents of a file, you can append the output of a program to a file by using the concatenate (>>), or *append*, redirection operator:

```
# cpio -o < trashfiles.txt >trash.cpio 2>>cpio.errors
```

This command line saves the previous contents of the cpio.errors file and appends any new errors to the end of the file. This approach keeps a log of errors when you run the cpio command. This method is used if you enabled system logging for Linux. Take a look (as the root operator) at the contents of the file called messages, found under the /var/log directory.

If you recall the simple cat command text editor example from Hour 4, "Reading and Navigation Commands," you remember that the standard output redirection operator was used with the cat command to read input from the terminal to create a text file:

```
# cat >file.txt
this is a line
this is another line
EOF
# cat file.txt
this is a line
this is another line
```

6

NEW TERM The end-of-file, or *EOF*, character is used to close the file and is entered by holding down the Ctrl key and pressing the D key. Add a new feature to this simple editor by using the <<, or *here*, redirection operator, which tells the shell that the EOF character is the character that immediately follows the << operator:

```
# cat >file.txt <<.
> This is a line of text.
> This is another line of text.
> .
# cat file.txt
This is a line of text.
This is another line of text.
```

Notice that the file is closed after typing a period (.) on a line by itself, which is handier than using a control key combination to close the file. You can use any character or combination of characters to represent EOF.

Now try using the here operator to build a simple, self-contained database file by combining the egrep command (discussed in Hour 5, "Manipulation and Searching Commands") and input redirection. First, use a favorite text editor (such as pico, included with the pine email program) to create a file called db. Type a list of addresses, then wrap the list by putting the egrep command at the beginning and the end-of-input character string at the end of the file. Create the file like so:

```
# pico db
```

 The pico editor might easily become your favorite text editor for OpenLinux because it is easy to use, fast, and extremely safe in saving text files. See Hour 14, "Text Processing," for details about this great little editor.

Next, type the egrep command, followed by a short list of addresses, and end the file with a string of characters to match the here operator, like this:

```
egrep -i $1 <<zzzz
Debby, 275 Collins Rd., Vestal NY 13850
Cathy, 1001 N. Vermont St., Arlington, VA 22003
Scotty, 2064 N. 16th St., Arlington, VA 22001
Bill, 4000 N. Pennsylvania Ave., Washington, DC 10000
Fred, Slip 417, N. Woodward Ave., Boca Raton, FL 46002
zzzz
```

Save the file by typing Ctrl+X. Finally, use the chmod command to make the text file an executable program, like this:

```
# chmod +x db
```

This creates a short address database. Test your database by typing db, followed by a name, city, state, or zip code, like this:

```
# db deb
Debby, 275 Collins Ave., Vestal NY 13850
```

The database works by using the egrep command to read the file until the end-of-input string zzzz. The -i command line option tells the egrep command not to distinguish between uppercase and lowercase characters. The $1 string is a shell variable (discussed in the next section) representing the command-line argument to be fed to the egrep command.

Input and output redirection with the shell can be used in many different ways. This discussion continues and you're introduced to shell variables and shown some handy tricks for customizing your shell.

Customizing Your Shell

NEW TERM When you use a shell, you're running the shell in an environment that contains *environment variables*. Environment variables are predefined values or pathnames in various resource text files, found under your home directory and the /etc directory. For the bash shell, the default, systemwide environment variables are defined in the /etc/profile file, whereas personal settings can be found in the file .bashrc in your home directory.

There are many different environment variables. Use the printenv or set command to see a list of the variables currently in use:

```
# printenv
...
PATH=/usr/local/bin:/bin:/opt/kde/bin:/usr/bin:.:/usr/X11R6/bin:/home/
➥bball/bin
HOME=/home/bball
SHELL=/bin/bash
...
```

This hour doesn't list all the environment variables you might find defined for your OpenLinux shell, but one of the most important is the $PATH variable. This variable tells the shell where to find executable programs. Without $PATH, you have to type the complete *path*, or directory hierarchy of a command, to run a program. For example, if you want to run the ifconfig command to check the status of your network connections, you might first try to type its name on the command line:

```
# ifconfig
bash: ifconfig: command not found
# whereis ifconfig
ifconfig: /sbin/ifconfig
```

6

As you can see, this doesn't mean that the `ifconfig` command doesn't exist or isn't installed on your system; it's just that your shell doesn't know where to find the program. To run the `ifconfig` command, you can type the full pathname before the command, but if you need to use this program repeatedly, include its directory in the list of known paths in your shell's `$PATH` environment variable.

Do this at the command line by adding the `/sbin` directory to your `$PATH` variable, using the `bash` shell's `export` command (which saves the new variable definition and makes it available to your shell):

```
# ifconfig
bash: ifconfig: command not found
# PATH=$PATH:/sbin ; export PATH
# ifconfig
lo          Link encap:Local Loopback
            inet addr:127.0.0.1  Bcast:127.255.255.255  Mask:255.0.0.0
            UP BROADCAST LOOPBACK RUNNING  MTU:3584  Metric:1
            RX packets:436 errors:0 dropped:0 overruns:0
            TX packets:436 errors:0 dropped:0 overruns:0
```

As you can see, your shell now knows where to find the `ifconfig` command. But this is temporary and only lasts as long as you're logged in or running a particular terminal. Make this change effective for each time you log in by adding the path to the file `.bash_profile` in your home directory or if you're the root operator and want all users to benefit, to the file `profile` under the `/etc` directory.

Look for the following line in the `.bash_profile` file:

```
PATH=$PATH:$HOME/bin
```

Using a text editor, add the `/sbin` directory:

```
PATH=$PATH:$HOME/bin:/sbin
```

If you're the root operator, add the `/sbin` directory in the following line in the profile file under the `/etc` directory:

```
PATH="/bin:/sbin:/usr/bin"
```

After making these changes, read in the new `$PATH` by using the `bash` shell's `source` command, like so:

```
# source /etc/profile
```

In the profile file, you also see a line like the following:

```
export PS1="[\u@\h \W]\\$ "
```

Although this line might seem somewhat cryptic, this is the prompt string definition for the $PS1 environment variable and is printed at the command line of your console or terminal window when you use a shell. You can change this string to define nearly any type of prompt string. The preceding definition is in the following form:

```
[username@host base_working_directory]$
```

The bash shell has 15 different prompts (tcsh has 18, and ksh has 35) you can combine with character strings to customize your prompt. For example, you can have the current date and time in your prompt. If you use the bash shell export command, you can test different prompts from the command line:

```
# PS1='Date: \d Time: \t-> ';export PS1
Date: Thu Dec 10 Time: 22:19:01->
```

The time is updated each time you enter a command or press the Enter key. If you want to have the shell's name, along with the current directory in the command line, try the \s and \w prompt characters:

```
# PS1='\s:\w> '; export PS1
bash:/usr/bin>
```

You also can use different escape characters and terminal sequences to control the attributes of your prompt strings. You can use underlining, boldfacing, blinking, or other modes for your prompt strings:

```
# PS1='[\033[4m\u\033[0m@\033[4m\h\033[0m]:';export PS1
[bball@localhost]:
```

This example uses the proper escape sequences for the xterm X11 terminal (found with the printenv command, and by looking at the $TERMCAP variable) to change the prompt by underlining the username and hostname in the prompt. You can find these definitions included in the file termcap under the /etc directory, and in the termcap manual page. For more examples and other prompt strings for specific shells, consult your shell's manual page.

NEW TERM Changing the prompt is only one way to customize how you work in your shell. You also can define command shortcuts, or *aliases*, to tailor how your favorite commands work. You can find at least one or two aliases defined for your system in the bashrc file under the /etc/directory.

Systemwide alias definitions are entered by the root operator. You can put your own definition in the .bashrc file in your home directory, but if you're the root operator, you want to put in at least these three for all your users:

```
alias rm='rm -i'
alias cp='cp -i'
alias mv='mv -i'
```

6

These three aliases cause delete, copy, and rename (move) operations to be done interactively and provide at least some element of safety when deleting, copying, or moving (renaming) files. Without the `-i`, or interactive option, users might not think before deleting or overwriting files.

You also can define aliases to build new commands or provide variations of familiar commands to avoid typing long command-line options. For example, the `ls` command has many different options, but you can define several variations to make life easier. Some alias definitions you might want to try include the following:

```
# list the current directory using color filenames
alias lsc='ls --color'
# long format listing
alias lsl='ls -l'
# show all files except . and ..
alias lsa='ls -AF'
# show all file except . and .. in color
alias lsac='ls -AF --color'
```

After you enter these changes into your `.bashrc` file in your home directory, you can use the aliases by again using the `bash` shell's `source` command:

 # source .bashrc

Now you can type `lsc`, `lsl`, `lsa`, or `lsac` without adding the command-line options. Just make sure that you don't redefine an existing command! If you come up with some really useful aliases, make sure they're defined for each of the shells active on your system.

Just because a shell is available on the system does not mean that a user can use a particular shell to log in. As the root operator, you can maintain a list of acceptable shells for your system by editing the file `shells` under the `/etc` directory. As a default, the following shells are listed for OpenLinux:

```
/bin/bash
/bin/sh (a symbolic link to the bash shell)
/bin/ash
/bin/tcsh
/bin/csh (a symbolic link to the tcsh shell)
/bin/ksh
/bin/zsh
```

If you don't want your users to be able to use a particular shell, simply remove it from the list! If you try to change your shell with the `chsh` command to use a particular shell for the next log in, the shell must be listed in the `/etc/shells` file. The `chsh` command complains and quits without making any changes:

```
# chsh -s /bin/zsh
Changing shell for bball.
Password:
chsh: "/bin/zsh" is not listed in /etc/shells.
chsh: use -l option to see list
```

Note that this doesn't restrict a user from running a shell after logging in. The only way to effectively manage who can run a particular shell is to change a shell's ownership or file permissions (see Hour 22, "Handling Files and Your File System," for details).

Running Programs in the Background

NEW TERM   Most shells also offer a way to start and then run programs as a *background* process. Starting a command in the background means that the command continues to run in memory while control of the shell's command line is returned to your console. This is a handy way to get work done, especially if you are working on a separate terminal, have limited screen space when working in X11, or have lots of memory. Operations such as sorting large files or searching directories and other file systems are good candidates for execution in the background.

Although Linux offers virtual consoles when not working with X (accessed through the Alt and Function keys) and many X11 window managers offer separate desktops, you'll probably run programs in the background many times while using Linux.

Programs are run in the background from the shell command line by using the &, or ampersand, operator at the end of a command. For example, to start another terminal program under X11, you want the program to run in the background so that your current terminal is free for further input:

```
# rxvt &
```

This command starts the rxvt terminal, and your command-line prompt returns. The program is assigned a process number you can see using the ps, or process status, command as in the following example:

```
# ps
...
  291   1 R    0:03 rxvt
...
```

In this example, to keep the list short, not all the running processes are listed. You can stop the program by using the shell's kill command with the program's process number:

```
# kill 291
[1]+  Terminated              rxvt
```

6

NEW TERM Using the `kill` command is a crude way to control background programs. There is a more refined approach that uses other shell commands. Depending on your current shell, you can put running programs in the background, suspend the program, continue to run the program in the background, kill the program, or bring the program back to the terminal display. This is known as *job control*.

If you're running the `bash` shell, put a running program into the background and suspend its operation by holding down the Ctrl key and pressing the Z key on your keyboard:

```
# pine
... program is running... (ctrl-z)...

Pine suspended. Give the "fg" command to come back.

[1]+  Stopped (signal)          pine
# fg
.... program returns
```

> In order to be able to suspend the `pine` mail program, you must enable sus-
> pension using the `pine` configuration menu. While running `pine`, press the S
> key to enter the Setup menu and then the C key to enter the Configuration
> menu. Then, scroll through the options until you highlight "enable-sus-
> pend," and press the X key to enable this feature. Next, press the E key to
> exit the configuration screen and then the Y key to save the changes. You
> are now able to suspend the `pine` mailer.

Sending a running program into the background and suspending its operation can be followed by the `fg` command to bring the running program back to your display or by the
`bg` command to continue to enable the program to run. This can be handy if you want to
start a program, such as a newsreader (discussed in Hour 11, "Configuring Internet
Email," and Hour 12, "Configuring Internet News"), and then suspend and continue to
run the program during lengthy operations (such as updating an internal list of newsgroups) while you run other programs in the foreground.

Using the `bash` shell, you can start, suspend, and run a number of programs and then
selectively bring a background program back to your display by the program's job number:

```
# pine
... program is running (ctrl-z)...

Pine suspended. Give the "fg" command to come back.
```

```
[1]+  Stopped (signal)        pine
# sc
.... program is running (ctrl-z)...

[2]+  Stopped                 sc
# fg %1
... pine program returns...
```

In this example, the pine mail reader is started and then suspended in the background to start the sc spreadsheet. Because pine is the first job suspended, the bash shell assigns a job number of 1 to the mail program. The sc spreadsheet is then suspended, assigned job number 2, and returned to the mail program by specifying its job number with the fg %1 command.

If you run and suspend many jobs in the background, you might not remember a program by its job number or remember which programs are suspended. You can get a list of the suspended programs by using the bash shell's jobs command:

```
# jobs
[1]   Stopped (signal)        pine
[2]-  Stopped                 sc
[3]+  Stopped                 emacs-nox
# fg %sc
... sc program is running ...
```

This shows that there are three jobs, the pine mailer, the sc spreadsheet, and the emacs editor, currently suspended in the shell. Note that instead of restarting the sc spreadsheet job by referring to its job number, the program is brought back to the foreground by using the fg % command with the name of the suspended job.

You also can stop programs using this same approach. Instead of using the ps command to find a program's process number and then issuing a kill command, you can use kill with the % operator:

```
# kill %1

[1]-  Stopped (signal)        pine
# kill %emacs-nox

[3]+  Stopped                 emacs-nox
```

Here you see how to use the kill command to stop a program by its number or name. This is much easier than using the ps command, especially if there are a large number of programs or other processes running in the background.

6

> Although not part of any shell, OpenLinux also includes the `killall` com-
> mand, which you can use to kill processes by name. To use the previous
> example, in which the `kill` command was used to stop the `rxvt` terminal
> emulator, instead of typing `kill`, followed by a process number, you can
> use:
>
> `# killall rxvt`
>
> After you press Enter, the terminal emulator process is stopped, and the
> window disappears. The `killall` command also has an `-i`, or interactive,
> option you can use to selectively stop programs, or you can specify a process
> number to kill.

Using your shell's job control facilities is a powerful way to work efficiently with multiple programs, especially if you use a single display or console. All the shells included on
your OpenLinux CD-ROM include job control in one form or another. In the next section, you're shown another powerful way to use your shell to run multiple programs on a
single command line.

How to Use Pipes

NEW TERM   You've already seen how to redirect the output of a program into a file and how
to then redirect the contents of that file into another program. But you can do this
all at once without the use of a temporary file by using the ¦, or vertical bar, character,
which is called a *pipe*. Using pipes to string commands together on the command line,
called pipelining, is a quick and powerful way to enhance the power of individual commands and represents a unique strength of Linux and other versions of UNIX.

You definitely use piped commands as you begin to learn how to use Linux. Not only do
pipes save you time, but you can use different combinations of piped commands to tackle
computing tasks particular to the way you work and the programs you run. At first, your
pipe commands might be simple, but as you gain confidence and understanding, you can
construct fairly complex pipelines.

NEW TERM   Pipes work well under Linux because many commands are also *filters*, which
accept some sort of input, optionally process or modify it in some way, and emit
the result as output to standard output or another command. Pipes can be used in nearly
any computing task and can be used to quickly find information, generate reports, transform data, or view results. First, look at four simple examples:

```
# ls ¦ lpr
# printenv ¦ fgrep EDITOR
# nroff -man mymanpage.1 ¦ less
# cat document.txt ¦ wc ¦ mail -s "Document.txt Report" bball
```

The first command line pipes a listing of the current directory through the line printer command to print a report. The second example searches through a listing of your current shell environment and prints the value of the default text editor. The third example prints the formatted output of a manual page to your display so you can browse the document to check for errors. The last example pipes a text document through the word count command, wc, and then electronically mails a report on the number of characters, words, and lines in the document to the user bball.

You can use pipes to confront and solve everyday problems not usually solved by individual programs. This is one of the secrets and power of using the shell with OpenLinux! For example, if you have a lot of documents on your system but can't remember which document contains a certain phrase, you can find this information quickly. Instead of running your word processor and opening each file, you could try typing the following:

```
# find /home -name *.doc ¦ xargs fgrep administration ¦ less
```

This command line uses the find command to search the /home directory for all files ending in .doc and then pipes each file's name into the xargs command. The xargs command then runs the fgrep command to search for the word "administration" in each file and pipes the results through the less pager. You also can use pipes to not only find information, but to process data and create new files.

```
# find *.doc ¦ xargs cat ¦ tr ' ' '\n' ¦ sort ¦ uniq ¦ tee dict ¦ less
```

The preceding command line builds a file called dict that contains a sorted list of unique words contained in all your word processing files. What do you call this type of file? A dictionary! To be honest, not all the dictionary words might be spelled correctly.

This command works by piping each found file through the tr command, which translates each character space into a carriage return to break the stream into one word per line. The stream of lines is sorted, and the uniq command removes all occurrences of similar lines except for one. Notice that the tee command is also used to save the output of the stream to a file.

6

The zsh shell contains some improvements on input and output redirection, so you might not need the tee command if you're using pipes on the zsh shell command line. See the zsh shell documentation for details.

The tee command is used to save the results of a pipe at a particular juncture. This is handy when you want to test your results when building pipes or save results in a complex pipe. Look at the following example:

```
# xwd -out wd.xwd
# xwdtopnm < wd.xwd ¦ ppmtogif ¦ tee wd.gif ¦ giftopnm ¦ tee wd.pnm ¦
➥ pnmtotiff >wd.tif
```

In this example, a window dump graphic is created using the X11 xwd command, which captures and saves the contents of an X window or desktop. Then, the xwdtopnm command is used to convert this graphic into a portable bitmap graphic. The output of the xwdtopnm command is then fed into the ppmtogif command. The tee command is used to save the output, in GIF format, to a file called wd.gif. At the same time, the GIF output is converted back into the portable bitmap format by the giftopnm command, and the tee command is again used to save the portable bitmap as the file wd.pnm. Finally, the pnmtotiff command saves the portable bitmap file as a TIFF graphic. That's one command line and four graphic conversions!

Using pipes with Linux is an easy way to get work done. As you continue to work with Linux, you can soon develop your own set of favorite command lines. When you develop your favorites, you can then build your own shell commands, which you'll read about in the next section.

Building Shell Scripts

NEW TERM You don't have to be a programmer to write commands for Linux. After you become familiar with different programs and find yourself typing the same command lines over and over, save these command lines into text files, and turn them into shell *scripts*. In the simplest form, a shell script is simply one or several command lines you frequently use. Look at the following example:

```
# rxvt -geometry 80x11+803+375 -bg white -fg black -e pico &
# rxvt -geometry 80x24+806+2 -bg white -fg black -e pine &
```

These two command lines start the pico editor and the pine mail program in two X11 rxvt terminal windows on the second desktop in an 800×600 pixel display. These certainly aren't command lines you want to type each time you want to run these programs. Although you can manually start the terminal windows after moving to the other desktop, it might take some time to correctly size the windows and then start the programs. Turn these command lines into an executable file by saving them into a file with your text editor, and then use the chmod command to make the file executable:

```
# chmod +x d2
```

Now when you want to run these programs, all you have to type is the following, which is certainly a heck of a lot easier:

 # d2

You can make this new command even more flexible by using the shell variables $1 and $2, which represent the first and second command-line arguments to a shell command. Edit the file you created, and change the program names to these variables:

```
rxvt -geometry 80x11+803+375 -bg white -fg black -e $2 &
rxvt -geometry 80x24+806+2 -bg white -fg black -e $1 &
```

Note that the order of the variables isn't important. Now when you run your command, you can supply the program names on the command line as in this example:

 # d2 pine pico

This has the same result, but from now on you're able to run nearly any program you want in the terminal windows.

This discussion of using the shell concludes with a simple shell script you can use to safely delete files. There's nothing special about the rmv script in Listing 6.1, but it demonstrates some of the power of shell scripts.

LISTING 6.1   THE rmv SAFE DELETE SHELL SCRIPT

```
#!/bin/bash
# rmv - a safe delete program
# uses a trash directory under your home directory
#
# when run, always create a directory called .trash
mkdir $HOME/.trash 2>/dev/null
cmdlnopts=false
delete=false
empty=false
list=false

# get any command-line options
while getopts "dehl" cmdlnopts; do
  case "$cmdlnopts" in
    d ) /bin/echo "deleting: \c" $2 $3 $4 $5 ; delete=true ;;
    e ) /bin/echo "emptying the trash..." ; empty=true ;;
    h ) /bin/echo "safe file delete v1.0"
        /bin/echo "rmv -d[elete] -e[mpty] -h[elp] -l[ist] file1-4" ;;
    l ) /bin/echo "your .trash directory contains:" ; list=true ;;
  esac
done
```

6

continues

LISTING 6.1   CONTINUED

```
# d - delete any files found on the command line
if [ $delete = true ]
then
  mv $2 $3 $4 $5 $HOME/.trash
  /bin/echo " rmv finished."
fi

# e - empty the trash?
if [ $empty = true ]
then
  /bin/echo "empty the trash? \c"
  read answer
  case "$answer" in
    y) rm -fr $HOME/.trash/* ;;
    n) /bin/echo "trashcan delete aborted." ;;
  esac
fi

# l - show any files in the .trash directory
if [ $list = true ]
then
  ls -l $HOME/.trash
fi
```

The first line of the script invokes the bash shell to run the script. After you type this script using your favorite text editor, make the script executable by using the chmod command:

 # chmod +x rmv

This script moves unwanted files to a directory called .trash in your home directory. When you're sure you want to delete the files, you can then verify the files and empty the trash. Because this script is supposed to act like a regular command, a short, built-in help command is included.

If you want to try the rmv script, make sure you type it correctly or change the line containing rm -fr $HOME/.trash/* ;; to rm -i $HOME/.trash/* ;;, which is much safer than an unconditional delete. If you don't type this line correctly, you might delete your entire home directory!

The script works by first creating a .trash directory in your home directory (found with the $HOME environment variable). If the directory exists, any error messages generated by the mkdir command are discarded by sending the standard error output to the /dev/null device. The /dev/null device is a handy place to send all complaints, as all input is discarded! This device (known as the 'ol bit bucket) is also used when you don't care about the output of a program and want to hide the output from the display.. Four internal script variables are then defined: cmdlnopts, delete, empty, and list.

The script uses the bash shell getopts command to look at your command line for any options. If a matching letter is found by the case statement, the script commands up until the two semicolons are executed. For example, if you want a reminder of how to use the script, you can use the -h, or help, option:

```
# rmv -h
safe file delete v1.0
rmv -d[elete] -e[mpty] -h[elp] -l[ist] file1-4
```

This prints a short help message because the script found the letter h on the command line, and then printed the message using the echo command. To delete files, you must use the -d, or delete, command-line option:

```
# rmv -d berries.jpg bowtie.jpg face.gif
deleting: berries.jpg bowtie.gif face.gif rmv finished.
```

This deletes the three files by moving them to the .trash directory in your home directory. The -d option is detected on the command line, and the script then prints a message, echoes the file names back to your display, and sets the delete variable to true. Because the delete variable is changed to true, the mv command found in the if ... then statement is executed.

You can verify that the files have been moved by using the -l, or list, option to see the contents of your trash:

```
# rmv -l
your .trash directory contains:
total 36
-rw-r--r--   1 bball     users        11967 Nov  6 14:18 berries.jpg
-rw-r--r--   1 bball     users        14010 Nov  6 14:18 bowtie.gif
-rw-r--r--   1 bball     users         8681 Nov  6 14:18 face.gif
```

As before, because the letter l is detected on the command line, the script sets the list variable to true and then executes the ls command to list the contents of your .trash directory. If you're sure you want to delete these files, you can then use the -e, or empty, command-line option:

```
# rmv -e
emptying the trash...
empty the trash? n
```

6

```
trashcan delete aborted.
# rmv -e
emptying the trash...
empty the trash? y
# rmv -l
your .trash directory contains:
total 0
```

The rmv script asks if you're sure you want to empty the trash. If you type an **n**, the delete is aborted. If you type a **y**, the trash is deleted. Because the letter e is found on the command line, the empty variable is set to true and the statements following the if ... then test line are run. The script prints a message to your display, and then, using the read command, waits for you to enter an answer. The answer is then tested, and if it is yes, the files in the .trash directory are deleted.

Using the shell, you can quickly build simple programs to accomplish major tasks. Feel free to improve this program by adding features or improving on how file names are handled at the command line. One such improvement might be to add the capability to handle wildcards or whole directories. Another improvement might be an interactive deletion of files. See the bash manual page for more information about other shell commands and operators you can use in your own shell scripts.

Summary

This hour introduced just the basics of using a shell with OpenLinux. Don't be intimidated by the command line! Mastery of the intricacies and idiosyncrasies of using any shell can take lots of practice. Make sure you practice safe computing: define aliases to force potentially harmful commands to act interactively; think twice before using wildcards when deleting files; and never use OpenLinux as the root operator all the time. The more you learn about OpenLinux, the more confidence you'll have in tackling problems and building custom solutions when using the shell.

Q&A

Q Help! I was using the shell, a program ran awry, and all of a sudden the screen is full of garbage characters?

A Try using the reset command. Chances are that your shell still understands your keyboard input. Type reset and press Enter to reset your terminal or console.

Q How can I get more information about bash?

A Besides the bash manual pages, you can find at least three additional files of information under the /usr/doc/bash directory. You can also try searching your favorite bookstore for books about this shell.

Q What's the best shell to use with OpenLinux?

A That's a hard question to answer, as each shell has particular strengths or weaknesses. However, the bash shell seems to be the most popular, and it is the default shell for other distributions of Linux. Most OpenLinux users are quite happy with this shell, and many shell scripts developed for Linux work with bash.

Exercises

1. Locate the default .bashrc settings for new users. Modify this file to include safe aliases of the rm, cp, and mv commands.

2. What file should you edit to add your own personal aliases?

3. Modify the rmv script to change the location or name of the trash directory.

4. If you use the -d option without any filenames on the command line, the mv command, through the rmv script, reports an error. How can you fix this?

6

HOUR 7

Using the X Window System

The X Window System installed on your computer, as you learned in Hour 3, "Configuring the X Window System," is a port of X11 from the XFree86 Project, Inc. This graphical interface includes about 3,500 files, with nearly 200 programs (clients), more than 500 fonts, and more than 500 graphic image files in nearly 50 megabytes of software. You can find almost everything (but not all files or programs) for X11 under the /usr/X11R6 directory.

This hour shows you several ways to start X11, discusses some of the different graphical interfaces, or window managers, you can use during your X sessions, and provides exercises for several terminal programs (or shell consoles) installed on your system. You'll also learn about some basic operations, such as copying and pasting text, adjusting your mouse pointer or cursor shape, and doing screen captures. The last section shows you a sampling of X11 clients you might want to try.

Note that many clients, such as text editors, graphics programs, and even other X11 window managers, are discussed throughout this book.

Starting X

When you first log in to OpenLinux, you see a short message like this:

```
Welcome to your OpenLinux system!
You can start X11 with 'startx' or KDE with 'kde'.
```

The startx and kde commands are almost identical shell scripts used to start an X11 session. startx is found under the /usr/X11R6/bin directory, whereas kde is found under the /opt/kde/bin directory. To start an X11 session using the fvwm window manager (discussed later this chapter in the section "X11 Window Managers") with the Looking Glass desktop client, type **startx** on the command line of your console, and then press Enter, like this:

```
# startx
```

If you properly configured X11 to work with your computer's graphics card (as described in Hour 3), your display clears, and after a few seconds, the X11 desktop appears, as shown in Figure 7.1.

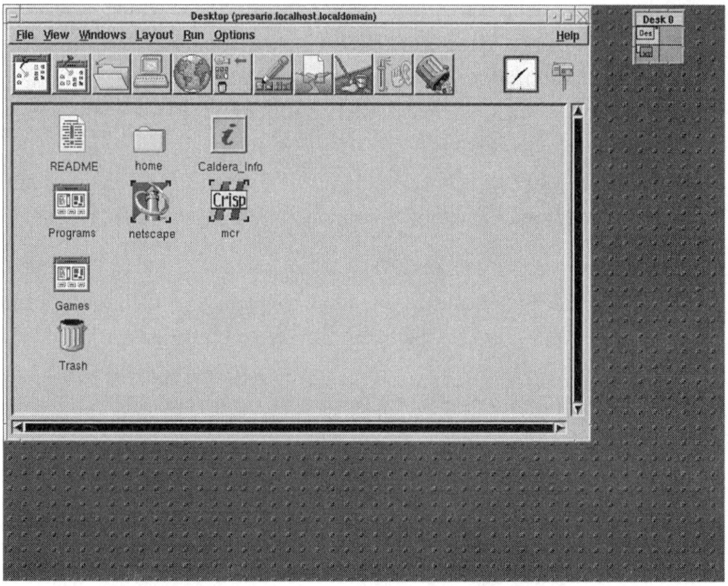

FIGURE 7.1

The fvwm *X11 window manager with the Looking Glass desktop client is one of several ways to use X with OpenLinux.*

To start an X session using the K Desktop Environment (discussed in Hour 8, "Exploring the K Desktop Environment), type **kde** at the command line, and press Enter, like this:

```
# kde
```

The screen clears, and you soon see KDE's default desktop appear, as shown in Figure 7.2.

FIGURE 7.2

The KDE desktop is a complete X11 environment and includes nearly all the features of a modern graphical interface.

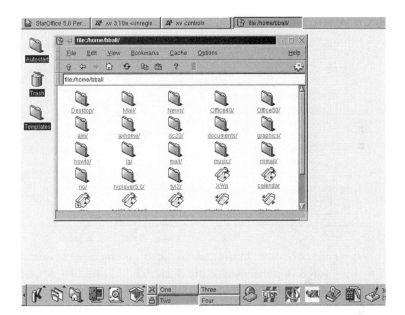

Starting X11 with Different Color Depths

When you start an X11 session with kde or startx, X11 uses 256 colors, or eight-bit planes (one byte, or eight bits per pixel). To start an X session using 16-bit planes (or two bytes, or 16 bits per pixel), use the -bpp option, followed by 16, like this:

```
# startx -- -bpp 16
```

or

```
# kde -- -bpp 16
```

The -bpp 16 option is passed on to the X server you selected when configuring X as an option to use 64,000 colors. Other color depths, such as 24 or 32, might be possible depending on the capabilities of your graphics card and how you configured your

7

XF86Config file. Although XF86Config, found under the /etc directory, is described in more detail in Hour 3, the pertinent part of this file is in the Screen section. A sample is shown in Listing 7.1.

LISTING 7.1   TYPICAL **XF86C**ONFIG SCREEN SECTION

```
Section "Screen"
    Driver      "svga"
    Device      "NeoMagic"
    Monitor     "Generic Multisync"
    Subsection "Display"
        Depth       8
        Modes       "1024x768"  "800x600"  "640x480"
#       Virtual  1024 768
    EndSubsection
    Subsection "Display"
        Depth       16
        Modes       "1024x768"  "800x600"  "640x480"
    EndSubsection
    Subsection "Display"
        Depth       24
        Modes       "800x600"  "640x480"
    EndSubsection
EndSection
```

Note the "Display" subsections in the listing (for a NeoMagic video graphics display). Each subsection starts with a Depth setting, and then lists different Modes, or resolutions. The Depth setting sets the display depth, or number of colors for the X session. If you always use X with 64,000 colors at a resolution of 800∞600 and don't want to have to type -- -bpp 16 every time you start X, edit your XF86Config file and simply use a "Screen" section, like this:

```
Section "Screen"
    Driver      "svga"
    Device      "NeoMagic"
    Monitor     "Generic Multisync"
    DefaultColorDepth 16
    Subsection "Display"
        Depth       16
        Modes       "800x600"
    EndSubsection
EndSection
```

The Modes line tells the X server to use a particular number of dots per inch horizontally and vertically. Your selected X server automatically uses the first available mode value (such as 800∞600) which matches corresponding *mode lines* in your XF86Config file. In Listing 7.1, if all modes are valid, your X session starts with eight bits per pixel and a display that is 1024 pixels wide and 800 pixels high. To switch to a lower resolution or mode during an X session (such as going from 1024×768 to 800×600), press Ctrl+Alt+KeyPad-. That is, press Ctrl+Alt, and then press the minus (-) key on your keyboard's keypad. To switch to a higher resolution, press Ctrl+Alt+KeyPad+.

The Virtual line in Listing 7.1. enables you to have a display larger than the physical area of your screen. This is handy if your computer's graphics card and monitor only support a lower resolution, such as 800×600, but you need to run an X11 client (program) at a higher resolution, such as 1024×768. The Virtual line in Listing 7.1 is disabled with a pound (#) sign, but you can enable it by removing the pound sign and then restarting X. Your display is then a scrolling window and moves about the larger, virtual display when your mouse pointer is dragged beyond the edge of the screen.

> Unfortunately, some X clients, such as the graphics drawing xfig or the arcade action game xboing, require larger display areas. Your screen resolution depends on how well your graphics card is supported by a particular X server, how much video memory is installed on your graphics card, the resolution capabilities of your computer's monitor or laptop's screen, and how you have configured your XF86Config file. You cannot, for example, use a 1024×768 display on a laptop that only supports a resolution of 800×600, but you might be able to use a virtual resolution of 1024×768 or greater if enough video memory is installed.

Using Virtual Consoles with X11

NEW TERM Although you can get to a shell command line during an X session when you use a terminal client, such as rxvt (discussed later this chapter in the section "Using X11 Terminal Programs"), you can also get to a OpenLinux console when using X on your desktop computer. OpenLinux supports six different *virtual consoles*, or login screens. When you don't use X, you can get to six different login prompts by pressing Alt+FX, where X is F1 through F6.

For example, when you first log in to OpenLinux, you're at the first virtual console. After you log in, press Alt+F2. You then see another login prompt, and you can log in as another user or start another OpenLinux session. To get back to your first login screen, press Alt+F1.

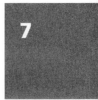

7

When you log in to OpenLinux and start an X11 session with `startx` or `kde`, X, by default, uses a seventh virtual screen. Because you started X from the first virtual console, this console is unavailable for use. However, you can get to another virtual console, such as the second, by pressing Ctrl+Alt+F2. You then see the OpenLinux login prompt. To go back to your X session, press Alt+F7. Using this approach, you can go back and forth between your X session and different consoles.

Starting Multiple X11 Sessions

Not only can you use multiple virtual consoles with OpenLinux during an X session, you can also start and use multiple X consoles during an OpenLinux session. This means that you can log in, start X using one window manager at a particular color depth, and then go to a different console, log in, and start another X session using a different window manager and color depth. Then, during your X session, switch between different consoles and X window managers!

Here's a step-by-step example that shows how to log and use the `startx` and `kde` commands at the same time:

1. Start OpenLinux and log in. At the command line, start an X session with KDE using 256 colors with:

    `# kde`

2. Press Enter to start the X session (which uses the seventh virtual screen).

3. After the KDE desktop appears, press Ctrl+Alt+F2. You're at the second virtual console and an OpenLinux login prompt. Log in to OpenLinux again.

4. At the command line, use the `startx` command to start an X session using 64,000 colors with the `fvwm` window manager and the Looking Glass desktop. Include the `:1` and `vt8` command-line options to start a second X11 session named `:1` using the eight virtual screen, like this:

    `# startx -- :1 -bpp 16 vt8`

    The screen clears, and the `fvwm` and Looking Glass desktop appears (like the one shown in Figure 7.1).

The Looking Glass desktop is an X11 client used to provide a graphical workspace during your X11 sessions. The Looking Glass client appears by default when you use `startx` to start an X session. When the desktop appears, click the Caldera or Netscape icon to read the Looking Glass manual. You can find all the information you need to use this client with X.

5. To go to your KDE session, press Ctrl+Alt+F7. To go to another virtual console, press Ctrl+Alt+F3 (because the first and second are being used). To go back to fvwm, press Ctrl+Alt+F8.

Logging in to OpenLinux and X11 with xdm

NEW TERM The default configuration of OpenLinux is to boot Linux to a login prompt for a console, or shell command line. You can, however, boot OpenLinux directly to an X11 login prompt. This can be done by passing a kernel *message*, or boot-prompt option, through the LILO boot prompt or by configuring OpenLinux to start X11 and the xdm, or X display manager client, after booting.

> You must properly configure X for your computer's graphics card before trying this, or you can lock up your system!

To boot directly to the xdm login screen, turn on your computer, and at the LILO boot prompt, type the following:

```
linux 5
```

After you press Enter, Linux boots and presents the xdm login screen, as shown in Figure 7.3. This method works by booting OpenLinux directly to a particular run level, as specified in the OpenLinux system initialization table, inittab, under the /etc directory. Run level 5 is defined in /etc/inittab as follows:

```
x:5:respawn:/usr/bin/X11/xdm -nodaemon
```

This line specifies that when OpenLinux is started, the login prompt is provided by xdm. To start your X session (which uses fvwm by default), type your username, press Enter, then type in your password, and press Enter again.

To configure OpenLinux to boot directly to this login screen, log in as the root operator, and then open /etc/inittab with your favorite text editor. Scroll through the file until you see the following:

```
# Default runlevel.
id:3:initdefault:
```

> Editing your system's initialization table is inherently dangerous! Make a backup copy first, and make sure to disable line-wrapping (such as using the -w option with the pico editor) when editing this file.

7

FIGURE 7.3

The xdm *client is the X
display manager and
provides a login
prompt to X.*

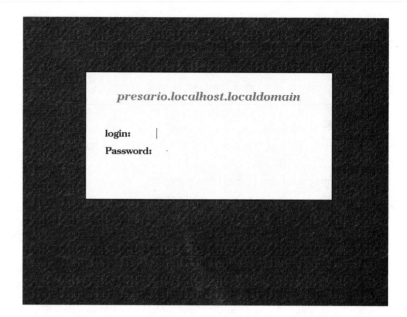

presario.localhost.localdomain

login:
Password:

The initdefault line tells OpenLinux what run level to use by default. To boot directly
to the xdm login screen, change the 3 to a 5, like this:

```
id:5:initdefault:
```

Save the file, exit your text editor, and either use the command **/sbin/telinit 5** or
reboot OpenLinux with the shutdown command. When you reboot to OpenLinux, you
see the xdm screen, as shown in Figure 7.3.

> A nice alternative to xdm is the K Display Manager, or kdm. This client offers
> more login choices and configurations than the stock xdm client. For details
> about how to configure kdm, see the section "Configuring kdm" in Hour 8.

X11 Window Managers

NEW TERM   One of the great things about X11 is that you have freedom of choice in how you
want to manage your windows and programs on your screen. All the hard work
of screen management is done by a *window manager*, which is simply another X11 program or client. Of course, you don't have to use a window manager with X. For example,
create a file called .xinitrc in your home directory with a single line:

```
xterm
```

Then use the `startx` command. This starts X11, but you only have a single terminal window with no window borders, scrollbars, buttons, or colors. The computing life in X is very drab without a window manager!

Although freedom of choice is good, one of the bad things about X11 is the possibly confusing choice and complexity of window managers: you might be initially overwhelmed by the array of configuration files, scripts, or resource settings.

Configuring the `fvwm` Window Manager

The `fvwm` window manager, by Evans and Sutherland Computer Corporation, the Massachusetts Institute of Technology, and Robert Nation, builds on an earlier window manager named `twm`. This window manager is used by default when you start an X session with the `startx` command and provides elements common to many window managers for X:

- Hierarchical root menus (menus and submenus)
- Graphics icons (when minimizing a window)
- 3D window buttons (using shading and color)
- 3D scrollbars (draggable and shaded)
- Customizable display colors and screen elements
- Window manager modules (for icon docks, pagers, and so on)
- Virtual desktops (multiple screens)

NEW TERM Although there is a `fvwm` configuration file, `system.fvwmrc`, in the `/etc/X11/fvwm` directory, the major elements of this window manager are found in the `wm1_modules` directory under the `/usr/X11R6/lib/X11` directory. Configuration and management of `fvwm` (and other window managers) is through a series of macro and configuration files under the `/etc/X11/wmconfig` directory that have been processed by the `wmconfig` (window manager configuration) command. Settings for menus, colors, borders, keyboard values, and other aspects of window management are processed and built from these files when you start an X11 session using `fvwm` (and other window managers). This is a complex system but one that provides a rudimentary form of *session management*, or the capability to save settings for use in the next X11 session. These files are listed in Table 7.1.

7

TABLE 7.1   X11 MACRO AND CONFIGURATION FILES

Name	Description
AfterStep.M4	Macros used by the AfterStep window manager
Common.M4	Macros and definitions for all window managers
Fvwm1.M4	Macros used for the fvwm window manager
WmConfig	Macros used to reconfigure a window manager's settings following a restart
desk	Startup functions for the Looking Glass client
rc	Macro definitions about how to process configuration files
rc.bindings	Mouse and keyboard settings
rc.config	Background and display font settings
rc.functions	Specialized mouse and window-handling functions
rc.goodstuff	Icon and application-launching definitions
rc.menus	Menu definitions
rc.menus.exclude	Clients excluded from menus
rc.modules	Module definitions for windows and pagers
rc.options	Window colors, focus, icons, appearance, placement, decoration, and pager size
rc.styles	Window decorations and icon assignments
xinitrc	Initial setup and settings for starting an X session
xsessionrc	Setup and settings used by xdm when starting an X session

For the best overview of how the wmconfig command works, read the file Fvwm-Config-Dokumentation.en.txt under the /usr/doc/wmconfig directory.

 Fortunately, you do not (and probably should not) edit these files. The settings and interaction of the macro definitions are quite complex. Unless you know *exactly* what you're doing, leave these files alone.

You can change how fvwm displays information through the use of numerous configuration menus in the root display. These menus, accessed by pressing Alt+C (or Alt+Shift+C) in a blank area of the desktop, enable you to change many of the following:

- Fonts for windows, icons, and menus
- Window colors (background and foreground)
- Focus policy (clicking in a window to activate it, or moving the cursor over it, and so on)
- Set how windows are handled and appear
- Set the default window manager to use
- Set the location of modules, icons, or desktop buttons
- Set which modules, icons, or desktop buttons appear

To save your settings, you must first select the Enable Autosave Topics item of the desktop menu. Press Alt+C in a blank area of the desktop. A menu appears, as shown in Figure 7.4.

FIGURE 7.4

You must first enable configuration saving with the fvwm *configuration menu before you can save X session settings.*

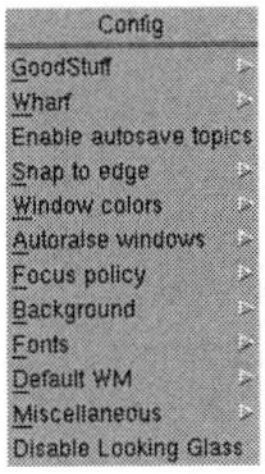

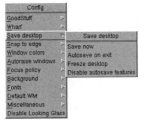

Click the Enable Autosave Topics item of the desktop menu. You can then change different settings through the Config menu. When you finish, again press Alt+C. You see that the Config menu has changed and now has a Save Desktop item, as shown in Figure 7.5.

FIGURE 7.5

Save your window manager's settings with the Config menu's save options.

7

Click the Save Now menu item to save your changes (they are put in the files desk and rc.config in the .wmconfig directory in your home directory.)

You can start different X11 clients from the command line of a terminal window or through fvwm's root menu. To use this menu, move your mouse cursor to a blank area of the desktop, click your left mouse button, and scroll down to a desired group of programs, as shown in Figure 7.6.

FIGURE 7.6

Use fvwm's *root menus to launch different X11 clients.*

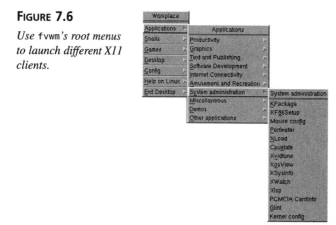

> If you accidentally click the Disable Looking Glass menu item in the root Config menu, you can always start Looking Glass by typing **lg&** in the command line of a terminal window.

The fvwm window manager also supports numerous keyboard commands to control the mouse pointer, menus, and the currently active window. Using these commands, it is possible to control windows or the mouse and select menu items without lifting your fingers from the keyboard. Table 7.2 lists some of the more common commands.

TABLE 7.2 COMMAND fvwm WINDOW AND POINTER KEYBOARD COMMANDS

Command	Description
Alt+A	Pops up Applications menu
Alt+C	Pops up Config menu
Alt+D	Pops up Desktop menu
Alt+Esc	Displays graphic list of windows

Command	Description
Alt+F	Pops up Graphics menu
Alt+G	Pops up Games menu
Alt+H	Pops up Help menu
Alt+I	Pops up Internet Connectivity menu
Alt+P	Pops up Productivity Tools menu
Alt+R	Pops up Amusement menu
Alt+S	Pops up Shells menu
Alt+T	Pops up Terminals menu
Alt+Tab	Activates next window
Alt+V	Pops up Software Development menu
Alt+X	Pops up Text and Publishing menu
Alt+Y	Pops up System administration menu
Ctrl+Alt+down arrow	Moves pointer down 100 pixels
Ctrl+Alt+left arrow	Moves pointer left 100 pixels
Ctrl+Alt+right arrow	Moves pointer right 100 pixels
Ctrl+Alt+up arrow	Moves pointer up 100 pixels
Ctrl+down arrow	Moves active window down to next desktop
Ctrl+left arrow	Moves active window to next left desktop
Ctrl+right arrow	Moves active window to next right desktop
Ctrl+up arrow	Moves active window up to next desktop
Shift+Alt+Tab	Activates previous window
Shift+Ctrl+Alt+down arrow	Moves pointer down 1 percent of screen
Shift+Ctrl+Alt+left arrow	Moves pointer left 1 percent of screen
Shift+Ctrl+Alt+right arrow	Moves pointer right 1 percent of screen
Shift+Ctrl+Alt+up arrow	Moves pointer up 1 percent of screen

If you like the fvwm window manager, you might also want to try AfterStep, a sophisticated customization of fvwm's configuration files.

Starting AfterStep

The AfterStep window manager, by Frank Fejes, Alfredo Kenji Kojima, and Dan Weeks, provides window management, controls, and other features similar to the commercial NEXTSTEP operating system (see Figure 7.7). These features include the following:

- 3D, configurable icons
- A "Wharf," or icon dock, for launching X11 clients
- Pop-up, multiple icon menus
- Window shade-type window controls (double-click a window's title bar to draw the shade up or down)
- Sophisticated title bars, buttons, and other decorations
- Styled, pop-up root menus

FIGURE 7.7

The AfterStep *window manager provides sophisticated window controls, icons, and an application "Wharf" for your X sessions.*

You can use AfterStep as the default window manager through the Default WM menu item in the root display Config menu. AfterStep uses the same menu and desktop configuration scheme as fvwm, so you can make changes to your desktop and save the settings for future use (changes are reflected in the rc.config file in the .wmconfig directory in your home directory).

Starting the twm Window Manager

The twm, or Tab window manager, found under the /usr/X11R6/bin directory, is one of the original window managers for the X Window System. The twm client, developed by Tom LaStrange and other authors, provides the most basic window operations, such as window titles, icons, root window menus, and other custom mouse or keyboard commands. Figure 7.8 shows a typical twm window management session.

FIGURE **7.8**

The twm, *or Tab window manager, provides basic X11 desktop displays with program lists, icons, and window controls.*

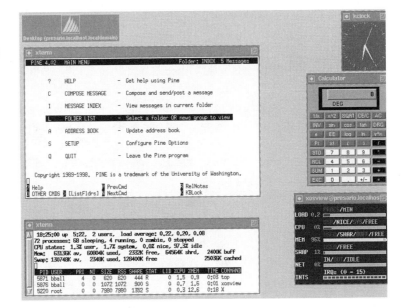

Start this window manager, like the others, by clicking the Default WM menu item in the root display Config menu. However, twm does not use the same menu and desktop configuration scheme as the fvwm or AfterStep window managers. If you make twm the default window manager, you can't go back to using any other manager until you edit the rc.config file in the .wmconfig directory in your home directory! Open this file with your favorite text editor, and look for the WINMGR setting, like this:

```
WINMGR="twm"
```

You can delete this setting or change it to another window manager, like this:

```
WINMGR="afterstep"
```

Save the file, and restart X11 to use the new window manager. The configuration file for the twm window manager, system.twmrc, is found in the /etc/X11/twm directory. If you're the root operator, you can customize this file to support features and programs of your system for all users. If you want to make your own custom twm features, copy this file as .twmrc, and save it in your home directory.

X11 Terminal Programs

X11 terminal clients provide a console with command-line access to the shell. Although you don't need to use a terminal during your X sessions, it might be a good idea to keep

7

at least one open (or iconified) so you can start other programs. Having several windows open at one time is also a convenient way to learn new commands because you can have the manual page displayed in one window while you try out the program in another window. You can also use multiple terminal windows to copy and paste information between programs.

This section introduces you to several terminal programs you might want to use with X11: cmdtool, rxvt, xterm, kvt, and kterm. Table 7.3 lists these various terminals.

TABLE 7.3   X11 TERMINAL CLIENTS INCLUDED WITH OPENLINUX

Name	Description
ansi-xterm	Symbolic link to xterm-color
cmdtool	Terminal window emulator included with Sun's OpenWindows
color-xterm	Symbolic link to xterm-color
kterm	Multilingual terminal emulator
kvt	Menu-enabled X11 terminal included with KDE
rxvt	Memory efficent, color-capable terminal
xterm	Standard X11 terminal included with XFree86
xterm-color	Shell script to run xterm as a color terminal (using the xterm-16color entry in the /etc/termcap database)

Changing the xterm Terminal Settings

The xterm client is a color-capable terminal emulator. When started, it displays an open window with a command line. You can run programs, do word processing, or perform nearly any function you normally do when you aren't running X11. Like most X11 terminal emulators, xterm features a resizeable window. Depending on the window manager you use, buttons on the window's title bar enable you to move, size, minimize, or maximize the window and might enable you to close or kill the window and any running programs started from the window. If you minimize an xterm window, an icon might appear on the desktop or be placed in an icon dock or taskbar, depending on the window manager.

NEW TERM   If you start xterm from another terminal, you can choose how and where to initially display the new window through the use of command-line options called *X11 Toolkit options*. These are discussed in the section "Learning X11 Basic Operations" later in this hour. One feature xterm shares with the kvt terminal emulators is the capability to change fonts on-the-fly.

For example, if you want your terminal to use a larger or smaller font, all you have to do is move the cursor inside the terminal window, hold down the Ctrl key, and press the right mouse button. A menu called VT Fonts with a list of sizes pops up from which you can select larger or smaller sizes.

> One really great feature of xterm's VT Fonts menu is the Selection option. Here's how it works: First, run the xterm client, and then start the xfontsel client from the command line. The xfontsel client displays different fonts in many variations, and you can see the effects of different point sizes or orientation on a selected font. After you find an extremely readable font for your display, click the Select button at the top of the xfontsel window. Then, move your mouse cursor to the xterm window, hold down the Ctrl key, press the right mouse button, and select the VT Fonts menu item Selection. Voilà! Your xterm window now uses the font you selected with the xfontsel client. This is handy for finding the best typeface to use for your terminal.

Although nearly all terminals support scrolling, not all terminal emulators have nicely drawn scroll bars. You can control whether scrolling is enabled and scroll bars are visible by holding down the Ctrl key and pressing the middle mouse button (for two-button mouse users, make sure you enable three-button emulation and depress both mouse buttons).

If you don't need all these features or need more memory to run programs, you might want to use the rxvt terminal emulator, discussed next.

Using the Memory-Efficient rxvt Terminal

The rxvt client, or terminal emulator, is a color-capable X11 console window with fewer, but possibly more useful, features than the xterm client, including the following:

- Smaller size, so this client uses less memory or swap space
- Color-capable terminal emulator
- Supports limited X Toolkit command-line options
- Does not have Tektronix 4014 emulation, which is not really needed for standalone Linux X11 workstations

rxvt supports at least one of the same command-line options as xterm—the -e option to run programs in a standalone X window. The -e option is useful if you want to run

7

programs under X that are normally run from a nongraphical environment (the console), for example:

```
# rxvt -e pico &
```

This command line runs the pico editor (part of the pine mail program) in a standalone window. You can create, open, edit, and save files, but when you quit the pico editor, the window disappears. This is a great way to run interactive console programs under X.

The rxvt client also supports a number of X Toolkit options, as you'll see in the next section. By using these options, you can start your rxvt terminal at any location of your desktop, with any available font, and with a selection of foreground and background colors.

Learning X11 Basic Operations

A number of basic operations are important for you to know about when using X11 and X11 clients. Many programs accept similar command-line options, so you can customize the size, color, and placement of client windows. This section introduces you to some of the more common command-line options and shows you how to use them.

Not all X11 clients support the same X11 options, known as X Toolkit command-line options. For a full discussion of these options, see the X manual page found under the /usr/X11/man/man1 directory or an individual client's manual page for details.

Using X11 Client Geometry Settings

You can use the geometry option, usually in the form of -geometry widthxheight+xoffset+yoffset, to manage how and where your client's window is displayed.

For example, if you want to start an rxvt terminal in the upper left corner of your screen, you use the following:

```
# rxvt -geometry 80x25+0+0 &
```

This command starts an 80 character, 25 line rxvt terminal, and places its window at the upper left corner of your display. Here's a neat trick: If you are using a virtual-window[nd]capable window manager and have several desktops available, you can start terminal emulators not only in your current desktop, but also in other desktops.

For example, if your current desktop is 800∞600, you can easily start other X11 clients in adjacent desktops by specifying the x and y offsets, as follows:

```
# rxvt -geometry 80x25+801+0
# rxvt -geometry 80x25+0+601
```

The first command line starts another terminal window, but at the upper left corner of the desktop immediately to the right. The second command line starts another terminal window, but at the upper left corner of the desktop immediately below. This is a handy feature to use if you want to set up not only your desktop, but others before you start X11. Using this approach, you can start word processing in one desktop, a Web browser in another, and a graphics program in a third (assuming you have enough memory).

Geometry specifications are useful for building organized, working screens from the command line. Build your desktop, starting clients from the command line or resizing windows, and then use the Save Desktop feature of the root display menu to save your window settings.

Setting Background and Foreground Colors for X11 Clients

You can also usually set the background and foreground colors of a terminal's window with the -bg and -fg color command-line options. You can find a list of colors supported by the XFree86 X11 servers in the file rgb.txt in the /usr/X11R6/lib/X11 directory. For example, to start the rxvt terminal emulator with a red background with yellow text for the foreground, you use the following:

```
# rxvt -bg red -fg yellow
```

If you're not using X11 in the 8-bpp (8-bits per pixel) mode (256 colors) with the XF86_SVGA server, you find a more limited selection of colors available. For example, you only have 16 colors available if you use the XF86_VGA16 server or black and white if you use the monochrome server, XF86_Mono. You can also try to see the available colors by using the xcolorsel client or xcmap client, which displays the colors in a grid and gives the rgb (red, green, and blue) values of the color in base 16, or hexadecimal. (See the X, xcolorsel, and xcmap manual pages for more information.) Another program to try is the showrgb client, which automatically lists the contents of the rgb database, rgb.txt.

7

Other color options include -bd for color choices of window borders and the -rv and +rv reverse video modes, which are useful for monochrome displays.

Setting X11 Client Resources

The X Window System also supports further client configuration through the use of client resources. These are text files that contain settings for different aspects of how a client looks or runs. You might also be able to set different resources of a client program when it first starts by using the -xrm command-line option to specify a resource string, but most programs only use a resource file.

In order to change resource settings, you need to know what resources an X11 client uses. You can find this information by either reading the program's manual page or looking for any installed settings in a file with (but not always) the client's name in the app-defaults directory under the /usr/X11R6/lib/X11 directory, as follows:

```
# ls -A /usr/X11R6/lib/X11/app-defaults
Axe                 Pixmap.No3d        XLogo              Xconq
Axinfo              Rosegarden         XLogo-color        Xconq-color
Beforelight         Rubik              XMailbox           Xditview
Bitmap              Seyon              XMixer             Xditview-chrtr
Bitmap-color        Seyon-color        XPaint             Xditview.No3d
Bitmap.No3d         Seyon.No3d         XPat               Xedit
Chooser             Skewb              XPat.No3d          Xfd
Chooser.No3d        Triangles          XPlaycd            Xfm
Clock-color         Velvet.ad          XPlaymidi          Xgc
Coolmail            Velvet.ad.No3d     XPostitPlus        Xgc.No3d
Cubes               Viewres            XPostitPlus.No3d   Xgopher
Dino                Viewres.No3d       XRn                Xgopher-color
Editres             XBlast             XScreenSaver       Xloadimage
Editres-color       XCalc              XShowimf           Xmag
Editres.No3d        XCalc-color        XShowimf-color     Xman
Fig                 XCalc.No3d         XSm                Xman.No3d
Fig-color           XClipboard         XSok               Xmessage
Freeciv             XClipboard.No3d    XSok.No3d          Xmessage.No3d
GV                  XClock             XSysinfo           Xmh
GXditview           XConsole           XSysinfo-color     Xmh.No3d
Ghostview           XDaliClock         XTar               Xmine
Ghostview.No3d      XDbx               Xterm              Xosview
HMan                XEvil              Xterm-color        Xtartan
Hexagons            XFontSel           XTrojka            Xtetris
KTerm               XFontSel.No3d      XWatch             Xtetris.bw
Knews               XFrisk             Xarchie            Xtetris.c
ML                  XGammon            Xbl                Xvidtune
Mball               XGetfile           XbmBrowser         netscape.cfg
Mlink               XISDNLoad          XbmBrowser-color   xnwdsadmin
Panex               XLoad              Xcolorsel
Pixmap              XLock              Xcolorsel-color
```

You can see that there are quite a few files with application default settings but that not all of the more than 370 programs for X11 installed on an OpenLinux system have settings installed. Each file contains resource strings for a particular X11 client. The resource strings can provide not only information that determines how a program is displayed, but the contents and handling of menus, buttons, or other parts of a program.

You can use X11 resource strings in the file Xdefaults in your home directory. Resource and configuration settings for selected KDE clients are stored in the .kde/share/config directory in your home directory.

The format of resource strings is defined in the X manual page, but many X11 client manual pages list different resources with examples for a particular client. For example, if you look at the resource settings for the xpaint drawing program's main toolbox (contained in the file XPaint in the /usr/X11R6/lib/X11/app-defaults directory), you see the following values:

```
...
!
!  The top level operation/toolbox menu
!
XPaint.width:                   232
XPaint.height:                  350
...
```

These values tell the xpaint client to draw a vertical toolbox. If you want a horizontal toolbox instead, you can resize the toolbox, note the dimensions shown by the window manager during the resize operation, and use the new settings to change the initial size of the toolbox in its default resource settings file, for example:

```
...
!  The top level operation/toolbox menu
!
XPaint.width:                   702
XPaint.height:                  122
...
```

For details about X resources, see the X man page. For details about different client resources, see the program's manual page or other documentation.

Make sure your changes reflect your supported screen size, or programs might start off-screen or with windows too large to be useful. Always use the exclamation character for comments, and if you edit the default, or original application resource file, copy the original settings first to a comment line.

Changing X11 Mouse and Cursor Modes

When you use X11, you might want to change the way your mouse works or switch the order of the mouse buttons. This is especially handy if you're left-handed or if your mouse responds differently from the desired setup. You can also change the type of cursor used by your window manager.

To change your root window cursor, you need to know what cursors are available. You can find a list of cursors in the cursorfont.h file under the /usr/X11R6/include/X11 directory, for example:

```
...
#define XC_exchange 50
#define XC_fleur 52
#define XC_gobbler 54
#define XC_gumby 56
#define XC_hand1 58
#define XC_hand2 60
#define XC_heart 62
#define XC_icon 64
...
```

As you can see, many types of cursors are listed in this file. Knowing these different types of cursors, use the xsetroot client, or root window utility program, to set your root cursor image, for example:

 # xsetroot -cursor_name hand1

This changes the root cursor to look like a right-pointing hand. If you are left-handed, you might want to use the left-pointing hand2 cursor!

An easy way to see all the cursors is to use the xfd, or X11 font display, client found under the /usr/X11R6/bin directory. Used with the -fn command-line option, the xfd client displays the entire character set of the cursor font, cursor, located in the /usr/X11R6/lib/X11/fonts/misc directory.

If you find the left and right mouse buttons inconvenient, change how these buttons are ordered on your mouse by using the xmodmap client (which can also change keyboard keys). For example, to reverse the order of your mouse buttons, you can try the following:

```
# xmodmap -e "pointer 3 2 1"
```

This example, from the xmodmap manual page, can help left-handed users.

> The xmseconfig client, which is part of the XF86Config setup program for XFree86, is a graphical mouse configuration utility. However, it does not reorder mouse buttons, and you must run the client as the root operator in order to save any changes.

You can also customize other mouse settings using the xset, or user preference, client. For example, if you want to speed up your mouse acceleration, or how fast it travels across the screen, you can try these settings:

```
# xset m "40 4"
```

If this is too fast for you, try the following:

```
# xset m "4 8"
```

Experiment with different settings. You can really slow down your mouse with the xset m "0 1000" command line. See the xset client manual page for other X11 settings you can change, and see if some of them work with your system.

How to Copy and Paste in X11

Copying and pasting information in X11 involves transferring text between terminal windows or graphics from one X11 client to another. For example, you can use the xmag program to select a portion of your desktop and then paste the copied graphic into an open xpaint drawing window (see Hour 16, "Graphics Tools"). To do this, first run the xpaint client, go to the File menu, and select New Canvas. Then start the xmag client. You see a tiny corner cursor. If you click an area of the screen you want to magnify, the xmag client displays the selection in a window. You then move your cursor to the xpaint drawing window, go to the Edit menu, and select Paste. Your selected graphic is pasted in the xpaint window.

7

Copy and paste operations using KDE are quite different. KDE-aware applications fully support copy and paste operation using Copy and Paste menu items from each client's Edit menu.

If you're running a word processor in one window and the command line in another terminal window, you can copy and paste text between the windows. Both the xterm and rxvt terminals support copy and paste operations using your mouse cursor and mouse buttons. To copy text, you must first highlight the desired text. If you just want a word, double-click the word with your left mouse button. If you want a line of text, triple-click the line. If you want more than a word or a line, you need to highlight regions of text.

Text regions in terminal windows can be selected in two ways (depending on the capabilities of your X terminal client). Move your cursor to the beginning or end of the text, and then drag up or down with the left mouse button held down to highlight the selected text. You can also click at the beginning of the text with your left mouse button and then, holding down the Shift key, click at the end of the text to highlight a selection.

After you highlight text, there are also two ways to paste the selection in another window. One way is to click in the desired window, hold down the Shift key, and press the Insert key. The other way is to click in the window and then press the middle mouse button (or the left and right mouse buttons simultaneously if you're using a two-button mouse to emulate three buttons).

The xcutsel client also copies from one window to another. When you run this client, you see two buttons called Copy PRIMARY to 0 and Copy 0 to PRIMARY. To copy text from one window to another, first highlight text in one window. Then click on the Copy PRIMARY to 0 button. You can then click on the Copy 0 to PRIMARY button, move to the window where you want to paste the text, and use either your keyboard or mouse to paste the text.

Yet another X11 client for copying and pasting text is the xclipboard client. This program is especially handy for copying sections of text from messages, FAQs, HOWTOs, or other files. Like the xcutsel client, xclipboard places the copied text into a buffer but has the added benefit of displaying the text, which you can then save into a file or copy into other windows or programs.

If you want to do more than just copy small bits of graphics or text, you can also capture pictures of whole windows or your desktop. The next section shows you how to capture, save, and display pictures from your X11 desktop.

Capturing and Dumping X11 Windows

You can capture pictures of windows or your entire desktop using several X11 clients included with X11. The first is xwd, or the X11 window dump program. You can use this client to take snapshots of your screen or any desired window.

The xwd program is easy to use. You want to redirect the output or specify a file on the command line because if you don't, the file is sent to the standard output and scrolls up your terminal window. To redirect the output, use xwd, like this:

```
# xwd > mydump.xwd
```

The xwd client also has an -out option that can be used to direct the output, like this:

```
# xwd -out mydump.xwd
```

After you press Enter, your cursor turns to a crosshair (+). If you click on the root desktop, the xwd client dumps, or captures, a picture of your entire screen. If you click in a window, the xwd client captures the contents of the window, even if it is hidden or overlapped by another window.

This is handy if you want to capture a series of pictures of a running client, show off high scores of games, or create quick slide shows. The captured file is in an X11 windows dump format, and you can find a number of clients you can use to view the image. One is the xwud (X11 window undump) client. To see your screenshot, you can use the following:

```
# xwud -in mydump.xwd
```

You can also create a slideshow of your images with the xloadimage client found under the /usr/X11R6/bin directory. For example, if you create a series of screen dumps, you can build a looping slideshow of the screenshots with the following:

```
# xloadimage -fit 1.xwd 2.xwd 3.xwd -goto 1.xwd
```

Using this command line, you can repeatedly page through the dump files by pressing the N character on your keyboard, or you can press the Q character on your keyboard to quit. The xloadimage client has many features and can also save your screen dump files in different graphics file formats. See the xloadimage manual page for more information.

> Many other graphic utilities are included on your OpenLinux CD-ROM. See Hour 16 for an overview of paint and drawing programs, graphics conversion utilities, and other image viewers, such as the xv client, which not only captures screenshots, but edits, converts, saves, and prints graphics.

7

Customizing the X11 Root Window and Using Screen savers

If you have a color monitor, you might want to change the default color or pattern of the root, or desktop, window. You can do this quickly and easily with several X11 clients. I'll also show you how to put pictures into your background and how to set up and use screen savers in X11.

Setting the Background Color

You can change the background color of your display with the xsetroot, or root window utility, which is found under the /usr/X11R6/bin directory. Your choice of color, as I mentioned previously, depends on the number of color depth of your X11 server. If you're using the SVGA server, you have a choice of 256 colors. For example, you can change the color with the following:

```
# xsetroot -solid red
```

Setting the Background Pattern

If a solid color is too hard on your eyes or too plain for your tastes, you can also use one of nearly 90 different bitmap graphics files from the /usr/include/X11/bitmaps directory to set a desktop pattern. For example, to get a red basket-weave pattern for your desktop, use the following:

```
# xsetroot -bitmap /usr/include/X11/bitmaps/wide_weave -bg red
```

This command line tells the xsetroot client to load the bitmap graphic file wide_weave from the X11 bitmap graphics directory and display the pattern with a background color. If you have a monochrome display, you're out of luck with colors. But you can change the pattern and apparent shade of your background display with different bitmap files. Try the dimple1, dimple3, or flipped_gray bitmap files.

Displaying Pictures on the Root Display

Many users like to display a favorite picture in the root window. If you have a favorite photograph you've scanned or a graphic you like, you can display your image on the desktop with the xsetroot client, but the image must be in the X11 bitmap format.

You can use a client that's already been discussed—xloadimage. See what graphics file formats the xloadimage client recognizes with the -supported command-line option, for example:

```
# xloadimage -supported
Type Name  Can Dump Description
---------- -------- -----------
```

niff	Yes	Native Image File Format (NIFF)
sunraster	No	Sun Rasterfile
gif	No	GIF Image
jpeg	Yes	JFIF-style JPEG Image
fbm	No	FBM Image
cmuraster	No	CMU WM Raster
pbm	Yes	Portable Bit Map (PBM, PGM, PPM)
faces	No	Faces Project
rle	No	Utah RLE Image
xwd	No	X Window Dump
vff	No	Sun Visualization File Format
mcidas	No	McIDAS areafile
vicar	No	VICAR Image
pcx	No	PC Paintbrush Image
gem	No	GEM Bit Image
macpaint	No	MacPaint Image
xpm	No	X Pixmap
xbm	No	X Bitmap

The file formats xloadimage can use are listed in the left column. If you have a graphic you want to display, you can use the following:

 # xloadimage -onroot cathy.gif

This loads the graphic file, cathy.gif, and displays it (depending on its size) in a tiled, or multiple-view, format. If you only want one large version of your graphic in the root display, use the -fullscreen command-line option, for example:

 # xloadimage -onroot -fullscreen cathy.gif

This causes the xsetroot command to load the graphic and zoom to fit the display. You have to experiment with different sized graphics to get the best effect for your graphics.

> The xv client can also be used to put images in your root display. If you use KDE, save your favorite image in JPEG format in the /opt/kde/share/wallpapers directory. You can then select the image as a default wallpaper for one of your desktops with the KDE Control Center's Desktop Background dialog box.

Screen Saver Settings and Programs

Although displaying a colored pattern or picture on your desktop can be fun, X11 screen savers also offer password control. Even though screen savers aren't needed to protect modern computer monitors from the "burn-in" effect of a continuous display, they are fun, and you can find an interesting variety installed along with X11.

7

KDE users can use the KDE Control Center's Desktop Screen savers dialog box to control screen saving.

Use the xset client, introduced earlier, to manage screen saving under X11. If you want to see the current settings, use the q command-line option (note that there is no hyphen used), for example:

```
# xset q
...
Screen Saver:
  prefer blanking:  yes     allow exposures:  yes
  timeout:  0    cycle:  600
...
```

You can turn on screen saving with the xset client by using the s command-line option, followed by the word on. To set the time in seconds, use the s option, followed by the number of seconds you want your X11 server to wait to blank the screen, for example:

```
# xset s 10
```

This sets the time out interval to 10 seconds before the X11 screen saver is activated (just to test screen saving). To enable the screen saver, which is built in to your X11 server, use the s option with the word on, for example:

```
# xset s on
```

After 10 seconds, X displays a blank screen. If you want to see graphics and a background pattern, you can use the noblank option for the xset s command-line option, for example:

```
# xset s noblank
```

As you can see, a large X is displayed on the screen. To turn off screen saving, use the s off command-line option (don't forget to change the screen saving interval to something more reasonable, such as **600** for 10 minutes, if you use xset). If this isn't your idea of a screen saver, you can try the xscreensaver clients.

The xscreensaver and xscreensaver-command clients, by Jamie Zawinski, are found under the /usr/X11R6/bin directory. The xscreensaver client has 16 command-line options. Although this hour doesn't cover all the options, the basic way to use this screen saver is to first run the xscreensaver client in the background, as follows:

```
# xscreensaver -timeout 5 &
```

This command sets the screen saver to run after five minutes of no keyboard or mouse activity. You can control this client with the `xscreensaver-command` client to turn the `xscreensaver` on or off or to activate it immediately. Although the `xscreensaver` client has a `-lock` option to password-protect your display, you have to recompile the program to enable this feature.

The `xscreensaver` client comes with nearly two dozen different screen savers, which can also be run as standalone programs. For example, you can run the fractal drawing program, `hopalong`, in a window, as follows:

 # hopalong

After you press Enter, a fractal image appears in a window (as shown in Figure 7.9), so you can see what it looks like.

FIGURE 7.9

The hopalong *client is part of a screen saver for X11.*

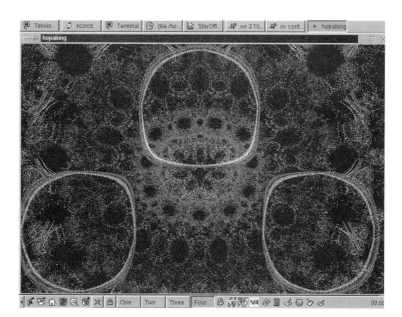

For a list of the screen savers that work with the `xscreensaver` client, read the file `XScreenSaver` in the `/usr/X11R6/lib/X11/app-defaults` directory. You can find other settings in the file, which is the X11 resources file for this client.

You might also be interested in the `xlock` client. Although it is not a screen saver, `xclock` is a sophisticated terminal-locking program with nearly 50 command-line options and more than 50 different displays built in. The `xlock` client is helpful if you want to password-protect your display to prevent others from using your computer while you're away.

By default, after you start the xlock program, you must enter your password before you can use your display again. You can use it as a simple screen saver without password protection to display a variety of animations, for example:

```
# xlock -duration 10 -nolock -mode random
```

This command line tells the xlock program to display a random selection of its animations, each of which runs for 10 seconds.

The xlock client can also make your desktop an animated display if you use the -inroot command-line option. This doesn't protect your system, but you might find the visuals stimulating!

Exploring X11 Programs

There's not enough room in this hour to discuss all the X11 clients on your CD-ROM. You can find discussions about different clients throughout the rest of this book, but this section shows you some helpful programs that give you more information about your system and some tips and tricks on how to use them.

Listing X11 Fonts with xlsfonts

If you want a list of all the fonts recognized by X11 on your system, you can use the xlsfonts client. Use a pager like less or more (discussed in Hour 4, "Reading and Navigation Commands") if you call the client without any options. You can also use wildcards or patterns to match font names. This can be handy to find a particular font on your system, for example:

```
# xlsfonts -fn *italic*
lucidasans-bolditalic-10
lucidasans-bolditalic-10
lucidasans-bolditalic-12
lucidasans-bolditalic-12
lucidasans-bolditalic-14
lucidasans-bolditalic-14
lucidasans-bolditalic-18
lucidasans-bolditalic-18
lucidasans-bolditalic-24
lucidasans-bolditalic-24
lucidasans-bolditalic-8
lucidasans-bolditalic-8
lucidasans-italic-10
lucidasans-italic-10
lucidasans-italic-12
```

```
lucidasans-italic-12
lucidasans-italic-14
lucidasans-italic-14
lucidasans-italic-18
lucidasans-italic-18
lucidasans-italic-24
lucidasans-italic-24
lucidasans-italic-8
lucidasans-italic-8
```

As you can see, this lists all the italic fonts installed or recognized by your X11 server. You can use the xlsfonts client to troubleshoot whether fonts are recognized or installed or to find a font name to choose as an X Toolkit option when starting a client.

Getting Window Information with the xwininfo Client

You can use the xwininfo client, or window information utility, to get helpful information about a window. When you use this command, you can click another window to get a detailed information listing, for example:

```
# xwininfo
 xwininfo: Please select the window about which you
          would like information by clicking the
          mouse in that window.
```

After you click on the desired window, you see a list of information, such as the following:

```
xwininfo: Window id: 0xc00002 "rxvt"

  Absolute upper-left X:  8
  Absolute upper-left Y:  397
  Relative upper-left X:  0
  Relative upper-left Y:  0
  Width: 574
  Height: 158
  Depth: 8
  Visual Class: PseudoColor
  Border width: 0
  Class: InputOutput
  Colormap: 0x21 (installed)
  Bit Gravity State: ForgetGravity
  Window Gravity State: NorthWestGravity
  Backing Store State: NotUseful
  Save Under State: no
  Map State: IsViewable
  Override Redirect State: no
  Corners:  +8+397   -218+397   -218-45   +8-45
  -geometry 80x11+3-40
```

7

This information can be helpful, for example, if you want to get the specifications about a window's geometry settings for the next time you run the program or if you want to change the default behavior of a window by editing its resource file.

Making a Sticky Note Calendar with the xmessage Client

The xmessage client, by Chris Peterson and Stephen Gildea, is a handy way to create quick notes as reminders while you work. This deceptively simple client is easy to use. For example, if you want to make a quick note of a phone number, you can use the following:

```
# xmessage "George called at 10:15; call him back at 555-1212" &
```

This command line displays the xmessage client window with the text of your message. Although this is a simple example, you can also use the xmessage client to display the output of program searches or use it in your personal schedules to automatically send reminders while you work. See Hour 18, "Personal Productivity Tools," or Hour 24, "Using Scheduling to Automate System Management," for details.

You can also use xmessage as a handy calendar display program if you need to keep a copy of the current calendar on the screen or if you want a calendar on your desktop when you start your X session. You can't find a simple X11 version of the cal calendar program, but here's one you can use:

```
# cal ¦ xmessage -file "-" &
```

This displays the output of the cal calendar program in a square xmessage client window.

> You can find the ical X11 client under the /usr/X11R6/bin directory, but this is a personal scheduling utility with a larger calendar display. See Hour 18 for details.

Keeping Time with X11 Clocks

If you're a habitual clock watcher, you're in luck using X11 as you can find several clocks. You're sure to find one you like.

Unfortunately, the rclock client, which usually accompanies the rxvt terminal, is not included with OpenLinux. This client is much more than just a clock; it's an appointment calendar and mail notification program, as in the following example:

```
# rclock -bg red -fg yellow -update 1 -geometry 80x80+718+0 &
```

This command line puts a square red clock with yellow hands (a second hand is created with the -update 1 option) in the upper right corner of an 800×600 desktop. A file called .rclock in your home directory is used create automatic reminders. The rclock client pops up a reminder message at the appointed time and can run programs at certain times (it checks the file every 10 minutes; when email arrives, rclock reverses its display). Look for this client on your favorite Linux archive Web site!

The xclock client displays time, by default, in a standard clock face, but you can make xclock look like a digital clock with the -digital option. You can also control the color of the standard clock hands or add a chime for the hour and half hour, for example:

```
# xclock -chime -hd red -hl red -update 2 -geometry 80x80 -bg yellow
```

This command displays an 80×80 pixel chiming xclock with a yellow face, red hands, and a sweeping second hand. If you want a digital version, you can use the following:

```
# xclock -chime -update 1 -digital -bg yellow
```

This command displays a digital chiming clock with a yellow background. If you like digital clocks, you might also like the xdaliclock client, which uses animation for its digits and has many options to control the digits, coloring, shape, or fonts used in the display, for example:

```
# xdaliclock -24 -cycle -font 9x15 -transparent -geometry +697+3
```

This command displays a transparent digital clock in the upper right corner of an 800×600 display with melting digits that constantly change color. If you click on the digital display, the current day, month, and year are displayed momentarily.

Summary

This hour introduced numerous initial topics relating to the X Window System, such as start up, using different color depths, navigating through virtual consoles, and starting multiple X11 displays. You then discovered several window managers for X11, saw how to configure and manage the X11 desktop, and learned copy and paste operations of text and graphics. Finally, you were introduced to several useful X11 utilties and clients to use to make your X session easier.

7

Q&A

Q **I still can't get X11 working with my computer's graphics card and monitor! What can I do?**

A If you have a troublesome graphics card (which usually happens with the latest equipment), try using a commercial X11 distribution for OpenLinux from a vendor such as MetroLink, Inc. (`http://www.metrolink.com`) or Xi Graphics, Inc. (`http://www.xig.com`). You can probably get much better support for newer cards.

Q **What is the best window manager to use for X11?**

A This is a religious question, and beyond the scope of this book. One good site to check for different window managers includes `http://www.PLiG.org/~xwinman/` where you can find links to at least 40 different GUIs for X.

Q **How many different window managers for X11 are there?**

A More than you'll ever want installed on your computer! There are more than 100. For example, if you want your desktop to look like an Apple Macintosh, try the `mlvwm` window manager at: `http://www.bioele.nuee.nagoya-u.ac.jp/member/tak/mlvwm.html`

Q **Hey! You haven't mentioned the GNU's Network Object Model Environment! What gives?**

A GNU GNOME development is moving along quite rapidly at the time of this writing. Like KDE, GNOME development is aimed at providing a quality environment and interface support for all versions of Linux. KDE is included with OpenLinux and has had the advantage of building increased popularity and adherents before GNOME's latest releases. You can find out more about GNOME by browsing to `http://www.gnome.org`.

Exercises

1. Create your own information display with the `xmessage` client. What kind of information should be shown?

2. Download and install a different window manager. How is it different? How are windows handled, and what do they look like?

3. See Hour 18 for information about using the `crontab` command. How can this command be used to configure your X11 display to mimic ambient light conditions?

HOUR 8

Exploring the K Desktop Environment

In this hour you'll learn about one of the newest desktop environments for the X Window System. Although there are more than 50 different window managers for X11, each with different themes, desktop colors, and decorations (for example, window controls), the K Desktop Environment, or KDE, reigns supreme in popularity with the OpenLinux crowd. You'll be especially pleased with KDE because Caldera Systems, Inc. has taken special pains to configure KDE's desktop to match programs in the OpenLinux distribution.

The hour will help you learn how to overcome the challenge of configuring KDE, and I think you'll soon agree—KDE is easy to use! Because choosing and using a window manager with X11 is a matter of personal preference, this hour will show you how to configure KDE using the KDE Control Center to change different settings, such as the background of the root display, fonts, the mouse, and the keyboard, and how window *decorations*, such as title bars, scrollbars, and buttons, appear.

KDE features some of the latest and most sophisticated features shared by commercial software libraries such as Motif, and the now fading Common Desktop Environment, or CDE (which is now only offered by one vendor, Xi-Graphics, for Linux). These features include:

- Drag-and-drop actions (such as copy, move, and delete) for files and devices
- Point-and-click dialog configuration of the desktop to display colors, window borders, and themes
- Programs and other data represented as icons on the desktop or in windows with folder icons
- Graphic configuration of your system's keyboard, mouse, and sound
- Single-click convenience to edit files, view graphics, or launch applications
- A desktop trash can for safer file deletions
- Pop-up menus and built-in help for nearly any desktop action and KDE client
- Network Transparent Access, or NTA, so you can click on a graphic document in an FTP listing and have a program on your computer automatically download and display the graphic
- "Sticky Buttons" to put an application or window on every desktop
- JPEG graphic formats for background wallpaper graphics for the root display
- Session management, so open applications and window positions are remembered between sessions (like CDE)
- A suite of personal productivity tools, such as disk and network utilities, crafted to take advantage of the desktop interface and the capability to import and export data to other tools

KDE is more than just an X11 window manager; it is a complete environment and comes with more than 100 clients with a consistent interface. Each client generally has a File and Help menu, so you can easily open files, quit, or get help. Pundits endorse this similarity, whereas some users prefer other X11 window and client management. Fortunately, because you're using OpenLinux, the choice is up to you!

Starting KDE

By default, you'll start KDE after logging into the kdm, or KDE display manager login. However, if you've disabled the login manager, you should know that there's another way to start KDE. When you log in to your OpenLinux console without X11, you're greeted with the following:

```
You can start X11 with 'startx' or KDE with 'kde'.
```

This is true, but if you've configured X11 with the xf86config command, and simply type **kde** and press Enter, your KDE and X session will start using only 256 colors, or an eight-bit pixel depth. To use a greater color depth, start your X sessions using the `-- -bpp`, or bits-per-pixel option. For example, to start KDE with thousands of colors, type **kde**, followed by the `-bpp` option, like so:

```
# kde -- -bpp 16
```

If you're fortunate enough to have a graphics card supporting millions of colors, try

```
# kde -- -bpp 24
```

or

```
# kde -- -bpp 32
```

The available color depths are defined in the XF86Config file found under the /etc directory. Look for the Depth settings in the Display subsection of the Screen section. If you configured X11 by editing XF86Config, use pound sign (#) characters to comment out lower color-depth settings. Another way is to use the DefaultColorDepth option, followed by 8, 15, 16, 24, or 32, in the Screen section. You can then just type **kde** to start X11 at higher color depths. For details about configuring X11, see Hour 3, "Configuring the X Window System and OpenLinux."

When you use xdm to log in to Linux and run X11, you might find that you're unable to run programs as the root operator from a terminal window. This is because you must use the xhost command to temporarily add the hostname of your computer to the access list of your X server. To do this, you can use this formula: xhost + localhost; su -c "rootcommand", where rootcommand is the name of the command you want to run as the root operator (such as the control panel or printtool). Afterwards, remove the access with: xhost - localhost to preserve your system's security.

Features of the KDE Desktop

As mentioned at the beginning of this hour, KDE has many of the features expected of a modern graphical computer interface. KDE builds on these features to provide an easy to use way of handling files to enable you to be more productive during X sessions. This section highlights some of the ways you can get work done when using the KDE desktop.

Performing Basic Desktop Actions

When you first start KDE, you see the kfm, or K file manager window, and a root display, or desktop, as shown in Figure 8.1.

The KDE desktop consists of several elements: a *taskbar* across the top of display, the root background (or *root display*), and the *desktop panel* along the bottom of your screen. In the panel, starting from the left, is the *Application Starter* button (the large 'K'), followed by several icons representing different applications, folders, and directories. There are four buttons representing the default four *virtual desktops*, or displays, followed by more application icons. (You may see ones for the CriSPlite editor, Netscape, BRU-2000, KDE help, and the Kcalc calculator.)

FIGURE 8.1

The KDE desktop is your introduction to point-and-click convenience during X sessions, and features a taskbar, root display area, panel with pop-up menus and client buttons, and a home directory.

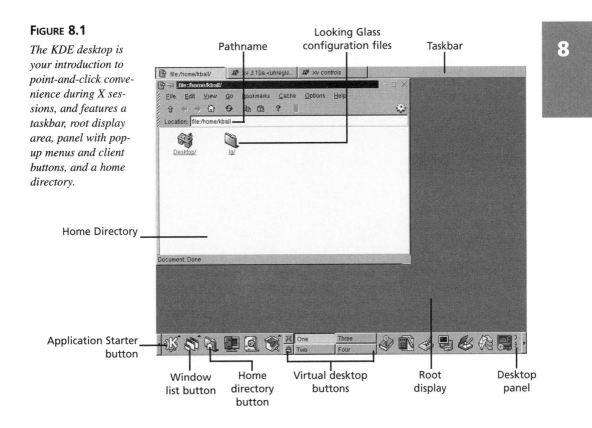

Pathname · Looking Glass configuration files · Taskbar · Home Directory · Application Starter button · Window list button · Home directory button · Virtual desktop buttons · Root display · Desktop panel

Using Desktop panel

The panel is used as a convenient tool for holding the Application Starter menu (accessed when you click the Application Starter menu), other application icons, the screen lock or logout button, virtual desktop buttons, and other program icons. To change the panel's size or orientation, click the Application Starter button, select Panel then click Configure.

A dialog box appears, as shown in Figure 8.2, from which you can select different settings. When you're finished, click Apply, then the Cancel button.

If you want to change how icons are placed or arranged on the panel, right-click a desired icon, and then select Remove (to delete the item) or Move from the small pop-up menu. If you click Move, you can drag the icon across the panel to a different place. If the panel is getting in the way during your KDE session, click the small button to the far left of the panel to temporarily hide the panel from your screen. To restore the panel, click the small button again, and the panel reappears.

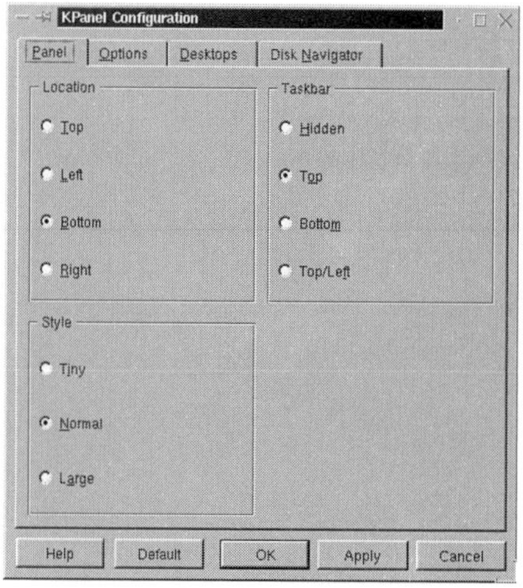

FIGURE 8.2

The Panel Configuration dialog box enables you to change how the panel and taskbar look and where they are placed on your desktop.

KPanel Configuration

| Panel | Options | Desktops | Disk Navigator |

Location
- ○ Top
- ○ Left
- ● Bottom
- ○ Right

Taskbar
- ○ Hidden
- ● Top
- ○ Bottom
- ○ Top/Left

Style
- ○ Tiny
- ● Normal
- ○ Large

| Help | Default | OK | Apply | Cancel |

Editing the KDE Panel Menu

To edit the desktop's panel menus, click the Application Starter button, select Panel, and then click Edit Menus. The KDE Menu Editor dialog box appears as shown in Figure 8.3. If you're logged in as the root operator, you can change and edit menu items on the panel menus by using drag-and-drop to shift items in the menu list or create items using the Empty menu item.

> If you're logged in as a regular user, you can only change menu items for which you have permission. If you right-click on a KDE panel item, you see the message "! PROTECTED Button !". You can, however, edit a single applink menu item in your desktop's panel. To this menu, you can add nearly any other command or client.

For example, to create a new menu item, right-click the Empty menu item, and then select New. A new Empty menu item appears. Right-click the new Empty menu item, then click Change, and the kmenuedit editor dialog box appears, as shown in Figure 8.4. Fill in the required fields, and select a large icon and menu icon for the menu item. When you finish, click Ok to save the changes. You can now drag and drop the new item anywhere in the panel menu's hierarchy.

FIGURE 8.3

The panel menu editor enables you to add or remove menu items from the panel's menus.

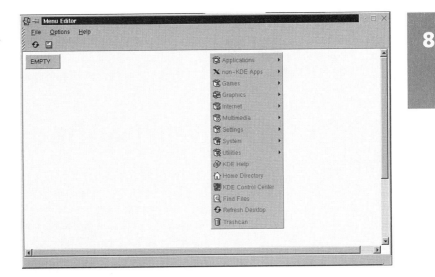

FIGURE 8.4

The kmenuedit dialog box is used to create or edit new individual menu items in your panel's menus.

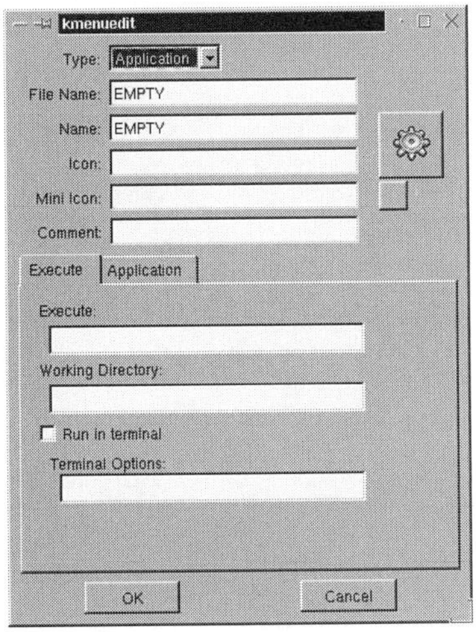

Using the kfm File Manager

The K file manager, or kfm, is near the center of the magic of KDE. This file manager, unlike Looking Glass (discussed in Hour 7, "Using the X Window System"), provides a usable desktop where you can drag, drop, multiple-select, copy, move, or delete icons of data files or programs. Many of the desktop actions supported by kfm become apparent when you drag or right-click a file's icon.

The kfm desktop, which includes your home directory and your root display (as shown in Figure 8.1), is represented by the directory named Desktop in your home directory. If you drag files to this folder, the files' icons appear on your root display. Similarly, if you drag a file from another folder or directory to the desktop, it appears in your Desktop directory.

Configuring KDE with the KDE Control Center

The KDE Control Center is the main dialog box through which you can change numerous settings of your desktop, get system information (such as the currently mounted devices and capacities), or (if logged in as the root operator) configure and control KDE's appearance, background, fonts, and sessions for all users.

Click the Application Starter button on your desktop's panel, and then click KDE Control Center to display the Control Center dialog box. The main dialog box appears, as shown in Figure 8.5.

FIGURE 8.5

The KDE Control Center dialog box provides access to many different controls of your system's KDE sessions.

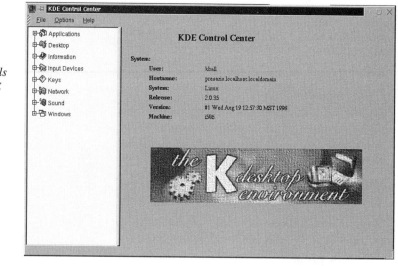

Using Display Manager Options

Click Applications and then Login Manager in the drop-down menu in the Control Center to change settings for the KDE Display Manager. You must be logged in as the root operator to access this portion of the Control Center. The Login Manager dialog box, shown in Figure 8.6, enables you to change how the kdm dialog box appears when you boot OpenLinux.

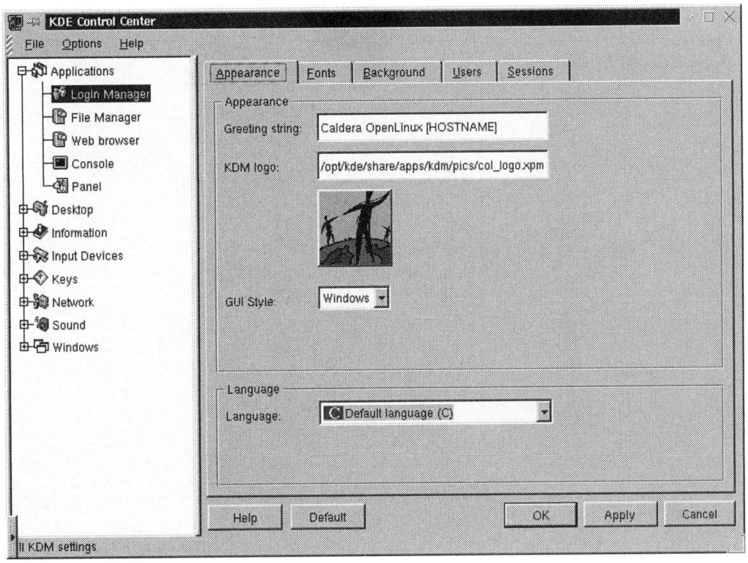

FIGURE 8.6

Use the Login Manager dialog box to change kdm's login screen and other settings, such as the type and number of X window managers or users allowed to log in.

By clicking on different tabs at the top of the dialog, you can change many different features of your kdm login screen:

- Appearance — the greeting strings, logo used in the login dialog, window style, and language
- Background — the wallpaper, background color, and tiling of images for the wallpaper
- Fonts — the greeting font
- Sessions — the type of shutdowns allowed, the commands used to shutdown or restart OpenLinux from kdm, and the types of "sessions" or window managers used for the X session after logging in
- Users — which system users are allowed to log in, whether the user list is sorted, and the icon used for each user (which may be substituted by a scanned photo!)

For example, to control which users are permitted to log in to OpenLinux directly to X, click the Users tab in the Login Manager dialog box. The Users dialog box appears, as shown in Figure 8.7. To selectively control user log-ins, click the Show only selected users button, and then click and add users to the Selected users section of the dialog using the >> button.

FIGURE 8.7

The Users dialog box can control who is permitted to log in to OpenLinux using X and KDE.

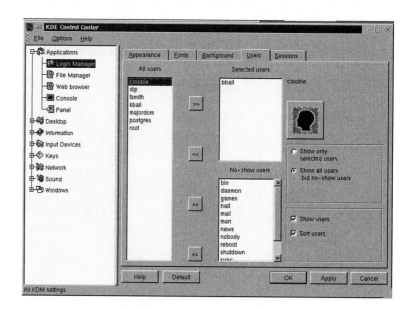

To control whether anyone can reboot or shutdown OpenLinux from the kdm login screen, when your system shuts down or reboots, and what window managers can be used after logging in, click the Sessions tab of the Login Manager dialog box. Click the Allow to shutdown drop-down menu shown in Figure 8.8, and select who is enabled to stop or restart OpenLinux. When finished, click the Apply button.

FIGURE 8.8

The Sessions dialog box can control who can shut down or restart OpenLinux and what X window managers can be used.

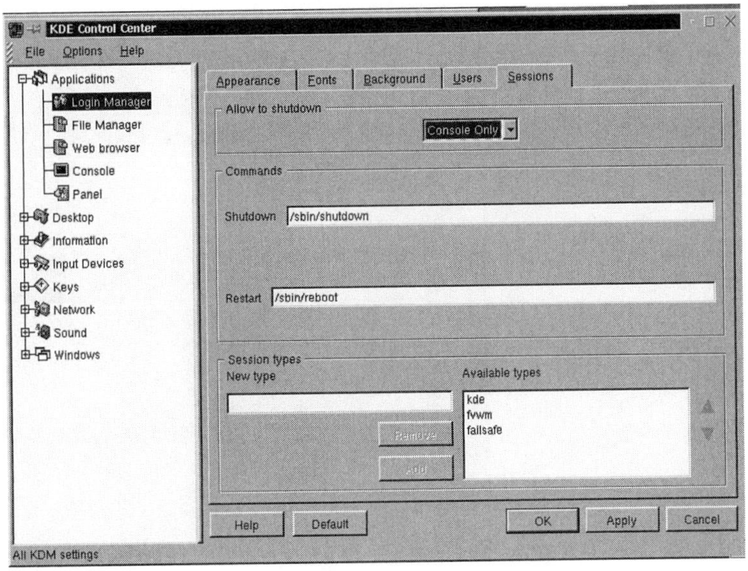

Changing Your Desktop's Wallpaper

KDE comes with nearly 150 different wallpapers you can use to fill the root display, or background of your desktop. To configure the current desktop's wallpaper, click the drop-down Desktop menu, and then click Background. You can also click the Application Starter button on the desktop panel, and select Settings, then Desktop, and then Screensaver.

The Background dialog box, shown in Figure 8.9, enables you to set the name of each desktop, each desktop's colors, and whether the desktop uses a wallpaper. To set a different wallpaper, click the Wallpaper pop-up menu in the Wallpaper section of the dialog box, and then click Apply.

> KDE wallpapers are graphics files in JPEG format. To add to the choice of wallpapers or to use your own wallpapers, log in as the root operator, and copy your favorite graphics (in JPEG format) to the `/opt/kde/share/wallpapers` directory. You can also select wallpaper graphics from any OpenLinux directory by clicking on the Browse button in the Background dialog box.

FIGURE 8.9

*Use the Background
dialog box to set
your desktop's name,
colors, and wallpaper.*

Changing Your Screensaver

KDE comes with 24 different screensaver settings. To configure the screensaver of your
KDE desktop, click Screensaver from the Desktop drop-down menu in the KDE Control
Center. You can also click the Application Starter button on the desktop panel, and then
select Settings, then Desktop, and then Screensaver.

The Screensaver dialog box, shown in Figure 8.10, has a number of settings, such as the
type of screensaver, the time delay before activating the screensaver, and whether you
want to require a password to go back to work. After you make your changes, click the
Apply button, and then click OK to close the dialog box.

> Right-click different corners of the sample display in the Screensaver dialog
> box to set automatic screen-saving or screen-locking! A small pop-up menu
> appears, and you can select Save Screen or Lock Screen for each corner. For
> example, if you set the lower-left corner of the sample display to start
> screen saving, the next time you move your mouse pointer into the left cor-
> ner of the display (and leave it there for a second), screen saving starts.

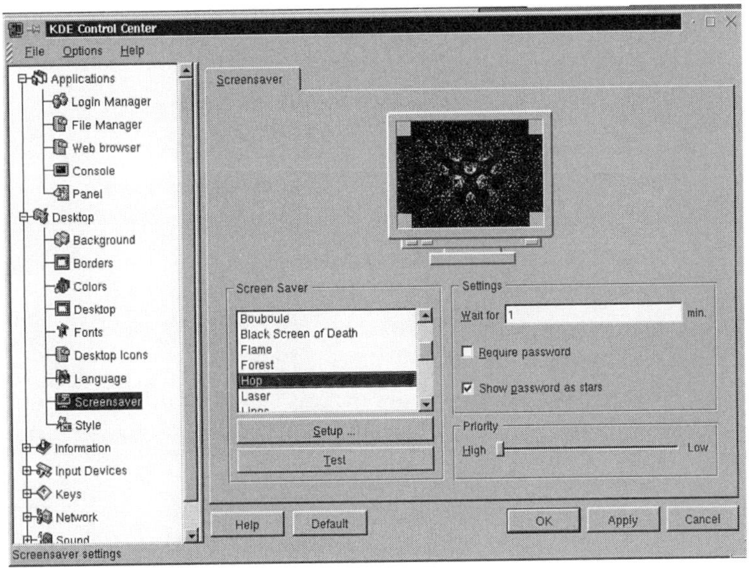

FIGURE 8.10

The Screensaver dialog box has different settings you can use to test a screensaver, set a time delay, or require a password.

8

Changing Default Fonts

KDE can also use different fonts for menus, buttons, the panel, or your panel's clock. To set the fonts of your KDE desktop, click the Application Starter button on the desktop panel, and select Settings, then Desktop, and then Fonts. You can also click KDE Control Center from the Application Starter menu, then click Desktop, and then click Fonts.

The Fonts dialog box, shown in Figure 8.11, shows a list of the different desktop fonts, along with a pop-up menu of typefaces. First, click a type of display item, such as the Panel clock font, and then select a typeface, type style (such as bold or italic), and a size. The sample text area of the dialog box changes. To effect your changes, click the Apply button, and then click OK to close the dialog box.

FIGURE **8.11**

The KDE fonts dialog box enables you to change the fonts used for menus, buttons, or the desktop panel's clock.

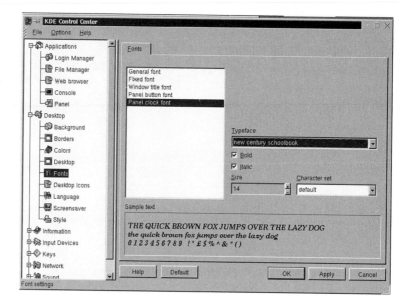

Installing System Sounds

Click the Sound drop-down menu in the KDE Control Center, and then click System Sounds to configure KDE to use sound during your X sessions. KDE recognizes 28 separate system events to which you can assign a sound. Table 8.1 shows a list of currently supported events, such as opening or closing windows. To have KDE play a sound when it first starts, in the Sound dialog box, as shown in Figure 8.12, first click enable systems sounds, and then click the Startup system event. Next, drag the icon of a sound file into the blank Sounds: area of the dialog, and click the Apply button. The next time you start KDE, you hear the sound file play.

TABLE 8.1   K DESKTOP ENVIRONMENT SYSTEM SOUND EVENTS

Desktop Element	Events
Desktop	Changing to 1-8
System	Startup, Logout, Logout Message
Window	Activate, Open new, Close, Shade Up, Shade Down, Iconify, DeIconify, Maximize, UnMaximize, Sticky, UnSticky, Trans New, Trans Delete, Move Start, Move End, Resize Start, Resize End

KDE sounds must be in WAV format. If you've installed StarOffice 5.0, a full directory of various sounds is located under the Office50/gallery/Sounds directory. Navigate to the Sounds directory through your home directory, then drag the file Applause.wav into the Sound dialog box, click the Startup event, and then click Apply. The next time you start KDE, you'll hear applause!

FIGURE 8.12

The Sound dialog box is used to assign sounds to KDE system events.

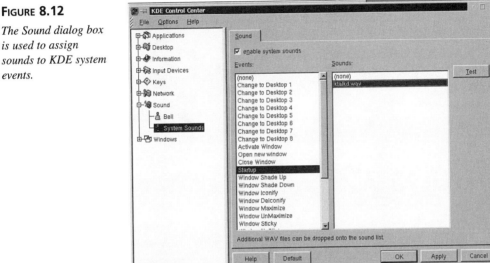

Changing Keyboard and Mouse Settings

Click Keyboard from the Input Devices drop-down menu in the KDE Control Center to toggle keyboard character repeat (repeated printing of a character when a key is held down), and whether each key-press generates a key-click sound. Click the Apply button, as shown in Figure 8.13, when you finish with your selection.

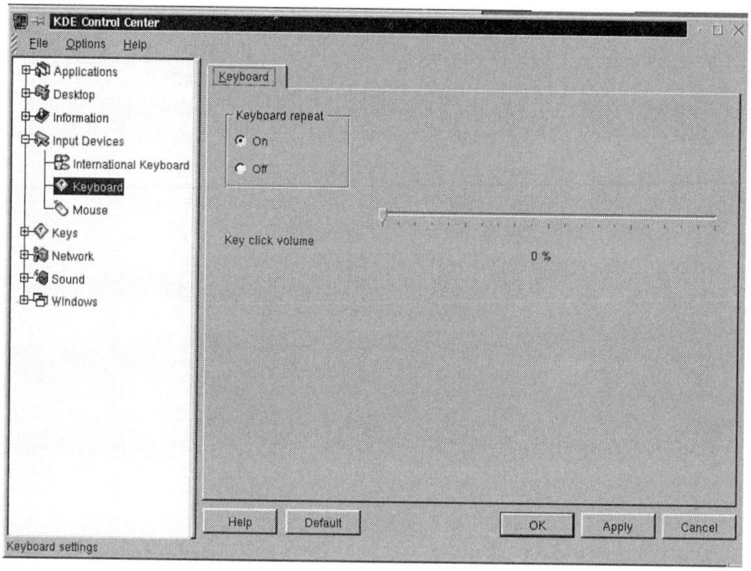

FIGURE 8.13

Use the Keyboard dialog box to toggle Keyboard repeat and key-click sounds.

Click Mouse to change how fast your mouse cursor moves across the screen and the sequence of mouse buttons for right- or left-handed users. You can also click the Application Starter button on the desktop panel, and select Settings, then Input Devices, and then Keyboard or Mouse to get to these settings.

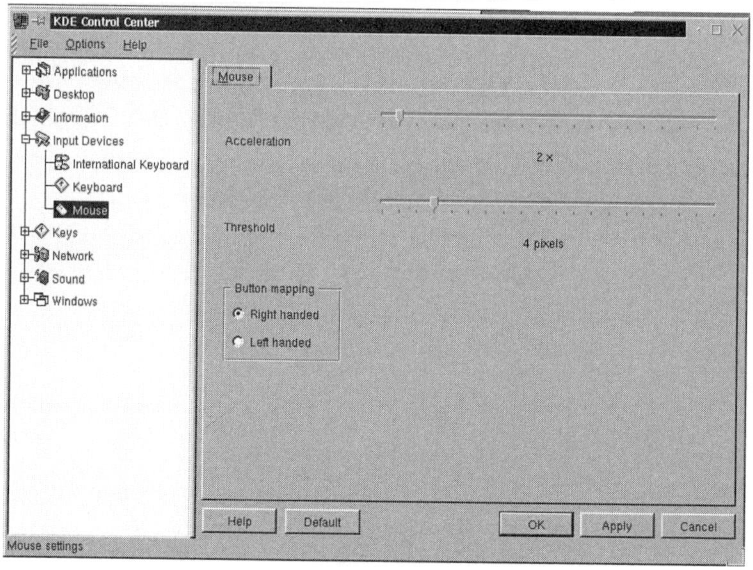

FIGURE 8.14

The Mouse dialog box can be used to make KDE sessions easier for left-handed mouse users!

8

Changing Window Buttons, Properties, and Title Bars

Click the Windows drop-down menu to access the Buttons, Mouse, Properties, and Titlebar dialog boxes. You can also click the Application Starter button on the desktop panel and then select Settings and Windows to get to these settings. Toggle each button under Left, Right, or Off in the Button dialog box shown in Figure 8.15 to add, remove, or place different window controls.

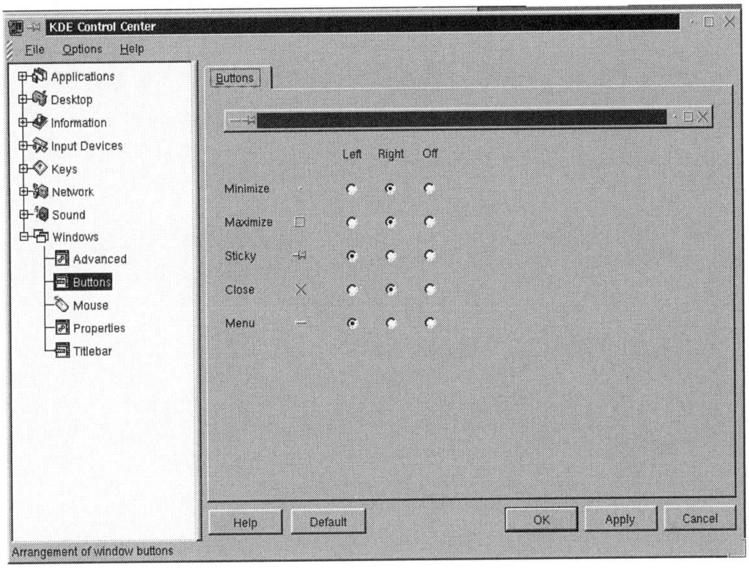

FIGURE 8.15

The Buttons dialog box is used to change the appearance of all windows during your KDE sessions.

In the Titlebar dialog box shown in Figure 8.16, click different buttons to change how KDE windows' title bars appear (controlling elements such as shading or whether a picture is used). Drag the Title Animation slider to change how fast a window's title moves back and forth for a KDE client (when the title is wider than the window's title bar). The Mouse action pop-up menu is used to set how windows react when you double-click in the title bar. (The default setting might use a "window shade" effect, but under X11, normally a window enlarges or shrinks)

For more complex window control, click Properties to use the Windows dialog box, shown in Figure 8.17, to tell KDE how to move, place, resize, or activate windows on your desktop. For example, the Focus Policy section tells KDE how to make a window active. The default action is that you must click on a window to activate it, or enable it to receive keyboard input; other policies make a window active when your mouse pointer is over the window.

FIGURE 8.16

The Titlebar dialog box sets how KDE windows act and look during your KDE sessions.

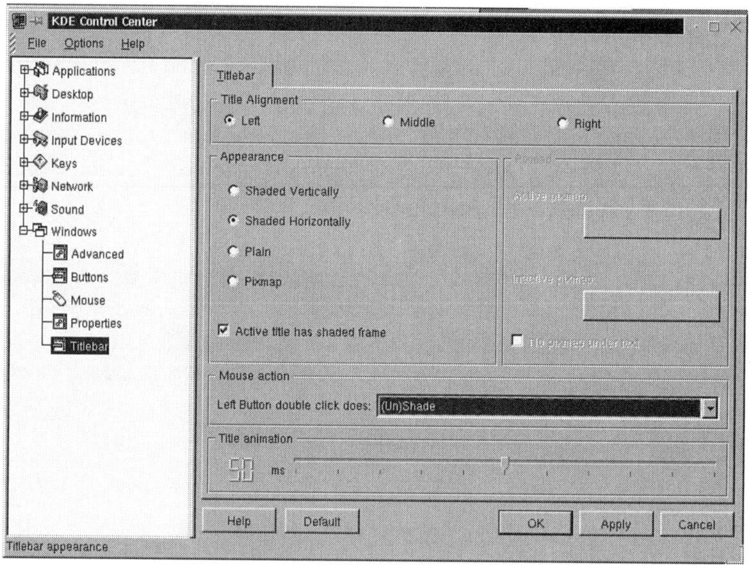

The Mouse dialog box under the Windows drop-down menu is used to set how you want KDE windows to react to your mouse clicks. You can find a dozen different mouse actions (such as left, middle, or right clicks on active windows) you can customize.

FIGURE 8.17

You can fine-tune how KDE handles windows on your desktop with the Windows dialog box.

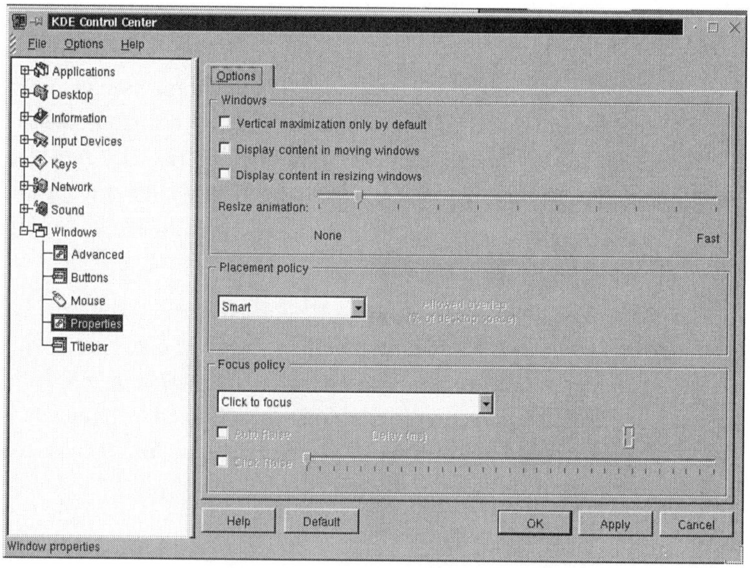

8

Controlling Cursor Movement Through Desktops

The Borders dialog box, which you can also access through the Settings and Desktop menu items from the Application Starter menu of your panel, is indispensable when controlling cursor movement between virtual desktops. By default, you have to click a virtual desktop button on your desktop's panel to move between desktops. But if you click the Enable active desktop borders item, and then click the Apply button, you move to a different desktop by moving your mouse cursor to the edge of the current desktop.

> Don't want to click the panel's desktop buttons or drag your mouse to move between desktops? Use the keyboard instead! Press Ctrl+Tab to walk through the desktops. Press Alt+Tab to walk through (activate) windows in the current desktop.

In the Borders dialog box, shown in Figure 8.18, drag the different sliders to set the time delay for desktop switching and the width of the sensitive edge of each desktop.

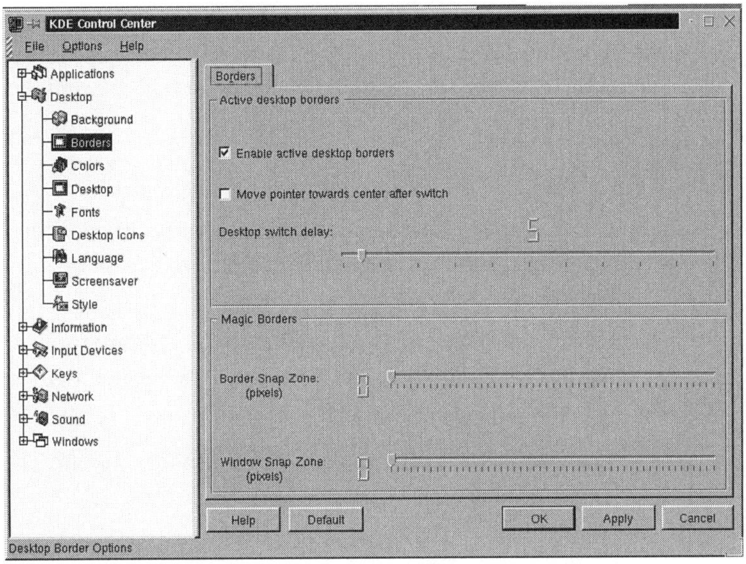

FIGURE 8.18

The Borders dialog box is used to tell KDE whether to use the mouse to move between desktops, how fast to make the switch, and when to make the change.

Summary

This hour introduced you to the basics of configuring the K Desktop Environment. There are many features and different programs specifically tailored to work with KDE, and more appear every day.

Q&A

Q **Where is KDE installed?**

A The major portion of KDE is installed under the `/opt/kde` directory in your OpenLinux file system. The various KDE clients are found under the `/opt/kde/bin` directory. Each user also has a `.kde` directory installed in the home directory, which is used to store personal settings and configurations.

Q **How can I find out more about KDE?**

A Click the KDE Help item on your panel's Application Starter menu. KDE's documentation is written in HTML and is displayed by the `kdehelp` client. The documentation files are found under the `/opt/kde/share/doc/HTML` directory in German, English, Spanish, Finnish, Italian, and Norwegian. The language used for all help files is determined by a symbolic file named `default`, which points to a designated language directory. Other languages can be used by changing the Locale setting in the Language item under the Desktop settings in the KDE Control Center.

Q **Where can I find more KDE applications?**

A Browse to `http://www.kde.org` for a list of the latest programs and application suites for KDE. A full office suite of productivity programs called K Office (which includes a word processor and spreadsheet) is currently under development.

Exercises

1. Create a new application link for a program, such as WordPerfect, Applixware, or StarOffice, and then install the icon into your desktop's panel. (Hint: read "The KFM Handbook" Usage section for details).

2. Download, create, scan, and edit a favorite picture for use as a background for one of your KDE desktops, and then install the picture as your wallpaper.

3. Add different sounds to KDE's system events.

4. Change the orientation of the panel and taskbar to offer the maximum screen real estate for your display.

PART III

Connecting to the Outside World

Hour

9 Using Communications Programs

10 Connecting to the Internet

11 Configuring Internet Email

12 Configuring Internet News

13 Internet Downloading and Browsing

HOUR 9

Using Communications Programs

In this hour, you'll learn about communicating with the outside world using programs installed from this book's CD-ROM. You'll learn how to set up your serial port or modem, configure and use two communication programs, and send and receive faxes with Linux.

Although your CD-ROM contains all the software you need to run Linux communications programs, you do need a serial communications port and modem to dial out with your Linux system. I assume you're familiar with modems, communication terms such as baud rate, parity, or stop bits, and how to connect your modem to your computer.

Setting Up and Testing Your Modem

Your first task is to find your spare serial port. You should be able to find the port on the back of your computer, and it most likely has 9 or 25 pins. If you're using a laptop, you might have a 9-pin male serial port, an RJ-11 telephone jack for an internal modem, or a PCMCIA modem card with an RJ-11 telephone jack.

You can find your serial port in Linux by looking in the device or /dev directory. Many devices are defined there, such as hard drives, floppies, and printers, but you should look for devices of type ttyS, for example:

```
# ls /dev/ttyS*
/dev/ttyS0   /dev/ttyS1   /dev/ttyS2   /dev/ttyS3
```

These devices correspond to the traditionally defined DOS serial ports (with addresses that might be similar or different for your computer), as shown in Table 9.1.

TABLE 9.1 DOS AND LINUX SERIAL PORTS AND ADDRESSES

DOS Port	Linux Device	Address
COM1	/dev/ttyS0	0x2F8 IRQ 4
COM2	/dev/ttyS1	0x2F8 IRQ 3
COM3	/dev/ttyS2	0x3E8 IRQ 4
COM4	/dev/ttyS3	0x2E8 IRQ 3

If you have a laptop with a PCMCIA modem card, you can't use your modem (or any other PCMCIA devices) until you enable those services and tell Linux to look for PCMCIA devices when it starts. To enable your PC card modem, make sure you're logged in as the root operator, and then edit the file named pcmcia in the /etc/sysconfig directory to look like this:

```
PCMCIA=yes
PCIC=i82365
PCIC_OPTS=
CORE_OPTS=
```

This tells Linux to install PCMCIA services. Save the file, and then reboot Linux. Your PC card modem (and other PC cards, if installed) should be recognized during the reboot.

If you have trouble with PCMCIA devices, read David Hinds' PCMCIA-HOWTO, which you can find under the /usr/doc/pcmcia directory. If you want the latest information about PCMCIA support for Linux, browse to

http://hyper.stanford.edu/HyperNews/get/pcmcia/home.html

To download the latest drivers (kernel modules) for OpenLinux, go to

ftp://csb.stanford.edu/pub/pcmcia

If you have trouble with setting up your serial ports, read Greg Hankins' Serial-HOWTO, also under the /usr/doc/HOWTO directory. There is a complete discussion on setting up your serial ports and troubleshooting installation. To read the document, which is a compressed text file, use the zless pager, like so:

zless /usr/doc/HOWTO/Serial-HOWTO.gz

You can check to make sure that your serial ports are enabled by checking portions of the Linux startup message with the dmesg command. Pipe the output of the dmesg command through the less pager to display the boot messages and look for the Serial driver message like this (press the Q key when you're finished to quit):

```
# dmesg ¦ less
...
Serial driver version 4.13 with no serial options enabled
tty00 at 0x03f8 (irq = 4) is a 16550A
tty03 at 0x02e8 (irq = 3) is a 16550A
...
```

A portion of the dmesg file is reproduced here, so you can see what to look for. The output here indicates that the system has serial ports of the MS-DOS equivalent of COM1 and COM4 at the IRQs enclosed in parentheses. If you do not see a serial driver or serial port listing, you must make sure that serial-line support is enabled for your Linux kernel. By default, OpenLinux comes with serial support, so this is probably not a problem.

Test your modem interactively with the minicom program discussed in the section "Dialing Out with Communications Programs."

Creating /dev/modem with the lisa Command

Use the lisa command to set up your modem. The lisa command creates a symbolic link, /dev/modem, after you select your modem type and modem serial port. Make sure you're running as the root operator, or use the su - command, and then start lisa with its --modem option, like this:

```
# su -c "lisa --modem"
```

After you press Enter, you see the lisa dialog box, as shown in Figure 9.1.

FIGURE 9.1

*The lisa administra-
tion program config-
ures the selected
modem.*

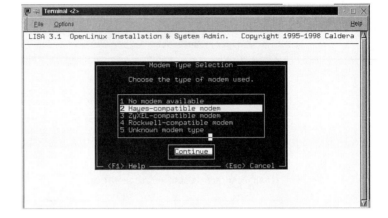

Scroll through the list of options to highlight the type of modem used with your computer (nearly all modems today are Hayes-compatible), and press Enter. The lisa command asks you to select the serial port used by the modem, as shown in Figure 9.2.

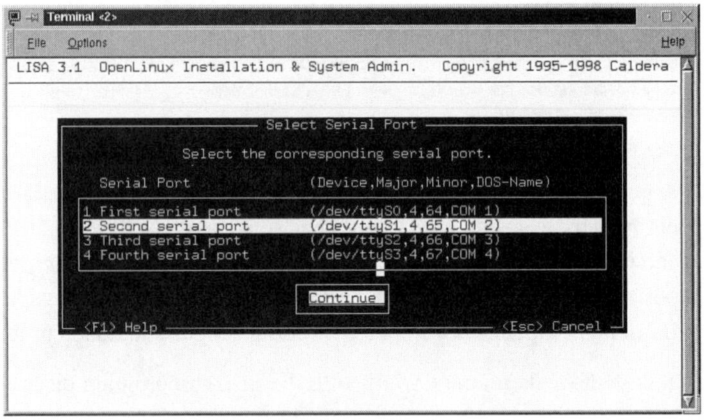

FIGURE 9.2

*Scroll through the list
of serial ports, and
press Enter to select
your modem's serial
port.*

Scroll through the list of serial ports to highlight the serial port for your modem. After
you press Enter, lisa asks you to select the highest speed used by your modem. If you
have a 33.6 modem, select 57600 bps. If you have a 56K modem, select 115200 bps (as
shown in Figure 9.3).

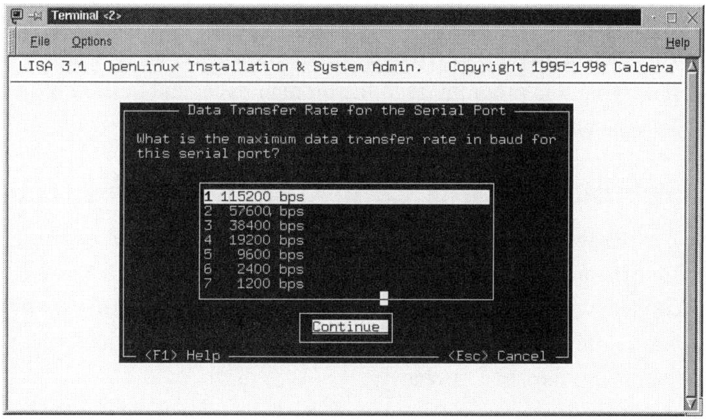

FIGURE 9.3

Scroll through the list of serial port speeds and press Enter to select the highest speed for your modem's serial port.

After you press Enter, you are asked to enter your fax number. Enter your fax number and press Enter, or just press Enter to finish configuring your modem. The lisa command quits and makes a symbolic link (discussed in Hour 5, "Manipulation and Searching Commands") from the selected device to a file called /dev/modem.

You can verify this operation by listing the file /dev/modem with the ls command, like so:

```
# ls -l /dev/modem
lrwxrwxrwx   1 root      root          5 Dec 29 15:43 /dev/modem -> ttyS0
```

> You can do the same thing as lisa from the command line using the ln command to create the symbolic link yourself. For example, if you have your modem connected to COM2, make sure you're running as root, and enter the following:
>
> ```
> # ln -s /dev/ttyS1 /dev/modem
> ```
>
> This creates a symbolic link, /dev/modem, which points to the serial port connected to your modem.

Dialing Out with Communications Programs

This section covers two communications programs that come with your OpenLinux distribution: minicom and seyon. The minicom program can be used either with or without running X11. The seyon program must be used while you're running the X Window System.

There is also an old communications program, called cu, under the /usr/bin directory. This program is not as friendly as minicom or seyon, but if you're interested in setting up and trying this program, read the cu man page, and definitely read the uucp software documentation under the /usr/doc/uucp directory.

Setting Up and Calling Out with minicom

The minicom program, created by Miquel van Smoorenburg and located under the /usr/bin directory, is a friendly communication program you can use to dial out and connect with other computers or BBSs. You can use minicom without running X11. If you're running X11, you can try to use the xminicom shell script, which is also located under the /usr/bin directory.

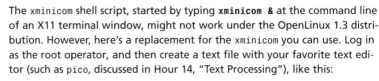

The xminicom shell script, started by typing **xminicom &** at the command line of an X11 terminal window, might not work under the OpenLinux 1.3 distribution. However, here's a replacement for the xminicom you can use. Log in as the root operator, and then create a text file with your favorite text editor (such as pico, discussed in Hour 14, "Text Processing"), like this:

 # pico -w xminicom

The -w option disables line-wrapping. Type in the following line:

```
xterm -bg black -fg green -cr red -n minicom -geometry 80x25
➥-e minicom
```

This command line starts an xterm terminal with a black background, green text, red cursor, the name minicom, use of 80 characters by 25 lines, and running the minicom program inside the window. If you're using pico, press Ctrl+X to save the file. Next, use the chmod command to make the text file an executable program, like this:

 # chmod +x xminicom

Finally, copy the new xminicom command to the /usr/bin directory with the same or a different name.

The first time you use minicom, make sure you're running as the root operator so you can set up and save minicom's default file, minirc.dfl, which is created and saved in the /etc directory. Assuming you're using X11, you can start minicom with the following:

 # xminicom &

This command runs the xminicom script and starts minicom in an X11 terminal window. To get help on how to use minicom, press Ctrl+A, and then press the Z key. Figure 9.4 shows the minicom help screen.

FIGURE 9.4

The minicom *communications program features built-in help for the user.*

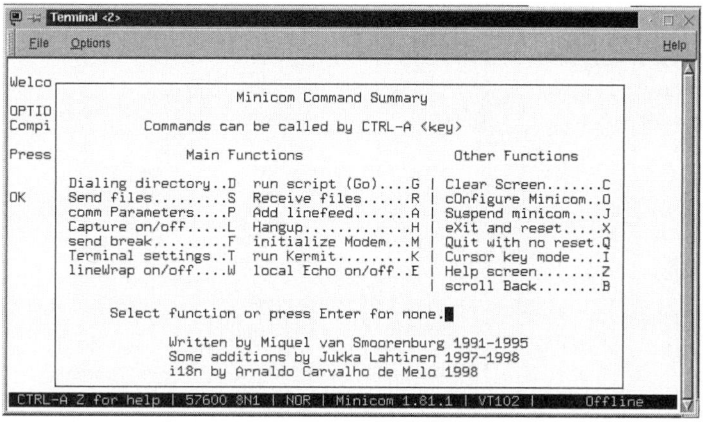

```
Terminal <2>
File  Options                                                          Help

Welco┌─────────────────────────────────────────────────────────────┐
     │                    Minicom Command Summary                    │
OPTIO│                                                               │
Compi│          Commands can be called by CTRL-A <key>               │
     │                                                               │
Press│              Main Functions                Other Functions     │
     │                                                               │
OK   │   Dialing directory..D   run script (Go)....G │ Clear Screen.......C │
     │   Send files.........S   Receive files......R │ cOnfigure Minicom..O │
     │   comm Parameters....P   Add linefeed.......A │ Suspend minicom....J │
     │   Capture on/off.....L   Hangup.............H │ eXit and reset.....X │
     │   send break.........F   initialize Modem...M │ Quit with no reset.Q │
     │   Terminal settings..T   run Kermit.........K │ Cursor key mode....I │
     │   lineWrap on/off....W   local Echo on/off..E │ Help screen........Z │
     │                                               │ scroll Back........B │
     │                                                               │
     │     Select function or press Enter for none.█                 │
     │                                                               │
     │        Written by Miquel van Smoorenburg 1991-1995            │
     │        Some additions by Jukka Lahtinen 1997-1998             │
     │        i18n by Arnaldo Carvalho de Melo 1998                  │
     └─────────────────────────────────────────────────────────────┘
CTRL-A Z for help | 57600 8N1 | NOR | Minicom 1.81.1 | VT102 |      Offline
```

To configure minicom, press Ctrl+A, and press the O key to get to the configure screen. Scroll down and select Serial Port Setup, and press the Enter key. You can then type in the Serial Device by pressing the A key. Type in the device your modem is connected to, such as /dev/ttyS1, or the symbolic link, /dev/modem, if you created the link. Figure 9.5 details the serial port setup screen.

FIGURE 9.5

Configure the serial port for minicom *by pressing a letter and typing a new value.*

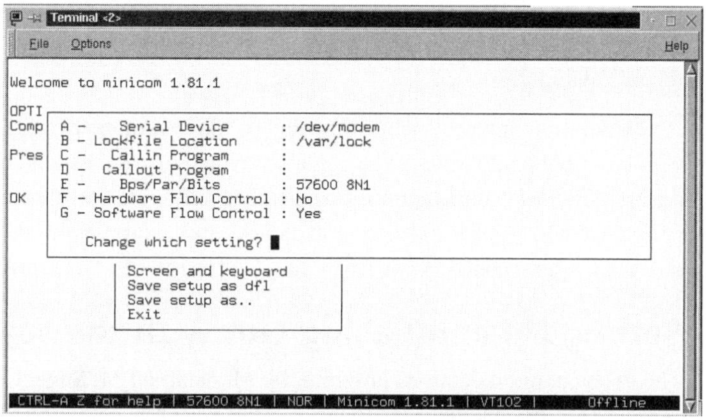

```
Terminal <2>
File  Options                                                          Help

Welcome to minicom 1.81.1

OPTI
Comp│ A -     Serial Device      : /dev/modem
    │ B - Lockfile Location      : /var/lock
Pres│ C -    Callin Program      :
    │ D -   Callout Program      :
    │ E -      Bps/Par/Bits      : 57600 8N1
OK  │ F - Hardware Flow Control  : No
    │ G - Software Flow Control  : Yes
    │
    │     Change which setting? █
    │
    │    ┌──────────────────────┐
    │    │ Screen and keyboard  │
    │    │ Save setup as dfl    │
    │    │ Save setup as..      │
    │    │ Exit                 │
    │    └──────────────────────┘

CTRL-A Z for help | 57600 8N1 | NOR | Minicom 1.81.1 | VT102 |      Offline
```

For example, to change your modem's speed, press the letter E. A new dialog box appears, as shown in Figure 9.6. To change the baud rate, press the key corresponding to the letter next to the desired baud rate. When you finish, press Enter to return to the serial setup dialog box.

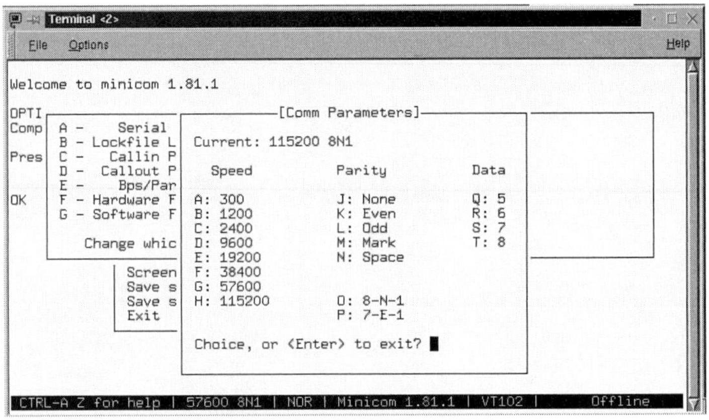

FIGURE 9.6

Set a new serial port speed for your modem by pressing a letter.

```
┌─────────────────────────────────────────────────────────────┐
│ 🖳 ⊣ Terminal <2>                                    ⊣ □ ✕   │
├─────────────────────────────────────────────────────────────┤
│  File   Options                                        Help  │
│                                                              │
│ Welcome to minicom 1.81.1                                    │
│ OPTI┌──────────────────[Comm Parameters]──────────────┐     │
│ Comp│ A -    Serial                                    │     │
│     │ B - Lockfile L  Current: 115200 8N1             │     │
│ Pres│ C -   Callin P                                  │     │
│     │ D -  Callout P    Speed        Parity      Data │     │
│     │ E -   Bps/Par                                   │     │
│ OK  │ F - Hardware F  A: 300      J: None      Q: 5   │     │
│     │ G - Software F  B: 1200     K: Even      R: 6   │     │
│     │                 C: 2400     L: Odd       S: 7   │     │
│     │   Change whic   D: 9600     M: Mark      T: 8   │     │
│     │                 E: 19200    N: Space            │     │
│     │         Screen  F: 38400                        │     │
│     │         Save s  G: 57600                        │     │
│     │         Save s  H: 115200   O: 8-N-1            │     │
│     │         Exit                P: 7-E-1            │     │
│     │                                                 │     │
│     │                 Choice, or <Enter> to exit? ▮   │     │
│     └─────────────────────────────────────────────────┘     │
│                                                              │
│ CTRL-A Z for help | 57600 8N1 | NOR | Minicom 1.81.1 | VT102 |   Offline │
└─────────────────────────────────────────────────────────────┘
```

Press the Enter key, select Save setup as dfl, and press the Enter key again, followed by the Escape key. Your system defaults should be set. You can then try to call out with the following (substituting the correct phone number for *XXX-XXXX*):

ATDTXXX-XXXX

This command uses the modem's AT command, DT, to dial out using a dial tone (for a full list of your modem's commands, consult your modem's manual). After you press Enter, your modem dials the phone number. To exit the program, press Ctrl+A, press X, and then press Enter.

If you have a number of phone numbers of other computers to call, you can enter them in minicom's phone directory. You can also set up minicom to send or retrieve files using different file transfer programs. For details about these and other features, read the minicom manual page. You can also find documentation under the /usr/doc/minicom directory, which contains extensive details of using other features of this program.

Setting Up and Calling Out with the seyon X11 Client

The seyon communications program, by Muhammad M. Saggaf, runs only under the X Window System and has an extensive list of features. Although seyon is not as simple or initially friendly as minicom, it does have the following:

- Built-in help
- A built-in telecommunications scripting language to automate calling up and logging in to other computer systems
- A built-in text editor for writing telecommunications scripts

- A command-line shell dialog box for running commands, which displays output in the main communication window
- Buttons to set up modem speed, parity, and stop bits

If you created a symbolic link to /dev/modem, the seyon program automatically recognizes and works with your modem. All you have to do to call out and connect with another computer is to type your AT command string with the phone number to dial out and connect.

If you need to tell the seyon client the specific device for your modem, click on the Set button in the seyon Command Center window (which appears automatically when you start the client) to bring up the Settings window. Click on the Port button in the Settings window, and type in the name of the device, /dev/cua1 for example, in the Values? window. Figure 9.7 shows seyon and its settings windows.

FIGURE 9.7

The X11 client, seyon, has point-and-click convenience for modem setup.

Main seyon window   Main seyon controls

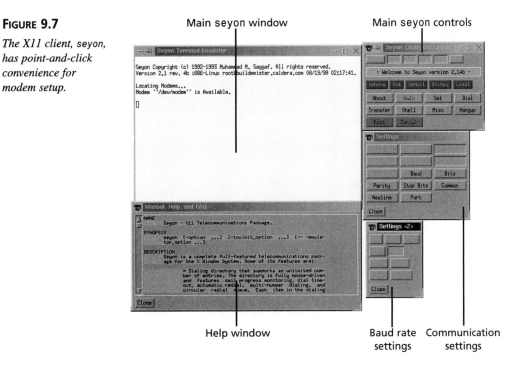

Help window   Baud rate   Communication
                     settings   settings

Click on the OK button, and click on the Close button of the Settings window. If you want to start the seyon program with a default modem speed, number of bits, or parity, edit the file $HOME/.seyon/. This directory is installed automatically when you install the seyon program. You can make changes to the following lines in the startup file:

```
...
# set baud
set baud 19200

# can be 5, 6, 7, or 8
# set bits 8
set bits 8

# can be 0 (= no parity), 1 (= odd parity), or 2 (= even parity)
# set parity 0
set parity 0

# can be 1 or 2
# set stopBits 1
set stopBits 1
...
```

If you need help when using the seyon program, you can click on the Help button in the seyon Command Center window. A window pops up with the seyon manual page, and you can scroll through the text for help (the help screen is shown in Figure 9.7).

Setting Up Your Linux System for Dialing In

You can also set up your OpenLinux system so that your computer's modem answers the phone and enables you to log in. You can then run a bulletin board system (BBS), word processors, and spreadsheet programs. You can even dial out on another line if you have at least two modems connected to your computer and two phone lines in your home.

Most of the details and custom configurations are in the Serial-HOWTO under the /usr/doc/HOWTO and /usr/doc/getty_ps directories, but the three basic steps outlined here should work for nearly any modem.

> Setting up your OpenLinux system to accept incoming calls involves editing the /etc/inittab file and can potentially hang your system if you make an error. Always have a backup boot disk handy, and make a copy of the /etc/inittab file before you make changes.

First, log in as the root operator, and run minicom. Use the AT command &V to display your modem's profile, or default setup, for example:

```
AT&V
ACTIVE PROFILE:
B1 E1 L1 M1 N1 Q0 T V1 W0 X4 Y0 &C1 &D2 &G0 &J0 &K3 &Q5 &R1 &S0
➡&T5 &X0 &Y0 ~Z0
```

```
S00:000 S01:000 S02:043 S03:013 S04:010 S05:008 S06:004 S07:045
➥S08:002 S09:006
S10:014 S11:095 S12:050 S18:000 S25:005 S26:001 S36:007 S37:000
➥S38:020 S44:020
S46:138 S48:007 S51:012 S52:012 S53:010 S54:010 S95:000
```

You might see other values for your modem's internal profile and registers, but you need to make sure that your modem is at least set to the following:

```
E1 Q0 V1 S0=1 &C1 &S0
```

You can set your modem to these values by using the AT command, for example:

```
ATE1Q0V1S0=1&C1&S0&W
OK
```

Note that at the end of the AT command string, using the &W AT command saves the modem configuration as a default. You can also see the OK prompt echoed back to you from your modem after entering the string, and you can again issue the AT&V command to verify the settings.

The second step is to create a directory named default under the /etc directory, like this:

```
# mkdir /etc/default
```

Then, use the cp command to copy the file uugetty.autoanswer from the /usr/doc/getty_ps directory, renaming the file to match your modem's serial port device, like so:

```
# cp /usr/doc/getty_ps-2.0.7h/Examples/uugetty.autoanswer
➥/etc/default/uugetty.ttyS0
```

This command line shows that the desired serial port is /dev/ttyS0, which corresponds to the DOS COM1 port. Now edit the copied file with your favorite text editor, and look for the following line:

```
ALTLOCK=cua2
```

Change the default values of cua2 to match the extension and serial port of your modem, like this:

```
ALTLOCK=ttyS0
```

Save the file and exit your editor.

The final step involves a one-line edit of /etc/inittab, the system initialization table. If you look in this file, you see these lines:

```
# less /etc/inittab
...
# Run gettys in standard runlevels
```

```
1:12345:respawn:/sbin/getty tty1 VC linux
2:2345:respawn:/sbin/getty tty2 VC linux
3:2345:respawn:/sbin/getty tty3 VC linux
4:2345:respawn:/sbin/getty tty4 VC linux
5:2345:respawn:/sbin/getty tty5 VC linux
6:2345:respawn:/sbin/getty tty6 VC linux
...
```

Each of the lines represents a different Linux `runlevel` documented at the beginning of the `/etc/inittab` file. This discussion doesn't cover `runlevels` or the details of how OpenLinux boots, but all you have to do to enable dial-in logins for your Linux system is to change the following line:

```
3:2345:respawn:/sbin/getty tty3 VC linux
```

Change it as follows:

```
3:2345:respawn:/sbin/uugetty ttyS0 38400 vt100
```

Save the file, and use the shutdown command to restart your system. This `inittab` entry tells OpenLinux to start the `getty` command after you boot and have `getty` monitor your `/dev/ttyS0` serial port for incoming calls. The value `38400` is not a modem baud rate but corresponds to an autobaud entry (which works at `38400` or lower speeds) in the `/etc/gettydefs` file. If you call in to your OpenLinux system, the modem synchronizes with your calling modem's speed and then presents a login prompt.

> When you log in to OpenLinux, the contents of the `/etc/issue` file are printed on your display right before the login prompt. This file is created by the startup script `rc.local` in the `/etc/rc.d` directory every time you start OpenLinux as part of the booting process. As the root operator, you can customize the `rc.local` script to change the contents of the `/etc/issue` file if you want a different login banner.

> If you set up your system to accept incoming calls and want to use `minicom`, run `minicom` as the root operator. Then configure the serial device name under serial port setup in the configuration menu to match the name of your modem's actual device, such as `/dev/ttyS1`, and make sure the name is not a symbolic link, such as `/dev/modem`.

Sending and Receiving Faxes

If your modem supports fax protocols, chances are that you can send and receive faxes using OpenLinux. Sending and receiving faxes under OpenLinux involves graphics translation of both received files and files you want to send. Your OpenLinux distribution on the CD-ROM contains the `efax` family of fax software and documentation. Have your modem's documentation on hand and read the `efax` manual pages and documentation under the `/usr/doc/efax` directory carefully before you start.

Faxing with the `efax` System

The `efax` system, by Ed Casas, is a simple and easy-to-use fax system that, according to its documentation, is best suited to a single-user, standalone Linux system. This software consists of a series of programs and scripts and supports Class 1 and 2 fax modems.

The system is made up of the following programs:

- `/usr/bin/efax`—The faxing program
- `/usr/bin/efix`—A graphics conversion program used to prepare text files for faxing or to convert files to different graphics formats
- `/usr/bin/fax`—A shell script used to create, send, receive, display, or print fax files

If you want to preview or fax PostScript graphics files, you also need to have the `gs` PostScript interpreter and companion viewer, `gv`, installed on your system. For viewing received faxes, you can use the X11 client `xv` (discussed in Hour 16, "Graphics Tools").

> You need to edit the `/usr/bin/fax` script to configure faxing. But before you make changes to the script, do yourself a favor and make a copy first. If you make errors or delete the file, you need a copy to reinstall the `efax` software.

Before you start sending or receiving faxes, take a look at the `/usr/bin/fax` shell script. This program is the front-end to fax service with `efax`, but you need to check several sections in the file to make sure the script is configured properly. For example, the first section lists the names of the `efax` programs:

```
FAX=/usr/bin/fax
EFAX=/usr/bin/efax
EFIX=/usr/bin/efix
```

These should not pose a problem because the programs are installed in the correct place when you installed the software. The next section lists your modem:

```
DEV=modem
```

You can use the word modem if you created a symbolic link. However, if you have Linux set up to answer incoming calls for logins, use the actual name of the device (such ttyS0, using our previous example). The next section to check is the type of faxing your modem supports:

```
# CLASS=1
CLASS=2
# CLASS=2.0
```

Comment or uncomment the proper support by using the pound sign (#), but make sure only one CLASS is listed. For example, if your modem supports the minimal Class 1 fax service, change these entries to look like the following:

```
CLASS=1
# CLASS=2
# CLASS=2.0
```

After this, you can customize your faxes with your phone number:

```
# Use only digits, spaces, and the "+" character.
FROM="0 000 000 0000"
# Your name as it should appear on the page header.
NAME="Your Name Here"
```

Enter your phone number in the FROM line, such as "1 202 555 1212", and change the NAME entry to your name, such as "Eric Goldfarb". Finally, set the default page size for faxing, for example:

```
 PAGE=letter
# PAGE=legal
# PAGE=a4
```

Comment or uncomment the different page sizes, but use only one. After you finish making your changes, try the fax command to test your configuration and modem, using the test command-line option, for example:

```
# fax test
- - - - - - - - - - - - - - - - - - - - - - - - - - - - - - - - - - - -

Please wait, this will take a minute...

- - - - - - - - - - - - - - - - - - - - - - - - - - - - - - - - - - - -
--- /usr/bin/fax ---
```

```
FAX=/usr/bin/fax
EFAX=/usr/bin/efax
EFIX=/usr/bin/efix
DEV=cua1
CLASS=2
...
```

You get a three-page listing of information about your configuration and your modem's response to the fax script's queries. If you want to see this information at your leisure, redirect the output of the text to a file, for example:

 # fax test > faxtest.txt

You can then read about any error messages or problems with missing software. Assuming everything is okay, you can then try faxing a document using the `fax` command:

 # fax send -l 8207442 faxtest.txt

The `-l` option tells the `fax` program to send a low-resolution (98 lines per inch) fax, using the fax testing information you created. To send a high-resolution (196 lines per inch) fax, no option is needed, for example:

```
# fax send 8207442 faxtest.txt
faxtest.txt.nnn is up-to-date
/usr/bin/efax: Tue Dec 29 21:38:02 1998 efax v 0.8a Copyright 1996
➥Ed Casas
efax: 38:02 opened /dev/modem
efax: 38:03 dialing T8207442
efax: 38:26 connected
efax: 38:32 session 196lpi  9600bps 8.5"/215mm 11"/A4 1D  -   - 0ms
efax: 38:32 header:[98/12/29 21:38   Eric Goldfarb (1 317 123 1234)
➥--> 8207442  p. 1/3]
efax: 39:06 sent 20+2156 lines, 38961+0 bytes, 34 s  9167 bps
efax: 39:09 sent -> faxtest.txt.001
efax: 39:10 header:[98/12/29 21:38   Eric Goldfarb (1 317 123 1234)
➥--> 8207442  p. 2/3]
efax: 39:37 sent 20+2156 lines, 32200+0 bytes, 27 s  9540 bps
efax: 39:40 sent -> faxtest.txt.002
efax: 39:41 header:[98/12/29 21:38   Eric Goldfarb (1 317 123 1234)
➥--> 8207442  p. 3/3]
efax: 39:50 sent 20+2156 lines, 9635+0 bytes, 9 s   8564 bps
efax: 39:55 sent -> faxtest.txt.003
efax: 39:56 done, returning 0
```

As you can see, the fax script automatically recognizes that your file is a text file because of the extension. You can also send PostScript graphics files by fax. If you want to test sending such a graphic, try this command line:

 # fax send 8207442 /usr/share/ghostscript/4.03/examples/tiger.ps

The fax shell script converts the PostScript graphic to fax format and sends it to the remote fax (albeit in black and white, not color).

To set your computer to automatically wait for incoming faxes, you can use the fax script's wait command-line option, for example:

```
# fax wait
running /usr/bin/fax answer
/usr/bin/efax: Tue Dec 29 22:38:02 1998 efax v 0.8a Copyright
➥1996 Ed Casas
```

You can also use the background operator to put the shell script in the background. You can check on the status of your Linux fax machine with the status command-line option, for example:

```
# fax status
USER    PID %CPU %MEM  SIZE  RSS TTY STAT START TIME COMMAND
root    785 1.8  0.6  1032  404 p2 S <  21:45 0:00 /usr/bin/efax -d/dev/

from: /var/spool/fax/modem.785

efax: 45:23 opened /dev/modem
efax: 45:25 waiting for activity
```

This shows that the efax command is waiting on the /dev/modem serial port for incoming faxes. To check whether you've received any faxes, you can use the fax command's queue command-line option, for example:

```
# fax queue

Fax files in /var/spool/fax :

-rw-r--r--  1 root     root        18449 Dec 29 21:51 1229215055.001
-rw-r--r--  1 root     root        15001 Dec 29 21:54 1229215350.001
-rw-r--r--  1 root     root        16229 Dec 29 21:54 1229215350.002
```

This output shows that two faxes have been received. The first is a one-page fax received at 9:51 p.m. The other is a two-page fax received three minutes later. These faxes are waiting in the /var/spool/fax directory (created automatically when you first run the fax command with the wait command-line option). Each page of a fax is saved as a separate file, and pages of the same fax have the same filename with the date and time, followed by the page number as an extension.

To view a fax, you can use the fax command's view option. For example, to view the one-page fax, as shown in Figure 9.8, use the fax command with the view option, followed by the fax's filename, like this:

```
# fax view 1229215350.001
/var/spool/fax/1229215055.001
1229215055.001 ...
```

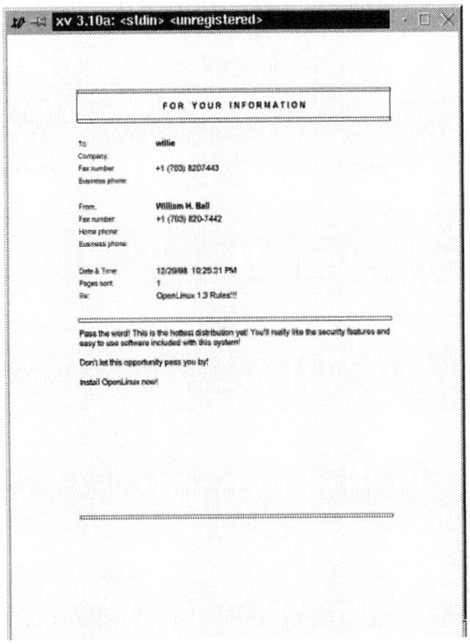

FIGURE 9.8

The fax *command automatically runs the X11* xv *graphic program to view or print your incoming faxes.*

9

To view all the pages of a fax, use a wildcard, such as an asterisk (*), with the first part of a multiple page fax name. To use the previous two-page fax as an example, type a command line like this:

```
# fax view 1229215350.*
```

The fax program cycles through the files and displays each page with the viewer you specified in the fax shell script. You can use the X11 xv client to print your faxes, or you can try the fax command's print command-line option to print your faxes, for example:

```
# fax print 1229215350.001
/var/spool/fax/1229215055.001
1229215055.001 ...
```

This prints the first page of the incoming fax. You can print all the pages of a multiple page fax with the following:

```
# fax print 1229215350.*
```

If you want to delete a fax, use the rm command, for example:

```
# rm /var/spool/fax/1229215350.*
```

If you want, you can try to use the fax command's rm command-line option. However, this is potentially dangerous and might delete files in the current directory, especially if you use a plain asterisk (*) as a filename. You should specify the fax filenames explicitly when using this command-line option.

The efax family of commands is a simple and versatile way to send and receive faxes with Linux. The fax command has more commands than are documented in the manual page, including support for voice modems and creating cover pages. Read the fax command itself for more details.

Sending Fax Documents with the ksendfax Client

If you use the K Desktop Environment, or KDE, you can use ksendfax to quickly select and send a fax. Although not included with the KDE distribution on your OpenLinux CD-ROM, you can download a copy from http://www.kde.org. Follow the links to the Applications section and download the file ksendfax-0.3.1.tar.gz. Building and installing ksendfax is easy. First log in as the root operator and decompress the file with the tar command, like this:

```
# tar xvzf ksendfax-0.3.1.tar.gz
```

Change the directory into the ksendfax directory, and then build and install the package by using the configure and make commands, like this:

```
# configure; make install
```

The ksendfax client is installed. If you're logged in as the root operator, start ksendfax by clicking the Application Starter button on your desktop's panel, selecting the Graphics menu, and then clicking the KsendFax menu item. However, if you're not logged in as the root operator, start the program from the command line of a kvt terminal window, like this:

```
# su -c ksendfax
```

The main dialog box appears. Type in a filename to send in the File Name section, or click the Browse button to choose a file. Next, type in the remote fax machine's number in the Fax no. field, as shown in Figure 9.9.

To configure ksendfax with your favorite fax program, such as efax, click the Preferences menu item under the Options menu. Next, type in the command string for ksendfax to use to send a fax (as shown in Figure 9.10). For example, to use the fax script with ksendfax, enter the following:

```
/usr/bin/fax send '@@Phone' '@@FName'
```

FIGURE 9.9

Using the ksendfax *client is an easy way to send a fax.*

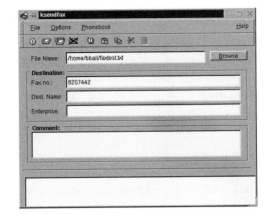

When you finish, click the OK button. To send the fax document, press Ctrl+S, click the Send Fax button, or click the Send Fax menu item under the File menu. A small dialog box appears, showing the communications progress of your faxing operation.

To find out how to configure ksendfax for other fax programs for OpenLinux, click the Help menu item under the ksendfax Help menu. There are tips and tricks on getting ksendfax to work with at least three different fax software packages.

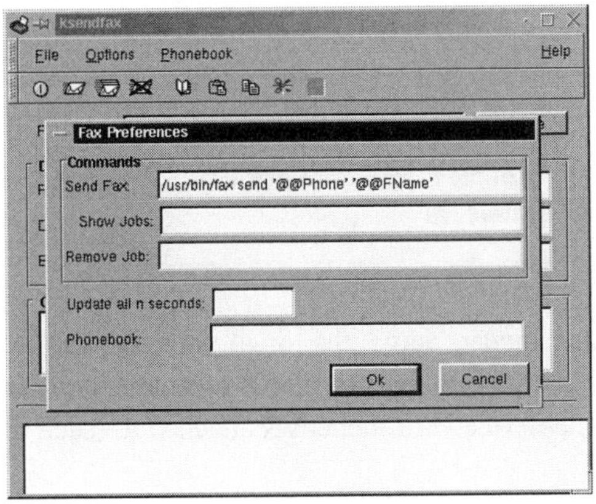

FIGURE 9.10

To use ksendfax *with your fax program, you must enter a command string in the Preferences dialog box.*

Sending Fax Documents with `mgetty+sendfax`

`mgetty+sendfax` is a package of software that uses the `mgetty` command, which you install in `/etc/inittab` much like the `uugetty` example shown previously, and the `sendfax` program, which is used to send faxes. The installation and configuration of this software is a little more complicated than setting up `efax`. This section shows you how to set up, configure, and use this software to send and receive fax documents with your modem.

This package of software includes many files (too many to list here). The examples in this section concentrate on the important ones and show you how to configure the `sendfax` software and quickly send a fax. Your first step is to make sure you're logged in as the root operator. You need to change the directory to the `mgetty+sendfax` directory under the `/etc` directory. You see a number of files there, for example:

```
# ls -A
dialin.config   fax.deny     faxrunq.config   mgetty.config   voice.conf
fax.allow       faxheader    login.config     sendfax.config
```

Your first job is to create the `fax.allow` and `fax.deny` files if they do not exist. In the `fax.allow` file, enter the names of users you want to enable to have fax service. Enter at least two names: root and your username.

Next, edit the `faxheader` file, and enter your name and phone in the sample header line, for example:

```
    FAX  FROM:  John H. Doe 1 202 555 1212    TO: @T@    PAGE: @P@ OF @M@
```

> You should use the comment character, #, when you make changes to the `sendfax` configuration files, and retype your changes on a new line. This saves you trouble if you make mistakes and need to return the file back to its original state.

The sample header line appears across the top of your faxed pages on the receiving fax machine. Next, edit the `sendfax.config` file, then look for the fax-devices section, and change the name of the device your modem is attached to (such as `/dev/ttyS1` for COM2), for example:

```
# which devices to use for outgoing faxes
#fax-devices tty4c:tty4d
fax-devices ttyS1
```

This tells the `sendfax` programs that your fax modem is attached to `/dev/ttyS1`. Next, enter your fax number, which is sent to the remote fax machine, for example:

```
# which fax number to transmit to the receiving station
#fax-id 49 89 xxxxxxxx
fax-id 1 317 123-1234
```

This identifies your fax machine to the remote fax. You also need to enter the type of dialing you want to use when sending a fax, for example:

```
# which command is used to dial out? (Could be ATD, ATDP, ATX3D0W...)
#dial-prefix ATD
dial-prefix ATDT
```

This tells the `sendfax` software that you want to dial out using tone dialing. Save the file, and exit your text editor. At this point, you're almost ready to start sending faxes.

To send a one-page fax using the `sendfax` program, you must first convert a text file into the Group 3 fax format. You can do this by using the graphics conversion program `pbm-text`, found under the `/usr/bin` directory with the `pbm2g3` program, for example:

```
# cat myfile.txt ¦ pbmtext ¦ pbm2g3 > myfile.g3
```

This pipes the file `myfile.txt` through the `pbmtext` command, which outputs a portable bitmap graphics format into the `pbm2g3` command, which then converts the piped stream of characters into the fax graphic format. After you do this, you can send the file (assuming you're the root operator) with the following:

```
# /usr/sbin/sendfax -v -l ttyS1 -C cls2 -r 5551212 myfile.g3
Trying fax device '/dev/ttyS1'... OK.
Dialing 5551212... OK.
sending 'myfile.g3'...
```

This runs the `sendfax` program. The `-v` command-line option tells `sendfax` to give some feedback during the faxing operation. I specify the `ttyS1` serial port with the `-l` option and send the fax through a Class 2 fax modem with `-C cls2` command-line option. The phone number 555-1212 is specified with the `-r` option, and the file, `myfile.g3`, is the file you created with the preceding command-line pipe.

Unlike `efax`, the `sendfax` command only supports Class 2 fax modems. If you have a Class 1 modem, use the `fax` shell script.

You can also set up your Linux system to automatically receive incoming faxes with the mgetty program. Used much like the uugetty program, mgetty also requires at least one change to its configuration file in the /etc/mgetty+sendfax directory. The change you can make (as the root operator) is to edit the phone identification entry in the file mgetty.config, for example:

```
# set the local fax station id
#fax-id 49 89 xxxxxxxx
fax-id 1 317 123 1234
```

This sets the local fax machine phone number. After you do this, edit the /etc/inittab file as described earlier, and use mgetty to listen to the serial port, for example:

```
3:2345:respawn:/usr/sbin/mgetty -s 38400 ttyS1
```

As mentioned before, any edits of the /etc/inittab file are potentially hazardous. Always have a spare boot disk and make a backup of the file first.

After you make this change, save the file, and reboot the computer. Now, not only are you able to receive faxes, but you can also dial in from an outside line and run Linux programs. To see if any faxes have arrived, you have to explicitly look at the /var/spool/fax/incoming directory, for example:

```
# ls -A /var/spool/fax/incoming
fn4878f9aS1-_IBM-APTIVA-M61-_.01   fn4878f9aS1-_IBM-APTIVA-M61-_.02
```

This shows that there is a two-page fax awaiting reading. You can read the faxes by first converting them to the portable bitmap file format, for example:

```
# cat /var/spool/fax/incoming/*.01 ¦ g32pbm > faxpage1.pbm
```

After you convert these fax files to the portable bitmap format, you can then use the X11 xv client or the ImageMagick display X11 program to read or print your faxes.

As you can see, you have several choices of software when faxing documents with OpenLinux. The sendfax program has many other options. Read its man page and documentation under the /usr/doc/mgetty+sendfax directory to find out the details.

Summary

This hour showed you how to configure your OpenLinux system to work with your computer's modem. You also learned how to set OpenLinux to answer incoming calls and how to send and receive fax documents.

Q&A

Q **I'd like to learn more about modems and faxing. What resources are there?**

A First, read the documentation for the efax and mgetty+sendfax programs to learn more about using these programs with OpenLinux. If you'd like to read a good, non-specific operating system overview of using modems and modem software, read Peter Chen's What You Need to Know about Modems, at http://www.vix.com/flexfax/Modems-PeterChen.

Q **I'd like to turn off the high-pitched squeal my modem makes when it connects. How do I do this?**

A Read your modem's documentation for the specifics, but in general, the ATM0 command turns off your modem.

Q **I want to hear the modem dial out and connect, but I don't want it to be so loud!**

A Try using the ATM1 command to enable sound, and then try to use the ATLx command, where x represents a number from 0 (low) to 3 (high) speaker volume. This feature is not supported by all modems.

Q **My modem sometimes disconnects during my on-line sessions!**

A If you have call waiting, it is possible that an incoming call can disrupt your modem. Try adding *70 to the front of any dial string (such as ATDT*70) to disable call waiting.

Exercises

1. Try to call a local Bulletin Board Service (BBS) and connect with the seyon or minicom program.

2. Create a graphic, then save it in PostScript format, and try to send it as a fax. See Hour 16 for more information on creating graphics during your OpenLinux sessions.

Hour **10**

Connecting to the Internet

In this hour, you'll learn how to set up your Linux system to connect to the Internet using the serial line Point-to-Point Protocol known as PPP. Connecting to the Internet is one of the biggest hurdles many new OpenLinux users face after installing OpenLinux, configuring OpenLinux to work with their computer's sound card, and configuring the X Window System to work with their computer's graphics card. After following the directions in this lesson, you can connect to the Internet through your Internet Service Provider (ISP), and do email, Web browsing, and file transfers.

This hour shows you how to connect to your ISP manually in the simplest, most basic way possible. I also point you to sources of information for more details so that you can troubleshoot or fine-tune your connection. You'll then learn how to use two easy-to-use graphical interface programs, kppp and xisp, to set up, start, and stop your PPP connection.

I'm recommending you use a PPP connection for a number of reasons:

- Although it's complex, it is easy to set up.
- You can find documentation and details on the protocol in a number of HOWTO documents.
- You can read the `comp.protocols.ppp` newsgroup about PPP and the `comp.os.linux.networking` newsgroup for specific Linux information.
- It offers security on both ends of the connection.
- It is a common protocol supported by nearly all ISPs.
- OpenLinux comes with several programs you can use to set up your PPP connection.
- It is flexible enough to accommodate different types of connections.

This hour starts by listing some of the hardware and software prerequisites for OpenLinux and then asks for some necessary information you need from your ISP. Using that information, you'll first create a set of customized scripts you can use to manually start or stop your connection. I'll then show you how to set up a PPP connection using two graphical interface programs: the `kppp` client for the K Desktop Environment and the `xisp` graphical interface client for X11.

You'll also learn about some handy utilities you can use to diagnose your connection and some other programs you can use to monitor your sessions.

Hardware You Need

You probably already have all the hardware you need: a modem, a modem cable if your modem is external, and a phone line. However, you must have a modem you can use with OpenLinux. You *cannot* use any of the following modems with OpenLinux:

- 3Com/U.S. Robotics 56K V.90 Winmodem
- 3Com/U.S. Robotics 56K Winmodem PC Card
- 3Com/U.S. Robotics Sportster 33.6 Winmodem
- Aztech Systems 56K PCI modem
- Cardinal 56K Windows Fax modem
- Diamond SupraMax 56K ISA/PCI modems
- Hayes 56K Accura V.90 PCI Win modem
- Motorola FM56 ISA/PCI modems
- Mwave adapters (but might work as sound card)

- Viking Components 56K ISA Windows modem

- WinStorm 56K PCI Data/Fax Speaker phone modem

- Zoltrix Phantom/Spirit 56K modems

- Any other modem requiring Windows-only software

> If you plan to purchase a modem to use with OpenLinux, do not buy any modem considered a *winmodem*. These useless pieces of junk were recently introduced into the computer industry by manufacturers to save money and increase profits in hardware production. Winmodems use fewer chips than "real" modems and depend on operating system-specific software drivers (and your computer's CPU) in order to work. Unfortunately, many computer manufacturers (especially those that make and sell laptop computers) do not tell you that a provided or built-in modem does not work with any operating system other than Windows. Beware! If you're not sure about what modem to buy, get an external modem that works with any operating system, not just Windows.

One of the great things about OpenLinux is that it runs well even on older computers. Although graphics-intensive applications such as X can tax the capabilities of older, slower PCs, you don't need X11, a fancy display monitor, or a 16MB VRAM accelerated 3D video card to use PPP. You do, however, need a working serial port and modem.

If you're able to use your modem under Linux to dial out and connect using the `minicom` program or C-Kermit, chances are you won't have any problems. If you're using a laptop with a PC Card modem and the cardmgr PCMCIA device manager recognizes and initializes your modem, you should be okay, as any recognized card is identified and listed when you boot OpenLinux.

One way to check for serial-port recognition is to use the `dmesg` program, which displays the boot messages shown when you start OpenLinux. Run the `dmesg` program (piped through the `less` command), and look for lines in the output describing serial ports similar to these:

```
# dmesg ¦ less
....
tty00 at 0x03f8 (irq = 4) is a 16550A
tty01 at 0x02f8 (irq = 5) is a 16550A
tty03 at 0x02e8 (irq = 3) is a 16550A
....
```

Using dmesg is convenient, especially if the boot messages scroll by too fast for you to read. These lines show that three serial ports were found using the devices ttyS0, ttyS1, and ttyS3. Another consideration is your modem's speed. You might remember when 2400- or 9600-baud modems were the greatest innovation since touch-tone dialing. If you're still using an older modem and refuse to upgrade to the newer V.90 modems until model prices drop, you can still connect to the Internet with PPP; most older modems automatically synchronize with the newer models lodged in your ISP's modem bank.

> Want to lessen the chances of problems when connecting with your ISP? Find out what modems your ISP uses, and buy the same model for your computer system.

If you want to listen to radio stations, watch live video, or upgrade your Red Hat Linux system through your phone connection, you want the fastest modem and Internet connection you can afford. Although I don't advocate you try to get any work done through a 1200- or (shudder) 300-baud connection (which borders on masochism, but can be done, as ATM machines prove), you can use email, FTP, and text-only Web browsing at 9600 speeds.

It's up to you, and besides, isn't that what OpenLinux is all about—freedom of choice?

Linux Software You Need

In order to set up your PPP connection, you need to make sure that your Linux kernel supports PPP. You might have PPP support compiled into the kernel or loaded as a module when you start Linux. One of the ways to check to see if PPP support exists on your system is to again use dmesg:

```
# dmesg ¦ less
...
PPP: version 2.2.0 (dynamic channel allocation)
TCP compression code copyright 1989 Regents of the University of
➥California
PPP Dynamic channel allocation code copyright 1995 Caldera, Inc.
PPP line discipline registered.
...
```

You see similar lines.

> By default, OpenLinux loads PPP support via a loadable Linux kernel module. If you do not see PPP, you must either recompile the kernel with built-in PPP support, build the PPP module and use the `insmod` command to load the driver, or make sure you have selected the proper Linux kernel during your OpenLinux installation (with the word "modular" in its filename). You also need networking support enabled, especially TCP/IP. See Hour 2, "Installing Linux," for details.

You also need the `chat` program, found under the `/usr/sbin` directory, and part of the pppd daemon software package. The `chat` program is used during the dialing process to dial out and connect to your ISP's modem. Along with `chat`, you need the `pppd` daemon, also installed in the `/usr/sbin` directory. If `pppd` is installed, you can find a `ppp` directory under the `/etc` directory containing some or all of the following files:

```
# ls /etc/ppp
chap-secrets      options         ppp-on-dialer
connect-errors    pap-secrets     ppp-on
ip-up             ppp-off
```

If you don't see the `ppp-on` or `ppp-on-dialer` files, you can copy them from the `/usr/doc/ppp-2.2.0f` directory.

The first setup you learn during this hour requires you to make changes to the `ppp-on` file, which is an executable script. Next, you might want to check to see if the file `resolv.conf` exists under the `/etc` directory. If it doesn't, don't worry; it's a short file containing one or two lines, and I show you what to type in the file.

Finally, you might want to see if you have the `ifconfig`, `minicom`, `netstat`, `ping`, and `route` commands on your system. You use these later in this chapter to run some tests on your connection.

> Need to look for a command? Try the `whereis` or `locate` commands like so: `whereis ifconfig` to see where the ifconfig command is located on your system or `locate ifconfig` to print a list of any files or directories using ifconfig.

10

Information You Need from Your ISP

In order to connect to the Internet using PPP through your ISP, you need to first, obviously, have a PPP account. When you sign up for your service, your ISP account representative most likely assumes you want a setup and software for either a Windows or Macintosh computer system. If you say "Neither. I'm using Caldera's OpenLinux," and the response you get is either a blank stare, dead air on the phone, or "What's Linux?" don't panic!

You might get lucky. Linux is growing in popularity, and many ISPs in the U.S. and around the world recognize and support Linux users. If your ISP is aware of Linux, ask for the minimum system requirements, any setup guides, or install tips. This book's CD-ROM contains the latest, stable releases of the software you need, so you don't have to worry anyway.

Assuming your ISP doesn't know about Linux, here's what you need from your ISP:

- Your account information, meaning your username (login name) and password, so you can log in to your ISP's computer.

- Your ISP's modem connect number(s), so you can dial out and connect.

- Whether your ISP assigns you a static Internet Protocol (IP) address or assigns your IP address dynamically (the examples in this hour assume dynamic addresses, but I show you where you can make changes for a static IP address).

- The IP addresses and names of your ISP's primary Domain Name Server and secondary Domain Name Server. This information goes into the /etc/resolv.conf file (as explained in this chapter's section "Editing the resolv.conf File") in the first example.

The DNS IP addresses are in the form of four 8-bit numbers, and look something like 205.198.114.1 or 205.198.114.20. These are the address or addresses of the servers used or maintained by your ISP that translate hostnames, such as metalab.unc.edu, into numeric IP addresses, so you can connect, query, or address other computers and users around the world. This section doesn't go into the details about the mechanics of IP addressing, and this book does not cover all aspects of networking under Linux. If you want more complete details, see the *Linux Network Administrators Guide* under the /usr/doc/LDP/nag directory.

- The name or IP address of your ISP's mail server, so you can send and retrieve mail (you might also need a separate username and password for your ISP's mail server). You need this information in Hour 11, "Configuring Internet Email."

- The name or IP address of your ISP's news server, so you can read Usenet news and subscribe to newsgroups. You need this information in Hour 12, "Configuring Internet News."

Finally, ask for the Uniform Resource Locator, or URL, of your ISP's World Wide Web home page and your home page, if your ISP provides this service. Your ISP's Web pages might provide technical bulletins, help files, or other information that helps in troubleshooting connections.

Setting Up a PPP Connection Manually

10

Armed with this information, you can now learn how to specify your ISP's DNS server and how to create or edit your connection script, `ppp-on`. Although specifying your ISP's DNS server (s) is not necessary to initiate or maintain your connection, you need this information later with the `kppp` and `xisp` clients and when you learn about Internet email and news.

Editing the `resolv.conf` File

This is a simple process. First, make sure you're logged in as the root operator. Then look in the `/etc` directory for a file called `resolv.conf`. If it's there, open it with your favorite text editor, such as `pico` (see Hour 14, "Text Processing"), and add the search keyword, followed by the domain name of your ISP, and the IP addresses of your ISP's DNS servers. If your ISP only has one, that's okay. If your ISP has more than one, that's okay too. Create and open the file, like so:

```
# pico /etc/resolv.conf
```

Enter the lines, using this format:

```
search erols.com
nameserver 205.198.114.1
nameserver 205.198.114.20
```

Close the file. That's all there is to do! Next, you create or edit a script you can use to start a PPP connection.

Editing the PPP Connection Scripts

Before you start, you should know that using this script is only one way to start a PPP connection. This approach requires you to be logged in as the root operator. You also learn a much simpler approach later in this chapter.

I don't go into the detailed methods because I want to get you online quickly. When you get a working connection, I suggest you take a look at the pppd manual pages, Robert Hart's PPP-HOWTO under the /usr/doc/HOWTO directory, Al Longyear's PPP-FAQ under the /usr/doc/FAQ/PPP-HOWTO directory, the ISP-Connectivity mini HOWTO, or any pertinent sections in the *Linux Network Administrators Guide* under the /usr/doc/LDP/nag directory.

The first thing to do is to make sure you're logged in as the root operator. Then, look in the /etc/ppp directory for a file called ppp-on. If it's there, first make a copy (you can call it anything you want), or rename ppp-on to ppp-on.org. If ppp-on isn't there, copy it from the /usr/doc/ppp-2.20f directory. Listing 10.1 shows you parts of the script, written by Al Longyear:

LISTING 10.1   THE *ppp-on* CONNECTION SCRIPT

```
...
TELEPHONE=555-1212      # The telephone number for the connection
ACCOUNT=username        # The account name for logon (as in 'George Burns')
PASSWORD=password       # The password for this account (and 'Gracie Allen')
LOCAL_IP=0.0.0.0        # Local IP address if known. Dynamic = 0.0.0.0
REMOTE_IP=0.0.0.0       # Remote IP address if desired. Normally 0.0.0.0
...
DIALER_SCRIPT=/etc/ppp/ppp-on-dialer
...
exec /usr/sbin/pppd lock modem crtscts /dev/modem 57600 \
    asyncmap 20A0000 escape FF $LOCAL_IP:$REMOTE_IP \
    noipdefault netmask $NETMASK defaultroute connect \
        $DIALER_SCRIPT &
```

You need to change several parts of this script. For the most part, you only need to make a few changes. Some of the critical elements are the following:

TELEPHONE—Enter your ISP's modem connect number here.

ACCOUNT—Enter your username or login name (usually assigned by your ISP).

PASSWORD—Enter your password here (usually assigned by your ISP).

DIALER_SCRIPT—Enter the complete pathname of your dialing script, which uses the pppd daemon's companion chat program. The chat program does the dialing, connecting, and login for you. If you can't find a copy of this script, which is called ppp-on-dialer, look under the /usr/doc/ppp-2.2.0f directory. (Listing 10.2 shows the ppp-on-dialer script.)

> If your ISP's computer does not present a login: and password: prompt, you have to change the ogin: and assword: strings in this script to match the ones from your ISP.

LISTING 10.2 THE *ppp-on-dialer* DIALING SCRIPT

10

```
...
exec /usr/sbin/chat -v                                    \
        TIMEOUT         3                                 \
        ABORT           '\nBUSY\r'                        \
        ABORT           '\nNO ANSWER\r'                   \
        ABORT           '\nRINGING\r\n\r\nRINGING\r'      \
        ''              \rAT                              \
        'OK-+++\c-OK'   ATH0                              \
        TIMEOUT         30                                \
        OK              ATDT$TELEPHONE                    \
        CONNECT         ''                                \
        ogin:--ogin:    $ACCOUNT                          \
        assword:        $PASSWORD
```

Next, examine the pppd command line in the ppp-on script, and change /dev/modem to match the device your modem is connected to. If you want, you can use the approach outlined in Hour 9, "Using Communications Programs," to make a symbolic link from your modem's serial port to /dev/modem.

> If you have a 14.4 modem, use 19200 as the numeric value; if you have a 28.8 or 33.6 modem, try 57600. If you have a 56K or V.90 modem, try using a value of 115200. You might be able to connect at a faster speed, especially with newer modems.

If your ISP assigns IP addresses automatically (dynamic IP addresses, or addresses that might be different each time you log in), you're all set. But if you must connect to a specific (static, or fixed) IP address, you need to remove the noipdefault option from the pppd command line in listing 10.1. You also need to change the $REMOTE_IP string to the IP address provided by your ISP (you can do this in the pppd command line or further up in the script in the $REMOTE_IP variable).

Finally, make sure both the ppp-on and ppp-on-dialer scripts are executable by checking with ls -l or modifying with the chmod program:

```
# chmod +x /etc/ppp/ppp-on*
```

You're now ready, assuming your modem is connected to your computer and your phone line is connected to your modem, to try a connection.

Manually Starting and Stopping PPP Connections

This section shows you how to connect to your ISP and start your Internet session. There are several ways to do this. The first way you see is the most basic way to connect with the minicom program without using the scripts you just created. Then, you learn how to use your PPP connection script, ppp-on.

The minicom program, discussed in Hour 9, is a communications program you can use to dial out and connect to other computers or information services, such as bulletin board systems, or BBSs. See the minicom manual page for more information.

Using minicom to Connect

Using minicom to connect with your ISP has an advantage in that your account information and password are not recorded in the system logs under the /var/log directory. You can use minicom each time you want to use the Internet, but you might find the process tedious. I'm showing you this approach first, because you might find it useful in verifying that the login and password entries you specified in your ppp-on-dialer script work.

Here is the step-by-step method. You can do this because one of `minicom`'s features is that it has the capability to quit without resetting your modem. This means you can use `minicom` to dial out, connect, and then quit, enabling you to start your PPP session with the `pppd` daemon. Make sure you enter your ISP's DNS server information in `/etc/resolv.conf` first! Here's how:

1. Run `minicom`.
2. Type **ATDT**, followed by your ISP's modem number.
3. Wait for the connection and your ISP's prompt, and then log in with your username and password. Note whether the login and password prompts are different. If so, write them down so you have the information you need to edit the `chat` program options in your `ppp-on-dialer` script. After you type your password and press Enter, you might see a string of garbage characters sent back from your ISP's computer; this is normal and indicates your ISP's computer has started PPP.
4. Press Ctrl+A, and then press Q to exit `minicom` without a modem reset.
5. From the command line, log in as the root operator, and then type the following:

```
# pppd -d detach /dev/modem &
```

After a second or so, you're connected! (Well, check first—try some of the programs discussed later.)

Using Your ppp-on Script to Connect

Using the `ppp-on` script to establish your PPP connection is easy. Make sure you're logged in as root, and type the following to start the connection:

```
# /etc/ppp/ppp-on
```

> You don't have to log in as the root operator to start a PPP connection with the `ppp-on` script. Use the `su` command instead, like so:
>
> `su -c /etc/ppp/ppp-on`
>
> Press Enter. After you enter the root password, the script runs.

Notice that you have to type the entire pathname to the script. If your connection works, you can either move the script to the `/usr/local/bin` directory or make a symbolic link to the script with the following (you can call it whatever you want; just don't use `pppd`):

```
# ln -s /etc/ppp/ppp-on /usr/local/bin/start-ppp
```

After you start the script, you can hear your modem connect to your phone line, dial out, and then connect with your ISP's modem. After several seconds, you are connected!

> Here's a tip: if you don't like the sound of your modem or find it disruptive (especially if you have to work in a quiet environment), use your modem's AT command set to turn off the modem's speaker. Run minicom, then type ATM0, hit the Enter key, and then type AT&W, followed by the Enter key to save the settings. Now you can start stealth PPP connections! The first command turns of the speaker; the second command saves this setting to the modem's NVRAM (nonvolatile RAM).

Stopping the PPP Connection

To stop your PPP session, use the ppp-off script, found in the /etc/ppp directory. To use it, type the following:

```
# /etc/ppp/ppp-off
```

This script works by finding your network interface, ppp0, which you can test by using some of the programs in the next section and then using the kill command to kill the process ID of ppp0 (the kill command is discussed in the next hour).

> If you're interested in the details on setting up other serial-line connections, such as Serial-Line IP, or SLIP, look under the /usr/doc/slip-login-2.1.2 directory.

Configuring a PPP Connection with kppp

The kppp client included with KDE is an easy-to-use graphical interface you can use to configure, start, and stop PPP connections. This section shows you how to configure kppp to work with an ISP. You must be running X11 to use kppp, but you can use kppp without KDE.

To start the kppp client, type **kppp**, and press Enter at the command line of an X11 terminal window. If you're using KDE, click the Application Starter button on your desktop's panel, and then click Kppp from the Internet submenu. The kppp dialog box appears, as shown in Figure 10.1.

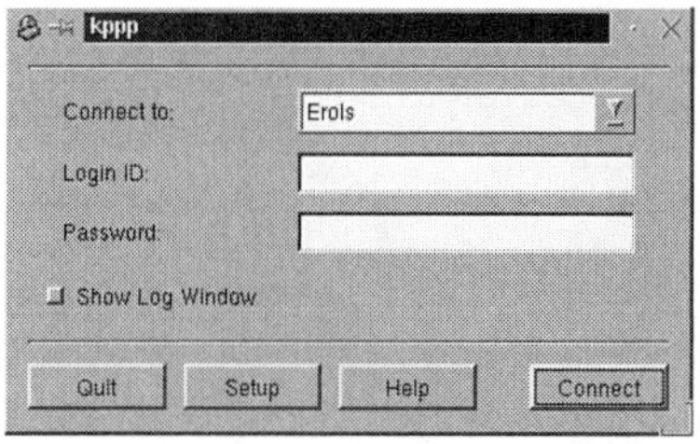

FIGURE 10.1

The kppp client can be used to set up, start up, and shut down PPP connections during X11 sessions.

Configuring Your kppp Connection

Click the Setup button (shown in Figure 10.1) to start your configuration. The kppp Configuration dialog box appears. To define a new connection, click the New button. In the New Account dialog box, as shown in Figure 10.2, type a connection name and phone number.

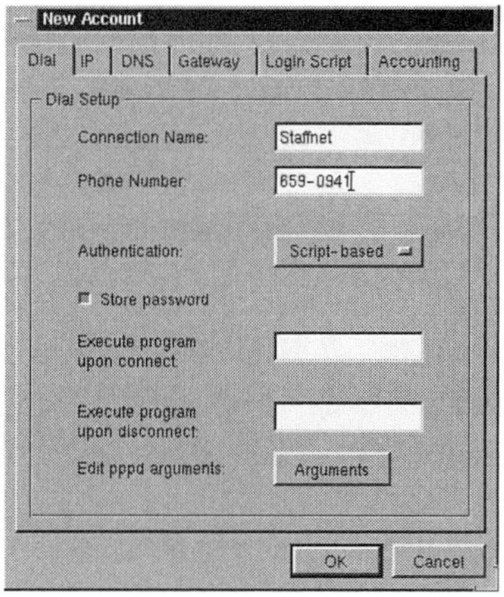

10

FIGURE 10.2

The kppp client's New Account dialog box is used to define PPP connections.

When you finish, click the IP tab at the top of the dialog box. If you have a static (assigned) IP address, click the Static IP Address button, and then enter the address. If you have a dynamic (randomly assigned) IP address, click Dynamic IP Address. When you finish, click the DNS tab to display the DNS Servers entry dialog box, as shown in Figure 10.3.

First, type your ISP's domain name, and then enter the first IP address of your ISP's DNS server. Next, click the Add button to add the IP address to the kppp list. Repeat this step until you enter all the DNS IP addresses. When you start a connection with kppp, the program temporarily adds these addresses to /etc/resolv.conf and then deletes the entries when you close the connection. When you finish entering the DNS addresses, click the Login Script tab in the dialog box.

FIGURE 10.3

*The kppp client's DNS
Servers dialog box is
used to define the
addresses of your
ISP's Domain Name
Service computers.*

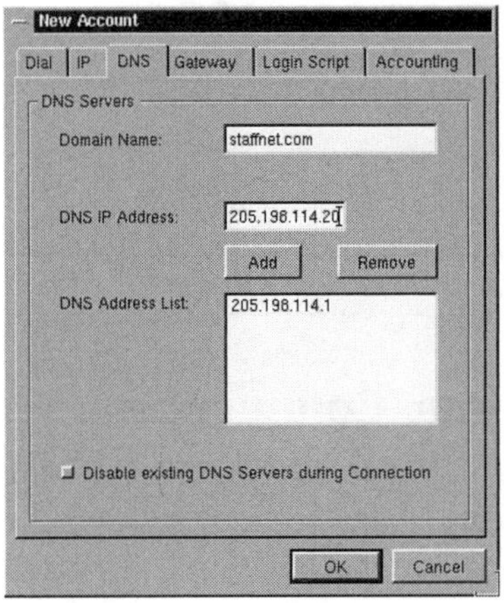

This is a critical step in configuring your PPP connection. Click in the blank field next to
the Expect button (as shown in Figure 10.4), type the phrase **ogin:**, and click the Add
button. This tells kppp to look for part of the phrase login: after it connects with your
ISP's computer.

FIGURE 10.4

*The kppp client's
Login Script dialog
box is used to define a
series of expected
phrases and responses
to log you into your
ISP's computer and
start your PPP
connection.*

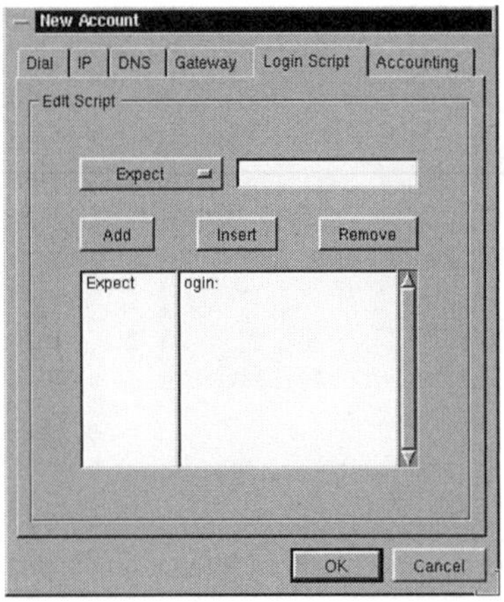

Next, click the Expect button, and select the Send item from the pop up menu (as shown
in Figure 10.5). Type your username (assigned by your ISP), and click the Add button.
This tells kppp to send your username when it detects the phrase ogin: during the
connection process.

FIGURE 10.5

The kppp client sends your username and password according to expected phrases in its login script.

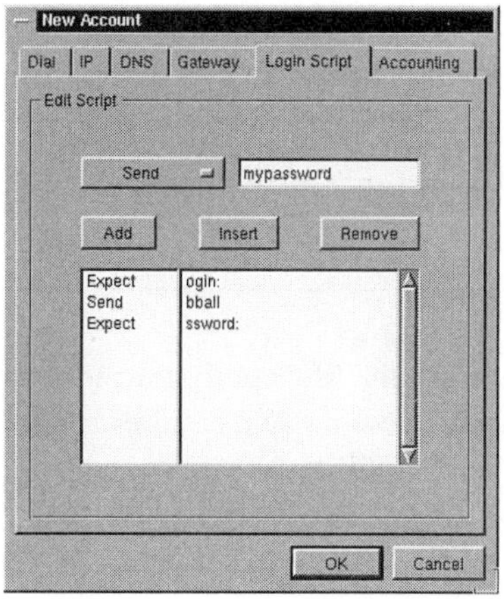

Next, again select the Expect item, type **ssword:** (to represent the phrase password: sent by your ISP's computer), and click the Add button. Finally, select the Send item, type your password (assigned by your ISP), and click the Add button. When you finish, click OK. You return to the kppp main Configuration dialog box. Click the Device tab to set the modem device you want kppp to use.

In the dialog box (as shown in Figure 10.6), click each pop-up menu to select the Modem Device, Flow Control, Line Termination, Connection Speed, Modem Lock File, and Modem Timeout. If you have a 56K or V.90 modem, the settings in Figure 10.6 work just fine. When you finish, click the Modem tab.

FIGURE 10.6

The kppp client's Device dialog box is used to define your modem, its speed, and other settings.

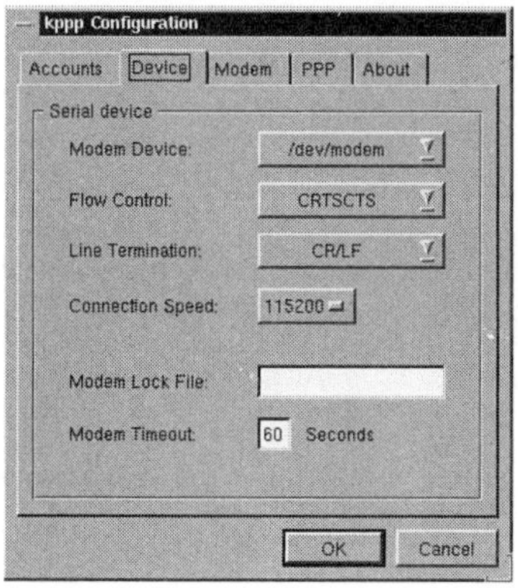

To see exactly what prompts are used by your ISP, follow the preceding steps in the section "Using minicom to Connect." Write down the prompts, and use them when you build your login script with kppp. This helps you later if you are having trouble and need to figure out what's going on during a connection.

In the Modem tab's dialog box, click the Modem Commands button to view the default modem commands used by kppp. If your modem requires any special settings, enter the proper commands in the Initialization String field as shown in Figure 10.7. When you finish, click the OK button.

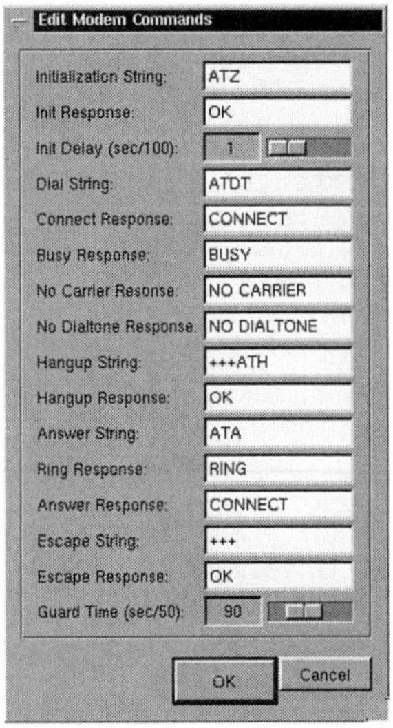

FIGURE **10.7**

Configure your modem in the kppp *Edit Modem Commands dialog box by entering AT commands or response strings.*

Edit Modem Commands

Initialization String:	ATZ
Init Response:	OK
Init Delay (sec/100):	1
Dial String:	ATDT
Connect Response:	CONNECT
Busy Response:	BUSY
No Carrier Resonse:	NO CARRIER
No Dialtone Response:	NO DIALTONE
Hangup String:	+++ATH
Hangup Response:	OK
Answer String:	ATA
Ring Response:	RING
Answer Response:	CONNECT
Escape String:	+++
Escape Response:	OK
Guard Time (sec/50):	90

OK   Cancel

To finish your kppp configuration, click the PPP tab to view the kppp Setup dialog box, as shown in Figure 10.8. Use the different settings in this dialog box to control how kppp acts after it starts or stops or when you stop your X11 session. For example, if you select Dock into Panel on Connect, a tiny modem icon with flashing red and green send and receive lights docks into the far right of your desktop's panel when you connect. When you finish, click OK. You're now done configuring kppp!

FIGURE 10.8

The kppp client's PPP dialog box is used to determine how kppp should act depending on where you are in your X11 session.

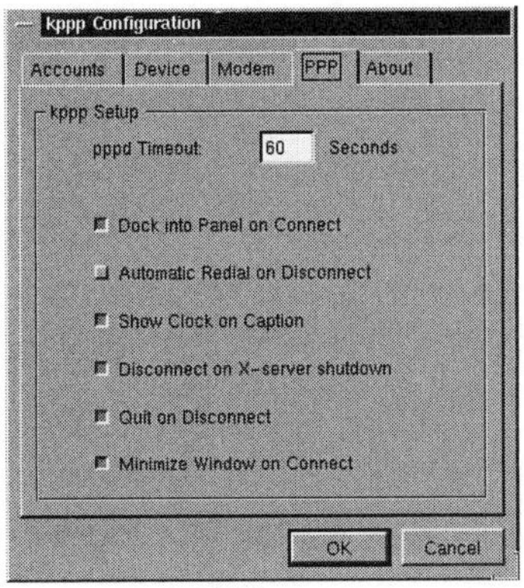

Starting and Stopping PPP with kppp

To start your PPP connection, select your ISP from the kppp drop-down menu, and then click the Connect button (as shown in Figure 10.9). If you select the Show Log Window, a window appears as kppp attempts the connection. This is a handy diagnostic tool you can use to watch the progress and conversation between kppp and your ISP's computer. When the PPP connection is made, kppp docks into your desktop's panel as a small modem icon. The kppp client also makes temporary *domain* and *name server* entries in your OpenLinux system's /etc/resolv.conf file.

FIGURE 10.9

Click the Connect button in the kppp client's main dialog box to start a PPP connection.

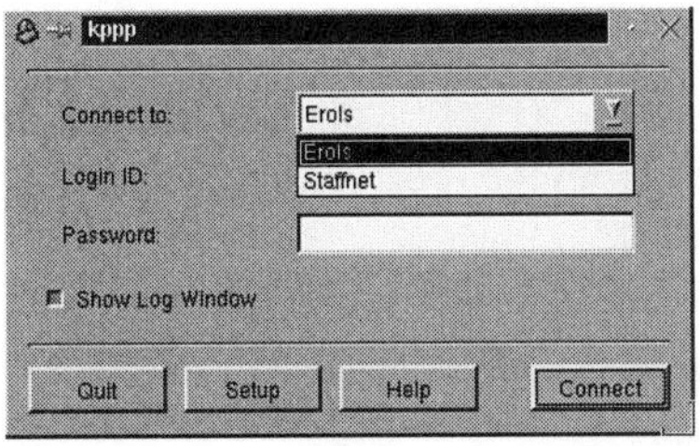

To get information about your PPP connection, right-click the modem icon on your desktop's panel, and then click the Restore menu item. A small dialog box appears with the name of your ISP. To view details about your connection, click the Details button, and a large dialog box appears, as shown in Figure 10.10.

FIGURE 10.10

The kppp client fea-
tures several dialog
boxes with information
about your PPP
connection.

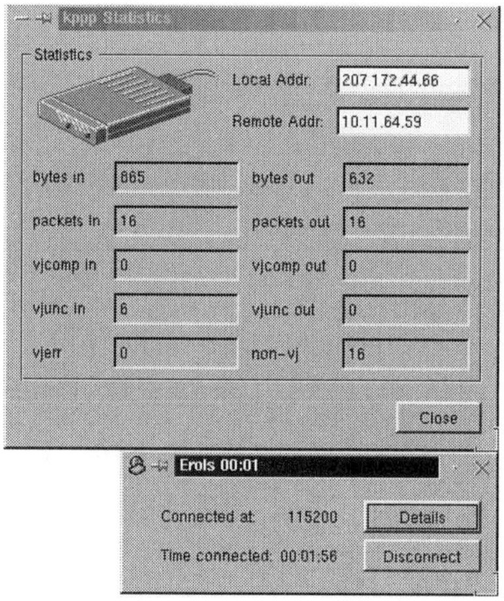

To shut down your PPP connection, either click the Disconnect button in the small dialog box or select Disconnect after right-clicking the kppp icon in your desktop's panel.

Configuring a PPP Connection with xisp

The xisp client included with OpenLinux is another easy-to-use graphical interface you can use to configure, start, and stop PPP connections. This section shows you how to configure xisp to work with an ISP. You must be running X11 to use xisp.

To start the xisp client type **su -c "xisp&"** and press Enter at the command line of an X11 terminal window. After entering the root operator password, the X-ISP dialog box appears, as shown in Figure 10.11.

FIGURE 10.11

The xisp client can be
used to set up, start up,
and shut down PPP
connections during
X11 sessions.

Configuring a New `xisp` Account

Select the Options menu and click Account Information to start your configuration. The `xisp` Account Information dialog box appears (as shown in Figure 10.12). To define a new account, click a blank line under ISP name. A small dialog box appears. Type your ISP's name, and click OK. Enter the ISP's phone number, your account name, and your account's password. Note that your password is not echoed on the screen, so make sure to type it in correctly! Also, if you need any other options, such as password authentication, click the appropriate buttons. When you finish, click OK.

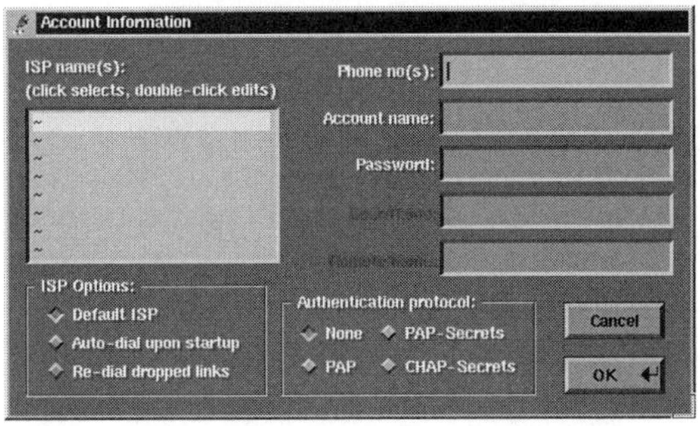

FIGURE 10.12

Use the `xisp` *client's New Account dialog box to define a new PPP account.*

Next, select the Options menu, and click the Dialing and Login menu item (as shown in Figure 10.11). The `xisp` Dialing and Login dialog box (similar to the `kppp` dialog box shown in Figure 10.5) appears. Enter the expected characters and responses for your ISP and select other desired options from the dialog box, as shown in Figure 10.13. Note that your password in the send column is echoed back to the screen (so make sure no one is looking over your shoulder)! When you finish, click the OK button.

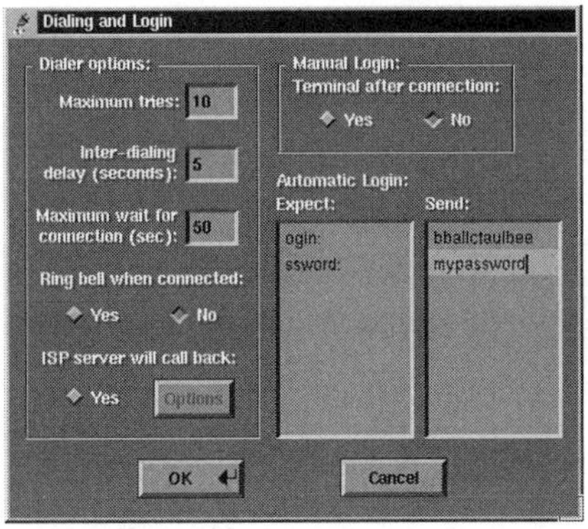

FIGURE 10.13

The `xisp` *client automates PPP connections with login scripts similar to those for the* `kppp` *client.*

Next, select the Options menu and click the Communications Options menu item (as shown in Figure 10.11). The Communications Options dialog box appears as shown in Figure 10.14. Select the appropriate modem device and baud rate. Most of other default settings can be used as is. When you finish, click the OK button.

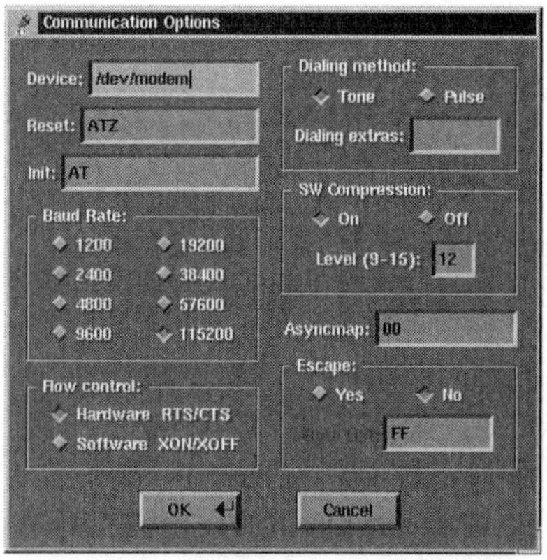

FIGURE 10.14

Select the appropriate communications options for your OpenLinux system when configuring a new account with the xisp *client.*

Now, select the Options menu again, and click the TCP/IP Options menu item (as shown in Figure 10.11). The TCP/IP Options dialog box appears as shown in Figure 10.15. If your ISP assigns IP addresses dynamically, simply click the Yes button for ip-if/up, and then type the primary and secondary DNS addresses for your ISP. When you finish, click the OK button. You're done!

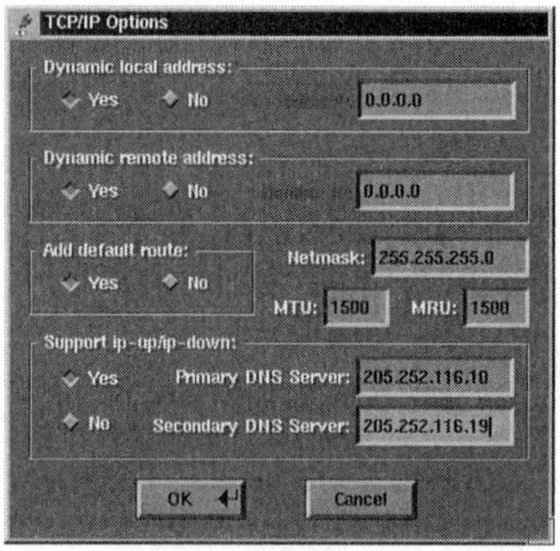

FIGURE 10.15

The TCP/IP xisp *dialog box is used to define the addresses of your ISP's Domain Name Service computers.*

> Although xisp is supposed to manipulate your system's /etc/resolv.conf file, it might not. You might have to put your ISP's DNS addresses in your /etc/resolv.conf before starting your connection. This information is absolutely necessary for Web browsing and other Internet activities.

Starting and Stopping PPP with `xisp`

To start your PPP connection, start `xisp`, and then click the Connect button. As `xisp` attempts to make the connection, the progress and status scroll by in the main `xisp` window (as shown in Figure 10.16). When you are logged in to the Internet, your IP address appears in the IP: field. The `xisp` client also keeps track of your time online and your connection speed.

FIGURE 10.16

Click the Connect button in the `xisp` *client's main dialog box to start a PPP connection and Internet session.*

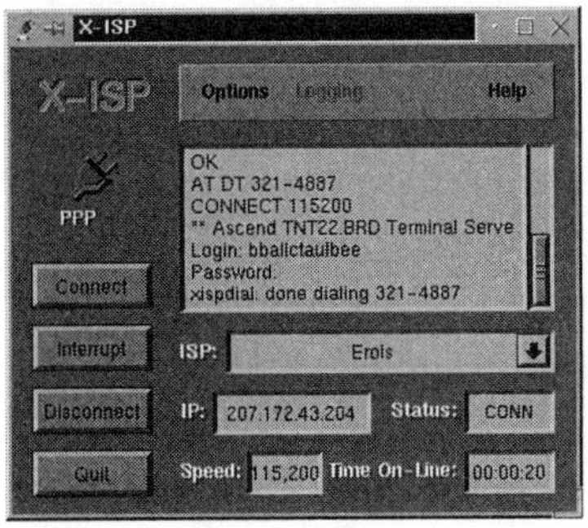

To shut down your PPP connection, click the Disconnect button. If you need help with `xisp`, read its manual page, select the General Info menu item from its main dialog box, or see the README files under the `/usr/doc/xisp` directory.

Checking the Connection

You can diagnose, troubleshoot, or get more information about your PPP connection in a number of ways. You can use networking utility programs during your connection to test, time, and diagnose the `ppp0` interface. You can also examine system logs to look for any problems occurring during startup, connecting, and disconnecting.

This section introduces you to a few of these networking programs and shows you where to look in your system logs for more information.

Using the `ifconfig` Command

Although the `ifconfig` command, found under the `/sbin` directory, is generally used in network administration by the root operator to configure network interfaces (a skill not covered in this book; see the *Linux Network Administrators Guide*), you can use `ifconfig` to see the status of your PPP connection.

This command can also be helpful when you're running programs, such as newsreaders, which appear "frozen" but are actually sending and receiving data without displaying updates on your screen. To use ifconfig, just enter the following:

```
# /sbin/ifconfig
lo        Link encap:Local Loopback
          inet addr:127.0.0.1  Bcast:127.255.255.255  Mask:255.0.0.0
          UP BROADCAST LOOPBACK RUNNING  MTU:3584  Metric:1
          RX packets:17257 errors:0 dropped:0 overruns:0
          TX packets:17257 errors:0 dropped:0 overruns:0

ppp0      Link encap:Point-Point Protocol
          inet addr:207.226.80.52  P-t-P:207.226.80.4
Mask:255.255.255.0
          UP POINTOPOINT RUNNING  MTU:1500  Metric:1
          RX packets:676 errors:0 dropped:0 overruns:0
          TX packets:545 errors:0 dropped:0 overruns:0
```

The command lists the current active network interfaces. Look at the ppp0 listing, and you can see the number of bytes received and transmitted (in the form of packets) over your PPP interface. Calling the program intermittently from another console or terminal window under X shows you the progress of data being sent and received.

Using the netstat Command

The netstat command is the definitive command for checking your network activity, connections, routing tables, and other network messages and statistics. Try this command if you're interested in a flexible listing of what's going on. For example, you can try the following (and the sample output is abbreviated here):

```
# netstat
Active Internet connections (w/o servers)
Proto Recv-Q Send-Q Local Address          Foreign Address         State
tcp    1      0 localhost:1644         localhost:1322          CLOSE_WAIT
tcp    0      0 localhost:2579         localhost:6000          ESTABLISHED
...
tcp    0      0 serial52.staffnet.:4216 megan.staffnet.com:pop  ESTABLISHED
Active UNIX domain sockets (w/o servers)
Proto RefCnt Flags       Type       State         I-Node Path
unix  2      [ ]         STREAM     CONNECTED     417
...
unix  2      [ ]         STREAM                   419      /dev/log
unix  2      [ ]         STREAM     CONNECTED     1982
unix  2      [ ]         STREAM                   1983     /dev/log
```

The netstat command has more than a dozen different command-line options. See the netstat manual page for more information.

Using the `ping` Command

The `ping` command is useful for verifying that your ISP's IP addresses are valid and for testing the response times of your ISP's host servers. `Ping` sends test packets of data and measures the time it takes for the host to send back the information, as in the following example:

```
# ping staffnet.com
PING staffnet.com (207.226.80.1): 56 data bytes
64 bytes from 207.226.80.1: icmp_seq=0 ttl=254 time=176.9 ms
64 bytes from 207.226.80.1: icmp_seq=1 ttl=254 time=180.0 ms
64 bytes from 207.226.80.1: icmp_seq=2 ttl=254 time=170.0 ms
64 bytes from 207.226.80.1: icmp_seq=3 ttl=254 time=170.0 ms
64 bytes from 207.226.80.1: icmp_seq=4 ttl=254 time=170.0 ms
64 bytes from 207.226.80.1: icmp_seq=5 ttl=254 time=170.0 ms
64 bytes from 207.226.80.1: icmp_seq=6 ttl=254 time=169.7 ms
...

--- staffnet.com ping statistics ---
7 packets transmitted, 7 packets received, 0% packet loss
round-trip min/avg/max = 169.7/172.3/180.0 ms
```

As you can see, the `ping` command sends each packet and reports the amount of time (in thousandths of a second) it takes for the packet to be echoed back. By default, `ping` continues to send and receive information until you tell it to quit with Ctrl+C. Using the `-f`, or flood, option is not a nice thing to do to your ISP (or any other host computer for that matter), as it creates network overhead and unnecessary network traffic. If you want to test the connection for a short period of time, use the `ping` command's `-c` option, followed by a number, to have `ping` only send a specific number of packets, like this:

```
# ping -c 10 staffnet.com
```

Using the `route` Command

The `route` command, generally used to set up or delete networking routes for interfaces, can also be useful in showing you what is going on with your ppp0 interface. You can try the following:

```
# /sbin/route
Kernel IP routing table
Destination     Gateway         Genmask         Flags Metric Ref    Use Iface
pm2.staffnet.co *               255.255.255.255 UH    0      0        0 ppp0
127.0.0.0       *               255.0.0.0       U     0      0        2 lo
default         pm2.staffnet.co 0.0.0.0         UG    0      0        3 ppp0
```

This listing (similar to the `netstat -r` command) shows that in addition to a normal loopback interface (127.0.0.0, defined in your `/etc/hosts` file), a ppp0 interface is currently active. For more details about the `route` command, see its manual page.

10

Reading Your System Log

If you want to read in detail about what is going on while your scripts are executing, take a look through your system log for a file called messages under the /var/log directory. Try the following (as the root operator):

```
# less /var/log/messages
```

Look for the start of the pppd daemon in the ppp-on script. Notice that your dialer script uses the chat program, which does most of the work and then quits, followed by pppd getting and setting the network IP addresses, as follows:

```
...
Nov  5 16:29:49 localhost pppd[370]: pppd 2.2.0 started by root, uid 0
Nov  5 16:29:51 localhost chat[371]: timeout set to 3 seconds
Nov  5 16:29:51 localhost chat[371]: abort on (\nBUSY\r)
Nov  5 16:29:51 localhost chat[371]: abort on (\nNO ANSWER\r)
Nov  5 16:29:51 localhost chat[371]: abort on
➥(\nRINGING\r\n\r\nRINGING\r)
Nov  5 16:29:51 localhost chat[371]: send (rAT^M)
Nov  5 16:29:51 localhost chat[371]: expect (OK)
Nov  5 16:29:51 localhost chat[371]: rAT^M^M
Nov  5 16:29:51 localhost chat[371]: OK -- got it
Nov  5 16:29:51 localhost chat[371]: send (ATH0^M)
Nov  5 16:29:51 localhost chat[371]: timeout set to 30 seconds
Nov  5 16:29:51 localhost chat[371]: expect (OK)
Nov  5 16:29:51 localhost chat[371]: ^M
Nov  5 16:29:51 localhost chat[371]: ATH0^M^M
Nov  5 16:29:51 localhost chat[371]: OK -- got it
Nov  5 16:29:51 localhost chat[371]: send (ATDT659-9041^M)
Nov  5 16:29:51 localhost chat[371]: expect (CONNECT)
Nov  5 16:29:51 localhost chat[371]: ^M
Nov  5 16:30:10 localhost chat[371]: ATDT659-9041^M^M
Nov  5 16:30:10 localhost chat[371]: CONNECT -- got it
Nov  5 16:30:10 localhost chat[371]: send (^M)
Nov  5 16:30:10 localhost chat[371]: expect (ogin:)
Nov  5 16:30:10 localhost chat[371]:  57600^M
Nov  5 16:30:12 localhost chat[371]: ^M
Nov  5 16:30:12 localhost chat[371]: ^M
Nov  5 16:30:12 localhost chat[371]: Staffnet PM0 login: -- got it
Nov  5 16:30:12 localhost chat[371]: send (username^M)
Nov  5 16:30:12 localhost chat[371]: expect (assword:)
Nov  5 16:30:12 localhost chat[371]: username^M
Nov  5 16:30:12 localhost chat[371]: Password: -- got it
Nov  5 16:30:12 localhost chat[371]: send (password^M)
Nov  5 16:30:12 localhost pppd[370]: Serial connection established.
Nov  5 16:30:13 localhost pppd[370]: Using interface ppp0
Nov  5 16:30:13 localhost pppd[370]: Connect: ppp0 <--> /dev/modem
Nov  5 16:30:16 localhost pppd[370]: local  IP address 207.226.80.171
Nov  5 16:30:16 localhost pppd[370]: remote IP address 207.226.80.214
,,,
```

You can look at portions of your log to troubleshoot whether your modem is working or your ISP's modems are working. Hopefully, everything goes well, but if you have a hard time connecting or setting up your scripts, take the time to read the chat and pppd manual pages, along with the PPP-HOWTO and PPP-FAQ.

> If you're still having trouble, make sure to read Robert Hart's PPP-HOWTO, along with Al Longyear's PPP-FAQ, which go into much more detail about setting up PPP connections. You can find a lot of handy hints about setting up, testing, and troubleshooting your connection. If security is a big issue for you, make sure to read these documents, too. You can also check with the comp.os.linux.networking, comp.os.linux.setup, or comp.protocols.ppp USENET newsgroups for specific information or tips on using PPP.

10

The next two hours show you how to set up your email and newsreader programs so you can send and receive email and read some favorite USENET newsgroups.

Summary

This hour you learned several ways to set up an Internet connection to your ISP using the PPP protocol. As you observed, OpenLinux comes with several connection and troubleshooting utilities that make getting connected to the Internet easier than ever before.

Q&A

Q My modem dials and connects to my ISP, but the connection dies almost immediately! What's going on?

A Make sure you have entered the proper log in sequence either in your ppp-on script, or in the appropriate dialog boxes for the kppp or xisp clients. Try manually connecting to your ISP with the seyon or minicom programs and note the prompt strings from your ISP's computer.

Q I manually connected with minicom, but after I log in to my ISP's computer and press Enter, I see strings of garbage characters echoed back!

A This is probably normal and shows that your ISP's computer has started PPP. Exit minicom without resetting your modem, and test your connection.

Q OK, I've established my connection. Now what?

A You should first try to `ping` a remote host computer, or attempt an FTP connection. For information about other Internet activities, see Hour 11, "Configuring Internet Email," Hour 12, "Configuring Internet News," or Hour 13, "Internet Downloading and Browsing."

Exercises

1. After establishing your PPP connection, try using other Internet utilities, such as the `whois` command, to get information about your ISP. At the command line of a terminal window, type `whois`, followed by the domain name of your ISP, and press Enter. What do you see?

2. Try using the `ping` command to see how fast packet information is returned to your computer. Test the speed with different host computers on the Internet and measure the difference.

Hour 11

Configuring Internet Email

This hour shows you how to set up your OpenLinux system to handle electronic mail. You'll also explore various programs you can use to read and send mail, such as the pine mail program and Netscape Messenger.

First you'll learn to set up your system to send and receive mail, building on your experience in setting up and connecting to your ISP using PPP.

Setting Up and Getting Your Email

There's not really much to do to set up your system to send and receive mail, although configuring the main mail daemon, sendmail, is complex enough to be considered a black art, suitable only for UNIX wizards. You shouldn't be intimidated though, because you can use email right after you install OpenLinux.

NEW TERM I can't discuss all the details about UNIX mail in this hour, but you should understand how electronic mail works in general. The main programs involved in email are, in technical terms, *transport agents* and *user agents*. A transport agent is a program, usually a daemon, that sends mail files from one computer to the next automatically. A user agent is a program, also called a mail reader, that you use to manage messages. You'll learn how to use these programs in this hour.

After you install OpenLinux, you can find nearly all the programs you need to compose, send, and receive mail. The transport agent used for OpenLinux is `sendmail`, and it is configured and run automatically when you boot the operating system. As far as user agents and electronic mail utilities, you have a wide choice from at least nine (listed in Table 11.1).

TABLE 11.1 ELECTRONIC MAIL PROGRAMS FOR OPENLINUX

Name	Description
biff	Mail notification utility
coolmail	3D animated mail notification utility for X11
elm	Interactive mail program
fastmail	Bulk email program
fetchmail	Essential POP, IMAP, or ETRN mail retrieval program
frm, nfrm	Handy mailbox message list utilities
mail	Basic mail program
messages	Handy mailbox message counting utility
ml	Mail user agent for X11
mush	Shell for electronic mail
mutt	Mutt mail user agent
Netscape Messenger	Mail user agent component of Netscape Communicator newmail, wnewmailMail notification utilities
pine	Program for Internet News and Email
printmail	Format utility to prepare mail for printing
procmail	Recipe-based mail processor
readmsg	Handy mail message extractionutility
xbiff	Mail notification utility for X11
xfmail	Mail user agent for X11
xmailbox	Mail notification utility for X11
xmh	Mail user agent for X11

Because you're probably connecting to the Internet with a PPP connection, the general approach to handling mail outlined in this hour is to do the following:

1. Log in and establish a PPP connection.
2. Retrieve mail using a retrieval utility or user agent.
3. Disconnect (or stay connected for a few quick replies).

This is a similar approach to other ways of handling mail. If you've experimented with free email dial-in account programs (such as Juno) for other operating systems, you know the general approach is to minimize connect time by composing and replying to mail offline, then connecting, sending and retrieving mail, and followed by logging off.

If you want details about Linux mail handling along with pointers to other sources of information, read Guylhem Aznar's Mail-HOWTO under the `/usr/doc/HOWTO` directory.

Retrieving Your Email with `fetchmail`

By now you're probably wondering how to get your email from your ISP. If you recall from the preceding hour, you need the IP address or name of your ISP's mail server. To get your mail, you need `fetchmail`, which can be found in the `/usr/bin` directory. The `fetchmail` program was written by Eric S. Raymond, an outstanding programmer, outspoken proponent of Open Source software, and all-around good guy (who wants to be known by his initials, *esr*).

NEW TERM This program has many features, including a *daemon* mode, or background mode, that periodically checks to see if you have mail while you're connected to your ISP. The `fetchmail` program can recognize and retrieve mail using all standard Internet mail-retrieval protocols, such as the following:

- POP2
- POP3
- RPOP
- APOP
- KPOP
- CompuServe POP3 with RPA
- SDPS
- IMAP
- ESMTP ETRN

11

To retrieve electronic mail, you need to know what protocol your ISP uses (most ISPs support POP3, APOP, or IMAP), along with your username and password on the mail server.

Put all this information together, connect to your ISP, and then grab all your waiting email with the fetchmail command. Include the -p option, followed by the type of protocol used, followed by the name of your ISP's mail server, and ending with the -u option and your username, like this:

```
# fetchmail -p POP3 pop.erols.com -u bball
Enter password for bball@pop.erols.com:
2 messages for bball at pop.erols.com (3524 octets).
reading message 1 of 2 (2335 octets) .. flushed
reading message 2 of 2 (1189 octets) . flushed
You have new mail in /var/spool/mail/bball
```

After you press Enter, fetchmail prompts for your password (so you can gain access to your ISP's mail server), then retrieves your mail, and flushes (or deletes) your mail from your ISP's mail server. If you want to keep copies of your mail on your ISP's mail server (not recommended), include the -k (keep) option on the command line.

> Unfortunately, the version of fetchmail (4.0.7) included with OpenLinux 1.3 is sadly out of date. The current version at the time of this writing is 4.7.4 and includes numerous improvements. To get a newer version, browse to ftp://metalab.unc.edu/pub/Linux/system/mail/pop. To get the latest version, browse to http://www.tuxedo.org/~esr/fetchmail. You can find .rpm and .tgz versions at both sites.

To make retrieving email easier, fetchmail uses the contents of a file called .fetchmailrc you can create in your home directory. In fact, if you use the —fetchmailrc option, followed by the name of a different file, you can easily retrieve mail from different accounts or ISPs. The contents of a .fetchmailrc file are spelled out in detail in the fetchmail man page but generally consist of the following:

```
poll mailserver protocol POP3 username yourusername password yourpassword
```

Use your favorite text editor to create your own .fetchmailrc, and replace *mailserver* with the name of your ISP's mailserver (such as pop.erols.com), *POP3* with your ISP's mail server protocol, *yourusername* with your username, and *yourpassword* with your password. Save the file, exit your editor, and then retrieve your mail, like so:

```
# fetchmail
```

If you want `fetchmail` to periodically check for waiting mail (say, every five minutes), use its daemon, followed by the number of seconds to specify the interval between checks. When you use this mode with the `-d` option, `fetchmail` runs as a background process. Start the command as follows:

```
# fetchmail -d 300
```

`fetchmail` also has a nifty option, `-c`, which merely checks to see if you have mail waiting and reports the number of messages, along with the size. For example:

```
# fetchmail -c
2 messages for bball at pop.erols.com (3435 octets).
```

By default, your mail goes into a single file with your username under the `/var/spool/mail` directory.

Remember: The `fetchmail` program is designed to work only one way; it retrieves your mail from your ISP's mail server and then tells your ISP's mail server to delete (or keep) your mail after messages are sent. Now that you've retrieved your mail, how do you send, read, or reply to messages? This is where user agents, or mail reading programs, come in.

> If you get an error when retrieving mail, make sure that the `sendmail` daemon has started. This service, listed as the Mail Transfer Agent under the `lisa` command's Configure daemon/server autostart menu, ensures proper receipt and delivery of mail (in addition to mail forwarding).

11

Sending Mail with Mail Programs

This section introduces you to three basic mail programs you can use under Linux. The explanations start with one of the oldest, the `mail` program, and then follow with two screen-oriented programs, `elm` and `pine`.

Using the `mail` Program

The `mail` program, found under the `/bin` directory, is the simplest mail program you can use. It is not screen-oriented, and works on a line-by-line basis with single-letter commands. However, this program is easy to use to create and send messages. For example, to create a quick message, call `mail` with an email address on the command line like this:

```
# mail tball@mcp.com
Subject: Howzit going?
Hope everything is OK with you.
Just wanted to drop a quick line!
.
EOT
```

The mail program responds by asking for a Subject: line. Enter your message subject, and then press Enter. Next, type each line of text in the body of your message. When you finish, put a period (.) on a line by itself, and press Enter. The mail program sends the message.

Retrieving your messages is easy. After you connect to your ISP and retrieve your mail using fetchmail, type mail on the command line, for example:

```
# mail
Mail version 8.1 6/6/93.  Type ? for help.
"/var/spool/mail/bball": 5 messages 1 unread
    1 MAILER-DAEMON@staffn  Thu Jan  7 18:51  12/510
➥"DON'T DELETE THIS MES"
    2 majordomo@rim.calder  Sun Nov  8 11:26  54/2067
➥"Welcome to caldera-us"
    3 majordomo@rim.calder  Sun Nov  8 11:26  25/982
➥"Majordomo results: Re"
    4 bball@staffnet.com    Thu Jan  7 18:23  69/2805
➥"Welcome to caldera-us"
>U  5 bball@staffnet.com    Thu Jan  7 18:23  40/1658   "test"
&
```

The mail program retrieves your mail from the /var/spool/mail directory, prints its version, lists information about each message, and presents the ampersand (&) as a prompt. Note that a right angle bracket (>) precedes the current message. The basic mail commands are as follows:

- t—Type, or list, the current message
- n—Go to the next message and list it
- +—Move to the next message and list it
- -—Move backwards to the previous message and list it
- h—Reprint list of messages (after listing a message)
- d—Delete the current message
- R—Reply to sender
- r—Reply to sender and all recipients
- q—Quit, saving messages in the default mailbox, mbox
- x—Quit, and don't save messages in mbox

One handy way to send a long message quickly is to use the command-line redirection operator of your shell. For example, if you compose a long message in your favorite text editor, you can send the message with the following:

```
# mail -s "How is it going?" myfriend@somewhere.com < mymessage.txt
```

Using this approach, the `mail` program creates a message with a subject you specify with the `-s` option (note that you must enclose the subject lines that contain spaces between quote marks) and then puts the file `mymessage.txt` into the body of the message. Be careful, though, because the message is sent right away without asking you if you really want to send it.

There are many different ways to use the `mail` program. You might find it useful. See the `mail` manual page for more information. Although using `mail` can be quick and convenient, the next two mail programs are a lot more interactive and offer features most people have become accustomed to when they send and receive mail.

Configuring and Using the `elm` Mail Program

The `elm` program, more than 10 years old, was originally developed by Dave Taylor and is now under cooperative development by a team of more than 40 programmers known as The Elm Development Group. This program features an interactive screen and can be used from the console or the command line of an X11 terminal window.

> Unlike `pine`, `elm` must be started in a window with at least 14 rows, or it complains and quits.

When you first start `elm`, you're asked if you want to create `elm`'s default mail folder, `Mail`:

```
# elm

Notice:
This version of ELM requires the use of a .elm directory in your home
directory to store your elmrc and alias files. Shall I create the
directory .elm for you and set it up (y/n/q)?
```

Press the Y key, and press Enter. `elm` has features similar to `mail` and `pine` (discussed in the next section). For example, you can, as in `mail`, send a message from the command line using the `mail` command example you saw earlier, for example:

```
# elm -s "How is it going?" bball@staffnet.com < author.msg
Sending mail...
Mail to bball@staffnet.com
Mail sent!
```

After you retrieve your mail, `elm` reads your messages and displays your them as shown in Figure 11.1.

FIGURE **11.1**

The elm mail program displays messages in a list.

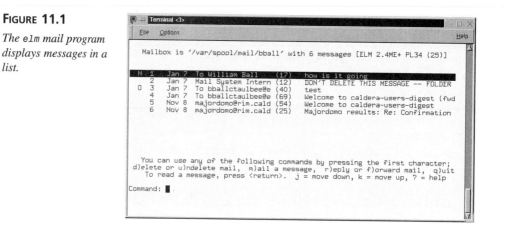

You can use `elm` to delete, forward, save, or compose messages. Customize some of its features by typing an **o** (for options) while in elm's main display (as shown in Figure 11.2). Type a letter, then type a new value for features such as the default editor (used when you compose or reply to messages), and press Enter. These custom features are saved in an `elmrc` file under the `.elm` folder in your home directory when you press the < key.

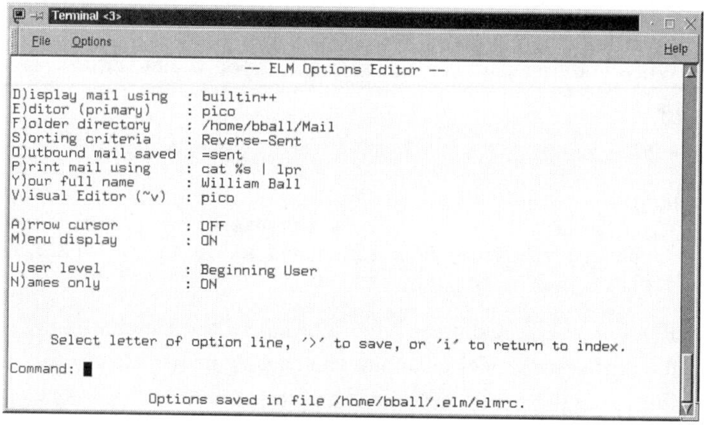

FIGURE **11.2**

The elm setup dialog is used to set various options.

Make sure to read the manual page for `elm` before you start using it. You can also find documentation under the `/usr/doc/elm` directory. If you want more information about `elm`, you can also check the following:

`http://www.myxa.com/elm.html`

Configuring and Using the `pine` Mail Program

The `pine` (Pine Is No longer Elm) mail program, which you can find under the `/usr/bin` directory, was developed by the University of Washington as an interactive mail and news reader. This means that not only can you use `pine` for sending or reading your mail, but you can also use it to read Usenet newsgroups. Usenet and different news readers are discussed in the next hour, "Configuring Internet News." This section focuses on configuring and using `pine` for electronic mail.

The `pine` program also comes with an extremely easy-to-use editor called `pico`, which might easily become your favorite Linux text editor because it can be used with any other program and not just `pine`. See Hour 14, "Text Processing," for more details about the `pico` editor.

The `pine` program is easy to set up and use. Most of the work is done for you automatically when you first start the program. The first time you use this program, it reports the following:

```
# pine
Creating subdirectory "/home/bball/mail" where Pine will store
its mail folders.
```

The `pine` program starts up and creates a directory called `mail` along with a `.pinerc` configuration file in your home directory. You see an initial greeting screen (as shown in Figure 11.3).

FIGURE 11.3

The pine mail program works with your console or through an X11 terminal window.

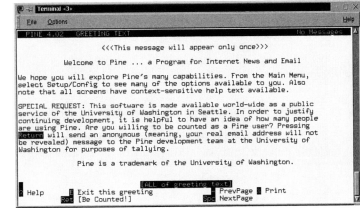

Before you start composing or sending mail, configure pine to recognize your username, your ISP's mail server, and, as you'll see later, your ISP's news server. Although you can compose mail and use pine's postpone feature to save your composed messages, you can't send mail until you tell pine who you are or the name of your ISP's mail server.

To do this, first start pine, and then type an **s** and then a **c** to get to pine's configuration screen (see Figure 11.4).

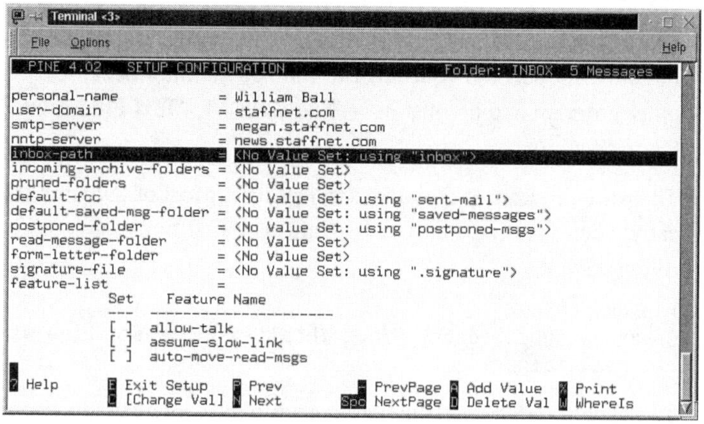

FIGURE 11.4

Specify the personal name, user domain, smtp server, and nntp server in the pine mailer configuration screen.

Enter your personal name, the domain of your ISP, the name of your ISP's mail server, and if you know it, the name of your ISP's news server. Then type an **e**, and pine asks if you want to save the changes. Your configuration is then saved in the .pinerc file in your home directory. Although you can edit this file in your favorite text editor, using pine is a lot easier.

To compose a message, press the **c** key, and you're in pine's compose mode (see Figure 11.5).

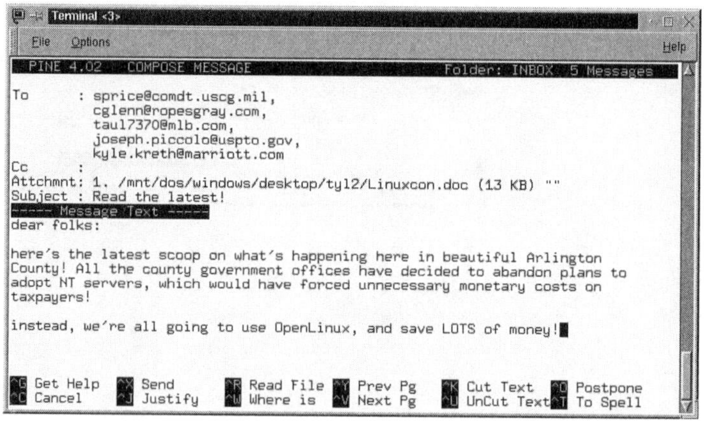

FIGURE 11.5

Composing a mail message with file attachments to multiple recipients in the pine compose mode.

You can specify multiple recipients to your message by typing a comma between names. You can also send file attachments by typing the name of the file in the Attchmnt: field (if it is in your home directory) or the complete path of your file (if it is somewhere else on your file system).

As you compose your message, use your cursor keys to move around the text. There are a number of editing keys you can use to change your text. Lines of text can also be deleted or undeleted for cutting and pasting. These keys, listed in table 11.2, correspond with the pico editor.

TABLE 11.2   PINE MESSAGE COMPOSITION EDITING COMMANDS

Action	Keystroke
Back one character	Ctrl+B
Backspace	Ctrl+H
Cancel message	Ctrl+C
Delete character	Ctrl+D
Delete line	Ctrl+K
Down one line	Ctrl+N
Forward one character	Ctrl+F
Help on editing	Ctrl+H
Insert text from file	Ctrl+R
Justify paragraph	Ctrl+J
Beginning of line	Ctrl+A
End of line	Ctrl+E
Next word	Ctrl+@
Page down	Ctrl+V
Page up	Ctrl+Y
Postpone (save) message	Ctrl+O
Spellcheck	Ctrl+T
Up one line	Ctrl+P
Word search	Ctrl+W

11

When you finish composing your message, send the message immediately by using Ctrl+X, or postpone the message by using Ctrl+O. Using this approach, you can create or reply to messages when you're not connected to your ISP and send them later.

When you retrieve your mail, `pine` looks in the `/var/spool/mail` directory, and then extracts the messages from your mail file and puts them into the default folder, `INBOX`, in the directory named `mail` in your home directory. You can also create other folders and save and delete messages in different folders to organize your mail. Of course, you can also use the `procmail` approach discussed in the section "Configuring `procmail` and Writing Recipes to Fight Spam" later in this chapter to automate some of this process for you.

The folder index of your messages is displayed in a list, and you can select messages by scrolling up and down with the cursor keys (see Figure 11.6). From the main list of messages, you can delete, undelete, save, read, and export messages to your directory. To read a message, just hit the Enter key.

Figure 11.6

You can select messages through the message list of a pine mail folder.

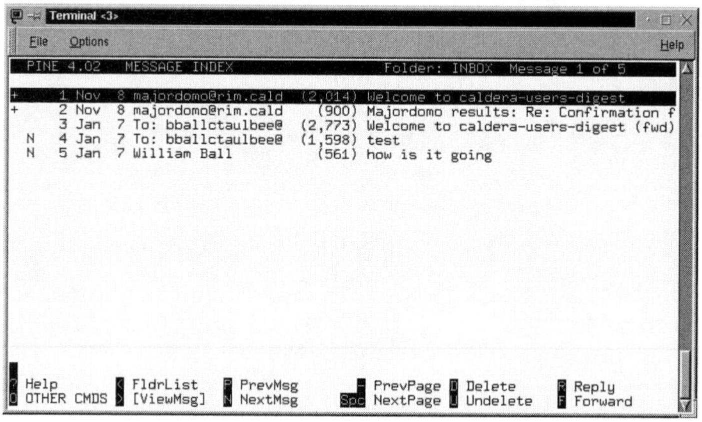

The `pine` program has a number of command-line options and other features, such as built-in help, which you access with the question mark (?) from the `pine` main menu.

Configuring and Using Netscape Messenger for Email

Netscape Messenger, a component of the Netscape Communicator suite of Internet clients, is a graphical electronic mail client for the X Window System. You can start this program from the Communicator menu in the Netscape Navigator window by clicking the Messenger button on Netscape's component bar. You can also start it through the use of the -mail option with the `netscape` command like this:

```
# netscape -mail &
```

When the client launches (as shown in Figure 11.7), select the Edit menu, and then click the Preferences menu item. When the Preferences dialog box appears, click the Mail & Groups item, and then click the Identity list item. Type in your name and email address, as shown in Figure 11.8.

FIGURE 11.7

Netscape Messenger is an easy-to-use interface to electronic mail in X11.

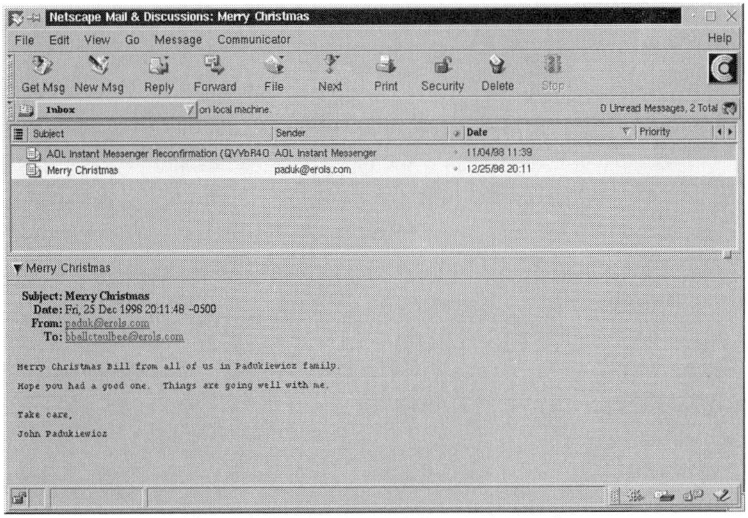

FIGURE 11.8

Enter your name and email address, along with any other desired information (such as your organization), in the Messenger Identity dialog box.

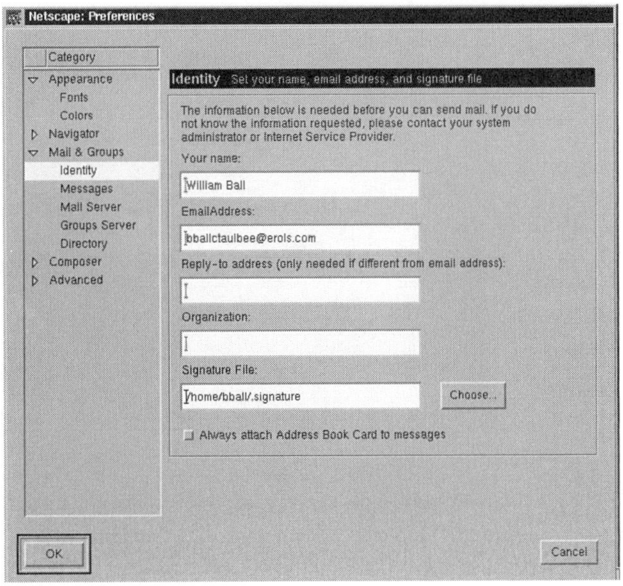

11

By default, Netscape Messenger sends the text of your email message for-matted in HTML. This is okay if you're sending mail to another Netscape user but is a messy way to communicate with others who use mail, elm, or pine. Turn off the HTML message format by clicking the Messages list item under Mail & Groups and then deselecting the HTML messages push button under the Message Properties section of the Messages dialog box.

Next, click the Mail Server list item. This dialog box (shown in Figure 11.9) is used to set several critical items, such as server names and your ISP's mail retrieval protocol. Type your username (usually the name you use to log in to your ISP), and then type the name of your ISP's mail server in the Incoming mail server field (leave the outgoing server entry set to localhost). Next, click to select the type of mail server protocol used by your ISP.

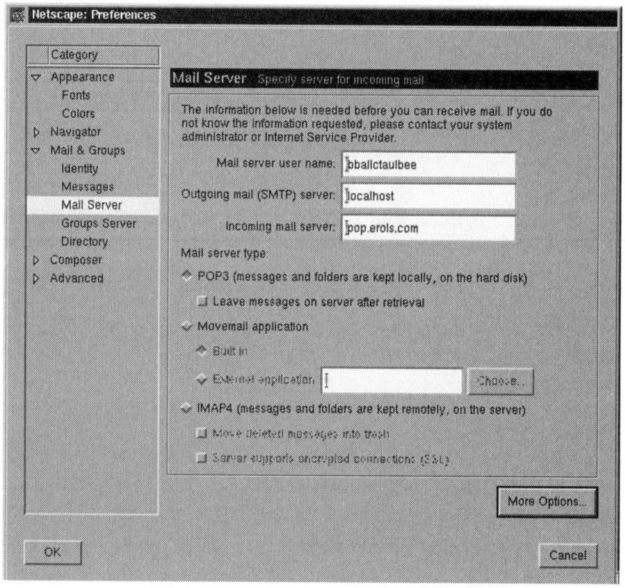

FIGURE **11.9**

You can use the Messenger Mail Server preferences dialog box to set critical informa-tion needed to retrieve and send mail.

Click the More Options button to change other settings, such as the default mail folder or how often you want Messenger to check for waiting email.

When finished, click OK to save your changes. In the main Messenger window, click the Get Msg button (shown in Figure 11.7). Messenger asks for your password. Click the OK button to retrieve your messages. New messages appear in a list in the Messenger window. To read a message, click the desired message in the message list, and its text appears in the bottom half of the Messenger window.

At this point, you can use the various Messenger buttons to reply to, forward, save, print, or delete the message. To compose a new message, click the New Msg button in Messenger's menu bar. The Messenger Compose window appears, as shown in Figure 11.10.

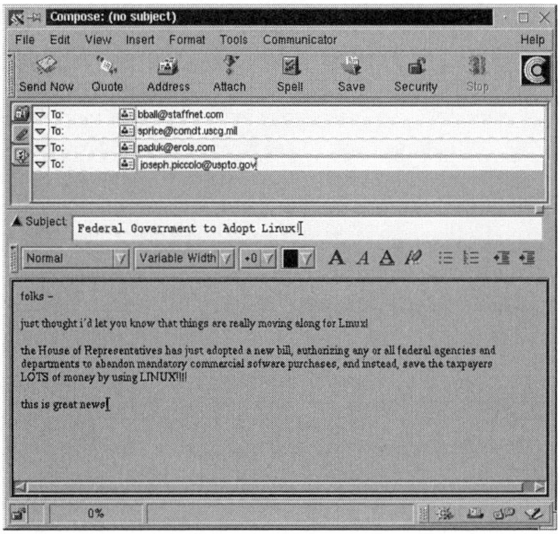

FIGURE 11.10

Compose new messages, address multiple recipients, and attach Web pages or files through Messenger's Compose window.

Click in the To: field to enter a recipient. To enter multiple recipients, press Enter after typing in an email address. Next, click in the Subject: field, and enter a subject. If you want to send an attachment with the message, click the Attach button in the compose window's menu bar, or select the File menu and the Attach menu item. Click your mouse in the blank area of the Compose window (below the formatting bar), and type in a message. When you finish, you can save the message as a draft, spellcheck the message, or send the message by clicking on the Send Now button.

Subscribing to Mailing Lists

When you feel confident that your mail system is working, you might want to subscribe to a mailing list. Mailing lists are handled by automatic mail servers and work by relaying messages generated to all members of a mailing list. One smart way to subscribe to mailing lists is to sign up for a digest version in which the day's message traffic is condensed into a mailing once or twice a day.

You can find out more about mailing lists by browsing to the following:

`http://www.lsoft.com/lists/listref.html`

Chances are that you can find a mailing list (the preceding site enables you to search more than 21,000 of the 135,000 available lists at the time of this writing) of interest to you. Have fun!

> To participate in discussions about OpenLinux using email and to exchange information with other OpenLinux users, send a message to `majordomo@rim.caldera.com` with the following line in the body of the message:
>
> **subscribe caldera-users youremailaddress@yourisp.com**
>
> An electronic mail message asks you to confirm your subscription. Reply to the message according to its directions. For more information about this service, send a message to `majordomo@rim.caldera.com` with the word **help** in the body of the message. You receive a reply with lots of details about using Caldera's mailing lists. For the digest version of Caldera's OpenLinux list, send a message to `majordomo@rim.caldera.com` with the following line in the body of the message:
>
> **subscribe caldera-users-digest youremailaddress@yourisp.com**

Configuring `procmail` and Writing Recipes to Fight Spam

NEW TERM We're all used to getting junk mail or telemarketing calls. Day after day, we receive offers for credit cards, home equity loans, new long-distance service, or great deals on prime cuts of pot roast at the local food market. You can do something about unwanted postal mail, junk faxes, and telemarketing calls, but there's no current nationwide regulation regarding junk email, otherwise known as *SPAM* (not to be confused with the famous canned meat product).

> Fortunately, many State's Attorney General offices around the United States are heeding the hue and cry against spammers, or junk emailers. Some states, such as California, now have civil penalties that are enforced against these bonehead spammers. This type of action is long overdue!

NEW TERM You can, however, use procmail, which is found under the /usr/bin directory, to filter your incoming mail. You need to create a directory, create several files, write a small script, and customize how your incoming mail is handled by writing short filters, or procmail recipes. It only takes you a minute or so to set up your system to organize incoming mail and dispose of junk mail.

The first step is to create a text file, called .procmailrc, in your home directory. Then, type in the following, specifying the name of your mail directory (if you use pine, the directory is mail), the location of the .procmail directory (which you'll soon create), and the name of your procmail filter file:

```
MAILDIR=$HOME/mail
PMDIR=$HOME/.procmail
INCLUDERC=$HOME/.procmail/rc.mailfilter
```

Save this file. Next, create a text file called .forward in your home directory. This file needs to contain the following line:

```
"|IFS=' ' && exec /usr/bin/procmail -f- || exit 75 #username"
```

This command line controls procmail, and you should use your username instead of "username." Now, make your .forward file world readable and your home directory world searchable with the chmod command. See the following example (making sure you're in your home directory):

```
# chmod 644 .forward
# chmod a+x .
```

You're almost done. Now, with the mkdir command, create a directory called .procmail, change directory into it, and create a text file called rc.mailfilter.

This file is to contain your procmail filters, or recipes. Although these recipes can be extremely complex (so complex, in fact, that you can write your own mail delivery service), this section presents simple recipes to get you started.

First, examine a sample message's mail headers (which contain the From:, To:, or Subject: lines). The British MG sports cars digest has the following subject line in each message:

```
Subject: mgs@autox.team.net digest #905 Mon Nov 17 10:09:07 MST 1997
```

Each digest message can contain almost 100,000 characters and is sent twice a day, so it is nice to have all these digests go into their own mail folder, which you can call mgdigest. To do this, you enter the following line in rc.mailfilter:

```
:0:
*^Subject:.*digest
mgdigest
```

11

This small recipe saves any incoming message with a subject line containing the word digest into a mail file called mgdigest in your mail program's mail directory (if you subscribe to other digests, such as Caldera's, you need to create separate recipes with more specific Subject line criteria). Note that you don't have to create this mail file yourself. It is created for you when you first retrieve mail and procmail finds a match. You can also use another recipe to have all mail files from your friends saved to a specific folder, for example:

```
:0:
*^From:.*aol.com
AOL
```

"Okay," you're asking, "but what about junk email?" Well, you know what you want to do with junk email—trash it! For Linux users, there's a special place to which you can send junk email: the old bit bucket, /dev/null. So if you get an unwanted message from a place like hotlips4u.com, you can send this type of garbage to the boneyard with the following:

```
:0:
^From:.*hotlips4u.com
/dev/null
```

Junk email is usually easily recognized because the message contains some form of clever subject line to interest you. Other clues include that you never requested the information in the message or that the sender, receiver, or reply-to sections of the message are forged (this is unethical and fraudulent behavior). Never reply to junk email, even if the mail contains a message such as "To never receive this message again, reply to bonehead@ spammers.com with a message containing the word UNSUBSCRIBE in the body of text." This is a trap to verify your email address, and you could end up receiving even more junk mail!

The mail message isn't stored on your hard drive, and you don't have to bother with any mail from that address again. Using this approach is simplistic, however, and if you get a lot of junk mail, you might want to experiment with more complex recipes that can filter out everything except people with whom you want to exchange mail.

If you want to add some more features to your procmail service, read the procmailrc manual page. For a great selection of procmail recipes, see the procmailex manual page, which details numerous examples, ranging from simple to complex.

Want more information about procmail, writing procmail recipes, and filtering your mail? Look for Nancy McGough's Filtering Mail FAQ, which is posted regularly to the comp.mail.misc, comp.mail.elm, comp.mail.pine, and other newsgroups. Reading news from Usenet also happens to be the next hour's subject!

Summary

This hour introduced you to just several of the electronic mail programs available for OpenLinux. You can find these programs, and many others, available on this book's CD-ROM.

Q&A

Q When I try retrieving mail from my ISP, fetchmail reports an error! What's going on?

A Make sure that you specified the correct protocol with fetchmail to match your ISP's mail server protocol. Make sure that sendmail is running. Also, make sure that you use the latest version of fetchmail. For additional troubleshooting information, see the fetchmail FAQ under the /usr/doc/fetchmail directory.

Q I want to receive mail from a Microsoft Exchange server or through my CompuServe account. How do I do this?

A See the fetchmail FAQ under the /usr/doc/fetchmail directory. There are tips and tricks you can use to get your mail and traps to avoid during your OpenLinux PPP sessions.

Q I've set fetchmail to retrieve mail periodically from my ISP. How can I tell if mail has been received?

A There are many different mail notification programs included with OpenLinux. Some work with the console, whereas others only function during X11 sessions. See the newmail or biff man pages to get started. (Others are listed in the table at the beginning of this hour)

Q When I use fetchmail, it reports that the "connection failed" and "failed: temporary name server error." What's going on?

A You must first establish a PPP connection with your ISP. Also make sure that you correctly entered the name of your ISP's mail server in your .fetchmail rc file.

11

Exercises

1. Experiment with different mail programs, such as xmh, mutt, or xfmail. How are these programs different? What do you like or not like about these programs?

2. Create different procmail recipes to organize or filter your incoming mail. Save all junk email in a folder called spam, and then later sort through the mail and forward pertinent copies to the appropriate State Attorney General's office with a complaint.

Hour 12

Configuring Internet News

This hour introduces you to Usenet news and shows you how to set up and use the tin, slrn, and K Desktop Environment's krn newsreader programs and the Discussions component of Netscape Communicator to read Usenet news during your PPP connection. Reading news can be an endless source of amusement, help, and even frustration (especially if the "signal-to-noise" ratio is low).

Usenet is an international network of computers around the world that share news and mail. Originally developed by Tom Truscott and James Ellis in 1979, Usenet was a collection of software that provided bulletin-board style communication between two university computer systems in North Carolina. In 10 years, Usenet grew to 10,000 computer systems, and although Usenet was originally started to support computer questions and answers, the number of different newsgroups, or discussion areas, grew to nearly 1,000 in the late 1980s.

Usenet newsgroups are organized in a hierarchy, usually by topic or type of discussion. For example, the Linux newsgroups are generally organized under the alt.os, comp.os.linux, or linux topics. Here is a partial list of Linux newsgroups of interest to U.S. readers; there are also many Linux newsgroups in other languages:

```
alt.os.linux.caldera
comp.os.linux.advocacy
comp.os.linux.announce
comp.os.linux.answers
comp.os.linux.hardware
comp.os.linux.misc
comp.os.linux.networking
comp.os.linux.portable
comp.os.linux.setup
comp.os.linux.x
```

This shows that most Linux subjects, such as setup, hardware, or X11, are organized under the topic of computers, operating systems, and Linux. You'll find many other subjects organized the same way. Although there's no guarantee you'll find the exact subject you're looking for, chances are you'll easily find a newsgroup discussing a subject you're interested in.

Today, there are dozens of different Usenet software transport programs and newsreaders and more than 50,000 different newsgroups.

All newsreaders offer these basic functions:

- Subscribing or unsubscribing to newsgroups
- Browsing messages and reading follow-up messages (threads)
- Directly mailing a reply to the author of a message
- Posting a follow-up message to a newsgroup message
- Saving the contents of a message (usually to a directory called News in your home directory)

The tin reader uses a newsgroup index file called .newsrc (whereas slrn uses a file named .jnewsrc), which is normally located in your home directory. These programs do not require the X Window System, so you can read news after connecting to the Internet through your Internet service provider (ISP). The krn newsreader, which requires X11, also uses an index file in your home directory but with a name beginning with .newsrc- followed by the name of your ISP's news server. You'll see how to configure krn later in this hour.

Although you can start both `tin` and `slrn` and tell the programs to retrieve a complete list of active newsgroups from your ISP's news server, you'll waste a lot of time while the programs retrieve the list (nearly 50,000 items at the time of this writing). Instead, create the `.newsrc` file with your favorite text editor and then enter the newsgroups you want to browse:

```
news.announce.newusers:
comp.os.linux.announce:
comp.os.linux.development.apps:
comp.os.linux.development.system:
comp.os.linux.hardware:
comp.os.linux.misc:
comp.os.linux.networking:
comp.os.linux.setup:
comp.os.linux.x:
comp.windows.x:
comp.windows.x.i386unix:
rec.autos.antique:
alt.humor.best-of-usenet:
rec.humor:
```

> Not all ISPs provide access to all existing Usenet newsgroups. Many newsgroups, especially those with prurient content, may be excised or filtered out. If your ISP doesn't offer a specific newsgroup you're interested in, you can use your favorite Web browser (discussed in Hour 13, "Internet Downloading and Browsing") to read news through http://www.dejanews.com.

12

Notice that the list does not have to be in alphabetical order. You must have a colon following the newsgroup. If you type in a newsgroup not supported by your ISP, both `tin` and `slrn` will ignore the name, and both programs will display the list of newsgroups in the same order in which you typed them in the `.newsrc` file.

Developing your own list of newsgroups will speed up your newsreading considerably.

Reading Usenet News with the `tin` Newsreader

Iain Lea's newsreader, `tin`, which is found in the `/usr/bin` directory, is a full-screen newsreader that reads a list of newsgroups from the `.newsrc` in your home directory. The `tin` reader is easy to use (see Figure 12.1). You can navigate through its display with cursor keys, read messages with the Enter key, and reply with a single keystroke.

FIGURE 12.1

The tin newsreader displays newsgroups in a cursor-driven list.

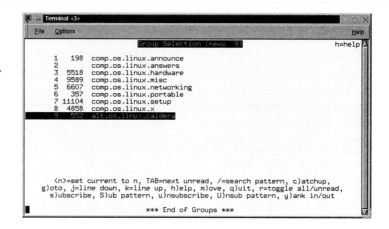

```
 Terminal <3>
 File   Options                                                          Help
                           Group Selection (news   9)              h=help
        1    198   comp.os.linux.announce
        2          comp.os.linux.answers
        3   5518   comp.os.linux.hardware
        4   9589   comp.os.linux.misc
        5   6607   comp.os.linux.networking
        6    357   comp.os.linux.portable
        7  11104   comp.os.linux.setup
        8   4858   comp.os.linux.x
        9    552   alt.os.linux.caldera




        <n>=set current to n, TAB=next unread, /=search pattern, c)atchup,
     g)oto, j=line down, k=line up, h)elp, m)ove, q)uit, r=toggle all/unread,
        s)ubscribe, S)ub pattern, u)nsubscribe, U)nsub pattern, y)ank in/out

                           *** End of Groups ***
```

To read Usenet news with `tin`, you must tell the program the name of your ISP's NNTP, or news server. You should have received this information when you signed up for service. Once you have the name, you can tell `tin` the NNTP server name in at least two ways: by creating an `nntpserver` file under the `/etc` directory, which will only work for `tin`, or by creating an environment variable named `NNTPSERVER`, which will work for `tin` and `slrn`.

> You do not have to create the `nntpserver` file or the `NNTPSERVER` variable if you use the `kppp` client to connect with your ISP. The `kppp` client will create temporary entries in the `hosts` file in your OpenLinux `/etc` directory.

To create the `nntpserver` file, first make sure you're logged in as root. Then, using a text editor (such as `pico`), create a file call `nntpserver` in the `/etc` directory. There's no special format to the file; all you have to do is type the name of the news server:

news.erols.com

Save the file and exit your editor. However, a better way to tell `tin` your ISP's news server is to define an environment variable named `NNTPSERVER`. Creating environment variables is discussed in Hour 6, "Using the Shell." One way to create the `NNTPSERVER` variable, if you always use the `bash` shell, is to log in as root and then edit a file named `profile` in the `/etc` directory. Enter the following into the file, and make sure the `NNTPSERVER` variable is placed in the export statement:

```
NNTPSERVER=news.erols.com
export NNTPSERVER
```

You can then read the variable into your environment with

```
# source /etc/profile
```

After reading the new variable from this file, you can check for the NNTPSERVER variable by piping the output of the env or printenv command through the fgrep command:

```
# printenv | fgrep NNTPSERVER
NNTPSERVER=news.erols.com
```

You can also log out, log back in, and check again. Once defined, the NNTPSERVER variable will work for tin and slrn.

After you have defined your NNTPSERVER, connect with your ISP and call tin with this command line:

```
# tin -nqr
```

The -n option tells the tin program that you want it to only load newsgroups from your .newsrc file, whereas the q option specifies a quick start without checking for any new newsgroups. Finally, the r option tells tin to read your news remotely from your ISP's NNTP server. Once tin reads the groups and gathers any new news, it will display the newsgroups in a list (see Figure 12.1). Read a group's messages by using the Up or Down cursor keys to highlight a newsgroup name and then pressing Enter. The list of messages will appear, as shown in Figure 12.2.

If you don't want to use tin with its -r option but need to retrieve your news from a remote server, use the rtin version of tin with remote retrieval compiled in.

12

FIGURE 12.2

Listing a newsgroup's messages with the tin newsreader.

```
 ⊟ ⊹  Terminal <3>                                                    ⌐ ▢ ✕
 File   Options                                                        Help
               alt.os.linux.caldera (209T(B) 552A OK OH R)        h=help
      129   +    2     4 download                             Markus Zettl
      130   +    2    16 OpenLinux 1.3 and laptop Installation. techie
      131   +          7 Neomagic VGA adapter support.         techie
      132   +    2    10 Boss's Linux Demonstration Box Network Steve Johnston
      133   +    4    12 Installation of Star Office 5.0 on Cal Joel
      134   +         11 Install packages after basic system in Paul Riemerman
      135   +         35 Dell Latitude laptop with Windows and  Extreme Sims
      136   +          6 set up printer                        Martinez's
      137   +          9 Samba & Win '95 printer                Jonathan A. Laub
      138   +         11 lpc problem                           Tom Bozack
      139   +   11    14 HTTPD                                 paul
      140   +    3    26 Ho Ho Ho                              Laura
      141   +          4 C350 LIFEBOOK                         TURBO1010
      142   +         24 Unresolved Symbols in modules          TURBO1010
      143   +         13 OmniBasic Web Site                    Michael L. Smith
      144   +    5     5 About PPP in Caldera Linux             Ntfs

      <n>=set current to n, TAB=next unread, /=search pattern, ^K)ill/select,
   a)uthor search, c)atchup, j=line down, k=line up, K=mark read, l)ist thread,
      |=pipe, m)ail, o=print, q)uit, r=toggle all/unread, s)ave, t)ag, w=post
 ▮
```

NEW TERM To read a message, scroll through the list (using the arrow keys) and press Enter. The message will appear. Although many OpenLinux Usenet readers like to *lurk*, or just read messages, you can reply directly by electronic mail to the person who posted the message by pressing the r key and composing a reply or follow-up to the message and post your comments by pressing the f key. Table 12.1 lists the main `tin` commands.

TABLE 12.1 COMMON `tin` COMMANDS

Action	Command
Backward search through articles	?
Follow up with post (when reading message)	f
Forward search through articles	/
List articles in highlighted group or read message	Enter
Post a new article to current group	W
Quit reading, quit listing, or quit tin	q
Read tin's help	h
Reply by email (when reading message)	r
Save current message to disk	s
Search for article author (in message list)	a
Subscribe to group (in group list)	s
Unsubscribe to group (in group list)	u

You can configure many `tin` settings, such as the default editor to use while posting or replying to messages. Edit the `tinrc` file under the `.tin` directory in your home directory. For other details about this newsreader, read the `tin` manual page.

Reading Usenet News with the `slrn` Newsreader

The `slrn` newsreader, by John E. Davis, in the `/usr/bin` directory, is a newsreader like `tin`. However, `slrn` has some nifty features not supported by the `tin` program:

- Message headers and messages are displayed at the same time.
- Extensive custom colors for different parts of the display and messages are available.
- Mouse-cursor–aware mode.
- Different NNTP servers can be specified on the command line.

Figure 12.3 shows the slrn screen.

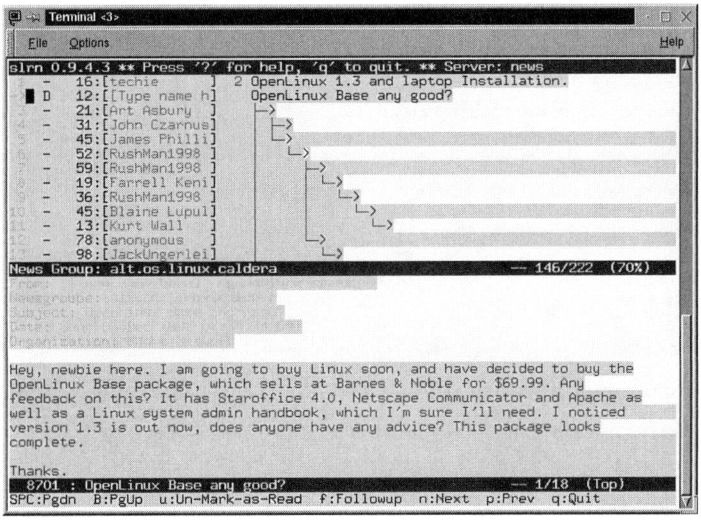

FIGURE 12.3

*The slrn newsreader
features mouse-aware
menus and split-screen
viewing of messages
and message contents.*

The slrn program features a split display once you're reading messages in a newsgroup. You can also run slrn without specifying an NNTPSERVER variable with the -h command-line option:

```
# slrn -h news.staffnet.com
```

You'll also be able to browse quickly once you learn most of its keystroke commands, which are listed in Table 12.2.

12

> Here's a tip on an undocumented feature you won't find in the slrn manual page: You can scroll up and down through messages by using the left or right mouse buttons of your mouse. Use slrn in a menu-driven mode by enabling mouse support. This is handy if you run slrn in an xterm or rxvt window under X11.

TABLE 12.2   COMMON slrn COMMANDS

Action	Command
Close current article	h
Follow-up post to current article	f
Forward copy of article by email	F
Go to next newsgroup	N
Mark all articles in group (or message list) as read	c
Post article to current group	p
Quit reading articles (in current group)	q
Quit slrn (from group list)	q
Read the next article in current group	n
Reply by email to current article	r
Save current article	o
Search for article (in message list)	/
Search for newsgroup name (in group list)	/
Subscribe to current group	s
Unsubscribe from current group	u

When you start slrn, the program looks under the /var/lib/slrn directory for a file called slrn.rc, which contains system-wide defaults for the program. You should copy this program as .slrnrc to your home directory and make your changes to this file. Although there are many different customizations you can perform, I cover a few here to get you started.

First, look for the hostname, username, realname, and replyto entries in the file. These entries look something like

```
%hostame "YOUR.HOSTNAME"
%set username "jd"
%set realname "John Doe"
%set replyto  "jd@somthing.com"
```

Change these entries to your username, your real name, and your email address:

```
hostname "erols.com"
set username "bball_NO_SPAM"
set realname "William Ball"
set replyto  "bballREMOVE_TO_REPLY@erols.com"
```

Note that you must remove the percent character (%) from the beginning of each of these lines to enable the options. I have also included the _NO_SPAM and REMOVE_TO_REPLY phrases in the username and replyto entries. These are to foil those insidious, nefarious, and insipid computer users who use "harvesting" software to extract email addresses and build spam lists from Usenet postings.

> Using an invalid but easily correctable email address in newsgroup posting (such as bball@_ALL_SPAMMERS_SHOULD_BE_HANGED_erols.com) is one way to protect yourself against ending up in a junk emailer's spam list. See Hour 11, "Configuring Internet Email" to see how to automatically trash any incoming junk mail. Fortunately, a number of state governments in the United States, such as California, now have a $500 penalty for each piece of unwanted junk email. I hope other states will follow with similar legislation to help stem this electronic plague.

To enable mouse support, also look in your .slrnrc file for

```
% Enable xterm mouse support: 1 to enable, 0 to disable
  set mouse 0
```

Change set mouse 0 to set mouse 1 to enable menu- and mouse-driven modes in slrn. Yet another change you might want to make concerns how slrn displays messages and menus. Look for the color section of the .slrnrc file:

```
%----------------------------------------------------------
% Colors
%----------------------------------------------------------
color header_number    "black"     "white"
color header_name      "black"     "white"
color normal           "black"     "white"
color error            "red"       "white"
color status           "yellow"    "blue"
color group            "blue"      "white"
color article          "blue"      "white"
color cursor           "black"     "white"
color author           "blue"      "white"
color subject          "black"     "white"
color headers          "black"     "white"
color menu             "yellow"    "blue"
color menu_press       "blue"      "yellow"
color tree             "red"       "white"
color quotes           "red"       "white"
color thread_number    "blue"      "white"
color high_score       "red"       "white"
color signature        "red"       "white"
color description      "blue"      "white"
color tilde            "black"     "white"
```

12

These lines are in the format of display item, foreground color, and background color. According to the slrn manual page, these colors can be

black	gray
red	brightred
green	brightgreen
brown	yellow
blue	brightblue
magenta	brightmagenta
cyan	brightcyan
lightgray	white

With a little bit of work, you can devise your own display.

Make your changes and then save the file. To use color during your newsreading sessions, start slrn with its -C or color option:

```
# slrn -C
```

When slrn starts, you'll have a color display and you can use your mouse to click menu items at the top of the screen, click a newsgroup to see lists of messages, or click a message in a message list to read the message.

The slrn newsreader is a flexible, customizable program that will work in black-and-white or color, with or without X11, and with the keyboard and your mouse.

Reading Usenet News with the krn Client

The krn client, included with KDE, is a graphical interface to reading Usenet news. You must run X11 in order to use the program (but you don't have to use KDE). If you use KDE for your X11 sessions, start krn by clicking the Application Starter button on your desktop's panel, selecting the Internet menu item, and then clicking the News client item. If you use some other window manager, you can start krn from the command line of a terminal window like this:

```
# krn &
```

After you press Enter, the krn main dialog will appear, as shown in Figure 12.4.

To configure krn, select the Options menu and then click Identity. The identity dialog will appear, as shown in Figure 12.5. Enter your real name, your email address (if you want, use the previous method for slrn to mask your address from spammers), and your Organization. (This field cannot be left empty, so you can use the default hyphen (-) entry.) This information will be used when you reply by email or follow up to a newsgroup posting. When finished, click OK to save your settings.

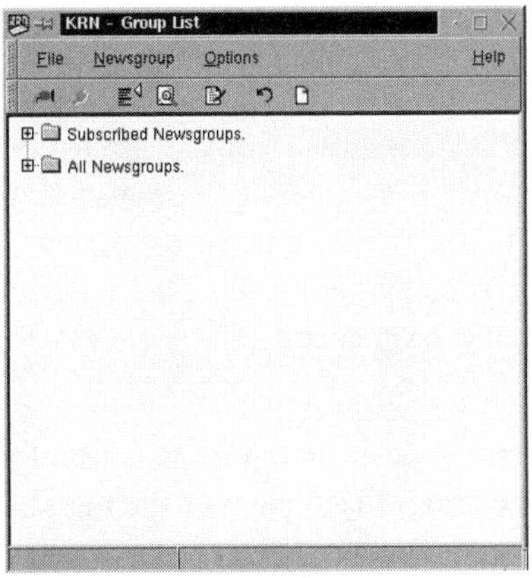

FIGURE 12.4

The krn newsreader features the familiar KDE graphical interface with a menu bar, buttons, and scrolling window.

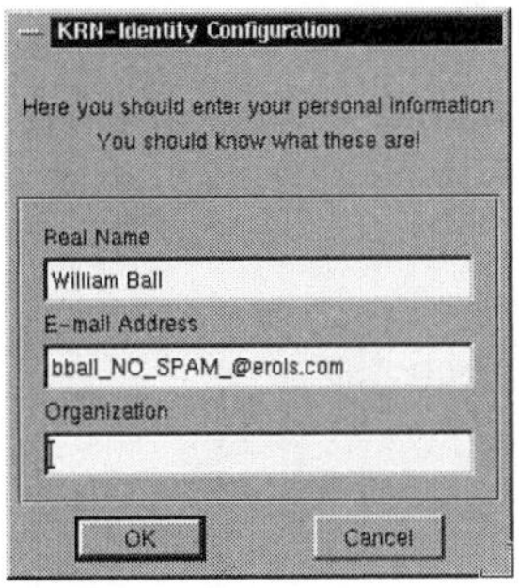

FIGURE 12.5

The krn identity dialog sets your username and email address.

Next, open the Options menu and click NNTP Options. In the dialog, shown in Figure 12.6, type the name of your ISP's mail server. Then, click in the NNTP Server field and type the name of your ISP's news server. If you want krn to connect to your ISP's news server as soon as it starts, select the appropriate option. If you need a username or password to access your ISP's news server, enter the correct username and password. These settings are used when krn connects to your news server and when you email a reply to a Usenet post. When finished, click OK to save your settings.

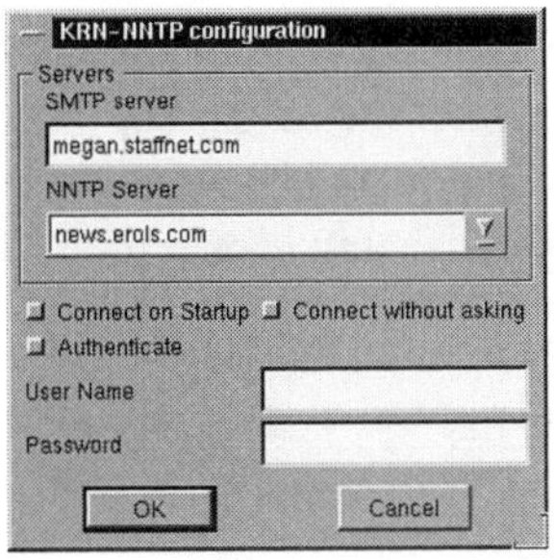

FIGURE 12.6

The krn NNTP options dialog is where you set access options for email and news service when newsreading.

12

You can set other options, such as how long you want to hold onto messages or how to print, through other menu items under the Options menu.

The main krn dialog features a row of buttons you can use to connect to or disconnect from your news server, list or find groups, subscribe or unsubscribe to groups, check for unread articles, or post new articles. To get an initial list of newsgroups from your ISP, click the Get list of active groups button (left of the Find group button with the small magnifying glass). krn will then ask whether it can connect to your ISP's news server. Click OK.

This operation might take several minutes as krn builds a list of newsgroups from your server. You'll see the size of the group file along with the message "Getting active list from server" at the bottom of krn's window. When krn is finished, click the small plus sign (+) to the left of the All newsgroups folder.

The folder will open and list each top hierarchy of Usenet's newsgroups as another series of folders. Scroll through the list, and continue to click open folders until you reach a desired newsgroup, such as alt.os.linux.caldera. The newsgroup will appear, as shown in Figure 12.7.

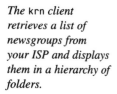

FIGURE 12.7

The krn *client retrieves a list of newsgroups from your ISP and displays them in a hierarchy of folders.*

Click and highlight a newsgroup name and then press the Subscribe button from krn's menu bar. The small, blank document icon of the newsgroup will change to a document with a small quill attached. Repeat this step to build your list of subscribed newsgroups. The next time you start krn, your newsgroups will appear in the Subscribed folder.

To retrieve all available messages in the newsgroup, double-click the newsgroup name. The krn main newsreading window will appear after all unread messages have been retrieved and will show a list of articles (messages). If you click an article, its text will appear in the lower half of the newsreading window, as shown in Figure 12.8.

Figure 12.8

The krn *newsreading window features scroll bars and a point-and-click interface for reading, replying to, or following up on newsgroup articles.*

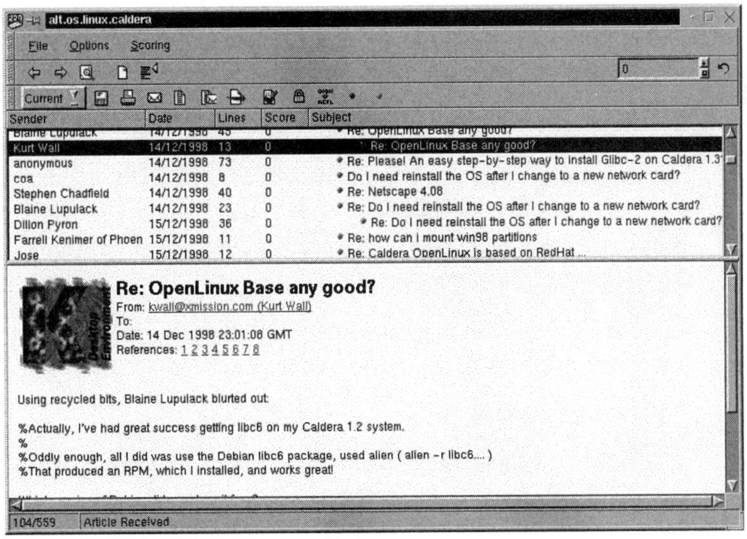

The numerous buttons in the window's menu bar let you

- Navigate through the newsgroup's articles
- Search for subjects
- Print
- Save to disk
- Reply to by email
- Follow up with a post
- Reply and follow up
- Forward by email
- Mark as read or unread

Click your mouse button on the Sender, Date, Lines, or Subject column headings to sort the article list.

12

Reading Usenet News with Netscape Discussions

Without a doubt, one of the most popular Internet software suites for OpenLinux is Netscape Communicator. You can use the Netscape Discussions component of Communicator to read Usenet news. If you're using KDE, click the Netscape icon in your desktop's panel to start Netscape, and then select the Communicator menu and click the Collabra Discussions menu item.

You can also start Netscape and jump right into Discussions from the command line of a terminal window by using the netscape command and the -news option:

```
# netscape -news &
```

After you press Enter, the Discussions window will appear. It looks similar to Netscape's Messenger, as shown in Figure 12.9.

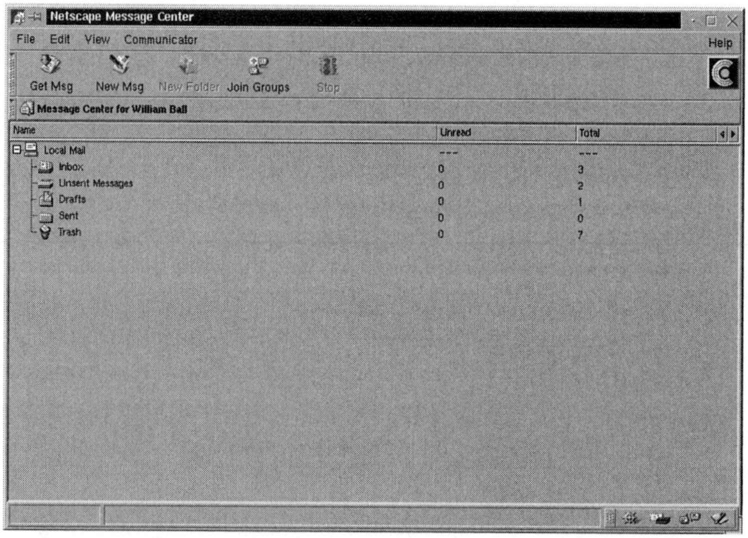

FIGURE 12.9

Before configuration to read Usenet news, Netscape Discussions looks very similar to Netscape's Messenger, or email window.

To configure Discussions to read news, first Open the Preferences menu and then click Preferences. Next, in the dialog shown in Figure 12.10, click the Groups Server under the Mail and Groups list item. Type the name of your ISP's news server, and specify the directory you'd like to use to save newsgroups messages. When finished, click OK.

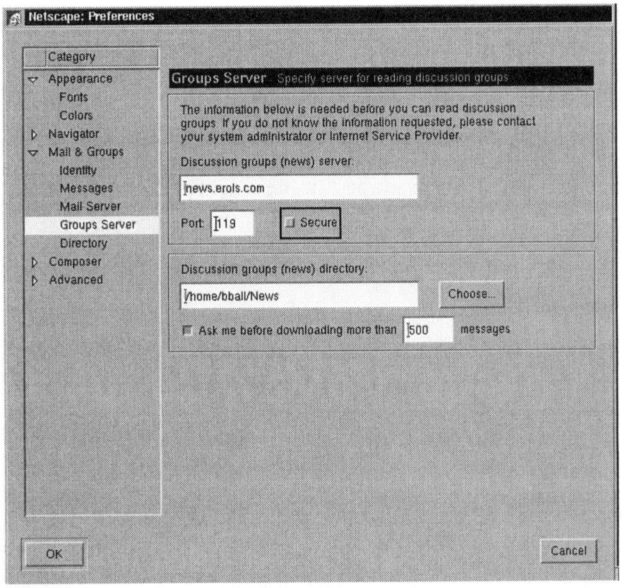

FIGURE 12.10

The Preferences dialog is where you set the name of your ISP's news server and your news directory.

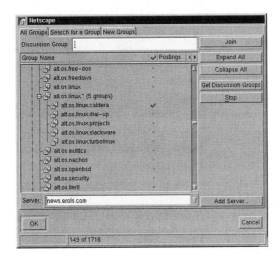

You'll be returned to the Discussions window. To get a list of newsgroups from your ISP, click the Join Groups button in the window's menu bar. A newsgroup dialog will appear, as shown in Figure 12.11. Make sure your ISP's news server is selected at the bottom of the dialog and then click the Get Discussion Groups button.

FIGURE 12.11

The newsgroup dialog is used to retrieve and subscribe to various Usenet newsgroups.

Discussions will retrieve the list of newsgroups available from your ISP. This operation, similar to that for krn, might take some time. When Discussions finishes, you'll see a list of newsgroups, sorted by hierarchy. Scroll through the list and open folders until you reach a newsgroup you like. Next, click the newsgroup and then click the Join button to subscribe. A small blue checkmark will appear to right of the newsgroup name. Repeat this step until you have subscribed to the desired number of groups. When finished, click the OK button.

> Instead of clicking the Join button, you can click the tiny ball to the right of each newsgroup name to make the checkmark appear and subscribe to the group.

You're returned to the main Discussions window. Click the small plus sign (+) next to the name of your ISP's news server in the list of folders in the window. The list of your subscribed (joined) groups will appear. To retrieve articles for a newsgroup, double-click the newsgroup's name in the list. Discussions will launch the newsreading window with the list of articles for the group, as shown in Figure 12.12.

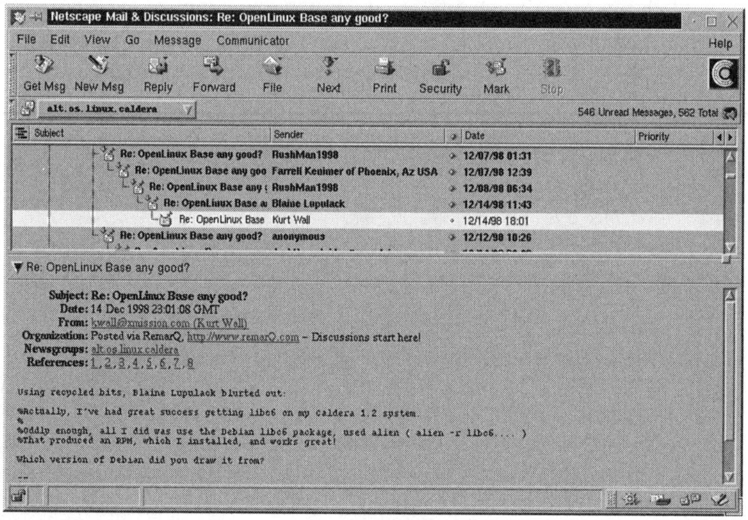

FIGURE 12.12

The Discussions news-reading window lists each newsgroups articles in a scrolling list.

Use the buttons on the newsreading window's menu bar during your group session.

> To quickly jump to a list of articles for a different newsgroup, click the drop-down menu at the current newsgroup's name (as shown in Figure 12.12) and select a new group.

Before Posting to a Usenet Group

You should keep in mind several things when you feel tempted to post a message to a Usenet newsgroup. First, it's much better to lurk for a while before posting. Chances are that you'll find the answers you need before you post a message. Make sure you're posting to the right newsgroup or newsgroups. Check to make sure you're not cross-posting, or sending messages that may be off topic in other groups. Make sure you ask the right question in the right newsgroup. Woe be to the unfortunate miscreant who asks for Windows 98 advice in `comp.os.windows`! At best, you'll be ignored, and at the worst, you'll be flamed unmercifully and termed a *luser* (a user who's a loser).

Keep in mind that Usenet is worldwide. Your comments, opinions, jokes, and observations might not be welcome, funny, or relevant to other members of the Usenet community. What is true in the United States might not be true in other countries.

If you're thinking about advertising your business or service in Usenet newsgroups, post your "advertisement" in the proper newsgroup (for example, if you have something to sell). Spamming newsgroups with your ads, in this author's opinion, should be cause for retribution worse than social ostracism. There are more than one or two of the 50,000-plus newsgroups where you can post messages to sell stuff.

Asking for help? You'll have much better success in getting help from other people if your subject line is a good summary of your request:

`Subj: Help! How do I recover my Linux filesystem?`

Finally, one of the things you should know about Usenet is that there are, for all practical purposes, no rules. You'll converse with all kinds of people from countries all over the world. Some people are nice, and others are, well, not so nice. The good news is that the good-hearted newsgroup posters are in the majority.

Every new Usenet person should subscribe to `news.announce.newusers`. This newsgroup contains FAQs, etiquette guidelines, and handy tips to help you find answers. You'll read about the history of Usenet and find interesting statistics and a copy of the latest, complete listing of newsgroups.

Summary

This hour introduced four different Usenet newsreaders for OpenLinux. As you probably learned, each program allows you to easily read news but offers different features and requires a different configuration. Reading Usenet news is an addictive pastime that can offer great rewards when you're looking for information or troubleshooting tips about nearly any subject.

Q&A

Q What other newsreaders are included on my OpenLinux CD-ROM?

A You'll find several other newsreaders for the console or the X Window System installed with OpenLinux. Try running the knews, trn, nn, or xrn readers from the command line of a terminal window. These programs are also capable newsreaders (although perhaps not as popular with the Linux crowd as with users of other variants of the UNIX operating system).

Q Are there any newsreading utilities included with OpenLinux?

A Yes. See the pnews, lmove, lpost, newsetup, and newsgroups commands.

Q I'd like to read my news articles after closing down my PPP connection with my ISP. Is there a program I can use to do this?

A Use the suck command. This program will download articles from your ISP and save the news feed according to the command line you specify, such as to a single file, separate files, or indexed file format suitable for other newsreaders. See the suck man page for details.

Q Is it true that I can use the pine email program to read Usenet news?

A Yes! The pine program is almost two programs in one. Although most people will use pine primarily as a mail handler, pine can be an efficient way to read news and can save you disk space if you don't have much room on your hard drive for other programs (especially if you're using a laptop computer). Specify your ISP's news server in the .pinerc file in your home directory or through pine's setup and config commands. To read news, make sure you're connected to your ISP and then run pine. Move to the folder list view, press the Enter key, and then move down to the news collection expanded list and press the Enter key.

Exercises

1. Use krn's search for newsgroup function to find a newsgroup about a topic when reading news. Which button in krn's window is used to search for a newsgroup?

2. Find out how many newsgroups your ISP supports. Are all newsgroups available through your service? Were any limitations on the number of groups spelled out in your service contract?

3. Editing a text list of groups (such as .jnewsrc or .newsrc) for reading news is a handy way to limit the availability of newsgroups for the younger crowd. How else can you limit or protect this list from being modified?

12

HOUR 13

Internet Downloading and Browsing

This hour introduces you to programs you use to get information and programs from the Internet. I assume that you are signed up with an Internet Service Provider (ISP) and that you configured your OpenLinux system to start and stop Point-To-Point Protocol network connections.

 If you already have an account with a local ISP but have not configured your Linux system to connect to the Internet, read Hour 10, "Connecting to the Internet," for instructions.

I first introduce you to two Internet file transfer programs and then cover some of the many World Wide Web browsers you can find for Linux.

Using File Transfer Protocol Programs to Get Files

NEW TERM   There are several ways to retrieve files from other computers on the Internet. You
             can use email or a Web browser, but if you're interested in just getting files into
your computer, you can use the ftp (file transfer) program. The ftp program is one of
the oldest programs to support the standard *File Transfer Protocol*, or FTP, and was the
original program designed to transfer files. The FTP protocol enables you to send and
receive files interactively with get and put commands.

The next section shows you how to use two FTP transfer programs, ftp and ncftp.

Retrieving Files with the ftp Command

The ftp command, found under the /usr/bin directory, has five different command-line
options but is most often used with a hostname, or name of a remote computer, for
example:

```
# ftp ftp.mcp.com
```

This command line specifies that you want to connect to the ftp server at Macmillan
Publishing. You don't have to specify a hostname on the command line because you can
run the ftp program interactively, repeatedly connecting to and disconnecting from different computers. The ftp command has more than 70 different built-in commands,
including a help facility. This hour doesn't cover all the different commands, but you can
get more information about these commands by reading the ftp program's manual page
or by using the built-in help command.

Some of the commands you're most likely to use, especially when all you want to do is
retrieve some programs or source code from Linux sites, are the following:

  !—Prompts for and runs a shell command. This is a handy way to view the contents
  of files, delete files you download, or check on how much hard drive space you have
  left.

  ascii—Downloads any specified files in text form.

  binary—Downloads any specified files in binary form. You must use this command
  before downloading most compressed Linux files.

  bye—Closes any open connection and exits the ftp program.

  cd —Changes directories, for example:

```
> cd ..
```

`close`—Closes the current connection.

`get`—Downloads a specific file from the current directory to your current directory, for example:

```
> get killbarney.tgz
```

`ls` —Lists files or directories in the current directory.

`mget`—Downloads several files, one after another, that match a specified pattern, for example:

```
> mget kill*.tgz
```

`open`—Opens a connection to a specified host, for example:

```
> open ftp.mcp.com
```

`prompt`—Toggles interactive prompting (such as the use of y or n when downloading multiple files).

For example, to run the `ftp` command interactively, all you have to do is type the following:

```
# ftp
ftp> help
Commands may be abbreviated.  Commands are:
```

!	debug	mdir	sendport	site
$	dir	mget	put	size
account	disconnect	mkdir	pwd	status
append	exit	mls	quit	struct
ascii	form	mode	quote	system
bell	get	modtime	recv	sunique
binary	glob	mput	reget	tenex
bye	hash	newer	rstatus	tick
case	help	nmap	rhelp	trace
cd	idle	nlist	rename	type
cdup	image	ntrans	reset	user
chmod	lcd	open	restart	umask
close	ls	prompt	rmdir	verbose
cr	macdef	passive	runique	?
delete	mdelete	proxy	send	

```
ftp> help exit
exit            terminate ftp session and exit
ftp> help bye
bye             terminate ftp session and exit
ftp> bye
#
```

13

> If you have a shell or login account with your ISP, you can run into problems when downloading large files if your ISP enforces disk quotas, which limit the amount information that can be stored in a user's directory. See if your ISP lets you first change the directory to a /tmp directory if using ftp, and then open a connection to download any large files. The /tmp directory is later cleaned out by any housekeeping crontab routines to make more storage room, and you can download large files without hitting hard limits on quotas.

To demonstrate the ftp program in action, I show you a sample session used to download a compressed file from the University of North Carolina's famous Linux repository (formerly known as sunsite, but now named MetaLab):

```
# ftp ftp.metalab.unc.edu
Connected to helios.metalab.unc.edu.
220-                   Welcome to UNC's MetaLab ftp archives!
220-             (at the site formerly known as sunsite.unc.edu)
220-
220-You can access this archive via http with the same URL.
220-
220-example:    ftp://metalab.unc.edu/pub/Linux/ becomes
220-            http://metalab.unc.edu/pub/Linux/
220-
220-For more information about services offered by MetaLab,
220-go to http://metalab.unc.edu
220-
220-WE'RE BACK TO USING WUFTPD.
220-You can still get tarred directories if you issue the following
➥command:
220-    get dirname.tar
220-You can also get gzipped or compressed tarred directories by
➥ following
220-the .tar with .gz or .Z, respectively.
220-
220-Have any suggestions or questions? Email ftpkeeper@metalab.unc.edu.
220-
220 helios.oit.unc.edu FTP server (Version wu-2.4.2-academ[BETA-13](6)
➥Thu Jul 1
7 16:22:52 EDT 1997) ready.
Name (ftp.metalab.unc.edu:bball): anonymous
331 Guest login ok, send your complete e-mail address as password.
Password:
230 Guest login ok, access restrictions apply.
Remote system type is UNIX.
Using binary mode to transfer files.
ftp> cd pub/Linux
```

```
250-README for
250-
250-Linux: A copylefted Unix-like operating system for 80[3456]86,
250-      DEC Alpha, Sun SPARC, Motorola 68k, PowerPC/PowerMac,
250-      ARM, Mips R[3,4]x00, Fujitsu AP/1000+ and more to come.
250-
250-Mirrors are better!  Look at the MIRRORS file to find one near you.
250-
250-Email linuxguys@sunsite.unc.edu with comments/complaints about this
➥archive.
250-
250-Please see HINTS for information on how to get most effective use
➥out of
250-this archive.  HINTS was last updated on 17 March 1997.
250-
250 CWD command successful.
ftp> cd apps
250-README for /apps
250-
250-What you'll find here: large useful packages and applications for
➥Linux
250-
250-
250 CWD command successful.
ftp> ls
200 PORT command successful.
150 Opening ASCII mode data connection for /bin/ls.
total 41
-rw-rw-r--    1 347      1002          1573 Jul 04  1998 !INDEX
-rw-rw-r--    1 347      1002          2697 Jul 04  1998 !INDEX.html
-rw-rw-r--    1 347      1002          2823 Jul 04  1998 !INDEX.short.
➥html
drwxrwsr-x   26 347      1002           512 Jul 19  1998 .
drwxrwsr-x   25 67       1002          1024 Jan 26 05:28 ..
drwxrwsr-x    2 347      1002           512 Mar 25  1997 MGR
-rw-rw-r--    1 347      1002            91 Jul 04  1998 README
drwxrwsr-x    2 347      1002           512 Sep 03 21:15 appliance
drwxrwsr-x    2 347      1002           512 Dec 27 18:59 cai
drwxrwsr-x    2 347      1002           512 Dec 24 19:44 chinese
drwxrwsr-x    4 347      1002          2560 Jan 25 22:44 circuits
drwxrwsr-x    2 347      1002           512 Apr 01  1997 conferencing
drwxrwsr-x    2 347      1002          1024 Nov 27 18:49 crypto
drwxrwsr-x   12 347      1002           512 Jul 04  1998 database
drwxrwsr-x    4 347      1002           512 Jan 25 21:14 doctools
drwxrwsr-x    7 347      1002           512 Mar 28  1998 editors
drwxrwsr-x    6 347      1002           512 Jul 15  1998 financial
drwxrwsr-x   13 347      1002           512 Jan 25 22:47 graphics
drwxrwsr-x    8 347      1002          1024 Sep 27 20:03 ham
drwxrwsr-x    7 347      1002          1024 Oct 20 20:34 math
drwxrwsr-x    2 347      1002          1536 Jan 25 22:55 misc
drwxrwxr-x    2 347      1002           512 Oct 22 19:10 office
```

13

```
drwxrwsr-x    2 347        1002              1024 Jan 22 21:05 religion
drwxrwsr-x    4 347        1002              1024 Dec 08 20:31 reminder
drwxrwsr-x    7 347        1002               512 Mar 28  1997 serialcomm
drwxrwsr-x   19 347        1002              1536 Jan 11 15:47 sound
drwxrwxr-x    6 347        1002              1536 Nov 19 21:37 tex
drwxrwsr-x    2 347        1002              2048 Jan 25 21:02 video
drwxrwsr-x    6 347        1002               512 Jul 09  1998 wp
drwxrwsr-x   13 347        1002               512 May 19  1997 www
226 Transfer complete.
ftp> cd appliance
250-README for apps/appliance
250-
250-What you'll find here: household appliance control
250-
250-
250 CWD command successful.
ftp> ls
200 PORT command successful.
150 Opening ASCII mode data connection for /bin/ls.
total 250
-rw-rw-r--    1 347        1002               634 Sep 03 21:15 !INDEX
-rw-rw-r--    1 347        1002              2454 Sep 03 21:15 !INDEX.html
-rw-rw-r--    1 347        1002              1197 Sep 03 21:15 !INDEX.short.
➡html
drwxrwsr-x    2 347        1002               512 Sep 03 21:15 .
drwxrwsr-x   26 347        1002               512 Jul 19  1998 ..
-rw-rw-r--    1 347        1002                79 Sep 03 21:15 README
-rw-rw-r--    1 754        1002               861 Aug 24 05:05 alarm-0.20b.lsm
-rw-rw-r--    1 754        1002              6559 Aug 24 05:05 alarm-0.20b.tar.gz
-rw-rw-r--    1 347        1002             14895 Aug 25  1997 cheaplightswitch
   ➡ -1.0.tgz
-rw-rw-r--    1 347        1002               666 Aug 25  1997 cheaplightswitch.
➡lsm
-rw-rw-r--    1 347        1002             29617 May 19  1998 irx-v0.1.tgz
-rw-rw-r--    1 347        1002               691 May 19  1998 irx.lsm
-rw-rw-r--    1 347        1002               469 Jun 16  1998 netlitng.lsm
-rw-rw-r--    1 347        1002             28081 Jun 16  1998 netlitng.tgz
-rw-rw-r--    1 347        1002              1007 Jul 14  1997 twd-0.2.lsm
-rw-rw-r--    1 347        1002             21903 Jul 14  1997 twd-0.2.tgz
-rw-rw-r--    1 347        1002               580 Jan 22  1996 x-automate
➡-1.00.lsm
-rw-rw-r--    1 347        1002            110006 Jan 23  1996 x-automate
➡-1.00.tgz
-rw-rw-r--    1 347        1002              1290 Mar 07  1997 x10-amh-v1.06.lsm
-rw-rw-r--    1 347        1002             12168 Mar 07  1997 x10-amh-v1.06.tgz
226 Transfer complete.
ftp> binary
200 Type set to I.
ftp> get netlitng.tgz
local: netlitng.tgz remote: netlitng.tgz
200 PORT command successful.
```

```
150 Opening BINARY mode data connection for netlitng.tgz (28081 bytes).
226 Transfer complete.
28081 bytes received in 8.35 secs (3.3 Kbytes/sec)
ftp> bye
221 Goodbye.
#
```

The session shows that I specified the ftp server at MetaLab as the host computer I wanted to connect to and retrieve files. By convention, many system administrators create and maintain a user called ftp and a directory called ft to accommodate the distribution of information, software, and software updates.

> An ftp user with a directory under the /home directory exists on your OpenLinux system. This directory (/home/ftp) is where you end up if you log in anonymously. If you log in to your computer with your username and password, you end up in your home directory.

By convention, when you use the ftp program to connect to other computers, you enter your username at the Name: prompt as **anonymous**, followed by a password in the form of a mail address, such as user@somewhere.com.

You can see that after I logged in, I changed the directory to the pub/Linux directory. I then changed to the apps directory and changed directory to the appliance directory. If I had known the full path to the directory I wanted, I could have specified that pathname in a single cd command, for example:

cd pub/Linux/apps/appliance

I then enabled the ftp command's binary transfer mode, retrieved the file netlitng.tgz with the get command, and then logged off and exited the ftp program with the bye command. As you can see, using the ftp command is not hard and is an easy way to retrieve files.

You can also open an anonymous ftp connection to your own computer to demonstrate how ftp works without having an Internet connection available. You can specify the hostname of your computer, which you can get with the hostname command or by using your computer's Internet Protocol address, for example:

```
# hostname
presario.localhost.localdomain
# ftp presario
Connected to presario.localhost.localdomain.
220 presario.localhost.localdomain FTP server (Version wu-2.4.2-academ
➥[BETA-17](1) Wed Aug 19 02:55:52 MST 1998) ready.
```

13

```
Name (presario:bball): anonymous
331 Guest login ok, send your complete e-mail address as password.
Password:
230-Welcome the OpenLinux 1.3 from Caldera Systems, Inc.!
230-
230-
230 Guest login ok, access restrictions apply.
Remote system type is UNIX.
Using binary mode to transfer files.
ftp> ls
200 PORT command successful.
150 Opening ASCII mode data connection for /bin/ls.
total 6
drwxr-xr-x    5 root      root           1024 Jan 11 16:11 .
drwxr-xr-x    5 root      root           1024 Jan 11 16:11 ..
d--x--x--x    2 root      root           1024 Oct 18 14:09 bin
d--x--x--x    2 root      root           1024 Oct 18 14:09 etc
drwxr-sr-x    2 root      ftp            1024 Jan 11 16:11 pub
-rw-r--r--    1 root      ftp              55 Jan 11 16:10 welcome.msg
226 Transfer complete.
ftp> bye
221 Goodbye.
#
```

Note that if you perform an ftp login without an existing username or password, you
end up in an ftp directory. You can also log in to other computers using an assigned
username and password, but for this example, I use my own system and the computer's
host IP address:

```
# ftp 127.0.0.1
Connected to 127.0.0.1.
220 presario.localhost.localdomain FTP server (Version wu-2.4.2-academ
➥ [BETA-17](1) Wed Aug 19 02:55:52 MST 1998) ready.
Name (127.0.0.1:bball): bball
331 Password required for bball.
Password:
230 User bball logged in.
Remote system type is UNIX.
Using binary mode to transfer files.
ftp> ls dos/mp3music
200 PORT command successful.
150 Opening ASCII mode data connection for /bin/ls.
total 40616
drwxr-xr-x    2 bball     users          4096 Jan 24 23:25 .
drwxr-xr-x    8 bball     users          4096 Jan 24 22:27 ..
-rwxr-xr-x    1 bball     users       5041544 Jan 25 00:24
➥Rippingtons-A Place for Lovers.mp3
-rwxr-xr-x    1 bball     users       4341612 Jan 25 00:48
➥Rippingtons-Carnival!.mp3
```

```
-rwxr-xr-x   1 bball    users      5704848 Jan 25 01:15
➥Rippingtons-Highroller.mp3
-rwxr-xr-x   1 bball    users      5480811 Jan 25 00:14
➥Rippingtons-Indian Summer.mp3
-rwxr-xr-x   1 bball    users      5538079 Jan 25 01:02
➥Rippingtons-Moka Java.mp3
-rwxr-xr-x   1 bball    users      5704686 Jan 25 09:55
➥Rippingtons-St. Tropez.mp3
-rwxr-xr-x   1 bball    users      4606027 Jan 25 00:01
➥Rippingtons-Vienna.mp3
-rwxr-xr-x   1 bball    users      5150057 Jan 25 00:48
➥Rippingtons-Weekend in Monaco.mp3
226 Transfer complete.
ftp> bye
221 Goodbye.
#
```

In this example, after logging in with my system username and password, I ended up in my home directory instead of the default ftp directory. I then listed the contents of a folder on another mounted file system (you can't tell from the pathname or the files). If you have an open PPP connection with your ISP and other users know your computer's IP address, you and other users can access your system's files and upload and download files.

Downloading with the ncFTP Program

The ncftp command, found under the /usr/bin directory, is much like the original ftp command but features some unique improvements, such as the following:

- A visual mode with colors
- A status bar with a separate command line and scrolling window
- Visual status of downloading—a progress meter to show elapsed and remaining time for file downloads
- Bookmarks and a bookmark editor, so you can use abbreviated hostnames of computers

Like the ftp command, ncftp also has built-in help. The ncftp command, by Mike Gleason of NCEMRSoft, also sports a number of interesting command-line options. If you know the hostname of the computer and the complete path to a desired file, you can retrieve the file with a single command line, for example:

```
# ncftp -a ftp://ftp.metalab.unc.edu/pub/Linux/apps/appliance/
➥netlitng.tgz
```

```
# nctp -a ftp.metalab.unc.edu/pub/Linux/apps/appliance/netlitng.tgz
```

13

Both command lines connect to the ftp.metalab.unc.edu host, log in anonymously, and then retrieve the file. This is a handy way to retrieve known files from remote computers. These command lines can also be used in shell scripts or combined with pipes to other commands to process the incoming files. You can, for example, automatically translate incoming graphics files and save them in a specified directory:

```
# ncftp -c rsd.gsfc.nasa.gov/pub/Weather/GOES-8/gif/mapped/color/
➡conus/latest.gif ¦ giftopnm ¦ ppmtopcx >/home/ftp/weather.pcx
```

This example downloads a .GIF format weather satellite image, translates the graphic into .pnm format and then .pcx format, and saves it in your system's ftp area. You can use this approach to download and update files automatically, especially when used in a crontab file. (For details about using crontab, see Hour 24, "Using Scheduling to Automate System Management," or Hour 18, "Personal Productivity Tools").

The ncftp status bar is helpful when interactively downloading files. Although I can't show you the animation of the progress meter, when you use ncftp to download files, you get information on how the downloading is going, for example:

```
wustl> get app-defaults.color

Receiving file: app-defaults.color
100%  0 ===================================> 6583 bytes. ETA:  0:00
app-defaults.color:  6583 bytes received in 5.77 seconds, 1.11 kB/s.
ftp.wustl.edu   /packages/NCSA/Web/Mosaic/Unix/binaries/app-defaults
wustl>
```

This shows a completed download of the X11 application defaults file for the Mosaic Web browser.

> If you do a lot of downloading via FTP using anonymous log in, create a file named .netrc in your home directory. Enter a single line like this:
>
> default login anonymous password *yourusername@yourISP.com*
>
> Use your email address for *yourusername@yourISP.com*. The next time you use the ftp or ncftp command, you're automatically logged in!

Browsing the World Wide Web with Linux Browsers

This section introduces you to several Web browsers for Linux. You can find these browsers on your OpenLinux CD-ROM included with this book.

You can find other browsers, such as Chimera, Mosaic, and qweb at
http://metalab.unc.edu/pub/Linux/apps/www/browsers.

This book doesn't have enough room to cover these browsers in detail. If you're interested in learning about Web browsers or writing your own Web pages, I suggest you look
at the following books:

HTML by Example, by Todd Staufer; Que

Using HTML, by Mark Brown, John Jung, and Tom Savola; Que

Fast Browsing with the `lynx` Command

The Lynx browser, originally sponsored by the University of Kansas, does not support
graphics, sound, or any of the other plug-in features of today's modern Web browsers.
You can really like Lynx anyway because it's fast, efficient, and does not take up a lot of
disk space.

Lynx was designed to run on regular displays, or terminals, so you don't need to run the
X Window System in order to use it. This program is ideal for quickly browsing Web
pages to get the information you need without the "World Wide Wait" of too-large
graphics or animations that just waste bandwidth.

NEW TERM The Lynx browser has 66 different command-line options, but it's easy to use. If
you properly set up your system and start your PPP connection, you can start
browsing by specifying a *Uniform Resource Locator* (URL), or Web address, on the
command line, for example:

```
# lynx http://www.mcp.com
```

Figure 13.1 shows the Lynx browser.

If you need to fine-tune some of the ways the `lynx` command works, you can edit its
configuration file, `lynx.cfg`, in the `/usr/lib` directory. I suggest that you make a copy
of this file and copy it to your home directory with `.lynxrc` as the filename. In this file,
you can set a number of Lynx features. For example, if you specify the name of your
ISP's news server, you can read news:

```
NNTPSERVER:your.ISPnewserver.com
```

After you make this change, you can try to browse news with this:

```
# lynx news://your.ISPnewserver.com
```

13

Figure 13.1

The Lynx text-only Web browser is a compact, efficient program you can use to quickly browse Web pages without waiting for graphics to load.

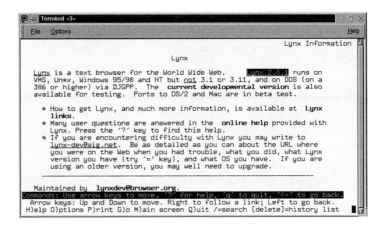

You can also use the Lynx browser to retrieve files without browsing. By using this approach, you can automatically research or get information on a regular basis:

```
# lynx http://www.yahoo.com/headlines/news -dump >news.raw
```

In this example, the content of the Web page is downloaded by the `lynx` command and then redirected to the file `news.raw`. Lynx also downloads files just like other browsers if you press the Enter key while your cursor has a file or link highlighted. The basic navigation keys for this browser are the cursors (to scroll up and down the current page, to go back to a previous page, or forward to the next), the Enter key (to load a link), and the Tab key (to go to the next link). To get help while using `lynx`, type the question mark (?) key.

Exploring Netscape Communicator

The Netscape Communicator Web browser, by Netscape Communications (soon to merge with America Online), is one of the most popular browsers for all computer systems. You can find a copy installed on your system that is specifically configured for OpenLinux (see Figure 13.4).

Netscape, like most well-behaved X11 clients, uses several X11 Toolkit options. For example, if you don't like the large initial window, you can specify a smaller starting window using geometric settings.

See Hour 7, "Using the X Window System," for a discussion of X11 toolkit options, such as geometry settings.

You can get a list of Netscape's initial command-line options with the `-help` option. Some common options are listed in Table 13.1.

TABLE 13.1 COMMON NETSCAPE COMMUNICATOR COMMAND-LINE OPTIONS

Description	Option
Display version	`-version`
Don't remember session settings	`-no-session-management`
Don't remember window settings	`-dont-save-geometry-prefs`
Don't show license page	`-no-about-splash`
Ignore saved window settings	`-ignore-geometry-prefs`
Launch to Composer	`-composer` or `-edit`
Launch to Discussions (newsreader)	`-discussions` or `-news`
Launch to Messenger	`-messenger` or `-mail`
Limit colors	`-install`
Set X11 *resource* (from the file `Netscape.ad` under the `/opt/netscape/communicator` directory)	`-xrm` *resource*
Show GUI help	`-nethelp`
Show help	`-help`
Start, and then iconify	`-iconic`
Start as a floating toolbar	`-component-bar`
Use black and white	`-mono`
Use server *svr*	`-display` *svr*
Use window of *WxH* at *X,Y*	`-geometry=WxH+X+Y`
Use *X* colors	`-ncols` *X*

Several of these options are useful if you start Netscape from the command line of a terminal window. For example, as I pointed out earlier in this hour, the geometry settings can help reduce the initial window size of your browser. A much better option, especially for laptop users with little screen real estate, is the `-component-bar` option, for example:

```
# netscape -component-bar &
```

This command runs Netscape, but the application and its additional components, which include Mailbox, Discussions, and Composer, appear in a short vertical floating window (shown in Figure 13.2) you can put off to one side of the screen. You can then run the desired component by clicking one of the icons in the small window.

13

FIGURE 13.2

*Netscape
Communicator offers a
convenient and com-
pact component bar
for small desktops that
can be used to launch
Navigator and other
components.*

If you need help using Netscape, use Netscape's Help menu information system. To get
help, open the Help menu, and click the Help Contents menu item. A help dialog box
appears, as shown in Figure 13.3. Unlike some browsers, Netscape comes with all the
help files you need to get started. You can find information about each component and
how to set up and use them, along with a full discussion of HTML page composition.

FIGURE 13.3

*Netscape
Communicator comes
with a complete help
and learning system.*

You can launch Netscape from the command line by clicking its icon in your Looking
Glass desktop or by clicking its icon on your desktop's panel in KDE. After Netscape
starts, the Navigator main window appears. If you click in Netscape's Location field or
on the Home button in Netscape's button bar, Netscape loads an introductory help page
on your system, using the address `file:/usr/doc/html/Caldera_Info` as shown in
Figure 13.4.

FIGURE **13.4**

*Netscape
Communicator auto-
matically displays
local links to
OpenLinux and Linux
documentation
installed on your
computer.*

This is a handy and convenient way to read much of the documentation included with OpenLinux and is a good place to start reading or searching if you want to learn more about your system.

To browse to an Internet address, make sure you have an active Internet connection, then click the Location field, and type a URL. Netscape accepts several types of URLs:

- `about:mozilla`   The Mozilla Easter egg
- `file://`   To read a local file or display a local graphic
- `ftp://`   To log in to and display a remote FTP server
- `http://`   To load and display a remote Web page
- `news:`*your.favorite.newsgroup*   To read Usenet articles

NEW TERM   The Linux version of Netscape Communicator also supports many different *plug-ins*, or additional programs that add features to the browser. Some of these plug-ins enable you to listen to live radio or watch recorded or live video. For more information about using plug-ins with Netscape, browse to the following:

`http://home.netscape.com/plugins/index.html`

An interesting plug-in is the RealPlayer application. This plug-in plays stereo music from live Internet radio stations around the world and can display video clips or live TV in a Netscape Web page or separate window. See Figure 13.5.

13

FIGURE 13.5

The RealPlayer plug-in from RealNetworks displays live video and audio over your PPP connection.

Netscape Communicator automatically displays local links to OpenLinux and Linux documentation installed on your computer.

To see a current list of live TV and radio stations, browse to the following:

```
http://www.timecast.com/stations/realvideo.html
```

For more information about getting the latest RealPlayer plug-in, browse to the following:

```
http://www.real.com/products/player/50player/downloadrealplayer.html
```

Chatting with Internet Relay Chat

The irc (Internet relay chat) command, found under the /usr/bin directory, is a program you can use to converse with other people on the Internet. When you run irc, you can use the built-in irc commands to connect to chat servers, see who is chatting, and set many other options.

The irc command has built-in help on more than 110 different commands and topics, many of which have further subtopic help. In order to use this program, you need an active Internet connection. By default, the irc program tries to connect to a default chat server (another computer supporting IRC).

After you connect, the screen splits into two parts. Ongoing discussions and responses are in the majority of the upper portion of the screen. You can use the lower portion of the screen to enter commands to the irc program or send keyboard sentences as messages to different active discussions.

Using irc is much different from reading and responding to USENET newsgroups (see Hour 11, "Configuring Internet Email," and Hour 12, "Configuring Internet News"). Discussions and comments are read and sent as you type. You should first browse through the `irc` command's help facility, and read all the available introductory information about the following topics: basics, commands, etiquette, expressions, intro, ircII, menus, news, newuser, and rules.

To start `irc`, type the command on the command line of your console or an X11 terminal window, like this:

```
# irc
*** Connecting to port 6667 of server irc-2.mit.edu
*** Welcome to the Internet Relay Network bball
*** If you have not already done so, please read the new user
information with
/HELP NEWUSER
...
```

After you press Enter, a lot of information scrolls by on the screen. Next, get a list of the help topics by using the `irc` /HELP command, for example:

```
> /HELP newuser
> /HELP etiquette
```

The next step is to see what chat groups are active. Use the /LIST command. You see a list of groups with different names. To join a chat group, use the /JOIN command, followed by the name of the chat group (which is preceded by a pound sign), like this:

```
> /JOIN #linux
```

After you press Enter, you join the group and might see a message such as:

```
*** bball (~bball@207-132-114-136.s196.tnt2.brd.erols.com) has joined
channel #linux
*** Users on #linux: bball whizzo KerNElDudE cathyt Scrotty
```

Messages and chat sentences scroll by on your screen. If you type a sentence and press Enter, your message is sent to all the users in the chat area. To quit the chat session, use the /LEAVE command, like this:

```
> /LEAVE
```

After you press Enter, you can /LIST other groups or use the /QUIT command to exit IRC.

To find out more about participating in `irc` chat sessions, read the built-in help files, the ircII man page, and the documentation for `irc` under the /usr/doc/irc directory. Another place to learn more about chatting on the Internet is http://www.irchelp.org.

13

Installing and Configuring AOL Instant Messenger

AOL's Instant Messenger, or IM, is a fun and easy-to-use X11 client for chatting with friends over the Internet. The service is free, and you don't have to pay for the software. This client constantly checks and then instantly notifies you when a friend logs in the service. You can then send an instant message!

You have to first register at AOL's Web site and then download and install IM. Navigate to http://www.aol.com/aim/home.html. and sign up for the service by selecting a screen name and a password and entering your email address (you receive a confirmation message by email from AOL). Next, go to the download section, and select the Java version. It takes you about 20 minutes to download the five-megabyte file called aim_linux.sh (a self-extracting shell script).

After downloading, start the installation like this:

```
# sh aim_linux.sh
AOL Instant Messenger(TM) Registration Agreement

Your use of AOL Instant Messenger(TM) service ("Service") constitutes
your acceptance, and agreement with America Online, Inc. ("AOL"), as
follows: You represent and warrant that you are eighteen years or older.
You understand and agree that your use of the Service does not constitute
membership in the AOL service.  You agree that you will not use the
Service to publish, post, distribute or disseminate any defamatory,
obscene, or other unlawful material or information.  You further agree
that you will not use the Service to transmit unsolicited commercial
messages or use the Buddy Info screens to collect or harvest personal
information about users of the Service to transmit unsolicited commercial
messages. You will not decompile, reengineer or otherwise copy the
Service.
...
```

After several screens of information, you're asked this question:

```
Do you accept the license? (y/n)
```

Type a y. The script then reports the following:

```
Uncompressing and Installing AOL Instant Messenger.
```

IM is installed in your home directory in a directory named aim. Start your PPP connection to your ISP, and then launch aim like this:

```
# aim/aim&
```

After you press Enter, you see the main IM dialog box, as shown in Figure 13.6.

FIGURE 13.6

AOL's Instant Messenger for Linux is an Internet notification and chat tool.

Enter your username in the Screen Name field, press the Tab key, and then enter your password. After you press Enter and your username and password are verified, the IM main dialog box appears. To configure IM, select the File menu, and then click Options and the Edit Preferences menu item. A dialog box, shown in Figure 13.7, appears next to IM's main window.

FIGURE 13.7

The main IM window shows you when friends log on to the Internet, AOL, or Instant Messenger, whereas the Setup dialog box is used to configure IM.

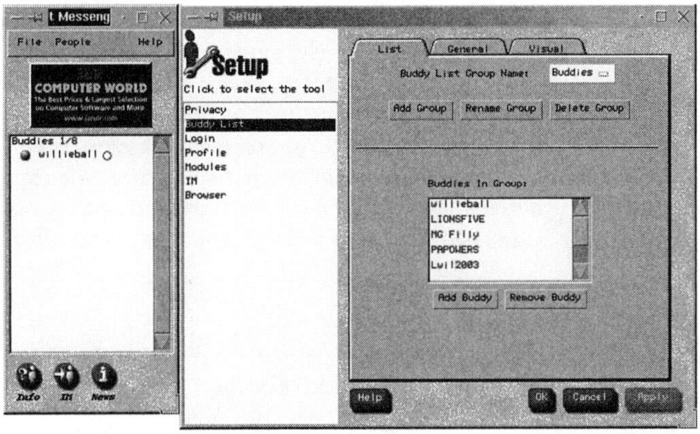

You can now add an IM Buddy and set other options. When a buddy logs on, his or her name appears in your IM's buddy list. To send an instant message, click your buddy's name, and then click the IM button in the main dialog box. Enter your message, and then click the Send button to chat.

Connecting with Other Computers with the `telnet` Command

You can use the `telnet` command to log in to remote computers to run programs, view files, or download data. The `telnet` command has a number of options but is generally used with a hostname or remote computer system's name on the command line to start a telnet session, for example:

```
# telnet computer.somewhere.com
```

This command connects you to the remote computer, and you receive a login prompt. You generally need to have a username and password in order to enter the remote system. For security reasons, few computer systems enable unknown users anonymous access. You might be able to find a list of computer systems providing access by using your favorite search engines, such as through a Web search site.

> If you "`telnet`" to a remote computer system through an active Internet connection or through a shell account through a direct dial-in to the computer, you can easily transfer programs using the `sz` and `rz` (send and receive) files (if those programs are resident on the remote computer). After you dial in to a remote computer directly through the phone line, you can transfer files to your computer with `sz -w 2048 filename.tgz`. This command sends the file `filename.tgz` using the ZMODEM communications protocol. Your communications program automatically starts receiving the file using this protocol (most communications programs, anyway). If you're connected through an Internet connection, the companion program, `rz`, automatically starts to receive the file. If not, you can start the `rz` program manually. See the `sz` and `rz` manual pages for more information.

You can also run the `telnet` command in an interactive mode, opening and closing sessions to different remote computers. Like the `ftp` command, the `telnet` command has built-in help. If you want to get a list of available help topics, you can use the question mark (?), for example:

```
# telnet
telnet> ?
Commands may be abbreviated.   Commands are:

close           close current connection
logout          forcibly logout remote user and close the connection
display         display operating parameters
mode            try to enter line or character mode ('mode ?' for more)
```

```
open            connect to a site
quit            exit telnet
send            transmit special characters ('send ?' for more)
set             set operating parameters ('set ?' for more)
unset           unset operating parameters ('unset ?' for more)
status          print status information
toggle          toggle operating parameters ('toggle ?' for more)
slc             change state of special charaters ('slc ?' for more)
auth            turn on (off) authentication ('auth ?' for more)
z               suspend telnet
environ         change environment variables ('environ ?' for more)
?               print help information
telnet>
```

If you want to experiment with this command without an active Internet connection, you can telnet to your own computer from a terminal window under X11 or through the console. As with the `ftp` command, first determine the hostname of your computer with the `hostname` command, and then either specify the hostname on the `telnet` command line or run `telnet` and use its `open` command to start the session, for example:

```
# hostname
presario.localhost.localdomain
# telnet presario
Trying 127.0.0.1...
Connected to presario.localhost.localdomain.
Escape character is '^]'.

Caldera OpenLinux(TM)
Version 1.3
Copyright 1996-1998 Caldera Systems, Inc.

login: bball
Password:
You have old mail in /var/spool/mail/bball
Last login: Mon Jan 25 15:28:01 1999 on tty2
You have mail.
#
```

As you can see, after entering the username and password at the login prompt, you're presented with the shell prompt command line.

Summary

This hour introduced you to downloading and browsing on the Internet. You learned how to use the `ftp` command to connect to a remote computer and download files. You also learned about several Internet browsers included with OpenLinux. Finally, you learned about Internet Relay Chat and the `telnet` command.

13

Q&A

Q I clicked a link to download a file while using Netscape, but all I got was a bunch of garbage characters in a new window. What happened?

A The version of Netscape included with OpenLinux is configured to recognize several file types automatically and act accordingly. However, if you click a link to download an unrecognized file type, Netscape attempts to download the file into a window. The safest approach to downloading a file is to first hold down the Shift key and then click the link to download a file. Netscape then shows a file save dialog box, so that you can confirm the file save and start downloading.

Q I started downloading a file with Netscape. Can I go back to browsing and start downloading other files?

A Yes. You can run multiple downloads at the same time.

Q Are any other Web browsers included with OpenLinux?

A Yes. You can try the amaya Web browser for X11. This browser, according to its developers, is "a work in progress."

Q If I'm downloading files with Netscape, is it safe to send or retrieve mail?

A Yes, because you're using a network connection. However, you might find things slowing down a bit (depending on the type of Internet connection you use.

Q I tried irc, but there were some people using foul language and who were really nasty!

A Unfortunately, chat discussions are generally not moderated, so there's no one in charge. In general, members of Linux chat groups tend to be a bit more civilized.

Q I tried running Instant Messenger, but the program complained about not being able to find "Oscar.main"?

A This is a conflict with an installed Java Development Kit, JDK. Use glint, lisa, or rpm to remove the JDK package, and then restart IM.

Exercises

1. Download and install the RealPlayer for Netscape, and then connect to an Internet site with a live TV broadcast. Relax.

2. Connect to the Internet, and then start the irc command. Join a chat group, and watch the conversations.

3. Try using ncftp to download a known file from an FTP site. How can this program be useful?

4. Try the Netscape (Mozilla) Easter egg. What else do you see besides a quotation?

PART IV

Using Linux Productively

Hour

14 Text Processing

15 Preparing Documents

16 Graphics Tools

17 Learning Math and Financial Tools

18 Personal Productivity Tools

19 Home Office Management with StarOffice

20 Relaxation and Playing Linux Games

HOUR **14**

Text Processing

This hour provides an overview of some word processing, or text editing, tools for OpenLinux. There are more than 100 text editors available for OpenLinux and more than one dozen on this book's CD-ROM. This hour shows you some of the highlights and features of using these editing tools. You'll find tips on installing and using some of the latest exciting software releases for OpenLinux, such as Corel's WordPerfect 8 and Star Division's StarOffice suite. Read on to learn the basics of using these tools and to see how to write and edit with OpenLinux.

Word Processors in the Linux Environment

Text editors are used by many different people in different vocations. Casual users, writers, programmers, and system administrators all use a text editor at one time or another in OpenLinux. You definitely need to know how to change your system's text configuration files to make OpenLinux work the way you want. What follows is an introduction to different word processors, text editors, and text tools you can use during your OpenLinux sessions.

Although how you use a computer dictates what type of software is important and should be installed, most people agree that more than half their time using a computer is spent using a text editor or word processor. This will change, of course, as computer software interfaces evolve and network communication becomes more integrated into our work environment, but in general, if you're using OpenLinux on your computer at home, you're probably going to be word processing or editing files a lot of the time.

The tools in this hour are interactive programs that enable you to enter text, move a cursor, or drop a menu. These programs and related files vary in size from more than 150 megabytes (such as the StarOffice suite) to fewer than 200,000 characters (such as the pico editor). Table 14.1 lists editors included with OpenLinux on this book's CD-ROM. You can also find more than two dozen text tools, such as line editors such as the ed or ex commands, that although not interactive, enable you to change, manipulate, or rearrange text.

TABLE **14.1**   TEXT EDITORS FOR OPENLINUX

Name	Description
aXe	X11 text editor
CRiSPlite	The CRiSP programmer's editor
ed	Line editor
edy	Text editor (German)
ee, easyedit	emacs in easy mode
elvis, xelvis	Clone of the vi text editor
jed, xjed	Programmer's editor for console and X11
joe, jmacs, jpico, jstar	The Joe's Own Editor and variants
kedit	Text editor included with the K Desktop Environment distribution
nex	Berkeley line editor clone
nvi	Berkeley vi editor clone
pico	Text editor (part of the pine electronic mail program's distribution)
red	Read-only line editor
sed	Stream editor
StarWriter	StarOffice word processor
textedit	Text editor for X11
uemacs	MicroEMACs text editor
vim	Vi IMproved, a programmers text editor
xedit	Text editor for X11

Features of the XEmacs Environment

What do you call a text editor that edits text, reads Usenet news, acts as a personal calendar and diary, sends electronic mail, is a programming language interpreter, plays games, is a Linux shell, and more? Why, emacs, of course!

Emacs, which stands for Editor Macros, was originally developed by Richard Stallman, the founder of the Free Software Foundation (FSF). The original emacs editor is distributed by the FSF as part of the GNU, or GNU's Not UNIX, project. XEmacs is a version of the original editor included with OpenLinux with improvements by companies such as Sun Microsystems and Lucid, Inc. and programmers, such as Ben Wing. Although there are some subtle differences (purist emacs users might insist that the only real version is from the FSF) between these versions, XEmacs is just as useful and capable as the FSF's GNU version.

Without a doubt, emacs is the most widely available and fully featured free editor and runs on more computer systems than any other text editor. There isn't enough time in this hour (or this book!) to cover all the features of this program.

Look at Table 14.2 to find most of the keyboard commands you can use to get started.

TABLE 14.2 BASIC EMACS COMMANDS AND KEYSTROKE COMBINATIONS

C-b=hold down Ctrl key, press b   M-v=Press Esc key, press v

Action	Key Combination
Abort current operation	C-g
Cursor backward	C-b
Cursor down	C-n
Cursor forward	C-f
Cursor up	C-p
Delete character	C-d
Delete line	C-k
Delete word	M-d
Go to beginning of file	M-<
Go to beginning of line	C-a
Go to end of file	M->
Go to end of line	C-e
Help	C-h
Open file	C-x C-f

14

continues

TABLE 14.2 CONTINUED

Action	Key Combination
Page down	C-v
Page up	M-v
Quit	C-x C-c
Save As	C-x C-w
Save file	C-x C-s
Tutorial	C-h t
Undo	C-_ or C-x, u

Emacs has 22 different command-line options but is easy to start. To run emacs and open a text file for editing, specify the file's name on the command line, like this:

```
# emacs myfile.txt
```

This loads the editor and opens your file. If you specify emacs on the command line by itself, the program starts, displays an opening screen, and then clears when you touch the keyboard. Starting the emacs tutorial is highly recommended if you're a beginner. Hold down the Control key and press the H key. You see a prompt on the emacs command line at the bottom of screen. Type the **T** key, and then press Enter to start the tutorial.

If you enter this command at the shell prompt of an X11 terminal window, the X11 version of emacs, xemacs, with mouse and menu support, automatically starts (see Figure 14.1). But what if you want to run the console, or non-X11 version, of emacs instead? In this case, use emacs with the -nw, or no-window, command-line option, like so:

```
# emacs -nw myfile.txt
```

This command runs emacs inside your X11 terminal window without a menu bar. xemacs also obeys most X11 Toolkit options, such as geometry settings. Some of the X11 options you might find helpful include the following:

- -geometry 80x24+400+200—start in a window 80 characters wide by 24 lines, at screen position X (400) Y (200)
- -fg *color*—set foreground to *color*
- -bg *color*—set background to *color*
- -cr *color*—set text cursor to *color*
- -mc *color*—set mouse cursor to *color*

> The colors you can use for the *color* settings are listed in the file `rgb.txt` under the `/usr/X11R6/lib/X11` directory.

Use these options, and others (such as X11 resource settings, discussed in Hour 7, "Using the X Window System") to customize how `emacs` looks when started in X11:

```
# emacs -geometry 80x24 -fg black -bg white blue -cr red
```

This starts `xemacs` in a window 80 characters wide and 24 lines high. The text is black with a white background. The cursor is red, and the mouse cursor is blue. Emacs also has 43 different X resource settings you can configure and enter into your `.Xresources` file in your home directory. You also can save editor defaults (such as word wrapping, or fill-mode on) in a file called `.emacs` in your home directory.

NEW TERM For example, you can automatically put `xemacs` into a text- and word-wrap mode, enable daily diary service, and put the current time in the *modeline*, a status bar in the main window. Create the `.emacs` file with `xemacs`, like this:

```
# xemacs .emacs
```

Next, type in the commands to customize `xemacs`:

```
(setq default-major-mode 'text-mode)
(setq text-mode-hook 'turn-on-auto-fill)
(require 'appt)
(display-time)
(appt-initialize)
```

Press Ctrl+X and Ctrl+S to save the file, and then press Ctrl+X and Ctrl+C to exit `xemacs`. The next time you start the editor, you see the time displayed in the modeline.

The `xemacs` program for OpenLinux comes in 14 different packages containing various files and utilities. If you install everything, `emacs` requires more than 60 megabytes of disk space. You can, however, save 45 megabtyes if you install the `xemacs` package, which contains the editor, documentation, and support routines.

You can find documentation for `xemacs` under the `/usr/info/xemacs` directory. You also can read the `xemacs` manual page for an overview.

Variants of the VIsual iMproved Editor —`vim`

14

The `vim` editor, by Bram Moolenaar, is a text editor that is compatible with the original Berkeley Software Distribution `vi` editor by Bill Joy. An X11 version is called `gvim` and sports multiple scrolling windows and menus.

FIGURE 14.1

The XEmacs editor features split windows, built-in help, a tutorial, and other tools to help you be more productive.

Menubar   Tutorial Mode   Button Toolbar

Split Window

Current Time

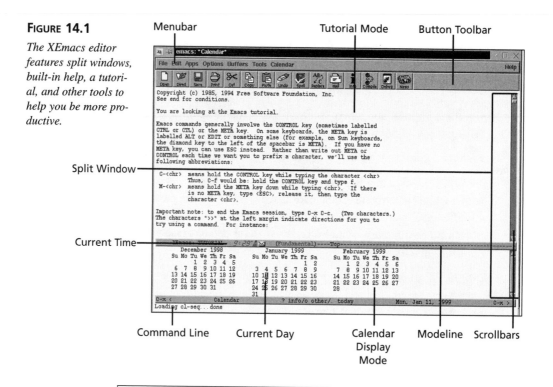

Command Line   Current Day   Calendar Display Mode   Modeline   Scrollbars

Although the vim :version command shows that the systemwide vimrc and gvimrc resource files are located under the /usr/share/vim directory, this is not true: these files aren't installed with the vim package. However, you can create your own resource file after making changes to vim while running the editor and then using the :mkvimrc command. A resource file called .vimrc (which you can copy to .gvimrc) is created in your home directory and contains your changes. You can then edit and add your own commands, configurations, and menus to these files.

Several files and symbolic links to the vim editor are created on your system when you install the vim package from your CD-ROM:

- /usr/bin/vi -> /bin/vi
- /bin/vi -> /bin/vim
- /bin/view -> /bin/vim
- /usr/bin/view -> /bin/vim
- /bin/vim
- /usr/X11R6/bin/gvim

The vim editor, shown in Figure 14.2, is used as a replacement for the ex, vi, and view editors and is a visual editor supporting features such as cursor movement.

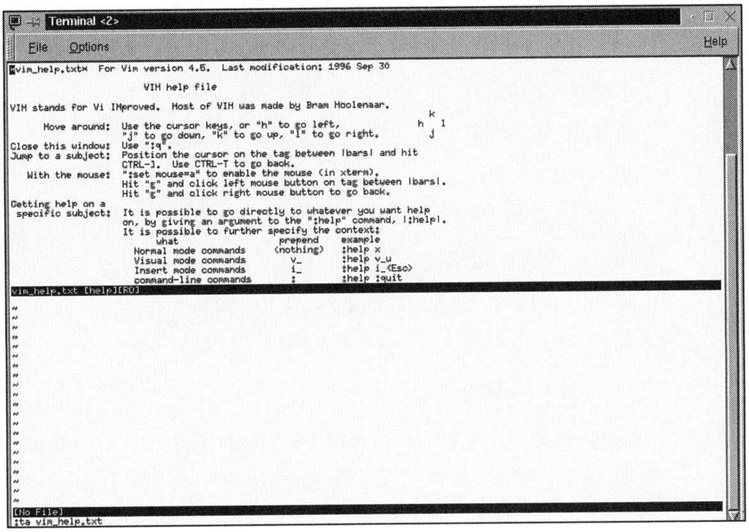

FIGURE **14.2**

The vim *editor features split windows and built-in help.*

The vim editor features a number of improvements over the traditional vi editor, and has 23 different command-line options. In vim you can find built-in help, split-screen windows, block moves, command-line editing, horizontal scrolling, and word wrapping for word processing.

The gvim version of vim, used under the X Window System, has custom colors, window sizes, scrollbars, and menus. You can create your own set of menus containing specific vim commands and generate different versions of vim by saving your features in different gvim resource files. You can then use the -u command-line option to load a custom version.

Creating new menus for gvim is easy. You can, for example, group related macros or custom commands you create in a separate menu. For details about building custom menus, read the files vim_menu.txt and vim_gui.txt under the /usr/share/vim directory.

Most of the documentation for vim is contained in its built-in help, and 21 text files in the /usr/share/vim directory contain extensive instructions.

Features of Pine's pico Editor

The pico editor, included with the University of Washington's pine electronic mail program, is a compact, efficient, and easy-to-use editor usually used to compose or reply to email messages. This editor is a nifty replacement for all your editing needs and is

14

especially handy if you need a reliable text editor but don't have a lot of hard drive space (for example, on a laptop).

Despite its relatively small size, the `pico` editor has most of the features you expect in a word processor, including:

- word wrap
- built-in help
- word search
- paragraph justification
- text block move, copy, and delete
- directory mode for file and text insertion
- mouse support
- spell checking

The `pico` editor, shown in Figure 14.3, has 16 different command-line options and rudimentary but secure crash protection. In the untimely event of a power outage (just about the only way to crash Linux) `pico` attempts to save any work in progress before exiting, saving your file with a name ending in `.save` or if unsaved, in a file named `pico.save`.

FIGURE 14.3

The pico *editor, part of the* pine *electronic mail program distribution, is a compact and easy-to-use editor with nearly all the basic features of a text editor.*

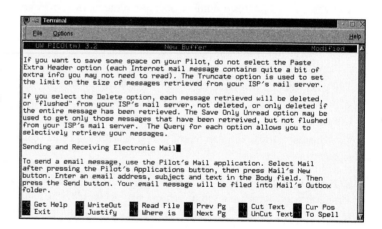

This editor is an excellent choice for your `$EDITOR` environment variable, as it is much friendlier and easier to learn than the default `$EDITOR` variable, which points to the `vi` (`vim`) command. To use `pico` as your editor, open the file `.profile` in your home directory, and then add this line:

```
EDITOR=/usr/bin/pico; export EDITOR
```

As the root operator, set the `$EDITOR` variable for all users by editing the `/etc/profile` file, and insert the same line.

In both cases, save the file, and then use the following to use the new $EDITOR variable:

```
# source /etc/profile
```

After you do this, any Linux command requiring a default system editor uses pico.

You can find documentation for pico in its manual page, or you can use the lynx Web browser to read the pine and pico technical documentation with the following:

```
# lynx /usr/doc/pine-4.02/tech-notes/index.html
```

Five Editors in One—joe

The joe editor, by Joseph H. Allen, comes in five different versions: jmacs, joe, jpico, jstar, and rjoe. The jmacs version emulates the emacs editor. The jpico version emulates the pine mailer's pico text editor. The jstar version uses WordStar-compatible keyboard commands, whereas the rjoe program is a restricted editor.

> For those of you who don't know about WordStar: this program was one of the first full-screen text editors with a spelling checker, originally developed and marketed for the CP/M operating system. In the early 1980s, WordStar was the most popular word processor for the DOS operating system, and its legacy is the Ctrl key "diamond." This meant that the user pressed the Ctrl key with the left pinky finger, and tapped the WER, ASDF, or XC keys to move within a document.

The joe configuration files (for each text mode) are found under the /usr/lib/joe directory. To create your own custom configuration, copy the file called joerc to your home directory, save it with the .joerc filename, and then edit this file to change the joe help menus, display, and keyboard commands.

You can find documentation for the joe editor, shown in Figure 14.4, in its manual page (which needs to be spell checked) and by using its built-in help (Ctrl+X, K).

Configuring the jed Editor

The jed editor (shown in Figure 14.5), by John E. Davis, comes in two versions: one for the console (jed) and the other tailored for the X Window System (xjed). This editor can also emulate other editors, such as WordStar or Brief, using those programs' keyboard commands.

14

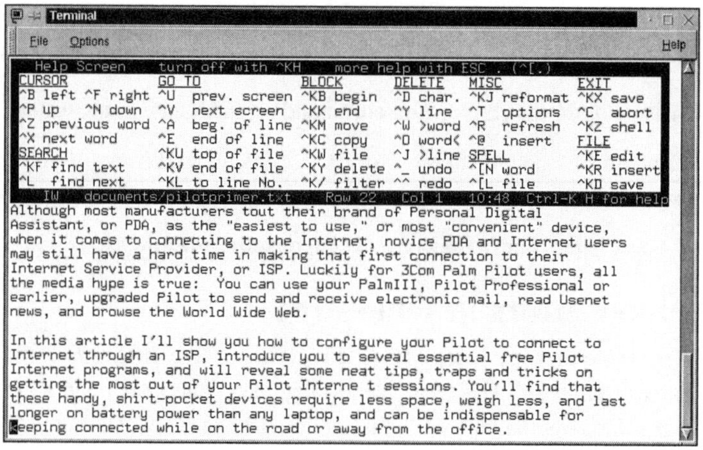

FIGURE 14.4

The joe *editor comes in five versions and can emulate the keyboard commands of several different editors, such as* pico *and* emacs.

The jed main configuration files can be found under the /usr/lib/jed/lib directory, and you can customize how jed runs by placing preferences in a .jedrc file in your home directory. Copy the file jed.rc from the /usr/lib/jed/lib directory to your home directory as .jedrc, and then edit to your taste.

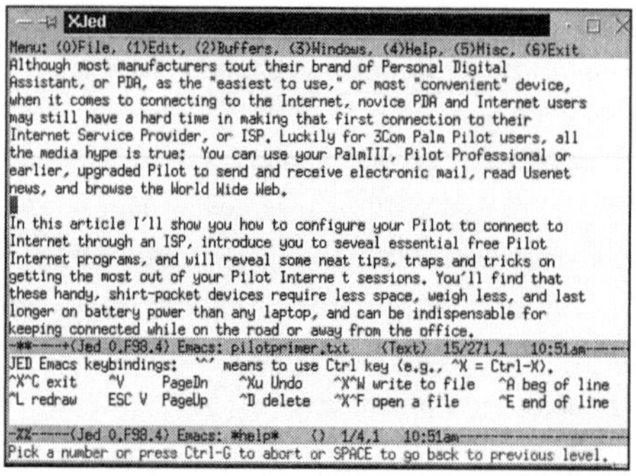

FIGURE 14.5

The jed *editor has built-in help and text menus you can use as a shortcut to keyboard commands.*

The jed editor has built-in help, but you can find information about jed under the /usr/doc/jed directory, in its manual page, and in info files under the /usr/lib/jed/info directory.

Using the kedit Editor Client

The kedit editor (shown in Figure 14.6) is included with the K Desktop Environment and has numerous features, including the following:

- A menu bar supporting file, editing, options and help
- A toolbar containing buttons for the following:

- Creating a new document
- Email
- Help
- Performing copy, paste, and cut operations
- Printing
- Opening a file
- Saving the current file

- Custom colors and fonts
- Insertion of the current date and time
- Retrieval of Internet documents via FTP
- Search and replace
- Sending of documents by electronic mail
- Text file insertion
- Word wrap

FIGURE 14.6

The kedit editor has many different features, such as search-and-replace, help, custom colors, and retrieval of text documents via the Internet.

You can test kedit's remote file retrieval by creating a file called welcome.msg with some sample text. Copy this file to the /home/ftp directory (as the root operator). Next, start kedit by clicking the Application Starter button on your desktop's panel, then selecting the Applications menu, and clicking the editor menu item. When the kedit window appears, select the File menu, and then click the Open URL... menu item. A retrieval dialog box appears (as shown in Figure 14.6). Click the OK button and the text of the welcome.msg file is inserted into kedit's editing window.

> To learn how to navigate the Internet and download files using the ftp command, see Hour 13, "Internet Downloading and Browsing."

14

Using the CRiSPlite Editor

The CRiSPlite editor, included with OpenLinux, is a programmer's editor used mainly to create and edit source code for programming. This editor (an extremely limited version of the commercial editor) sports a graphical interface under the X Window system and features buttons and menus you can use while you work.

Start CRiSPlite by clicking the editor's icon on your desktop's panel if you're using the K Desktop Environment. You can also find an icon in the initial Looking Glass desktop after you start an X session with the fvwm2 window manager. Start the editor from the command line of a terminal window with the mcr command, like this:

```
# mcr
```

The editor appears with its window, as shown in the Figure 14.7.

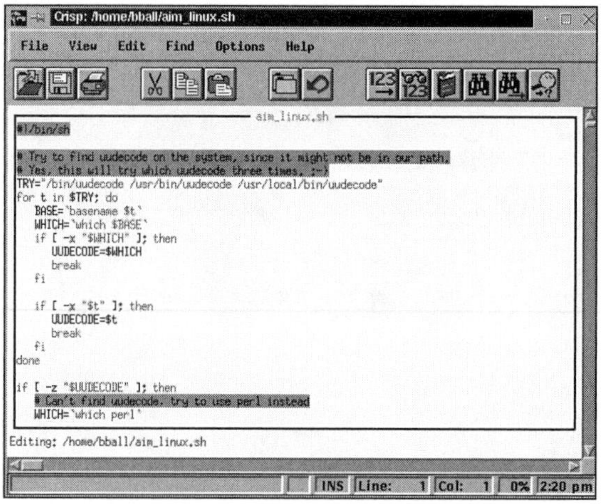

FIGURE **14.7**

The CRiSPlite editor for OpenLinux is mainly a programming editor.

You can also use this editor from the command line of your console with the cr command, like this:

```
# crg
```

Press Enter to launch CRiSPlite without the X Window System.

StarOffice's StarWriter

The StarWriter component of the StarOffice suite of productivity programs (shown in Figure 14.8) for OpenLinux is a professional and capable word processor. This program (used, in part, to write this book) is installed along with StarOffice from this book's CD-ROM. This editor supports nearly all the features found in more expensive word processors for other operating systems.

FIGURE 14.8

The StarWriter component of the StarOffice suite of tools for OpenLinux is a professional word processor.

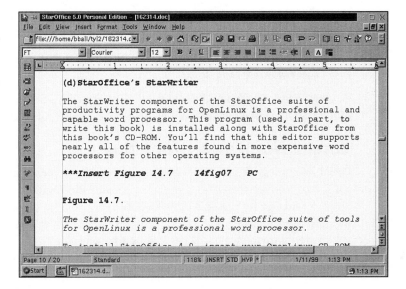

To install StarOffice 4.0, insert your OpenLinux CD-ROM, and then mount the CD-ROM like so:

```
# su -c "mount /mnt/cdrom"
```

Navigate to the StarOffice installation directory on the CD-ROM, like so:

```
# cd /mnt/cdrom/Star*/english/prod_lnx
```

At the command line, use the StarOffice setup command to start the installation, like this:

```
# setup
```

Press Enter to start the installation.

If you receive the newer StarOffice 5.0 suite, first browse to http://www.stardivision.com to obtain a customer number and registration key. You need to enter your customer name, customer number, and registration key exactly as shown on the StarDivision registration page in order to install and enable StarOffice 5.0. See Hour 19, "Home Office Management with StarOffice," for more details about installing and using StarOffice.

14

StarOffice installs in an OfficeXX directory in your home directory, where *XX* represents the version of StarOffice installed (40 for 4.0 or 50 for 5.0). Start StarOffice by typing the following:

```
# Office50/bin/soffice &
```

To create a new StarWriter document, click the StarOffice Start menu (at the bottom left of the StarOffice desktop). StarWriter appears, as shown in Figure 14.8).

Corel's WordPerfect for Linux

OpenLinux is a great Linux distribution to use, and now there's an even better reason to use Linux: In December 1998, Corel, Inc. released the WordPerfect version 8 word processor for free for personal use with the Linux operating system. WordPerfect, one of the most mature and capable word processors on the market today (for any operating system) can be downloaded, installed, and used for free.

> You should definitely register your copy of WordPerfect, even if you only use it occasionally. Corel, Inc. needs to have an accurate idea of the potential of the Linux software market, and your registration helps encourage development of new commercial software for Linux. Corel, Inc. is to be applauded for making this software available at little cost to the casual Linux user.

To get your copy, browse to http://www.linux.corel.com/linux8/index.htm. Follow the links, read the installation instructions, and then download and install the file GUILG00 (nearly 24 megabytes in size). You can then start WordPerfect by typing the complete path to the executable file (using the installation directory specified during your WordPerfect installation), like so:

```
# /opt/wp/wpbin/xwp &
```

The WordPerfect splash screen appears, along with a control dialog box and the blank WordPerfect document window, as shown in Figure 14.9.

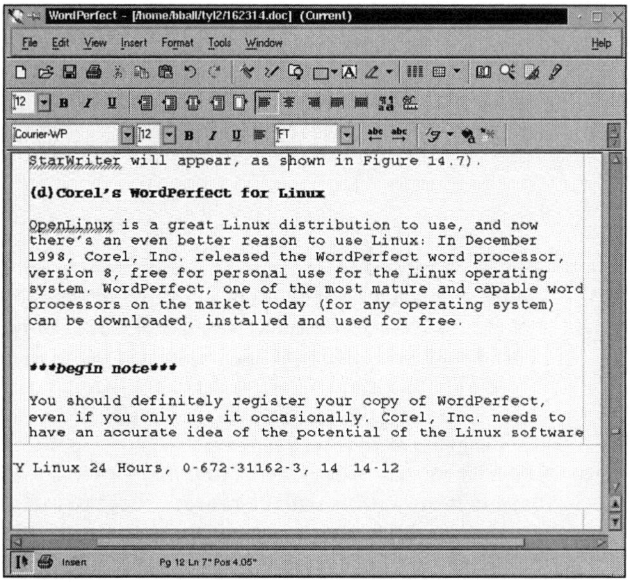

FIGURE **14.9**

The distribution of the WordPerfect 8 word processing system for OpenLinux represents Corel, Inc.'s concerted investment and confidence in the worldwide Linux user community.

Applix Words

There are many other Linux word processing programs besides the text editors installed on your system. These programs are in the public domain, distributed as shareware, or sold commercially. One word processor, Applix Words by Applix, Inc., has many different features:

- It is an integrated part of the Applixware suite of office tools, including a spreadsheet, graphics, mail, and presentation program and supporting frames, linked objects, and pasted graphics.

- It provides a WYSIWYG view of your documents and comes with two dozen fonts.

- It imports and exports 20 different word processing file formats.

- It supports extensive editing macros.

- It includes a spelling dictionary and thesaurus.

- It includes extensive built-in and context-sensitive help.

- It creates and edits hypertext markup language, or HTML documents.

- It can be completely customized with new menus or keyboard commands.

- It builds indexes, tables, tables of contents, and glossaries.

14

Applix Words requires the X Window System. The Applixware suite needs about 135 megabytes of your hard drive space and 16 megabytes of your computer's memory to run comfortably. After installing Applix Words from the Applixware CD-ROM, run it with the following:

```
# applix -wp
```

> The latest version of Applixware (4.4.1 at the time of this writing) has an installation and execution problem related to OpenLinux 1.3. This problem involves Caldera's use of older versions of shared software libraries. Fortunately, you can install Applixware and then configure its libraries to work with OpenLinux 1.3. First, log in as the root operator, and then navigate to the `/opt/applix/jre115/lib/i386/green_threads` directory. Use the `mv` command to rename the library file `libdl.so.1` to `libdl.so.1.dontuse`. Next, open your `.bashrc` file in your home directory, and enter this new environment variable definition: **export LD_PRELOAD=/lib/libdl.so.1**. Log out and log back in to OpenLinux to use the new definition. You can now use Applixware!

This command line starts the word processor component as shown in Figure 14.10. Applix Words also has a tutorial, like emacs. To start learning, select the Help menu, and then pull down the Tutorial menu item. (You also can hold down the Alt key, and then press H, followed by the T key.)

FIGURE 14.10

The Applix Words program is a WYSIWYG word processor including a customizable interface and professional editing tools for writers.

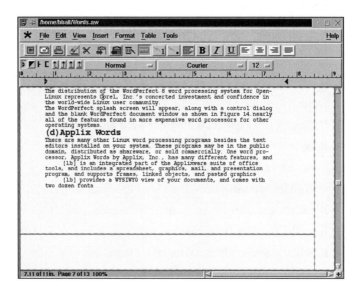

Find out more about Applix Words and the Applixware productivity suite for Linux by browsing to the following site:

`http://www.applix.com.`

Changing Text with `sed` and Other Filters

Until now, this hour has discussed interactive editors featuring cursor movement, menus, or other keyboard commands. There are several other programs, such as text filters, or stream editors, included with your system that can edit text.

If you read the discussion in Hour 6, "Using the Shell," you'll recall that many Linux programs can use your shell's standard input and standard output. By using shell operators, such as pipes or redirection operators, you can use Linux commands to filter text through pipelines to manipulate or change the text stream. There also are several other programs, such as `ex` and `sed`, that are specifically designed to edit filtered text and are called stream editors.

Thanks to the FSF folks, the GNU `text-utils` package of two dozen text utilities is also installed on your system. This collection includes `cat`, `cksum`, `comm`, `csplit`, `cut`, `expand`, `fmt`, `fold`, `head`, `join`, `md5sum`, `nl`, `od`, `paste`, `pr`, `sort`, `split`, `sum`, `tac`, `tail`, `tr`, `unexpand`, `uniq`, and `wc`.

Some of these formatting commands, such as `fmt` and `pr`, are discussed in the next hour, "Preparing Documents," but this section shows you how you can use several others to manipulate text. For example, the `tr`, or transliterate, command can be used to work on streams of text to translate, squeeze, or delete characters.

The `tr` command works by taking sets, or lists of characters on the command line, and using them to translate input text. If you have a document containing uppercase and lowercase but want to change the text to all uppercase, you can tell the `tr` command to do this by specifying the two sets of characters. A public domain software license (found in the `/usr/doc/shadow-misc` directory) is used in the following example:

```
# cat LICENSE
...
1.  You may make and give away verbatim copies of the source form of the
Standard Version of this Package without restriction, provided that you
duplicate all of the original copyright notices and associated
disclaimers.

2.  You may apply bug fixes, portability fixes and other modifications
derived from the Public Domain or from the Copyright Holder.  A Package
modified in such a way shall still be considered the Standard Version.
...
```

14

You can change this document to all uppercase with the following:

```
# cat LICENSE ¦ tr a-z A-Z
...
1.  YOU MAY MAKE AND GIVE AWAY VERBATIM COPIES OF THE SOURCE FORM OF THE
STANDARD VERSION OF THIS PACKAGE WITHOUT RESTRICTION, PROVIDED THAT YOU
DUPLICATE ALL OF THE ORIGINAL COPYRIGHT NOTICES AND ASSOCIATED
DISCLAIMERS.

2.  YOU MAY APPLY BUG FIXES, PORTABILITY FIXES AND OTHER MODIFICATIONS
DERIVED FROM THE PUBLIC DOMAIN OR FROM THE COPYRIGHT HOLDER.  A PACKAGE
MODIFIED IN SUCH A WAY SHALL STILL BE CONSIDERED THE STANDARD VERSION.
...
```

The document has been piped, using the `cat` command, through the `tr` command, specifying that you want the set of lowercase letters, from a to z, to be translated to uppercase, or A to Z. The `tr` command can also be used to translate individual characters. For example, notice that two spaces are used following each number and a period in the sample text. You can replace multiple occurrences of characters with a single character by using the `-s`, or squeeze, command-line option:

```
# cat LICENSE  ¦ tr -s " "
...
1. You may make and give away verbatim copies of the source form of the
Standard Version of this Package without restriction, provided that you
duplicate all of the original copyright notices and associated
disclaimers.
...
```

As you can see, the two spaces have been replaced with a single space. The `tr` command also filters input to other commands, such as `cut`, to quickly generate custom reports. For example, if you don't need all the information from the `ls` command's `-l`, or long, format listing and only want certain columns of the output, you can get any column you want by filtering the listing through several pipes:

```
# ls -l
...
-rw-r--r--  1 root     root         1898 Jan 29  1998 ANNOUNCE
-rw-r--r--  1 root     root        28796 Jul 23 18:13 CHANGES
-rw-r--r--  1 root     root        68500 Mar 16  1997 HOWTO
-rw-r--r--  1 root     root         5040 May  1  1997 LICENSE
-rw-r--r--  1 root     root          850 Dec 14  1997 LSM
-rw-r--r--  1 root     root        11535 May  1  1997 README
...
```

This is a lot of information, but if you only want the permissions, size, and name of each file, you can quickly generate a custom listing with the following:

```
# ls -l ¦ tr -s " " ¦ cut -d" " -f1,8,9
...
-rw-r--r-- 1998 ANNOUNCE
-rw-r--r-- 18:13 CHANGES
-rw-r--r-- 1997 HOWTO
-rw-r--r-- 1997 LICENSE
-rw-r--r-- 1997 LSM
-rw-r--r-- 1997 README
...
```

The listing now only shows the first, eighth, and ninth columns of the original listing because the `tr` command squeezed multiple spaces into a single space. The output is piped through the `cut` command, specifying a field delimiter using the `-d` option (in this case, a space). Notice that although the first and second columns look okay, the third is a little ragged. If this still isn't what you want, cut different fields or clean it up by again using the `tr` command to replace the space delimiter with a tab:

```
# ls -l ¦ tr -s " " ¦ cut -d" " -f1,5,9 ¦ tr " " '\t'
...
-rw-r--r--          1898      ANNOUNCE
-rw-r--r--          28796     CHANGES
-rw-r--r--          68500     HOWTO
-rw-r--r--          5040      LICENSE
-rw-r--r--          850       LSM
-rw-r--r--          11535     README
...
```

The listing now shows the permissions, file size, and name of each file. You can use these filters to change text in your documents, but stream editors, such as the `sed` command, offer more capable approaches to editing text from the command line. For example, the sample license document uses the phrase `this Package` to describe a software package. If you are the software developer of a new game, *Nano-Warrior*, and need to save time writing copyright licenses, you can change all occurrences of `this Package` to `Nano-Warrior` easily and quickly without using a text editor:

```
# cat LICENSE ¦ sed 's/this Package/Nano-Warrior(TM)/g'
...
1.  You may make and give away verbatim copies of the source form of the
Standard Version of Nano-Warrior(TM) without restriction, provided that
you duplicate all of the original copyright notices and associated
disclaimers.
...
```

The `sed s`, or substitute, command is used to search for all instances of the first string and replaces each instance with the second because of the `g`, or global, command. The original text file is not changed, and you can save a new version by redirecting the output.

14

The `sed` command also is designed to work using editing scripts. To make numerous, regular changes to files, create an editing script, and use your script to edit files. Use the `sed` command's `-f`, or script file, command-line option to use the script:

```
# sed -f myscipt.sed < form.ltr >output.ltr
```

There are too many text filters included with your OpenLinux distribution to discuss in this hour; see the manual pages for the filter commands listed near the beginning of this section. You also might want to experiment with the `wc`, or word count, program, which reports the number of characters, words, and lines in your text documents.

Spell Checking Your Documents

Misspelled words in your documents can be embarrassing, especially if other people read your text. Correct spelling is an important part of writing and word processing. Just as errors in syntax can cause programming errors, spelling errors can cause problems in miscommunication, loss of a potential job or customer, or the respect of a supervisor.

Fortunately, your Linux distribution comes with the `ispell` spelling checker, so you don't have to suffer the embarrassment of misspelling! This section shows you how to correct documents and fix your spelling errors.

Correcting Documents with the `ispell` Command

The `ispell` command, found under the `/usr/bin` directory, is an interactive spelling program you can use alone or with your text editor to correct spelling mistakes. Several editors included with your Linux distribution, such as `emacs` and `pico`, are set up to automatically use this program for spell checking, but using `ispell` by itself is easy. For example, to check the spelling of the file `myfile.txt`, use the following:

```
# ispell myfile.txt
```

The `ispell` program loads the text and then displays the first found error in context, along with a single or several suggested replacements, as in this example:

```
MERCHANTIBILITY                    File: LICENSE

WARRANTIES, INCLUDING, WITHOUT LIMITATION, THE IMPLIED WARRANTIES OF
MERCHANTIBILITY AND FITNESS FOR A PARTICULAR PURPOSE.

 0: MERCHANTABILITY
[SP] <number> R)epl A)ccept I)nsert L)ookup U)ncap Q)uit e(X)it or ?
➥for help
```

Correct the spelling by either typing 0, the number of the suggested replacement word, or R, which you can use to replace the word by retyping it.

Look up other words with L, the lookup command, which searches the system dictionary, called words, located under the /usr/dict directory. If you use I, or the insert command, ispell creates a personal dictionary in your home directory, using .ispell_english as a filename.

You also can specify multiple documents on the ispell command line:

```
# ispell *.txt
```

This command line causes ispell to load each file ending in .txt for spell checking. If you prefer to use ispell as the more traditional UNIX spell command, which reads a document and then prints out a list of suspected words, use the -l, or list, option on the command line:

```
# ispell -l < LICENSE
...
Julianne
Haugh
uunet
uu
MERCHANTIBILITY
...
```

Note that the < redirection operator is used because in the -l mode, the ispell command acts as a spelling filter, checking the input text stream against its dictionary (located under the /usr/lib/ispell directory). You can redirect this list to a file or use the -f command-line option:

```
# ispell -l -f errors -a <LICENSE
```

This sends all misspelled words to the file called errors. The ispell program has 15 different command-line options. Use the -L option to change the amount of context, or text displayed before and after a suspected error. The -b option creates a backup file of your original document, which is a good idea if you make the mistake of entering a wrong correction (this is the default for your version of ispell).

The ispell package includes nine other programs you can use to build your own dictionaries or to add lists of words from your personal dictionary into the ispell dictionaries. For details about these programs, see the ispell manual page. For details about building your own dictionaries, read the ispell manual page under the /usr/man/man5 directory. You can do this with the following command:

```
# man 5 ispell
```

Documentation for ispell is in its two manual pages and under the /usr/doc/ispell directory.

Single Word Lookup and Other Tricks

When all you need is quick confirmation of the spelling of a single word, you don't have to run your word processor or text editor to get the answer because you can use the look command, found under the /usr/bin directory.

Although the look command is normally used to search files and print all lines matching a given string pattern, the look command quickly looks up a word in the system dictionary. If you don't specify a file to search on the look command line, look automatically searches the system dictionary, called words, which is located in the /usr/dict directory. See the following example:

```
# look consci
conscience
consciences
conscientious
conscientiously
conscious
consciously
consciousness
```

> The system dictionary, words, is a symbolic link to the file called linux.words, also located in the /usr/dict directory. This dictionary, a 400,000 character, plain ASCII list of sorted words, contains 45,402 words. You can find an even larger dictionary, called web2, which is more than two megabtyes and contains more than 234,000 words, by searching your favorite Linux Internet sites or browsing to ftp://ftp.digital.com/pub/BSD/net2/share/dict.

All you have to do is type several characters of the beginning of a word, and the look command prints any matches found in the system dictionary. You also can use the ispell command's -a command-line option to check spelling interactively or quickly look up a single word or several words at the keyboard. Lookups are performed on the ispell dictionary, not the system dictionary. See the following example:

```
# ispell -a
@(#) International Ispell Version 3.1.20 10/10/95
seperate
& seperate 1 0: separate

mispell
& mispell 2 0: ispell, misspell
```

```
mississippi
& mississippi 1 0: Mississippi

truncate
*
[Ctrl-d]
#
```

Notice that ispell starts, prints a short version message, and then waits for your input. When you enter a misspelled word, ispell echoes the word back and if a suggested replacement is found, prints the replacement with a number. Also note that ispell even corrects words spelled correctly but not properly capitalized. Finally, if you enter a correct word, ispell merely echoes back an asterisk. To quit, enter an end of text character by pressing Ctrl+D.

Summary

This hour introduced you to a number of word processors, editors, and text utilities for OpenLinux. You now also know how to spellcheck text documents using the ispell command and how to quickly look up words from the command line.

Q&A

Q I found that I made a lot of incorrect changes to a document when using xemacs. I know about the undo command, but is there are faster way to quickly fix things?

A The good news is the xemacs creates a backup file of your document. However, you can revert back to the original form of the document with the revert-buffer command. Press the Esc key, and then type the **x** key. At the command prompt (at the lower left of the xemacs window), type **revert-buffer**, and press Enter.

Q Help! I can't get printing to work with WordPerfect!

A Don't panic. See Hour 15, "Preparing Documents," for step-by-step directions on how to print with WordPerfect.

Q I entered a misspelled word into my personal dictionary when using ispell. How can I fix this?

A The personal dictionary is a simple text file. Open the file with your favorite text editor and remove or correct the word.

14

Q I accepted an incorrect word when using `ispell`, and the file has been written to disk! How can I fix this?

A Fortunately, `ispell` saves a copy of your original document with the extension `.bak` appended. Use the `mv` command to replace the incorrect file or to rename the backup file.

Q StarOffice 5.0 won't let me install or finish its installation after I enter my name, customer number, and personal key!

A Make sure you enter your name, customer ID and registration number exactly as entered when you registered StarOffice. You can later change your personal information through the Configuration menu.

Q I want words to wrap around in the `kedit` editing window. How do I do this?

A Select the Options menu, and then click the `kedit` Options menu item. Next, click the Set Fill-Column At button, and type in the number of characters you want to use for a line width.

Q How do I print with the CRiSPlite editor?

A Open the Setup Options dialog box and select Printer. In the Print to file field, type ¦ `lpr`, and then click the Apply button.

Exercises

1. Experiment with the Search and Replace dialog box in the `kedit` editor. If you're not the root operator, try opening a text file under the `/usr/doc` directory and then saving the file with a different name. Why can't this be done?

2. Create a blank StarWriter document, and then in a separate terminal window, highlight the output of a program, such as `ls`. How should you paste the highlighted text in the StarWriter document? (Hint: You can't use the middle mouse button!)

3. Try using cut and paste operations in the `pico` editor to move different paragraphs inside a document. How do you move blocks of text with `pico`?

HOUR 15

Preparing Documents

Hour 14, "Text Processing," discussed text editing tools and programs used to create, edit, and save documents. This hour introduces you to programs and utilities used to format and print your text documents. It starts off with a discussion of different text formatting programs and shows you how to easily format your documents for printing without using complicated formatting commands. It then shows you how to use more complex programs using simple command lines.

The hour concludes with a discussion of the basics of document printing under OpenLinux, as well as detailed information about how to configure your printer to get the best possible output.

Formatting Text

Although you can do basic formatting of text documents using a text editor, most of these basic editing programs for OpenLinux lack the necessary features to add page numbering, boldfacing, font changes, indenting, or other fancy text layout.

The programs discussed in this hour are used to prepare, format, convert, and print text documents. To create professionally typeset documents with a word processor, try StarOffice's StarWriter or Corel's WordPerfect 8 for Linux. See Hour 14 to learn more about these programs.

Producing nicely typeset documents using the text utility programs included with OpenLinux is usually a three step process. First, you create the document using a text editor and intersperse your text with typesetting commands to create certain effects when you filter your document through a formatting program. The second step is to process your document through a typesetting program and produce formatted output. The third step is to either check your formatting by previewing the document or if you're confident about your formatting, to print the document.

This section shows you how to use formatting programs to produce nicely organized documents. It also discusses the basic syntax, or commands, that these programs recognize.

Formatting Text Using Text Filters

In Hour 14, you were introduced to some text filters that change the output of different programs or the contents of a document. The text filters discussed here can help you quickly format your documents if you don't want to learn a complex formatting program or use complicated typesetting commands. You can find these programs useful to quickly build formatted documents with headers, footers, margins, and page numbers.

Sending directory listings or short text files directly to your printer without formatting might be okay, but printing larger text files usually requires better formatting. One command you can use is the pr command, found under the /usr/bin directory. The pr command has 19 different command-line options to format documents, as shown in Table 15.1.

TABLE 15.1   COMMON *pr* COMMAND-LINE OPTIONS

Option	Action
+x	Begin printing at page *x*
-a	Print columns across the page
-b	Balance columns (on last page)
-c	Use ^c notation to make control characters visible
-d	Use double spacing

15

`-e[x[y]]`	Convert tabs (or x) to spaces, use y tab character width
`-f, -F`	Output form feed between pages
`-h str`	Use str as page header instead of filename
`-i[x[y]]`	Convert spaces (or x) to tabs, use y spaces in tabs
`-l xx`	Page length set to xx
`-m`	Print multiple files in parallel columns on page
`-n[x][y]]`	Use line numbers (with a following character x), and y digits for the numbers
`-o x`	Set left margin to x
`-r`	Turn off warning messages
`-s[x]`	Use character x to separate columns
`-t`	Turn off default headers and footers
`-v`	Show unprintable characters in base 8 (octal) notation
`-w xx`	Set page width to xx characters
`-x`	Format page into *x* columns

Look at the following example:

```
# pr +4 -h "Draft Number 1" -o 8 <pilotprimer.txt ¦ >output.txt
```

This command line formats the file `pilotprimer.txt`, starting at page 4, with a header containing the date, time, page number, and the words `Draft Number 1`; the left margin is 8 spaces. Using the > redirection operator, the formatted output is then saved to a file called `output.txt`, which you can print at a later time.

> Pipe the output through the `less` pager to preview your formatting before printing.

The `pr` program also formats selected streams of text. One handy use is to create formatted columns. For example, if you have a paragraph, you can quickly create columns of text by combining several filter programs and then formatting the text with the `-COLUMN` command-line option (a hyphen, followed by the number of columns; `-3` in the following example):

```
# cat cities.txt
Cincinnati, San Francisco, Philadelphia, Chicago, Miami, Norfolk,
Savannah, Seattle, Pittsburgh, St. Louis, Phoenix, Nashville, Las Vegas,
Atlantic City, Raleigh
# cat cities.txt ¦ sed 's/, /#/g' ¦ tr '#' '\n' ¦ sort ¦ pr -l 1 -3
Atlantic City          Chicago             Cincinnati
Las Vegas,             Miami               Nashville
Norfolk,               Philadelphia        Phoenix
Pittsburgh             Raleigh             San Francisco
Savannah               Seattle             St. Louis
```

The preceding example uses a list of cities separated by commas. By using several filters, including the pr command, the text is formatted as a readable list, sorted alphabetically. The command line works by first using the sed stream editor (discussed in Hour 14) to change each comma and space to a pound (#) sign. The pound sign is translated to a carriage return by the tr command (also discussed in Hour 14). The text, now a list of words, one per line, is fed into the sort command. The sorted text is fed into the pr command to produce three columns of text (the -l (or page length) option, with a value of 1, is used to inhibit the page header).

You also can use the fmt command with the pr command to change the word wrap, or width, of your text documents. The following example is part of a public-domain software license (found under the /usr/doc/shadow-misc directory):

```
# cat LICENSE
...
1.  You may make and give away verbatim copies of the source form of the
Standard Version of this Package without restriction, provided that you
duplicate all of the original copyright notices and associated
disclaimers.

2.  You may apply bug fixes, portability fixes and other modifications
derived from the Public Domain or from the Copyright Holder.  A Package
modified in such a way shall still be considered the Standard Version.
...
```

Although this text might be okay when printed on the screen or by using the default settings with the pr command, the text overruns lines if you use a left margin of 10 spaces. Look at the following example:

```
# pr -o 10 <LICENSE
...
          1.  You may make and give away verbatim copies of the source fo
rm of the
          Standard Version of this Package without restriction, provided
that you
          duplicate all of the original copyright notices and associated
          disclaimers.
```

```
        2.  You may apply bug fixes, portability fixes and other modifi
cations
        derived from the Public Domain or from the Copyright Holder.  A
    Package
        modified in such a way shall still be considered the Standard V
ersion.
...
```

The preceding example certainly doesn't look nice when printed! To fix this, use the `fmt` command to format the text with a smaller line width before formatting with the `pr` command:

```
# cat LICENSE ¦ fmt -w 60 ¦ pr -o 10
...
        1.  You may make and give away verbatim copies of the
        source form of the Standard Version of this Package
        without restriction, provided that you duplicate all of
        the original copyright notices and associated disclaimers.

        2.  You may apply bug fixes, portability fixes and other
        modifications derived from the Public Domain or from the
        Copyright Holder.  A Package modified in such a way shall
        still be considered the Standard Version.

...
```

As you can see, the text now fits nicely on your page when printed. You can also create more sophisticated effects by combining the output of `fmt` with the multiple-column option of the `pr` command. For example, to format the previous example document, `pilotprimer.txt`, use the `fmt` command to reformat the text into a thin column of 26 characters, and then send the text through the `pr` command to format the text into multiple columns, like this:

```
# fmt -26 <pilotprimer.txt ¦ pr -2 -s\¦ -o 2 -t -w 60
  HACKING THE 3COM PALM      ¦Information You Need
  PILOT PERSONAL DIGITAL     ¦to Connect
  ASSISTANT                  ¦
                             ¦There are several things
  Although most              ¦you need to know before
  manufacturers tout their   ¦you can starting web
  brand of Personal Digital  ¦browsing, Usenet news
  Assistant, or PDA, as the  ¦reading, or sending and
  "easiest to use," or most  ¦receiving email on your
  "convenient" device, when  ¦Pilot. When you signed
  it comes to connecting     ¦up for your Internet
  to the Internet, novice    ¦service, you should have
  PDA and Internet users     ¦received an information
  may still have a hard      ¦packet from your
  time in making that        ¦ISP. This information
  first connection to        ¦should include:
...
```

Not all the output is shown, but as you can see, the `fmt` command is used to convert the text stream into a 26-character wide column. This output is then fed to `pr`, which formats the text in two columns. The `-s` option is followed by a backslash (\) and a vertical bar (¦) to specify the vertical bar as a column separator. The `-o` option sets the left margin to two spaces, and the `-t` option turns off headers and footers. The `-w 60` option sets a page width of 60 characters, which is certainly suitable for most printers.

But what if you want to save paper and see at least two pages of output on a single page? In this case, use the `mpage`, or multiple page, command to print several sheets of paper on a single page. Look at the following example:

```
# mpage -2 myfile.txt >myfile.ps
```

This command line uses the `mpage` command, found under the `/usr/bin` directory, to create a PostScript file you can later print that contains the contents of the `myfile.txt` document as two side-by-side pages on each sheet of paper. To preview the PostScript file during an X11 session, use the `gv` previewer, like this:

```
# gv myfile.ps
```

> You can use the `mpage` command's `-O`, `-E`, or `-R` options to print full-duplex (back-to-back) documents. This can be handy for producing small booklets using letter-size paper with a printer that's not capable of printing on both sides of each sheet. You also can set different margins, fonts, and the order of printed pages. See the `mpage` manual page for details.

Using the `fmt`, `pr`, or `mpage` commands, along with other text filters, you can perform quick and dirty rudimentary text formatting. If you want to try more complex formatting, use a text formatting program.

Formatting Text with the `groff` Formatter

If you've used OpenLinux for the past several hours and have read some manual pages, you're probably familiar with at least one complex formatting program: `groff`. When you read a manual page with

```
# man ls
```

it is equivalent to the following:

```
# nroff -man /usr/man/man1/ls.1 ¦ less
```

NEW TERM   Notice that the `nroff` command is used on the command line instead of `groff`. This is because the `nroff` command installed on your system is a shell script, written to use the GNU `groff` formatting program to emulate the `nroff` command. All OpenLinux man pages are written using a special set of `nroff` commands called *man macros*. You can use the `groff` command to use man macros to format your own manual pages. For example, if you create a manual page for a new game called `nw`, the manual page, called `nw.6`, might look like the following:

```
.TH Nano-Warrior 6  Games 1/1/98 Linux
.SH NAME
nw - play Nano-Warrior
.SH SYNOPSIS
nw
.B -d
.PP
-d = play deathmatch mode
.SH DESCRIPTION
.PP
The nw command is used to play a game of Nano-Warrior on your Linux
console. Play continues until you are wiped out by hordes of alien
invaders swarming down the screen.
.PP
Don't give up the fight!
.SH FILES
/usr/games/nw
.PP
$HOME/.nw_scores
.SH BUGS
Probably too many.
```

You can process this manual page and send it to your display with the following:

```
# groff -Tascii -man nw.6
Nano-Warrior(6)                 Linux                 Nano-Warrior(6)


NAME
        nw - play Nano-Warrior

SYNOPSIS
        nw -d

        -d = play deathmatch mode

DESCRIPTION
        The  nw  command is used to play a game of Nano-Warrior on
        your Linux console. Play continues until you are wiped out
        by hordes of alien invaders swarming down the screen.

        Don't give up the fight!
```

15

```
FILES
        /usr/games/nw

        $HOME/.nw_scores

BUGS
        Probably too many.
```

Notice that the man page macros boldface the sections and format the following text automatically. A list of these and other manual page macros are found in the man.7 manual page under the /usr/man/man7 directory. You can read this manual page with the following:

 # man 7 man

The groff formatting program also comes with other sets of typesetting macros, such as the me, mm, or ms manuscript macros used to format text files. You generally need to specify the macro set on the groff command line if you use these commands:

 # groff -Tascii -mm myfile.txt

Documentation for several of these macros is on various manual pages related to groff. One of the best documented sets included with your OpenLinux distribution is the collection of mm manuscript macros on the groff_mm manual page. Table 15.2 lists some common macros you can use to produce formatted documents.

TABLE 15.2 COMMON *groff mm* MACROS

Action	Macro Name
Center justify	.ds C
End text box	.b2
Justification off	.sa 0
Justification on	.sa 1
Line fill off	.ds N
Line fill on	.ds F
New paragraph with x indent	.p x
No indents	.ds L
Right justify	.ds R
Start bold text	.b
Start text box	.b1
Use columns	.mc
Use one column	.1c
Use two columns	.2c

15

Some of the more common commands that don't require a macro set are listed in Table 15.3. Experiment with them to see their effect on your documents before printing.

TABLE 15.3   COMMON *groff* TYPESETTING COMMANDS

Action	Command Name
Begin new page	.bp
Begin new paragraph	.pp
Center next *x* lines	.ce *x*
Center text *x*	.ce *x*
Insert (space) *x* inches down	.sp *x*i
Insert *x* inches down	.sv *x*i
Set font bold	.ft B
Set font roman	.ft R
Set line spacing to *x*	.ls *x*
Temporary indent *x* inches	.ti *x*i
Turn off line fill	.nf
Turn on centering	.ce
Turn on indenting *x* inches	.in *x*i
Turn on line fill	.fi
Underline next *x* lines	.ul *x*

When you're ready to produce a formatted document, use the groff command's -T command-line option to produce a document in several different document formats. The groff formatter produces PostScript, TeX dvi (discussed next), text, HP printer-control language, or PCL formats. Look at the following example:

```
# groff -Tascii -mm myfile.txt >myfile.txt
# groff -Tps -mm myfile.txt >myfile.ps
# groff -Tdvi -mm myfile.txt >myfile.dvi
```

You can preview these documents before printing by using several different programs, such as gv for PostScript (.ps) or xdvi for dvi files (.dvi).

The gv program is discussed in Hour 16, "Graphics Tools."

Formatting Text with TeX

The TeX typesetting system, originally by Donald E. Knuth, is a collection of programs and other utilities used to produce professionally formatted documents. It is a much more sophisticated system than the groff distribution and includes more than 65 programs, along with such related support files as libraries, macros, fonts, and documentation.

If you install TeX on your system with the lisa or rpm commands, you need at least 30 megabytes for the main distribution, 10 megabytes for a series of related macros called LaTeX, and eight megabytes for 50 different fonts. Obviously, describing the entire system and how to use each different program in the TeX system is beyond this hour. But this section shows you how to get started with a sample document.

> Previewing TeX dvi documents requires a preprocessing step that can take several minutes before the pages are even displayed. Files must first be processed by the MakeTeXPK program, and related processes can eat up your system resources. A much better approach is to convert the file to PostScript with the dvips command, found under the /usr/bin directory with the following:
>
>   dvips -f < texdoc.dvi >tex.ps
>
> Now use the gv program with gv tex.ps to read the file.

You can find documentation for TeX in a variety of places. You can read the manual pages for related files, check the /usr/info directory for TeX information files, and browse to the /usr/TeX/texmf/doc directory. There are 10 different directories of documentation files, but the easiest way to read about your TeX distribution is to use the lynx Web browser with the following:

```
# lynx ls /usr/TeX/texmf/doc/index.html
```

The TeX distribution files are displayed in an organized list that you can browse through to download sample files and guides directly to your home directory. Beginning users should definitely read the TeX Frequently Asked Questions (FAQ) document.

Like the groff program, TeX uses formatting commands inserted in your text files to manipulate how your file looks when printed. You create your file, insert appropriate commands or macros to format text, and then process your document through TeX to create an output file, usually in dvi format, that you can preview or print.

To see a sample of TeX using the LaTeX macros, try processing a sample file in the TeX directories:

```
# latex  /usr/TeX/texmf/doc/generic/pstricks/samples.tex
```

This creates a file called `samples.dvi`. First, convert the file to PostScript with the `dvips` command, like this:

```
# dvips -f <samples.dvi >samples.ps
```

You see quite a bit of output from this command. When the command finishes, use the `gv` client to preview the `sample.ps` document, like so:

```
# gv samples.ps
```

You can use TeX to produce complex diagrams and text, but you have to make the effort to learn TeX first!

> There are many different macros and macro sets included with the TeX formatting system. Covering the details of complex formatting is beyond the scope of this book, but you're encouraged to experiment, starting with simple commands, to get a feel for typesetting documents. There are nearly 100 books about using TeX on the market. If you're serious about learning how to use TeX, a good book is indispensable.

Printing Text Documents

After you finish formatting your text files, using either a series of filters or inserted typesetting commands, you can print your file to produce a typeset hard copy. To control the printing of your documents, you need to understand how OpenLinux handles printing and how to start, stop, cancel, and control the printing process.

There are several printing commands you can use to control the printing process on your system. This section first shows you how your printer is described under OpenLinux and where the important printer files are located. Because most OpenLinux users at home have a parallel printer attached to their computers, this hour's discussion is limited to parallel printers.

Printers are known as character mode devices and are listed under the `/dev` directory. Look at the following example:

```
# ls /dev/lp*
/dev/lp0 /dev/lp1 /dev/lp2
```

This shows the three parallel printer devices that are installed on your system by default.

> Serial printers are serial devices and have names such as /dev/ttySX, where
> X is a number from 0 to 3 (similar to your modem ports). Read the setserial
> command's manual page to learn how to set your serial port to the fastest
> baud rate your printer supports. Read Grant Taylor's Printing-HOWTO under
> the /usr/doc/HOWTO directory for additional pointers on using serial printers.

To determine if your printer is working, first make sure your printer is plugged in,
attached to your computer's parallel port, and turned on. Next, boot OpenLinux, and log
in. For a clue about which printer parallel port and printer device are used, pipe the output of the dmesg command through the less pager, and look for output similar to the following:

```
lp1 at 0x0378, (polling)
```

Then, using the specified device (in this case, lp1) try sending a directory listing to your
printer with the following:

```
# ls >/dev/lp1
```

> You might also hear your printer activate or reset as OpenLinux boots and
> loads the lp.o parallel printer kernel module.

If you specified the right printer device, your printer activates and prints the current
directory list. If nothing happens, try looking at any listed devices in the OpenLinux
process directory, like so:

```
# cat /proc/devices
```

See if the printer device driver was loaded or compiled in your kernel. You see something
like the following:

```
Character devices:
...
 6 lp
...
```

If you don't see an lp device listed, make sure that the parallel printing lp.o module is
listed in the OpenLinux module file (with the pathname returned by uname -r and uname
-v commands) under the /etc/modules directory.

Printing Documents with the LPRng Printing System

If you installed a printer during the initial Linux installation process, you can find your printer defined in the /etc/printcap file. This file is an ASCII database of your system's local and network printers and describes the capabilities of each printer.

OpenLinux uses Patrick Powell's line printer spooling system, named LPRng, which is an updated and improved version of the lpr spooling system used by other Linux distributions. It features networking and security enhancements. When you first boot, OpenLinux starts lpd, the line printer daemon. The lpd program runs in the background, waiting for printing requests. You start a printing request with the lpr command:

```
# lpr mydocument.txt
# lpr myfile.ps
```

This command line spools, or sends, your documents to a file in the /var/spool/lpd directory. You also can use the lpr command as a printing filter to print outgoing streams of formatted text:

> In general, files sent to your printer are converted to PostScript according to a set of configuration rules in files called *print filters* under the /var/spool/lpd/lp directory. Under OpenLinux, your printer is designated as a PostScript printer (with the name ps), which enables a wide variety of UNIX and Linux programs to work transparently to print your documents.

```
# groff -Tascii -mm myfile.txt ¦ lpr
```

This command line sends the output of the groff formatting program through the line printer spooler. You also can spool multiple files and then track your print *jobs*, or printing requests, by using the lpq command. See the following example:

```
# lpr mes.txt
# lpr test.txt
# lpq
Printer: ps@presario
 Queue: 2 printable jobs
 Server: pid 797 active
 Unspooler: pid 798 active
 Status: printed all 16543 bytes at 14:30:05
 Rank    Owner/ID                 Class Job  Files          Size Time
active  bball@presario+796          A  796 (stdin)        16543 14:30:05
2       bball@presario+804          A  804 kdmfix.txt      1500 14:30:10
```

The output of the lpq command in the preceding example shows that there are two jobs created by the user bball for the printer ps@presario. If you don't want to print various spooled files, use the lprm command to remove a waiting print job. For example, to delete the print job for the kdmfix.txt document in the preceding example, use the following:

```
# lprm 804
```

You also can (as the root operator) disable or enable printers or reorder jobs with the lpc command. When you start lpc by itself on the command line, you see a prompt like this:

```
# lpc
>
```

This command has built-in help. To see a list of commands, use a question mark (?), like this:

```
# lpc
> ?
usage: %s [-A] [-Ddebuglevel] [-Pprinter] [-V] [command]
 with no commands, reads from stdin
  -A              - use authentication
  -Pprinter       - specify printer
  -V              - increase information verbosity
  -Ddebuglevel  - debug level
 commands:
abort    (printer[@host] ¦ all)  - stop server
disable  (printer[@host] ¦ all)  - disable queueing
debug    (printer[@host] ¦ all) debugparms - set debug level for printer
enable   (printer[@host] ¦ all)  - enable  queueing
hold     (printer[@host] ¦ all) (name[@host] ¦ job ¦ all)* - hold job
holdall  (printer[@host] ¦ all)  - hold all jobs on
kill     (printer[@host] ¦ all)  - stop and restart server
lpd [HUP]  - get LPD PID, signal it to reread printcap and configuration
lpq (printer[@host] ¦ all) (name[@host] ¦ job ¦ all)*      - invoke LPQ
lprm (printer[@host] ¦ all) (name[@host]¦host¦job¦ all)*  - invoke LPRM
move printer (user¦jobid)* target - move jobs to new queue
noholdall (printer[@host] ¦ all)  - hold all jobs off
printcap (printer[@host] ¦ all) - report printcap values
quit                            - exit LPC
redirect (printer[@host] ¦ all) (printer@host ¦ off )*   - redirect jobs
release  (printer[@host] ¦ all) (name[@host] ¦ job ¦ all)* - release job
reread                          - LPD reread database information
start    (printer[@host] ¦ all)  - start printing
status   (printer[@host] ¦ all)  - status of printers
stop     (printer[@host] ¦ all)  - stop  printing
topq     (printer[@host] ¦ all) (name[@host] ¦ job ¦ all)* - reorder job
lpc>
```

Documentation for your OpenLinux printing system can be found in various man pages of the LPRng software distribution and under the /usr/doc/LPRng directory. Table 15.4 lists the major components and programs used.

TABLE 15.4   PRINT SPOOLING SYSTEM UTILITIES

Name	Description
lpc	The line printer control program
lpd	The line printer daemon
lpd.conf	Description of the LPRng configuration file
lpd.perms	Description of the LPRng permissions control file
lpf	A printer filter (used in printer definition files)
lpq	Show the printer spool queue
lpr	Start print jobs
lpraccnt	Printer accounting information utility
lprm	Delete print jobs from the spool queue
monitor	Log information from the lpd daemon

Configuring Your Printer with the `lisa` Command

Installing, changing, or deleting local printers with your OpenLinux system is a snap thanks to the Linux Installation and System Adminisration utility called `lisa`. This program is located under the /bin directory. This program can be used with or without the X Window System to set up your printer so you can print from the command line or through various X11 clients.

Because `lisa` is a system administration tool, you have to make sure you're the root operator and then type the following at your console or terminal command-line to configure your printer:

```
# lisa --printer
```

The screen clears, and you see a dialog box, as shown in Figure 15.1.

This dialog box lists nearly 40 different printers. Scroll through the list, and then pick a printer that matches your printer (or has the same capabilities).

FIGURE 15.1

The lisa *program provides an easy-to-use interface when you need to configure a printer for OpenLinux.*

If you have a printer that appears to be unsupported, check Caldera System's Web site at http://www.calderasystems.com/support/techguide.html to see if additional support has been created for your printer. Users of Epson Stylus color printers definitely need to read about support for these printers. If you want to print over a network or install a network printer, definitely read the "Local Filter for Remote Printer" document. If you have a PostScript printer, see the document "Setting Up a Real PostScript Printer."

When you finish, press Enter. You see a dialog box (in Figure 15.2) that lists several parallel-printer ports. Scroll through the list, pick your computer's parallel port, and press Enter.

FIGURE 15.2

After you select your printer, lisa *asks you to select the appropriate parallel-printer port for your computer's printer.*

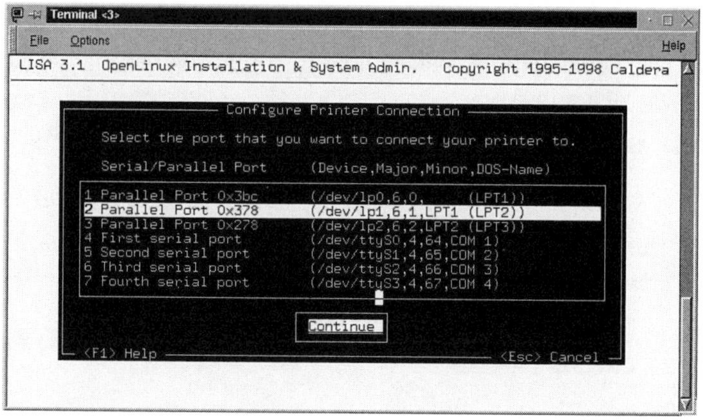

Your next step is to select the default resolution supported by your printer. This value is in horizontal and vertical dots per inch. If you're not sure about your printer, check the manufacturer's manual included with your printer. Scroll through the list of resolutions (shown in Figure 15.3), and pick one that matches your printer's capabilities.

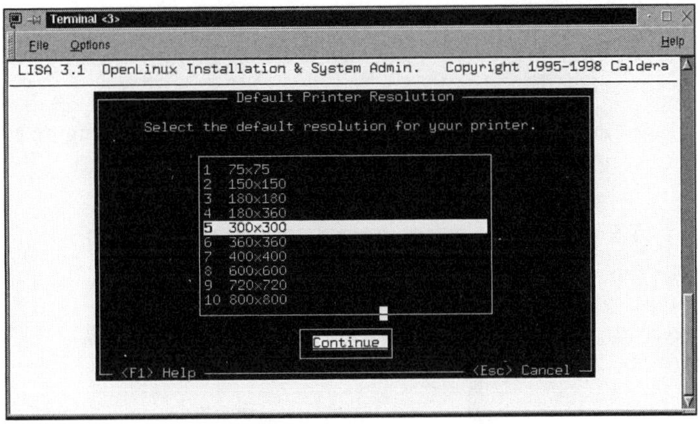

FIGURE 15.3

Select the proper resolution when configuring a printer for OpenLinux.

When you finish, press Enter. As the last step, you now see a dialog box asking for the default paper size used with your printer. These capabilities are all used to build and configure a proper print filter for your printer. Scroll through the list of paper sizes (shown in Figure 15.4), select the right size, and press Enter to finish configuring your printer.

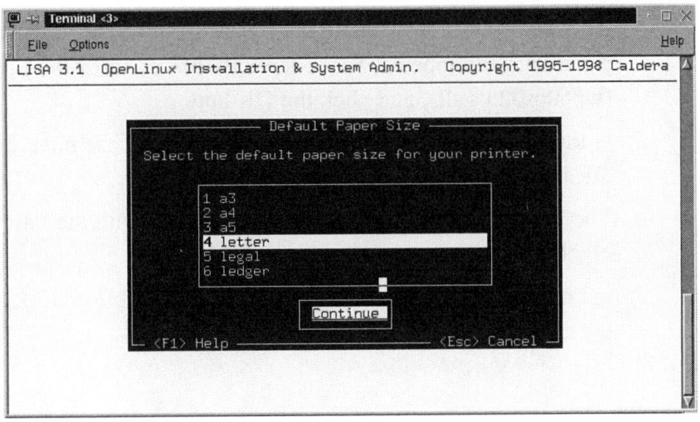

FIGURE 15.4

You must also select a default paper size when you configure a printer for OpenLinux.

Configuring WordPerfect for Printing

If you downloaded and installed the free-for-personal-use edition of Corel's WordPerfect 8 for Linux from http://www.linux.corel.com/linux8/index.htm, you need to follow several steps to print. This involves adding and selecting a printer driver as the default printer.

1. Start WordPerfect, and then press the F5 key. In the WordPerfect Print dialog box, click the Select button.

2. A Select Printer dialog box appears, as shown in Figure 15.5. Click the Printer Create/Edit button.

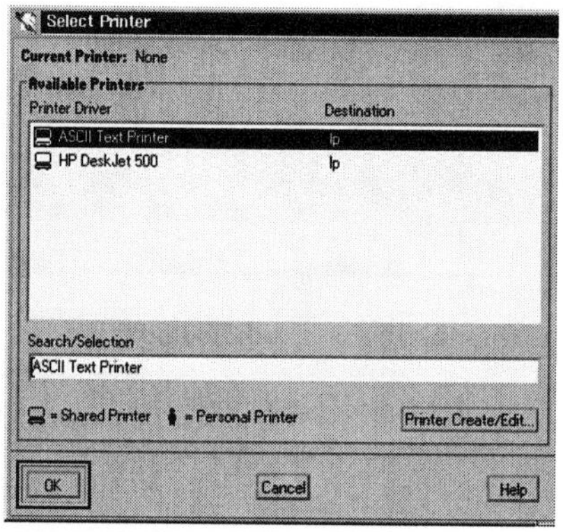

FIGURE 15.5

The WordPerfect Select Printer dialog box is used to create or edit printers.

3. A Printer Create/Edit dialog box appears. Click the Add button.

4. An Add Printer Driver dialog box (shown in Figure 15.6) with a scrolling list of printer drivers appears. Scroll through the list, click the Passthru PostScript driver (wp60ps02.us.all), and click the OK button.

5. A tiny Create Printer dialog box appears, using the name passpost.prs. Click the OK button.

6. The Printer Create/Edit dialog box reappears with the Passthru PostScript printer highlighted. Click the Setup button.

7. A Printer Setup dialog box appears, as shown in Figure 15.7. Near the bottom of the dialog box, click the Destination button.

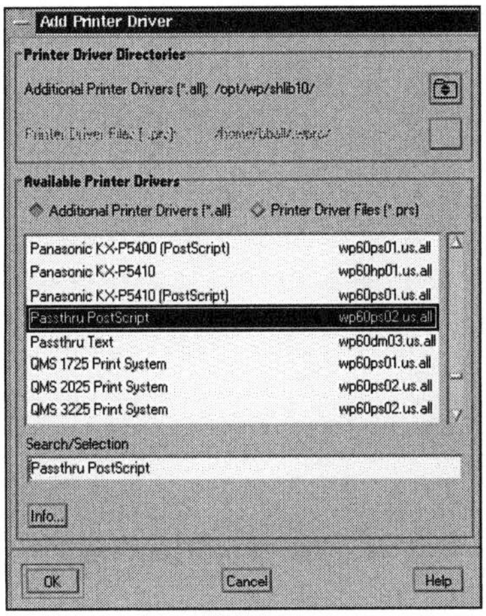

FIGURE 15.6

Select the Passthru PostScript WordPerfect printer driver to create a printer for OpenLinux.

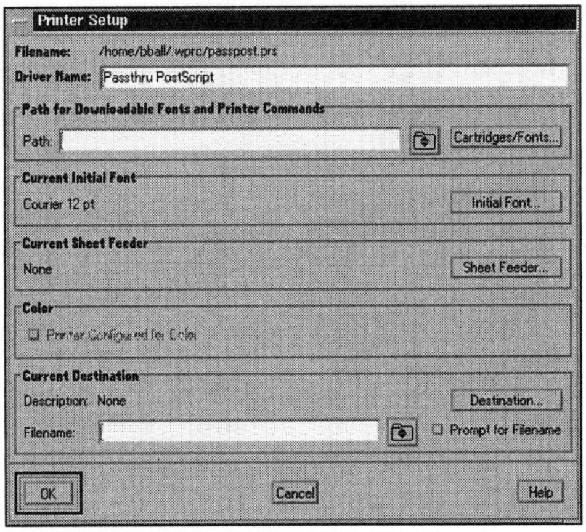

15

FIGURE 15.7

In the Printer Setup dialog box, click the Destination button in the Current Destination section to select a document destination.

8. A Select Destination dialog box appears (as shown in Figure 15.8), listing $PRINTER, Disk, lp, and ps. Click ps, and then click the OK button.

9. In the Printer Setup dialog box, click the OK button. In the Printer Create/Edit dialog box, click the OK button. In the Select Printer dialog box, click the OK button. You're now at the main Print dialog box. Click OK to print the current document or Cancel to cancel the printing operation. (You won't lose the new printer you created.)

If you set up printing to work correctly under OpenLinux before starting these steps, you can now print WordPerfect documents to your printer!

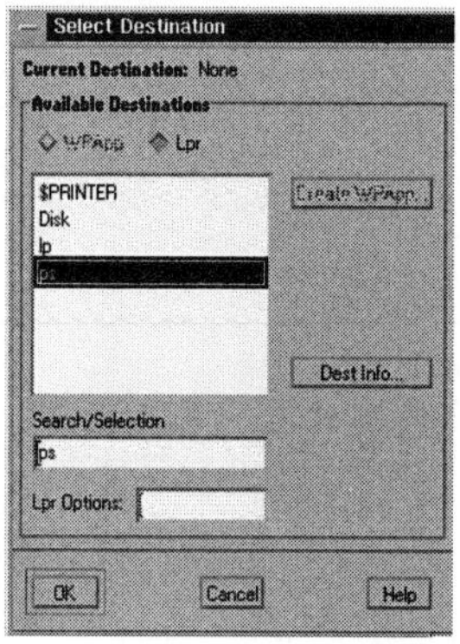

FIGURE 15.8

*In the Select
Destination dialog
box, you complete your
printer setup.*

Summary

This hour details some of the programs you can use to format and prepare text documents for printing. You also learned a little about some of the more complex typesetting systems included with OpenLinux. Finally, you learned how to start, list, and control print jobs from the command line. You also learned how to create and configure a printer to use with OpenLinux.

Q&A

Q What other formatting utilities are included with OpenLinux?

A There are quite a few, especially for converting text file documents to PostScript. Try using the enscript command to convert text documents, and then read about the eqn utility for formatting equations for typesetting, the pic command for typesetting pictures from text, and the makeindex command for creating document indexes.

Q What other typesetting systems are included with OpenLinux?

A Read the man pages for the amstex system, which uses macros to extend the power of the TeX system. Another system, named latex, is included with OpenLinux.

Q Typesetting using these macro languages seems tedious! Is there an easier way to create these documents?

A Try using the Lynx editor. This is a quasi-What-You-See-Is-What-You-Get editor that creates documents styled similarly to latex.

Q **I try printing, and the `lpr` command responds with an error like "connection to ps@localhost.localdomain failed—Network is unreachable"! What's going on?**

A Make sure that your `/etc/hosts` file contains a definition for the loopback device and local host. Also, make sure that you do not have any incorrect hostname definitions in the file.

15

Exercises

1. Try printing several files and then removing remaining jobs from the print queue.

2. Use `lisa` to try to reconfigure your printer to use a higher resolution. What happens?

3. Create your own man page using several of the man macros. Try using the `nroff` script and the `groff` program. Which works better?

HOUR 16

Graphics Tools

This hour introduces a variety of graphics programs and utilities for OpenLinux. I'll start with a short discussion of different graphics formats used with OpenLinux and then show how you can convert graphics using filter programs and other graphics utilities. These programs are useful for creating, editing, and translating graphics imported from other computer programs or operating systems.

You can find a treasure trove of great graphics programs on this book's CD-ROM, and you're likely to be impressed with their usefulness and versatility. At the end of this hour, you'll be able to translate nearly any type of graphics file and perform sophisticated operations to transform your graphic files.

Understand Linux Graphics File Formats

There are many different types of graphics file formats, and examples of several types are installed in your system. You might already be familiar with several different formats, especially if you've used other computer operating systems. However, if OpenLinux is new to you, expect to run into graphics files in formats you've never seen before.

Many graphics file formats can be recognized by the file name's extension, or letters following a period in the file name. For example, you might recognize .GIF, .PCX, .TIF, or .JPG as common extensions. More than 5,000 graphics are installed on your computer if you do a full installation of OpenLinux!

Table 16.1 lists numerous graphics formats, along with relevant conversion programs included on your system. Read on to learn how to convert a graphics image from one format to another.

TABLE 16.1 LINUX GRAPHICS FORMATS AND CONVERSION PROGRAMS

Format	Type	Conversion Program
.10x	Gemini 10X	pbmto10x
.3d	Red/Blue 3D pixmap	ppm3d
.asc	ASCII text	pbmtoascii
.atk	Andrew Tookit raster	atktopbm
		pbmtoatk
.avs	AVS X image	convert
.bie	Bi-level image expert	convert
.bg	BBN BitGraph graphics	pbmtobbnbg
.bmp	Windows, OS/2 bitmap	bmptoppm
		cjpeg
		convert
		gimp
		ppmtobmp
		xv
.bmp24	Windows 24-bit bitmap	convert
		xv
.brush	Xerox doodle brush	brushtopbm
.cgm	Computer graphics metafile	convert
.cmu	CMU window manager bitmap	cmuwmtopbm

Format	Type	Conversion Program
		pbmtocmuwm
.dcx	ZSoft Paintbrush	convert
.ddif	DDIF image	pnmtoddif
.dib	Windows bitmap image	convert
.dxb	AutoCAD database file	ppmtoacad
		sldtoppm
.dvi	TeX printer file	dvips
		dvilj4
		dvilj4l
		dvilj2p
		dvilj
.eps2	Encapsulated PostScript Level II	convert
.epsf	Encapsulated PostScript	convert
.epsi	PostScript preview bitmap	pbmtoepsi
		convert
.epson	Epson printer graphics	pbmtoepson
.fax	Group 3 fax	convert
.fig	TransFig image	convert
.fits	Flexible Image Transport	fitstopnm
		pnmtofits
		convert
		gimp
		xv
.fpx	FlashPix	convert
.g3	Group 3 fax file	g3topbm
		g32pbm
		g3cat
		pbm2g3
		pbmtog3
.gif	Graphics Interchange	cjpeg

continues

16

TABLE 16.1 CONTINUED

Format	Type	Conversion Program
		giftopnm
		gif2tiff
		gimp
		ppmtogif
		convert
		xv
.gif87	Graphic Interchange	convert
		xv
.go	Compressed GraphOn	pbmtogo
.gould	Gould scanner file	gouldtoppm
.icn	Sun icon	icontopbm
		pbmtoicon
.ico	Microsoft icon	convert
.ilbm	IFF ILBM file	ilbmtoppm
		ppmtoilbm
.img	GEM image file	gemtopbm
		pbmtogem
		imgtoppm
.icr	NCSA ICR raster	ppmtoicr
.jbig	Joint Bi-level Image Group	convert
.jpeg	Joint Photographic Experts	cjpeg
	Group	djpeg
		jpegtran
		convert
		gimp
		xv
.lj	HP LaserJet data	pbmtolj
.ln03	DEC LN03+ Sixel output	pbmtoln03
.mgr	MGR bitmap	mgrtopbm
		pbmtomgr
.miff	MNG multiple-image network	convert
.mitsu	Mitsubishi S340-10 file	ppmtomitsu

Format	Type	Conversion Program
.mpeg	Motion Picture Group	convert
.mtv	MTV ray tracer	mtvtoppm
		convert
.pbm	Portable bitmap	pbm*
		convert
		xv
.pcd	Photo CD	convert
.pcl	HP PaintJet PCL	ppmtopjxl
		convert
.pcx	PCX graphics	pcxtoppm
		ppmtopcx
		convert
		gimp
		xv
.pdf	Portable Document Format	convert
		xpdf
.pgm	Portable graymap	pbmtopgm
		pgmtoppm
		ppmtopgm
		convert
		cjpeg
		xv
.pi1	Atari Degas file	pi1toppm
		ppmtopi1
.pi3	Atari Degas file	pbmtopi3
		pi3topbm
.pict	Macintosh PICT file	picttoppm
		ppmtopict
		convert
.pj	HP PaintJet file	pjtoppm
		ppmtopj

continues

16

TABLE 16.1 CONTINUED

Format	Type	Conversion Program
.pk	PK format font	pbmtopk
		pktopbm
.plasma	Plasma fractal	convert
.plot	UNIX plot file	pbmtoplot
.png	Portable Network Graphic	pngtopnm
		pnmtopng
		convert
		gimp
		xv
.pnm	Portable anymap	pnm*
		convert
		gimp
.pnt	MacPaint file	macptopbm
		pbmtomacp
.ppm	Portable pixmap	ppm*
		cjpeg
		convert
		xv
.ps	PostScript (lines)	pbmtolps
		pnmtops
		convert
		xv
		gimp
		gv
.psd	Abode PhotoShop bitmap	convert
.ptx	Printronix printer graphics	pbmtoptx
.qrt	QRT ray tracer	qrttoppm
.rad	Radiance image	convert
.ras	Sun rasterfile	pnmtorast
		rasttopnm
		gimp

Format	Type	Conversion Program
		xv
.rla	Alias/Wavefront image	convert (read-only)
.rle	Utah run-length encoded	convert (read-only)
		xv
.sgi	Silicon Graphics image	pnmtosgi
		sgitopnm
		convert
.sir	Solitaire graphics	pnmtosir
		sirtopnm
.sixel	DEC sixel format	ppmtosixel
.spc	Atari Spectrum file	spctoppm
.spu	Atari Spectrum file	sputoppm
.sun	Sun rasterfile	convert
		gimp
.tga	TrueVision Targa file	ppmtotga
		tgatoppm
		convert
		gimp
		xv
.tiff	Tagged File Format	pnmtotiff
		tifftopnm
		ppmtotiff
		tiff2ps
		convert
		gimp
		xv
.tiff24	Tagged file Format (24-bit)	convert
		xv
.tim	PSX TIM	convert
.ttf	TrueType font file	convert
.txt	text file bitmap	pbmtext
		convert (read-only)

16

continues

TABLE 16.1 CONTINUED

Format	Type	Conversion Program
.uil	Motif UIL icon	ppmtouil
		convert
.upc	Universal Product Code	pbmupc
.uyvy	16-bit YUV format	convert
.vicar		convert (read-only)
		xv
.viff	Khoros Visualization image	convert
.x10bm	X10 bitmap	pbmtox10bm
.xbm	X11 bitmap	pbmtoxbm
		xbmtopbm
		convert
		xv
.xim	Xim file	ximtoppm
.xpm	X11 pixmap	ppmtoxpm
		xpmtoppm
		convert
		gimp
		xv
.xv	xv thumbnail	xvminitoppm
.xvpic	xv thumbnail file	xvpictoppm
.xwd	X11 Window Dump	pnmtoxwd
		xwdtopnm
		convert
		gimp
		xv
.ybm	Bennet Yee face file	pbmtoybm
		ybmtopbm
.yuv	Abekas YUV file	ppmtoyuv
		yuvtoppm
		convert
.zeiss	Zeiss confocal file	zeisstopnm
.zinc	Zinc bitmap	pbmtozinc

Converting and Viewing Graphics

There are a number of ways to convert graphic files to different formats using the programs installed on your system. Several of the painting or drawing programs discussed in this hour translate graphics, and many programs in Table 16.1 also work as filters in piped commands (see Hour 6, "Using the Shell," for details) to translate graphics.

You can use different combinations of these commands to convert files. OpenLinux users, such as graphics artists or system administrators, convert files for different reasons. Artists or casual users might want to import or export graphics for use by different drawing programs. System administrators might look for a side benefit of converting graphics to save disk space. In some instances, the savings can be considerable. Look at the following example:

```
# xwd >graphic.xwd
# xwdtopnm <graphic.xwd ¦ convert - graphic.jpg
xwdtopnm: writing PPM file
# ls -l graphic.*
-rw-r--r--   1 bball     users          11003 Jan 27 14:21 graphic.jpg
-rw-r--r--   1 bball     users         851523 Jan 27 14:17 graphic.xwd
```

The first command line uses the xwd client to create an X11 window dump graphics file (.xwd) after you select a window and press your left mouse button. The window dump file is converted to .pnm format with the xwdtopnm command, and the output stream is fed into the convert command to create a .jpg graphics file. The hyphen (-) following the convert command specifies that the standard input should be used in lieu of an input filename. As you can see, the .jpg graphics file is more than 77 times smaller than the X11 window dump graphics file!

Results and benefits of file compression vary, depending on the size of the graphics file and compression settings. See the convert man page for details.

There are also many graphics programs not listed in Table 16.1 that can be used to alter graphics images. For example, the pnmrotate, pnmsmooth, and pnmscale commands rotate, smooth, and resize graphics images. You can use a variety of these programs to not only convert graphics, but change their appearance or orientation.

If you're using pipes to convert graphics, you also can change the images on-the-fly by applying these filter programs. For example, if you have a graphics file in .xpm format but want to quickly flip it upside down and save it in `.gif` format, apply a filter program such as the `pnmflip` command:

```
# xpmtoppm penguin.xpm ¦ pnmflip -topbottom ¦ convert - penguin.gif
```

Here the file `penguin.xpm` is converted from `.xpm` format to `.ppm` format. The output of the `xpmtoppm` command is fed to the `pnmflip` command, which flips the graphics file upside down with the `-topbottom` option. The output of the `pnmflip` command is fed to the `convert` command, which reads the standard input and saves the graphics stream in `.gif` format.

Combinations of different filters achieve different effects. For other effects, see such commands as `pnmcrop`, `pnminvert`, `pnmrotate`, `pnmscale`, `pnnsmooth`, or `pnmtile`.

> Not all graphics conversion programs included with your Linux distribution read the standard input and write to the standard output. Read the manual pages for any desired conversion programs before experimenting with pipes on the command line.

> Preview or print the results of your conversions before discarding original files to make sure you achieve the effect you want and that the resulting graphics file does not suffer loss of image quality.

If you experiment with complex pipes, use the `convert` command, one of seven programs in the ImageMagick package (discussed later in the section "Graphics Editing with ImageMagick") for easier file conversions. This command, found under the `/usr/bin` directory, translates more than 75 different graphics file formats (even some not listed in Table 16.1).

The `convert` program normally works by recognizing different file extensions on the command line, as shown in the following example:

```
# xwd >graphic.xwd
# convert graphic.xwd graphic.tiff
```

Here, the `xwd` client is used to create an X11 window dump graphics file. The `convert` command then creates a `.tiff` file by specifying the `.tiff` extension on the second, or output, file on the command line. For details about using the `convert` command, see the `ImageMagick` and `convert` command man pages.

Graphics Editing with GIMP

You can change or manipulate graphics from the command line, but if you use X11, it's a lot more fun to interactively work with files using an image-processing program. One of the best and newest graphics tools for Linux is the GNU Image Manipulation Program, or the GIMP, by Spencer Kimball and Peter Mattis.

This capable and complex program, shown in Figure 16.1, has many features. If you've worked with commercial software image-editing programs on other operating systems (such as Adobe PhotoShop), you'll appreciate the GIMP's tools and filters. The GIMP features the following:

16

- 9 program operation menus
- 21 different editing tools
- 81 brushes
- 168 patterns
- 123 different plug-in filters and tools to create image effects or perform operations
- Import and export of 24 different graphics formats
- Multiple image windows, handy for cutting and pasting or multiple views of a file
- Multiple layers for each image, so that effects can be superimposed
- Multiple undo levels, handy if you make mistakes
- Six floating windows and dialog boxes for selecting tools, brushes, colors, or patterns

NEW TERM You need nearly 23 megabytes of hard drive space to install GIMP and its software libraries, support files, and related directories. The main GIMP files are installed under the /usr/X11R6/share/gimp and /usr/X11R6/lib/gimp/X.X directories, where X.X is the current version (1.0 at the time of this writing). The library directory contains GIMP's *plug-ins*, which are compiled modules run by GIMP from different menus that create effects or alter an image or image selection.

This program has 11 different command-line options (such as -help to show the list of options) but does not support X11 Toolkit options, such as geometry settings. When you specify a graphics file on the command line, GIMP attempts to load and interpret the file according to the file's extension. Starting GIMP is easy; simply type the following:

```
# gimp &
```

Unless you use the --nosplash option, you see a small window that provides details about various GIMP resource files while loading.

The file `gimprc` under your `.gimp` directory can contain settings for default brushes, patterns, palettes, and temporary directories. This file is initially empty, but you can copy the default systemwide `gimprc` file and then edit the various settings according to your needs. Table 16.2 lists some common settings you can change. For example, to create your own copy in your home directory, use the following:

```
# cp /usr/X11R6/share/gimp/gimprc $HOME/.gimp/gimprc
cp: overwrite `.gimp/gimprc'? y
```

If you edit large image files, you can quickly run out of disk space because GIMP initially uses 10 megabytes of system memory and creates large temporary files during editing sessions (this is not unusual, as even commercial image editing applications typically require swap storage three times larger than system memory). If you have a separate hard drive with a lot of room, change the swap path (which is not the same as your Linux swap partition!) setting in the `gimprc` file to point to a directory on that drive. If you're really tight on memory and hard drive space, you can uncomment the `stingy-memory-use` option in your `gimprc` file. Open `gimprc` with your favorite text editor, delete the pound sign (#) in front of `stingy-memory-use`, and then save the file. On the other hand, if you have a lot of system memory, change the tile-cache size to force GIMP to use less swap space and run faster.

Your `.gimp` directory is searched first for available default brushes, tools, patterns, and other settings. Customize how GIMP runs by copying the defaults from the various `/usr/X11R6/share/gimp` directories into your home directory.

TABLE 16.2 COMMON GIMP RESOURCES SETTINGS AND DEFAULTS

Name	Value	Description
allow-resize-windows	off	Automatic resizing of window during image resize
default-brush	19fcircle.gbr	Default brush
default-gradient	German_flag_ smooth	Default gradient
default-palette	Default	Default palette
default-pattern	wood2.pat	Default pattern
dont-auto-save	off	Autosaving is not functional in GIMP 1.0
dont-confirm-on-close	off	Disable image close without saving
dont-show-rulers	off	No initial display of rulers
dont-show-tool-tips	off	Disable help text
install-colormap	off	Color setting for 8-bit displays
ruler-units	pixels	Measurement in inches, centimeters, or pixels
stingy-memory-use	off	Setting for small memory systems
swap-path	~/.gimp	Swap file location
temp-path	~/.gimp/tmp	Temporary file location
tile-cache-size	10m	Default cache (in megabytes)
undo-levels	5	Number of available Undo steps

When GIMP is running, you can tear off different dialog boxes and windows by using the dialog menu item under the GIMP File menu. If you have an active image window, access the complete GIMP menu system by pressing your right mouse button while the cursor is over your image. The various menus cascade, and you can select the file, edit, or other menu operations by dragging your cursor through the menus. Common editing keys are listed in Table 16.3.

TABLE 16.3 COMMON GIMP KEYBOARD COMMANDS

Action	Key
Clear selection	Ctrl+K
Close file	Ctrl+W
Copy selection	Ctrl+C
Cut selection	Ctrl+X
Fill selection	Ctrl+.
Lower layer	Ctrl+B
Merge layer	Ctrl+M
Open file	Ctrl+O
Paste clipboard	Ctrl+V
Quit	Ctrl+Q
Raise layer	Ctrl+F
Redo	Ctrl+R
Save file	Ctrl+S
Select airbrush	A
Select all	Ctrl+A
Select Bezier	B
Select blur/sharpen tool	V
Select clone tool	C
Select elliptical tool	E
Select eraser	Shift+E
Select eyedropper	O
Select fill tool	L
Select lasso	F
Select magic wand	Z
Select move tool	M
Select next tool	Tab
Select paintbrush	P
Select pencil	Shift+P
Select rectangular select tool	R
Select text tool	T

Action	Key
Show brushes dialog box	Ctrl+Shift+B
Show palette dialog box	Ctrl+P
Show patterns dialog box	Ctrl+Shift+P
Show rulers	Ctrl+Shift+R
Undo	Ctrl+Z
Zoom in	=
Zoom out	-

16

You can't find much information about the GIMP included with OpenLinux with the exception of a manual page. For the latest news and details about this program, browse to the following site:

`http://www.gimp.org`

This is the best place to find copies of the latest version of GIMP, links to GIMP Frequently Asked Questions lists, a GIMP tutorial, and new plug-ins.

Graphics Editing with ImageMagick

The ImageMagick package, by John Cristy, is a collection of seven programs you can find installed on your system. Some of these commands require the X Window System, whereas others can be used from the command line. The convert command has already been discussed in this hour, but you might find some of the other utilities useful when you want to manipulate graphics:

- animate—Displays a series of graphics; requires X11
- combine—Combines and overlays multiple images into a single image
- convert—Converts or changes graphics files
- display—Displays program with menus for manipulating images; requires X11
- import—Window capture utility; requires X11
- mogrify—Converts or changes and then overwrites multiple graphics files
- montage—Combines several graphics into a larger image

ImageMagick's display command has more than 75 different features and effects you can use to edit or change graphics. One interesting feature is the capability to load images into a visual directory so you can see thumbnails of all images in a directory.

Although most applications and the X11 desktop (such as the background, window frames, and program borders) look colorful, if you load and try to display a color image with lots of colors, the displaying client (such as the `display` command) reduces the number of colors used for the image if not enough colors are found in X's colormap table. This is a technical problem and limitation in X11. There are two things you can try to do: first, try to use at least 16-bit color for your X sessions (with the `-- -bpp 16 startx` option); next, see a client's man page to see if there is a private colormap option. Using a private colormap when you launch an application causes the client to display better color for its windows. The downside (which you can readily see when you use a client such as `quake.x11` or `xboing`) is that when your mouse pointer moves in the client's windows, the surrounding desktop's colors are thrown out of whack.

Using the `display` command is easy, but you must be running the X Window System. To load a graphics file from a terminal command line, type the following:

```
# display nat.jpg &
```

This loads the file and starts the program. When the graphics file loads, it is displayed in a window. Click the graphics window to see the `display` command's menu, as shown in Figure 16.2. To see a visual directory of your graphics, type the following:

```
# display 'vid:*.gif' &
```

This command line loads all `.gif` graphics in the current directory. After the program starts, access its menus by pressing the left mouse button when your cursor is over the images window. The `display` command imports and exports 58 different graphics formats. The program features built-in help and can also create slide shows of graphics.

For more information about ImageMagick, see its manual page and the manual pages for the other programs in the distribution. Comprehensive documentation is available at `http://www.wizards.dupont.com/cristy/ImageMagick.html`.

Using the xv Command to View Graphics

The xv command, shown in Figure 16.3, is a handy previewer used to review, crop, scale, edit, or convert graphics. This command offers many sophisticated sizing and color controls and more than 100 command-line options. You also can use xv, found under the `/usr/X11R6/bin directory`, to capture windows of your X11 session.

FIGURE 16.2

The display X11 client, part of the ImageMagick software package, can be used to make changes to many different types of graphics.

 The xv client is not free software. If you use this program for commercial purposes or institutional or government use, you should send a registration fee to the author, John Bradley. Press Ctrl+A in the xv controls dialog box to see how to register.

The xv command loads a single file or series of graphics if you use a wildcard on the command line, as in the following example:

```
# xv *.jpg
```

This command line loads all files ending in .jpg in the current directory. After the files are loaded, scroll through a list of files to make your changes, or use a graphics directory to select your files.

 The xv client does not function well on 24-bit displays. If you need to use a lot of colors during your X sessions, start X11 with 16- or 24-bit color.

FIGURE 16.3

The xv command is an X11 client that loads, edits, captures, saves, or prints images and features sophisticated color controls.

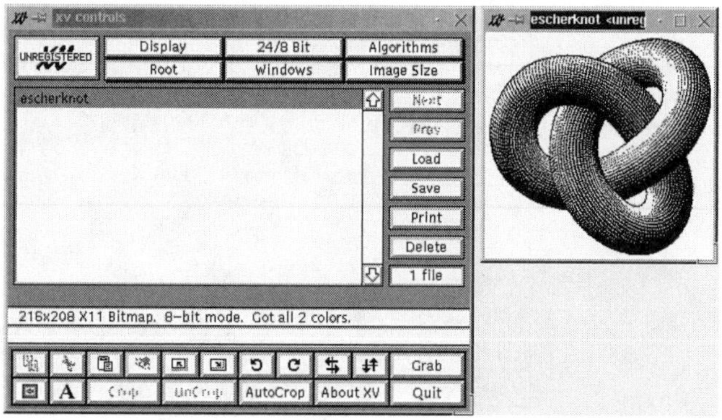

The xv command can import and export 18 different graphics file formats and also can print graphics. For more information about using xv, see its man page and read its definitive documentation. This file is 128 pages in PostScript format. See the next section to learn how to easily read this documentation.

Using the gv Command to View PostScript Files

The gv command is a PostScript previewer used to examine or read PostScript graphics or documents before printing. You must run the X Window System to use this program. This command, found under the /usr/X11R6/bin directory, is a much-improved previewer by Johannes Plass and is based on the older ghostview program by Tim Theilson (installed under the /usr/X11R6/bin directory).

The gv command (shown in Figure 16.4) has more than 36 different command-line options and uses a number of X11 Toolkit options, such as geometry settings. You can start gv by itself or specify a file on the command line, along with its options:

```
# gv -geometry 640x480 myfile.ps
```

This command line starts the gv command in a 640∞480 pixel window displaying the file myfile.ps.

Use the gv command to read X11 client or program documentation in PostScript format. For example, to quickly browse and read the xv documentation, use gv like this:

```
# gv -geometry 640x480 /usr/doc/xv-3.10a/xv.docs.ps.gz
```

The gv client reads compressed PostScript documents!

Another great feature of the gv command is that it reads portable document format, or
.pdf, files. This is a handy way to read .pdf documents without installing an additional
.pdf reader, such as Adobe Acrobat or xpdf.

FIGURE 16.4

The gv X11 client displays PostScript or PDF documents and graphics and provides an easy-to-use interface to previewing files before printing.

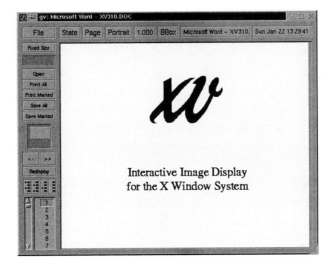

The gv command also uses a unique scrolling mechanism; instead of scrollbars alongside
or below the document window, a rectangular button controls the document viewing area.
You also can print whole documents or selected pages by using different commands.

You can find a comprehensive manual page, along with a hypertext series of .html files,
under the /usr/doc/gv directory.

> An easy way to read gv's documentation is with the lynx or netscape Web
> browsers as in the following example:
>
> ```
> # lynx /usr/doc/gv-doc-html-3.5.8/gv.html
> ```

A Word About Digital Cameras and Scanners

Although Linux runs on many different computers and supports many different hardware
devices, the state of digital camera and scanner support is still in its infancy. Before you
buy a digital camera or scanner with the express purpose of using it with OpenLinux,
carefully check all Linux Internet sites for different scanning software, and then read as
much documentation as possible.

You can find scanner support for many models from Nikon, Epson, Genius, Hewlett-Packard, and Mustek. Although most scanners for Linux require a Small Computer System Interface, or SCSI interface, you can find support for the Connectix series of QuickCams using your computer's parallel port or the Kodak DC20 and DC25, which use a serial-port interface. Beware: there are variations between models of scanners even from the same manufacturer, and not all models in a particular series of scanners might be supported.

The best place to check for support before buying is the SANE, or Scanner Access Now Easy Web pages. You can browse to `http://www.mostang.com/sane/` and find a tutorial on how to install the sane scanner drivers for OpenLinux. To help you in making a decision, Table 16.4 lists manufacturers and the number (not models) of scanners from the manufacturer that are supported.

TABLE 16.4 MANUFACTURERS AND NUMBER OF CAMERAS OR SCANNERS FOR SANE

Manufacturer	Number of Cameras or Scanners
Abaton	2
Agfa	8
Apple	3
Artec	4
Canon	3
Epson	1
Hewlett-Packard	11
Kodak	2
Linotype	1
Microtek	17
Mustek	7
Nikon	3
Plustek	3
Polaroid	1
Tamarack	3
Umax	19
Vobis	2

Another place to look for scanner software, documentation, and support is in the small collection of graphics application capture software packages at the following site:

`http://metalab.unc.edu/pub/Linux/apps/graphic/capture`

For QuickCam support, try the following site:

`http://www.quickcam.com/developer.html`

If you want to scan documents using the xv X11 client, look for the xvscan software at the following site:

`http://www.tummy.com`

16

Summary

This hour introduced you to graphics conversion programs for use with OpenLinux. You also learned about several X11 clients you can use to create and edit graphic files. There are many additional graphics programs included with OpenLinux, but support for scanners is still somewhat limited.

Q&A

Q What other drawing and graphics editing programs come with OpenLinux?

A The classic graphics editor included with X11 is the bitmap client. For editing more complex bitmaps, try the xpaint client. For technical drawing, such as blueprints, try the object-oriented editors tgif and xfig. However, you need a display with a resolution of at least 1024∞768 in order to use these clients.

Exercises

1. Look under the /usr/X11R6/include/X11 directory, and then load some images from the bitmap and pixmap directories. What clients did you use?

2. Try converting a favorite graphics file into another graphics format. What programs did you use?

3. If you have a dual-boot computer running another operating system, mount the other file system and search for graphic images. What file extensions did you use as a search criteria, and how many images did you find?

HOUR 17

Learning Math and Financial Tools

This lesson is an introduction to some of the mathematical and financial tools available for Linux. This hour shows you calculators, spreadsheets, and graphic modeling programs and points you to sources where you can find even more programs. Whether you're only interested in setting up simple single-screen spreadsheets or would rather plot detailed maps using 200 megabytes of cartographic data from the U.S. Geologic Survey, you'll find Linux tools to help you get started.

The hour begins with a discussion of some calculators and calculating languages, introduces you to some of the Linux spreadsheet programs, and finishes with a discussion of modeling programs, such as gnuplot. This hour can't cover all the more than 1,500 scientific applications for Linux, but if you have an interest in other fields, such as artificial intelligence, astronomy, biology, chemistry, database systems, electronics, linear algebra, physics, or raytracing, you can find tools for Linux to help you.

Calculators

This section introduces you to several Linux calculators. You'll find some of these handy when you pay bills, cook, or even travel. Some of these calculators work from the command line, and others run under the X Window System.

Doing Desk Calculations with the dc Command

The dc (desk calculator) command is a command-line calculator that uses reverse Polish notation, or RPN, to perform calculations and has more than 30 different operators and internal commands. The dc command, found under the /usr/bin directory, is easy to use:

```
# dc44 55 + p
99
q
```

The example shows that to add two numbers, you first enter the numbers, then enter the operator, and then use the p command to print the value placed on the stack by the addition operator. The q command quits the dc program. This method of performing calculations is not as inconvenient as you might think. For example, suppose that you're going through the checks you've written during the month and that you want to check your written calculations. Using the dc command, you can enter the following:

```
# dc
2500.00
49.95
-
p
2450.05
32.18
-
p
2417.87
q
```

You start by entering a $2500.00 balance, and then enter $49.95 as the first check, followed by the subtraction operator (–). The p command prints the result, and the next current balance of $2450.05 is maintained on the *stack* (a temporary storage area in memory). You can also use the dc command to read files of calculations instead of typing commands at your terminal, and it has 256 different *registers*, or temporary storage areas, for your calculations. See the dc command's manual page for more information and other features.

Calculating with the X11 `xcalc` Client

The `xcalc` client is one of the more familiar graphic calculators (see Figure 17.1) and comes with the XFree86 X Window System. The `xcalc` command, found under the /usr/X11R6/bin directory, has only two command-line options, -stipple and -rpn. The -stipple option merely colors the background of xcalc's face, whereas the -rpn option tells the `xcalc` command to use `rpn` for doing calculations and changes its appearance.

You must be running X11 to use the `xcalc` command. You can use your mouse or the keyboard to enter numbers and perform calculations. To use it in its normal mode with the -stipple option, type the following:

```
# xcalc -stipple &
```

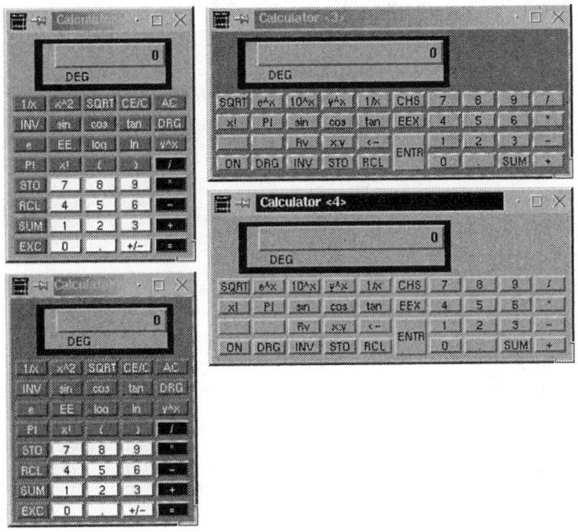

FIGURE 17.1

The xcalc calculator has two options that can also be used together: -stipple *(for a mottled background) and* –rpn *(to emulate a Texas Instrument's calculator).*

To use the `xcalc` command as an `rpn` calculator, type the following:

```
# xcalc -rpn -stipple &
```

You can customize nearly any aspect of `xcalc` by editing its defaults file, Xcalc, which is found under the /usr/X11R6/lib/X11/app-defaults directory. See the `xcalc` manual page for more information.

Calculating with the `kcalc` Client

The `kcalc` client, included with the K Desktop Environment, or KDE, is available through the Utilities menu on your desktop's control panel or can be started from the command line of an X11 terminal window, like this:

```
# kcalc &
```

After you press Enter, the kcalc dialog box appears as shown in Figure 17.2. To customize the kcalc display, click the kCalc button. A dialog box appears, as shown in Figure 17.3. To change the background and foreground colors, click the Change buttons. To change a font, click the Display Font tab.

> If you need quick access to the command line but find the process of opening a terminal window tedious, use KDE's minicli client: press Alt+F2, and a small command-line window appears. Type in your command, such as xcalc, and press Enter. The command-line window disappears, and the X11 client runs.

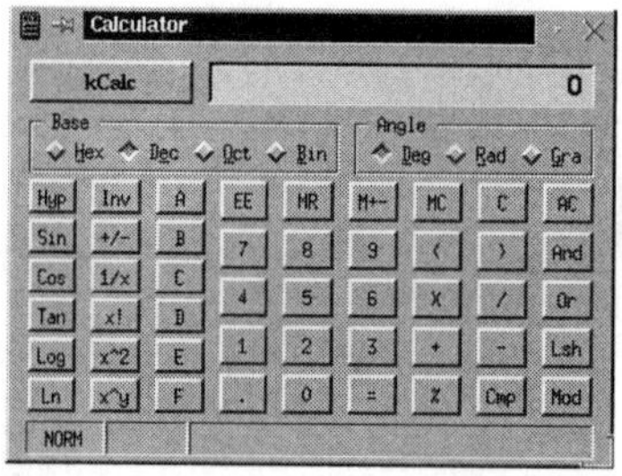

FIGURE 17.2

The kcalc *calculator performs calculations in several numerical bases.*

This calculator, created by Bernd Johannes Wuebben, sports a trigonometric and statistical mode and can perform calculations in base 16, 10, 8, and 2. You can use your number keys, numerical keypad, or Num Lock key to enter calculations.

> The precision for base 16, 8, and 2 might be limited. Click the About tab after pressing the kCalc button for more details. You might be able to increase kcalc's precision by rebuilding the program. If the source code is not included on your OpenLinux CD-ROM, you can download the source to KDE's utilities distribution through http://www.kde.org or one of this site's mirrors.

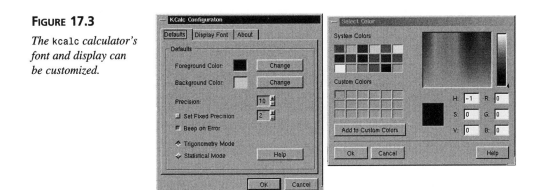

FIGURE 17.3

The kcalc *calculator's font and display can be customized.*

This calculator is also handy for performing quick conversions of numbers in different base values. To convert a number, click a base to use, enter the number, and click a different base. The number is converted automatically.

Performing Unit Conversions with the units Command

If you've ever had trouble remembering the formulas to convert miles to meters or cups to gallons, you'll really like Adrian Mariano's units command, which you can find under the /usr/bin directory. Want to know how many furlongs per mile? How about how many acres are in a square mile?

One way to use the units command is from the command line, for example:

```
# units floz gallon
        * 0.0078125
        / 128
```

This simple example shows how to find out how many fluid ounces are in a gallon. You see that there are 128 and that a fluid ounce is less than one hundredth of a gallon. Although using the command line is handy for quick conversions, you can also run a series of queries, as follows:

```
# units
501 units, 41 prefixes

You have: mile*mile
You want: acre
        * 640
        / 0.0015625
You have: mile2
You want: acre
        * 640
```

```
        / 0.0015625
You have: mile^2
You want: acre
        * 640
        / 0.0015625
You have: mile
You want: furlong
        * 8
        / 0.125
You have: 100 fathoms
You want: feet
        * 600
        / 0.0016666667
...
```

In the interactive mode, you can ask units for any number of conversions. The units command works by reading its database of conversions from the file /usr/share/units.dat. You can also copy this file to your home directory and add your own custom conversions to it. As you can see, you can use different notations to indicate amounts to be converted. Another interesting feature is that units can also perform currency conversions, for example:

```
# units dollar yen
        * 107.52688
        / 0.0093
```

Note that this might not be entirely true, as currency values change daily. You can edit the units.dat file and insert not only current currency values, but also prices for gold, silver, platinum, or pork bellies. See the units manual page for more information.

Programming Calculators with the bc Language Interpreter

The bc command is an interpreter for a calculator language. You can use this command, by Philip Nelson, to write calculator programs while bc is running or have bc run the program after it starts. The bc language has nearly 40 operators, functions, and programming logic keywords. Although this section doesn't go into how to program in bc, if you're interested in the bc language, try the simple checkbook balancing program from bc's manual page. The program can work like the previous example for the dc command. Read the bc manual page, and then type the program into a file using your favorite text editor. You can run it with the following:

```
# bc nameofyourfile
```

The bc command starts by reading in the program in the file **nameofyourfile** and presents the following:

```
...
Initial balance? 2500.00

current balance = 2500.00
transaction? 49.95
current balance = 2450.05
transaction? 32.18
current balance = 2417.87
transaction?
...
```

This is only one way to use the bc command's language. With a little effort, you can write your own programs. If you need to perform more complex calculations, use a spreadsheet application. The next section discusses the variety of spreadsheets for Linux.

17

Spreadsheets

Spreadsheet programs offer a convenient way to store and manipulate financial or scientific data. You can use these programs to help manage your home or business. Typical uses involve personal finance, such as tracking loans and investments, or running business inventory control, personnel worksheets, or accounting tasks.

You can also use these programs to do forecasting, or "what if" calculations. This can help you create estimates you can use for home mortgages, auto loans, and even home construction. You're limited only to your imagination with most of these programs, and many not only offer the capability to work as a whiz-bang calculator, but also create graphic charts so you can visually see your data.

Several of these programs are on your CD-ROM. After you connect to your ISP (see Hour 10, "Connecting to the Internet"), you can use the Lynx Web browser or Netscape Navigator to search for other spreadsheet or financial programs. If you need to have a spreadsheet program to use with OpenLinux, you're in luck because at least a dozen are available. Nearly half come with source code, so you can make changes, add features, or fix problems. Recent releases of free-for-personal-use spreadsheets are as feature rich as many commercial programs costing lots of money.

Using the Public Domain sc Spreadsheet

The sc (spreadsheet calculator) command (see Figure 17.4) is a freely available, public domain spreadsheet program. This program is a collective work of nearly 60 programmers, and runs on many different UNIX systems. With a little effort in learning its commands, you can build very capable spreadsheets. The sc program is free, and it comes with source code. A short tutorial and manual page documenting its features is included.

This program is especially handy if you're running OpenLinux on a small hard drive and disk space is at a premium. The sc program requires only about 120 kilobytes of disk space but provides a lot of features.

Using the sc program is easy. You can load programs from the command line when you start it, or you can load and save programs while it's running. You can run this program as follows:

```
# sc
```

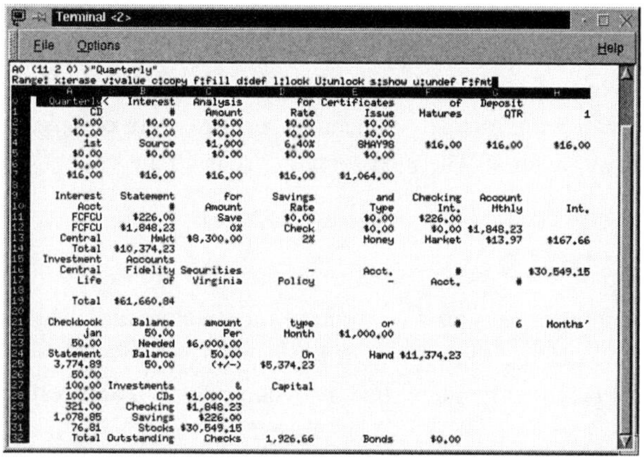

FIGURE 17.4

The sc spreadsheet calculator works with or without the X Window System, and it comes with a short tutorial.

If you want a quick reference to the sc commands, use the scqref command (found under the /usr/bin directory) and pipe the output through the nroff and less commands. Then either read at your leisure or redirect to a file you can edit and print, for example:

```
# scqref ¦ nroff -man ¦ less > scref.txt
```

To learn how to use the sc spreadsheet program, load the sc program's tutorial, which you can find under the /usr/doc/sc directory:

```
# sc /usr/doc/sc*/tutorial.sc
```

This runs sc and loads the tutorial. An included program, called psc, can help you import text-only data files by converting word processor or other spreadsheet program files. For example, to prepare exported spreadsheet text for input to sc, use the psc command like this:

```
# psc <mysheet.txt >mysheet.psc
```

The sc program has more than 60 built-in functions, and because you get the source code, you can add your own.

Using the `slsc` Spreadsheet

The `slsc` spreadsheet calculator command (see Figure 17.5) is an improved version of `sc`. This program sports many new features such as improved menus, the use of color (with the `-C` command-line option), a resource file for customizing colors and keys, improved printing support, and information hiding.

Like `sc`, the `slsc` program is free and comes with source code. A short tutorial and manual page documenting its features is included. You can use this program with or without the X Window System.

You can load programs from the command line when you start `slsc`, or you can load and save programs while it's running. To start this program with color, type the command as follows:

```
# slsc -C
```

For color support in X11, you must start `slsc` in a color-capable terminal window. You can also customize the default, systemwide settings by copying the file `slsc.rc` to your home directory with the name `.slscrc`. Then edit this file in your favorite text editor to change the settings.

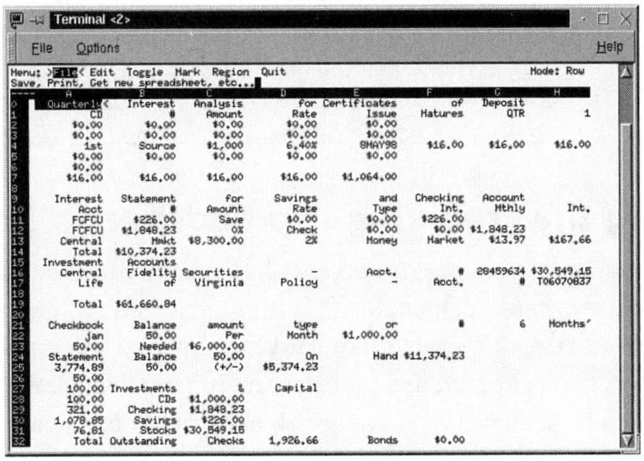

FIGURE 17.5

The `slsc` spreadsheet calculator is an improved version of `sc` and also works with or without the X Window System.

17

To learn how to use the slsc spreadsheet program, load the slsc program's tutorial, which you can find under the /usr/lib/slsc directory:

```
# slsc /usr/lib/slsc/tutorial.sc
```

This runs slsc and loads the tutorial. An included program, called vprint (included under the /usr/lib/slsc directory) can be used to print spreadsheet files. For more information, see the slsc man page, various files in the /usr/lib/slsc directory, and documentation under the /usr/doc/slsc directory.

If you like sc or slsc but want to try other spreadsheet programs for OpenLinux, look for the oleo spreadsheet, which is included on this book's CD-ROM. You might also want to try the X11 xspread program created by software engineering teams at the University of Wisconsin-Milwaukee. This program requires that you're running X11, but offers mouse support, the capability to import Lotus 1-2-3 format files, and can generate and display line, bar, stacked-bar, and pie chart graphics from spreadsheet data. Look for this program at ftp.cdrom.com in the /pub/linux/slackware_source/xap/xspread directory.

Another alternative spreadsheet is the teapot (table editor and planner) spreadsheet program by Michael Haardt. This spreadsheet works under X11 or your console, and features import of sc and .WK1 (one of the old Lotus formats) spreadsheet files, export of CSV, HTML, LaTeX, or ASCII file formats, three-dimensional spreadsheets, support of custom keyboard function keys, great documentation, and availability in German, English, or Dutch language versions. You can get a copy at: ftp://cantor.informatik. rwth-aachen.de/pub/unix/teapot-1.0.3.tar.gz.

Finding the Free Wingz Spreadsheet

The Wingz spreadsheet, from Investment Intelligence Systems Corporation, is a freeware spreadsheet program for OpenLinux. This program, which comes in two versions, requires more than six megabytes of hard drive space when installed. Wingz has nearly any feature you could need in a spreadsheet program, including a built-in scripting language called HyperScript. You can use HyperScript to build custom interfaces and programs to present your spreadsheet data. There isn't much documentation, but there are some impressive example sheets you can load and examine, and Wingz has built-in, context-sensitive help.

You can generate many different types of 3D graphics, and spreadsheets can be linked or previewed before printing. To read more about `Wingz`, browse to `http://www.wingz-us.com`. To get a free copy, go to `http://metalab.unc.edu/pub/Linux/apps/financial/spreadsheet`.

Features of the `StarCalc` Spreadsheet Program

The `StarCalc` spreadsheet program (see Figure 17.6) is part of the free-for-personal-use StarOffice suite of programs for OpenLinux. This spreadsheet program is integrated with the other StarCalc applications. You can copy, paste, or use spreadsheet data and graphics as linked objects, like those for Applixware.

This is a capable program with all the features of a commercial title. Like all other programs in the StarOffice suite, `StarCalc` has print previews, 3D graphics, and drag-and-drop cell movement.

17

If you're using StarOffice 4.0, press Ctrl+N to open the StarOffice Templates dialog box, and then scroll down the list of Categories and click on the Spreadsheets item. There are seven ready-made spreadsheet documents you can use. If you're using StarOffice 5.0, press Ctrl+N to open the Templates dialog box, and then scroll down and select the Financial Documents item. There are six different specialized spreadsheets, such as a Household Budget, a Stock Portfolio, and a Car Financing document.

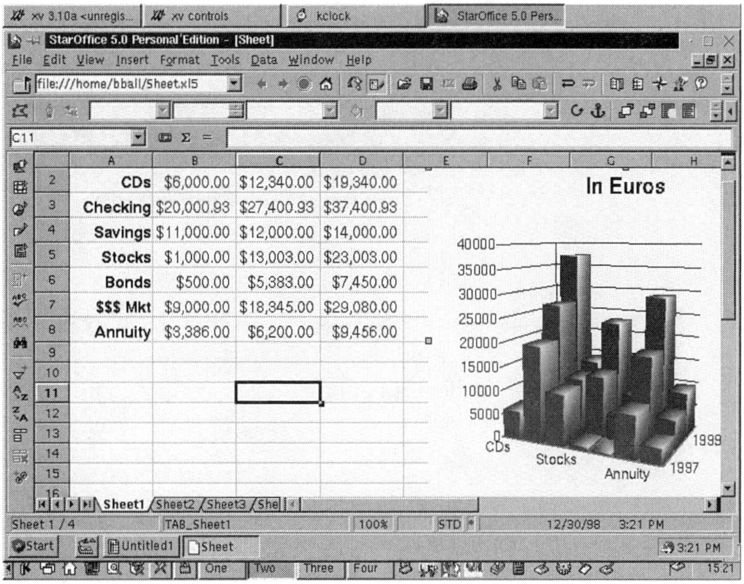

FIGURE 17.6

The StarCalc *spreadsheet, like Applix Spreadsheets, has style sheets and mouse-driven toolbars and supports multiple ways of viewing spreadsheet data graphically.*

You can import and export many different types of spreadsheet formats, as shown in Table 17.1.

TABLE 17.1   StarCalc Spreadsheet Import and Export Formats

Import	Export
MS Excel 4, 5, 95, 97	MS Excel 5, 95, 97
Lotus 123 DOS/WIN	
DIF	DIF
CSV	CSV
SYLK	SYLK
dBase	dBase
text	text

To import a spreadsheet document into StarCalc, use the Open menu item from the StarCalc File menu. To export a spreadsheet document, use the Save As menu item from the File menu. A dialog box appears as shown in Figure 17.7. Click the drop-down menu next to the File type field, and a scrolling list of file types appears. Scroll through the list, and click the desired format. To save the file, click the Save button.

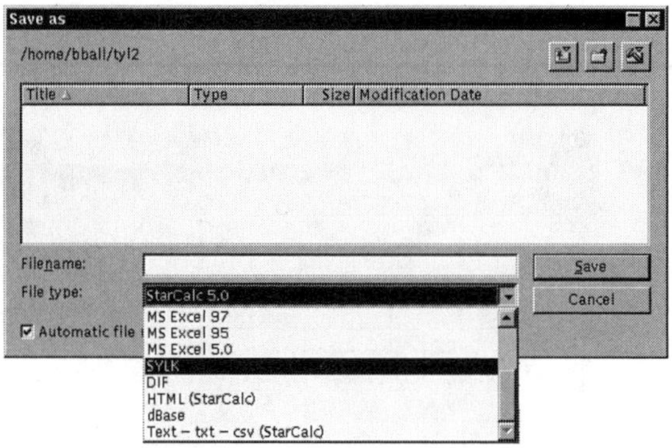

FIGURE 17.7

The StarCalc spreadsheet can export documents in 13 different formats.

Find out more about the StarCalc spreadsheet program by browsing to http://www.stardivision.com. Also see Hour 19, "Home Office Management with StarOffice" for more detailed information about how to use StarOffice and StarCalc.

Commercial Features of the Applixware Spreadsheet Program

The Applixware spreadsheet program (see Figure 17.8) is part of the commercial Applixware suite of 10 programs for Linux (see Hour 14, "Text Processing," for more information). This spreadsheet program is integrated with the other Applixware programs using linked objects. This means that if you change the data in your spreadsheet file, the data or chart used in a word processing document also changes.

As you might expect with a commercial program, this spreadsheet offers all the features of competing titles. Besides such features as integration with the other programs in its suite, print previews, or 3D graphics, this spreadsheet program has drag-and-drop cell movement, multiple views, and numerous database functions.

17

FIGURE 17.8

The Applixware spreadsheet has style sheets and mouse-driven toolbars and supports multiple graphics.

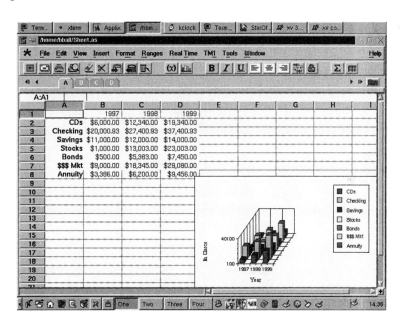

You can import and export many different types of spreadsheet formats, as shown in Table 17.2.

TABLE **17.2**   APPLIXWARE SPREADSHEET IMPORT AND EXPORT FORMATS

Import	Export
XLS	XLS3, XLS4, XLS5
WKS, WK1, WK3, WK4	WK1, WK3
DIF, XDIF	DIF
CSV	CSV
SYLK	SYLK
Text	Text

You can find out more about the Applix spreadsheet program by browsing to
`http://www.applix.com`.

Using gnuplot to Graph Mathematical Formulas

This section shows you how to use gnuplot, an interactive plotting program by Thomas Williams and Colin Kelley. This program supports nearly 40 different printers and output devices, although you'll probably want to experiment with gnuplot using the X Window System and print your graphics using PostScript (see Hour 15, "Preparing Documents," for more information on how to do this).

Although gnuplot (no relation to GNU software, but supported and distributed by the Free Software Foundation under the GNU General Public License) is not the only mathematical modeling and plotting program available for Linux, it is included on your CD-ROM. You can find the gnuplot program under the /usr/bin/X11R6 directory.

The gnuplot program (see Figure 17.9) is a complete, interactive plotting program and was originally designed to graph math functions and data. In this regard it is somewhat similar to other commercial formula-interpretation and plotting programs. It can read and save files and has built-in help, so you can query the program while you use it.

Using gnuplot is simple. The program has five different command-line options (such as -mono or -gray to force monochrome or grayscale plots, and -clear and -tvtwm to clear the window first or place the window relative to the desktop), but many aspects of the program can be controlled interactively or as commands in a loaded gnuplot data file. One common use of the command line option is to control the point size (in pixels) of drawing lines using the -pointsize option, as in the following example:

```
# gnuplot -pointsize 2
```

You can use and plot many types of mathematical expressions, and according to the gnuplot documentation, any C, Pascal, Fortran, or BASIC language mathematical statement can be used. For example, start the program at the command line of an X11 terminal window like this:

```
# gnuplot
```

After you press Enter, type in some variable values, such as the following:

```
gnuplot> y = -5
gnuplot> x = 8
```

FIGURE 17.9

The gnuplot program can help you visualize mathematical formulas, spreadsheet data, and yes, even whales.

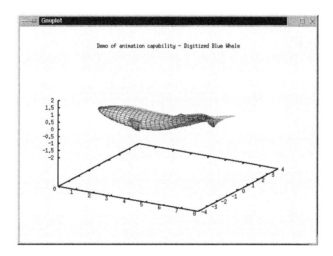

To plot an expression, such as (x*y)-(x+y), use the plot command, followed by the expression, like so:

```
gnuplot> plot (x*y)-(x+y)
```

After you press Enter, a new gnuplot window appears with a graphic of your expression. When you finish, type quit at the gnuplot prompt to exit the program. To load and plot sample datafiles, change directory to /usr/X11R6/lib/gnuplot/demo. Then, to display the data (as shown in Figure 17.9), use gnuplot followed by the name of a demo file, like this:

```
# gnuplot animate.dem
```

After you press Enter, you see a picture of the digitized whale, which starts swimming around the plot area of the gnuplot window. You can find more documentation, the gnuplot FAQ, and updates to the gnuplot program at http://www.cs.dartmouth.edu/gnuplot_info.html.

Many, many different financial and math applications are available for Linux. This hour barely scratches the surface. You can find financial applications that can help you manage investment portfolios, track stock prices, or aid in developing cost estimates for construction projects. You can also find hundreds of specialized programs you can use in solving special computing needs for other sciences. One of the best sites for perusing some of the best of these applications is `http://SAL.KachinaTech.COM`. You can also find a number of financial tools for Linux, along with source code, at `http://metalab.unc.edu/pub/Linux/apps/financial`.

Summary

This hour introduced you to a number of calculators and financial tools available for OpenLinux. Most of these programs are included on this book's CD-ROM.

Q&A

Q I tried running the `bc` and `dc` calculators, but the shell returns "`bash: dc: command not found`".

A Use `lisa`, `glint`, or `kpackage` to install the programs. Look under the `Scientific/Math` package folders.

Q What other calculators, scientific programs, or math utilities are included with OpenLinux?

A If you're interested in other advanced programmable calculators with a built-in programming language, try the `gp` command. Another language-type calculator is the `yorick` interpreter, which features syntax similar to BASIC or Lisp and includes an interactive graphics package for plotting results. Other programs include the following:

- `rasmol`   This program is for viewing molecular graphics
- `felt`   This program is for finite element analysis, which includes a CAD-like companion X11 client named `velvet`
- `xmgr`   This X11 client can generate high-quality visualizations of complex data.
- `mxp` and `xfractint`   These clients for X11 compute and display fractal images.

Q **I tried using StarOffice 5.0's File menu to create a new spreadsheet document, but can't find these types of files listed!**

A This used to be possible with StarOffice 4.0. If you're using StarOffice 5.0, click the Start menu button in the lower left corner of StarOffice's desktop, and then scroll up and click Spreadsheet to create a new spreadsheet document.

Q **I tried running the `gnuplot` demo, but it stopped with an error after showing several plots. What happened?**

A There's an error in the one of the plot files. Try running the demo plots separately.

Exercises

1. Start `gnuplot` and try plotting your own math expressions.

2. Copy a spreadsheet file from another operating system or application, and try importing the data into StarCalc. Experiment with importing and exporting different formats. What formats work best?

3. Start the `dc` calculator. Enter two 10-digit numbers, then an asterisk, and then the P key. What happens?

4. Compare the `sc` and `slsc` spreadsheet calculators. How are these programs similar? In what ways are they different?

17

Hour **18**

Personal Productivity Tools

In this hour I'll show you some calendars, commands, and X11 clients you can use to help your personal productivity. Whether it's keeping a diary or creating reminders, you'll learn how to use these tools under OpenLinux to keep you on track and on schedule with your life.

Each program or technique discussed in this hour can be accomplished with software you'll find on the CD-ROM that comes with your book. After reading this discussion, you'll find additional ways to use these programs to craft your own set of tools and techniques for personal productivity.

Scheduling Personal Reminders and Tasks with the at Command

If you need to keep track of important schedules, set reminders, or run programs unattended, you can use the at command. This command, found under the /usr/bin directory, schedules commands, or jobs, to be run at a time you specify. For example, if you are working on a project but need to remember to catch your car pool, you can enter a quick at job from the command line.

> Your system should enable you to use the at commands by default. If it does not, see Hour 24, "Using Scheduling to Automate System Management," on how to enable at command facilities for your system.

For example, to send a pop-up reminder to your screen at the appropriate time, use the following:

```
$ at 16:15
at> xmessage -display :0.0 "The car pool is leaving in 15 minutes."
at> <EOT>
warning: commands will be executed using /bin/sh
job 12 at 1998-12-18 16:15
```

This tells the at command to run the xmessage program to display the text of your message about your car pool on the specified X11 display, as shown in Figure 18.1. The end-of-text (EOT) in the listing means you should press Ctrl+D to close the command to enter the job. If you make a mistake in the syntax of the command, you receive a mail message at the scheduled time. The -display command-line option tells the xmessage command which screen to show the message on, usually 0.0, which you can find with the following:

```
# printenv ¦ fgrep DISPLAY
```

This command line pipes the output of the printenv command through fgrep to search your environment variables (discussed in Hour 6, "Using the Shell") for the value of your $DISPLAY environment variable.

You can also use the at command to provide a visual reminder, if you're using X11, by controlling the color of your desktop, for example:

```
# at 16:15
at> xsetroot -display :0.0 -solid Red
at> xmessage -display :0.0 "The car pool is leaving in 15 minutes."
at> <EOT>
warning: commands will be executed using /bin/sh
job 14 at 1998-12-18 16:15
```

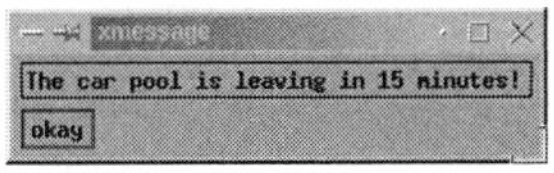

FIGURE 18.1

The at *command can be used to run any OpenLinux program or X11 client, such as* xmessage, *as a reminder.*

This turns your desktop, or root display, a solid red color at the appointed time and then displays your message. As you can see, you can combine multiple commands to do a number of things simultaneously. If you find this approach convenient, you can also type these commands into a text file called `carpool` and run the commands by using the `-f` option, followed by the name of the file, with the following:

```
# at 16:15 -f carpool
warning: commands will be executed using /bin/sh
job 13 at 1998-12-18 10:19
```

The at command reads the commands from your text file and responds with a confirmation. As a further convenience, you can place this command line in your `.xintrc` script in your home directory to schedule the job after you start X11 at the beginning of the day.

See Hour 7, "Using the X Window System," for more information about configuring your `.xinitrc` file.

Use the `atq` command to see a list of all your scheduled jobs, like this:

```
# atq
14      1998-12-18 12:00 a
15      1998-12-18 13:00 a
16      1998-12-18 14:00 a
17      1998-12-18 15:00 a
18      1998-12-25 16:15 a
```

This shows that four jobs are scheduled for December 18 with another scheduled for December 25. When you schedule jobs with the at command, a shell script containing each command is created in the `/var/spool/atjobs` directory. The atq command looks in this directory for your jobs and then prints them to your display.

18

You can use the at command to schedule a job minutes, hours, days, weeks, or even years in advance. If you want to run your car pool reminder file in three hours, you can use the at command's plus sign (+) command-line option, for example:

```
# at +3 hours -f carpool
```

This runs your job three hours from the current system time. You can also use the time and date (in the form of *mm*/*dd*/*yy*) to schedule jobs, like so:

```
# at 16:15 12/25/00
at> xmessage -display :0.0 "The car pool is leaving in 15 minutes."
at> <EOT>
warning: commands will be executed using /bin/sh
job 21 at 2000-12-31 16:15
```

As you can see, the at command is Y2K-compliant! Use the atrm command to control your at jobs. You can selectively delete specific jobs by number. For example, using your job queue from the earlier example, you can type the following:

```
# atrm 16 18
```

This removes jobs 16 and 18 but leaves the other two intact. Using the at command is a handy way to program one-time reminders for specific times. In the next section, I'll show you how to schedule other jobs to run at regular intervals.

You can also use Rob Nation's X11 clock client, rclock, to schedule reminders or run programs at a selected day or time. To build a reminder, create a file called .rclock in your home directory, and enter reminder command lines. For example:

```
11:30 mtwtf Time for lunch!
```

This displays a reminder for lunch during the week. The rclock client is usually distributed with the X11 rxvt terminal, but does not come with OpenLinux. You can get the latest version from http://babyaga.math. fu-berlin.de/~rxvt/, or you can also get both rxvt and rclock in an .rpm file from http://metalab.unc.edu/pub/Linux/X11/terms/. For a diverse listing of different clocks (many with alarms) for OpenLinux and X11, browse to http://metalab.unc.edu/pub/Linux/X11/clocks.

Scheduling Regular Reminders with the crontab Command

Although the `at` command is helpful for scheduling one-time jobs, you can use Paul Vixie's `crontab` command if you need regular tasks completed at regular intervals. The `crontab` command, found under the `/usr/bin` directory, is used to enter your desired times and commands into a personal file.

The `crontab` command works by looking for `crontab` schedules by username in the `/var/spool/cron` directory. The `crontab` file for your Linux system is called `crontab` and is located in the `/etc` directory. The program that runs the system and the user `cron` schedules is the `cron` daemon, which is started when you boot Linux and wakes up each minute to check the system and user files.

To create your own `crontab` file, you must use the command's `-e` option, for example:

```
# crontab -e
```

> Make sure you enable `crontab` use for your system. See Hour 24, "Scheduling" for details on how to do this. You can also define the default `$EDITOR` environment variable to your favorite text editor when you create or edit your `crontab` files. See Hour 6, "Using the Shell," on how to set environment variables, and Hour 14, "Text Processing," for information about using various text editors.

18

This command launches the default text editor defined in your shell's `$EDITOR` environment variable, so you can create or edit your personal `crontab` file. But before you get into the format of your `crontab` entries, think about configuring your default editor.

If your default editor is `vi` and you want to use a different editor, you can temporarily change the `$EDITOR` variable using your shell. For example, if you're using the `bash` shell and want to use the `pico` text editor, you can use the following:

```
# EDITOR=/usr/bin/pico; export EDITOR
```

This sets the default editor to the `pico` editor. You can confirm this by searching your environment variables, for example:

```
# printenv | fgrep EDITOR
EDITOR=/usr/bin/pico
```

If you've never created a crontab file, you're initially presented an empty file where you can enter crontab settings, regardless of which editor you use. Before you can enter your own schedule, you need to know how to format a crontab request.

The format of a crontab entry looks like that in Table 18.1. Step values can be used in different fields, such as */3 for every three minutes or hours. Ranges can also be used, such as 7-10 for 7, 8, 9, and 10 a.m. Note that numbers (0 or 7 for Sunday) or names (the first three letters) can be used for month and day of the week fields.

TABLE 18.1   FORMAT OF A crontab ENTRY

Minute	Hour	Day	Month	Day of Week
0-59	0-23	0-31	0-12 (or names)	0-7 (or names)

You can find the format of crontab requests and some sample entries in the crontab manual page under the /usr/man/man5 directory. You can read this manual page as follows:

```
# man 5 crontab
```

Your crontab file can contain settings to start programs you want to run at regular and even not so regular times, for example:

```
* * * * * somecommand
0,15,30,45 * * * * somecommand
0 * * * * somecommand
```

The first example shows you want to run a program every minute. The second crontab entry runs a program every 15 minutes. The third example runs a program once an hour, on the hour.

To run a program once a day at an appointed time, you can use the following:

```
30 7 * * * somecommand
30 0 * * * somecommand
15 16 * * * somecommand
```

The first example runs at 7:30 a.m. The second example runs at 30 minutes past midnight. The third example runs at 4:15 p.m. each day. You can also run a program on a specific day of the month or the week, for example:

```
30 16 1 * * somecommand
30 15 * * mon somecommand
```

The first example runs at 4:30 p.m. on the first day of each month, and the second runs at 3:30 p.m. each Monday. To round out these examples, you can also specify a particular month, for example:

```
30 7 25 12 * somecommand
```

This example runs the command at 7:30 a.m. on each Dec. 25. The commands you specify can be system utilities or even your own shell scripts. You can use the `crontab` command's `-l` (list) option to print your `cron` settings, for example:

```
# crontab -l
# DO NOT EDIT THIS FILE - edit the master and reinstall.
# (/tmp/crontab.XXXXa02274 installed on Fri Dec 18 13:20:49 1998)
# (Cron version -- $Id: crontab.c,v 2.13 1994/01/17 03:20:37
➥vixie Exp $)
0,30 * * * * /usr/local/bin/saytime
0 8 * * * /usr/local/bin/ppp on
3 8 * * * /usr/bin/fetchmail -u bball -p mypasswd staffnet.com
```

This shows a `crontab` file that speaks the time every half hour, starts a PPP connection at 8 a.m. every day, and downloads the day's mail three minutes after the PPP connection starts. You can remove your `crontab` file with the `crontab` command's `-r` (remove) option, for example:

```
# crontab -r
```

Using the `crontab` command is an easy way to create, run, and manage regular tasks. Even though you can create your own reminders, you might want to use a calendar for short- or long-range planning.

Creating Appointment Reminders with the X11 `ical` Client

You can use Sanjay Ghemawat's `ical` calendar to store appointments and reminders in a personal calendar. The `ical` client, found under the `/usr/X11R6/bin` directory, has a number of unique features and improvements over the `cal` or `gcal` calendar printing programs:

- Custom graphical X11 interface with menus, dialogs, sliding controls, and buttons
- Copy and paste, drag-and-drop notes, and appointments
- Alarms for upcoming events
- Multiple calendar views
- Import, export, and autosaving of calendar files

- Group sharing of calendar files
- Printing of different calendars
- cron-type scheduling of appointments, notes, or reminders
- To-do checklists
- Built-in help

When you first run ical, the program shows the current month, set to the current day, along with a note, or appointment entry list, on the right. Start ical by using its -calendar option, followed by the name of a calendar file you want the program to create, like this:

```
# ical -calendar $HOME/.calendar &
```

This starts ical, which then creates a calendar file named .calendar in your home directory.

> Unless you define an environment variable named CALENDAR that points to an ical-calendar file, you need to specify what calendar file to use every time you start ical (it periodically complains with an error message if it cannot open a calendar file). To define your CALENDAR environment variable, open your .bashrc file with a text editor and add the following:
>
> export CALENDAR=$HOME/.calendar
>
> Now save the file. To use this value right away, use the bash shell's source command, like so:
>
> source .bashrc and press Enter.

The ical client also uses many of the standard X Toolkit command-line options, so you can start the ical client as an icon, for example:

```
# ical -iconic
```

You can also change geometry settings to set the initial calendar size, as follows:

```
# ical -geometry 800x600
```

Figure 18.2 shows the ical client.

FIGURE 18.2

The ical X11 client features notices, appointments, to-do lists, and reminder alarms.

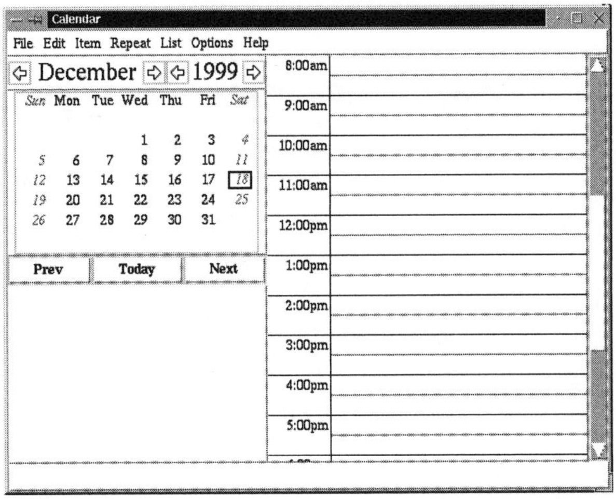

Notices are created by selecting a day and then clicking on and typing in the box below the calendar. Appointments for the day are created by clicking on a specific time and typing in the name of the appointment. You can drag appointments anywhere during the day to rearrange your schedule by holding down the middle mouse button (or both left and right mouse buttons if you're using a two-button mouse).

After you have set your notice or appointment, you can also set an alarm to have the ical client warn you of the upcoming event. To set a reminder alarm, first click the appointment, and then select the Item menu's Properties item to set an alarm for an appointment. You can also just double-click the appointment to bring up the alarm dialog.

You can tell ical to remind you from 1 to 15 days in advance, with up to 60 warnings the hour before an appointment. The ical alarm notice window pops up at the previously selected times as a reminder.

18

> The ical client must be running in order to receive alarms. You can, however, use the ical command and its -popup command-line option in a crontab entry. If you use -popup, ical lists all the day's appointments in a window and then exits after you press the Okay button.

Figure 18.3 shows the `ical` client's alarm dialog.

FIGURE 18.3

The `ical` client's alarm dialog features multiple, cascading alarms with drag-and-drop controls.

Item Properties			
Plant new Leyland Cypress	Start Time	◀◀ ◀	1:00pm ▶ ▶▶
	Finish Time	◀◀ ◀	1:30pm ▶ ▶▶

Calendar | Highlight | Early Warning

Main Calendar

◆ Always
/ Never
/ Until Expiration
/ As Holiday

0
1
5
10
15

Days

⌐ Todo Item

Select set of alarm times in minutes. Create an alarm by dragging a marker out of the well at the right of the scale. You can also drag existing markers to change alarm times. If you drag a marker far enough up or down so that it turns dim, it will be deleted when you release the mouse button.

0   5   10 15 20 25 30 35 40 45 50 55 60
Alarms (in minutes)

Cancel   Okay

If you select an appointment or notice, you can also make it repeat daily, weekly, monthly, or annually by selecting the pertinent Repeat menu item. When you cause an item to repeat, it is automatically duplicated in your calendar.

Appointments can also be made to-do items by clicking on the appointment and selecting the Todo Item from `ical`'s Item menu. A box appears at the beginning of the text. Until you complete the item by clicking in the box with your left mouse button to place a check mark, the to-do item will reappear on the next day's list of appointments.

You can list your appointments and notices by using `ical`'s List menu. If you want a hard copy of your calendar, you can print six different built-in calendar formats or specify a range of days. Before you print, you can also preview your calendar.

The `ical` client is a convenient way to organize personal or group tasks. You can take a look at some of `ical`'s companion shell scripts and programs under the `/usr/lib/ical/contrib` directory to find tips and hints on how to customize `ical` to suit your needs.

You can find the latest version (v2.2) of `ical` at `http://www.research.digital.com/SRC/personal/Sanjay_Ghemawat/ical/home.html`.

Checking the Calendar and Keeping Appointments with emacs

The emacs text editor, more fully discussed in Hour 14, "Text Processing," has a number of features that can help your personal productivity or even keep you amused. You can check the current calendar, see a list of holidays (and more), and keep a diary with appointment reminders.

If you're using X11, you automatically run the X11 version of emacs unless you use the -nw command-line option on the command line to run emacs in your terminal window, for example:

```
# emacs -nw
```

After you start the X11 version of emacs, you can view a calendar of the previous, current, and next months by clicking Apps, then Calendar, and then 3-Month Calendar on the main menu. The emacs editor also offers you a Diary, Holidays, Phases of the Moon, and Sunrise/Sunset times. You can also use the non-X11 emacs command, ESC-x-calendar. Press the Escape key, type an x, then type the word **calendar**, and press Enter. emacs displays a three-month calendar as shown in Figure 18.4.

18

FIGURE 18.4

The emacs editor features a built-in calendar with an assortment of calendar tools, including a diary and appointment reminder.

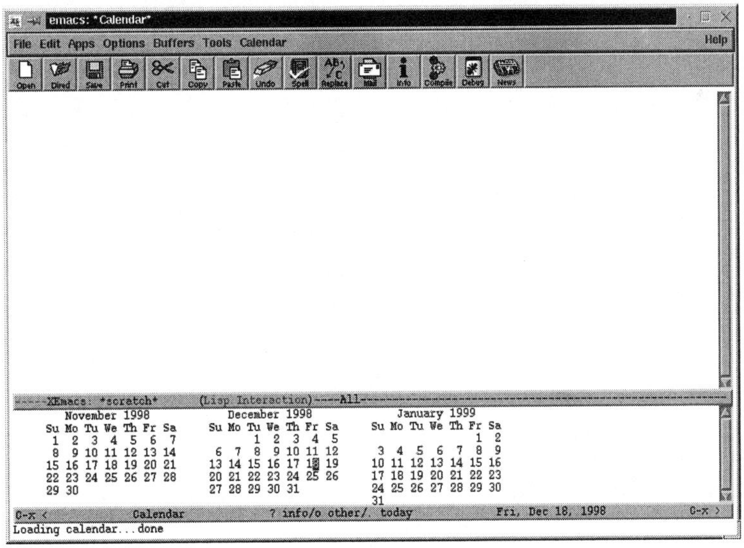

You can get help on using emacs' calendar tools by typing the question mark after clicking in the calendar window. A help menu of calendar items appears. After you start the calendar mode in emacs, a Calendar menu item will appear on the emacs menu bar.

Use the Calendar menu item's Goto sub-menu to advance the calendar forward or backward, or jump to nearly 20 different types of dates, such as Julian, Islamic, and even Mayan! The Holidays sub-menu either lists all the holidays for a range of days or months displayed by the calendar listing at the bottom of the screen or marks the holidays by highlighting days of the calendar listing. The Moon menu lists the different phases of the moon.

More than 100 different calendar commands (other than obvious menu items) are available in emacs. In order to receive appointment reminders, emacs must be running. For more information, first try calendar's help, and then use the apropos command from emacs' Help menu to get more detailed information.

You can also use emacs to remind you of important events by using Neil Mager's emacs appointment commands. To set appointment reminders, you must first create a .emacs file in your home directory containing the following:

```
(require 'appt)
(display-time)
(appt-initialize)
```

Use the File menu to save this file. Quit, and restart emacs. To create an emacs diary, start the calendar mode. Click the Apps menu, then click the Calendar item, and finally click the 3-Month Calendar item. After you enable the emacs calendar mode, click in the calendar window on a specific day. Then go to the Calendar menu, click the Diary sub-menu, and select Insert Daily. Your scratch buffer changes to "diary," and you find your cursor following text containing the selected date. Make some diary entries, then save the buffer (through the File menu), and exit and restart emacs.

The emacs appointment function is written in the LISP programming language (much of emacs and many of its functions are in LISP). You can learn more about the specifics of setting appointments by reading the source code to the emacs appointment functions, like so:

```
less /usr/lib/xemacs-19.16/lisp/calendar/appt.el
```

Entering Appointments

After you restart emacs, you can enter appointment reminders in your diary with the emacs appt-add command. First, enter the calendar mode, and click your left mouse button on a specific day. Next, press and release the Escape key, type an **x**, then type **appt-add**, and press Enter. You're asked, at the command line at the bottom of the emacs window, for an appointment time in hours and minutes, like so:

```
Time (hh:mm[am/pm]):
```

Enter the time in the form of a 24-hour clock (such as 15:00) or a 12-hour clock (such as 3:00 pm). After you press Enter, you're prompted for a message, like so:

```
Message:
```

Type in a reminder message (such as "Wake up!"), and press Enter again.

Five minutes before the appointment time, emacs beeps and then displays a new mode line, informing you of the appointment. Two minutes later, the same thing happens. You can also manually add reminders to your diary file, for example:

```
 8:00am Jogging with dog
12:00am Lunch with Cathy
15:00pm Check with car repair shop
```

You can save these reminders following each date in your diary files to set future appointments. If you want to delete appointments, use the appt-delete command after selecting a specific day. You're asked interactively to delete various appointments from your diary.

By using the emacs calendar mode and appointment functions, you can build a history of your appointments in your personal diary. Experiment with different modes, and read the emacs info files for more information.

Setting Alarms with the knotes Client

You don't need to run large programs or word processors in order to set alarms when you use the K Desktop Environment, or KDE. If you want to try an easy-to-use utility to set reminders or alarms during your X sessions, try the knotes client, included with the KDE utilities distribution.

Click the Utilities menu on your KDE desktop's panel and select knotes. A small Post-It™-like window will appear on your desktop. Type in some text, and then right-click in the knotes window. From the pop-up menu, scroll down, select the Operations menu, and then click the Alarm menu item, as shown in Figure 18.5.

18

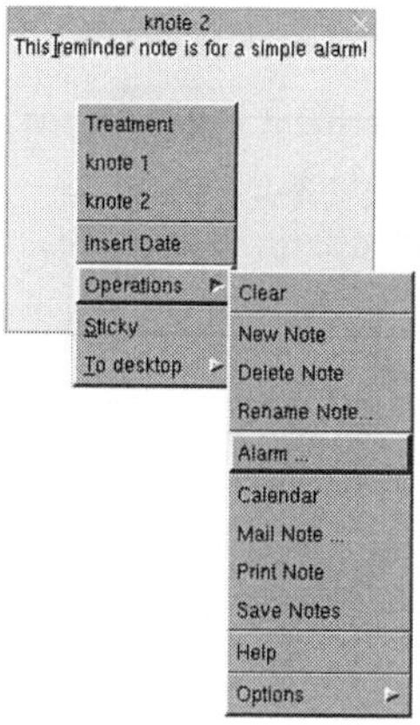

FIGURE **18.5**

*The knotes client,
besides sporting
easy-to-uses
note-taking features,
also includes alarms
and reminders.*

An alarm dialog box, as shown in Figure 18.6, appears. Click the up and down arrows for the day, month, and year to set the alarm dates. Click AM or PM, and then choose the hour and minute to set the alarm time. When finished, click Set to set the alarm.

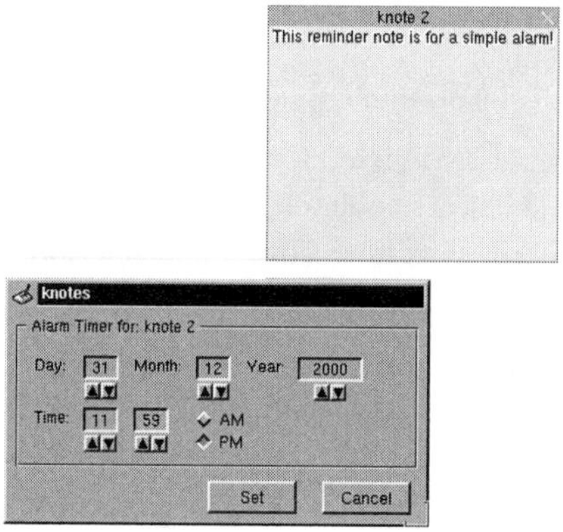

FIGURE **18.6**

Setting knotes *alarms
is an easy task with its
alarm dialog box.*

Summary

This hour introduced you to a number of personal productivity programs and X11 clients you can use to track your time, set appointments, and document your day.

Q&A

Q My cursor was on a date in the 3-month calendar, but when I tried to insert a diary entry, `emacs` reported `not on a date`.

A Try double-clicking the date in the calendar view. When a date is correctly selected, you should see a full list of diary items in the Diary submenu.

Q I tried running `crontab` with its `-e` option, but the screen cleared and then listed a bunch of apostrophes down the left side of the screen. What's going on?

A By default, `crontab` uses the `vi` editor. See the `vim` man page for more information on using this editor. Better yet, create and use your own `EDITOR` environment variable to point to the `pico` editor (included with the `pine` email program).

Q I defined the `EDITOR` environment variable, but when I use `crontab -e`, the program exits with an error. What's going on?

A Make sure you install the `pine` email program from your OpenLinux CD-ROM or that you include the full pathname to `pico` in your `EDITOR` definition. The shell reports an error and `crontab` also exits with an error.

Exercises

1. Examine this `crontab` entry:

   ```
   15 0 4 * * echo "What day is it?"
   ```

   When and how often will this entry run?

2. Try setting several appointments in `emacs`. What does `emacs` do as the time for an appointment draws near? What happens if you set an appointment and then quit `emacs`?

3. Try setting an alarm or appointment with the `crontab` command. Then try setting an alarm or appointment with the `at` command. Which command is better to use and why?

18

HOUR 19

Home Office Management with StarOffice

NEW TERM This hour shows you how to get started with StarOffice from Star Division GmbH. This is an office-automation productivity suite, or *office suite*, available for download from http://www.stardivision.com. An office suite is a collection of integrated programs, such as a word processor, spreadsheet, and presentation graphics client that can easily share data such as blocks of text, tables of figures, or graphic images.

A good office suite uses many of the same menu commands and has an integrated "look and feel" to help you more easily learn its component programs. A great office suite makes your computing experience more efficient and productive. I think you'll like StarOffice, which is one of the latest and best office suites for OpenLinux. It is free for personal use, but if you use the program for commercial purposes, you must pay a registration fee (see the following note).

This program, combined with the power of your OpenLinux system, provides a great home office productivity solution. You can use StarOffice to produce professionally type-set color documents with very little effort.

In this hour, you'll learn how to install and use StarOffice to create word processing and spreadsheet documents.

> This hour describes using StarOffice 5.0. You can download its 50-megabyte compressed archive for free from http://www.stardivision.com. You must obtain a customer number and personal key by registering before you can even begin installation of the software.

Installing and Configuring StarOffice

StarOffice is not installed when you install OpenLinux. Unlike other Linux programs, you must install StarOffice through a separate procedure. This involves running an instal-lation script to copy the software to your OpenLinux file system.

The installation is pretty painless, but you need to run X11. You do not have to be logged in as the root operator. When you install StarOffice on a standalone OpenLinux worksta-tion, the installation process installs StarOffice in a directory named Office50 in your home directory.

> You can also perform a network installation or an installation to support multiple users from the same StarOffice install. Read the 36-page StarOffice installation guide. The documentation manual, install_guide.pdf, is in Portable Document Format, but you can use the xpdf client (which reads .pdf files) to read it like this (substituting *path_to_the_guide* with the direc-tory path either on CD-ROM or on your hard drive):
>
> # xpdf /*path_to_the_guide*/install_guide.pdf

To start the installation, use the cd command to navigate to the StarOffice setup directory, and use StarOffice's setup command by typing ./**setup** and pressing the Enter key. The StarOffice 5.0 Installation dialog box appears. Click the Next button to start the install. You then see a Software License Agreement dialog box. Scroll through the agreement, and then click the Accept button to continue. A dialog box appears, asking you to enter your personal information. Type in your personal information, such as name, address, phone number, and email address, and then click the Next button. You're then asked to enter a Media Key (or registration information if you're installing a downloaded copy). Type in the key or registration, and click the Next button.

> You can change your personal information later. See this chapter's section, "Customizing StarOffice".

You then see a dialog box (as shown in Figure 19.1), asking you to choose a type of installation.

FIGURE 19.1

Choose a type of installation when you install StarOffice 5.0.

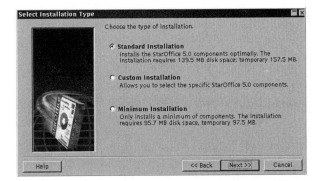

The Standard installation requires nearly 140 megabytes of hard drive space, along with an additional 20 megabytes for temporary files. If you do not have this much space, choose a Minimum installation, which only requires a maximum of little more than 100 megabytes during the install.

> You can also choose a Custom installation, but this is not recommended. The best approach is to perform a minimum install and then add any missing components with the Custom installation later.

Click the button next to a desired type of installation. You're then asked where you want StarOffice to be installed, as shown in Figure 19.2.

19

FIGURE 19.2

*Choose a location for
the StarOffice 5.0
installation.*

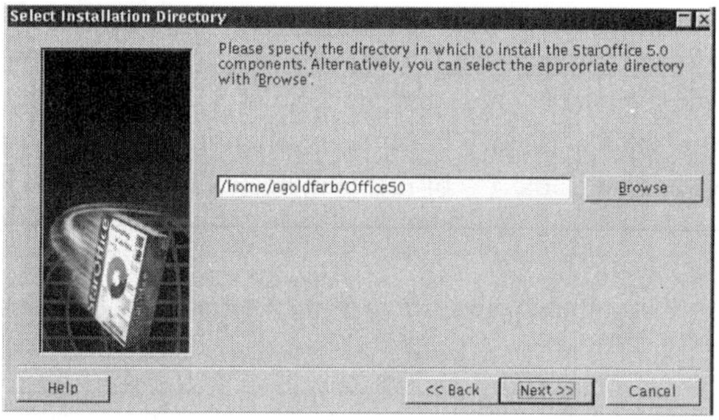

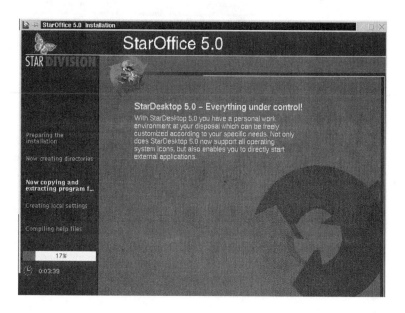

The default is the Office50 folder in your home directory. If you choose another location, make sure you have read and write permission (see Hour 22, "Handling Files and
Your File System"). After you click the Next button and confirm creation of the directory, click the Complete button. You see the install window, as shown in Figure 19.3, displaying the progress of the install. This installation typically takes less than five minutes
with a late-model computer.

FIGURE 19.3

*StarOffice 5.0 tracks
and displays the
progress and time
remaining of the
installation process.*

After the software is installed, click the Complete button to exit the `./setup` script.

Make sure to read the text file displayed in the final installation dialog box or the file README under the `Office50` directory after installing StarOffice. This text file contains some important hints about installing StarOffice over a network and configuring email, fonts, and printers; it also has a license and short FAQ section about OpenLinux and StarOffice.

Starting StarOffice

StarOffice 5.0 is started by the `soffice` script in the `$HOME/Office50/bin` directory. If you are in your home directory, start StarOffice by using the `soffice` command like this:

```
# Office50/bin/soffice &
```

After a minute or so, the StarOffice desktop appears, as shown in Figure 19.4.

Don't forget to register your copy of StarOffice at
http://www.stardivision.com!

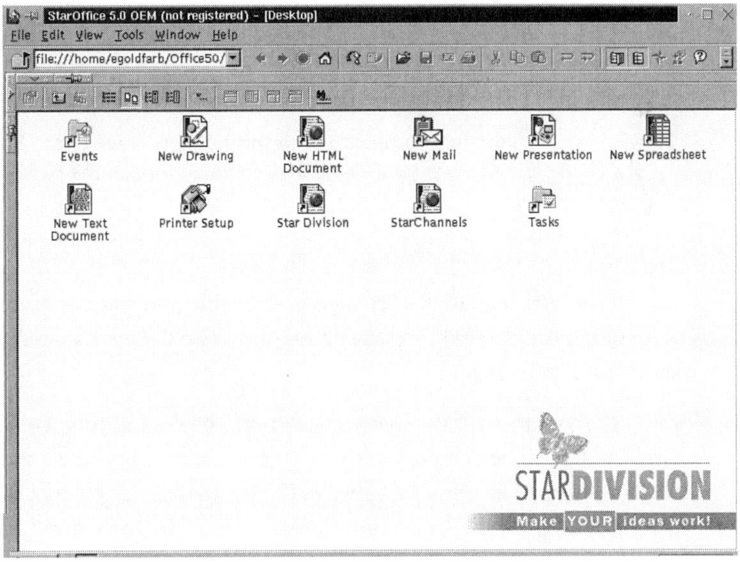

FIGURE 19.4

The StarOffice 5.0 desktop features menus, several tool-bars, and a Work area with icons for creating new documents or getting help.

19

StarOffice performs best on an OpenLinux system with at least 32 megabytes of RAM, or system memory. However, even having twice that much memory can't make it start faster.

Customizing StarOffice

If you made a mistake or want to change the personal information you entered when you installed StarOffice, open the Tools menu, select the Options menu item, and then click General. A dialog box appears, as shown in Figure 19.5, offering you the capability to change a number of default StarOffice features.

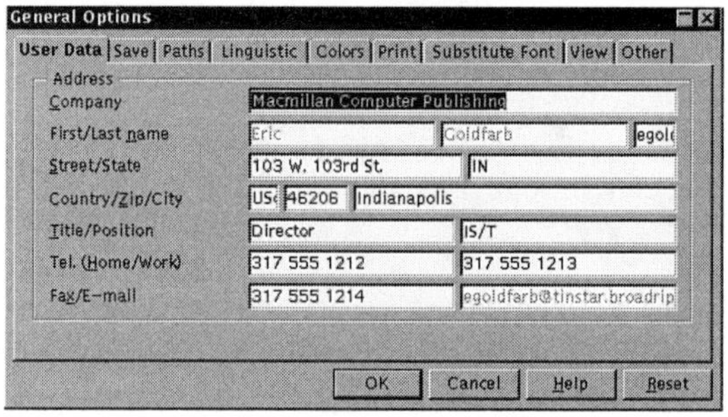

FIGURE 19.5

Set various StarOffice options with the General Options dialog box.

Although not discussed in this hour, in order to use StarOffice Mail, you must enter your name and email address in the personal information dialog box.

One of the first functions to change is to enable auto-saving of documents. Click the Save tab in the General Options dialog box. The defaults Save dialog box appears, as shown in Figure 19.6.

Click the Automatic Save Every checkbox. The default time between saves is 15 minutes, but this value can be set from 1 to 60 minutes. If you want a backup copy made of a working document, click the Always Create Backup Copy checkbox. Also, note that the default number of the Undo scroll box levels is 20. You can set StarOffice to use as many as 100 levels of undo.

FIGURE 19.6

Set automatic saving defaults to ensure documents are routinely saved during StarOffice sessions.

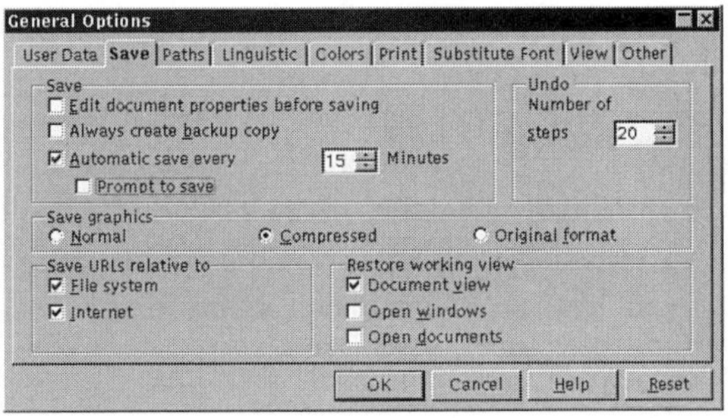

![General Options dialog box with Save tab selected]

If you select Automatic Save Every, uncheck the Prompt to Save checkbox (shown in Figure 19.6) to avoid having to respond to a dialog box each time StarOffice tries to save your current document.

Other tabs in the General Options dialog box offer settings for spell checking, colors, toolbar button sizes, printer warnings, and languages.

Installing a Printer for StarOffice

Fortunately, if you configured your printer to work with OpenLinux (using the `lisa` command; see Hour 15, "Preparing Documents"), you don't have to change printer settings for StarOffice. If you do need to make changes or want to set up StarOffice to use a different printer than the default generic PostScript printer, click the Printer-Setup icon in StarOffice's work area.

Using StarOffice

The StarOffice *desktop*, or main window, is your entry and launch pad to a number of StarOffice programs. This office suite is a large, capable and complex program with a lot of interface elements. To enlarge the desktop window, double-click the desktop window's title bar (or click the maximize window button, if available).

If you use KDE and need even more room for the StarOffice desktop, use the KDE desktop panel's minimize button, or configure the panel to hide automatically (using the panel's configuration dialog box). To get the absolute most use of your screen real estate, press Shift+Ctrl+J to zoom the current StarOffice work area to full screen. See Table 19.1 for other keyboard commands.

19

The StarOffice desktop (shown in Figure 19.4) consists of several elements, such as a menu bar with the File, Edit, View, Tools, and other menus. Below the menu bar is the function bar, a toolbar with buttons and other controls. If you click the right-pointing triangle in the upper-left corner of the Work area, an open area on the left side of the desktop appears (and the triangle now points to the left). This button controls the display of the Explorer, which provides quick access to different StarOffice folders (directories), such as the Gallery of artwork or sample documents folder.

> The Gallery is installed during a Standard installation, not a minimal installation. If you performed a minimum install, restart the setup script, and then choose a Custom installation to install the artwork.

To see a list of installed artwork, open the Explorer, and then click on the small plus sign (+) in front of the Gallery icon in the Explorer. A list of graphics categories drops down. Double-click a category, such as Flags, and the first several files appear in the *Beamer* (as shown in Figure 19.7).

FIGURE 19.7

The Beamer in the StarOffice desktop displays the graphics or files in a directory.

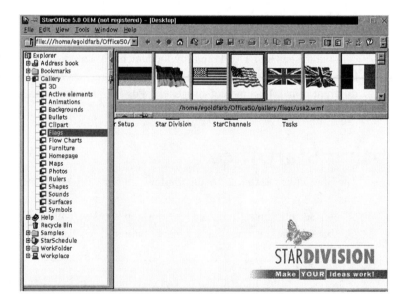

The Beamer is used to view the contents of directories or graphics files listed in the Explorer window (and also for placing graphics into documents; see the following section "Creating Documents with StarWriter"). Note that the Beamer shows the currently selected file's pathname. Click the minus sign(-) in front of the Gallery icon in the Explorer to close the Gallery and the Beamer.

The *work area* is the largest part of the StarOffice desktop. It contains icons that represent *links* to different documents or help files. Your first step is to create a project folder to organize your work.

Right-click a blank area of the work area. A pop-up menu appears. Select the New menu item, and then click Folder. The folder appears in the work area. Type a name for the folder, such as MyProjects. Hold down your left mouse button on the folder, drag the folder to the Explorer window, and drop it—the folder disappears from the work area and is now in the Explorer.

Creating Documents with StarWriter

StarWriter is the word processor portion of the StarOffice office suite. This program is integrated into the StarOffice desktop and can share information with other parts of StarOffice, such as StarCalc (see the section "Calculating with StarCalc," later in this hour). StarWriter has all the features of a modern word processor, which include the following:

- Automatic spelling checking and correction
- Building of tables, footnotes, and indexes
- Complete search and replace capabilities, including styles
- Complete style controls
- Complex text and font control, including kerning and spacing
- Cut, copy, paste, and draggable text selections
- Document-creation wizards (AutoPilot)
- Drag-and-drop of StarOffice document items (such as data or graphics)
- Drawing tools, fields, and graphic insertions
- Hyphenation controls
- Import and export of different file formats (see Table 19.2)
- Insertion of hyperlinks
- Macro support
- Multiple views, including layout and outline

19

- Multiple zoom levels for enlargement/reduction
- Revision control
- Templates for documents and layouts
- Thesaurus support

Start by creating a StarWriter document in your new project folder. Double-click your project folder in the Explorer, and the work area clears.

There are several ways to create a new document:

- Click the Start button in the lower left corner of the desktop, and then click the Text Document menu item.
- Open the File menu, select the New item, and then click the Document submenu item.
- Press Ctrl+N and select a document type from a list of 70 different template documents.
- Open the File menu, select AutoPilot, and then click Letter, Fax, Agenda, or Memo

For now, double-click your project folder in the Explorer, hide the Explorer, and then right-click in your project's work area. Select New from the pop-up menu, click Documents, and then click the Text Document menu item. A StarWriter text document window appears in the work area, as shown in Figure 19.8.

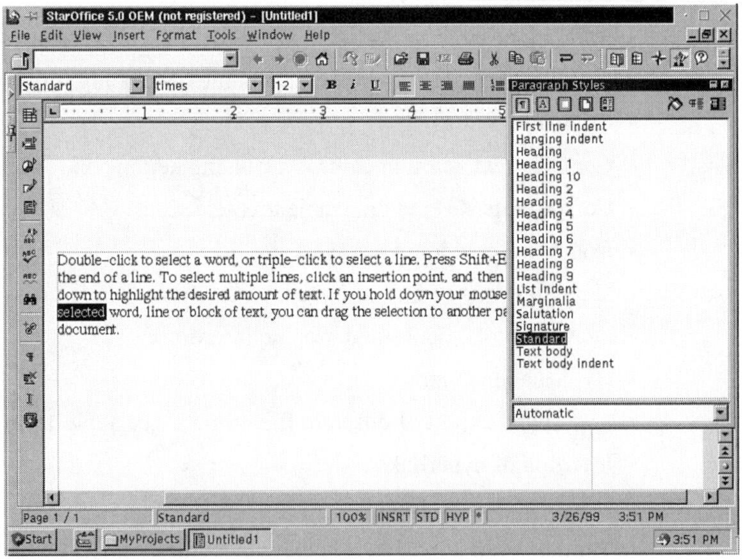

FIGURE 19.8

The current StarWriter document appears in the StarOffice work area.

Note that StarOffice has a taskbar similar to KDE's at the bottom of the desktop window. To quickly navigate back to the initial desktop, click its button (between the Start button and the MyProjects folder's button) in the taskbar. For now, click in the blank page, and type a paragraph or so.

> StarWriter's document work area has a horizontal rule and formatting tool-bar above it and a vertical toolbar to the left of it. The ruler is used to set margins and tab stops, whereas the formatting toolbar is used to set font attributes and justification. The vertical toolbar can be used for a number of actions, such as table, field, or graphics insertions, spell checking, or search and replace procedures.

Double-click to select a word, or triple-click to select a line. Press Shift+End to select to the end of a line. To select multiple lines, click an insertion point, and then drag up or down to highlight the desired amount of text. If you hold down your mouse button on a selected word, line, or block of text, you can drag the selection to another part of your document.

To format text, select the appropriate toolbar icon, or right-click the text and select attributes from a pop-up menu. Character formatting from the Format menu can be used to access more complex controls, such as font effects, style, size, or color.

StarWriter has many different keyboard commands you can use while creating documents. See Table 19.1 for a list of common commands (also shared by StarCalc) and their actions.

TABLE 19.1 STARWRITER COMMON KEYBOARD COMMANDS

Action	Keyboard Command
Abort menu operation	Esc
Check spelling	F7
Copy	Ctrl+C
Cut	Ctrl+X
Edit menu	Alt+E
File menu	Alt+F
Format menu	Alt+O
Function Navigator	F5
Help menu	Alt+H

continues

TABLE 19.1 CONTINUED

Action	Keyboard Command
Insert menu	Alt+I
New file	Ctrl+N
Open file	Ctrl+O
Paste	Ctrl+V
Print	Ctrl+P
Quit	Ctrl+Q
Search & Replace	Ctrl+F
Select All	Ctrl+A
Thesaurus	Ctrl+F7
Toggle full-screen mode	Ctrl+Shift+I
Tools menu	Alt+T
Undo	Ctrl+Z
View menu	Alt+V
Window menu	Alt+W

Spellchecking and Saving StarWriter Documents

Checking the spelling of documents is an important task. Misspelled words can have a detrimental effect on your professional image and even your career. Fortunately, StarOffice comes with a built-in spelling checker that not only works with StarWriter documents, but any StarOffice document, including graphic images with embedded text!

Open the Tools menu, select Spelling, and then click the Check menu item to start the spelling checker. If you don't want to use a menu or your mouse, press F7.

The Spelling dialog box appears, as shown in Figure 19.9.

The spelling checker highlights and displays the first misspelled word found after the current insertion point in your document. Continue through the document, and click the appropriate button to ignore, replace, or globally ignore the word in your document. Correctly spelled but unrecognized words can be added to your personal dictionary by clicking the Add button. When you finish, click the Close button.

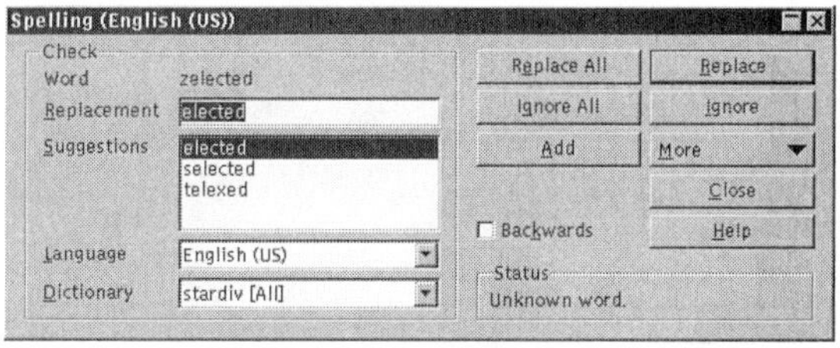

FIGURE 19.9

StarOffice spell checks all document types and not just StarWriter documents.

Spelling (English (US))

Check			Replace All	Replace
Word	zelected		Ignore All	Ignore
Replacement	elected		Add	More ▼
Suggestions	elected			
	selected			Close
	telexed			
		□ Backwards	Help
Language	English (US) ▼		Status	
Dictionary	stardiv [All] ▼		Unknown word.	

You can also use automatic spell checking while you work. Enable Auto Spellcheck to have StarWriter automatically underline any misspelled or suspect words. Open the Tools menu, select Spelling, and then click Auto Spellcheck. You can also click the small ABC icon underlined in red on the vertical toolbar to the left of the work area to enable automatic checking.

> To set StarOffice and its components to always use automatic spell checking, open the Tools menu. Select Options, and then click the General menu item. In the General Options dialog box, click the Linguistic tab, and check the Check Spelling as You Type check box. Press the OK button to save your changes.

To save your document, press Ctrl+S, or open the File menu and click the Close menu item. StarWriter can open (import) and save (export) a variety of file formats, as shown in Table 19.2.

19

TABLE 19.2   STARWRITER 5.0 FILE FORMATS

Name	Type
MSWord 6.0/95, 97	Microsoft Word for Windows 6.0, 95, 97
Rich Text Format	RTF
StarWriter 1.0 (read-only), 2.0, 3.0, 4.0, 5.0	StarOffice
StarWriter HTML	Hypertext Markup Language
Text (ANSI, DOS, Mac)	Text format

FIGURE 19.10

*StarWriter can read
and save documents in
a number of formats.*

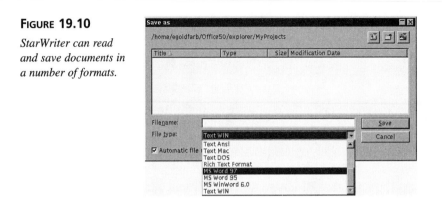

To save your document in a different format, click the drop-down File Type menu (as shown in Figure 19.10), and then click the OK button.

Calculating with StarCalc

StarCalc is the spreadsheet component of StarOffice. Like StarWriter, this program integrates with the StarOffice desktop and can share information, such as tables of data or graphics, with other StarOffice components. For example, you can create a spreadsheet and then paste the data in a StarWriter document.

When you work with StarCalc, you quickly see that it's easy to create even complex spreadsheets. As you probably know from Hour 17, "Learning Math and Financial Tools," spreadsheets are handy for storing, tracking, visualizing, and forecasting data. In this section you learn the basics of creating and saving a StarCalc spreadsheet.

There are several ways to create a StarCalc spreadsheet:

- Double-click the New Spreadsheet icon in the StarOffice desktop's work area.
- Open the File menu, select New, and then click Spreadsheet.
- Click the Start menu, and then click the Spreadsheet menu item.
- Type Ctrl+N, and then select a spreadsheet type from a template dialog box.

For now, double-click your project folder in the Explorer.

You can also click the drop-down menu on the StarOffice toolbar (below the menu bar), and then click a previously visited document or folder.

Next, right-click your mouse in a blank spot in your work area. From the pop-up menu, select the New menu, select Documents, and then click the Spreadsheet menu item. The work area clears, and you see a familiar blank spreadsheet grid with row and column headers (as shown in Figure 19.11).

> Note that the toolbar above the work area includes a cell selection and data entry field.

Enter some data into columns and rows by clicking an insertion point and typing a number. Press the Tab key to enter the data and move right. Press the Enter key to enter the data and move down.

FIGURE 19.11

StarCalc is a comprehensive and capable spreadsheet calculator that can share data and graphics with other StarOffice components.

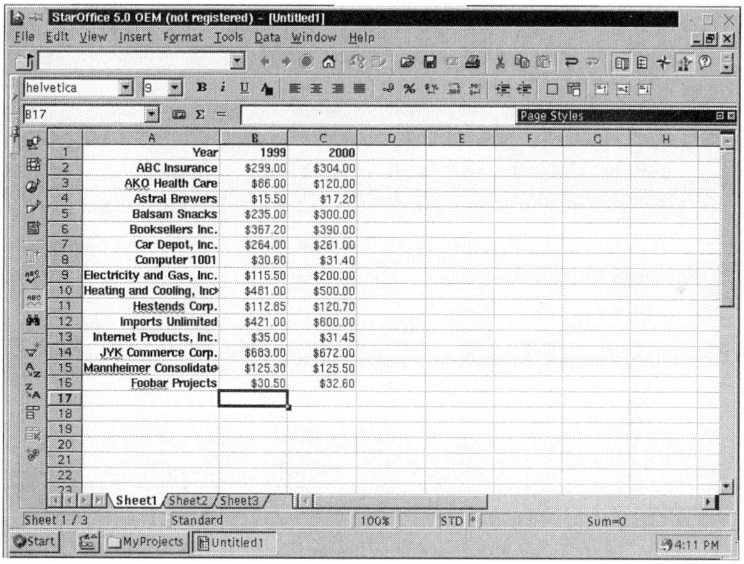

NEW TERM Numbers and text can be formatted like those in a StarWriter document. Single cells are selected by a mouse click. Multiple cells are selected by selecting a cell and then dragging with the left mouse button held down. An ingenious feature is a *discontiguous* selection, where multiple selections are made without the selected regions adjoining. You can use discontiguous selection to format two or more areas of your spreadsheet at the same time. Click the first cell, and then drag to select the first area. Hold down the Ctrl key and click and drag to select another area (see Figure 19.12). You can now format the cells as needed.

19

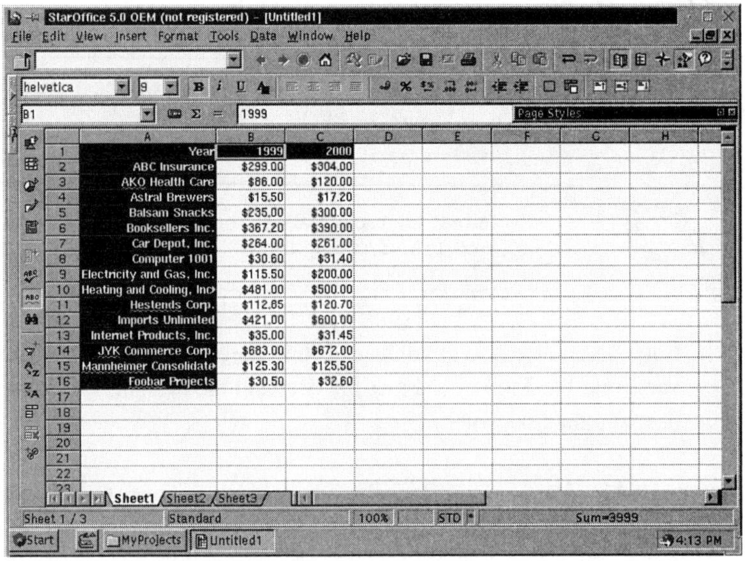

FIGURE 19.12

StarCalc supports advanced formatting features, such as discontiguous selection.

To perform quick totals of your data, click in the bottom cell of a column of numbers, and then click the Sum button (the Σ) next to the equal(=) sign in the data entry field above your work area. An X and a check mark appear next to the data entry field, which has the SUM formula inserted. Click the check mark to accept the entry, or click the X button to cancel.

When you finish, press Ctrl+S, or open the File menu and click Save to save your work. StarCalc can import and export a variety of spreadsheet document formats, as shown in Table 19.3.

TABLE 19.3 STARCALC SUPPORTED SPREADSHEET FORMATS

Type	Name
dBase	Dbase database
DIF	Document Interchange Format
HTML	Hypertext Markup Language
MSExcel 5.0/95, 97	Microsoft Excel for Windows 5.0, 95, 97
StarCalc 3.0, 4.0, 5.0	StarCalc
SYLK	Symbolic Link format
Text, CSV	Text, cell values

StarCalc supports all the keyboard commands listed in Table 19.1. You can also select and move blocks of highlighted data around the sheet using the same drag-and-drop mechanism as with StarWriter text.

Graphing with StarCalc

StarCalc can easily create complex graphs of your spreadsheet's data. The first step is to click and drag to select the desired spreadsheet data.

To start drawing a graph, click the Insert Object button (the third button down) on the vertical toolbar to the left of your chart's work area. A small toolbar appears. Click the tiny chart icon, and your cursor turns into a plus sign (+) with a tiny chart. Click and drag on a blank area of your spreadsheet to set the initial size of your graph. When you release your left mouse button, the AutoFormat Chart dialog box appears, as shown in Figure 19.13.

You can also open the Insert menu and click the Chart menu item to start the AutoFormat Chart dialog box.

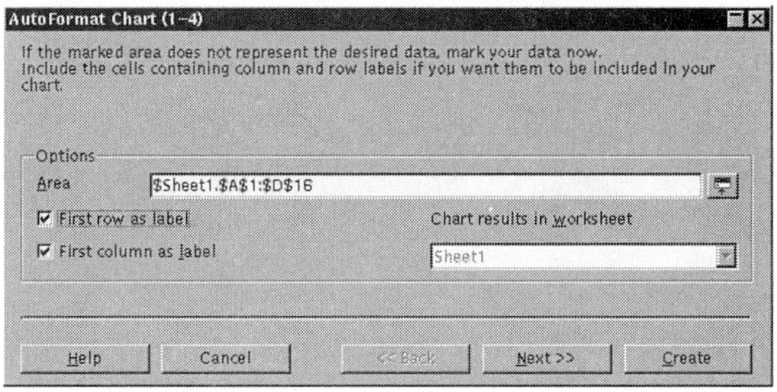

FIGURE 19.13

StarCalc's AutoFormat Chart dialog box is an easy way to start creating chart graphics of your spreadsheet's data.

19

To build your chart, select any desired options and click the Next button. Continue through the AutoFormat dialog boxes until you arrive at a final dialog box with a button labeled Create (as shown in Figure 19.14).

FIGURE 19.14

A single click of a button creates a chart graphic of your spreadsheet's data.

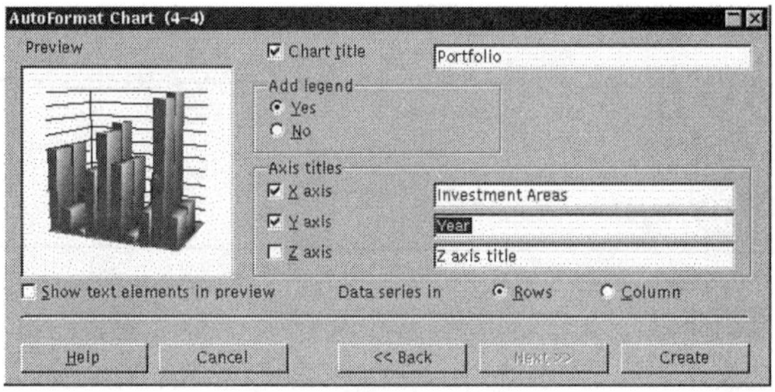

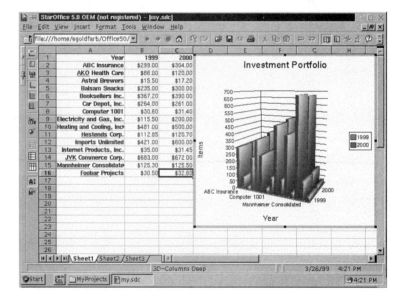

Your chart appears in the previously selected area of your spreadsheet (as shown in Figure 19.15). You can then move, resize, or edit the chart. If you click the chart and then press Ctrl+C, you can paste the chart into another StarCalc or StarWriter document.

FIGURE 19.15

StarCalc can create professional chart graphics of your spreadsheet's data.

Summary

This hour introduced you to StarOffice for OpenLinux. This office suite provides a professional set of programs you can use to be more productive. You learned how to install StarOffice, and then start StarWriter and StarCalc to create great-looking documents. StarOffice comes with several other programs, such as a database, graphics, and presentation package. Read the StarOffice user's guide to learn more about this great set of programs from Star Division.

Q&A

Q I started installing StarOffice but got an error!

A Carefully read any error messages, and then look at the StarOffice installation guide. The installation script requires X11! Upon a serious error, the StarOffice installation aborts and returns you to your shell prompt. It is possible to get an installation error if you repeatedly choose an installation type, cancel, and then reattempt an installation without quitting the installation script first. Try reinstalling again.

Q I've installed StarOffice from CD-ROM, but how do I eject my CD-ROM?

A Use the umount command. See Hour 22, "Handling Files and Your File System."

Q Where are documents saved when I use StarOffice?

A Look under the Office50/explorer directory for any folders you created.

Q I want to learn more about using StarOffice. What other documentation is included?

A Look for the file user_guide.pdf included with the StarOffice distribution. Then, use the xpdf client to read or print the document.

Q Why doesn't my Backspace key work?

A Check to see if you disabled the XKEYBOARD extension in your XF86Config file (see Hour 3, "Post-Installation Issues"). You can also try the xmodmap command, like this:

```
# xmodmap -e "keycode 22 = BackSpace"
```

19

Exercises

1. Create a StarWriter document, and then type multiple paragraphs. Triple-click a line of text, hold your left mouse button down on the highlighted text, and drag down to the end of your document. Release your mouse button. What happens?

2. Leave your StarWriter document open. Click the Desktop button in the lower left corner of the StarOffice desktop. Double-click the New Spreadsheet icon in the StarOffice work area. Create a spreadsheet, enter some data, and create a graphic. When the graphic appears, click the graphic, and then press Ctrl+C. Select the Window menu, and click your StarWriter document. Click an insertion point, and press Ctrl+V. What happens?

3. Highlight some data in your StarCalc spreadsheet. Press Ctrl+C. Navigate to your StarWriter document, click an insertion point, and press Ctrl+V. What happens?

HOUR **20**

Relaxation and Playing Linux Games

Now it's time to sit back, relax, and have some fun. Chances are that you skipped the rest of the book and are reading this chapter first. Well, that's okay because we all know the real reason we bought our computers, right? To zap hordes of alien invaders streaming across the screen!

In this hour you'll learn how to play music CDs with the amazing kcsd client. You'll also learn about some of the more than 70 games included with OpenLinux.

Playing Music CDs with the `kscd` and `xplaycd` Clients

Using your computer as a stereo system might seem a bit extravagant, but it's nice to be able to listen to music while you work. Besides, playing music CDs with OpenLinux is not only easy; it's convenient and fun!

If your sound card works with Linux, great! You can start playing music

CDs right away. You can find several music CD player clients installed with OpenLinux that you can use during your X sessions.

One of the best CD players is the kscd client that comes with KDE. This program not only plays CDs, but if you have an active Internet connection, kscd goes out in the Internet, queries a remote computer with your music CD's serial number, and retrieves the name of your music CD, the artist's name, the number of tracks, and the name of each track. You can save this information in a database on your hard drive.

Before you begin, use the chmod command to set the permissions of your CD-ROM so that anyone can read your CD, like this:

```
# su -c "chmod 664 /dev/cdrom"
```

You don't have to use KDE to use the kcsd player. However, you must have KDE installed on your system.

Start your Internet connection, and then start kcsd. If you're using KDE, click the Application Starter button on your desktop's panel, scroll up to Multimedia, and click the CD Player menu item. If you're using another window manager, type kcsd & at the command line and press Enter. The kcsd dialog box appears as shown in Figure 20.1.

The kscd player automatically goes out in the Internet and tries to locate your CD's artist and title. If you need to configure kcsd, such as what Internet database to query or colors and fonts to use in its display, click the Configure kscd button (the one with the hammer and screwdriver).

FIGURE 20.1

The kcsd audio CD player connects to Internet databases to show you information about your audio CD.

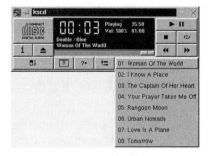

The Configuration dialog box appears, as shown in Figure 20.2. Note that the Enable Remote CDDB (CD database) button is selected. If kscd has trouble connecting to a particular remote Internet database, click a different CDDB server in the CDDB server list. Deselect the Enable Remote CDDB button if you don't want kscd to use the Internet.

FIGURE 20.2

The kscd *Configuration dialog box is used for communications and display settings.*

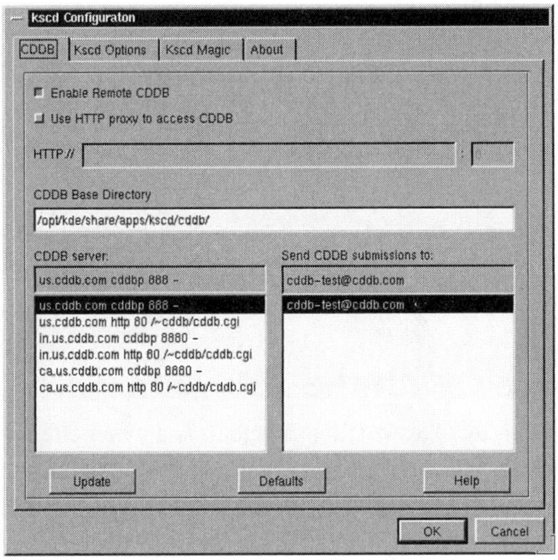

Use the CDDB Base Directory field to specify the pathname to your system's audio CD database. As you use kscd, you can save each CD's information in this database. To access kscd's database controls, click the CDDB dialog box button in kscd's main window (immediately to the right of the player's power button).

The CD Database Editor dialog box appears, as shown in Figure 20.3. kscd fills out most of the information about your CD from information retrieved by the remote Internet server (this happens almost instantaneously, as only a small amount of information is sent and received). Click the Save button, and you're asked to pick one of 10 different categories of music.

20

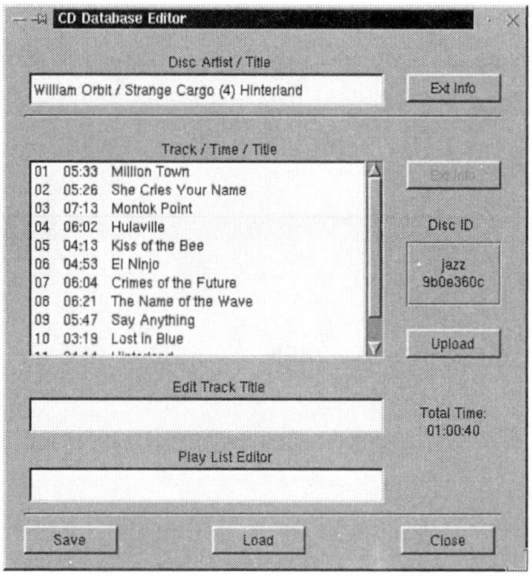

FIGURE 20.3

The kscd *database dialog box is used to save information about your audio for use the next time you play the CD.*

Playing Music with the xplaycd Client

The xplaycd client, by Olav Woelfelschneider, is another client you can use to play music CDs. The program appears in a small window with the standard music CD controls, along with horizontal stereo volume bars and a list of buttons representing the tracks on the CD. You can raise or lower your music's volume by clicking your left mouse button ahead of or behind the horizontal bars.

Start this player from the command line of a terminal window, like this:

```
# xplaycd&
```

The player appears, as shown in Figure 20.4.

One great feature of this program is the capability to reorder tracks and even play a track multiple times. By clicking a track number and dragging, you can rearrange the play sequence of the tracks on your CD. To play a track multiple times, click a track number with your mouse's middle button and drag the track along the CD track sequence. When you release your mouse button, the track number is duplicated.

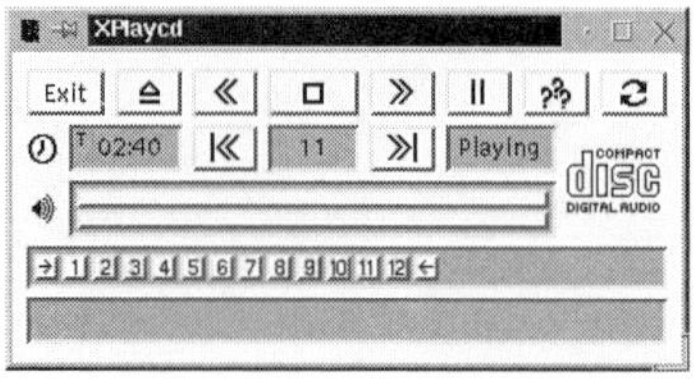

FIGURE 20.4

The xplaycd *player features draggable track numbers to reorder or repeat playing of music tracks.*

Not using X? Don't worry—you can play music CDs with Sariel Har-Peled's `cdp` command, found under the `/usr/bin` directory. This command is a text mode program and is started from the command line of your console, like this:

```
# cdp
```

When `cdp` starts, you see a list of the tracks on your CD. Turn on the NumLock key of your keyboard to control how to play your CD. Table 20.1 lists the controls for playing CDs from your keyboard's keypad.

TABLE 20.1   THE *cdp* COMMAND KEYPAD CONTROLS

Action	Keypad Key
Soft exit (music continues)	0
Help	.
Back 15 seconds	1
Hard abort (eject CD)	2
Forward 15 seconds	3
Previous track	4
Replay CD	5
Next track	6
Stop	7
Toggle pause/resume	8
Play	9

The `cdp` command has a number of command-line options. A symbolic link, called `cdplay`, can be used to play music without `cdp`'s interactive screen. Tell `cdplay` to start playing music at a certain track with the `play` option, followed by a track number, like this:

```
# cdplay play 3
```

This command line starts the `cdp` program, and your music CD starts playing from the third track.

20

Games for the Console

If you don't use X11, you also can have fun at the console because you can find an assortment of nearly 60 classic games you can play. Look under the `/usr/games` directory.

One of the classics is the `adventure` game. This features an interactive text screen where you enter simple commands to try to delve into a cave, retrieve treasures, and escape in one piece. Start the game by typing the full pathname to the program, like this:

```
# /usr/games/adventure
```

```
Welcome to Adventure!!  Would you like instructions?
yes

Somewhere nearby is Colossal Cave, where others have found fortunes in
treasure and gold, though it is rumored that some who enter are never
seen again.  Magic is said to work in the cave.  I will be your eyes
and hands.  Direct me with commands of 1 or 2 words.  I should warn
you that I look at only the first five letters of each word, so you'll
have to enter "northeast" as "ne" to distinguish it from "north".
(Should you get stuck, type "help" for some general hints.  For
information on how to end your adventure, etc., type "info".)
                                - - -
This program was originally developed by Will Crowther.  Most of the
features of the current program were added by Don Woods.  Address
complaints about the UNIX version to Jim Gillogly (jim@rand.org).

You are standing at the end of a road before a small brick building.
Around you is a forest.  A small stream flows out of the building and
down a gully.
```

Enter commands such as `inven`, `look`, `go west` (or n, w, s, e, up, or down). Type `quit` to exit the game.

Want the challenge of a good chess game? Try the `gnuchess` program, which plays an extremely strong game of chess. You can find several versions of this game installed on your system. The `gnuchess` version uses cursor addressing to provide a basic graphic display. The `gnuchessr` version scrolls each board after successive moves and uses reverse video and cursor addressing for a fancier display.

Moves are entered by specifying the column and row as a letter and number, as in the following example:

```
# gnuchess
Enter [moves] minutes[:sec] [increment][+]:
Computer                                    GNU Chess
```

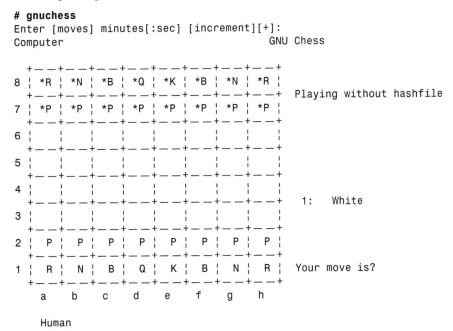

```
   +—─+—─+—─+—─+—─+—─+—─+—─+
 8 ¦ *R ¦ *N ¦ *B ¦ *Q ¦ *K ¦ *B ¦ *N ¦ *R ¦
   +—─+—─+—─+—─+—─+—─+—─+—─+    Playing without hashfile
 7 ¦ *P ¦ *P ¦ *P ¦ *P ¦ *P ¦ *P ¦ *P ¦ *P ¦
   +—─+—─+—─+—─+—─+—─+—─+—─+
 6 ¦    ¦    ¦    ¦    ¦    ¦    ¦    ¦    ¦
   +—─+—─+—─+—─+—─+—─+—─+—─+
 5 ¦    ¦    ¦    ¦    ¦    ¦    ¦    ¦    ¦
   +—─+—─+—─+—─+—─+—─+—─+—─+
 4 ¦    ¦    ¦    ¦    ¦    ¦    ¦    ¦    ¦
   +—─+—─+—─+—─+—─+—─+—─+—─+    1:   White
 3 ¦    ¦    ¦    ¦    ¦    ¦    ¦    ¦    ¦
   +—─+—─+—─+—─+—─+—─+—─+—─+
 2 ¦ P  ¦ P  ¦ P  ¦ P  ¦ P  ¦ P  ¦ P  ¦ P  ¦
   +—─+—─+—─+—─+—─+—─+—─+—─+
 1 ¦ R  ¦ N  ¦ B  ¦ Q  ¦ K  ¦ B  ¦ N  ¦ R  ¦    Your move is?
   +—─+—─+—─+—─+—─+—─+—─+—─+
     a    b    c    d    e    f    g    h

   Human
```

If you don't want to specify a timer, just press Enter after starting the game. To move the pawn up two squares from the lower rank, enter **e2e4**, and press the Enter key. The computer then makes its move, and new piece positions are updated on your display. The gnuchess program has more than 23 command-line options and features display play modes, hints, and timed games. For more information, see the gnuchess manual page.

Playing emacs Games

The venerable emacs editor (discussed in Hour 14, "Text Processing") not only edits text, reads mail, and handles your appointments, but also comes with 18 wacky games and modes that you can use to pass the time, such as doctor, dunnet, psychoanalyze-pinhead, and yow.

To play dunnet, a text adventure, use emacs from the command line:

```
# emacs -batch -l dunnet
Dead end
You are at a dead end of a dirt road.  The road goes to the east.
In the distance you can see that it will eventually fork off.  The
trees here are very tall royal palms, and they are spaced equidistant
from each other.
```

20

```
There is a shovel here.
>
```

This command line starts the game. At the > prompt, enter commands such as inventory, look, or go east. To end the adventure, enter the word quit.

Games for the X Window System

In this section you'll be introduced to several games for X11. There are more than two dozen you can play, but rather than discussing them all, the following pages highlight several of the best games for strategy and action.

If you like playing board games, you're in luck! There are several good board games for the X Window System on this book's CD-ROM. Want more action? Try some of the video arcade games—you're sure to find some you like. The following is a list of just a few of those that are included:

- abuse—futuristic combat game for X
- acm—aerial combat simulator for X
- koules—smash balls into the wall game for X
- paradise—a networked combat game
- scavenger—Lode-runner for X11
- xchomp—classic Pac-Man-like game
- xdemineuer—minesweep-type game
- xjewel, xtrojka, xbl—Tetris-like games
- xlander—a lunar lander game
- xpilot—networked combat game
- xpuzzles—a series of puzzle games for X11

Playing Chess with the xboard Client

Chess is a classic game, and one of the major challenges you can face is playing chess against your computer. To play chess in X11, use the xboard client. This program uses the GNU chess engine and can play chess over the Internet or through electronic mail.

The xboard client (shown in Figure 20.5) recognizes many X11 Toolkit options, such as geometry settings, and has 54 different command-line options. If you have a display smaller than 1024×768 pixels, use the -size or -boardSize small command-line option to fit the board on your screen, like this:

```
# xboard -size small &
```

FIGURE 20.5

The xboard X11 client plays chess on your display, over the Internet, or through email.

This command line starts xboard using smaller chess pieces. For more details about using xboard, see the xboard and gnuchess manual pages.

Playing X11 Solitaire

If you enjoy playing card solitaire games, you'll like the xpat2 X11 client. This program (shown in Figure 20.6) features 14 different solitaire games with scoring, hints, built-in help, and sound. Start the game from the command line of a terminal window, like this:

```
# xpat2 &
```

FIGURE 20.6

The xpat2 solitaire game for X11 features 14 different card games.

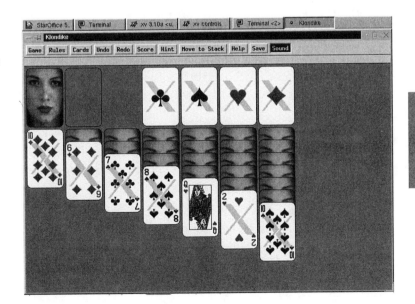

20

The xpat2 game, created by Heiko Eissfeldt and Michael Bischoff, is found under the /usr/X11R6/bin directory. For more details, read the xpat2 manual page.

Playing Backgammon for X11

For backgammon fanatics, the xgammon client (shown in Figure 20.7) produces hours of fun and practice. This game, by Lambert Klasen and Detlef Steuer, requires the X Window System and runs comfortably on an 800×600 pixel display.

Start xgammon from the command line of a terminal window, like this:

```
# xgammon&
```

FIGURE 20.7

The xgammon game for X11 features several types of play, such as computer against human, and provides a challenging game.

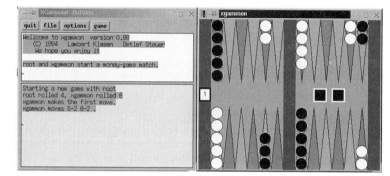

The xgammon client has 21 different command-line options. For an interesting variation, try watching your computer play itself:

```
# xgammon -g cvc &
```

This starts the xgammon game so you can watch the action. You also can create your own challenging games by editing the board and placing backgammon stones in different positions before play. For details about xgammon, read its manual page.

Playing Galaga for X11

Video action arcade games can be a lot of fun, especially if they have great graphics and sound. If you like shoot-em-ups, you'll love the xgal game by Joe Rumsey. This X11 client features a simple keyboard interface.

The xgal game (shown in Figure 20.8) has six different command-line options, but you can start the program without any at a terminal window by typing the following:

```
# xgal &
```

FIGURE 20.8

The xgal *game for X11 features spiffy arcade action and good sound.*

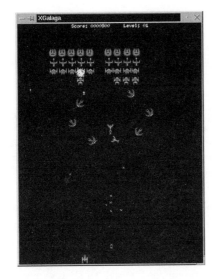

To start playing, press your spacebar. Use the right and left cursor keys to move your ship across the screen, and use your Spacebar to fire.

Breakout the Fun with the X11 Client xboing

xboing, by Justin C. Kibell, is a fast-paced, arcade-quality paddle and ball game for the X Window System. This game sports great graphics and sound and provides hours of fun. You can start the xboing program from the command line of a terminal window. You need a display of at least 1024×768 pixels to play.

By default, xboing does not use sound, so if you want to hear sounds when you play, you must use the -sound command-line option. Set the speed of the ball's action after playing a game to fine-tune the challenge by using the -speed option:

```
# xboing -sound -speed 7
```

This command line starts xboing with sound enabled and a very fast ball speed. Another good option to use is -grab, which keeps your cursor within the xboing X11 window, preventing you from accidentally activating other windows and missing any action. For more details about playing this game, see the xboing manual page.

Playing Quake for X Windows

Quake, by id Software, is a follow-up game to Doom, one of the most popular arcade games to hit the personal computer scene in recent years. You can't find a copy on this book's CD-ROM, but you can download Quake in a version for Linux and X11.

20

You need to download the `quake106.zip` shareware resource file (unless you own a copy of Quake) from `ftp://www.cdrom.com/pub/idgames/idstuff/quake/`, and the `quake.x11-1.0-i386-unknown-linux2.0.tar.gz` file from `http://www.mikrus.pw.edu.pl/lds/quake/files.html`.

Follow the installation instructions to install this version of Quake for OpenLinux. Quake II fans and Linux users interested in setting up a Quake server for Internet or network games can check out the `xqf` Quake server browser and launcher. Browse to `http://www.linuxgames.com/xqf/`.

Navigate to the directory where you installed quake, and start `Quake` from the command line, like this:

```
# quake.x11
```

The game starts playing in demo mode (Figure 20.9 shows some of the action). The window can be resized with your mouse or dragged around the desktop.

FIGURE 20.9

Don't lose your head while playing Quake *for Linux!*

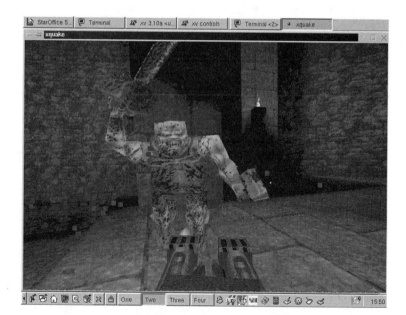

If you have the shareware or commercial Quake CD inserted in your computer, you get the Quake soundtrack. If you have any music CD inserted, different tracks play as you play the game.

Summary

This hour introduced you to just a fraction of the games available for OpenLinux and the X Window System. You're sure to find some favorites installed on your system.

Q&A

Q How can I find out how many games are installed with OpenLinux?

A Try using the `apropos` command, like this:

```
man apropos
```

Q I want to record sound from my audio CD to a disk file? How can I do this?

A Try the `cdda2wav` command.

Q I want to convert sounds from another operating system and use them with OpenLinux. What conversion tools are included?

A Try the `sox` command.

Q I want to play `.mp3` files. What program should I use?

A Try the `mpg123` command.

Q I like simulation games. Is one included with OpenLinux?

A Yes. A very good city-building simulator is `xlincity`. You can also find the X11 client `Freeciv`, a free Civilization clone (which uses the `civserver`, `civclient`, and `civ` commands for play).

Q I know there are more games than that installed. Is there a better way?

A Try using the `kpackage` client included with KDE, and then look under the `Recreation` folder.

Q Speaking of KDE—how many games are included with KDE?

A You can find nearly a dozen at the time of this writing. Of course, you can always check `http://www.kde.org` to find the latest selection.

20

Exercises

1. Download and install the Quake for X11 programs for OpenLinux. Are there any other Web sites supporting Quake and Linux? How do you find out?

2. Use the `xmixer` command to experiment with the sound input and output controls of your computer's sound system. Try recording some sounds with the sound recording script in Hour 3.

3. From the command line of a terminal window, start the `xteddy` client. What happens?

Part V

Administering Your System

Hour

21 Basic System Administration

22 Handling Files and Your File System

23 Backing Up and Restoring Your System

24 Using Scheduling to Automate System Management

HOUR 21

Basic System Administration

This hour introduces you to the basics of system administration. You'll learn how to use the su command, how to get information about your system, how to manage other users, and how to use file tools to keep your OpenLinux system running in top form. Although much of what's discussed in this hour consists of common-sense guidelines, you'll also get some valuable tips on squeezing the best performance out of Linux. You'll use this knowledge in the next three hours, which cover handling files, archiving, and scheduling.

Even if you're the only person who uses your computer, you should still learn basic system administration skills, for at least some of the following reasons:

- To back up or restore your system, or at the least, important files
- To conserve disk space
- To install new software or upgrade your Linux system
- To teach someone else about OpenLinux, such as a coworker, friend, spouse, or child
- To troubleshoot problems

Although some of the tasks described in this chapter require root permission (you must run a command as the root operator), you should not always log in and use OpenLinux as the root operator. Here's a good reason: Always running as root can be dangerous because you have access to all files on the system and can delete, move, or copy any file at will. You can wipe out your OpenLinux system (remember the warning in Hour 5, "Manipulation and Searching Commands," about the rm command) and any other mounted filesystem with this command:

```
# rm -fr /*
```

If you run Linux from your own account, this problem won't happen because rm will complain with "Permission denied" and quit. What if you're logged in under your account but need to do things to your system as the root operator? This is where the su command comes into play.

Running as the root Operator with the su Command

The su command, or substitute user command, allows you to run a command as any user on your system. Found in the /bin directory, su has seven different command-line options. Several of the most common are covered here. Although you'll most likely use su to become root, this command can be handy if you want to become another user and troubleshoot problems with email or printing. Using the su command is easy; for example, to become the root operator, use su like so:

```
# su -
Password:
su: incorrect password
```

By default, the su command will allow you to become the root operator if you call it without a username. (Use the hyphen command-line option to make sure you run as the root operator with root's environment variables.) You'll be asked to enter a password, and su will complain and quit if you enter the wrong one. If you enter the right password, you'll be logged in as root. To return to your shell, use your shell's exit command:

```
$ su -
Password:
# whoami
root
# exit
exit
$ whoami
bball
```

This example, using the whoami command, shows that after you execute the exit command, you're returned to your normal user status. Another handy feature of the su command is the -s command-line option to run a different shell. If you want to try a different shell without using the chsh command to permanently change your shell, you can use the following:

```
$ printenv ¦ fgrep SHELL
SHELL=/bin/bash
$ su -s /bin/ksh
Password:
# printenv ¦ fgrep SHELL
SHELL=/bin/ksh
# exit
$
```

This example (showing the output of the printenv command piped through the fgrep command) shows that although the default shell is bash, the su command allows you to temporarily use the pdksh, or public domain Korn shell. Unless you specify your own username, you'll run the new shell as the root operator. A better approach is

```
$ su -s /bin/ksh yourusername
```

Finally, you can also use the su command to execute a single command when you use the -c command-line option. This can be handy to perform tasks only permitted for the root operator, such as mounting a flash memory card:

```
# su -c "mount -t vfat /dev/hde1 /mnt/flash"
Password:
```

This command line mounts the /dev/hde1 device, a SunDisk flash card with a VFAT (long-filename) filesystem, at the /mnt/flash directory mount point. If you need to temporarily mount or unmount diskettes, CD-ROMs, Zip disks, or other devices, you'll find this a convenient approach. Hour 22, "Handling Files and Your File System," covers mounting and unmounting other filesystems.

If you're using Linux in the console mode (not running X11), you can use the console keys (Alt+F1 and so on) to run a virtual console as the root operator to do root operator tasks. This is a bad convenience, however, because you might be tempted to run as root all the time. At least using the su command makes you think about why you're running as root. Be careful!

The next section introduces you to tools you can use to determine how your system is working.

21

Getting Disk Space Information

When you installed Linux, you installed your system onto a partition, designated by a specific device, such as /dev/hda1, /dev/sdb1, and so on. I hope you made the partition large enough to accommodate your present and future needs. How do you check to see how much room you have left on disk or for that matter, how many disks you have? Although Linux can support partition sizes up to 4 terabytes and maximum file sizes up to 2 gigabytes, not many of us are wealthy enough to own, or even need, that much storage. Even though disk storage is getting cheaper, it is still at a premium when you have a lot of software installed or need the work space.

Getting Filesystem Statistics with the df Command

The df (free disk space) command, found in the /bin directory, will gather and summarize some important statistics about all currently mounted filesystems. The df command is easy to use:

```
# df
Filesystem        1024-blocks   Used Available Capacity Mounted on
/dev/hda3             497699   443871     28124    94%   /
/dev/hda1             509856   469632     40224    92%   /mnt/dos
/dev/hdc1               3868     2596      1272    67%   /mnt/flash
/dev/hdb              644324   644324         0   100%   /mnt/cdrom
```

This output shows four different filesystems on three different devices mounted under Linux. The first is the root partition at the / directory on /dev/hda3; the second is a DOS partition under /mnt/dos on /dev/hda1; the third is a flashcard under /mnt/flash on /dev/hdc1; and the fourth is a CD-ROM, mounted under /mnt/cdrom on /dev/hdb. The df command also lists the size of the storage device, how much has been used, how much is available, and the current capacity of the device. Notice that the CD-ROM has no space left. This is because it is mounted read-only, meaning you can't save or delete files on this device. The command shown in the next example will let you know.

One handy way to find out about the different filesystems you have mounted is to use the mount command. This command is usually used during startup by the root operator to mount and unmount filesystems, but any user can use mount to show what type of filesystems are in use and how the filesystems are mounted:

```
# mount
/dev/hda3 on / type ext2 (rw)
/dev/hda1 on /mnt/dos type msdos (rw)
none on /proc type proc (rw)
/dev/hdc1 on /mnt/flash type msdos (rw)
/dev/hdb on /mnt/cdrom type iso9660 (ro)
```

This shows that your root partition, on the / directory, is a Linux ext2 filesystem mounted read-write, whereas /mnt/dos and /mnt/flash contain DOS partitions, also read-write. (The /proc filesystem is a special directory Linux uses for process reporting, such as running applications, system state, and so on.) Finally, mount reports that your CD-ROM is mounted as a read-only iso9660 filesystem.

You can use this information from mount to get specific information with the df command, by using the df command's -t, or filesystem, option:

```
# df -t ext2
Filesystem          1024-blocks  Used Available Capacity Mounted on
/dev/hda3              497699   443873    28122     94%   /
```

This tells df to only show information about any mounted ext2 filesystems. You can get a list of valid filesystems to specify with the df command by looking at the mount manual page. The mount command is covered in more detail in Hour 22, "Handling Files and Your File System." You can see that by using the df and mount command, you can get reports on the type of mounted devices, how the devices are mounted, and how much room you have left on each.

Getting Filesystem Disk Usage with the du Command

The du (disk usage) command, found in the /usr/bin directory, conveniently summarizes how your disk is being used by reporting the amount of space required by each directory or specified path. Although the du command has more than 20 command-line options, this section presents some of the common ones and leaves it up to you to experiment. You can use the du command by itself, or specify a directory or path:

```
# du
904       ./book
12080     ./mail
1         ./.tin/.mailidx
1         ./.tin/.index
10        ./.tin
...
589       ./News
9         ./.index
7         ./.procmail
5         ./.ncftp
418       ./reading
778       ./documents
27199     .
```

21

This report (for brevity, not all the directories are listed) shows the contents of a home directory, with a total for 27199 1KB blocks. If you find this hard to understand, you can have du report the size in bytes:

```
# du -b
897606   ./book
12294410        ./mail
1024     ././tin/.mailidx
1024     ././tin/.index
9382     ././tin
561715   ./News
4033     ././index
4139     ././procmail
2791     ././ncftp
424037   ./reading
784216   ./documents
26785752        .
```

If this is too much information for you, then you can use the --summarize option to get the total in either kilobytes (with the --kilobytes or -k option) or bytes (with the -b or --bytes option):

```
# du -b --summarize
26786903        .
```

The du command can also help you keep track of directories which, unattended, sometimes grow out of control or use a lot of disk space. If you specify a path, du will report on the different size of the directories underneath that path, which might help you pinpoint those containing too much information:

```
# du --summarize -b /var/* ¦ sort -nr
6474535 /var/lib
2336494 /var/log
868163 /var/catman
76362 /var/spool
14591 /var/dt
2385 /var/run
2048 /var/lock
2048 /var/local
1024 /var/tmp
1024 /var/preserve
1024 /var/nis
```

Here, I've combined the du command, which has been instructed to summarize the number of bytes in each directory, with the sort command, which has been set to use a numerical sort in reverse order. This one-liner, which uses pipes (discussed in Hour 6, "Using the Shell"), will automatically print the largest directories at the top of the output list. You can see that the /var/log directory is getting pretty big. The /var/lib directory will be large because it contains the rpm databases. (rpm is discussed in Hour 22.)

Although the du command does not, like the df command, have a -t option to specify which filesystem to report on, you can use the -x option to exclude other filesystems. This is handy to avoid including other mounted filesystems such as DOS or Windows. You can have du report on other filesystems by specifying a usage report at the mount point. For example, du will merrily chug along and summarize how much room your Windows directories take up:

```
# du -b --summarize /mnt/dos/* ¦ sort -nr
129486405        /mnt/dos/windows
23929345         /mnt/dos/msoffice
20811654         /mnt/dos/photoenf
7744046 /mnt/dos/tranxit
6828902 /mnt/dos/org2
6647520 /mnt/dos/laplink
5556496 /mnt/dos/acrobat3
4041127 /mnt/dos/pcdr
3753962 /mnt/dos/psp
3603469 /mnt/dos/insync
3176769 /mnt/dos/antvirus
2669335 /mnt/dos/airlite
2408920 /mnt/dos/winfax
...
```

This (shortened) report shows that next to the Windows operating system, the largest space is consumed by certain Windows applications. This information can be helpful in making a decision on what applications to uninstall if you need more disk space.

Checking Symbolic Links with the symlinks Command

The symlinks command checks symbolic links in designated directories. The symlinks command has several command-line options you might find useful, including the -r or recursive option you can use to check whole directories. For example, to check your entire file system, use the -r option:

```
# symlinks -r /
dangling: /etc/rc.d/rc0.d/K30diald -> ../init.d/diald
dangling: /etc/rc.d/rc1.d/K30diald -> ../init.d/diald
dangling: /etc/rc.d/rc2.d/K30diald -> ../init.d/diald
dangling: /etc/rc.d/rc3.d/S70diald -> ../init.d/diald
dangling: /etc/rc.d/rc4.d/S70diald -> ../init.d/diald
dangling: /etc/rc.d/rc5.d/S70diald -> ../init.d/diald
dangling: /etc/rc.d/rc6.d/K30diald -> ../init.d/diald
absolute: /etc/mta/sendmail -> /usr/libexec/sendmail/sendmail
absolute: /etc/mta/rmail -> /usr/libexec/sendmail/rmail
dangling: /boot/System.map-2.0.35 -> /usr/src/linux-2.0.35/System.map
absolute: /usr/doc/html/lg -> /usr/doc/lg-doc-1.0
absolute: /usr/doc/bool-1.1/COPYING -> /usr/doc/Copyrights/GPL
...
```

21

You can see that this `symlinks` command output shows at least two types of diagnostics for dangling and absolute symbolic links. (There are six: absolute, dangling, lengthy, messy, other_fs, and relative.) Dangling links, or links that point to a non-existent file, might be a cause of concern because OpenLinux cannot determine whether the designated file exists.

 See the `symlinks` man page for definitions of the absolute, lengthy, messy, relative, and other_fs link diagnostics.

As a beginning sysadmin, you can use `symlinks` to look at file directories recursively and then print reports about the status of your file system. Here's one handy command line you can use to check all the symbolic links in your Linux filesystem (excluding others, such as Windows):

```
# symlinks -vr / ¦ fgrep "dangling" >symlinkstatusreport.txt
```

This command line uses the `symlinks` command to recursively descend through your OpenLinux file system and report on dangling links. The `fgrep` command then prints all matches when `symlinks` finds a dangling symbolic link and creates your report. As you become a more proficient sysadmin, you'll devise your own bag of tricks to help diagnose your system.

Saving Disk Space

This section gives you some tips on saving disk space. Part of being a sysadmin is maintaining the health of your filesystem and performing cleanup operations occasionally to free disk space. Once you've found some techniques or approaches that work for your system and the way you work on your system, you'll find that you can routinely trim and recover many megabytes of disk space.

One good way to save disk space is not to install a lot of software. For example, how many different word processors do you really need? How many graphics programs do you need? If you find a capable program, delete others that do the same thing. Make sure to read Hour 22 to see how the `rpm` command can help you free disk space and customize your Linux installation by deleting packages of programs and supporting software.

You can often trim the size of your directories by looking for less frequently used programs or collections of graphics or text you don't need. You've already seen one way to find directories that may be candidates for cleanup. You should also consider some other file types that can be deleted.

For example, some Linux programs create backup files with the tilde (~) prefix. You can search for these as follows:

```
# find / -name ~* -xdev
```

Once you feel comfortable with the results, you can pipe the filenames into the rm command, using the xargs command to build a cleanup command line (although you can also use the find command's -exec command-line option):

```
# find / -name ~* -xdev ¦ xargs rm -f
```

You should also search for files named core. These are *core dumps*, or dumps of program memory created if a program abnormally aborts. Some of these files can be huge! You can use the bash or pdksh shells' ulimit command to limit the size of these core files. To see the current allowable size of core files, use the ulimit command's -c option:

```
# ulimit -c
1000000
```

> Fortunately, the default bash shell ulimit setting for the size of core dumps under OpenLinux is 0. If you're a Linux programmer and need core files (for debugging), change this setting.

This doesn't mean that core dumps are limited to 1MB, but 1,000,000 512-byte blocks. You can limit the size of core files with the -c option, as in

```
# ulimit -c 1000
```

This sets the maximum size of core files to 512,000 bytes. If you're using the csh shell, use

```
# limit coredumpsize 1000
```

Limiting the size of these files is one way to save disk space in the future. Other candidates for removal include

*.bak, *.BAK—Backup files

*.o—Object files created during compiling operations

#*—Backup files

*.1, *.2, *.3—File extensions for system log files under the /var/log directory. Some logs can grow quite large, and unless you really need them, they should be deleted.

21

> Be careful about deleting files with file-number extensions, such as .1, across your system: You will delete a lot of libraries and manual pages if you automate a search-and-destroy mission starting at the root, or /, directory.

If you feel uncomfortable with letting the find command run through your file system and deleting files, have the command generate a report of candidate files as follows:

```
# find / \( -name core -o -name *.o \) -xdev > deletelist.txt
```

Note that you can also set this command to run unattended, at regular intervals, and have the report emailed to you as an automatic reminder. See Hour 24, "Using Scheduling to Automate System Management," for details.

If you experiment with your own combination of commands, you'll soon design your own customized reports and cleanup actions. You now know how to get information about your drive space. You'll also learn about managing disk space, using quotas (software limits on hard drive usage) in the section "Managing User Access" later in this chapter. For now, you'll learn how to find out more about what's going on in your computer's memory when you run Linux.

> Compressing unused files or directories or archiving and then deleting these directories is another way to conserve disk space. See Hour 5, "Manipulation and Searching Commands" for information about using compression utilities. Also, see Hour 23, "Backing Up and Restoring Your System" for details about backing up or restoring OpenLinux files and directories.

Getting Memory Information

NEW TERM Although the industry trend has been to offer more hard drive space and more system memory, or RAM, for less money, many people don't like to outlay more cash to expand their systems. The good news is that Linux is efficient at using memory because even a 16MB system provides enough room (with an equal amount of swap space) to run X11 and most programs well. The bad news is that programs are getting larger all the time, especially with *feature creep*, in which more and more functions creep into programs. (This is true of the Linux kernel, which has tripled in size over the past few years.) This section introduces you to some programs you might find helpful in understanding your system's memory and gives you some tips on conserving memory.

Memory Reporting with the `free` Command

The `free` command shows breakdowns of the amounts and totals of free and used memory, including your swapfile usage. This command, in the /usr/bin directory, has several command-line options, but is easy to run and understand:

```
# free
            total       used       free     shared    buffers     cached
Mem:        63136      60064       3072      53664      11080      26992
-/+ buffers/cache:     21992      41144
Swap:      130748       2616     128132
```

This shows a system with 64MB RAM and 131MB of swap space. Notice that nearly all the system memory is being used (normal) and almost 3MB of swap space (great!) has been used.

By default, the `free` command displays memory in kilobytes, or 1024-byte notation. You can use the `-b` option to display your memory in bytes or the `-m` option to display memory in megabytes. You can also use the `free` command to constantly monitor how much memory is being used through the `-s` command. This is handy as a real-time monitor if you specify a .01-second update and run the `free` command in a terminal window under X11. For example, to monitor your disk space in an X11 terminal window, use the free command like so:

```
# /usr/bin/free -b -s1
```

This will print a scrolling report, updated each second, in your terminal window.

Virtual Memory Reporting with the `vmstat` Command

The `vmstat` command, found under the /usr/bin directory, is a general-purpose monitoring program, which offers real-time display of not only memory usage and virtual memory statistics, but also disk activity, system usage, and central processing unit (CPU) activity. If you call `vmstat` without any command-line options, you'll get a one-time snapshot:

```
# vmstat
procs                    memory     swap        io    system        cpu
r b w  swpd  free  buff cache  si  so   bi  bo   in  cs  us sy  id
0 0 0  7468  1060  4288 10552   1   1   10   1  134  68   3  2  96
```

The major types of activity reported by `vmstat` are processes (`procs`), memory (in kilobytes), swap space (in kilobytes), input/output from block devices (hard drives), system interrupts (number per second), and percentages of central processing unit (CPU) time spent on users, the system, and idling.

21

If you specify a time interval in seconds on the vmstat command line, you'll get a continuously scrolling report. Having a constant display of what is happening with your computer can help you if you're trying to find out why your computer suddenly slows down or why there's a lot of disk activity.

Viewing Your Shell's "Ulimit"ations

You've already seen how you can limit the size of core dump files in this hour. There are other settings you can set in your shell. If you're using the bash or pdksh (ksh) shell, you can use the ulimit command's -a option to print your current settings:

```
# ulimit -a
core file size (blocks)    0
data seg size (kbytes)     unlimited
file size (blocks)         unlimited
max memory size (kbytes)   unlimited
stack size (kbytes)        8192
cpu time (seconds)         unlimited
max user processes         256
pipe size (512 bytes)      8
open files                 256
virtual memory (kbytes)    2105343
```

If you're using the tcsh or csh shell, you can use the limit command to list the current settings:

```
$ limit
cputime         unlimited
filesize        unlimited
datasize        unlimited
stacksize       8192 kbytes
coredumpsize    0 kbytes
memoryuse       unlimited
descriptors     256
memorylocked    unlimited
maxproc         256
```

NEW TERM These limits are different from limits for the root operator. The limits shown in this example are known as *soft limits* (limits that may be changed by any user). To view the shell's *hard limits* (limits that may only be raised by root), log in as the root operator, and use the -a limit option (use -Ha for bash or ksh's ulimit command):

```
$ su
Password:
# limit -h
cputime         unlimited
filesize        unlimited
datasize        unlimited
stacksize       8192 kbytes
```

```
coredumpsize    unlimited
memoryuse       unlimited
descriptors     256
memorylocked    unlimited
maxproc         256
```

As you can see, viewing the limits as the root operator in the tcsh shell shows a much different situation. This is another good reason not to run as the root operator. As a sysadmin, you can use these settings to limit the amount of memory or number of processes available to each user. This is extremely handy if you have a number of people working on your computer at the same time and you want to conserve system memory. For using Linux on a standalone computer under your normal login and working conditions, you'll find the default limits quite reasonable.

Reclaiming Memory with the kill Command

As a desperate measure if you need to quickly reclaim memory, you can stop running programs using the kill command. To kill a specific program, you should use the ps command to list current running processes and then stop any or all of them with the kill command. By default, the ps command lists processes that you own and you can kill:

```
# ps
 PID TTY STAT   TIME COMMAND
 367 p0  S     0:00 bash
 581 p0  S     0:01 rxvt
 582 p1  S     0:00 (bash)
 747 p0  S     0:00 (applix)
 809 p0  S     0:18 netscape index.html
 810 p0  S     0:00 (dns helper)
 945 p0  R     0:00 ps
```

The ps command will list the currently running programs and the program's process number, or PID. You can use this information to kill a process with the -9, or SIGKILL signal:

```
# kill -9 809
```

However, if you need to reclaim memory efficiently, you should use the ps command's m option, which also lists the memory usage of each process:

```
# ps m
 PID TTY MAJFLT MINFLT   TRS   DRS  SIZE  SWAP   RSS  SHRD   LIB  DT
➡COMMAND
 747 p0      0      3    16   208   364   140   224   224     0   0
➡(applix)
 582 p1    151    274   124   184   436   128   308   268     0  10
➡(bash)
 959 p0     89     20    28   376   404     0   404   320     0  21 ps m
```

21

```
  367  p0    305    826   220   316    600     64   536   428    0   27 bash
  810  p0    313     38   164   696    968    108   860   596    0   47 (dns
➥helpe
  581  p0    212    508    28   960   1280    292   988   304    0  171 rxvt
  809  p0   2615   1205  3900  3692   8684   1092  7592  4644    0  699
➥netscape
```

Using this information, you can see that if you want to reclaim the most memory, you should stop the Netscape Web browser because it is using nearly 9MB of system memory. Although you wouldn't normally use the kill command to stop programs, the kill command can be helpful to stop runaway or unresponsive programs. The kill command works by sending a signal to the Linux kernel, along with the PID, so the kernel can act on the process. There are various signals you can use, although the -9, or SIGKILL option, is the most abrupt and drastic. You can see a list of different signals by using the kill command's -1 option:

```
# kill -1
 1) SIGHUP        2) SIGINT        3) SIGQUIT       4) SIGILL
 5) SIGTRAP       6) SIGIOT        7) SIGBUS        8) SIGFPE
 9) SIGKILL      10) SIGUSR1      11) SIGSEGV      12) SIGUSR2
13) SIGPIPE      14) SIGALRM      15) SIGTERM      17) SIGCHLD
18) SIGCONT      19) SIGSTOP      20) SIGTSTP      21) SIGTTIN
22) SIGTTOU      23) SIGURG       24) SIGXCPU      25) SIGXFSZ
26) SIGVTALRM    27) SIGPROF      28) SIGWINCH     29) SIGIO
30) SIGPWR
```

For more details on these signals and the kill command, see its manual page.

The ps command has nearly two dozen command-line options, and you can also list all running processes. See the ps manual page for more information. You can also use the top command, discussed next, to find and kill processes.

Getting System Load Information with the top and xload Commands

The top command, in the /usr/bin directory, is a system monitor that displays statistical information about how Linux is currently handling your memory, swap file, and processes. The top program also shows how long your system has been running, the status of your CPU, the size of each process, and more. You'll typically use the top command by running it on a spare console or separate X11 terminal window (see Figure 21.1).

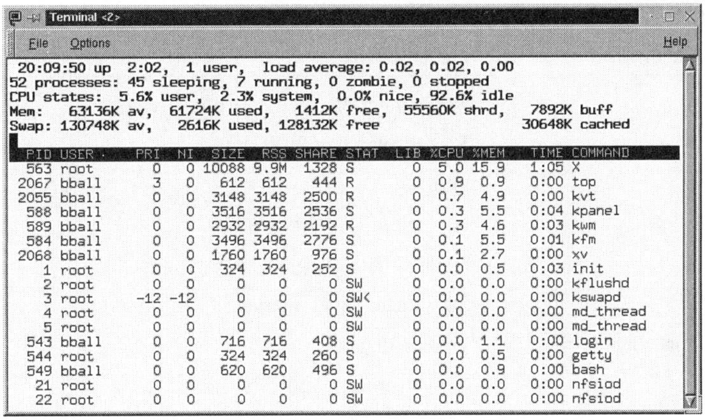

FIGURE 21.1

*The top command
provides an ongoing
display of your system.*

```
  Terminal <2>                                                        □ ×
 File  Options                                                        Help
 20:09:50 up  2:02,  1 user,  load average: 0.02, 0.02, 0.00
52 processes: 45 sleeping, 7 running, 0 zombie, 0 stopped
CPU states:  5.6% user,  2.3% system,  0.0% nice, 92.6% idle
Mem:   63136K av,  61724K used,   1412K free,  55560K shrd,   7892K buff
Swap: 130748K av,   2616K used, 128132K free                  30648K cached

  PID USER     PRI  NI  SIZE  RSS SHARE STAT LIB %CPU %MEM   TIME COMMAND
  563 root       0   0 10088 9.9M  1328 S      0  5.0 15.9  1:05 X
 2067 bball      3   0   612  612   444 R      0  0.9  0.9  0:00 top
 2055 bball      0   0  3148 3148  2500 R      0  0.7  4.9  0:00 kvt
  588 bball      0   0  3516 3516  2536 S      0  0.3  5.5  0:04 kpanel
  589 bball      0   0  2932 2932  2192 R      0  0.3  4.6  0:03 kwm
  584 bball      0   0  3496 3496  2776 S      0  0.1  5.5  0:01 kfm
 2068 bball      0   0  1760 1760   976 S      0  0.1  2.7  0:00 xv
    1 root       0   0   324  324   252 S      0  0.0  0.5  0:03 init
    2 root       0   0     0    0     0 SW     0  0.0  0.0  0:00 kflushd
    3 root     -12 -12     0    0     0 SW<    0  0.0  0.0  0:00 kswapd
    4 root       0   0     0    0     0 SW     0  0.0  0.0  0:00 md_thread
    5 root       0   0     0    0     0 SW     0  0.0  0.0  0:00 md_thread
  543 bball      0   0   716  716   408 S      0  0.0  1.1  0:00 login
  544 root       0   0   324  324   260 S      0  0.0  0.5  0:00 getty
  549 bball      0   0   620  620   496 S      0  0.0  0.9  0:00 bash
   21 root       0   0     0    0     0 SW     0  0.0  0.0  0:00 nfsiod
   22 root       0   0     0    0     0 SW     0  0.0  0.0  0:00 nfsiod
```

The top command also has a number of interactive controls, including a help screen, accessed with the question mark or the H key. You can also toggle various modes of the display, such as listing processes by memory usage or limiting the number of processes displayed. This can be helpful if you want to monitor only the top five processes that require the greatest amount of your system's memory, and it can help you diagnose problems if your computer starts unusual disk or swap file activity.

You can also use top to interactively kill processes, using the K key, or change a process's priority (how much time the CPU devotes to a task) with the R key. The top program has 19 different interactive commands, and you can customize its display by adding or removing different information fields and lengthening or shortening the number of processes. See Table 21.1 for more information.

TABLE 21.1 SINGLE-KEY INTERACTIVE COMMANDS FOR top

Command	Description
c	Display command name or full command line.
Ctrl+L	Redraw the display.
f	Add or remove display fields.
H	Sort display by memory usage.
h, ?	Show help.
i	Toggle display of idle or zombie processes.
k	Kill a process by its process number (PID).
l	Toggle load average and uptime display.
m	Toggle memory information display.

21

continues

TABLE 21.1 SINGLE-KEY INTERACTIVE COMMANDS FOR `top`

Command	Description
n, *x*	Set number of processes (n is interactive).
P	Sort display by CPU usage.
q	Quit.
r	Change priority of a process.
S	Change CPU usage display.
s	Set update delay interval.
Spacebar	Update display.
t	Toggle process and CPU state display.
W	Save current settings to `$HOME/.toprc`.

The `xload` client, used under X11, provides a running graph of your system's load, instead of the `top` command's statistics. System loads vary from computer to computer, but you can generally tell when your system is overloaded by inordinate disk activity because processes are swapped back and forth from your swap file. The `xload` command can give you a visual warning if you're running too many programs and might be especially helpful if you're running X11 on a 8MB or 16MB Linux system.

The `xload` command has eight different command-line options, and you can customize the color of the moving graphic, scale lines, or background.

> OpenLinux comes with a number of other helpful utilities you can use to graphically monitor your system. Try the `tload` command if you're using the console. If you use X11, try the `xosview` client, which can also display the status of your computer's network and serial ports.

Determining How Long Linux Has Been Running with the `uptime` and `w` Commands

The `uptime` command, in the `/usr/bin` directory, shows you how long Linux has been running, how many users are on, and three system load averages:

```
# uptime
  12:44am  up  8:16,  3 users,  load average: 0.11, 0.10, 0.04
```

If this is too little information for you, try the w command, which first shows the same information as the uptime command and then lists what currently logged-in users are doing:

```
# w
 12:48am  up  8:20,  3 users,  load average: 0.14, 0.09, 0.05
USER     TTY      FROM           LOGIN@   IDLE   JCPU   PCPU  WHAT
bball    ttyp0    localhost.locald 9:47pm 15.00s 0.38s  0.16s bash
bball    ttyp2    localhost.locald 12:48am 0.00s 0.16s  0.08s w
```

The w command gives a little more information, and it is especially helpful if you want to monitor a busy system with a number of users.

Getting Network and Mail Information with the pppstats and mailstats Commands

The pppstats command, in the /usr/sbin directory, will give you a running statistical display on the status and activity of your PPP connection. The information is similar to the output of the ifconfig command (discussed in Hour 10, "Connecting to the Internet"). To use the pppstats program, specify the PPP interface (usually 0) on the command after you have connected to your ISP:

```
# /usr/sbin/pppstats 0
    in  pack  comp uncomp   err |   out  pack  comp uncomp    ip
 24791    93    74      5     0 |  1922    72    54      4    14
    78     4     3      0     0 |    80     4     3      0     1
   129     2     0      0     0 |   160     3     0      1     2
  1169    23    21      1     0 |   842    23    20      2     1
 12748    28    27      1     0 |   730    27    18      9     0
  9582    18    13      5     0 |   375    13     6      7     0
  9399    18    16      2     0 |   268    12     8      4     0
    71     3     2      0     0 |    80     4     3      0     1
...
```

This shows the pppstats command in action after displaying a line of statistics every five seconds during startup of a newsreading session.

The mailstats program, part of the sendmail distribution, is in the /usr/sbin directory. You can use this program to generate reports about your system's mail usage. This command works by reading a file called sendmail.st under the /var/log directory. To create and use this file, you must use the -O StatusFile=/var/log/sendmail.st option with the sendmail daemon or set the appropriate option in the /etc/sendmail.cf file. As a test, you can try this command on an empty sendmail log file in the /var/state directory:

21

```
# mailstats -f /var/state/sendmail.st
Statistics from Wed Dec 23 20:48:29 1998
 M msgsfr bytes_from  msgsto   bytes_to  Mailer
========================================
 T    0        0K      0         0K
```

Monitoring Your Serial Ports with the `statserial` Command

The `statserial` program, originally by Jeff Tranter, can be used to show the status of your serial ports and can be a lifesaver if you need to troubleshoot modems or serial ports. To use `statserial` (in the `/usr/bin` directory), you must specify the device on the program's command line. You can, for example, tell `statserial` to monitor your modem by specifying its symbolic link:

```
# ln -s /dev/ttyS1 /dev/modem
# statserial /dev/modem
Device: /dev/modem
```

```
Signal  Pin  Pin  Direction   Status  Full
Name    (25) (9)  (computer)          Name
-----   ---  ---  ---------   ------  -----
FG       1    -    -            -      Frame Ground
TxD      2    3    out          -      Transmit Data
RxD      3    2    in           -      Receive  Data
RTS      4    7    out          1      Request To Send
CTS      5    8    in           1      Clear To Send
DSR      6    6    in           0      Data Set Ready
GND      7    5    -            -      Signal Ground
DCD      8    1    in           0      Data Carrier Detect
DTR     20    4    out          1      Data Terminal Ready
RI      22    9    in           0      Ring Indicator
```

You must be the root operator to use the `statserial` program. Try using statserial like so:

`su -c "statserial /dev/modem"`

Managing User Access

One of your main jobs as a sysadmin is to manage the users on your system. This involves creating accounts for new users, assigning home directories, specifying an initial shell for the user, and possibly restricting how much disk space, memory, or how many processes each person can use. This section shows you how to use different command-line programs to manage users (such as `lisa`), although you can do these and other tasks with graphical utilities while running the X Window System.

Creating Users with the `adduser` Command

One of the first things you should do after installing OpenLinux is to create user accounts for other family members. (You created a user account for yourself during your OpenLinux installation.) You should do all your work in OpenLinux through your user account and do your system management using the `su` command. There are several ways to create new users in Linux, but this section shows you the easy way, using a trio of commands: `adduser`, `passwd`, and `chfn`.

The first step in creating a new user is to use the `adduser` command, in the `/usr/sbin` directory. You must be the root operator to run this program. If you try to run `adduser` as a regular user, the command will report an error:

```
# adduser
Only root may add users to the system.
```

The `adduser` program also requires you to specify a username on the command line:

```
# adduser cloobie

Looking for first available UID... 502
Looking for first available GID... 502

Adding login: cloobie...done.
Creating home directory: /home/cloobie...done.
Creating mailbox: /var/spool/mail/cloobie...done.

Don't forget to set the password.
```

The command will create an account, assign a user identification (UID) and a group identification (GID), and then create a directory called `cloobie` under the `/home` directory. As a reminder, the `adduser` program tells you to set a password for your new user.

Managing Users with the `lisa` Command

The `lisa` command is an essential system administration tool for OpenLinux. You can use `lisa` to create and manage users through its graphical interface. In fact, you can jump right into `lisa`'s user screen with the `-useradm` command-line option:

```
# lisa --useradm
```

After you press Enter, the `lisa` command will display as shown in Figure 21.2.

21

FIGURE 21.2

The lisa *command provides an easy-to-use interface to OpenLinux user administration.*

Scroll through the lisa menu with the Up and Down cursor keys and then press Enter to display, add, or delete users.

Changing Passwords with the passwd Command

NEW TERM After creating your new user, you must assign a password with the passwd command. This command will create a default entry of x in the passwd text database in the /etc directory. The real passwords, in encrypted form, are in the /etc/shadow file, which has different *read permissions* than the /etc/passwd file. (Although anyone can read the /etc/passwd file, only the root operator has permission to view /etc/shadow.) To show you how this works, the following example first shows the passwd and shadow file entry for the user, cloobie. Then, after creating a new password for the new user, the example shows you the new user's entry in the shadow password file:

```
# fgrep cloobie /etc/passwd
cloobie:x:503:504:Caldera OpenLinux User:/home/cloobie:/bin/bash
```

You can see that although an account has been created and contains a username, UID, PID, name, directory, and default shell, the password field is represented by an x. The shadow password file shows

```
# fgrep cloobie /etc/shadow
cloobie:*notset*:9000:0:10000::::
```

To add a password, type the passwd command, along with the new user's name:

```
# passwd cloobie
New UNIX password:
Retype new UNIX password:
passwd: all authentication tokens updated successfully
```

You'll be asked for a password and then asked to retype it to verify. If all goes well, the password will be recorded in /etc/shadow:

```
# fgrep cloobie /etc/shadow
cloobie:hQSxtwq7CvJ3.:10584:0:10000:-1:-1:-1:1073917872
```

The /etc/shadow entry contains the user's name, an encrypted password, and a series of numerical values that detail

- The minimum and maximum number of days before mandatory password changes
- When to warn of a required password change
- How long after a warning a user can change the password
- How long before an account will expire

Later, users can change their own passwords using the passwd command, and you should encourage frequent password changes.

> You should know that not all Linux distributions use the shadow password system. This system of protecting passwords provides a slight increase in system security by making the system's passwords unreadable by all except the root operator. As the sysadmin, you can change anyone's password if they forget it. Don't forget yours!

Finally, you'll also want to use the chfn command to enter formal information about users or have your users enter this information. The chfn command, in the /usr/bin directory, is used with a username and will prompt you for four lines of information:

```
# chfn cloobie
Changing finger information for cloobie.
Name [Caldera OpenLinux User]: Heronimous J. Cloobie
Office []: Maritime Science Historian
Office Phone []: 703 555-1234
Home Phone []: 703 555-1235

Finger information changed.
```

If you now examine the /etc/passwd entry, you'll see

```
# fgrep cloobie /etc/passwd
cloobie:x:503:504:Heronimous J. Cloobie,Maritime Science Historian,
703 555-1234,703 555-1235:/home/cloobie:/bin/bash
```

21

This information is used by the `finger` command. The formal name may also be used along with the username in mail messages:

```
# finger cloobie
Login: cloobie                      Name: Heronimous J. Cloobie
Directory: /home/cloobie            Shell: /bin/bash
Office: Maritime Science Historian  Office Phone: 703 555-1234
Home Phone: 703 555-1235
Never logged in.
No mail.
No Plan.
```

The `finger` command will extract the user's information from the `/etc/passwd` file and print it in a nice format. One of the other things you should note in a user's `/etc/passwd` entry is the name of a shell at the end. This can be a unique way not only to specify the type of shell used (your Linux system is set up to assign the `bash` shell by default), but also to restrict the user to a particular program.

Restricting Logins

Your users normally can change the shell used after login through the `chsh` command, in the `/usr/bin` directory. You can list the currently available shells by using the `chsh` command's `-l` (list shells) option:

```
# chsh -l
/bin/bash
/bin/sh
/bin/ash
/bin/ksh
/bin/csh
/bin/tcsh
/bin/zsh
```

The `chsh` command looks in a file called `shells` under the `/etc` directory and prints a list. This does not mean that these shells are available (installed), just "acceptable." You can edit this file, adding or removing shells that can be specified by your users. You should make sure that the shells listed in this file are available on your system. To change shells, you can type

```
# chsh -s /bin/ksh
Changing shell for root.
Shell changed.
```

You can also use the `chsh` command to specify a program, other than a shell, to use as the program to run when the user logs in:

```
# chsh -s /usr/bin/pico cloobie
Changing shell for cloobie.
Warning: "/usr/bin/pico" is not listed as a valid shell.
Shell changed.
```

The chsh program will complain if the program is not listed as a shell in the /etc/shells file. Then, you check whether the change was made:

```
# fgrep cloobie /etc/passwd
cloobie:x:503:504:Heronimous J. Cloobie,Maritime Science Historian,
703 555-1234,703 555-1235:/home/cloobie:/bin/bin/pico
```

The preceding example specified the text editor pico, which allows a user to do word processing, printing, or spell-checking, but that's all! As soon as the user logs into Linux, the user is right in the text editor. After quitting the text editor, the user is logged out. This is a handy technique you can use to restrict users, especially children, if you only want them to play a game.

If you want to set the default shell or home directory for all new OpenLinux users, use the lisa command like so:

```
# lisa --useradm
```

After you press Enter, scroll down the menu (as shown in Figure 21.2) to Set default values and press Enter. You'll see the lisa menu as shown in Figure 21.3.

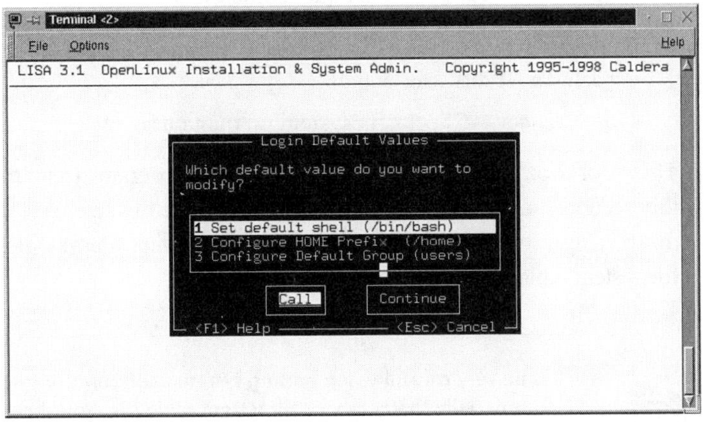

FIGURE 21.3

The lisa command can set the default shell and directories for all your new OpenLinux system users.

You can put other system-wide settings or restrictions in place. The next section shows you how you can limit how much of your system's hard drive can be used.

Setting Disk Quotas

NEW TERM On a large, multiuser systems, *disk quotas* (hard drive storage space limits for users) are not only a way of life, but also a necessity. You can impose disk quotas on your Linux system, and you should, especially if you worry about your disk space or if you're afraid the users will create huge files and overrun your hard drive. You can also use disk quotas as a warning device (and maybe justification for a new hard drive). This section explains how to start, set, and stop disk quotas.

21

Quota Manipulation with the `quota`, `quotaon`, and `quotaoff` Commands

Disk quotas limit the amount of hard drive space in several ways. You can set quotas for a group of users, using the GID, or impose limits on individual users. To manage disk quotas, you'll use some or all of these commands:

> The default Linux kernel included with OpenLinux does not support disk quotas. You must configure, rebuild, and install a new Linux kernel with quota support. For complete and definitive directions on rebuilding your OpenLinux kernel to support disk quotas, browse to `http://www.calderasystems.com/support/techguide/COL12-Kernel-Rebuild-1.html`.

- `quota`—Reports disk quotas
- `quotaon`—Turns on and sets disk quotas for users
- `quotaoff`—Turns off disk quotas for users
- `repquota`—Also reports on quotas
- `edquota`—Edits user quotas
- `quotacheck`—Checks filesystem on quota usage

This book won't discuss all the details of these programs (read the manual pages), but this section shows you how to set a disk quota for the new user you created. The first thing you must do is to enable quotas for your Linux filesystem. This involves editing the filesystem table, `fstab`, in the `/etc` directory.

> Be very careful when editing system configuration files in the `/etc` directory, especially the `fstab`, or filesystem table file. You should always first make a backup copy and then make sure you don't make incorrect changes, or you could cause boot problems. You have been warned!

Make sure you're logged in as root, and then use your favorite text editor to open the `fstab` file and edit the line containing the entry for your Linux partition:

```
# <device>      <mountpoint>    <filesystemtype> <options> <dump> <fsckorder>
/dev/hda3            /                           ext2    defaults 1 1
```

Add a comma and the word usrquota to the word default:

```
/dev/hda3                    /                    ext2
defaults,usrquota 1 1
```

Save the /etc/fstab file. Next, use the touch command to create a file called
quota.user, and make the file read-write enabled:

```
# touch /quota.user
# chmod 600 /quota.user
```

After you have done this, reboot your computer using the shutdown command with the -
r, or restart, option. Log back in as root, and use the edquota command, in the
/usr/sbin directory, along with the -u option, to edit quotas for your new user:

```
# edquota -u cloobie
```

The edquota command will read in the user.quota file under your root, or /, directory.
This file is normally a binary file, but edquota will open the file using the text editor
defined in your EDITOR environment variable. If you don't like the default editor, you can
first specify your own temporarily:

```
# EDITOR=/usr/bin/pico;export EDITOR
```

This will make the edquota command use the pico text editor. When edquota runs,
you'll end up in your editor with the following text:

```
Quotas for user cloobie:
/dev/hda3: blocks in use: 58, limits (soft = 0, hard = 0)
        inodes in use: 41, limits (soft = 0, hard = 0)
```

Although it is not important to understand all the information here (see Albert M.C.
Tam's mini-HOWTO, Quota, in /usr/doc/HOWTO/mini for details), you can easily set
both the maximum number of files and the maximum size of your user's directory. To set
limits to 3 to 5MB for disk space (blocks) and between 500 and 1000 files (inodes),
change the values for the soft and hard limits for the blocks and inode listings:

```
Quotas for user cloobie:
/dev/hda3: blocks in use: 58, limits (soft = 3000, hard = 5000)
        inodes in use: 41, limits (soft = 500, hard = 1000
```

Save the file. Then, as a last step, you must set a grace period using edquota again, but
this time with the -t option. Your new user will be warned if the lower, or "soft," limit is
exceeded:

```
# edquota -t cloobie
```

21

You can then set the grace-period warnings for exceeding either the number of files or disk use:

```
Time units may be: days, hours, minutes, or seconds
Grace period before enforcing soft limits for users:
/dev/hda3: block grace period: 1 days, file grace period: 1 days
```

If you want to warn your user right away, use a grace period of one day. (You can also use minutes or seconds.) Finally, you can use the quota command to check the new quota:

```
# quota cloobie
Disk quotas for user cloobie (uid 502):
     Filesystem  blocks   quota   limit   grace   files   quota   limit
grace
        /dev/hda3     58    3000    5000              41     500    1000
```

Using disk quotas might sometimes be necessary. If your disk space is at a premium, this could be one way to manage your hard drive resources.

Summary

This hour introduced you to some of the basic system administration skills you need to maintain a computer running OpenLinux. You also learned how to get information about what is going on inside your computer's memory while Linux runs and how to control background processes, users, and system resources, such as hard drive space.

Q&A

Q I tried to define pico as my default editor, but I either get an error message or vi runs anyway.

A Make sure you have installed the pine email program (using lisa, rpm, or glint) from your OpenLinux CD-ROM. The pico editor is part of the pine distribution.

Q I used lisa to remove a user from my system, but the user's directory under /home is still there.

A Utilities such as lisa do not remove a user's directory. If you use X11, run the Red Hat usercfg client. When you click a user's name and then click the Remove button in usercfg's dialog, you see an option to delete the user's home directory. Alternatively, log in as root and use the rm command to delete the user's files and directory. You'll also need to remove the user's mail files (in the /var/spool/mail directory).

Q **What other utilities come with OpenLinux to administer users?**

A To handle the administrative chore of creating dozens or hundreds of new users at one time, see the `newusers` command. This command reads a text file containing new users' names and passwords and can create many users with a single command line. To modify a user's account, use the `usermod` command. You can also remove users with the `userdel` command.

Exercises

1. View your system processes with other X11 utilities such as `xosview`, `xload`, or `perf`. How are these clients different?

2. The `/home` and `/var/spool` directories might contain files belonging to your OpenLinux system's users. How can you easily find all files on your system that belong to a user?

21

HOUR 22

Handling Files and Your File system

This hour continues with the basics of system administration and introduces you to handling files under Linux. You'll learn how to mount filesystems, manage the filesystem table (fstab), and format floppies. You'll see how you can protect files and directories. You'll also learn how to install or uninstall software from the command line or during your X sessions.

You will use this knowledge to administer your Linux system. Knowing how to manage file ownership is an important Linux skill and can help you overcome problems later.

One great reason to get up to speed about file access and ownership concerns security. There are some important files in your Linux system that, as root operator, you don't want all users to access. If you've set up your system to handle dial-in calls, you want to make sure that important files, and even other mounted filesystems, such as DOS or Windows, are protected. If you share your computer, you normally wouldn't want other users to have access to your files, but on the other hand, you might want to share files with other people but don't know how.

NEW TERM   This hour starts with a discussion of the Linux file system. There's a difference
between a file system and a filesystem. A *file system* is the layout of the directories and hierarchy of files on a partition. A *filesystem* is the layout of the lower-level format of a storage device, such as a hard drive. OpenLinux recognizes more than a dozen filesystems. You can find a list in the fstab, or filesystem table, manual page in the /usr/man/man5 directory, but it's best to look at the current list of supported systems in the mount command manual page. Why? The mount command is used to mount the filesystem at a *mount point*, or path, you specify. For now, take a look at the Linux filesystem.

How OpenLinux Is Organized

The software that comes with the Linux kernel comes from a variety of different UNIX systems. Some programs, utilities, and commands, such as mail, come from a UNIX distribution called the Berkeley Software Distribution, or BSD. Other programs and methods of organizing software, such as startup scripts and the organization of files used during startup, come from either AT&T System V UNIX or later variants. Because of this mixed heritage, Linux has a mix of directories, and although most pundits say Linux leans towards being System V-ish, you'll find elements of BSD and System V.

To give you a better idea, Listing 22.1 contains an edited directory listing, courtesy of the tree command.

LISTING 22.1   THE BASIC OPENLINUX FILE SYSTEM, OR DIRECTORY TREE

```
/ - the root directory
|-- bin - programs considered necessary
|-- boot - Linux boot image
|-- dev - devices, like serial ports, printers, hard drives
|-- etc - configuration files for network, X11, mail, etc.
|-- home - where users live (including root as a user)
|-- lib - software libraries, kernel modules
|-- lost+found - recovered files (from e2fsck)
|-- mnt - where you mount other filesystems
|    |-- cdrom (CD-ROMs)
|    |-- dos (DOS filesystems)
|    |-- flash (flash memory)
|    |-- floppy (floppy diskette)
|    `-- zip (Zip drives)
|-- opt - optional software (such as Applix, KDE, Netscape, or WordPerfect)
|-- proc - kernel, device, process status files
|-- root - where the sysadmin works
|-- sbin - system binaries (many root-only)
|-- tmp - temp files stored, deleted from here
```

22

```
¦-- usr - hosts much, much software, libraries
¦   ¦-- X11R6 - X Window System software
¦   ¦-- bin - more software
¦   ¦-- dict - dictionaries
¦   ¦-- doc - FAQs, HOW-TOs, software documentation
¦   ¦-- etc - software configuration files
¦   ¦-- games - fun, fun, fun!
¦   ¦-- i386-linux - development utilities
¦   ¦-- include - header files for programming
¦   ¦-- info - GNU information
¦   ¦-- lib - more software libraries
¦   ¦-- libexec - sendmail, news configuration files
¦   ¦-- local - locally developed programs
¦   ¦   ¦-- bin
¦   ¦   ¦-- doc
¦   ¦   ¦-- etc
¦   ¦   ¦-- games
¦   ¦   ¦-- info
¦   ¦   ¦-- lib
¦   ¦   ¦-- man
¦   ¦   ¦-- sbin
¦   ¦   `-- src - source code to local programs
¦   ¦-- man - manual pages
¦   ¦   ¦-- man1..9n
¦   ¦-- sbin
¦   ¦-- share
¦   ¦-- src - source for the Linux kernel!!!
¦   ¦   ¦-- linux -> linux-2.0.35
¦   ¦   ¦-- linux-2.0.35
¦   `-- tmp -> ../var/tmp
`-- var - system logs, spool directories, compressed manual pages
```

As you can see, the main directory structure is not that complicated. What is important to understand here is that you should know where you are as you navigate the file system. When you install software using package-management utilities such as Red Hat's rpm, KDE's kpackage, or the lisa command (all covered later in this hour), you won't know where software is installed unless you have a basic knowledge of your file system.

Knowing generally where different software should reside on your system might help you track down or troubleshoot difficulties if a problem should arise. Many programs will require different software components to be installed in different parts of your OpenLinux file system.

If you look at the file system listing, you see a /mnt, or mount, directory. Although you don't have to use this directory as a gateway to other filesystems, this is traditionally where other systems are mounted. The next section discusses how to make these other systems appear under the mount directory.

Using the `mount` Command to Access Other Filesystems

The `mount` command, found in the `/bin` directory, is an essential program used not only by system administrators, or sysadmins, but also by OpenLinux during startup and shutdown. This command is used to mount filesystems and make them available in your OpenLinux directory tree. During startup, the primary Linux partition, an `ext2` filesystem, is mounted at the root, or `/`, directory.

You can have other filesystems automatically mounted when OpenLinux starts, or you mount and unmount filesystems, using the `mount` and the `umount` commands, while you work. The Linux `mount` command recognizes and will mount (depending on how your kernel's modules are configured) more than a dozen different filesystems. This section concentrates on the most common, such as `ext2` for Linux, `msdos` or `vfat` for DOS or Windows, and `iso9660` for CD-ROMs.

Support for different filesystems, such as `vfat` (which provides long filenames for Win9x filesystems), is contained in loadable kernel modules.

Understanding the Filesystem Table, `/etc/fstab`

NEW TERM   When you start Linux, one of the first scripts to run is the `rc.boot` script under the `/etc/rc.d` directory. This script first mounts the *swap* partition (created when you first installed OpenLinux and used to temporarily hold portions of system memory) and then mounts your OpenLinux partition as read-write after it checks the partition for errors. If everything is okay, it will mount all filesystems described in the filesystem table, `fstab`, in the `/etc` directory with the following command:

```
# mount -avt nonfs
```

This mounts all filesystems described in the `/etc/fstab` (excluding those not meant to be automatically mounted, such as CD-ROMs), which is a short text file:

```
# <device>      <mountpoint>    <filesystemtype> <options> <dump> <fsckorder>

/dev/hda2       /               ext2             defaults 0 1
/proc           /proc           proc             defaults 0 0
/dev/hda3       none            swap             defaults 0 0
/dev/fd0        /mnt/floppy     ext2             defaults,noauto 0 0
/dev/hdc        /mnt/cdrom      iso9660          ro,noauto 0 0
/dev/hda1       /mnt/dos        vfat             noauto,dev,exec,suid 0 0
/dev/sda4       /mnt/zip        vfat             noauto,dev,exec,suid 0 0
/dev/hde1       /mnt/flash      vfat             noauto,dev,exec,suid 0 0
```

22

The fstab columns show the device name, where the filesystem will be mounted, the type of filesystem, any mount options, whether the dump command (discussed in Hour 23, "Archiving") needs to check for files to be archived, and the order in which the filesystem is checked during reboot.

> Your filesystem table will look different from the example shown here, especially if your computer uses a SCSI interface. The filesystem table described here is only an example.

The fstab rows show a Linux ext2 filesystem; the /proc or kernel process directory; the OpenLinux swap directory; a floppy diskette drive (/dev/fd0); the CD-ROM device (in this listing, the OpenLinux CD-ROM device, /dev/cdrom, is a symbolic link to /dev/hdc); a DOS filesystem partition on the same hard drive as the Linux ext2 partition (because both filesystems use the /dev/hda device); an entry for an Iomega Zip drive (/dev/sda4); and a DOS VFAT filesystem on a flash RAM card.

> You should know that editing the filesystem table is inherently dangerous. You learned to add quotas in Hour 21, "Basic System Administration." Always make a backup copy before adding a hard drive, new partitions, and so on. Make sure you have your OpenLinux boot disk on hand (created during installation). If things go awry, you can boot with your floppy, use the mount command to mount your OpenLinux partition on your hard drive, and then copy and restore the original /etc/fstab file.

Normally, the root operator mounts and unmounts filesystems. If you take my advice and don't run Linux as root all the time, you'll have to use the su command to mount and unmount filesystems:

```
# su -c "mount /mnt/cdrom"
```

This command will mount an inserted CD-ROM at the /mnt/cdrom directory. The more formal version of this command (depending on what the symbolic link /dev/cdrom points to in your system) is

```
# su -c "mount -t iso9660 /dev/hdc /mnt/cdrom"
```

This command uses the mount command to specify the filesystem type iso9660 and the device hdc (yours may be different) to be mounted at the /mnt/cdrom directory.

Does this seem like a lot of typing? If you want to make this process easier, use the `user` option of the `mount` command. You won't have to use the `su` command to mount CD-ROMs, enter passwords, or type long command lines. For example, open the `/etc/fstab` file with your favorite text editor (as the root operator), and change the original `fstab` entries to

```
/dev/hdc        /mnt/cdrom              iso9660  noauto,ro,user,dev,exec  0 0
```

The `ro` option specifies that the device is mounted read-only. The `exec` option will allow anyone to run programs from the CD-ROM. Save the file after making your changes. You'll be able to mount CD-ROMs without having to be the root operator, by using

```
# mount /dev/hdc
```

or

```
# mount /mnt/cdrom
```

This will automatically mount your CD-ROM's filesystem at the `/mnt/cdrom` path. You'll also be able to switch your disks with the `umount` command, for example:

```
# umount /dev/hdc
```

or

```
# umount /mnt/cdrom
```

Although you should enable this type of convenience only if you're using Linux on a standalone computer, and only for certain types of filesystems, such as CD-ROMs, it is convenient, especially for removable filesystems (such as Iomega Zip disks or flash memory cards). Another type of removable filesystem is the venerable floppy drive. The next section discusses floppy drives and follows with a discussion of a package of floppy utilities that might make life easier when you're dealing with floppies under Linux.

Formatting a Floppy

This section introduces you to four programs you can use to format a floppy from the Linux command line. I also take you step-by-step through the process. You might find this information useful if you want to back up files or use the floppy to install and test new software. You'll also learn how to format and then mount your floppy in Linux-native format using the `ext2` filesystem.

Floppy devices are located under the /dev directory; there are quite a few of them. You'll find a device corresponding to just about any type of floppy device ever made. You can look at the /dev directory for floppy devices:

```
# ls /dev/fd*
/dev/fd0          /dev/fd0h880     /dev/fd0u3520    /dev/fd1h1494
➡/dev/fd1u1743
/dev/fd0CompaQ    /dev/fd0u1040    /dev/fd0u360     /dev/fd1h1600
➡/dev/fd1u1760
/dev/fd0H1440     /dev/fd0u1120    /dev/fd0u3840    /dev/fd1h360
➡/dev/fd1u1840
/dev/fd0d360      /dev/fd0u1440    /dev/fd0u720     /dev/fd1h410
➡/dev/fd1u1920
/dev/fd0h1200     /dev/fd0u1600    /dev/fd0u800     /dev/fd1h420
➡/dev/fd1u2880
/dev/fd0h1440     /dev/fd0u1680    /dev/fd0u820     /dev/fd1h720
➡/dev/fd1u3200
/dev/fd0h1476     /dev/fd0u1722    /dev/fd0u830     /dev/fd1h880
➡/dev/fd1u3520
/dev/fd0h1494     /dev/fd0u1743    /dev/fd1         /dev/fd1u1040
➡/dev/fd1u360
/dev/fd0h1600     /dev/fd0u1760    /dev/fd1CompaQ   /dev/fd1u1120
➡/dev/fd1u3840
/dev/fd0h360      /dev/fd0u1840    /dev/fd1d360     /dev/fd1u1440
➡/dev/fd1u720
/dev/fd0h410      /dev/fd0u1920    /dev/fd1h1200    /dev/fd1u1600
➡/dev/fd1u800
/dev/fd0h420      /dev/fd0u2880    /dev/fd1h1440    /dev/fd1u1680
➡/dev/fd1u820
/dev/fd0h720      /dev/fd0u3200    /dev/fd1h1476    /dev/fd1u1722
➡/dev/fd1u830
```

The most common devices for 3.5-inch, 1.44MB floppies are

   /dev/fd0—Drive A

   /dev/fd1—Drive B

A number of supported floppy formats are listed in the fdprm, or floppy drive parameter file, in the /etc directory. Take a look at a portion of the file:

```
# /etc/fdprm  -  floppy disk parameter table

# Common disk formats. Names are of the form
#   actual media capacity/maximum drive capacity
# (Note: although 5.25" HD drives can format disks at 1.44M, they're
listed
#         as 1200 because that's the common maximum size.)

#              size sec/t hds trk stre gap  rate spec1 fmt_gap
360/360         720    9   2   40    0 0x2A 0x02 0xDF     0x50
```

```
1200/1200    2400    15    2    80    0    0x1B  0x00  0xDF    0x54
360/720       720     9    2    40    1    0x2A  0x02  0xDF    0x50
720/720      1440     9    2    80    0    0x2A  0x02  0xDF    0x50
720/1440     1440     9    2    80    0    0x2A  0x02  0xDF    0x50
360/1200      720     9    2    40    1    0x23  0x01  0xDF    0x50
720/1200     1440     9    2    80    0    0x23  0x01  0xDF    0x50
1440/1440    2880    18    2    80    0    0x1B  0x00  0xCF    0x6C
...
```

The format you'll most likely be interested in is the 1440/1440 description of today's 3.5-inch high-density drives. If you don't have a 1.44MB floppy diskette, you can use a name (such as 360/360) from this file with the setfdprm (set floppy disk parameter) command (found in the /usr/bin directory) to associate your drive A: floppy with a device, such as /dev/fd0:

```
# setfdprm -p /dev/fd0 360/360
```

After that, you can proceed with a low-level format of your drive. To do this, you use the fdformat (floppy disk formatting) command (found in the /usr/sbin directory). To perform this operation on the default floppy device, a 1.44MB diskette, insert a blank diskette in your drive and then use

```
# fdformat /dev/fd0
Double-sided, 80 tracks, 18 sec/track. Total capacity 1440 kB.
Formatting ... done
Verifying ... done
```

Here, you've told the fdformat command to do a low-level format of the /dev/fd0 device. Be careful! Be sure to specify the correct device.

> You should also know that you can alternatively use a specific floppy device to do the low-level format, for example:
>
> ```
> # fdformat /dev/fd0H1440
> ```
>
> This tells fdformat to use the specific floppy device for high-density drives, in this case, the A: drive.

The next step is to create a filesystem on the floppy. You'll use the mke2fs command to make a Linux second extended filesystem on the floppy. The mke2fs command, found in the /sbin directory, has at least two dozen command-line options, but you'll only use a few, for example:

```
# /sbin/mke2fs -c -v -L "Linux1" /dev/fd0
mke2fs 1.10, 24-Apr-97 for EXT2 FS 0.5b, 95/08/09
Linux ext2 filesystem format
Filesystem label=Linux1
```

```
360 inodes, 1440 blocks
72 blocks (5.00%) reserved for the super user
First data block=1
Block size=1024 (log=0)
Fragment size=1024 (log=0)
1 block group
8192 blocks per group, 8192 fragments per group
360 inodes per group

Running command: badblocks -s /dev/fd0 1440
Checking for bad blocks (read-only test): done
Writing inode tables: done
Writing superblocks and filesystem accounting information: done
```

The preceding example uses the `-c` option to check the diskette for any bad blocks and the `-L` option to give the floppy a name. To see what's going on, it also used the `-v` (verbose mode) option. The `mke2fs` command will automatically determine the size of your floppy, check it using the `badblocks` command, found in the `/sbin` directory, and then create your Linux filesystem. You might also want to use the `-m` option with a value of `0` to have the most room available and specify the high-density floppy device (to override `mke2fs`'s default behavior of reserving five percent of the filesystem for the root operator):

 # mke2fs -m 0 /dev/fd0H1440 1440

As a final step, you can mount the floppy, using the `mount` command, and then check the floppy's size, for example:

```
# mount -t ext2 /dev/fd0 /mnt/floppy
#  df /dev/fd0
Filesystem          1024-blocks  Used Available Capacity Mounted on
/dev/fd0                   1390    13      1377       1%  /mnt/floppy
```

> I've shown you the formal `mount` command line to mount a floppy. However, because the floppy device is defined in the default OpenLinux filesystem table, `/etc/fstab`, you can simply mount a floppy with `mount /mnt/floppy`.

Knowing how to format floppy drives is important. If you use the K Desktop Environment, read the next section and learn how to use the KFloppy utility.

Formatting Floppies with the KFloppy Client

If you use X11 and KDE, you can format floppy diskettes with a point-and-click client called KFloppy. To start this client, click the Utilities menu on your desktop's panel and then click KFloppy on the pop-up menu. The KFloppy dialog will appear as shown in Figure 22.1.

> You can also start KFloppy from the command line of a terminal window by typing **kfloppy &** and pressing Enter.

FIGURE 22.1

Use the KFloppy client to format floppies for the ext2 or DOS filesystems.

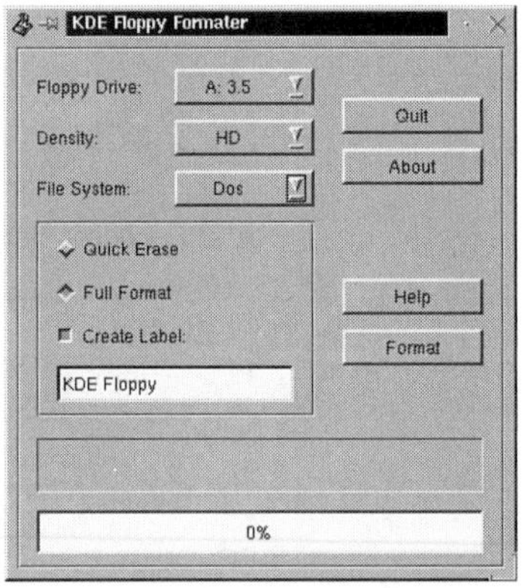

To format a floppy for Linux, click the File System pop-up menu and select ext2fs. The KFloppy dialog will automatically select a Full Format. Insert a floppy diskette and click the Format button to start formatting. A progress indicator will appear, as shown in Figure 22.2. Click the Abort button if you want to cancel formatting.

FIGURE 22.2

The KFloppy client shows a progress bar when formatting floppies.

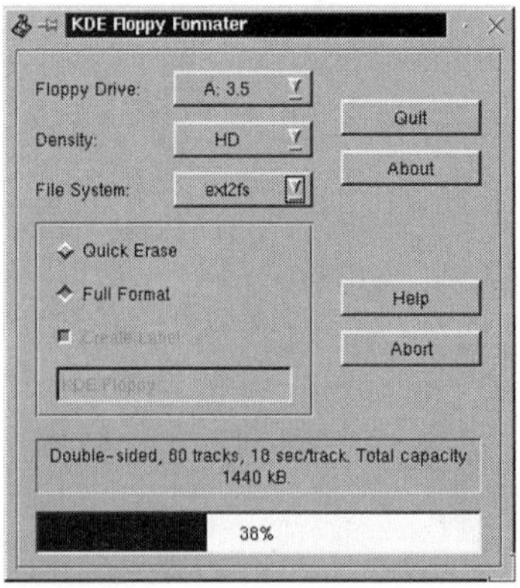

When KFloppy finishes, it will display a dialog reporting whether the floppy was formatted, how many bad blocks, if any, were found, and the raw capacity (in bytes) of the formatted diskette. (Bad floppies should be discarded.) To format a floppy for DOS, click the File System pop-up menu and select DOS. You can then click Quick Erase (for already formatted disks) or Full Format for the diskette. You can also type a volume label of up to 11 characters. Click the Format button to start the format.

> Fortunately, the `kfloppy` client will report an error if you try to format a mounted floppy. You must unmount your floppy with `umount /mnt/floppy` before attempting to format additional floppies.

If you're only interested in DOS floppies, you'll want to explore the `mtools` package, discussed next.

The `mtools` Package

The `mtools` package is a set of programs you can use in just about any operation on MS-DOS floppies. These commands are useful because you don't need to mount the floppy in order to read, write, or make changes to the floppy's contents. These utilities include

- `mattrib`—Change file attributes
- `mbadblocks`—Floppy testing program
- `mcd`—Change directory command
- `mcheck`—Check a floppy
- `mcopy`—Copy files to and from diskette
- `mdel`—Delete files on diskette
- `mdeltree`—Recursively delete files and directories
- `mdir`—List contents of a floppy
- `mformat`—Format a floppy
- `minfo`—Categorize and print floppy characteristics
- `mkmanifest`—Restore Linux filenames from floppy
- `mlabel`—Label a floppy
- `mmd`—Create subdirectory
- `mmount`—Mount floppy
- `mmove`—`mv` command for floppy files and directories

- mpartition—Make DOS filesystem as partition
- mrd—Delete directories
- mren—Rename a file
- mtoolstest—Test mtools package installation
- mtype—Types (lists) a file
- mzip—Zip/Jaz drive utility
- xcopy —Copy one directory to another

This hour won't cover all these utilities, but from the list, you should be able to see that the most often used are the mformat, mdir, mcopy, and mdel commands. The mformat command will format nearly any type of floppy device. One nice feature of this package of software is that you don't have to remember the specific names of floppy devices, such as /dev/fd0, and you can use the (possibly) familiar A: or B: drive designators. For example, to format a floppy in your drive A:, you would use

 # mformat a:

This will automatically format your diskette. After the mformat command has finished, you can copy files to and from the diskette with the mcopy command, for example:

 # mcopy *.txt a:

This will copy all files ending in .txt to your diskette. To copy files from your diskette, just reverse the arguments (in DOS form) to the mcopy command:

 # mcopy a:*.txt

This will copy all files ending in .txt to the current directory or a directory you specify. To see what is on the diskette, use the mdir command, for example:

```
# mdir a:x*.*
 Volume in drive A has no label
 Directory for A:/

xena      msg      8708 11-21-1997  12:14p xena.msg
xgames    msg      2798 11-21-1997  12:14p xgames.msg
xrpm      msg      3624 11-21-1997  12:14p xrpm.msg
        3 file(s)              15 130 bytes
                            1 067 008 bytes free
```

To label the diskette, you can use the mlabel command, for example:

```
# mlabel a:
 Volume has no label
Enter the new volume label : LINUX
```

You can also use special shell command-line quoting to label the diskette from the command line:

 # mlabel a:'DOS DISK'

This is a handy way to use spaces in a diskette's label. If you want to delete files on your diskette, use the mdel command:

 # mdel a:*.txt

This will delete all files ending in .txt on the diskette in the A: drive. If you need to perform more than these basic operations (such as use the floppy as a destination in an OpenLinux command line), you can also mount your diskette. For details, see the mmount manual page, along with the mount command manual page.

Now that you know how to manage different filesystems, the next section covers how to manage your files.

Managing File Ownership and Permissions

Managing files in Linux means more than moving files around the file system or keeping files grouped by similar behavior or topic. You can change which user or group owns a file or directory and whether you, your group, or others can read, write, or execute (run) your files.

The chmod (change access permissions) command, found in the /bin directory, is used to give or take away permission of groups or others to your files. Before you can begin to use the chmod program, you should understand Linux files and how Linux handles file permissions. In Hour 4, "Reading and Navigation Commands," you learned how to get a long-format directory listing using the -l option with the ls (list) command. This option shows the mode and permissions flags of files, for example:

```
# ls -l book/*doc
-rw-r--r--   1 bball     bball       78073 Nov 16 19:58 book/24hr06or.doc
-rw-r--r--   1 bball     bball       52287 Nov 16 19:57 book/24hr11or.doc
```

The mode and permissions flags for directories and files are listed in the first 10 columns and consist of a sequence of 10 letters. (See the section "Reading File Permissions Flags" later in this chapter.) The first letter tells you the type of file.

Understanding Linux File Types

There are at least eight file types in Linux, but these are the four most common ones:

- b—Block device (such as a hard drive)
- c—Character device (such as a serial port)
- d—Directory (also a file)
- l—Symbolic link (a small file pointing to another)

You'll usually find block and character devices in the /dev directory. Your modem or printer port on your PC will probably be a character device, whereas your floppy drive is a block device, for example:

```
# ls -l /dev/lp0 /dev/ttyS1 /dev/fd0
brw-rw-rw-  1 root     root      2,   0 Aug 19 04:22 /dev/fd0
crw-rw----  1 root     lp        6,   0 Aug 19 04:22 /dev/lp0
crw-rw-rw-  1 root     uucp      4,  65 Nov 24 13:46 /dev/ttyS1
```

As you can see, the different devices have either a b or a c in front of the permissions flags (denoting a block or character device). You can also use the ls command to list the permissions of a directory, using the -d (directory) option, for example:

```
# ls -ld book
drwxrwxr-x  2 bball    bball         1024 Nov 18 19:35 book
```

The d in the permissions flag denotes a directory. Symbolic links will also have designated type l in the ls -l listing, for example:

```
# touch file1
# ln -s file1 file2
# ls -l file2
lrwxrwxrwx  1 bball    bball            5 Nov 23 11:14 file2 -> file1
```

Now that you understand some of the basic file types, the next section shows you how to read the permissions flags.

Reading File Permissions Flags

Although the permissions sequence of letters might seem cryptic and mysterious at first, you can easily decipher what these mean. To do this, break the sequence of nine characters into three groups of three. Each group of characters represents (from left to right)

r—The file can be read.

w—The file can be written to.

x—The file can be executed, or run, or in the case of a directory, searched.

The first group of three characters is for the owner. If you create the file, you can change any of these permissions. The next group of three characters is for the group. If you recall the discussion of the /etc/passwd file in Hour 21, "Basic System Administration," you know that by default, you are assigned to two groups when your account is first created, one with your name and the other to the group users. As the system administrator, or sysadmin, you can organize users on your system by assigning users to different groups.

You'll find a list of groups for your Linux system in the group file in the /etc directory. This file contains a text database of groups. Here are a few sample entries:

```
root::0:
wheel::10:
bin::1:bin,daemon
daemon::2:bin,daemon
sys::3:bin,adm
adm::4:adm,daemon
...
users::100:bball,cloobie
bball::500:bball
cloobie::502:cloobie
```

The format of the /etc/group file is group, password, group number, and a comma-delimited list of users who belong to the group. This means that you can assign read, write, or execute permissions to your group and allow or deny access to your files. As the root operator, or sysadmin, you can organize your users into different groups. This is important and is one of the reasons you might need to use the chown (change ownership) command, as you'll see later in this hour.

The final set of three characters denotes the read, write, and execution permissions you grant all other users. Now that you know how to read the permissions, take a look at some examples before moving on to the chmod program.

When you create a file, by default, you and the members of your group have read and write permissions on that file. You can change the default of file creation permissions with your shell's umask command. (See your shell's manual page for details.) Here's a simple example:

```
# touch myfile
# ls -l myfile
-rw-r--r--   1 bball     users          0 Dec 26 09:29 myfile
```

This shows that only you (rw-) can read and write the file myfile, whereas your group (r--) and all others (r--) can only read the file. If myfile were available to everyone on your system, the permissions would look like this:

```
-rw-rw-rw-  1 bball    users          0 Dec 26 09:29 myfile
```

Now, anyone (rw-) can read or write this file. If myfile were only available for reading and writing to you, the permissions would look like this:

```
-rw-------  1 bball    users          0 Dec 26 09:29 myfile
```

This shows that you (rw-), but not your group (---) or others (---), can read the file. How do you change these settings? You use the chmod command.

Changing File Permissions with the chmod Command

You can use the chmod command in several ways to change file or directory permissions. Learning how to use this command is not as easy as 1-2-3, but it is as easy as 4-2-1!

You can use the chmod command in at least two different ways. Although you can use chmod to create simple commands from text files, using the +x command-line option (as you learned in Hour 6, "Using the Shell"), you might want to set exact permissions of certain files in your home directory, or as the sysadmin, of critical files on your system. The chmod command uses octal, or base eight, notation in modifying file or directory permissions. The 4-2-1 sequence corresponds to the three rwx sequences in the permissions flags.

How does this work? Well, suppose you want to make one of your files private so that no one else (except the root operator, of course) can read or write your file. When you first create the file, perhaps you and your group can read and write the file, whereas others can only read it. Knowing that 4-2-1 matches rwx, and knowing that the group and others permissions follow your permissions in the permissions flag, you can use chmod with the octal number 600 to change the permissions:

```
# chmod 600 afile
# ls -l afile
-rw-------  1 bball    users          0 Dec 26 14:50 afile
```

This makes the file readable and writable only by you because you've enabled read (4) +
write (2) for yourself and no one else. To change the file permissions back to the original
access permissions, you would want to enable read (4) + write (2) for you (6) and your
group (6) and read-only permissions for all others (4), and use the octal number 664:

```
# chmod 664 afile
# ls -l afile
-rw-rw-r--  1 bball    users            0 Dec 26 14:50 afile
```

You can also change file directory permissions and either let other people list the contents of your directory or have access only to the files in a directory and not be able to
list the directory contents. For example, to protect a directory from prying eyes (again,
from everyone but the root operator), you can try

```
# mkdir temp
# cd temp
# touch file1 file2 file3
# cd ..
# chmod 700 temp
# ls -ld temp
drwx------  2 bball    users         1024 Dec 26 14:52 temp
```

If anyone else tries to look into your directory, they will see

```
# ls /home/bball/temp
ls: /home/bball/temp: Permission denied
```

What if you want to allow others to read files in the directory without being able to list
the contents? To do this, you can enable execute permission of your directory:

```
# chmod 711 temp
# ls -ld temp
drwx--x--x  2 bball    users         1024 Dec 26 14:52 temp
```

Now, no other users will be able to list the contents of your directory but can read files
that you tell them are within. For example:

```
# ls -l /home/bball/temp
ls: /home/bball/temp: Permission denied
# ls -l /home/bball/temp/file1
-rw-r--r--  1 bball    users            0 Dec 26 14:52
/home/bball/temp/file1
```

As you can see, using the chmod command's octal notation is not hard. What you have to
decide is to whom you want to grant access and what kind of access you'd like your files
to have. The chmod command also has a command-line form:

```
ugoa +-= rwxXstugo
```

This book doesn't go into all the details of this notation (you can read the chmod command's manual page for more details), but the next few examples duplicate chmod's actions using the previous examples. You can protect a file from anyone else with

```
# ls -l file1
-rw-r--r--   1 bball     users              0 Dec 26 14:52
/home/bball/temp/file1
# chmod go-rwx file1
# ls -l file1
-rw-------   1 bball     users              0 Dec 26 14:52 file1
```

As you can see, the file is now readable and writable only by you because you have specified that your group (g) and others (o) do not (-) have read, write, or execute (rwx) permission. Now, you can protect your directory from prying eyes as follows:

```
# chmod go-rwx temp
```

To mimic the last example, to enable others to read files in the directory but not list the directory contents, you can use

```
# chmod go+x temp
```

You're now familiar with file and directory permissions and using the chmod command. The next section shows how you can change ownership of files or directories using the chown command.

Changing File Ownership with the chown Command.

The chown (change ownership) command, found in the /bin directory, is used to change, either permanently or temporarily, the ownership of files or directories. If you recall the previous discussion of the /etc/group file in this hour, you'll remember that your users can be assigned to different groups. Using the chown command, you can assign ownership to different users or groups, permitting reading, writing, or deletion of files and directories.

For example, if you've created a text file, you can share it with members of your group or others with the chmod command. By using chown, you can tell Linux specifically what other users or groups can have access to your file. You can use the groups command to find out what groups you belong to:

```
# groups
users
```

This shows that the user, bball, belongs to the group users. As the root operator, you belong to the group root, for example:

```
# groups
root
```

To find out who belongs to a group, look at the /etc/group file, or use the name of a user:

```
# groups cloobie
cloobie : users
```

This shows that cloobie belongs to at least one group, called users. To assign one of your files to the users group, and give cloobie access, you can use the chown command's syntax of *user:group*:

```
# chown :users myfile
# ls -l myfile
-rw-r--r--   1 bball     users          0 Dec 26 15:19 myfile
```

You might think that to assign specific ownership, you can use the following:

```
#  chown cloobie:users myfile
chown: myfile: Operation not permitted
```

What happened? This shows why Linux has groups. You can assign access of one of your files to a group, but unless you're the root operator, you cannot assign one of your files to appear to have been either created by or owned by another user. Make sure you're logged in as the root operator, and use

```
# chown cloobie:cloobie myfile
# ls -l myfile
-rw-rw-r--   1 cloobie  cloobie        0 Dec 26 15:19 myfile
```

As you can see, even though the file myfile was created by the user bball, as the sysadmin, you can assign ownership to any users and any group. If you just want to change the group ownership of a file or directory, you can use the chgrp command, and if you want to change your users or your own group, you can use the newgrp command.

Changing Groups and Ownerships with the chgrp and newgrp Commands

The chgrp (change group) command, found in the /bin directory, is used only to change group ownerships. In this regard, it is not as flexible as the chown command, which can do both. The chgrp command accepts a group name or group ID (GID), for example:

```
# ls -l myfile
-rw-r--r--   1 bball     users          0 Dec 26 15:26 myfile
```

This shows that the file belongs to user bball and group users. To change the group ownership and grant access to other members of the group, use

```
# groups bball
bball : bball users
# chgrp users myfile
# ls -l myfile
-rw-rw-r--   1 bball    users            0 Nov 23 14:16 myfile
```

Now, other members of the users group can access the file. Along with the chgrp command, you can use the newgrp command, which is found in the /usr/bin directory. Although the chgrp command will change group ownership of one of your files or directories to a group you belong to (or if you're the root operator, any group), you can use newgrp to shift your current group membership:

```
# groups
bball users
# touch file1
# ls -l file1
-rw-rw-r--   1 bball    bball            0 Nov 23 14:53 file1
# newgrp users
# groups
users bball
# touch file2
# ls -l file2
-rw-rw-r--   1 bball    users            0 Nov 23 14:54 file2
# newgrp bball
```

This shows that the user bball originally belonged to the default group bball. This was verified by creating a file showing the current user and group ownership. Next, the user bball changed to the users group, created a file, and verified that the created file has the new group's access. Finally, the user bball changed back to the original group, bball.

> The newgrp command will launch a new shell, and you must use the shell's exit command to return to your original prompt. If you only need to run a single command as the member of a different group, use the sg command, which will not replace your shell.

As you can see, Linux offers you a great deal of flexibility in assigning file ownerships and permissions. By using different combinations of directory and file ownership and permissions, you can organize your system along lines of types of work, types of users, or types of files.

Managing Linux Software with `rpm`, `lisa`, and `kpackage`

22

NEW TERM Software installation and removal under OpenLinux is accomplished with the Red Hat Package Manager, or `rpm` command. The `rpm` command works by using *software packages* and databases of installed software for your system under the `/var/lib/rpm` directory. A software package is an archive of files, information, and scripts used before and after files are decompressed and saved into your file system. The `rpm` command, its databases, and the format of the software packages are the *backend* system for *front-end* utilities such as `lisa` and the `kpackage` client.

This section introduces you to the `rpm` command and then shows you how to use the `kpackage` client and the `lisa` command to install or remove software.

Using the `rpm` Command

You use the `rpm` command to install, query, upgrade, uninstall, and verify software. What makes `rpm` so handy is that you can use it to easily track what software is installed and which version of a software package is installed and then upgrade the software package, and if desired, uninstall the software—all with a single command line!

The `rpm` command has many different command-line options, but most users will only use five of its options, or modes:

- `-i`, or install
- `-e`, or uninstall
- `-q`, or query
- `-U`, or upgrade
- `-V`, or verify

To install a software package (usually with a filename ending in `.rpm`), use the `-i` option, followed by the name of a software package. Software package names usually include the name of the program, its version, what computer platform the software is designed for, and an `.rpm` extension. You must be logged in as the root operator or have root permission before installing or removing software. For example, to install the `taper` backup software package from your OpenLinux CD-ROM, insert and mount the CD-ROM and then use `rpm`:

```
# rpm -i /mnt/cdrom/Packages/RPMS/taper-6.8.2-2.i386.rpm
```

To have `rpm` report on what it is doing, using the `-v` or verbose secondary option. If you'd like to see a progress indicator, which prints hash signs (#) (hence the `-h` name for the option) during the installation, also use the `-h` option like this:

```
# rpm -ivh /mnt/cdrom/Packages/RPMS/taper-6.8.2-2.i386.rpm
taper                   #################################################
```

The software package components will be extracted and copied to the proper directories in your OpenLinux file system. After a successful installation, the `rpm` databases will then be updated to include the new software. To verify that the taper software has been installed, use the `-V`, or verify option:

```
# rpm -V taper
```

Everything is okay if nothing happens. However, if any files in the taper package have changed in size, ownership, or permission, you'll receive various error messages. To find out more about a package, either before or after installing the software, use `rpm`'s `-q`, or query option. For example, to see a description of the taper software package after installation, use the `-q` option, along with the secondary `i` or information option:

```
# rpm -qi taper
Name        : taper                  Distribution: OpenLinux 1.3
Version     : 6.8.2                  Vendor: Caldera, Inc.
Release     : 2                      Build Date: Wed Aug 19 06:11:40
1998
Install date: Mon Dec 28 14:02:03 1998     Build Host:
buildmeister.caldera.com
Group       : Administration/Archiving     Source RPM: taper-6.8.2-
2.src.rpm
Size        : 425903
Packager    : Raymund Will <ray@lst.de>
URL         : http://www.multiline.com.au/~yusuf/
Summary     : Menu driven backup system with support for compression.
Description :
This is a tape backup and restore program that provides a friendly user
interface to allow backing/restoring files to a tape drive. Alternatively,
files can be backed up to hard disk files. Selecting files for backup and
restore is very similar to the Midnight Commander interface and allows
easy
traversal of directories. Recursively selected directories are supported.
Incremental backup and automatic most recent restore are defaults
settings.
SCSI, ftape, zftape, and removable drives are supported

WARNING: Please note that this is BETA software.
```

To query a software package before installation, use the -q option along with -i and the -p, or package file option, followed by the pathname to the package like this:

```
# rpm -qpi /mnt/cdrom/Packages/RPMS/taper-6.8.2-2.i386.rpm
```

You'll see the same information as shown in the previous example. Do you want to see what commands, files, or documentation are included in a package before installation? Use -q along with the -l option:

```
# rpm -qpl /mnt/cdrom/Packages/RPMS/taper-6.8.2-2.i386.rpm
/sbin/bg_backup
/sbin/bg_restore
/sbin/taper
/usr/doc/taper-6.8.2
/usr/doc/taper-6.8.2/BUGS
/usr/doc/taper-6.8.2/CHANGES.html
/usr/doc/taper-6.8.2/COMPRESSION
/usr/doc/taper-6.8.2/COPYING
/usr/doc/taper-6.8.2/CREDITS
/usr/doc/taper-6.8.2/FAQ.txt
/usr/doc/taper-6.8.2/VERSION6.8
/usr/doc/taper-6.8.2/WARNING
```

You can also use rpm's -U, or upgrade option, to upgrade, overwrite, and replace existing software with newer versions. For example, to upgrade to a new version of the taper command, use the -U option:

```
# rpm -U taper-6.8.4-2.i386.rpm
```

Deleting software can be a daunting task; many programs have configuration files, support libraries, or documentation scattered about the file system. However, if you use rpm, you can easily remove software with a single command line. For example, to remove the package for taper, use the -e, or erase option, followed by the name of the program:

```
# rpm -e taper
```

Note that this is not the same as the name of software's .rpm file! The rpm command will also check, before removing software, whether the software you're going to remove will cause problems for other software packages. If this is the case, rpm will report a *dependency* error. This occurs because another package may depend on the installed software.

If you're worried about installing or removing software, use rpm's --test option. To see exactly what rpm will do, also include the vv, or ultra-verbose, option. For example, to see exactly what rpm will do when it removes the taper software without removing the software, use a command like this:

```
# rpm -test -evv taper
D: counting packages to uninstall
D: opening database in //var/lib/rpm/
D: found 1 packages to uninstall
D: uninstalling record number 88728
D: will remove files test = 1
D: /usr/doc/taper-6.8.2/WARNING - removing
D: /usr/doc/taper-6.8.2/VERSION6.8 - removing
D: /usr/doc/taper-6.8.2/FAQ.txt - removing
D: /usr/doc/taper-6.8.2/CREDITS - removing
D: /usr/doc/taper-6.8.2/COPYING - removing
D: /usr/doc/taper-6.8.2/COMPRESSION - removing
D: /usr/doc/taper-6.8.2/CHANGES.html - removing
D: /usr/doc/taper-6.8.2/BUGS - removing
D: /usr/doc/taper-6.8.2 - removing
D: /sbin/taper - removing
D: /sbin/bg_restore - removing
D: /sbin/bg_backup - removing
D: removing database entry
```

Using kpackage

The kpackage client, included with the K Desktop Environment, or KDE, is a graphical interface to the rpm program and runs under the X Window system. You must be logged in as the root operator in order to use kpackage to install and remove software. As with other root-permission commands, if you're not logged in as the root operator, start the client from the command line of an X11 terminal window:

```
# su -c kpackage
```

This will start kpackage, and its window will list the groups of packages installed on your system (as shown in Figure 22.3).

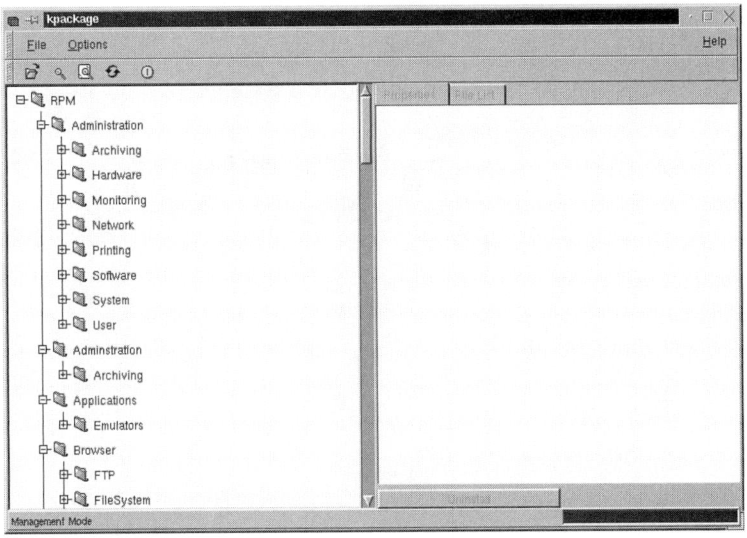

FIGURE 22.3

The kpackage *client, included with KDE, runs under X11 and uses the* rpm *command's databases to display installed software in your OpenLinux system.*

Note that your OpenLinux software is grouped under separate folders. Click the small plus (+) sign in front of the Archiving folder under Administration and then click the taper icon. A description of the package will appear, as shown in Figure 22.4.

FIGURE 22.4

The kpackage *client displays information about an installed package from your system's* rpm *database.*

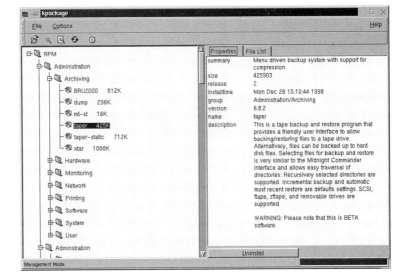

If you click the File List tab, a listing of each file in the taper package and the file's location in your Linux file system will appear, as shown in Figure 22.5. To uninstall the software, click the Uninstall button at the bottom of the file information or file list.

FIGURE 22.5

The kpackage *client displays the name of each file in an installed package and offers a one-click Uninstall button to remove software.*

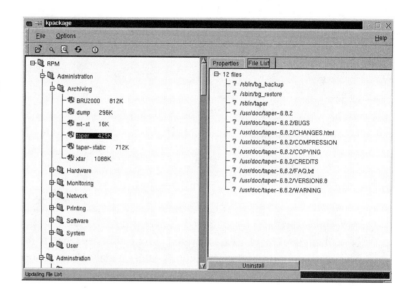

To install a package, select the File menu and then click the Open menu item. The kpackage file selection dialog will appear as shown in Figure 22.6. If your OpenLinux CD-ROM is inserted and mounted, you can navigate to the RPMS directory and install by double-clicking its name.

FIGURE 22.6

The kpackage *client installs software using drag-and-drop or through a file selection dialog.*

Using the `lisa` Command

The `lisa` command is not only a graphical interface program to most OpenLinux system administration tasks, but also can install or remove software. Again, you must be logged in as the root operator in order to install and remove software using `lisa`. However, you do not need to run X11.

To jump right into software package management, start `lisa` from the command line with its `--pkg` option:

```
# lisa --pkg
```

The `lisa` dialog will appear as shown in Figure 22.7.

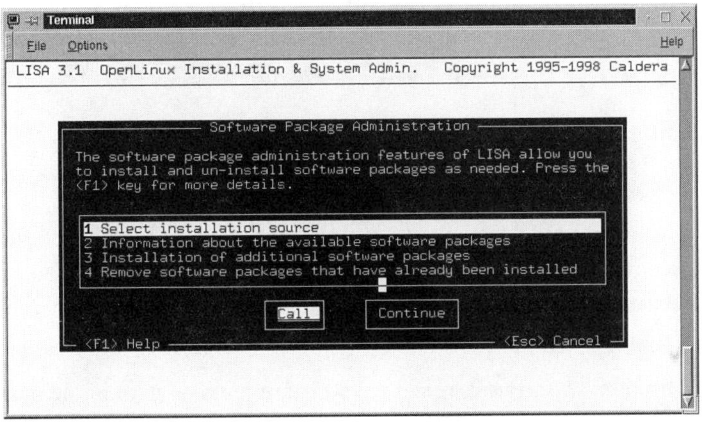

FIGURE 22.7

You can also use the lisa *command to install or remove OpenLinux software.*

To install a software package, you must first select the directory or filesystem. Press Enter to choose where the software package is located. A selection dialog will appear, as shown in Figure 22.8.

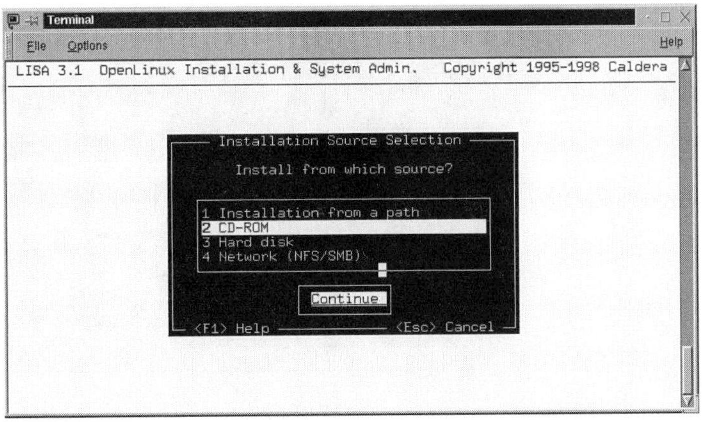

FIGURE 22.8

To install software with lisa, *you must first choose where the package is located.*

If you select CD-ROM, `lisa` will try to first detect your CD-ROM (you should mount the CD-ROM first), confirm your CD-ROM, and then present the initial dialog (as shown in Figure 22.7) with the software installation line (line number 3) highlighted. Press Enter to go to the Installation dialog, shown in Figure 22.9.

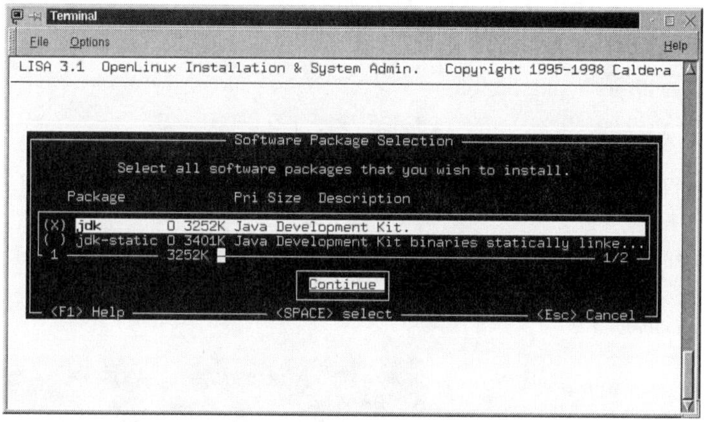

FIGURE 22.9

The lisa *command uses a scrolling list of files in its software installation selection dialog.*

A list of available packages is displayed after the list of .rpm files on your CD-ROM are compared against the list of installed .rpm files in your OpenLinux system's rpm database. To select a file, scroll through the list and press the spacebar. When finished, press Enter to install the software.

To remove software, select the software removal item in the main software administration dialog (as shown in Figure 22.7) and press Enter. You'll see a list of installed packages on your system (as shown in Figure 22.10). To remove a package, scroll through the list and press the spacebar. When finished, press Enter to remove the software.

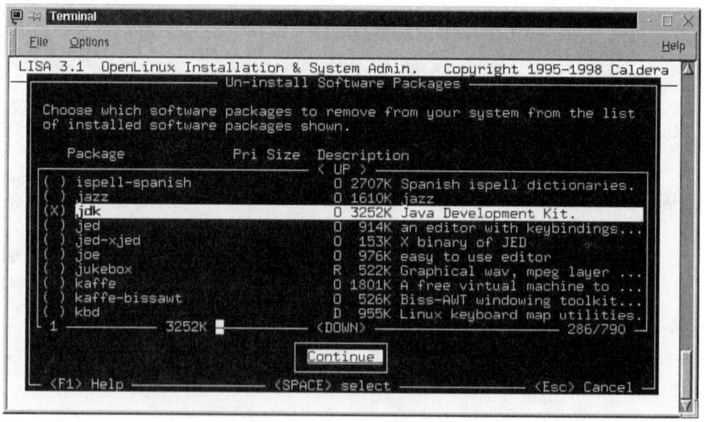

FIGURE 22.10

The lisa *command uses a scrolling list of files in its software removal dialog.*

To get information about a package, select the information line item in the main software package administration dialog (as shown in Figure 22.7) and press Enter. The lisa command will then query your system's rpm database and show a list of package names, as shown in Figure 22.11.

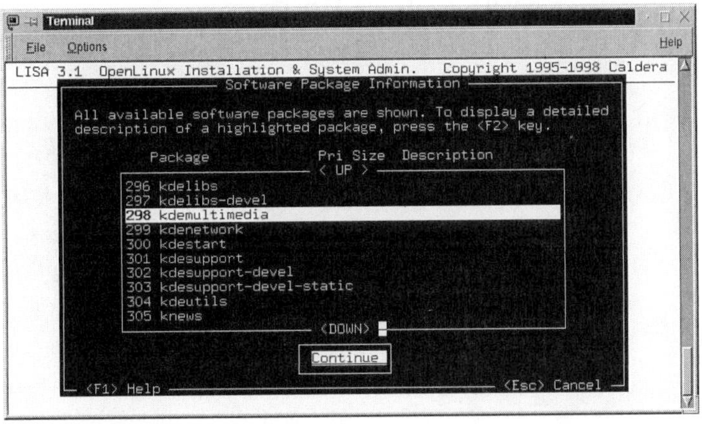

FIGURE 22.11

To get information about a package, scroll through the list of installed software, select a file, and press Enter.

Scroll through the list and select a package with the spacebar, and then press Enter to see the package information. This information is exactly the same as shown by the rpm command's -qi options.

OpenLinux also includes the Caldera Open Administration System, which features, another graphical interface to your system's rpm database. COAS requires X11, and uses a large window you can use to install and remove software.

Summary

This hour introduced you to the concept of the OpenLinux file system, or the organization of directories and files for Linux. You also learned about different filesystems and how to read your OpenLinux filesystem table, fstab in the /etc directory. In addition, you learned how to read and change file ownership and permissions. You also found out how to query, install, and remove software from your system using three different utilities. All these skills are an important part of knowing how to administer, maintain, and troubleshoot OpenLinux.

Q&A

Q I tried formatting a floppy with the `fdformat` command. After I inserted a floppy, typed the command, and specified the `/dev/fd0` device, the command reported `Could not determine current format type: No such device.` I know my floppy works. What's going on?

A It's possible that you didn't have a floppy inserted in the drive. If you get this error with an inserted floppy, the floppy was not blank and was previously formatted. The best approach to use when performing a low-level format is to specify the exact type of device (such as `/dev/fd0H1440`) as in `fdformat /dev/fd0H1440`.

Q How do I create a folder for my KDE desktop xe "KDE (K Desktop Environment):desktop" xe "K Desktop Environment (KDE):desktop" that, when opened, shows the contents of my Windows partition?

A Mount your Windows partition xe "Windows partition:mounting" and then create a symbolic link xe "symbolic links" with a name such as dos inside the Desktop folder in your home directory. Make sure this link points to the Windows desktop folder—for example, `ln -s /mnt/dos/windows/desktop $HOME/Desktop/dos`.

Exercises

1. Format a floppy and then prepare the diskette with the Linux ext2 filesystem . Mount the floppy and copy files from your home directory to the diskette. What utilities did you use?

2. Make a backup of your system's filesystem table and copy it to a diskette. Then, edit your filesystem to allow others to mount and unmount CD-ROMs.

3. Open the KDE help application from your desktop's panel and then click the Using Templates to access Applications and Devices item. Follow the directions and create a desktop icon for your floppy drive. After you finish, copy files to your floppy by dragging them from your home folder.

Hour **23**

Backing Up and Restoring Your System

This hour continues the discussion of basic system administration skills and shows you how, as the root operator, to back up and restore your system using several different Linux utilities. With a little practice, you can easily perform these system administration tasks.

Considerations Before Performing Backups and Restores

There are several things to consider before backing up or restoring your system. Although one ideal time to back up is after you install Linux and make sure all your devices (such as the sound card, graphics card, or tape drive) are working, there are other considerations. For example, if the kernel supplied on the CD-ROM works well for your system, you can simply rely on the CD for your initial backup if you have to do a full restore.

There is a difference between a backup and an archive. Backups are performed at regular intervals to save important documents, files, or complete systems. Archives are made to save important documents, files, or complete systems for long periods of time. This means that you should first devise a backup strategy and ask yourself the following questions:

- Do I need to use a formal backup strategy?
- Do I need to back up the entire system each time?
- Do I need to back up selected files or whole directories?
- How often should I back up?
- How long do I need to keep my archived copies?
- Do I need reports or statistics on the backups?
- What media (such as floppy, tape, or removable hard drive) should I use?
- What software format (such as tar or dump) should the backup be in?
- Do I need to use any specialized software tools, such as backup scripts, or can I perform the backups by hand?
- Should compression, straight copy, or encryption be used?

You can answer some of these questions by looking at the way you use OpenLinux. If you just use Linux for word processing or running spreadsheets, you can probably get away with only backing up certain files or directories. If you use Linux to learn programming, keep original copies of your programs, along with different versions. If you have other users on the system, save not only copies of their directories, but the /etc/passwd file, portions of the file system that take a long time to recreate (such as the entire /etc directory), or even the whole system. Do this so that you can quickly restore the system in the event of a hard drive crash (unlikely) or system operator error (more likely).

The size of your system and the capacity of your hard drives or other storage devices might be determining factors in approaching a backup strategy. If your Linux system is small enough (around 200MB), you can quickly back up everything to another hard drive or a tape drive. You also can use a removable media drive, such as an Iomega Zip or Jaz drive or Syquest EZ-flyer. If you only have to save copies of a small number of small files, you might even be able to use high-density floppies for storage.

You'll probably decide on a combination of archiving and regularly scheduled full or incremental backups. You need to choose software to use and explore how to automate as much of the process as possible, perhaps by using crontab entries (discussed in Hour 24, "Using Scheduling to Automate System Management"). Whatever you do, when you decide on your strategy, stick to it! The worst time to create and use a backup strategy is after you run into problems or lose files.

Configuring the BRU Backup System for Backups and Restores

You can download a free copy of Enhanced Software Technologies' BRU 2000 PE by browsing to http://www.estinc.com. This is a complete personal edition of a commercial software backup application you can use to back up your system or files using nearly any tape drive, removable hard drive, and even floppies. This section shows you how to configure BRU 2000 PE and highlight selected features of this software, which provides data verification, error detection, data compression, and selective backup and restores.

The BRU 2000 PE software included with this book's CD-ROM is exactly the same as the commercial version of BRU 2000 but does not support the same features (such as network backups). The personal edition is quite adequate for backup operations on a desktop OpenLinux system.

FIGURE 23.1

The BRU 2000 backup and restore utility features menus and buttons to manage Linux system backups.

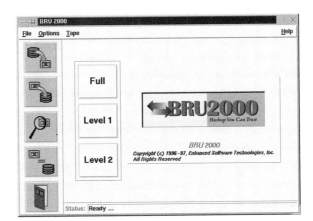

Install the BRU software by using the lisa, rpm, glint or kpackage programs (see Hour 22, "Handling Files and Your File System"). The software is installed into the /bru directory in your file system.

You can use the BRU software from the command line or during an X11 session. Using BRU with X is a lot easier, but you can perform backup operations from the command line of a console. BRU has more than 50 command-line options you can use to specify for your backup process. To use BRU at the command line, type bru [options]. To start the X interface, type xbru in an xterm window. See BRU's man page for details.

When you first run BRU, you must also tell BRU which device to use to back up your files. First, pull down the File menu with your mouse, and then select the Configure BRU menu item. A window called BRU Configuration Utility appears, as shown in Figure 23.2.

You must run BRU as the root operator in order to configure the software.

FIGURE 23.2

*The BRU
Configuration Utility
features several
windows, including a
tape device selection
list.*

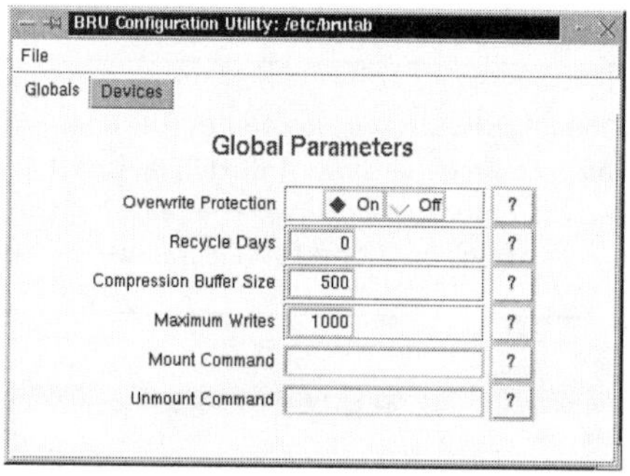

Click the Devices button in this window, and then click the New button. A New Device window, as shown in Figure 23.3, with a scrolling list of different devices appears.

FIGURE 23.3

*You can create new
backup devices to use
with BRU 2000 PE.*

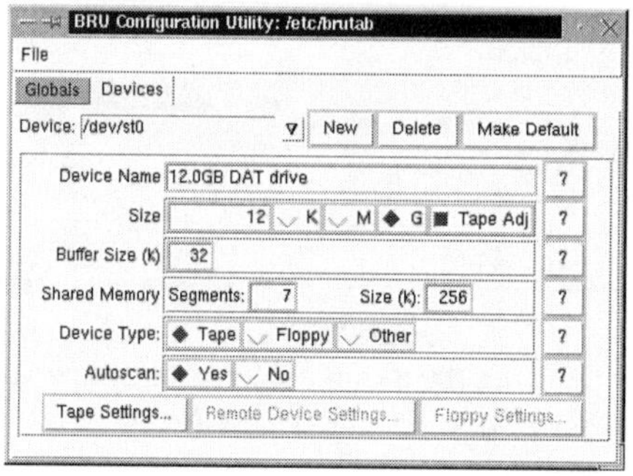

Click the New button to select a new device from BRU's built-in list, as shown in Figure 23.4.

FIGURE 23.4

BRU lists 37 different devices in its tape device selection list.

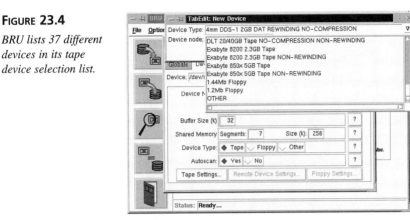

23

There are 37 different devices listed, including floppy drives. If you don't see a device you have in the list, select the OTHER device option to create your own. For example, if you have an older, floppy-based tape drive that uses the QIC-80 format, select OTHER and specify the tape device (most likely /dev/rft0, the rewinding tape device).

To create a backup device using a Zip drive, first select OTHER. After you select the backup device, type in the Zip drive's device (/dev/sda4 for a parallel-port Zip drive). To complete your Zip backup device definition, click in the Device Name field, enter Zip Disk, then click the Size field, and enter 100 (make sure to click M to specify the size in megabytes), as shown in Figure 23.5.

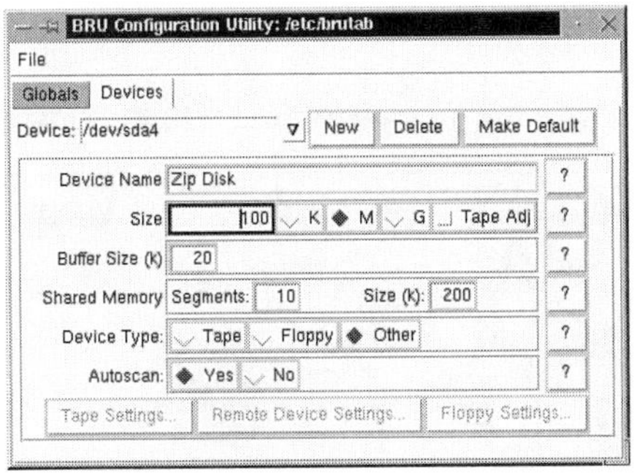

FIGURE 23.5

You can create your own BRU device definition for an Iomega Zip drive backup device.

To finish the definition, click Save and Exit from the File menu items of the BRU Configuration window. To begin a backup, insert a Zip disk into your computer's Zip drive.

You don't have to mount the Zip disk with the `mount` command; BRU automatically uses the disk through the `/dev/sda4` device. If you start a backup without first inserting a Zip disk, BRU reports an error!

To start a backup, first click New Device from BRU's File menu, and then select `/dev/sda4` from the list of devices, as shown in Figure 23.6.

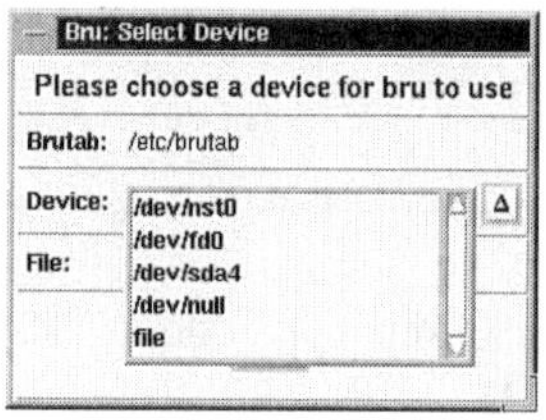

FIGURE 23.6

Select a backup device, such as /dev/sda4, for the Zip disk before beginning backup operations.

Select Backup from the BRU program's File menu, or click the top icon in the main BRU dialog box (showing an arrow going from the disks to a tape).

A file selection dialog box appears, as shown in Figure 23.7, which enables you to select whole files or directories to back up. After you finish selecting and adding the directories or files, click the Options button to select file compression or other options, or click the Begin Backup button to start your backup. BRU asks for a backup name or volume label and then starts backing up your data. If multiple volumes, or disks, are required, you're prompted to insert them when needed.

FIGURE 23.7

The BRU directory and file selection dialog box offers selective backup sets for archiving directories and files.

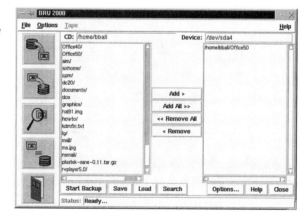

The BRU program has many different features, including compression, scheduling, and tape archive verification. You can find out more about this program by browsing to the following site:

`http://www.estinc.com`

Backing Up Your System with the `tar` Command

Although use of the `tar` command is discussed in Hour 5, "Manipulation and Searching Commands," as the system administrator, you need to explore some of the more complex `tar` command-line options and experiment with creating backups before implementing your backup strategy.

The `tar` command creates a tape archive. You can write the archive to your hard drive, a tape drive, or nearly any other Linux device. To create a quick backup of your users' home directories, use `tar` to create the archive as in the following example:

```
# tar cPfC users.tar / home
```

This command line creates the tape archive `users.tar` in the current directory. To save disk space, an even better approach is to use compression when creating your tape archive. The `tar` command supports `gzip` compression with the z command-line option. Just include z in the tape creation command line and revise the archive's name, like so:

```
# tar czPfC users.tar.gz / home
```

One easy way to regularly back up these directories is to save them on a different file system. If you have a DOS or Windows partition mounted (see Hour 22), automate the backup process with an `/etc/crontab` entry:

```
30 17 * * * root tar czPfC /mnt/dos/windows/desktop/users.tar.gz / home
```

> Only the root operator can create or modify entries in `/etc/crontab`.

This entry, in the `/etc/crontab` file, backs up your users' directories at 5:30 p.m. each day and saves the archive in the Windows desktop folder. As you can see, automating the backup process isn't that hard and has the benefit of working in the background without your attention; this type of process is called an *unattended* backup. If you save your data on a separate file system, make sure to mount the drive before trying to restore your information. If you use compression, don't forget to include the z option when you restore with the `tar` command's x, or extract, option:

```
# cd /
# tar xzvf /mnt/dos/windows/desktop/users.tar.gz
```

These command lines restore your users' directories and files, starting at the /, or root directory. The v option lists each file as it is restored. Although backing up files to another file on your hard drive is easy, you can also use the tar command with tape drives by specifying the tape device on the tar command line.

> Unfortunately, there are no utilities to format tapes under Linux. Although you must still use a DOS or Windows utility to do this, you don't have to bother with formatting if you make sure to purchase preformatted tapes.

This hour does not detail all the ins and outs of installing or using different tape devices, but it does show you the general approach and some examples you can try. To use a tape drive with the tar command, you must find the tape device under the /dev directory. There are a number of them, but I'm using the general floppy tape driver, /dev/ftape, as an example.

Although most tape drives can rewind a freshly inserted tape, you can use the mt, or magnetic tape, command to rewind or retension your tape. Insert the tape, and then use the following:

```
# mt -f /dev/ftape rewind
```

After the tape rewinds, erase it with the mt command's erase option:

```
# mt -f /dev/ftape erase
```

After the tape is erased, you can write a tar archive to the tape by specifying the /dev/ftape device:

```
# cd /
# tar cf /dev/ftape /home
```

This command creates a tape archive of all the files and directories under the /home directory. To restore your tape archive, you must use the tar command's x option:

```
# cd /
# tar xf /dev/ftape
```

There are many more options with the tar command. Explore some of them, such as the d option to test archives. For more information, see the tar manual page and read the ftape HOWTO under the /usr/doc/HOWTO directory.

Using the `cpio` Command to Backup and Restore

The `cpio`, or copy in and out, command can be used in much the same way as the `tar` command, but with several differences, especially with archive creation or extraction command-line options. For example, to create a `cpio` archive, you must use the `-o`, or create, option. The `cpio` command also requires a list of filenames, with paths, to build an archive. To do this, use the `find` command, which handily creates the required names for you.

For example, if you have a directory called x11 that contains a number of files you want to archive, you can combine the output of the `find` command with the `cpio` command to build the archive, as follows:

```
# find x11 ¦ cpio -ov >x11.cpio
cpio: x11: truncating inode number
x11
x11/xfree86faq.txt
x11/xappsfaq.txt
x11/x11faq.txt
x11/disaster.txt
x11/XHints1.txt
1082 blocks
```

This command line shows that the `cpio` command has been fed the names of the files inside the x11 directory, creating an archive with the `-o` option and showing you the files being added with the `-v` option. The name of the archive is x11.cpio, and it is created using the greater than, or >, redirection operator.

To restore a `cpio` archive, use the `cpio` command's `-i`, or extract, command-line option:

```
# cpio -i < x11.cpio
1082 blocks
```

This command line shows that to extract a `cpio` archive, you can use the less then, or <, redirection operator in conjunction with the `cpio -i` extract option. The `cpio` program recreates the directory and finishes by printing the number of 512-character blocks that were written to your hard drive.

You also can use the combination of the `find` command and `cpio` to create archives of any directory or even different files on your system. To back up all files in your directory that belong to you and have been created or modified during the current day, you can use the `find` command's `-user` and `-mtime` command-line options:

```
# find /home/bball -user bball -mtime -1 -print ¦ cpio -o >today.cpio
```

This command line creates a cpio archive called today.cpio that contains all files you've modified in the last 24 hours. You're only limited by your imagination in how to devise your backups and how to back up your system. For more information on the cpio command, read its manual page. For more information about the find command, see Hour 5, or read the find manual page.

Using the taper Script for Tape Drive Backups and Restores

The taper program, by Yusaf Nagree, is a backup and restore program used to create compressed or uncompressed archives of selected files or directories. This program provides a nice interface to create and maintain tape archives. You also can use other types of media to do your backups.

Using the taper command is easy. Specify the type of media to use with the -T media option. According to the latest documentation, the taper command supports the following options:

- ftape—floppy drive:tape driver that is included with your system and is used for tape drives that attach to the floppy interface
- zftape—more recent floppy drive tape driver that handles additional tape formats
- scsi—driver for tape drives using a scsi interface
- ide—driver to support ide tape drives
- removeable—driver to support floppies, or removeable hard drives

If you don't have a tape drive but would like to try the taper program to test a backup of a directory to floppy diskettes, use the -T command-line option with the removable option:

```
# taper -T removeable
```

This starts the taper program, as shown in Figure 23.8. taper uses the default removeable device, /dev/fd0, which is the floppy. To change the type of device to use a Zip disk, scroll down to the Change Preferences item, and press Enter. In the following dialog box, press Enter at the Tape Drive Preferences item.

In the Tape Drive Preferences dialog box, as shown in Figure 23.9, change both instances of /dev/fd0 to /dev/sda4, which is the default Zip disk device. Press Esc, and return to the main menu. In the main menu, press Enter at the Backup Module item.

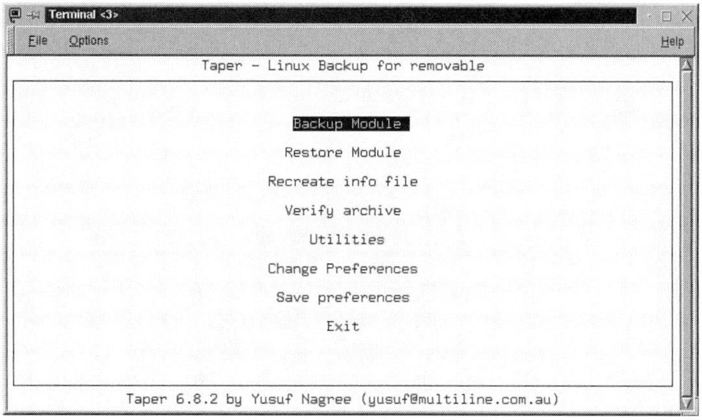

FIGURE 23.8

The taper *script provides a graphic interface for archives or backup operations of directories and files.*

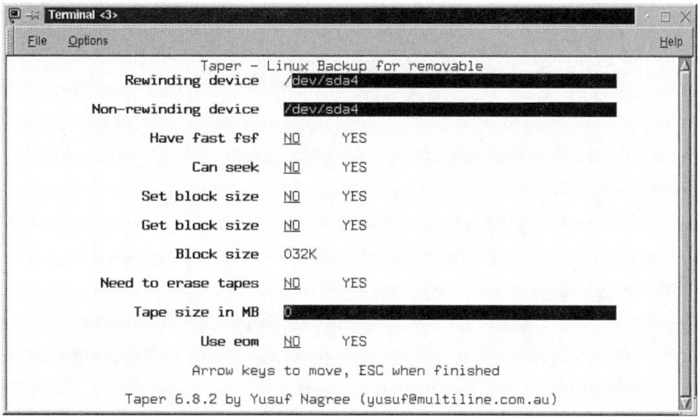

FIGURE 23.9

You can use different backup devices, such as /dev/sda4, *for a Zip disk during your* taper *backup operations.*

In the taper selection dialog box, as shown in Figure 23.10, you're asked to select files or directories before you start the backup. Scroll through the list of directories and files, and select items by pressing the I key. To get help, press the H or ? keys. When you finish, press the F key to start the backup operation.

The taper program has many different features. Its documentation is under the /usr/doc/taper directory in the file FAQ.txt.

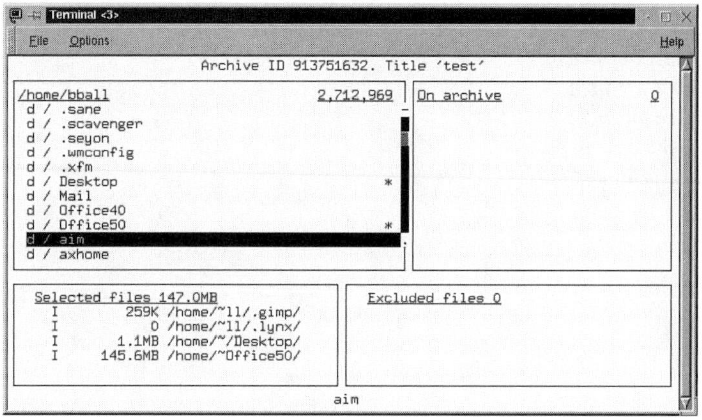

FIGURE 23.10

Scroll through the taper selection dialog box, selecting files or directories to back up with the I key.

Summary

This hour introduced you to different programs and ways to back up your OpenLinux system. Performing periodic backups is an important role for a system administrator, and perfecting the practice of preserving your system and important files enhances your computing experience.

Q&A

Q I don't want to use floppies to back up my system. I don't have a removeable hard drive. I also don't have a tape drive. What's the safest approach I can take to back up important files?

A You can at least back up your /etc directory. This directory probably contains fewer than 2.5 megabytes of files, which can be backed up to two floppy disks. Another method you can use is to back up important files to another partition (such as a mounted msdos or vfat partition). If you have the hard drive space, you can also create a small spare Linux ext2 partition to hold periodic backups of your system's configuration files. If something happens to your root partition, you can then restore from this spare partition.

Q Help! My system has crashed! I didn't back up my files! What can I do?

A First, don't panic! You did back up your important files, right? Do you have an emergency boot disk on hand? It might be possible to recover some files by booting with the emergency boot disk and then attempting to mount your OpenLinux partitions with the boot disk's mount command. If your Linux partitions still exist, it might also be possible to dump the contents of a partition to a compressed file on another volume and then extract pertinent files by hand (although this is tedious and not guaranteed). Always have a boot disk with recovery utilities on hand!

Q What's the best backup medium to use?

A There are many different types of removeable media on the market today. In the last 10 years, the price and cost per megabyte (a possible yardstick) of removeable optical drives has come down quite a bit. You have to decide on a balance of cost, speed, and reliability. You already have a wonderful backup included with this book—your OpenLinux CD-ROM, which is a working archive of nearly all the software used in this book. If you carefully preserve your /home and /etc directories, you can recover from a hard drive disaster to a working system within minutes.

23

Exercises

1. Use the tar command to create a compressed archive of your /etc and /home directories. How large is the file?

2. Use the du command to estimate the size of your OpenLinux system. How else can you find out how much space is required?

3. Investigate ways to prepare for a hard drive disaster. If your hard drive crashes, what files do you most fear losing? What steps can you take to prevent losing these files?

Hour 24

Using Scheduling to Automate System Management

In this hour, you'll finish by learning basic system administration skills. By now you know most of the commands used by sysadmins and are familiar with most of the tasks you have to perform to maintain your system for yourself or other users. This hour shows you how to put all this knowledge together in order to automate these tasks using the cron daemon and other OpenLinux scheduling programs.

By using the programs and techniques outlined in this hour, you can automate many different system administration jobs and maintain a healthy, well-running system. The first topic is the cron daemon, and then you'll learn how to administer the at command facilities for different users on your system.

Using the cron Daemon

The cron daemon, crond, is a program that starts after you boot Linux by the cron script in the /etc/rc.d/init.d directory on your system. This is done automatically, so you don't have to worry about starting the cron daemon every time you boot Linux. The crond program runs in the background and checks several files. The first is the crontab file in the /etc directory. A portion of this file reads as follows:

```
...
03  3  1  *  * root [ -x /usr/sbin/cronloop ] && /usr/sbin/
➥cronloop Monthly
04  4  *  *  6 root [ -x /usr/sbin/cronloop ] && /usr/sbin/
➥cronloop Weekly
05  5  *  *  * root [ -x /usr/sbin/cronloop ] && /usr/sbin/
➥cronloop Daily
42  *  *  *  * root [ -x /usr/sbin/cronloop ] && /usr/sbin/
➥cronloop Hourly
...
```

As you can see, this is a list of commands that runs tasks hourly, daily, weekly, and monthly. The cronloop command is a shell script that looks in the /etc/cron.d directory and then runs assigned tasks (in the form of shell scripts) according to files found in the Monthly, Weekly, Daily, and Hourly directories under /etc/cron.d. The actual shell scripts are found in the lib directory under the /etc/cron.d directory.

For example, if you look at the contents of the Daily directory, you find a file called 50update-locatedb that is linked to a shell script called update-locatedb in the /etc/cron.d/lib directory. This shell script, according to the preceding Daily /etc/crontab entry, builds a new database for the locate command at 5:50 a.m. each day:

```
#!/bin/bash
# Make/update the file name database

. /etc/cron.d/lib/functions

TMPDIR=$(cronloop_mk_TMPDIR)
declare -rx TMPDIR

# remove TMPDIR on exit
trap cronloop_rm_TMPDIR EXIT

OMIT="/tmp /proc /mnt /var/tmp /var/spool /dev /net /auto /amd /NetWare"

/usr/bin/updatedb --prunepaths="$OMIT" --netuser=nobody 2> /dev/null
exit 0
```

You can see that this script executes the `updatedb` command to build your system's `locate` database (see Hour 4, "Reading and Navigation Commands").

The `cron` command also searches the `/var/spool/cron` directory for personal `crontab` files with users' names. These files are created with the `crontab` command, found under the `/usr/bin` directory, and are used by your users to schedule their own regular tasks. How do you tell `cron` when to run these scripts, and how do you know that that `locatedb` script is run at 5:50 a.m. each day? Read on to see the format of the `cron` commands.

Managing User `cron` Scheduling

The `/etc/crontab` file is for scheduling regular, systemwide tasks. However, OpenLinux enables users to create their own `cron` schedules. As the root operator, if you want to enable your users to use the `crontab` command to create personal `cron` files under the `/var/spool/cron` directory, you first create two files: `/etc/cron.allow` and `/etc/cron.deny`. Under the `/etc/cron.allow` file, insert the root operator name, root, and the names of any users you want to enable access to the `cron` daemon. Because neither of these files exists in the default OpenLinux installation, all users have access to personal `cron` files. You can create files for your users with the `crontab` command, or users can create their own.

Always use the `crontab` command's `-u` command-line option. If you run `crontab` while running as root (after using the su command) and don't use this option, you receive a usage error message.

The next section shows you the format of the `crontab` file and the difference between the format of a `cron` entry for your Linux system and for individual users.

Setting Schedules with the `crontab` Command

The format of `crontab` entries is detailed in the `crontab` manual page under section 5. To see the manual page, use the following:

```
# man 5 crontab
```

This page provides specifications for `crontab` entries. However, to make things simpler, I'll give you some examples and at the end of this hour, some samples you can use. In general, the fields of an entry are as follows:

```
minutes    hour    day of month    month    day of week    command
```

Entries are usually separated with a space. However, cron entries in the /etc/crontab file must have a username inserted between the day of week entry and the command. A username field is not needed for personal crontab entries.

For example, if you run OpenLinux on a laptop but find that OpenLinux loses time after you wake up your laptop from a battery-saving sleep, edit the /etc/crontab file as root, and insert a command to update OpenLinux's time every minute from the laptop's hardware clock. Use the hwclock commmand in your crontab entry like so:

```
* * * * * root /sbin/hwclock --hctosys
```

Another handy entry can be used to build the database for the whatis command. For example, if you know that few users are present on your system early in the morning, schedule the makewhatis command to run at 2 a.m. with this setting:

```
30 2 * * * root /usr/sbin/makewhatis
```

On the other hand, as a regular user, you can have OpenLinux tell you the time every 15 minutes by first calling the crontab command with the -e command-line option, and then adding the following:

```
0,15,30,45 * * * * /usr/local/bin/saytime %
```

By default, OpenLinux launches the vim editor when you use crontab with its -e option. See Hour 18, "Personal Productivity Tools," for a tip on how to use the pico editor instead.

This tells the cron daemon to execute the saytime command to speak the time every 15 minutes. You can find the saytime command at the following:

```
http://metalab.unc.edu/pub/Linux/apps/sound/speech/saytime.tgz
```

If you want to hear the time every minute (though it might drive you crazy!), you can use this:

```
* * * * * /usr/local/bin/saytime %
```

Note that if you don't use a carriage return at the end of the line in your entry, you should use a percent (%) sign.

Here are some more sample entries:

```
* 22 * * 1-4 /usr/bin/wall 'Time for bed! Finished your homework yet?' %
0 1 * * * /usr/bin/find / -xdev -name core -exec /bin/rm {} \; %
0,30 * * * /usr/bin/tput bel >/dev/console %
* 12 25 12 * /bin/echo 'Happy Holidays' ¦ /bin/mail -s Greetings root %
```

The first example broadcasts a gentle reminder to all your users using the `wall` command at 10 p.m., Monday through Thursday; the number `22` represents the hour in 24 hour format, whereas the digits `1-4` represent Monday through Thursday. The second example (probably best suited for an `/etc/crontab` entry) runs the `find` command to search your system at 1 a.m. each morning for core files and deletes any found. The third rings your terminal's bell on the hour and half hour (`0` and `30` minutes), using the `tput` command to output. The last example sends a mail message at noon on December 25th to the root operator.

> The format and details of the fields in a `crontab` setting are explained in detail in Hour 18. These settings are also outlined in the `crontab` man page in section 5 of the man pages. See this man page for other sample settings.

24

Experiment with different tasks and times. Use OpenLinux to directly search results for files, reports of users online, and uptime reports to log files. Or use OpenLinux to email the information to you. You can also use `cron` to schedule backups when you're away or have your system shut down at a preselected time.

Managing User Scheduling with the `atrun` Command

The `cron` daemon is useful for scheduling regularly run programs or performing regular tasks, as you found out in Hour 18. The `at` command is useful for onetime or reminder jobs. Even though your Linux system is set up automatically after installation to handle user `at` scheduling requests, you should know how to manage the `at` command facilities.

By default, when a user uses the `at` command, the command is run with a default CPU priority. If too many users start running tasks with higher priorities or CPU-intensive programs in the background, your system's performance can be affected. Read on to learn to manage your system's `at` command facilities to provide the best performance and control possible.

Your system's `at` command facilities are enabled by the `cron` daemon, which, after starting when you boot Linux, checks the `/etc/crontab` file and sees the following entry:

```
...
# Run any at jobs every minute
* * * * * root [ -x /usr/sbin/atrun ] && /usr/sbin/atrun
...
```

As you can see, this is why the at command depends on the cron command: the cron command runs the atrun command, found under the /usr/sbin directory, each minute your system is up. The atrun command, in turn, searches the /var/spool/atjobs directory to look for jobs to run. For example, if the root operator creates a job at 14:46 for that day (2:30 p.m.), you see the following:

```
# at 14:46
at> echo Hello
at> <EOT>
warning: commands will be executed using /bin/sh
job 11 at 1998-12-14 14:46

# ls -l /var/spool/atjobs
total 1
-rwx------   1 root      root          842 Dec 14 14:43 a0000b00e85b62
```

To create an at command, use the word at, followed by a time. After you press Enter, the at > prompt appears. You can then enter a command and press Enter. To quit entering commands and save your job, press Ctrl+D. The at command then tells you the job number and the date and time the command executes. As you can see in the atjobs directory listing after entering the command, there is a job waiting for the root operator.

> You can get more specific information about waiting at jobs with the atq command. If you're the root operator, you see all the jobs your users have scheduled, instead of just the ones you've scheduled.

Controlling the batch and at Commands

Now that you know how the at facilities run, how do you control how at works, and for whom, on your system? One way to control how at works on your OpenLinux system is to use the atrun command's -l (load average) option. This option controls any jobs submitted by users using the batch command (discussed in Hour 18 with the at command). You can limit when batch jobs are run by specifying a number lower than 1.5 (the default), which tells atrun to run batch jobs only when the system load average is low. The load average is determined by a value in the /proc/loadavg file while the system is running.

You can see the current load average with the following:

```
# cat /proc/loadavg
0.20 0.11 0.03 2/50 1228
```

This shows the load average for the last 5, 10, and 15 minutes. You can also get the load average by using the uptime command, for example:

```
# uptime
  7:40pm  up  2:44,  3 users,  load average: 0.13, 0.08, 0.02
```

To enable your users to use batch nearly any time, change the value of the -1 option in the atrun command entry in your system's /etc/crontab file to a number higher than the default 1.5 value.

How do you control whether users are enabled to use the at command on your system? By default, after you install OpenLinux, anyone on your system can use the at command. There are four ways to control who can use the at command. Look in your /etc directory, and find a file called at.deny.

For security reasons, the at.deny file contains a list of OpenLinux users, including daemons or other processes, who are not enabled to use at. However, everyone else can use the at command to schedule jobs. If you want to prevent a user from using the at command, put the user's username in /etc/at.deny. If you don't want anyone on your system to use the at command (of course, this doesn't apply to you because you're the root operator), either create an empty at.allow file or delete the at.deny file from your /etc directory. If you want to enable only certain users to use the at command, create a file called at.allow in the /etc directory, and put the user's username in the file. If the at.allow and at.deny files are removed from the /etc directory, only the root operator can use the at command.

As a final, desperate measure to control at jobs as the root operator, list all at jobs scheduled on your system with the atq command, and if you see too many jobs scheduled, delete them with the atrm command, for example:

```
#  atq
Date                 Owner    Queue    Job#
20:00:00 11/26/97    bball    c        12
20:10:00 11/26/97    bball    c        13
20:15:00 11/26/97    bball    c        14
20:30:00 11/26/97    bball    c        15
...
# atrm 12 13 14 15 ...
```

Here, I'm assuming you see a long, long list of job numbers, and delete them. This is an abrupt, rude way to handle enthusiastic users. A better method might be to email the user to find out if there are tasks being run that can be automated during off-hour or off-peak times.

24

As the system administrator, you have complete control of scheduling commands for the users of your OpenLinux system. Think about tasks you should run hourly, daily, weekly, and monthly. With a little imagination, you can soon automate any custom tools, command lines, and reports you've created to help you manage your system. You can end up with more disk space, a better running system, and happier users.

Summary

This hour introduced you to a valuable skill required of all system administrators—the capability to schedule and automate complex tasks at any required date or time. This is one of the secrets to becoming a successful system administrator—to initially spend the time crafting a general-purpose approach or tool for system maintenance that can be used over and over again.

Q&A

Q I'd like to have my computer automatically connect to the Internet during the early morning hours and then download the day's news and email the news to me. Is this possible?

A Yes. Use the name of a shell script in your system's `crontab` file to initiate the connection, temporarily sleep, wake up, and then download and mail the news. For example, the `lynx` browser's `dump` option can be used with the `mail` command like this:

```
lynx http://some.newsource.com/news.html -dump ¦ mail
➡-s "news" root
```

Exercises

1. Create personal `crontab` settings to remind you several days in advance of important dates, such as anniversaries or birthdays. What do you think is the best way to have OpenLinux notify you?

2. Draw up a list of some important tasks to automate. How can you do this? When do you run the tasks?

INDEX

Symbols

% operator, 133
? option, 76
$EDITOR
    environment, 403
    variable, 320, 403
$HOME environment
    variable, 139
$PATH
    environment variable,
        128
    variable, 127
$PRINTER, 355
$PS1 environment vari-
    able, 129
$REMOTE_IP
    string, 232
    variable, 232
$TERMCAP variable,
    129
'ol bit bucket, 139
+rv (reverse video)
    option, 162
+x option, 494

-- -bpp (bits per pixel)
    option, 179
-- -bpp 16 option, 146
-- -bpp 16 startx option,
    374
-9 option, 464
–9 signal, 463
-a limit option, 462
-a option, 79, 334, 462
-atime option, 74
-b (backup) option, 99,
    101
-b option, 99, 333, 456
-bd option, 162
-bg option, 161
-boardSize small option,
    442
-bpp 16 option, 145
-bpp option, 145
—bytes option, 456
-C (color) option, 278
-C cls2 option, 219
-C command-line option,
    389
–c option, 245, 253, 453,
    459, 487

-calendar option, 406
–clear option, 394
—color option, 80
-COLUMN option, 339
-component-bar option,
    301
-d (decompress) option,
    82, 91, 114
-d (delete) option, 139
-d (directory) option, 492
–d option, 141, 253, 331
-digital option, 175
-display command, 400
-e (empty) option, 139
-e (erase) option, 501
-e (uninstall) option, 499
-E option, 110, 159, 342,
    403, 413, 526
-exec option, 459
-f (flood) option, 245
-f (script file) option, 332
-F option, 79-80, 96, 109,
    112, 333, 401
—fetchmailrc option, 252
-fg option, 161

-fr option, 96-97
—full-time option, 94
-fullscreen option, 169
-grab option, 445
–gray option, 394
-h (halt) option, 38
-h (help) option, 139
-h option, 275, 499
-Ha option, 462
-help option, 76, 84, 301, 369
-i (extract) option, 517
-i (install) option, 499-500
-i (interactive) option, 95, 99-101, 130, 134
-inroot option, 172
-k (keep) option, 252
-K option, 78, 456
—kilobytes option, 456
-l (list shells) option, 472
-l (list) option, 114, 139, 333, 405
-l (load average) option, 528
-l (long) format listing, 330
-l mode, 333
–l option, 213, 333, 340, 487, 491, 501
    usage, 464
-lock option, 171
-M command-line option, 88
-m option, 79, 487
-mail option, 260
—modem option, 201
–mono option, 394
-mtime option, 74, 517
-n 2 option, 89
-n option, 84, 91, 273
-news option, 282
—nosplash option, 369
-nw (no-window) option, 316
-nw option, 409

-o (create) option, 517
-O option, 342
-out option, 167
-p (package file) option, 500
-p (parent) option, 97
-p option, 98, 102, 252
—pkg option, 503
-pointsize option, 394
-popup option, 407
-q (query) option, 89, 499-500
-qi options, 505
-r (reboot) option, 38
-r (recursive) option, 95-96, 101, 457
-r (remove) option, 405
-r (restart) option, 475
-r option, 50, 82, 219, 273, 342
—remove-files option, 111
–rpn option, 383
-rv (reverse video) option, 162
-s (squeeze) option, 330
-s command, 461
-s option, 103, 118, 255, 453
-size option, 442
-sound option, 445
-speed option, 445
-stipple option, 383
—summarize option, 456
-T media option, 518
-t option, 114, 342, 345, 455, 457, 475, 518
—test option, 501
-topbottom option, 368
-tv option, 114
–tvtwm option, 394
-U (upgrade) option, 499, 501
-u option, 252, 319, 475, 525
-update 1 option, 175

-user option, 517
-useradm option, 469
-v (verbose mode) option, 487
-V (verify) option, 499
-v option, 112, 219, 517
-w 60 option, 342
-w option, 149, 204
-x (extract) option, 79, 112
-x option, 457
-xdev option, 75
-xrm option, 162
-z option, 110
.GIF, 360
.GIF format, 298, 368
.GIF graphics, 374
.html files, 377
.JPG, 360
    file, 375
    graphics file creating, 367
.PCX, 360
.pdf documents, 377
.pdf files, 377, 416
.ppm format, 368
.TIF, 360
.tiff file, creating, 368
.xpm format, 367
/boot directory, 50
/dev/modem, creating, lisa command usage, 201
/etc/fstab, 482
/JOIN command, 305
/LEAVE command, 305
/LIST command, 305
/proc directory, 483
/QUIT command, 305
0x224, 13
0x382, 13
3Com Palm Pilot Professional, 12
3Com/U.S. Robotics, 224
3D graphics, 391, 393
    generation, 391

3D scrollbars, 151
3D video card, 225
3D window buttons, 151
4-2-1 sequence, 494
490-based AMD CPUs, 11
56K ITU V.90 modems, 12
9-pin male serial port, 200

A

abbreviated hostnames, 297
about\ mozilla, 303
abuse, 442
accelerated video graphics, 43
account expiration, 471
account information, 228
account name, 241
account programs, dial-in, 251
acm, 442
Acrobat (Adobe), 377
active image window, 371
active Internet connection, 304, 308, 436
adduser command, 469
    usage, 469
Adobe Acrobat, 377
Adobe PhotoShop, 369
adventure game, 440
AfterStep, 155
    starting, 155
    usage, 156
    window manager, 152, 155, 157
agents, 250
    transport, 250
    user, 250, 253
        usage, 251

AIM (AOL Instant Messenger), 306
alarm dialog, 408
    box, 412
alarms setting
    knotes client usage, 411
Albanowski, Kenneth, 12
Almquist, Kenneth, 119
Alpha chip, 9
amaya Web browser, 310
ambient light conditions, 176
America Online (AOL), 300
    Web site, 306
America Online Instant Messenger (AIM)
    configuring, 306
    installing, 306
amstex system, 356
animation
    usage, 175
    selection, 172
anonymous access, 308
anonymous ftp connection, 291
AOL (America Online), 300, 306
    Web site, 306
APOP, 252
appearance, 152
append redirection operator, 125
Apple Macintosh, 176
appliance directory, 295
application
    default settings, 163
    resource file, 164
Application Starter, 184, 216, 234, 278, 323
    button, 180, 189, 192
    menu, 189, 195
application-launching definitions, 152
Applix, spreadsheets, 391
Applix Words, 327-328

Applix, Inc., 327
Applixware, 327-328, 391
    productivity suite, 329
    spreadsheet program, commercial features, 393
Appointments
    calendar, 175
    cron-type scheduling, 406
    entering, 411
    keeping, emacs usage, 409
    listing, 408
    reminders, 409
        creating, X11 ical client usage, 405
    time, 411
appt-delete command, 411
apropos command, 77-78, 410, 447
    usage, 72
apropos program, 71
ar command, 79
archived copies, keeping, 510
archives
    cpio archives, creating, 113
    creating, tape archive (tar) command usage, 110-113
archiving, 509
    Exercises, 521
    Q&A, 520
    Summary, 520
Artwork, installed, list, 422
as command, 79
ASCII
    command, 290
    database, 349
    file formats, 390
    list, 334

ash shell, 118-119
at (AT) command, 79,
  206, 208, 238, 400-401,
  403, 413
    controlling, 528
    creating, 528
    string, 207, 209
    usage, 400, 527, 529
at scheduling requests,
  527
AT&T System V UNIX,
  480
AT&V command, 209
ATA/IDE card drives, 57
ATA/IDE CD-ROM
  interfaces, 57
ATAPI, 13
ATDT, 233
ATI Rage II, 14
atjobs directory, 528
ATLx command, 221
ATM machines, 226
ATM0, 234
    command, 221
ATM1 command, 221
atq command, 401,
  528-529
atrm command, 402, 529
atrun command, 529
    usage, 527
Attorney General, 264,
  268
Auto Spellcheck
    enabling, 427
AutoFormat Chart
    StarCalc, 431
    dialog box, 431
AutoPilot, 423
    selecting, 424
Aztech Systems, 224

B

b file type, 492
backend system, 499
backgammon, playing,
  X11, 444
background, 374
background colors, 160,
  278
    setting, 168
background installation,
  23
background operator,
  214
background pattern, set-
  ting, 168
background processes,
  119, 131
background settings, 152
backspace key work, 433
backup
    BRU backup system
      configuring, 511
    cpio command usage,
      517
    device, 513
    devices creating, 512
    full, 510
    incremental, 510
    medium usage, 521
    name, 514
    network, 511
    performing considera-
      tions, 509
    scripts, 510
    strategy, 510
      devising, 510
      need, 510
    taper Script usage, 518
    tar (tape archive) com-
      mand usage, 515
    unattended, 515
    utility
      BRU 2040, 511

backup (-b) option,
  99-101
backup (BAK) files, 459
backup copy, 474
badblocks command, 487
BAK (backup) files, 459
bash (Bourne Again
  Shell), 30
    manual page, 140, 141
bash (Bourne Again
  Shell) shell, 121, 124,
  127-128, 138, 272, 403,
  406, 459, 462, 472
    features, 120
    running, 132
    usage, 139
BASIC, 396
    language, 395
basic system administra-
  tion, 451
batch command, control-
  ling, 528
baud rate, 199, 205, 210,
  348
bball, 497
    user, 135, 498
bball user, 350
BBS (Bulletin Board
  Service), 221
BBS (bulletin board
  system), 204, 208, 232
bc calculator, 396
bc command, 387
    language, 387
bc language interpreter
    usage, 386
bc manual page, 386
Beamer, 422
    usage, 423
BeOS, 35
Berkeley Software
  Distribution (BSD), 317,
  480
bg command, 132
biff man pages, 267
binary command, 290

binary transfer mode, 295
BIOS, 15, 19
  manager, 24
Bischoff, Michael, 444
bitmap client, 379
bitmap directories, 379
bitmap file format, 220
bitmap graphics files, 168
bits, number, 207
bits per pixel (-- -bpp) option, 179
block device, 492
block devices, input/output, 461
block moves, 319
blueprints, 379
boldfacing, 337
bookmarks, 83, 297
  editor, 297
boot device, 24
boot disk, emergency, 520
boot diskette, 17
boot problems, 474
boot-prompt option, 149
BootMagic, 18, 32, 38
  installing, 19, 33
  setup window, 32
borders, settings, 151
Bourne Again Shell (bash) shell, 120-121
Bradley, John, 375
Brief, 321
Brown, Mark, 299
Browsing, files, less command, 87-88
BRU
  built-in list, 512
  configuration utility, 512
  configuration window, 513
  device definition, 513

directory, 514
file selection, 514
software, 511
BRU 2040, 511
  restore utility, 511
BRU 2040 PE, 511-512
  software, 511
BRU backup system, configuring, 511
BRU-2040, 113, 180
brushes, 369-371
BSD (Berkeley Software Distribution), 42, 480
built-in calendar, 409
built-in help, 178, 318-320, 322, 327, 406
  command, 138, 290
built-in list, BRU, 512
built-in telecommunications scripting language, 206
built-in text editor, 206
builtins command, 122
Bulletin Board Service (BBS), 221
bulletin board system (BBS), 204, 208, 232
burn-in effect, 169
BusMouse, 46
buttons, 151, 156
  mouse, 159
bye command, 295, 291
bzip2 command, 115

C

c (create) option, 111
c file type, 492
C language, 395
C-Kermit, 225
CAD-like companion, 396

cal (calendar), 405
  program, 174
calculating
  kcalc client usage, 383
  X11 xcalc client usage, 383
calculator programming, bc language interpreter usage, 386
calculators, 382
Caldera, 7, 11, 23, 34, 148, 228, 264, 266, 328
  splash screen, 24
Caldera Open Administration System (COAS)
  System menu, 64
  usage, 53, 61
Caldera System, 9, 177
  Web site, 352
calendar (cal), 405
  appointment, 175
  built-in, 409
  checking, emacs usage, 409
  display program, 174
  mode, 410-411
  printing, 406
  program, 174
  size, 406
  views, 405
calendar files
  autosaving, 405
  group sharing, 406
  importing/exporting, 405
candidate files, 460
Canon BJC80, 12
capture software packages, 379
Card Services, 58
Cardinal, 224
carriage return, 340
Casas, Ed, 211
case statement, 139

cat (concatenate) command, 84-86, 88, 91, 116, 125, 329
  usage, 80-81
cd (change directory) command, 73, 79, 105, 118, 290, 295
  usage, 72, 91, 416
CD Database (CDDB), 437
CD music playing
  kscd client usage, 435
  xplaycd client usage, 435
CD-ROM controller type, 13
CD-ROM drive interfaces, 10
  ATA/IDE, 57
cdda2wav command, 447
CDDB (CD Database), 437
  Editor dialog box, 437
CDE (Common Desktop Environment), 178
cdp
  starting, 439
  command, 439
cdplay, 439
cell movement, drag-and-drop, 391, 393
cell selection, 429
Central Processing Unit (CPU), 8-9, 12, 225, 464
  activity, 461
  type, 13
change access permissions (chmod)
  command, 56, 126, 136, 204, 491, 495
    usage, 138, 436, 494
  program, 493
change directory (cd) command, 73, 79, 105, 118, 290, 295
  usage, 72, 91, 416

change group (chgrp) command, 497
change ownership (chown) command, 105, 493, 496
channel number, DMA, 47
character device, 492
character mode devices, 347
chart graphics, 432
chat
  discussions, 310
  manual pages, 247
  program, 227, 231, 246
Chen, Peter, 221
chess playing, xboard client usage, 442
chfn command, 469
  usage, 471
chgrp (change group) command, 105, 497
child directory, 97
Child subdirectory, 97
Chimera, 299
chipset, 14
chmod (change access permissions)
  command, 56, 126, 136, 204, 491, 495
    usage, 138, 436, 494
  program, 232, 493
chown (change ownership) command, 105, 493, 496
chsh command, 118, 130, 453, 472
Cirrus Logic, 14
civ command, 447
civclient command, 447
civserver command, 447
cksum command, 329
cleanup operations, 458
Client buttons, 181
client
  configuration, 162
  program, resources, 162

  resources, 162
  windows, customization, 160
clock client, 402
clockchips, 45, 47
cloobie, 497
  directory, 469
  user, 470
close command, 291
cmdlnopts, 139
cmdtool program, 158
COAS (Caldera Open Administration System)
  system menu, 64
  usage, 53, 61
code modules, 50
  loadable, 50
Collabra Discussions, 282
color, 151, 421, 425
  background, 160
    setting, 168
  custom, 319, 323
  foreground, 160
  image, 374
  monitor, 168
  name, database, 46
  printers, Epson Stylus, 352
  server, 48
  settings, 151, 317
  visual mode, 293
  window, 153
color (-C) option, 278
color depth, 45, 48, 148
  capability, 14
  usage, 145
  X11 server, 168
color-capable terminal
  emulator, 158-159
  window, 389
color-capable X11 console window, 159
colormap
  option, 374
  table, 374

column separator, 342
comm command, 329
comma-delimited list, 493
command interpreter, 118
command line, 296
  terminal, 374
command summary, getting
  apropos command usage, 76
  whatis command usage, 76
command-line access, 157
command-line argument, 127, 137
command-line editing, 119, 319
command-line editor, 122
command-line history, 119
command-line operators, 119
command-line option, 119-122, 130, 139, 158-162, 169-171, 212, 214, 219, 244, 275, 290, 299, 301, 316, 319-320, 330, 332-334, 338-339, 345, 374, 376, 389, 394, 400, 402, 406-407, 409, 442, 445, 452-453, 455, 457, 459, 461, 466, 469, 494, 515, 517-518, 525-526
command-line programs, 468
command-line prompt, 121
  options, 123
  usage, 119
command-line redirection operator, 254

command-line shell dialog box, 207
Common Desktop Environment (CDE), 178
communications program
  calling out
    minicom program usage, 204
    seyon X11 client usage, 206
  dialing out, 203
  setting up
    minicom program usage, 204
    seyon X11 client usage, 206
  usage, 199
    Exercises, 221
    Q&A, 221
    Summary, 220
component programs, 415
compress command, usage, 114
compressed text file, 201
compressing files, 110-112
  compress command, 114
  gzip command, 114
compression, 515
  usage, 510
  utilities, 115
computer
  abbreviated hostnames, 297
  connection, telnet command usage, 308
  memory, 460
  monitors, 169
  programs, 359
  software, interfaces, 314

concatenate (cat) command, 84-85
concatenate redirection operator, 125
config command, 286
configuration
  dialog box, 235
  menus, 152
  rules, 349
configuration file, 119, 151, 501
  fvwm, 151, 155
  processing, 152
configure command, 216
Connect button, 239
connection speed, 237
Connectix, 378
console
  games, 439
  keys, 453
  programs, interactive, 160
consoles, virtual, 9
context-sensitive help, 327
controller type, 13
conversion programs, 360
  graphics, 368
convert
  command, 367-368, 373
    man pages, 368
    usage, 368
  man page, 367
  program, 368
copy, straight usage, 510
copy in and out (cpio)
  archive, 517, 518
  command usage, 517
copying, files, cp command usage, 100-102
Copying/pasting operations, KDE usage, 166
core dump, 45, 459, 462

Corel, 338, 354
WordPerfect 8.0, 313, 326
cp command, 48, 96, 101-102, 105, 141, 209
usage, 100-102
CP/M operating system, 321
cpio (copy in and out)
archive, 517-518
creating, 113
command, 124
usage, 517
program, 109
CPU (Central Processing Unit), 8-9, 12, 225, 464
activity, 461
priority, 527
type, 13
CPU-intensive programs, 527
create (-o) option, 517
Create (c) option, 111
CRiSPlite editor, 180
printing, 336
usage, 324
Cristy, John, 373
cron command, 95, 525
cron daemon (crond), 403, 525-527
usage, 524
cron scheduling, 113
managing, 525
cron settings, 405
cron-type scheduling, 406
crond (cron daemon), 403, 525-527
usage, 524
cronloop, command, 524
crontab, 413
command, 405, 525
usage, 176, 403565
entries, 510, 525
file, 298, 404, 524
creating, 403
editing, 403

man page, 527
requests, 404
setting, 527
settings, creating, 530
cross-posting, 285
csh shell, 120, 459
usage, 462
csh-compatible shell features, 122
csplit command, 329
CSV files formats, 390
cu man page, 204
cu program, 204
currency conversions, 386
cursor fonts, 164
cursor modes, X11, changing, 164
cursor movement, 319, 329
control, desktop usage, 195
cursor shape, 143
cursor-driven list, 272
custom colors, 274, 319, 323
custom fonts, 323
custom keyboard function keys, support, 390
customer ID, 336
customized scripts, 224
cut and paste operations, 336
cut command, 329, 331
Cyrix CPUs, 11

D

d file type, 492
d option, 516
daemon, 231, 233, 246, 249, 253, 529
line printer, 349
mode, 251
software package, 227

dangling links, 458
data entry, field, 429-430
database
controls, 437
testing, 127
date/time (current), insertion, 323
Davis, John E., 274, 321
dc (desk calculator), 396-397
command, 382
program, 382
dd command, usage, 56
Debian, 7
debugging, 459
decompress (-d) option, 82, 91, 114
decoration, 152, 156, 177
default CPU priority, 527
default fonts, changing, 189
default graphical interface, 42
default Linux Shell, features, 120
default paper size, 353
default resolution, selection, 353
default resource settings file, 163
default settings, 340
default shell, 470, 473
default system editor, 321
default text editor, 403
default wallpaper, 169
default window manager, 153, 156-157
delete, 139
delete (-d) option, 139
deleting files, rm command usage, 95-96
delimiter, field, 331
desk calculations, dc (desk calculator) command usage, 382

desk calculator (dc), 396-397
  command, 382
  program, 382
desktop
  buttons
    appearance, 153
    location, 153
  client, Looking Glass, 144
  configuration scheme, 156
  display options, usage, 185
  menu, 153
  panel, 180, 189
    usage, 181
  pattern, 168
  trash can, 178
  wallpaper, changing, 187
device
  driver, printer, 348
  identifiers, list, 48
  name, showing, 483
  options, list, 48
df (free disk space) command, 79, 457
  usage, 454
dial string, 221
dial-in, account programs, 251
dialer script, 231, 246
dialing out, communications program usage, 203
dialog box
  command-line shell, 207
  installation, 23
Diamond SupraMax, 224
diary, 409
  emacs, 410
  entry, 413
  file, 411
dict file, 135

dictionary, personal, 426
digital cameras, 377
digital clock, transparent, 175
dir command, 82, 84
directory, 492
  archiving, 460
  backup, 510
  command-line option, 91
  compressing, 460
  creating, mkdir command usage, 96
  (-d) option, 492
  deleting, 460
  hierarchy, 127
  listing, 348
    dir command, 82
    long directory listing, 80
    sending, 338
    specification, 81
    vdir command, 82
  listing, ls command usage, 78-79
  manipulating, 93
  movement, cd command usage, 72
  reading, 78
  removing, rmdir command usage, 97
  searching, find command usage, 74
  tracking, 456
Disconnect button, 243
discontiguous selection, 429
discussion areas, 269
disk activity, 461
disk quota, 292
  setting, 473
  support, 8
disk space, 460, 468, 475
  conserving, 451
  freeing, 458

information
  getting, 454
  saving, 458
disk usage (du) command, usage, 455
display colors, customizable, 151
display command, 373
  menu, 374
  usage, 374
display font, settings, 152
display item, 278
display manager client, X, 149
dma, 52
DMA channel number, 51
DMA fields, 56
DMA values, 13
dmesg, 226
  command, 59, 201
  file, 201
  program, 225
DNS (Domain Name Server), 30, 228
  address, 242
  server, 229, 233, 236
doctor, 441
document
  auto-saving, enabling, 420
  correction, ispell command usage, 332
  creating, 425
    StarWriter usage, 423
  icon, 280
  preparing, 335
    Exercises, 357
    Q&A, 356
    Summary, 356
  printing, LPRng Printing System usage, 349
  spell checking, 332

templates, 424
viewing area, 377
document-creating wizards, 423
documentation, 346
domain entry, 239
domain name, 235
Domain Name Server (DNS), 28, 228
address, 242
server, 229, 233, 236
DontZap feature, 46
DontZoom feature, 46
DOS COM1 port, 209
DOS filesystem, 104, 488
partition, 483
DOS floppies, 489
DOS form, 490
DOS operating system, 321
DOS partition, 17, 32, 74, 95, 104, 454, 515
DOS rebooting, 16
DOS serial ports, 200
DOS utility, 516
DOS VFAT filesystem, 483
down command, 440
downloading, visual status, 297
DR-DOS, 10, 12
drag-and-drop actions, 178
drag-and-drop cell movement, 391, 393
drag-and-drop controls, 408
drag-and-drop icons, 36
drag-and-drop notes, 405
draggable track numbers, 438
drawing editing programs, 379
drawing programs, 367
drawing tools, 423

drive designators, 490
drive space, 460
drivers
downloading, 201
software, 225
drop-down menu, 185
DT command, 206
du (disk usage) command, 79, 521
directory tracking, 456
usage, 455
du report, 456-457
dual-boot computer, 18, 35, 379
dump, 510
dump command, 124, 483
dump files, screen, 167
dump format, X11 windows, 167
dump graphics file, X11 window, creating, 367-368
dump option, 530
dunnet, 441
dvi files, 345
dvips command, 346
dynamic IP address, 232, 235

E

e command, 440
echo command, 139
ed command, 106, 314
editing
keys, 371
macros, 327
sessions, 370
tools, 369
editor, 335
defaults, 317

EDITOR environment, 413
variable, 475
Editor Macros (Emacs), 315
edquota, usage, 475
edquota command, usage, 475
efax
command, 214, 216
manual pages, 211
setting up, 218
software, 211
system, usage, 211
egrep command, 108-109, 126
Eissfeldt, Heiko, 444
electronic mail, 252, 257, 261, 274, 442
documents, sending, 323
program
distribution, pine, 320
pine, 319
utilities, 250
Ellis, James, 269
elm
mail program, 256
configuring, 255
usage, 255
program, 253, 262
Elm Development Group, 255
Emacs/emacs (Editor Macros), 87, 315, 316, 328, 413
appointment
commands, 410
functions, 410
calender mode, 411
command, 409
diary, 410
editor, 71, 133, 315, 322, 332, 409, 441
games, playing, 441

non-X11 version, 316
text editor, 409
usage, 409
users, 315
X11 version, 316
email, 223, 249
address, 277, 278, 298,
420
configuration, 419
configuring, 249
getting, 249
message, 262
program, 476
retrieving
fetchmail usage, 251
setting up, 249
usage, 226
embedded text, 426
emergency boot disk, 516
empty, 139
empty (-e) option, 139
Empty menu, 182
emulator, terminal, 134
encryption, usage, 510
End Horizontal Retrace
value, 47
End Vertical Retrace
value, 47
end-of-file (EOF) charac-
ter, 126
end-of-input character,
126
end-of-input string, 127
end-of-text (EOT), 400
Enhanced Software
Technologies, 511
enlargement/reduction,
424
env command, 273
environment variable, 76,
117, 127, 129, 139, 272,
400, 452, 475
$EDITOR, 320
environmental variables,
115

EOF (end-of-file) charac-
ter, 126
EOT (end-of-text), 400
Epson, 378
printer, 13
Stylus, color printers,
11, 352
eqn utility, 356
equipment, inventory, 13
erase (-e) option, 501
erase option, 516
error messages, 499
esr (Raymond, Eric S.),
251
ESS, 13
EtherFast 10/100 card
(Linksys), 60
Ethernet
cards, 11
interface, 53, 57
configuring, 61
Interface Configuration
dialog box, 62
network interface, con-
figuring, 41
PC card, 59
Ethernet/modem combi-
nation cards, 57
Evans and Sutherland
Computer Corporation,
151
events, alarms, 405
ex command, 314
ex editor, 319
exec option, 484
executable programs, 121
exit command, 452, 498
expand command, 329
Expect button, 236
Explorer window, 423
export command,
128-129
export statement, 272
ext2 filesystem, 455,
482-484, 488, 508
ext2 partition, 483

extended filesystem, 486
extended partition, 18
extract (-i) option, 517
extract (-x) option, 79,
112
extract (x) option,
515-516

F

f (file) option, 111-112
Falstad, Paul, 122
FAQs (Frequently Asked
Questions), 71
fast browsing, Lynx com-
mand usage, 299
Fast Ethernet interface,
57
FAT16, 18
FAT32, 18
fax
class support, 13
filenames, 216
graphic format, 219
machine, phone num-
ber, 220
number, 203
protocols, 211
receiving, 211
sending, 211
shell script, 214-215,
219
software/documenta-
tion, 211
fax command, 214
trying, 212
usage, 213, 216
fax documents, sending,
218
ksendfax client usage,
216
mgetty+sendfax usage,
218

fax script, 216
  queries, 213
**faxing, efax system
  usage, 211**
**fdformat (floppy disk
  formatting) command,
  486**
**fdprm, floppy drive
  parameter file, 485**
feature creep, 460
Fejes, Frank, 155
felt, 396
fetchmail
  command, 252
  FAQ, 267
  program, 253
  running, 253
  usage, 251
fg % command, 133
fg command, 132
fgrep, 400
  command, 108-109,
    273, 453, 458
  search, 118
field delimiter, 331
field insertions, 425
fields, 423
File (f) option, 111-112
**file compressing/com-
  pression, 110-112, 367**
  compress command
    usage, 114
  gzip command usage,
    114
file formats, 423
  opening/saving, 427
  word processing, 327
file handling, 479
  Exercise, 507-511
  mc (Midnight
    Commander) Program
    usage, 104
  Q&A, 507
  Summary, 505
file ownership, 479
  changing, chown com-
    mand usage, 496

  managing, 491
file permissions, 131, 491
  changing, chmod com-
    mand usage, 494
  flags, reading, 492
file reading, 78
  head command usage,
    88, 90
  more command usage,
    86
  tail command usage,
    88, 90
**File Transfer Protocol
  (FTP)**
  document retrieval, 323
  listing, 178
  programs, usage, 290
  server, remote, 303
  usage, 226
filename, 141
  completion, 116
**file-number extensions,
  460**
files
  access, 479
  attachments, 258
  backup, 510
  browsing, less com-
    mand usage, 87-88
  combining, cat (con-
    catenate) command
    usage, 84-85
  conversions, 368
  copying, cp command,
    100-102
  creating, touch com-
    mand usage, 94
  deleting, rm command
    usage, 95-96
  extensions, 368, 379
  finding, whereis com-
    mand usage, 75
  insertion, directory
    mode, 320
  linking, 102-103
  listing, cat (concate-
    nate) command usage,
    84-85

  locating, locate com-
    mand usage, 76
  manipulating, 93
  matching, find com-
    mand usage, 74
  names, extension, 360
  procurement, File
    Transfer Protocol
    (FTP), programs
    usage, 290
  renaming, mv command
    usage, 98-99
  retrieval, 290
    ftp command usage,
      290
  searching, 105
    grep command
      usage, 108-109
    regular expressions,
      106-108
  selection, 514
  size, 331
  transfers, 223
    programs, 206
  uncompressing,
    110-112
**filesystem, 18, 53, 69,
  131, 454**
  access, mount com-
    mand usage, 482
  creating, 486
  definition, 480
  disk usage, getting
    du command usage,
      455
  DOS, 488
  ext2, 484, 488, 511
  extended, 486
  mounted, 479
  mounting, 479, 482
  mounting/unmounting,
    482-483
  navigating, 72, 481
  OpenLinux, 481
  option, 455
  pop-up menu, 488

removable, 484
rows, 483
searching, 72
statistics, getting, df
  command usage, 454
support, 9
vfat, 482
Win9x, 482
filesystem handling, 479
Exercise, 507-511
Summary, 505
**filesystem table (fstab),
474, 479, 507**
columns, 483
editing, 483
entries, 484
understanding, 482
file\, //, 303
filter, 134
commands, 332
programs, applying,
  367
usage, 329, 331, 347
writing, 265
Filtering Mail FAQ, 267
**financial applications,
396**
financial tools
Exercises, 397
learning, 381
Summary, 396
**find command, 74-75, 82,
105, 135, 459-460, 517,
527**
usage, 74
finding, files, 75
**finger command, usage,
472**
flash card, 453-454
flash memory, 13
card, 453, 484
flash RAM card, 95, 483
floating windows, 369
flood (-f) option, 245
**floppies formatting,
KFloppy client usage,
488**

floppy device
high-density, 487
location, 485
type, 485
floppy disk
formatting, 484
  (fdformat) com-
    mand, 486
unmounting, 489
**floppy drive, 10, 24, 484,
510, 513**
parameter file (fdprm),
  485
tape driver, 518
floppy utilities, 484
flow control, 237
**fmt command, 329,
340-342**
focus, 152
policy, 153, 193
fold command, 329
follow-up message
posting, 270
reading, 270
font, 342, 346
attributes, 425
changes/changing, 158,
  335
configuration, 419
control, 423
custom, 323
effects, 425
internalization, 8
italic, 173
X11 listing, xlsfonts
  usage, 172
footnotes, building, 423
forecasting, 387
**foreground color, 160,
278**
**formatted text, streams,
349**
**formatting commands,
329**
TeX, 346
formatting program, 338
formatting toolbar, 425

formatting utilities, 356
Fortran, 395
Fox, Brian, 120
**fractal drawing program,
171**
fractal image, 171
**free command, display-
ing, 461**
**free disk space (df) com-
mand, 457**
usage, 454
free editor, 315
**free graphical interface,
38**
**Free Software
Foundation (FSF), 71,
114, 315, 329, 394**
**Free Wingz spreadsheet,
finding, 390**
**free-for-personal-use
spreadsheets, 387**
Freeciv, 447
**freeware spreadsheet
program, 390**
front-end utilities, 499
**FSF (Free Software
Foundation), 71, 114,
315, 329, 394**
**fstab (filesystem table),
474, 479, 506**
columns, 483
editing, 483
rows, 483
understanding, 482
ftape driver, 518
**FTP (File Transfer
Protocol)**
document retrieval, 323
listing, 178
programs, usage, 290
server, remote, 303
usage, 226
**ftp command, 291,
293-293, 308**
running, 291
usage, 290

ftp connection, anony-
mous, 291
ftp directory, 292
ftp login, 292
ftp program, 291
   demonstration, 392
   usage, 291
ftp server, 291
ftp user, 291
ftp\, //, 303
full backup, 510
fvwm
   command, 149
      display process, 152
   configuration file, 151
      customization, 155
   configuration menu,
   153
   root menu, 154
   window manager, 152,
   154-155, 157
      configuring, 151
   X11 window manager,
   144
fvwm2, window manager,
324

G

g (global) command, 331
Galaga, playing, X11,
444
games
   console, 439
   emacs, playing, 441
   simulation, 447
   X Window System ,
   442
   X11, 442
garbage characters, 140,
233, 247
Gateway, 28
gcal calendar, 405

General Public License
(GPL), 9, 71, 394
Genius, 378
geometric settings, usage,
300
geometry
   option, 160
   settings, 174, 316, 369,
   376
      usage, 160
   specifications, 161
get command, 290-291,
291
getopts command, 139
getty command, 210
Ghemawat, Sanjay, 405
GID (group ID/identifica-
tion), 469, 474, 497
GIF format, 136
giftopnm command, 136
Gildea, Stephen, 174
GIMP (GNU Image
Manipulation Program)
   Frequently Asked
   Questions (FAQs),
   373
   image editor, 370
   information, 373
   installation, 369
   menu system
      accessing, 371
   resource files, 369
   running, 371
   usage, 369
Gleason, Mike, 293
glint, 396
   command, 310, 505
   program, 511
   usage, 476
global (g) command, 331
GNU, 9, 315
   text-utils package, 329
GNU chess engine, 442
GNU file utilities pack-
age, 94
GNU GNOME, develop-
ment, 176

GNU Image
Manipulation Program
(GIMP)
   Frequently Asked
   Questions (FAQs),
   373
   image editor, 370
   information, 373
   installation, 369
   menu system, access-
   ing, 371
   resource files, 369
   running, 371
   usage, 369
GNU software, 394
   packages, 71
GNU text, 88
gnuchess manual page,
441, 443
gnuchess program, 440
gnuplot
   documentation, 395
   FAQ, 395
   program, 381, 394-395
   usage, 394
go west command, 440
GPL (General Public
License), 9, 71, 394
grace-period warnings,
476
graphic configuration,
178
graphic conversions, 136
graphic files, 379
   converting, 367
graphic images, 426
graphic insertions, 423
graphic interfaces, 520
graphic utilities, 167
graphical interface, 12,
23, 143, 145, 234, 502
   default, 42
   free, 42
graphical interface pro-
gram, 118, 223, 502

**graphical mouse configu-
  ration utility, 165**
graphics
  application capture soft-
    ware packages, 379
  artists, 367
  card, 15, 46, 144-145,
    147, 149, 176, 509
    detection, 24
    type, 14
  chipsets, 43
  conversion, 374
    program, 219, 369,
      379
  converting/viewing, 367
  directory, usage, 375
  editor, 379
  formats, 211, 359, 374
  hardware, 42
  icons, 151
  images, 367
  insertions, 425
  manipulation
    filters usage, 370
  monitor, 147, 176
  package, interactive,
    396
  pads, 45
  programs, 144
  services, 42
  stream, 368
  translating/translation,
    211, 359
  viewing, xv command
    usage, 374
graphics editing
  GIMP (GNU Image
    Manipulation
    Program) usage, 369
  ImageMagick usage,
    373
  programs, 379
graphics file, 373
  .jpg, creating, 367
  conversion, 379

  formats, 368, 376
    Linux, understand-
      ing, 360
    types, 360
  image quality, 368
  loading, 374
  translation, 293
graphics tools, 359
  Exercises, 379
  Q&A, 379
  Summary, 379
grep command, 109, 112
  usage, 108-109
grep programs, 105
groff command, 343
  line, 344
groff distribution, 346
groff formatter, 345
  usage, 342
**groff formatting pro-
  gram, 344, 349**
groff program, 346
  usage, 357
group
  command, 496
  membership, 498
  ID/identification (GID),
    469, 474, 497
  ownerships, changing,
    497
  root, 497
group, changing
  chgrp usage, 497
  newgrp usage, 497
Groups Server, 282
**gs PostScript, inter-
  preter/companion view-
  er, 211**
gunzip program, 114
gv client, 347
gv command, 376-377
  usage, 376
gv previewer, 342
gv program, 345-346
gvim, 317
gvimrc resource files, 318

**gzip command, 70, 110,
  115**
  usage, 114
gzip compression, 515

H

Haardt, Michael, 390
hackers, 9
halt (-h) option, 38
Hankins, Greg, 201
Har-Peled, Sariel, 439
hard disk, interfaces, 10
**hard drive, 24, 38, 370,
  461**
  adding, 483
  controller, type, 13
  crashes, 521
  dividing/mapping, 18
  partitioning, 14, 19, 23
  partitions, 14
  preparing, 18
  removable, 510, 518,
    516
  size, 13
  space, 10, 13, 369, 417,
    460, 474, 476
    amount, 22
  storage space limits,
    473
hard limits, 462, 475
hard link, 102-103
  creating, ln (link) com-
    mand usage, 102-103
hardware devices, 377
hardware vendors, 17
Hart, Robert, 230, 247
harvesting, software, 277
hash signs, 499
Hayes 56K Accura, 224
**Hayes-compatible
  modem, 202**
head command, 89, 329
  usage, 88-90

header line, 218
help
    built-in, 406
    command, 121, 290
    man command usage,
        69
help (-h) option, 139
here redirection operator,
    126
Hewlett-Packard, 11, 378
hierarchical root, 151
high-density drives, 486
high-density floppy
    device, 487
high-end network server
    operations, 9
highlighting, 87
Hind, David, 58, 61, 201
home directory, 138, 154,
    163, 181, 270, 293, 317,
    321, 494
home office management,
    StarOffice usage, 415
    Exercises, 433
    Q&A, 433
    Summary, 432
hopalong
    client, 171
    program, 171
horizontal rule, 425
horizontal scrolling, 319
horizontal sync ranges,
    26, 45
host IP (Internet
    Protocol) address, 292
hostname, 228, 276, 290,
    308
    abbreviated, 293
    command, 64, 309
    definitions, 357
    resolution, 53
HOSTNAME entry,
    changing, 64
HP 344Cbi, 12
HP printer, 13

HP printer-control lan-
    guage, 345
HPCL, font type, 13
HTML (HyperText
    Markup Language)
    documents, 327
    file formats, 390
    format, 72
    message format, 262
    page composition, 302
http\, //, 303
hwclock commmand, 526
hyperlinks, insertion, 423
HyperScript scripting
    language, 390
hypertext links, 34
HyperText Markup
    Language (HTML)
    documents, 327
    file formats, 390
    format, 72
    message format, 262
    page composition, 302
hyphenation controls,
    423

I

i (information) option,
    500
I/O address fields, 52
ical calendar, 405
ical client, 406-407
    usage, 405
ical X11 client, 174
icon, 152, 157
    appearance, 153
    assignments, 152
    definitions, 152
    dock, 151, 156, 158
    drag-and-drop, 33
    fonts, 153
    location, 153
    menus, 156

id Software, 445
IDE, 10, 13
ide driver, 518
ide tape drives, 518
if ... then statement, 139
ifconfig command, 62,
    127, 227, 467
    usage, 243
IM (Instant Messenger),
    306
    buddy, 307
    running, 310
image
    files, editing, 370
    quality, graphics file,
        368
    thumbnails, 373
image window, 369, 374
    active, 371
image-processing pro-
    gram, 369
ImageMagick
    information, 374
    man pages, 368
    package, 368
    software package, 375
    usage, 373
IMAP, 252
incremental backup, 510
indenting, 335
indexes, building, 423
info command, 121
information
    display, 152
    fields, 465
    hiding, 389
    option (i), 500
    prompt, 87
infrared (IR) port, 12, 13
initdefault line, 150
Initialization String,
    field, 238
initialization table, 149
inittab, 149
inodes, 475
    listings, 475

input/output, 461
inserted typesetting commands, 347
insmod command, 52, 227
    usage, 64
install (-i) option, 499-500
INSTALL.148, 16
installation dialog boxes, 23
installation script, 433
installed artwork, list, 422
Instant Messenger (IM), 306
    buddy, 307
    running, 310
interactive (-i) option, 95, 99-101, 130, 134
interactive commands, 465
interactive console programs, 160
interactive controls, 465
interactive editors, 329
interactive graphics package, 396
interactive mode, 386
interactive prompting, 291
interactive spelling program, 332
interface
    computer software , 314
    graphic, 520
    serial-port, 378
    usage, 352
internal IDE drive, 64
internal modem, 200
internal script variables, 139
Internet, 251, 443
    active connection, 304, 308, 436
    activities, 242

address, 303
browsing, 289
    Exercises, 310
    Q&A, 310
    Summary, 309
clients, 260
    starting, 436
    type, 310
database, 436
documents, FTP retrieval, 323
downloading, 289
    Exercises, 310
    ncFTP program usage, 293
    Q&A, 310
    Summary, 309
email
    configuring, 249
    Exercises, 268
    Q&A, 267
    Summary, 267
file transfer programs, 289
links, 37
logging on, 307
navigation, 323
news
    configuring, 269
    Exercises, 287
    Q&A, 286
    Summary, 286
sites, 334
    Linux, 377
Internet connecting, 223
    Exercises, 248
    hardware, 224
    minicom command usage, 232
    OpenLinux usage, 15
    ppp-on script usage, 233
    Q&A, 247

Summary, 247
connection, 226, 291
Internet Protocol (IP), 53
    address, 28, 63, 229, 232, 235, 243, 246, 251, 295
    static, 228
    addressing, 228
Internet Relay Chat (IRC), 309
    chatting, 304
Internet Service Provider (ISP), 223, 226, 249, 251-253, 258-259, 267, 270-273, 279-280, 283, 286, 289, 392, 293, 306, 387, 467
    connecting, 232, 254
    Hookup HOWTO, 15
    host servers, 245
    mail retrieval protocol, 262
    name, 241
    needed information, 228
    phone number, 241
interpreter/companion, viewer, 211
Interrupt Request (IRQ), 47, 201
inven command, 440
Investment Intelligence Systems Corporation, 390
io, 52
Iomega Zip, 510
    disks, 484
    drive
        backup device, 513
        usage, OpenLinux usage, 64
    Plus drive, usage, 65

IP (Internet Protocol), 53
  address/addressing, 28,
    228, 229, 232, 235,
    243, 246
    static, 228
IR (infrared) port, 12, 13
**IRC (Internet Relay
  Chat), 309**
  chatting, 304
irc /HELP command, 305
irc command, 304, 310
  help facility, 305
irc program, 304
ircII, man page, 305
irq, 52
**IRQ (Interrupt Request),
  51, 201**
  sound card, 13
IRQ 5, 13
IRQ fields, 56
ISA/PCI modems, 224
Islamic dates, 410
iso9660, 482-483
iso9660 filesystem, 455
**ISP (Internet Service
  Provider), 223, 226, 249,
  251-253, 258-259, 267,
  270-273, 279-280, 283,
  286, 289, 392, 293, 306,
  387, 467**
  connecting, 232, 254
  Hookup HOWTO, 15
  host servers, 245
  mail retrieval protocol,
    262
  name, 241
  needed information,
    228
  phone number, 241
**ISP-Connectivity mini
  HOWTO, 230**
ispell
  command, usage, 332
  dictionary, 334
  manual page, 333
  package, 333

  program, 332-333
  spelling checker, 332
italic fonts, 173

J

**Java Development Kit
  (JDK), 310**
Jaz drive, 510
  utility, 490
**JDK (Java Development
  Kit), 310**
**jed, configuration files,
  322**
**jed editor, configuration,
  321**
jmacs editor, 321
job control, 8, 119, 132
  facilities, 134
jobs command, 133
**joe configuration files,
  321**
joe editor, 321
join command, 329
Joy, Bill, 317
Joy, William, 122
JPEG format, 169, 187
**JPEG graphic formats,
  178**
jpico editor, 321
jstar editor, 321
Julian dates, 410
Jung, John, 299
junk
  email, 264, 266, 268
  mail, 264-266, 277
Juno, 251
justification, 425

K

**K Desktop Environment
  (KDE), 28, 53, 54, 62,
  72, 96, 216, 224, 269,
  302, 322, 324, 383-384,
  411, 487, 501**
  applications, locating,
    192
  configuration manager,
    35
  configuring, KDE
    Control Center usage,
    184
  Control Center, 177,
    184, 189, 191, 192
    usage, 184
  cursor movement con-
    trol, desktop usage,
    195
  default fonts, changing,
    189
  desktop, 188
    actions, performing,
      180
    panel, usage, 181
  desktop, features, 180
  Exercises, 192
  exploring, 177
  fonts dialog box, 190
  help, 180
  keyboard/mouse set-
    tings, changing, 191
  menu editor, 182
  panel, menu, editing,
    182
  properties, changing,
    193
  Q&A, 192
  screensaver, changing,
    188
  sessions, 193
  starting, 179
  Summary, 195

system sounds,
  installing, 190
themes, 32
title bars, changing, 193
usage, 145
wallpaper, changing,
  187
window buttons, chang-
  ing, 193
windows, 190
**K Development
  Environment (KDE),
  12, 53, 158, 176, 234,
  278, 282, 383, 436, 447,
  481**
  clients, 163
  Control Center, 169
  graphical interface, 279
  session, 38, 149
  taskbar, 425
  usage, 148, 166, 169,
    421
  users, 170
**K Display Manager
  (KDM), 32, 150**
  Display Manager
    Options, usage, 185
**K display manager
  (kdm), login screen, 186**
**K file manager (kfm),
  180**
  usage, 183
kcalc
  calculator, 384
    font/display, 385
  client, usage, 383
  dialog box, 384
kCalc button, 384
Kcalc calculator, 180
kcsd
  client, 435
  dialog box, 436
  player, 436

**KDE (K Desktop
  Environment), 28, 49, 54,
  62, 72, 96, 216, 224, 269,
  302, 322, 324, 383, 384,
  411, 487, 501**
  applications, locating,
    192
  configuration manager,
    35
  configuring, KDE
    Control Center usage,
    184
  Control Center, 177,
    184, 189, 191, 192
    usage, 184
  cursor movement con-
    trol, desktop usage, 195
  default fonts, changing,
    189
  desktop, 188
    actions, performing,
      180
    panel, usage, 181
  desktop, features, 180
  Exercises, 192
  exploring, 177
  fonts dialog box, 190
  help, 180
  keyboard/mouse settings,
    changing, 191
  menu editor, 182
  panel, menu, editing,
    182
  properties, changing,
    193
  Q&A, 192
  screensaver, changing,
    188
  sessions, 193
  starting, 179
  Summary, 195
  system sounds,
    installing, 190
  themes, 35
  title bars, changing, 193
  usage, 145

  wallpaper, changing,
    187
  window buttons, chang-
    ing, 193
  windows, 190
**KDE (K Development
  Environment), 12, 53,
  158, 176, 234, 278, 282,
  436, 447, 481**
  clients, 163
  Control Center, 169
  graphical interface, 279
  session, 38, 149
  taskbar, 425
  usage, 148, 166, 169,
    421
  users, 170
**kde command, 49,
  144-145, 148**
**KDE-aware applications,
  166**
kdehelp client, 192
**kdm (K display manag-
  er)**
  client, 35
  login screen, 38, 186
kdm graphical login
  bypass process, 41
  display, usage, 48
**KDM (K Display
  Manager), 35**
  Display Manager
    Options, usage, 185
kedit editing window, 336
kedit editor, 322
  client, usage, 322
keep (-k) option, 252
Kelley, Colin, 394
kernel, 8, 50, 118, 226
  message, 149
  process directory, 483
**kernel module, 58, 201,
  227, 348, 482**
  boot-time control, 53
  configuring, 55
  sound, 52
  support, loading, 64

kerning, 423
key character, layout, 46
keyboard, 24
    activity, 171
    configuration, 45
    internalization, 8
    server shutdown, 45
    settings, 152
    type, 13
    values, settings, 151
    X86Config, 46
keyboard commands, 154, 156, 327, 421, 425, 431
    shortcut, 322
    WordStar-compatibile, 321
keyboard/mouse settings, changing, 191
keys, number, 13
KFloppy
    utility, 487
    client usage, 488
kfm (K file manager), 180
    usage, 183
Kibell, Justin C., 445
kill command, 131, 134, 234
    usage, 133, 463
killall command, 134
Kimball, Spencer, 369
Klasen, Lambert, 444
kmenuedit editor dialog box, 182
kmix, 57
knews, program, 286
knotes alarms, 412
knotes client
    note-taking features, 412
    usage, 411
Knuth, Donald E., 346
Kodak DC20/DC25, 378
Kojima, Alfredo Kenji, 155

koules, 442
kpackage, 396, 481
    client, 447, 501
    command, usage, 499
    file selection, 502
    program, 511
    usage, 501
Kpilot client, 12
kppp, 223
    client, 15, 224, 229, 234, 247, 272
    command, usage, 234
    configuration, finishing, 238
        dialog box, 234
    Configuration dialog box, 235
    connection, configuring, 235
krn
    client, 280
        usage, 278
    configuring, 278
    dialog, features, 280
    identity dialog, 279
    newsreader, 270
        features, 279
        programs, 269
    newsreading, window, 281
    program, 279, 284
    search, 287
kscd client, usage, 435
ksendfax client, 216
    usage, 216-217
ksendfax directory, 216
ksh, manual page, 122
ksh shell, 120, 129
    command, 122
kterm program, 158
kvt program, 158
kvt terminal
    emulators, 158
    window, 216

L

L (lookup) command, 333
l file type, 492
language type, 46
languages, 421
laptop users, 10, 46
LaStrange, Tom, 156
LaTeX file formats, 390
LaTeX macros, 346
latex system, 356
layouts, templates, 424
Lea, Iain, 271
less command, 87-88, 91, 116, 225, 388
    usage, 87-88
less pager, 91, 135, 201, 339, 348
lesskey option, 87
letter-size paper, 342
libraries, 346
    software, 369
lilo command, 17, 34
LILO (Linux loader), 17, 21, 32
    boot prompt, 49, 120, 149
    installation, 39
    message screen, 34
limit command, 462
line editors, 314
line printer
    command, 135
    daemon (lpd), 351
        starting, 349
    spooling system, 349
line termination, 237
line wrapping, 204
    disabling, 46, 149
link (ln) command, 102, 105
    usage, 102-103
linked objects, 327
links, 423

Linux
archive Web site, 175
booting process, 8
calculators, 382
chat groups, 310
console mode, 453
custom partitioning
  scheme, 21
definition, 8
distribution, 9, 326, 332,
  368
documentation, 303
environment, word
  processors, 313
evolution, 50
fax machine, 214
file system, 502
file types, 492
filesystem, 474, 480
games
  relaxation/playing,
    435
  Exercises, 448
  Q&A, 447
  Summary, 447
graphics file formats,
  understanding, 360
installation, 458
  beginning, 24
  finishing, 28
  guide, 39
  HOWTO, 25
installation preparation, 7
  Exercises, 22
  Q&A, 22
  Summary, 21
installing, 23, 454
  Exercises, 39
  Q&A, 39
  Summary, 38
Internet sites, 377
kernel, 118, 201, 226,
  460, 464, 474, 480
  module, 227
Laptop Pages, 11

logging, 473
logging in, 35
native format, 484
newsgroups, 270
programs, 220, 349,
  416, 459
rebooting, 35
repository, 392
required software, 226
root partition, 22
runlevel, 210
running determination
  uptime command
    usage, 466
  w command usage,
    466
shell, features, 120
shutting down, 35
sites, 290
software management
  kpackage command
    usage, 499
  lisa command usage,
    499
  rpm command
    usage, 499
subjects, 270
swap partition, 13, 24,
  370
system, 121, 210-211,
  226, 289, 466,
  472-473, 479, 493
  backups, 511
  dialing in, 208
  setting up, 208
  upgrade, 451
text editor, 257
users, 7, 266
utilities, 509
**Linux Basic Installation
  Guide, 108**
Linux browsers
  usage, 293
**Linux Installation and
  System Adminisration
  (lisa)**
  utility, 351

**Linux loader (LILO), 17,
  21**
**Linux Network
  Administrators Guide,
  228, 243**
**Linux partition, 7, 17, 26,
  32, 474, 482**
  creating, 20
  information, 26
**Linux System
  Administrator's Guide,
  98**
**Linux User Group
  (LUG), 17**
**lisa (Linux Installation
  and System
  Administration), 396,
  468**
  administration program,
    202
  command, 253, 310,
    346, 481
    usage, 201, 351, 469,
      473, 499, 502
  menu, 470
  program, 511
  usage, 357, 476
  utility, 351
Lisp, 396, 410
list, 139
**List (-l) option, 114, 139,
  333, 405**
list (ls) command, 491
**list files/directories (ls)
  command, 291**
list shells (-l) option, 472
list variable, 139
listing
  directories, 78-79
    dir command, 82
    directory specifica-
      tion, 81
    long directory list-
      ing, 80
    vdir command, 82
  files, cat command,
    84-85

lmove, command, 286
ln (link) command, 102, 105, 203
    usage, 102-104
lo (loopback) interface, 63
lo option, 63
load average (-l) option, 528
loadable code modules, 15, 50
loadable code sound modules, 50
LOADLIN program, 17
LOADLIN.EXE, 17
local printers, 349
locate
    command, 76-77, 82, 524
        usage, 76
    database, 525
    ifconfig command, 227
locatedb script, 525
locating, files, 76
lock file, 237
log information, 351
logged-in users, 467
login entries, verifying, 232
login name, 228, 230
login prompt, 147, 309
login screen, 31, 147
login script, 235
    building, 238
    dialog box, 236
logins, restricting, 472
long (-l) format listing, 330
long directory listing, 80
long-filename filesystem, 453
Longyear, Al, 230, 247
look command, 334, 440

Looking Glass, 183
    client, 148, 152
    desktop, 148, 302, 324
        client, 144
    menu item, 154
lookup (L) command, 333
loopback (lo) interface, 63
loopback device, 357
loopback interface, 245
Lotus 1-2-3 format files, 390
Lotus formats, 390
low-level format, 486
low-level SCSI protocol, 65
lp device, 348
lp.o module, 348
lp.o parallel printer kernel module, 348
lpc commands, 350
lpd (line printer daemon), 351
    starting, 349
lpost command, 286
lpq command, 349
lpr command, 349, 357
lpr spooling system, 349
lprm command, 350
LPRng, 349
    configuration file, 351
    permissions control file, 351
    Printing System, usage, 349
    software distribution, 351
ls (list files/directories) command, 291
ls (list) command, 491
ls -aF option, 82
ls -l listing, 492
ls -l option, 80, 83, 232
ls -R option, 82

ls command, 79, 82, 105, 107, 123, 130, 203, 330, 492
    usage, 78-79
ls man page, 80, 84
ls program, 336
lsa, 130
lsac, 130
lsc, 130
lsl, 130
lsmod command, 52
LS_COLORS, 80
Lucid, Inc., 315
LUG (Linux User Group), 17
lurk, 274
luser, 285
Lynx
    browser, 299, 530
        usage, 300
    command, usage, 299
    editor, usage, 356
    features, setting, 299
    Web browser, 321, 346, 377, 387

M

m option, 463
Macintosh, Apple, 176
MacOS, 35
macros, 152, 346
    definitions, 152
    documentation, 344
    files, 151
    inserting, 346
    languages, 356
    LaTeX, 346
    man page, 344
    mm manuscript, 344
    set, 345
    support, 423
    typesetting, 344
Mager, Neil, 410

magnetic tape (tp) command, 516
mail, 53, 255
  command, 255, 530
  daemon, 249
  message, 266, 472
    composing, 258
  retrieval protocol, 262
  sending, mail programs usage, 253
  server, 229, 251-253, 258, 262, 263, 279
    protocol, 267
  utilities, 250
mail information, getting
  mailstats command usage, 467
  pppstats command usage, 467
mail program, 262, 268
  message creating, 255
  responding, 254
  usage, 253
Mail Transfer Agent, 253
mail-retrieval protocols, 251
mailer configuration screen, 258
mailing list, 263
mailstats command, usage, 467
mailstats program, 467
make command, 216
makeindex command, 356
MakeTeXPK program, 346
makewhatis command, 77, 526
makewhatis program, 71
man command, 69-71, 73, 78, 87
  usage, 69
man macros, 343
man page macros, 344

manipulating
  directories, 93
  files, 93
manipulation commands, 93
  Exercises, 116
  Q&A, 115
  Summary, 115
manual page, 70
  creating, 343
manual sound configuration, 57
margins, 342
Mariano, Adrian, 385
Massachusetts Institute of Technology (MIT), 42, 151
Master Boot Record (MBR), 17, 32
math applications, 396
math co-processor, emulation, 8
math tools
  Exercises, 397
  learning, 381
  Summary, 396
mathematical formulas graphing, gnuplot usage, 394
Mattis, Peter, 369
mattrib, 489
Mayan dates, 410
mbadblocks, 489
MBR (Master Boot Record), 17, 32
mc (Midnight Commander)
  command, 95-96
  Program, features/usage, 104
mcd, 489
McGough, Nancy, 267
mcheck, 489
mcopy, 489
mcr command, 324
md5sum command, 329

mdel, 489
  command, 491
mdeltree, 489
mdir, 489
  command, 490
media
  removable, 521
  usage, 510
Media Key, entering, 417
memory
  card, 453
  information, getting, 460
  protection, 8
  reclaiming, kill command usage, 463
  space, 159
  usage, 461
  virtual, 9
memory reporting
  free command usage, 461
  vmstat command usage, 461
memory-efficient rxvt terminal, usage, 159
menu-enabled X11 terminal, 158
menus
  fonts, 153
  settings, 151
message, 246
  author, 270
  browsing, 270
  contents saving, 270
  creating, 255
  display, 274, 277
  file, 89
  headers, display, 274
  list, 260
  posting, 270
  reading, 270
  reminder, 411
MetaLab, 292, 295
mformat, 489
mgdigest, 265
mget command, 291

mgetty command, 218
mgetty program, 220
mgetty+sendfax, usage,
 218
mgetty+sendfax pro-
 grams, 221
Microchannel-based PCs,
 11
Midnight Commander
 (mc), 118
 command, 96
 Program
  features, 104
  usage, 104
minfo, 489
minicli client, 384
minicom
 command, 227
  usage, 232
 communications pro-
  gram, 205
 manual page, 232
 phone directory, 206
 program, 201, 203, 221,
  225, 232, 247
  running, 204
  usage, 204
 running, 210
MIT (Massachusetts
 Institute of Technology),
 42, 151
mkdir command, 97-98,
 102, 105, 139, 265
 usage, 96
mke2fs command, 486
mkmanifest, 489
mlabel, 489
 command, 490
mm manuscript macros,
 344
mmd, 489
mmount, 489
 manual page, 491
mmove, 489
mode lines, matching,
 146
mode value, usage, 146

modeline, 317
 fine-tuning, 47
 parts, 47
 time display, 317
 understanding, 47
modems, 11, 13, 57
 56K ITU V.90, 12
 bank, 226
 card, 200
 connect number, 228,
  230
 connection, 205, 226
 device, 237
 Hayes-compatible, 202
 internal, 200
  profile, 209
 port, 348, 492
 setting up, 199-200
 speed, 207
  setting, 207
 supports, 212
 testing, 200
 troubleshooting, 468
 type, 13
modules
 appearance, 153
 location, 153
MODULES.148, 16
monitoring program, 461
monitors
 horizontal refresh, 14
 maximum resolution,
  14
 resolution capabilities,
  147
 settings, 45
 specifications, 46
 vertical refresh, 14
monochrome display,
 162, 168
monochrome server, 48,
 161
Moolenaar, Bram, 317
more command, 86
 usage, 86

Mosaic, 299
Mosaic Web browser, 298
Motorola FM56, 224
mount
 manual page, 455
 point, 457
mount command, 454,
 516
 manual page, 480
 usage, 482-483
mount directory, 481
mount options, 483
mount point, 480
mounted filesystem, 452,
 454, 457
mouse acceleration, 165
mouse activity, 171
mouse button, 159, 164,
 166, 371, 425, 433
mouse commands, 156
mouse configuration, 41
 utility, graphical, 165
mouse cursor, 154, 166
mouse modes, X11,
 changing, 164
mouse pointer, 143, 147,
 154
mouse pointing devices,
 10
mouse settings, 152
 customization, 165
mouse settings, changing,
 191
mouse support, 320
 enabling, 277
mouse type, 13
Mouse-cursor aware
 mode, 274
mouse-driven toolbars,
 393
mouse-handling func-
 tions, 152
Mozilla, 310
mpage (multiple page)
 command, 342
mpartition, 490
mpg127 command, 447

MPU, 13

mrd, 490

mren, 490

MS-DOS (MSDOS), 12, 201
  floppies, 489
  partition, 516

mt (magnetic tape) command, 516

mtools package, 489

mtoolstest, 490

mtype, 490

multiuser runlevel, 45

multilingual terminal emulator, 158

Multimedia, 436

multiple page (mpage) command, 342

multiple-column option, 341

multiple-view format, 169

multitasking, 8

multiuser systems, 473

music playing, xplaycd client usage, 438

Mustek, 378

mutt, 268

mv command, 96, 99-101, 105, 139, 141
  usage, 98-99

Mwave adapter, 17, 224

mxp, 396

mzip, 490

N

n command, 440

Nagree, Yusaf, 518

name server entry, 239

naming, files, 98-99

Nano-Warrior, 331

Nation, Rob (Robert), 151, 402

native format, 484

navigation
  file system, 72
  keys, 300
  pwd (print working directory) command usage, 72

navigation commands, 69
  Exercises, 91
  Q&A, 91
  summary, 90

NCEMRSoft, 297

ncftp
  command, 297-298
  status bar, 298
  usage, 298, 310

ncFTP program, usage, 297

Nelson, Philip, 386

NeoMagic, video graphics display, 146

netcfg tool, 15

Netmask, 28

Netscape, 148, 180
  command, 260
  Discussions, 282
  newsreading, window, 282
  web browser, 377, 464

Netscape Communications, 300

Netscape Communicator, 260, 269, 282, 303-304
  exploring, 300
  Linux version, 303
  Web browser, 300

Netscape Messenger, 249, 261
  email configuring, 260
  email usage, 260
  mail server, 262
  text sending, 262

Netscape Navigator, 387

Netscape Web page, 303

netstat command, 227
  usage, 244

netstat manual page, 244

netstat –r command, 245

NetWare 3.x, utilities, 10

NetWare 4.x, utilities, 10

NetWare NDS client, 10

network, 13
  backups, 511
  connection, 127, 289, 310
  installation, 416
  IP addresses, 246
  ports, 466
  printers, 349
  server operations, 9
  services, 53
  traffic, 245
  windowing system, 42

Network Information
  configuring, COAS (Caldera Open Administration System) usage, 61
  getting
    mailstats command usage, 467
    pppstats command usage, 467
  Service, 53

Network Object Model Environment, 176

Network Transparent Access (NTA), 178

networking cards, 10

networking enhancements, 349

networking protocols, 8

new group (newgrp) command, 497-498

newgrp (new group) command, 497-498

newmail, man pages, 267

news readers, 257

news server, 229, 258, 272, 279, 282

newsetup, command, 286

newsgroups, 247, 257, 271, 285, 287
  articles, navigating, 281
  command, 286
  index file, 270
  list, developing, 271
  message, 270
  posters, 285
  posting, 278
  subscribing/unsubscribing, 270
newsreader, 132, 244
  functions, 270
newsreading, 279
  session, 278, 467
  utilities, 286
  window, 281-282, 284
newusers command, 477
NEXTSTEP, operating system, 155
Nikon, 378
nl command, 329
nn, program, 286
NNTP (nntp), 272
  options, 279
  server, 258, 273, 274, 279
NNTPSERVER (nntpserver), 272
  file, 272
  variable, 275
no-window (-nw) option, 316
noblank option, 170
non-X11, emacs command, 409
non-X11 version, emacs, 316
nongraphical environment, 160
nonvolatile RAM (NVRAM), 234
Not UNIX project, 315
notes, cron-type scheduling, 406
notices, listing, 408
nroff command, 343, 388

nroff script, usage, 357
nroff text formatting program, 71
NTA (Network Transparent Access), 178
NVRAM (nonvolatile RAM), 234

O

object files, 459
object-oriented editors, 379
octal notation, 495
od command, 329
off-hour times, 529
off-peak times, 529
office suite, 415
  definition, 415
office-automation productivity suite, 415
Office50 folder, 418
oleo spreadsheet, 390
open command, 291
  usage, 309
Open Sound System (OSS), 57
  drivers, 15
Open Source, software, 251
OpenLinux, 80, 90, 102, 110, 113, 175, 178, 249, 267, 274, 282, 286, 384, 387, 390, 399, 402, 525, 527
  1.3, 252
    distribution, 204
  boot disks, 23
  booting, 24
    planning, 17
  booting process, 8
  command, 70, 87, 115
    line, 491

configuring, 149, 223
console, 147
default configuration, 149
definition, 9
directory, 187, 460
discussions, 264
distribution, 116, 177, 203
document printing, 335
documentation, 303
editing programs, 335
equipment
  problems, 11
  requirement, 10
  support, 10
file, 460
  deletion, 96
  system, 103, 192, 416, 458, 481, 499
full installation, 51, 360
graphics programs, 359
installation/installing, 61, 223, 249, 469, 511
  best way, 22
  booting alternatives, 17
  CD-ROM booting, 15
  creating, 22
  decision, 15
  floppy booting, 16
  planning, 14
Internet connection, 15
kernel, 474
kernel modules, opening, 54
logging in, 72, 144, 148, 186
  xdm command usage, 149
modems usage, 224
module file, 348
organization scheme, 480
partition, 482, 516

Preparation, dialog box, 19
printer, 353
printing
   handling, 347
   system, documentation, 351
program, 401
rebooting, 150
running, 476
scheduling programs, 523
session, 34, 118, 147, 313
shutting down, 38
software, 18, 504
sound configuration, 50, 57
sound utilities, 53
system, 76, 80, 99, 123, 163, 208, 220, 239, 242, 249, 295, 416, 420, 451, 502-503, 511, 516-521, 528, 530
   initialization table, 149
   log, 60
   users, 473, 477
usage, 64, 510
users, 223, 264, 347, 367, 473
utilities, 359
workstation, 416
operating system, 9, 11, 14, 17-18, 42, 225, 250, 270, 286, 324, 359-360, 457
   CP/M, 321
   DOS, 321
   kernel, 8
operating system-specific drivers, 11
OSS (Open Sound System), 57
   drivers, 15

output redirection, 84
output stream, 367
ownerships, changing
   chgrp usage, 497
   newgrp usage, 497

P

p command, 382
package file (-p) option, 500
Package Manager, 499
page composition, HTML, 302
page length option, 340
page numbering, 335
pagers, 86, 151
   module definitions, 152
   saving, 342
   size, 152
painting programs, 367
palettes, 370
Palm III, 12
Palm Pilot Professional (3Com), 12
Panel Configuration dialog box, 182
paper size
   default, 353
   list, 353
paradise, 442
paragraph justification, 320
Parallel Line (PLIP) interface, 15
parallel port, 378
   assignment, 13
parallel printer, 347
   devices, 347
   kernel module, 348
parallel-port devices, 64
parallel-printer ports, 352
parent (-p) option, 97

parent directory, 97
parent subdirectory, 97
parity, 199, 207
   setting up, 207
partition
   adding, 483
   DOS filesystem, 483
   ext2, 483
   extended, 18
   primary, 18
   sizes, 454
   swap, 482
Partition Magic, 24-25
partitioning
   hard drive, 23
   scheme, 25
PartitionMagic, 18, 22
   Caldera Edition
      hard drive recognition, 21
      setup program, 20
   commercial version, 22
Pascal, language, 395
Passthru PostScript printer, 354
passwd
   file entry, 470
   text database, 470
passwd command, 469-470
passwords, 27, 149, 228-230, 240, 252, 295-296, 309, 452, 469
   authentication, 241
   changing, passwd command usage, 470
   entering, 172, 484
   entries, verifying, 232
   field, 470
   mandatory changes, 471
   protection, 171
paste command, 329
pasted graphics, 327
path hierarchy, 127
pathname, 72, 233, 295, 413, 437, 440

pattern, 370-371
  options, 87
  usage, 172
pbm2g3 program, 219
pbmtext command, 219
pbmtext program, 219
PC card, 13
  controller, 58
  modem, 225
  slot, Type II/TypeIII, 57
  Winmodem, 58
PC notebook, 46
PCDOS, 12
PCL (Printer Control
  Language), formats,
  345
PCMCIA, 16
  card, 10
    enabling, 57
    service, enabling, 41
  controller, 59
    type, 13
  device, 201
    manager, 225
  modem card, 200
  support, 58
PCMCIA-HOWTO, 201
PDF documents, 377
pdksh (public domain
  Korn shell), 121, 453,
  459, 462
  shell, 91
perf, 477
peripheral controls, 53
permissions, 331
  appearance, 494
  changing, 493-494
  files, 491
  flags, 491, 494
    reading, 492
  managing, 491
  root, 499
personal dictionary, 333,
  335, 426
personal name, 258

personal productivity,
  399
  tools, learning, 399
personal productivity
  tools, 178
  Exercises, 413
  Q&A, 413
  Summary, 412
personal reminders,
  scheduling, at command
  usage, 400
personal tasks, schedul-
  ing, at command usage,
  400
Peterson, Chris, 174
PhotoShop (Adobe), 369
pico, 204
  editor, 126, 149, 160,
    257, 259, 314, 322,
    332, 336, 413, 526
    features, 319
  text editor, 126, 136,
    229, 257, 272, 403,
    473, 475-476
PID (process number),
  463, 470
pilot-xfer command, 12
pine
  compose mode, 258
  distribution, 476
  electronic mail pro-
    gram, 319
    distribution, 320
  email program, 126,
    286, 413, 476
  mail folder, 260
  mail program, 132, 136,
    249
    configuring, 257
    usage, 257
  mail reader, 133
  mailer, 132, 321
    configuration screen,
      258
  program, 253, 255, 257,
    262, 265

Pine features, 319
ping command, 227
  usage, 63, 245, 248
pipelines, 329
pipelining, 134
pipes, 298, 329-330
  experimenting, 368
  usage, 134, 367
pixmap directories, 379
placement, 152
Plass, Johannes, 376
platforms, multiple, 8
play option, 439
PLIP (Parallel Line)
  interface, 15
plot command, 395
plug-in features, 299
plug-in filters/tools, 369
plug-ins, 303, 369
pnews, command, 286
pnmcrop command, 368
pnmflip command, 368
pnminvert command, 368
pnmrotate command,
  367-368
pnmscale command,
  367-368
pnmsmooth command,
  367
pnmtile command, 368
pnnsmooth command,
  368
point-and-click client,
  488
point-and-click dialog
  configuration, 178
point-and-click interface,
  117, 281
Point-to-Point Protocol
  (PPP), 223, 225, 249
  connections, manual
    start/stop, 232
  HOWTO, 15
  interface, 467
  manual setup, 229
  network connections,
    289

protocol, 247
sessions, 267
starting
    kppp command
        usage, 239
    xisp command
        usage, 243
stopping
    kppp command
        usage, 239
    xisp command
        usage, 243
support, 227
**Point-to-Point Protocol
(PPP) connection, 224,
226, 233, 251, 267, 269,
289, 293, 304**
    checking, 243
    configuring
        kppp command
            usage, 234
        xisp client usage,
            240
    scripts, editing, 230
    starting, 299, 306
    stopping, 234
**Pop-up menus, 156, 178,
181, 188**
pop-up reminder, 400
pop-up root menus, 156
POP3, 252
ports
    infrared (IR), 12
    parallel-printer, 352
**PostScript, 345-346, 349,
356**
    documents, 377
        compressed, 376
    driver, 354
    font type, 13
    format, 221, 376
    graphic, 214, 376
        files, 211, 213
    previewer, 376
    printer, 349, 352, 421
    usage, 394

PostScript file, 70
    conversion, 347
    creating, 342
    viewing, gv command
        usage, 376
Powell, Patrick, 349
PowerQuest, 19, 22
PowerQuest Corp, 18
ppa module, 65
ppmtogif command, 136
**PPP (Point-to-Point
Protocol), 15, 223, 225,
249**
    interface, 467
    manual setup, 229
    network connections,
        289
    protocol, 247
    sessions, 267
    starting, kppp command
        usage, 239
    stopping, kppp com-
        mand usage, 239
    support, 227
**PPP (Point-to-Point
Protocol) connection,
224, 226, 233, 251, 267,
269, 289, 293, 304, 405**
    checking, 243
    configuring
        kppp command
            usage, 234
        xisp client usage,
            240
    manual start/stop, 232
    scripts, editing, 230
    starting, 299, 306
    stopping, 234
ppp-off script, 234
ppp-on file, 227, 230
**ppp-on script, 231-232,
246-247**
    usage, 233
ppp-on-dialer file, 227
**ppp-on-dialer script,
231-232**

ppp0 interface, 245
    diagnosis, 243
ppp0 listing, 244
pppd
    command line, 231
    manual pages, 247
**pppd daemon, 231, 233,
246**
    software package, 227
pppstats command
    usage, 467
pppstats program, 467
**pr command, 329, 338,
340-342**
pr program, 339
preformatted tapes, 516
**presentation graphics,
client, 415**
previewer, 374
    PostScript, 376
**primary DNS address,
242**
primary partition, 18
print filters, 349
print jobs, 349, 351
    deleting, 351
print option, 215
print previews, 391, 393
**print working directory
(pwd), 118**
    command, 105
    usage, 73
printed pages, order, 342
printenv
    command, 400
**printenv command, 127,
129, 273, 453**
printer, 11
    accounting information
        utility, 351
    activating/resetting, 348
    capabilities, 349, 353
    configuration, 419
        lisa command usage,
            351
    device driver, 348

disabling/enabling, 350
filter, 351
installation, 421
model/type, 13
Passthru PostScript, 354
port, 492
PostScript, 421
reconfiguring, 357
spool queue, 351
warnings, 421
**Printer Control
Language (PCL), for-
mats, 345**
printing
commands, 347
operation, cancelling,
355
requests, 349
support, 389
WordPerfect configura-
tion, 354
process, 8
number (PID), 131,
134, 463, 470
reporting, 455
status (ps) command,
131
processes (procs), 461
processors, multiple, 8
procmail, 266
approach, 260
configuring, 264
filters, 265
recipes, 266, 268
writing, 265
service, 266
usage, 265
procs (processes), 461
**productivity programs,
324**
productivity tools, 399
profile file, 128
profile resource file, 117
program
borders, 374
documentation, reading,
376

lists, 157
memory, dumps, 459
names, 137
operation, menus, 369
running, background,
131
programmers, 313
programming
constructs, support, 119
editor, 324
project folder, 424
creating, 423
prompt command, 291
prompt string, 129
**prompting, interactive,
291**
properties, changing, 193
**ps (process status) com-
mand, 79, 131, 133,
463-464**
manual page, 464
PS/2 keyboard, 13
ps@presario printer, 350
psc command, 388
**psychoanalyze-pinhead,
441**
**public domain Korn shell
(pdksh), 121, 453, 459,
462**
**public domain sc
(spreadsheet calculator)
spreadsheet, usage, 387**
**public domain software
license, 329, 340**
put command, 290
**pwd (print working
directory), 118**
command, 73, 79, 105
usage, 73

Q

q command, 382
Q key, 88
q option, 170, 273

QIC-80 format, 513
Quake, 50
playing, X Windows,
445
server browser, 446
quake.x11, 374
**query (-q) option,
499-500**
queue option, 214
Quick Erase, 489
QuickCam, 378
support, 379
quota
command, usage, 476
hard limits, 392
quota manipulation
quota command usage,
474
quotaoff command
usage, 474
quotaon command
usage, 474
qweb, 299

R

r option, 273
r— option, 494
**RAM (random access
memory), 45, 47**
amount, 13
**RAM (Read Access
Memory), 41, 43, 420**
Ramey, Chet, 120
rasmol, 396
**RAWRITE3 program,
starting, 16**
**RAWRITE3.COM pro-
gram, 16**
Raymond, Eric S., 25
esr, 251
rc.boot script, 482
rclock, client, 175, 402

Read Access Memory (RAM), 45, 47, 420
read command, 140
read permissions, 470
read write execute (rws), sequences, 494
read write execute (rwx), permission, 496
read-only iso9660 filesystem, 455
read-write enabled file, 475
reading
directories, 78
files, 78
head command, 88, 90
more command, 86
tail command, 88, 90
reading commands, 69
Exercises, 91
Q&A, 91
summary, 90
README files, 243
real-time monitor, 461
realname, 276
RealNetworks, 304
RealPlayer
application, 303
downloading, 310
installing, 310
plug-in, 304
reboot (-r) option, 38
receive (rz) files, 308
recipes, writing, 264
recording script, 56
recursive (-r) option, 95-96, 101, 457
Red Hat, 7, 15, 226, 476, 481, 499, 505
redirection operator, 123, 125, 254, 329, 333, 339, 517
registers, 382
registration number, 336

regular expressions, 82
definition, 106-108
regular reminders scheduling, crontab command usage, 403
reminder
creating, 405
cron-type scheduling, 406
message, 411
scheduling, 403
remote computer, 290, 293, 308
remote fax machine, 216
remote FTP server, 303
remote host computer, 248
remote retrieval, 273
remote server, 273
remote shell (rsh), 119
remote Web page, 303
removable filesystems, 484
removable hard drive, 95, 510
remove (-r) option, 405
removeable driver, 518
removeable hard drives, 518, 516
removeable media, 521
removing, directories, 97
renaming, files, 98-99
reply, direct mailing, 270
replyto, 276-277
resolution
capabilities, monitor, 147
support, 48
virtual, 147
resolv.conf file, resolving, 229
resource file, 121-122, 162, 319
resource settings, 151, 162
file, default, 163

resource string, 162
format, 163
X11, 163
resources file, X11, 171
restart (-r) option, 475
restores
BRU backup system configuring, 511
cpio command usage, 517
performing considerations, 509
taper Script usage, 518
utility, BRU 2040, 511
restricted editor, 321
retrieval utility, usage, 251
reverse Polish notation (RPN/rpn), 382
calculator, 383
reverse video (+rv/-rv) option, 162
revert-buffer command, 335
revision control, 424
rgb (red, green, and blue) values, 161
RJ-11 telephone jack, 200
rjoe editor, 321
rm command, 97, 100-101, 105, 141, 215, 452, 459
usage, 95-96, 476
rmdir command, 96, 98, 105
usage, 97
rmv script, 137, 140
modifying, 141
trying, 138
ro option, 484
rodentiometers, 10
root, 77
cursor, image, 164
directory, 516
menus, pop-up, 156
partition, 454

permission, 499
display, 152, 157, 169, 180, 401
   pictures display, 168
window, utility, 168
   program, 164
root operator, 46, 52, 125, 128-129, 140, 149, 201, 204, 208, 216, 219, 229-230, 233, 240, 320, 323, 328, 336, 350, 416, 452-453, 462, 468, 470-471, 479, 483-484, 487, 493, 495, 497-498, 527
   running, su (substitute user) command usage, 452
root-permission commands, 502
route command, 227
   usage, 245
rpm, 481
   command, 310, 346, 458, 501
      usage, 58, 499
   database, 456, 499, 502, 504
   program, 110, 511
   usage, 476
RPMS directory, 502
RPN/rpn (reverse polish notation), 382
   calculator, 383
rsh (remote shell), 119
rtin, program, 273
Rumsey, Joe, 444
run configuration file, 121
runlevel
   multiuser, 49
   X11, 49
rw- option, 494
rwx (read write execute)
   permission, 496
   sequences, 494

rxvt
   window, 275
   client, 159-160
   program, 158
rxvt terminal, 131, 136, 166, 175, 402
   emulator, 134, 159
   starting, 160, 161
   usage, 159
rz (receive) files, 308

S

s button sizes, 421
s command, 440
s off option, 170
s option, 170
S.U.S.E., 7
Saggaf, Muhammad M., 206
SANE (Scanner Access Now Easy), Web pages, 378
Savola, Tom, 299
saytime command, 526
sc (spreadsheet calculator), 389, 397
   commands, 388
   program, 387-388
   usage, 387
sc spreadsheet, 133
scale lines, 466
Scanner Access Now Easy (SANE), Web pages, 378
scanners, 377
   drivers, 378
   software, 379
   support, 377
scavenger, 442
schedules setting, crontab command usage, 525

scheduling, 515, 523
   Q&A, 530
   programs, OpenLinux, 523
   requests, 527
   Summary, 530
   Workshop, 530
scotty, 119
scqref command, 388
screen
   captures, 143
   elements, customizable, 151
   size, 45, 48, 164
   space, 131
screen dump
   creating, 167
   files, 167
screen resolution, 147
   label, 47
screen savers
   settings/programs, 169
   usage, 168
   X11, 169
screen-oriented programs, 253
screensaver, changing, 188
screenshot
   capturing, 167
   seeing, 167
script, 151
   customized, 224
   file (-f) option, 332
   shells, 136
   variables, internal, 139
scrollbars, 151, 281, 377
   3D, 151
scrolling, 87
   list, 284
   window, 147, 279, 293
SCSI (Small Computer System Interface), 10, 13, 378
   drive, 64
   driver, 518

interface, 57, 483, 518
protocol, low-level, 65
support, loading, 65
**search and replace, 323,
336**
  capabilities, 423
  procedures, 425
search criteria, 379
**search-and-destroy mis-
sion, 460**
searching
  directories, 74
  file, 105
    grep command,
      108-109
    locate command, 76
    regular expressions,
      106-108
    system, 72
    whereis command,
      75
  less command, 87
searching commands, 93
  Exercises, 116
  Q&A, 115
  Summary, 115
**secondary DNS address,
242**
**security enhancements,
349**
sed command, 331
sed filter, usage, 329
**sed s (substitute) com-
mand, 331**
**self-extracting shell
script, 306**
send (sz) files, 308
sendfax
  configuration files, 218
  command, 219
  program, 218-220
  software, 218-219
sendmail, 249
  daemon, 253
  distribution, 467
  program, 267

**serial boards, supported,
10**
**serial communications
modem/port, 199**
serial interfaces, 57
serial mouse, 46
**serial port, 24, 220, 225,
348, 466, 492**
  9-pin male, 200
  assignments, 13
  configuring, 205
  DOS, 200
  list, 202
  monitoring, statserial
    command usage, 468
  number, 13
  recognition, 225
  setup, 199, 210
  speed, 203
    setting, 206
  troubleshooting, 468
serial printers, 348
**serial-line connections,
234**
**Serial-Line IP (SLIP),
234**
serial-line support, 201
serial-port interface, 378
server browser, 446
server operations, 9
**ServerFlags,
  XF86Config, 46**
**session management, 151,
178**
set command, 127
**set floppy disk parameter
(setfdprm) command,
486**
**setfdprm (set floppy disk
parameter) command,
486**
**setup command, 286,
325, 416**
setup script, 422

seyon
  client, 207
  communications pro-
    gram, 206
  manual page, 208
  program, 203, 207, 221,
    247
  X11 client, usage, 206
sg command, 498
sh shell command, 122
shadow
  entry, 471
  file entry, 470
  password, system, 471
shared libraries, 8
**shared software libraries,
328**
shareware, 9
shell, 157
  availability, 118
  built-in commands, 119
  changing, 472
  command-line quoting,
    491
  consoles, 143
  customizing, 127
  definition, 117
  initialization script, 121
  launching, 498
  manual page, 493
  operators, 329
  ownership, 131
  programming, 113
  prompt, 316
    command line, 309
  standard input, 329
  startup file, 121
  support, 119
  UNIX, 117
  usage, 117, 140
    Exercises, 141
    Q&A, 140
    Summary, 140
  variable, 127, 137

shell command, 131, 136
line, 147, 149
understanding, 123
prompting, 290
running, 290
**shell script, 144, 158, 204,
211, 214-215, 219, 293,
401, 408, 524, 530**
self-extracting, 306
building, 136
showrgb client, 161
**shutdown command, 38,
150, 210**
usage, 475
SIGKILL option, 464
SIGKILL signal, 463
simulation games, 447
single word lookup, 334
**single-click convenience,
178**
**single-letter commands,
253**
single-user mode, 120
size, 425
slideshow, creating, 167
**SLIP (Serial-Line IP),
234**
slrn
manual page, 275, 278
message display, 277
newsreader, 278
usage, 274
program, 271-272, 278
usage/setup, 269
starting, 276, 278
slsc spreadsheet, 397
calculator, 389
command, 389
usage, 389
slsc program, 389
**Small Computer System
Interface (SCSI), 378**
smtp server, 258
soffice script, 419
soft limits, 462, 475

software
drivers, 11, 225
format, choice, 510
installation/installing,
451, 499
libraries, 369
shared, 328
license, public domain,
329, 330
management, 53
package, 499
administration, dia-
log, 504
removing, 499
tools, need, 510
transport programs, 270
**solitaire, playing, X11,
443**
sort command, 329, 456
sound
easy configuration, 57
kernel modules, 52
support, 50
utilities, 53
sound card, 15, 51, 509
I/O address, 13
IRQ, 13
support, 50, 57
testing, 53
type, 13
usage, 41
**sound configurating/con-
figuration, 15**
COAS usage
manual, 57
OpenLinux, 50
testing, 53
sound module, 51, 55
loadable code, 50
loading, 50
SoundBlaster, 13, 52
**SoundBlaster-compatible
card kernel modules,
configuring, 56**

**source code, 8-9, 324,
384, 387-388, 396, 410**
retrieval, 290
**source command, 128,
130, 406**
sox command, 447
spacing, 423
spam, 268
fighting, 264
lists, 277
spammers, 264, 278
spamming, 285
SPARC, 9
**spell checking, 320, 332,
421, 425**
spell command, 74
spelling checker, 321
correction, 423
ispell, 332
starting, 426
spelling dictionary, 327
spelling errors, 332
spelling filter, 333
**spelling program, inter-
active, 332**
split command, 329
split windows, 318
split-screen windows, 319
spool queue, 351
spooled files, 350
**spreadsheet, 387, 415,
428**
documents, creating,
416
StarCalc, 433
creating, 428
data, 431
graphing, 431
documents
formats, 430
files, 390
free-for-personal-use,
387
programs, 208
running, 510
three-dimensional, 390

spreadsheet calculator (sc), 389, 397, 429
  commands, 388
  program, 387-388
  usage, 387
squeeze (-s) option, 330
stack, 382
Stallman, Richard, 315
standalone computer, 463
standalone Linux system, 211
standalone window, 160
standard input redirection operator, 119
standard output redirection operator, 119
Star Division, 313, 432
  GmbH, 415
StarCalc, 423, 425
  applications, 391
  AutoFormat Chart, 431
  calculations, 428
  document, 432
  graphing, 431
  spreadsheet, 391, 433
    creating, 428
StarCalc Spreadsheet Program, features, 391
StarDivision, registration page, 325
StarOffice, 96, 191, 324, 336, 338, 391-392
  4.0, 391, 397
  components, 428-429
  customization, 420
  default features, 420
  desktop, 326, 419, 421-422, 428
  document, 423
  documents, location, 433
  folders, 422
  installation
    configuration, 416
    directory, 325
    error, 433
    guide, 416

  office suite, 10, 423
  options, 420
  post-installation, 419
  printer installation, 421
  programs, 421
  sessions, 421
  setting, 420, 427
  setup directory, 416
  starting, 419
  suite, 313, 324
  taskbar, 425
  templates dialog box, 391
  usage, 415, 416, 421
    learning, 433
StarOffice 5.0, 325, 336, 391, 397, 416
  installation, 417
    dialog box, 416
    location, 418
    process, 418
StarOffice Mail, usage, 420
Start Horizontal Retrace value, 47
Start Vertical Retrace value, 47
startup files, 119, 123
startup script, 210
startx command, 49, 144-145, 148
  usage, 148, 151
StarWriter, 324, 338, 423
  document, 336, 424, 427-429, 432-433
    creating, 326, 336, 424, 433
    saving, 426
    spell checking, 426
  text, 431
    document window, 424
  usage, 423
static IP (Internet Protocol) address, 228, 235

statserial command, usage, 468
statserial program, 468
status bar, 293
status option, 214
Staufer, Todd, 299
Steuer, Detlef, 444
Sticky Buttons, 178
sticky note calendar, making, xmessage client usage, 174
stingy-memory-use option, 370
stop bits, 199
  setting up, 207
storage device, 454, 510
straight copy, usage, 510
stream editors, 329, 331
strings command, 116
style, 425
  controls, 423
  sheets, 393
su (substitute user)
  command, 451
    usage, 452
su command, 90, 233, 483, 525
  usage, 453, 469
su - command, 201
subjects, searching, 281
substitute (sed s) command, 331
substitute user (su) command, 451
  usage, 452
suck command, 286
sum command, 329
Sun Microsystems, 9, 315
SunDisk, 453
sunsite, 392
support files, 346, 369
support routines, 317
supported serial boards, 10
SVGA server, usage, 168
swap file, 464, 466
  usage, 461

swap partition, 13, 24, 482
  Linux, 370
swap space, 22, 159, 461
swap storage, 370
symbolic link, 102-103, 121, 158, 205, 210, 318, 439, 468, 483, 492, 507
  checking, symlinks command usage, 457
  creating, 203, 207
    ln (link) command usage, 102-103
  dangling, 458
symlinks command, usage, 457
sync ranges, 26
  horizontal, 26, 45
  vertical, 45
sync values, entering, 28
syntax errors, 332
Syquest EZ-flyer, 510
sysadmin (system administrator), 458, 463, 468, 482, 493, 497, 523
sysconfig file, 60
system
  administrator (sysadmin), 313, 367, 482, 493, 497, 516
  configuration files, editing, 474
  crash, 516
  dictionary, 333-334
  editor, default, 321
  fonts, 46
  initialization table, 209
    OpenLinux, 149
  interrupts, 461
  log, reading, 246
  management, 469
  memory, 13, 19, 370, 420, 460-461, 464-465
  RAM, amount, 13

  resource information, 53
  services, 53
  sounds, installing, 190
  usage, 461
system administration, 451
  basics, 479
  Exercises, 477
  Q&A, 476
  Summary, 476
  tool, 469
  tools, 351
system backup
  restore, 451
  tar (tape archive) command usage, 515
System Commander, 18
system load
  averages, 466
  information, getting
    top command usage, 464
    xload command usage, 464
System V, 480
system-specific software drivers, 225
system-wide settings, 473
systemwide alias definitions, 129
sz (send) files, 308
sz -w 2088 filename.tgz command, 308

T

t option, 116
Tab window manager (twm)
  client, 156
  starting, 156
  window management session, 156

table editor and planner (teapot) spreadsheet program, 390
table insertions, 425
tables, building, 423
tac command, 329
tail command, 89, 329
  usage, 88, 90
tape archive (tar)
  archive, 516
  command, 111-113, 116, 515, 521
    usage, 110-113, 515
  options, 112
  program, 116
  verification, 515
tape drive, 10, 509-510, 516, 518
  backups, taper Script usage, 518
  ide, 518
  restores, taper Script usage, 518
tape driver, floppy drive, 518
taper
  backup software package, installing, 499
  command, 501
    usage, 518
  program, 518
  Script, 520
    usage, 518
  software, 499, 501
tar (tape archive), 510
  archive, 516
  command, 111-113, 116, 124, 216, 515, 521
    usage, 110-113, 515
  options, 112
  program, 116
  verification, 515
target diskette, 16
taskbar, 158, 180, 425
Taylor, Dave, 255

Tcl interpreter, 119
tclsh shells, 119
TCP/IP (Transport Control Protocl/Internet Protocol), 227, 242
tcsh, 30
tcsh shell, 118, 129
  features, 122
  usage, 462
teapot (table editor and planner) spreadsheet program, 390
tee command, 135
Tektronix 4054 emulation, 159
telecommunications scripting language, built-in, 206
telecommunications scripts, writing, 206
telnet command
  running, 308
  usage, 308
telnet session, 308
termcap, manual page, 129
terminal client, usage, 147
terminal command line, 374
terminal emulator, 134, 159
  color-capable, 158-159
  kvt, 158
  multilingual, 158
  rxvt, 159
    starting, 161
  starting, 160
  X11, 158
terminal programs, 143, 158
  X11, 157
terminal settings
  xterm, changing, 158

terminal window, 44, 129, 137, 151, 158, 165, 166, 204, 240, 244, 248, 282, 286, 438, 443-444, 461, 488, 502
  command line, 154, 301, 324, 444, 448
  emulator, 158
  text regions, 166
test option, 212
TeX
  directories, 346
  distribution, 346
    files, 346
  documentation, 346
  formatting commands, 346
  formatting system, 347
  Frequently Asked Questions (FAQ) document, 346
  information files, 346
  system, 356
  typesetting system, 346
  usage, 346-347
TeX dvi, 345
  documents, previewing, 346
text, 345
  block, 320
  configuration files, 313
  control, 423
  editing tools, 335
  insertion, directory mode, 320
  menus, 322
  mode program, 439
  selections, 423
  stream, 329, 342
  tools, 314
  utilities, 329, 335
text change
  filter usage, 329
  sed filter usage, 329
text documents, 332
  conversion, 356
  formatting, 335

  printing, 347
  spellchecking, 335
text editor, 46, 56, 64, 126, 136, 144, 149, 209, 219, 229, 252, 254, 257, 271-272, 313, 317, 332, 335, 406, 409, 473, 475, 484
  built-in, 206
  default, 403
  features, 320
  pico, 403
  usage, 128, 338, 474
text file, 45, 87, 162, 204, 331
  compressed, 201
  formatting, 347
  insertion, 323
  opening, 316
  sending, 338
text filters, 329, 332
  usage, 338
text formatting, 335, 342
  groff formatter usage, 342
  TeX usage, 346
  text filters usage, 338
text printing, 313
  Exercises, 336
  Q&A, 335
  Summary, 335
text processing, 313
  Exercises, 336
  Q&A, 335
  Summary, 335
text-based interface, 43
text-only data files, importing, 388
text-only Web browser, 300
text-only Web browsing, 226
text-wrap mode, 317
tgif, 379
TGUI9680, 14
Theilson, Tim, 376

themes, K Desktop Environment, 35
thesaurus, 327
  support, 424
threads, reading, 270
three-button emulation, 159
three-button emulator, enabling, 46
three-dimensional spreadsheets, 390
TIFF graphic, 136
tile-cache size, 370
tiled format, 169
time, keeping, X11 clocks usage, 174
timeout, 237
  interval, 170
tin
  calling, 273
  commands, 274
  manual page, 274
  newsreader, 271
  program, 269-273
  reader, 270
  settings, 274
tinrc file, 274
title bar, 156, 158
  changing, 193
tload command, 466
to-do checklists, 406
Token-ring interface, 57
toolbar, 419
  formatting, 425
  icon, 425
  vertical, 425, 427, 431
tools, 371
top command, 464
  usage, 464
top program, 464
Torvalds, Linus, 8
touch command, 94
  usage, 94, 475
touch-tone dialing, 226
tput command, 527

tr (transliterate) command, 329
  usage, 331
transfer mode, binary, 291
transliterate (tr) command, 329
transparent digital clock, 175
transport agents, 250
Transport Control Protocl/Internet Protocol (TCP/IP), 227, 242
transport programs, 270
Tranter, Jeff, 468
trash directory, 141
tree command, 101, 480
trn, program, 286
Truscott, Tom, 269
ttyS0, 226
ttyS1, 226
ttyS1 serial port, 219
ttyS3, 226
twm (Tab window manager), 151
  client, 156
  window management session, 156
  window manager, starting, 156
two-button mouse, users, 42
Type II PC card slot, 57
Type III PC card slot, 57
typeset documents, 338
typesetting
  commands, 338
    inserted, 347
  macros, 344
  program, 338
  systems, 356

U

UID (user identification), 469-470
ulimit command, 459, 462
ulimit setting, 459
ulimit shell, viewing, 462
ultra-verbose (vv) option, 501
umask command, 493
umount command, 433, 484
  usage, 61
uname -r command, 348
uname -v command, 348
uname command, 50
unattended backup, 515
uncompressing files, 106-108
undo command, 335
undo levels, 369
undump, X11 windows, 167
unexpand command, 329
Uniform Resource Locator (URL), 229, 299, 303
uninstall (-e) option, 499
uniq command, 135, 329
unit conversions performance, units command usage, 385
units
  command, 385-386
    usage, 385
  manual page, 386
Universal Serial Bus (USB), 13
University of Helsinki, 8
University of Kansas, 299
University of North Carolina, 392
University of Washington, 319

University of Wisconsin-Milwaukee, 390
UNIX, 134
AT&T System V, 480
distribution, 122, 480
experience, 9
mail, 250
operating system, 286
programs, 349
shells, 117
systems, 387, 480
wizards, 249
UNIXC, 249
UNSUBSCRIBE, 266
unused files, compressing, 460
up command, 440
up option, 63
updatedb command, 76-77, 525
upgrade (-U) option, 499, 501
uptime command, 529
usage, 466
URL (Uniform Resource Locator), 229, 299, 303
USB (Universal Serial Bus), 13
drive, 64
USENET/Usenet, 229, 267
articles, 303
group, preposting, 285
news, 269, 286
Netscape
Discussions usage, 282
news reading
krn client usage, 278
slrn newsreader usage, 274
tin newsreader usage, 271
newsgroups, 247, 257, 270-271, 280, 283, 304
FAQs, 285

postings, 277
readers, 274
software transport programs, 270
user
access, managing, 468
account, 469
agent, 250, 253
usage, 251
bball, 135
cloobie, 470
creating, adduser command usage, 469
comma-delimited list, 493
cron scheduling, managing, 525
domain, 258
group, 498
hard drive storage space limits, 473
identification (UID), 469-470
management, 49
lisa command usage, 469
multiple, 8
option, 484
preference, 165
scheduling managing, atrun command usage, 527
usermod command, 477
username, 118, 149, 218, 228-230, 252, 276-277, 279, 295-296, 309, 452-453, 469-470, 472, 526
usrquota, 475
utilities distribution, 384
uucp software documentation, 204
uudecode command, 115
uuencode command, 115
uugetty program, 220

V

v option, 111, 116, 516
van Smoorenburg, Miquel, 204
vdir command, 82, 84
velvet, 396
verbose mode (-v) option, 487
verify (-V) option, 499
Vertical Display End value, 47
vertical sync ranges, 45
vertical toolbar, 425, 427, 431
Vertical Total value, 47
VFAT/vfat filesystem, 453, 482, 483
vfat partition, 516
vi command, 320
vi default editor, 403
vi editor, 317, 319, 413
video card, 10, 65
selecting, 26
video chipset, 10, 45, 47
video frequency, 47
video graphics, display, NeoMagic, 146
video memory, 147
amount, 14, 46
video modes, 43
video monitors, 43
video RAM, 47
amount, 27
video resolution, 45-46
video sync pulse, 47
video tuning, 45
video-mode switching, 45
videomode, 28
VideoRam setting, 47
view editor, 319
view option, 214
Viking Components, 225
vim (visual improved)
documentation, 319
command, 319-320

editor, 318, 526
   variants, 317
   package, 318
vimrc resource files, 318
virtual console, 9, 48,
131, 148, 453
   usage, X11 usage, 147
virtual desktops, 151, 180
virtual memory, 9
   command, vmstat com-
      mand usage, 461
   statistics, 461
virtual resolution, 147
virtual screen, 45, 48, 148
   size, support, 48
visual improved (vim)
   command, 319, 320
   documentation, 319
   editor, 318
      variants, 317
visual improved (vim)
package, 318
Vixie, Paul, 403
vmstat command, usage,
461
vprint program, 390
VRAM, 225
VT Fonts, 159
vv (ultra-verbose) option,
501

W

w command, 79, 440
   usage, 466
w option, 111-112
wait option, 214
wall command, 527
wallpaper
   default, 169
   pop-up menu, 187
WAV format, 191
wc (word count) com-
mand, 88, 135, 329

wc (word count) pro-
gram, 332
Web, text-only browsing,
226
Web address, 299
Web browser, 161, 271,
298, 310, 377, 464
   amaya, 310
   lynx, 321, 346
   text-only, 300
Web browsing, 223
Web page, 229, 299
   browsing, 299
   content, 300
   Netscape, 303
   remote, 303
Web site, 448
   Linux archive, 175
web2 (dictionary), 334
Weeks, Dan, 155
Wharf dock, 156
What is OpenLinux,
usage, 7
What-You-See-Is-What-
You-Get (WYSIWYG)
   editor, 356
whatis command, 72,
76-77, 526
whatis database, 77-78
whatis program, 71
whereis command, 77
   usage, 75
whereis ifconfig com-
mand, 227
whoami command, 453
whois command, 248
wildcard, 84, 215
   usage, 172, 375
Williams, Thomas, 394
Win9x filesystems, 482
window borders, 151
window buttons
   3D, 151
   changing, 193
window capture utility,
373

window colors, 152-153
window controls, 157
   window shade-type,
      156
window dump
   file, 367
   program, X11, 167
window emulator
   terminal, 158
window frames, 374
window information, get-
ting, xwininfo client
usage, 173
window manager, 143,
148, 151, 158, 164, 176
   AfterStep, 155
   configuration, 151
   default, 153, 156-157
   fvwm, 152, 154-155
      configuring, 151
   modules, 151
   settings, 153
   twm, 151
      starting, 156
   X11, 150
window operations, 156
window settings, 161
window shade-type win-
dow controls, 156
window-handling func-
tions, 152
windowing shell (wish),
119
windowing system, net-
work, 42
Windows, 35
   98, 285
   9x, 12
   applications, 457
   decorations, 152
   desktop, 19
   fonts, 153
   information utility, 173
   module definitions, 152
   NT, 9

operating system, 457
partition, 74, 104, 515
  mounting, 507
utility, 516
Wing, Ben, 315
Wingz, 390
spreadsheet, finding,
  390
WINMGR setting, 157
Winmodem, 11-12, 225
PC cards, 58
winprinters, 11
WinStorm, 225
**Wireless network inter-
faces, 57**
**wish (windowing shell),
119**
wmconfig command, 152
**Woelfelschneider, Olav,
438**
**word count (wc) com-
mand, 135**
**word count (wc) pro-
gram, 332**
**word processing, 161,
319, 332, 510**
documents, creating,
  416
file formats, 327
**word processor, 135, 166,
208, 324, 326, 334, 335,
338, 415, 423**
component, 328
features, 320
Linux environment, 313
WYSIWYG, 328
word search, 320
word-wrap mode, 317
**word wrapping, 317, 319,
320, 323, 340**
WordPerfect
configuration, 354
document window, 326
documents, 355
installation, 326

**WordPerfect 8.0 (Corel),
313, 326, 338, 354**
WordStar, 321
**WordStar-compatible
keyboard commands,
321**
work area, 423
**World Wide Web
(WWW)**
browsers, 289
browsing, 298
Linux browsers, usage,
  298
**Wuebben, Bernd
Johannes, 384**
**WWW (World Wide
Web)**
browsers, 289
browsing, 298
Linux browsers, usage,
  298
**WYSIWYG (What-You-
See-Is-What-You-Get),
327**
editor, 356
word processor, 328

X

X
configuring, 149
server, options, 46
starting, 144
**x (extract) option,
515-516**
**X display manager(xdm),
150, 180**
client, 149
X interface, 511
X man page, 163
X manual page, 160
X resources, 163

X server, 46, 48, 146
usage, 48
Xfree86, 46
**X session, 143, 147-148,
157, 181, 190, 374-375,
411, 436, 479**
colors, 146
exiting, 46
mode, 147
resolution, 147
settings, 153
starting, 145, 148-149,
  151, 324
startup, setup/settings,
  152
usage, 148
X terminal client, 166
X Toolkit, 406
command-line options,
  159-160
options, 160, 173
**X window managers,
148, 187**
**X Window System, 10,
18, 26-27, 35, 42, 72, 94,
117, 156, 162, 175, 177,
179, 203, 206, 223, 260,
286, 319, 321, 324, 328,
351, 373-374, 382-383,
388-389, 444-445, 468,
502**
configuring, 15, 41
  Exercises, 66
  process, 42
  Q&A, 65
  Summary, 65
games, 442
post-installation issues,
  41
running, 299, 376
usage, 143, 394
  Exercises, 176
  Q&A, 176
  Summary, 175
**X Windows, Quake, play-
ing, 445**

X-ISP dialog box, 240
X11, 42, 72, 80, 119, 224, 261, 270, 275, 278, 310, 466, 502
  application defaults, 298
  backgammon, playing, 444
  basic operations, learning, 160
  bitmap format, 168
  bitmap graphics directory, 168
  color support, 389
  configuring, 14, 42
  console window, color-capable, 159
  cursor modes, changing, 164
  cutting/pasting process, 165
  display, 175, 176
  distribution, 65, 176
  environment, 145
  Galaga, playing, 444
  games, 442
  ical client, usage, 405
  interface, 405
  login, bypass process, 41
  limitation, 374
  logging in, xdm command usage, 149
  mouse modes, changing, 164
  needing, 225
  nonusage, 439
  requiring, 505
  restarting, 157
  root window, customization, 168
  runlevel, 49
  running, 203-204, 234, 390, 416, 453, 503

  rxvt terminal, 136, 402
  screen savers, 169
  server, 11, 42
  settings, fine-tuning, 66
  solitaire, playing, 443
  usage, 61, 131, 147, 204, 369, 409, 466, 476, 488
  utilities, 175, 477
  workstations, 159
  xcalc Client, usage, 383
  xspread program, 390
  xwd command, 136
X11, starting, 143, 149
  color depths usage, 145
X11 client, 143, 148, 154, 160, 162, 165-166, 207, 211, 300, 306, 351, 375, 379, 384, 396, 399, 401, 407, 444, 447
  xboing, 445
  documentation, reading, 376
  geometry settings, usage, 160
  launching, 156
  manual pages, 163
  resources, setting, 162
  running, 147
  usage, 167
  xpat2, 443
X11 clock
  client, 402
  usage, 174
X11 desktop, 166, 374
  displays, 157
X11 fonts
  display, 164
  listing, xlsfonts usage, 172
X11 program, 220, 448
  exploring, 172
X11 resource
  file, 171
  settings, 317
  strings, 163

X11 server, 170, 173
  color depth, 168
X11 sessions, 46, 235, 267, 278 342, 374, 511
  starting, 49, 66, 144, 148, 151
X11 terminal, 129, 158
  emulators, 158
  menu-enabled, 158
  programs, 157
  window, 48, 204, 234, 240, 255, 305, 309, 316, 383, 395, 461, 464
X11 Toolkit options, 158, 300, 316, 376, 442
  support, 369
X11 windows
  capturing/dumping, 167
  dump format, 167
  dump graphics file, creating, 367-368
  dump program, 167
  manager, 131, 144, 150, 178
  undump, 167
X11 xv
  client, 215, 220
  graphic program, 215
x86 architecture, 9
xargs command, 135, 459
xbl, 442
xboard client
  usage, 442
xboing, 147, 374
  manual page, 445
  X11 client, 445
xcalc
  calculator, 383
  client, 383
  command, 383
    usage, 383
  manual page, 383
xchomp, 442

xclipboard client, 166
xclock program, 171
xcmap client, 161
xcolorsel client, 161
xcopy, 490
xcutsel client, 166
xdaliclock client, 175
xdemineuer, 442
xdm
    alternative, 150
    login screen, 149-150
xdm (X display manager), 180
    client, 150
    command, 149, 152
        usage, 149
xdvi files, 345
xemacs, 316, 335
    customization, 317
Xemacs/xemacs
    environment, features, 315
    editor, 318
    package, 317
    program, 317
    starting, 317
XF86Config/xf86config
    command, 43-44
    file, 45-46, 146, 179, 433
        understanding, 47
    keyboard, 46
    Screen, 48
    ServerFlags, 46
    settings, 46
    usage, 46
XF86_Mono, 48, 161
XF86_SVGA, 48
    server, 161
        mode, 48
    X11 server, 27
XF86_VGA16, 42
    server, 48, 161
xfd client, 164
xfig, 147, 379

xfmail, 268
xfontsel client, 159
xfontsel window, 159
xfractint, 396
XFree86, 158, 165
    user, 47
    X server, 46
Xfree86 Project, Inc., 42, 143
XFree86 X Window System, 383
XFree86-Video-Timings-HOWTO, 47
xgal game, 444
xgammon client, 444
Xi-Graphics, 178
Xircom ethernet cards, 11
xisp, 223
xisp account
    client, 15, 229, 247
    command, usage, 243
    configuring, 241
xjed, 321
xjewel, 442
XKEYBOARD extension, 433
xlander, 442
xload, 477
    client, 466
    command, 466
        usage, 464
xloadimage
    client, 167-168
    formatting, 169
    manual page, 167
xlock client, 171
xlsfonts
    client, usage, 172
    usage, 172
xmag client, 165
xmag program, 165
xman command, 72
xmessage, 401
    command, 400
    program, 400

xmessage client, 176
    usage, 174
    window display, 174
xmgr, 396
xmh, 268
xminicom
    command, 204
    script, 204
    shell script, 204
xmixer, 53, 57
    command, 448
xmodmap
    client, 165
    command, 433
    manual page, 165
xmseconfig client, 165
xosview, 477
    client, 466
xpaint
    client, 163, 379
    drawing program, 163
    drawing window, 165
    window, 165
xpat2
    manual page, 444
    solitaire game, 443
    X11 client, 443
xpdf, 377
    client, 416
xpilot, 442
xplaycd
    client, usage, 435, 438
    player, 438
xpmtoppm command, output, 368
xpuzzles, 442
xqf Quake server browser, 446
xrn, program, 286
xscreensaver client, 170, 171
xscreensaver-command clients, 170
xset
    usage, 165

xset client
manual page, 165
usage, 170
**xset command, usage,
170**
xset m \, 165
xset s option, 170
xsetroot
client, 164, 168
command, 169
xspread program, 390
XT, 10
xteddy client, 448
xterm
client, 158-159
program, 158
running, 158
starting, 158
terminal, 80, 166, 204
settings, changing,
158
window, 158-159, 275
X11 terminal, 129
xtrojka, 442
xv client, 167, 375
function, 375
xv command, 376
usage, 374
xv documentation, 376
xv X11 client, 379
**xvidtune client, starting,
66**
xwd client, 367-368
xwd command, 136
xwd program, 167
**xwdtopnm command,
136**
**xwininfo client, usage,
173**

Y

Y2K compliance, 402
yorick interpreter, 396
yow, 441

Z

z option, 515
Zawinski, Jamie, 170
zftape driver, 518
Zip 254 drive, 64
usage, 65
Zip backup device, 513
Zip disk
device, 518
mounting/usage, 64
unmounting, 65
Zip drive, 64, 513
usage, 41
utility, 490
**Zip parallel-port drive,
usage, 65**
Zip Plus drive, 64
zless pager, 201
**ZMODEM communica-
tions protocol, 308**
**Zoltrix Phantom/Spirit,
225**
zoom levels, 424
zsh, 30
zsh shell, 122, 135
documentation, 135

GNU GENERAL PUBLIC LICENSE

Version 2, June 1991

Copyright © 1989, 1991 Free Software Foundation, Inc.

675 Mass Ave, Cambridge, MA 02139, USA

Preamble

The licenses for most software are designed to take away your freedom to share and change it. By contrast, the GNU General Public License is intended to guarantee your freedom to share and change free software—to make sure the software is free for all its users. This General Public License applies to most of the Free Software Foundation's software and to any other program whose authors commit to using it. (Some other Free Software Foundation software is covered by the GNU Library General Public License instead.) You can apply it to your programs, too.

When we speak of free software, we are referring to freedom, not price. Our General Public Licenses are designed to make sure that you have the freedom to distribute copies of free software (and charge for this service if you wish), that you receive source code or can get it if you want it, that you can change the software or use pieces of it in new free programs; and that you know you can do these things.

To protect your rights, we need to make restrictions that forbid anyone to deny you these rights or to ask you to surrender the rights. These restrictions translate to certain responsibilities for you if you distribute copies of the software, or if you modify it.

For example, if you distribute copies of such a program, whether gratis or for a fee, you must give the recipients all the rights that you have. You must make sure that they, too, receive or can get the source code. And you must show them these terms so they know their rights.

We protect your rights with two steps: (1) copyright the software, and (2) offer you this license which gives you legal permission to copy, distribute and/or modify the software.

Also, for each author's protection and ours, we want to make certain that everyone understands that there is no warranty for this free software. If the software is modified by someone else and passed on, we want its recipients to know that what they have is not the original, so that any problems introduced by others will not reflect on the original authors' reputations.

Finally, any free program is threatened constantly by software patents. We wish to avoid the danger that redistributors of a free program will individually obtain patent licenses, in effect making the program proprietary. To prevent this, we have made it clear that any patent must be licensed for everyone's free use or not licensed at all.

The precise terms and conditions for copying, distribution and modification follow.

GNU GENERAL PUBLIC LICENSE

TERMS AND CONDITIONS FOR COPYING, DISTRIBUTION AND MODIFICATION

0. This License applies to any program or other work which contains a notice placed by the copyright holder saying it may be distributed under the terms of this General Public License. The "Program", below, refers to any such program or work, and a "work based on the Program" means either the Program or any derivative work under copyright law: that is to say, a work containing the Program or a portion of it, either verbatim or with modifications and/or translated into another language. (Hereinafter, translation is included without limitation in the term "modification".) Each licensee is addressed as "you".

Activities other than copying, distribution and modification are not covered by this License; they are outside its scope. The act of running the Program is not restricted, and the output from the Program is covered only if its contents constitute a work based on the Program (independent of having been made by running the Program). Whether that is true depends on what the Program does.

1. You may copy and distribute verbatim copies of the Program's source code as you receive it, in any medium, provided that you conspicuously and appropriately publish on each copy an appropriate copyright notice and disclaimer of warranty; keep intact all the notices that refer to this License and to the absence of any warranty; and give any other recipients of the Program a copy of this License along with the Program.

   You may charge a fee for the physical act of transferring a copy, and you may at your option offer warranty protection in exchange for a fee.

2. You may modify your copy or copies of the Program or any portion of it, thus forming a work based on the Program, and copy and distribute such modifications or work under the terms of Section 1 above, provided that you also meet all of these conditions:

   a) You must cause the modified files to carry prominent notices stating that you changed the files and the date of any change.

   b) You must cause any work that you distribute or publish, that in whole or in part contains or is derived from the Program or any part thereof, to be licensed as a whole at no charge to all third parties under the terms of this License.

   c) If the modified program normally reads commands interactively when run, you must cause it, when started running for such interactive use in the most ordinary way, to print or display an announcement including an appropriate copyright notice and a notice that there is no warranty (or else, saying that you provide a warranty) and that users may redistribute the program under these conditions, and telling the user how to view a copy of this License. (Exception: if the Program itself is interactive but does not normally print such an announcement, your work based on the Program is not required to print an announcement.)

   These requirements apply to the modified work as a whole. If identifiable sections of that work are not derived from the Program, and can be reasonably considered independent and separate works in themselves, then this License, and its terms, do not apply to those sections when you distribute them as separate works. But when you distribute the same sections as part of a whole which is a work based on the Program, the distribution of the whole must be on the terms of this License, whose permissions for other licensees extend to the entire whole, and thus to each and every part regardless of who wrote it.

   Thus, it is not the intent of this section to claim rights or contest your rights to work written entirely by you; rather, the intent is to exercise the right to control the distribution of derivative or collective works based on the Program.

   In addition, mere aggregation of another work not based on the Program with the Program (or with a work based on the Program) on a volume of a storage or distribution medium does not bring the other work under the scope of this License.

3. You may copy and distribute the Program (or a work based on it, under Section 2) in object code or executable form under the terms of Sections 1 and 2 above provided that you also do one of the following:

   a) Accompany it with the complete corresponding machine-readable source code, which must be distributed under the terms of Sections 1 and 2 above on a medium customarily used for software interchange; or,

   b) Accompany it with a written offer, valid for at least three years, to give any third party, for a charge no more than your cost of physically performing source distribution, a complete machine-readable copy of the corresponding source code, to be distributed under the terms of Sections 1 and 2 above on a medium customarily used for software interchange; or,

c) Accompany it with the information you received as to the offer to distribute corresponding source code. (This alternative is allowed only for noncommercial distribution and only if you received the program in object code or executable form with such an offer, in accord with Subsection b above.)

The source code for a work means the preferred form of the work for making modifications to it. For an executable work, complete source code means all the source code for all modules it contains, plus any associated interface definition files, plus the scripts used to control compilation and installation of the executable. However, as a special exception, the source code distributed need not include anything that is normally distributed (in either source or binary form) with the major components (compiler, kernel, and so on) of the operating system on which the executable runs, unless that component itself accompanies the executable.

If distribution of executable or object code is made by offering access to copy from a designated place, then offering equivalent access to copy the source code from the same place counts as distribution of the source code, even though third parties are not compelled to copy the source along with the object code.

4. You may not copy, modify, sublicense, or distribute the Program except as expressly provided under this License. Any attempt otherwise to copy, modify, sublicense or distribute the Program is void, and will automatically terminate your rights under this License. However, parties who have received copies, or rights, from you under this License will not have their licenses terminated so long as such parties remain in full compliance.

5. You are not required to accept this License, since you have not signed it. However, nothing else grants you permission to modify or distribute the Program or its derivative works. These actions are prohibited by law if you do not accept this License. Therefore, by modifying or distributing the Program (or any work based on the Program), you indicate your acceptance of this License to do so, and all its terms and conditions for copying, distributing or modifying the Program or works based on it.

6. Each time you redistribute the Program (or any work based on the Program), the recipient automatically receives a license from the original licensor to copy, distribute or modify the Program subject to these terms and conditions. You may not impose any further restrictions on the recipients' exercise of the rights granted herein. You are not responsible for enforcing compliance by third parties to this License.

7. If, as a consequence of a court judgment or allegation of patent infringement or for any other reason (not limited to patent issues), conditions are imposed on you (whether by court order, agreement or otherwise) that contradict the conditions of this License, they do not excuse you from the conditions of this License. If you cannot distribute so as to satisfy simultaneously your obligations under this License and any other pertinent obligations, then as a consequence you may not distribute the Program at all. For example, if a patent license would not permit royalty-free redistribution of the Program by all those who receive copies directly or indirectly through you, then the only way you could satisfy both it and this License would be to refrain entirely from distribution of the Program.

If any portion of this section is held invalid or unenforceable under any particular circumstance, the balance of the section is intended to apply and the section as a whole is intended to apply in other circumstances.

It is not the purpose of this section to induce you to infringe any patents or other property right claims or to contest validity of any such claims; this section has the sole purpose of protecting the integrity of the free software distribution system, which is implemented by public license practices. Many people have made generous contributions to the wide range of software distributed through that system in reliance on consistent application of that system; it is up to the author/donor to decide if he or she is willing to distribute software through any other system and a licensee cannot impose that choice.

This section is intended to make thoroughly clear what is believed to be a consequence of the rest of this License.

8. If the distribution and/or use of the Program is restricted in certain countries either by patents or by copyrighted interfaces, the original copyright holder who places the Program under this License may add an explicit geographical distribution limitation excluding those countries, so that distribution is permitted only in or among countries not thus excluded. In such case, this License incorporates the limitation as if written in the body of this License.

9. The Free Software Foundation may publish revised and/or new versions of the General Public License from time to time. Such new versions will be similar in spirit to the present version, but may differ in detail to address new problems or concerns.

   Each version is given a distinguishing version number. If the Program specifies a version number of this License which applies to it and "any later version", you have the option of following the terms and conditions either of that version or of any later version published by the Free Software Foundation. If the Program does not specify a version number of this License, you may choose any version ever published by the Free Software Foundation.

10. If you wish to incorporate parts of the Program into other free programs whose distribution conditions are different, write to the author to ask for permission. For software which is copyrighted by the Free Software Foundation, write to the Free Software Foundation; we sometimes make exceptions for this. Our decision will be guided by the two goals of preserving the free status of all derivatives of our free software and of promoting the sharing and reuse of software generally.

NO WARRANTY

11. BECAUSE THE PROGRAM IS LICENSED FREE OF CHARGE, THERE IS NO WARRANTY FOR THE PROGRAM, TO THE EXTENT PERMITTED BY APPLICABLE LAW. EXCEPT WHEN OTHERWISE STATED IN WRITING THE COPYRIGHT HOLDERS AND/OR OTHER PARTIES PROVIDE THE PROGRAM "AS IS" WITHOUT WARRANTY OF ANY KIND, EITHER EXPRESSED OR IMPLIED, INCLUDING, BUT NOT LIMITED TO, THE IMPLIED WARRANTIES OF MERCHANTABILITY AND FITNESS FOR A PARTICULAR PURPOSE. THE ENTIRE RISK AS TO THE QUALITY AND PERFORMANCE OF THE PROGRAM IS WITH YOU. SHOULD THE PROGRAM PROVE DEFECTIVE, YOU ASSUME THE COST OF ALL NECESSARY SERVICING, REPAIR OR CORRECTION.

12. IN NO EVENT UNLESS REQUIRED BY APPLICABLE LAW OR AGREED TO IN WRITING WILL ANY COPYRIGHT HOLDER, OR ANY OTHER PARTY WHO MAY MODIFY AND/OR REDISTRIBUTE THE PROGRAM AS PERMITTED ABOVE, BE LIABLE TO YOU FOR DAMAGES, INCLUDING ANY GENERAL, SPECIAL, INCIDENTAL OR CONSEQUENTIAL DAMAGES ARISING OUT OF THE USE OR INABILITY TO USE THE PROGRAM (INCLUDING BUT NOT LIMITED TO LOSS OF DATA OR DATA BEING RENDERED INACCURATE OR LOSSES SUSTAINED BY YOU OR THIRD PARTIES OR A FAILURE OF THE PROGRAM TO OPERATE WITH ANY OTHER PROGRAMS), EVEN IF SUCH HOLDER OR OTHER PARTY HAS BEEN ADVISED OF THE POSSIBILITY OF SUCH DAMAGES.

END OF TERMS AND CONDITIONS

Linux and the GNU system

The GNU project started 12 years ago with the goal of developing a complete free UNIX-like operating system. "Free" refers to freedom, not price; it means you are free to run, copy, distribute, study, change, and improve the software.

A UNIX-like system consists of many different programs. We found some components already available as free software—for example, X Windows and TeX. We obtained other components by helping to convince their developers to make them free—for example, the Berkeley network utilities. Other components we wrote specifically for GNU—for example, GNU Emacs, the GNU C compiler, the GNU C library, Bash, and Ghostscript. The components in this last category are "GNU software". The GNU
system consists of all three categories together.

The GNU project is not just about developing and distributing free software. The heart of the GNU project is an idea: that software should be free, and that the users' freedom is worth defending. For if people have freedom but do not value it, they will not keep it for long. In order to make freedom last, we have to teach people to value it.

The GNU project's method is that free software and the idea of users' freedom support each other. We develop GNU software, and as people encounter GNU programs or the GNU system and start to use them, they also think about the GNU idea. The software shows that the idea can work in practice. People who come to agree with the idea are likely to write additional free software. Thus, the software embodies the idea, spreads the idea, and grows from the idea.

This method was working well—until someone combined the Linux kernel with the GNU system (which still lacked a kernel), and called the combination a "Linux system."

The Linux kernel is a free UNIX-compatible kernel written by Linus Torvalds. It was not written specifically for the GNU project, but the Linux kernel and the GNU system work together well. In fact,adding Linux to the GNU system brought the system to completion: it made a free UNIX-compatible operating system available for use.

But ironically, the practice of calling it a "Linux system" undermines our method of communicating the GNU idea. At first impression, a "Linux system" sounds like something completely distinct from the "GNU system." And that is what most users think it is. Most introductions to the "Linux system" acknowledge the role played by the GNU software components. But they don't say that the system as a whole is more or less the same GNU system that the GNU project has been compiling for a decade. They don't say that the idea of a free UNIX-like system originates from the GNU project. So most users don't know these things.

This leads many of those users to identify themselves as a separate community of "Linux users", distinct from the GNU user community. They use all of the GNU software; in fact, they use almost all of the GNU system; but they don't think of themselves as GNU users, and they may not think about the GNU idea.

It leads to other problems as well—even hampering cooperation on software maintenance. Normally when users change a GNU program to make it work better on a particular system, they send the change to the maintainer of that program; then they work with the maintainer, explaining the change, arguing for it and sometimes rewriting it, to get it installed.

But people who think of themselves as "Linux users" are more likely to release a forked "Linux-only" version of the GNU program, and consider the job done. We want each and every GNU program to work "out of the box" on Linux-based systems; but if the users do not help, that goal becomes much harder to achieve.

So how should the GNU project respond? What should we do now to spread the idea that freedom for computer users is important?

We should continue to talk about the freedom to share and change software—and to teach other users to value these freedoms. If we enjoy having a free operating system, it makes sense for to think about preserving those freedoms for the long term. If we enjoy having a variety of free software, it makes sense for us to think about encouraging others to write additional free software, instead of additional proprietary software.

We should not accept the splitting of the community in two. Instead we should spread the word that "Linux systems" are variant GNU systems—that users of these systems are GNU users, and that they ought to consider the GNU philosophy which brought these systems into existence.

This article is one way of doing that. Another way is to use the terms "Linux-based GNU system" (or "GNU/Linux system" or "Lignux" for short) to refer to the combination of the Linux kernel and the GNU system.

Copyright 1996 Richard Stallman

(Verbatim copying and redistribution is permitted without royalty as long as this notice is preserved.)

The Linux kernel is Copyright © 1991, 1992, 1993, 1994 Linus Torvaldis (others hold copyrights on some of the drivers, file systems, and other parts of the kernel) and and is licensed under the terms of the GNU General Public License.

The FreeBSD Copyright

All of the documentation and software included in the 4.4BSD and 4.4BSD-Lite Releases is copyrighted by The Regents of the University of California.

Copyright 1979, 1980, 1983, 1986, 1988, 1989, 1991, 1992, 1993, 1994 The Regents of the University of California. All rights reserved.

Redistribution and use in source and binary forms, with or without modification, are permitted provided that the following conditions are met:

1. Redistributions of source code must retain the above copyright notice, this list of conditions and the following disclaimer.

2. Redistributions in binary form must reproduce the above copyright notice, this list of conditions and the following disclaimer in the documentation and/or other materials provided with the distribution.

3. All advertising materials mentioning features or use of this software must display the following acknowledgement:

   This product includes software developed by the University of California, Berkeley and its contributors.

4. Neither the name of the University nor the names of its contributors may be used to endorse or promote products derived from this software without specific prior written permission.

THIS SOFTWARE IS PROVIDED BY THE REGENTS AND CONTRIBUTORS "AS IS" AND ANY EXPRESS OR IMPLIED WARRANTIES, INCLUDING, BUT NOT LIMITED TO, THE IMPLIED WARRANTIES OF MERCHANTABILITY AND FITNESS FOR A PARTICULAR PURPOSE ARE DISCLAIMED. IN NO EVENT SHALL THE REGENTS OR CONTRIBUTORS BE LIABLE FOR ANY DIRECT, INDIRECT, INCIDENTAL, SPECIAL, EXEMPLARY, OR CONSEQUENTIAL DAMAGES (INCLUDING, BUT NOT LIMITED TO, PROCUREMENT OF SUBSTITUTE GOODS OR SERVICES; LOSS OF USE, DATA, OR PROFITS; OR BUSINESS INTERRUPTION) HOWEVER CAUSED AND ON ANY THEORY OF LIABILITY, WHETHER IN CONTRACT, STRICT LIABILITY, OR TORT (INCLUDING NEGLIGENCE OR OTHERWISE) ARISING IN ANY WAY OUT OF THE USE OF THIS SOFTWARE, EVEN IF ADVISED OF THE POSSIBILITY OF SUCH DAMAGE.

The Institute of Electrical and Electronics Engineers and the American National Standards Committee X3, on Information Processing Systems have given us permission to reprint portions of their documentation.

In the following statement, the phrase "this text" refers to portions of the system documentation.

Portions of this text are reprinted and reproduced in electronic form in the second BSD Networking Software Release, from IEEE Std 1003.1-1988, IEEE Standard Portable Operating System Interface for Computer Environments (POSIX), copyright © 1988 by the Institute of Electrical and Electronics Engineers, Inc. In the event of any discrepancy between these versions and the original IEEE Standard, the original IEEE Standard is the referee document.

In the following statement, the phrase "This material" refers to portions of the system documentation.

This material is reproduced with permission from American National Standards Committee X3, on Information Processing Systems. Computer and Business Equipment Manufacturers Association (CBEMA), 311 First St., NW, Suite 500, Washington, DC 20001-2178. The developmental work of Programming Language C was completed by the X3J11 Technical Committee.

The views and conclusions contained in the software and documentation are those of the authors and should not be interpreted as representing official policies, either expressed or implied, of the Regents of the University of California.

www@FreeBSD.ORG

What's on the CD-ROM?

The included CD-ROM contains Caldera's OpenLinux 2.2 which is freely available from Caldera's FTP site. This software includes the following:

- KDE 1.1
- WordPerfect 8
- Netscape Communicator 4.51
- LIZARD, the grapical installation wizard

The following are commercial upgrades which are also available on the included CD-ROM:

- PartitionMagic, Caldera Edition
- BootMagic, Caldera Edition

The following are available in Caldera's commercial package of OpenLinux 2.2:

- StarOffice 5.0
- BRU